How to use management ratios

For Wendy, Rachel and Robert

**Other publications by C.A. Westwick:**

*A study of profitability in the hosiery and knitwear industry*, National Economic Development Office, 1971.

*Accuracy of profit forecasts in bid situations*, Institute of Chartered Accountants in England and Wales, 1972.

*Investment appraisal for the clothing industry*, HMSO, 1973.

*Accounting for inflation: A working guide to the accounting procedures*, Institute of Chartered Accountants in England and Wales, 1973.

*Investment appraisal and inflation*, Research Committee Occasional Paper No. 7, Institute of Chartered Accountants in England and Wales, 1976 (with P.S.D. Shohet).

*Property valuation and accounts*, Institute of Chartered Accountants in England and Wales, 1980.

*Sources of British business comparative performance data*, Institute of Chartered Accountants in England and Wales, 2nd edition, 1986 (with W.J. Westwick).

*Current cost accounting*, Oyez Publishing, 1980 (with P.R. Hinton).

*Do the figures make sense?: A practical guide to analytical review*, Institute of Chartered Accountants in England and Wales, 1981.

*Profit Forecasts: how they are made, reviewed and used*, Gower, 1983.

*Accounting for overseas operations*, Gower, 1986.

# How to use MANAGEMENT RATIOS

Second edition

C.A. WESTWICK

A Gower Workbook

First published 1973 by Gower Press Limited

Reprinted 1973, 1974, 1978, 1979, 1981, 1983, 1987

Second edition published 1987 by

Gower Publishing Company Limited,
Gower House,
Croft Road,
Aldershot,
Hants GU11 3HR,
England

**British Library Cataloguing in Publication Data**

Westwick, C.A.
　How to use management ratios. (A Gower Workbook)
　1. Ratio analysis
　I. Title
　658.4′033　HF5681. R25

ISBN 0-566-02425-X

Typeset in Great Britain by
Graphic Studios (Southern) Ltd., Godalming, Surrey.
Printed and bound in Great Britain by
Robert Hartnoll (1985) Ltd., Bodmin, Cornwall

# Contents

# Illustrations

*ix*

**Tables**

# Acknowledgements

**For the First Edition**

This book is based on long practical experience of selecting ratios for management, including nine years at the Centre for Interfirm Comparison. Accordingly, my first and chief expression of indebtedness is due to the Centre and in particular to Herbert Ingham and Leslie Taylor Harrington.

This book owes much, both in some general principles and in matters of detail, to the body of knowledge painstakingly developed by the Centre. Certain topics appearing in the text and illustrations of this book are based on or are similar to material which was prepared by the Centre, and in such cases I have made specific and, I hope, adequate acknowledgements in the course of the book. I should like to thank the Centre for its permission to reproduce the material in question. There are other inevitable resemblances of a more general nature between the contents of the present volume and the work done by the Centre; I trust that such general resemblances will serve as a practical tribute to the Centre's principles and achievements.

I hope, however, that the book may be seen as reasonably broadly based and drawing on a variety of sources of knowledge about ratio analysis. Accordingly, I would like to thank the many people with whom I have had fruitful discussions on the subject of ratios over the past twelve years or more, including Herbert Ingham and Leslie Taylor Harrington in the first instance, and Professor W.T. Baxter, Peter Helps, W.J. Haydn Everitt, Tom Price, Richard Williams, Richard Deeley, Errol Bishop, Walter Stewart, Guenter Steinitz, D.R.C. Halford, R.S. Cutler, C.J. Platt and many others.

I am grateful to Miss M. Brownlow and Maria Rzysko of Inbucon/AIC's Group Information Department, to Kathleen Bolton and Brenda Goddard of the Library of the Institute of Chartered Accountants in England and Wales, and to Graham Rigby for help in compiling the list of suggestions for further reading.

I should particularly like to thank John Pleming and Bob Price, both of Inbucon/ AIC Management Consultants Ltd, for giving me the time and the generous encouragement that got me well on the way to writing this book, and Michael Renshall of the English Institute of Chartered Accountants for help and encouragement in completing it.

Finally I should like to thank my wife Wendy for believing that I could not only start to write a book but that I could finish it as well.


**For the Second Edition**

Many individuals and organisations have helped in the production of this second edition and I would like to thank them all for their valued contributions. They include:

Bill Capps, CIPFA; Gordon Cryne; Vic Francis, British Printing Industries' Federation; I.R. Fraser (Fisons); Dr E. Gualandi; R.G. Hollister; Mr McMorris (Raelbrook); B.R. Nixon, University of Exeter Agricultural Economics Unit; Sir K.J. Sharp; Phil Shohett, ICAEW; A. Short, Newspaper Society; A.A. Smith, HMSO; Lord Weinstock, GEC; Richard Williams, London Borough of Haringey.

The following colleagues at Arthur Andersen & Co: Ian Burns, Brian Currie, Ray Hinton, David Kaye, Keith Pitkin, Alec Rabarts, Philip Randall, Vincent Watts.

The following civil servants for help with Chapter 14.4.3: Mrs A. Case, Myra Chapman, Kate Collins, P.R. Cook, Norma Fenton, Dr R. Gibbs, A. Hardman, Andre P.G. Hare, R.C. Heron, R.A. Hirst, Dr A.A. Holt, L.E. Jaundoo,

T. Kent, A. Laurance, Sue Lewis, D.P.E. Mason, M. Matthews, Dr L.D. Mayhew, M. Meredith, S. McCarthy, A.G. Muir, M. Taylor and others who preferred to remain anonymous.

The following librarians and their staff: Michael Bywater, ICAEW; M.J. Campbell, City of London; A.L. Smyth and A. Gallimore, City of Manchester; Pat Thomson, Arthur Andersen & Co., for help with obtaining material, especially for Chapter 2, and with the bibliography.

All the organisations which contributed information for Appendix 2-2.

My wife Wendy for help with updating Chapter 2 and revising the Suggestions for Further Reading and the two indexes.

I am grateful to the following individuals and organisations for permission to reproduce the material indicated:

(a)  The editor of *The Accountant* Appendix 1-1 which is based on an article of mine published in the 23 December 1967 issue

(b)  Extel Statistical Services Ltd – Table 2-2

(c)  The editor, *Management Today* – Table 2-3 and Diagrams 8-1 and 8-7 which originally appeared in my article 'Analysing return on equity capital' (January, 1965)

(d)  Inter Company Comparisons Ltd – Table 2-4

(e)  Times Newspapers Ltd – Table 2-5

(f)  Jordan & Sons Ltd – Table 2-6

(g)  The Financial Times – Table 2-7

(h)  National Economic Development Office and the Controller of Her Majesty's Stationery Office – Table 2-8, material on pages 16 and 17 which originally appeared in my book *A Study of Profitability in the hosiery and knitwear industry* and the list of ratios in Chapter 11-5

(i)  The Centre for Interfirm Comparison – for tables and diagrams on which acknowledgements to the Centre appear

(j)  A.L. Smyth and A. Gallimore, Manchester Public Libraries – Appendix 2-1

(k)  M.J. Campbell, City of London Library – material in Appendix 2-2

(l)  *Times Business News* – part of Appendix 4-1

(m)  Lord Weinstock – part of Appendix 4-1

(n)  British Standards Institution – Appendix 9-1

(o)  British Printing Industries' Federation – material in Chapter 11-6

(p)  Newspaper Society – material in Chapter 11-7

(q)  University of Exeter Agricultural Economics Unit – material in Chapter 11-8

(r)  M.H. Cabourn Smith – Diagram 11-10

(s)  The Institute of Chartered Accountants in England and Wales – Diagrams 11-11, 11-12 and Table 11-2

(t)  Auditing Practices Committee – Diagram 13-1

(u)  The Controller of Her Majesty's Stationery Office – Appendix 13-3

(v)  Central Electricity Generating Board – Diagram 14-4

(w)  Department of Health & Social Security – Diagram 14-6

Views expressed in this book are my own and are not necessarily those of Arthur Andersen & Co, The Institute of Chartered Accountants in England & Wales, Inbucon/AIC Management Consultants or The Centre for Interfirm Comparison.

# Introduction

## Objective of the Book

The objective of this book is to help directors and managers run their companies or departments more profitably or efficiently. It describes what information executives should have, where and how to get it, and how to interpret it once it has been obtained.

This book differs from the many others on the subject of management information in that it is based on the belief that the information is more useful if it is in the form of a ratio rather than an absolute figure.

Perhaps an illustration of this point from outside the world of business may help. Next time you are sitting in your car look at the dashboard. You will probably see instruments which measure speed over the ground, engine speed, oil pressure, engine temperature, and rate of charge/discharge of battery. These instruments help you to drive quickly and safely to your destination. You will no doubt have noticed that of the five instruments mentioned four are giving readings in *ratio* form (miles per hour, revolutions per second, pounds per square inch, amperes per hour); only temperature is an absolute figure. It is perhaps not surprising therefore that this book, which is about controlling a business, should also measure events by using ratios. Your business will have cost many times more than your car. Many more people are involved. Has your business got the right instruments on its dashboards and control panels? Are your staff trained to read them and interpret their messages correctly? If you are not entirely happy with the answers to these questions then reading this book should help.

Before we leave the dashboard analogy there is another point worth making. It is a matter of judgement to interpret the readings of a car's instruments and to decide what to do. A suitable speed depends on the objective of the journey, the nature of the road and of the weather, and so on. So it is with management ratios. They tell you what is happening but you have to make up your own mind what to do about it. This is why it is not possible to lay down hard and fast rules applicable to all firms at all times as to what value a ratio should have. But guidance is given as to how and where to get such information for your firm for the period you are dealing with.

## How Ratios can help Management

Ratios are a tool that enables management to analyse business situations and to monitor the performance of their own and their competitors' firms. Armed with the information provided by ratio analysis, management can take action that is relevant to the problems revealed, and can refrain from irrelevant (and perhaps costly and damaging) action which they otherwise might have taken in the absence of this information. Ratio analysis has three main uses:

1    To help diagnose a situation
2    To monitor performance
3    To help plan forward

Diagnosis is not restricted to the manager's own firm; ratio analysis helps management to study the performance of suppliers, customers, competitors, and even prospective subsidiaries and affiliates, in a systematic way.

## What is new in the Second Edition

Since the first edition was published in 1973, it has been reprinted several times and translated into a number of overseas languages. It is now widely recognised as the major practical book on its subject.

The objectives of the second edition remain the same as for the first – to give practical help and guidance in the choice and use of management ratios – but it includes a number of topics not covered in the first edition, and deals with the many developments that have occurred over the last dozen years or so. The main changes and additions are as follows:

Chapter 2, 'Standards of Comparison', has been completely revised and updated. Discontinued sources have been deleted and new sources added. In general there has been an increase in the number of sources and the quantity of information they provide. There have however been a few notable casualties in this area. Also noticeable is the increase in the amount of information which is available electronically as opposed to the conventional printed paper.

Although still by no means ideal, the quantity and quality of published accounts has improved so much that it seemed desirable to include a new chapter (Chapter 13) on using published accounts. The approach adopted with its emphasis on a structured and analytical use of ratios is, I believe, unique.

There has been a considerable increase in the use of ratios in the public sector and accordingly there is a new chapter (Chapter 14) on this subject. As well as general comments on the difficulties of measuring efficiency, effectiveness and economy within the public sector, and the desirability of an interchange of experience between the public and the private sectors, there are separate sections on nationalised industries, local authorities and (the most recent to adopt the use of ratios) central government. This chapter will be of interest to MPs, Councillors, tax and rate payers, and the users of the services of National Industries, as well as to those working in the public sector.

A new section (1.4) on the effect of changes in volume on ratios and another (5.4) on break even charts, has been added.

Lord Weinstock has kindly agreed to let me publish his comments to me on his yardsticks of efficiency (Appendix 4.1).

For marketing management there are two new sections: 6.2 on market shares and 6.4 on sales promotions. There is also some new material on measuring advertising effectiveness.

For financial, purchasing and marketing management there is a new section on the use of Z scores (a technique for identifying companies with incipient financial difficulties) (section 8.4).

For financial management there are new sections on measuring debtors' turnover (8.5), pension funds and costs (8.9), and the company's auditors (8.10). There is also new material on risk and earnings per share.

Four new sections have been added to Chapter 11, 'Operating ratios for non-manufacturing organisations': ratios for the owner managed business (11.4); for printers (11.6); for newspapers (11.7); and for farms (11.8). New material on the later developments of the inter-firm comparison for accountants has also been added.

There are also various other relatively minor changes and updates.

## How to make the Best Use of this Book

How can you get the best out of this book? It is assumed that your time is limited and that there are many other things you must do. Everyone should read, or at least skim through, Chapters 1 to 3. Then, each reader should study the chapter relating to his function, such as Chapter 4 for the managing director or Chapter 9 for the production manager. You should select which ratios you are going to use. It will help to re-read Chapter 1 and your own functional chapter. Then you should select your standards after consulting Chapter 2 again. After you have done this you should use the work sheets at the end of your 'own' chapter to assemble the information and calculate your own and the standard ratios. You should then compare them and ask yourself what the differences mean, what they suggest you do, what other information they indicate might be helpful. Then you should act and monitor the results of your actions by using the same ratios (see Table 1).

Firms and managers differ and the same ratios will not suit all of them. Those described may need to be modified to particular circumstances. It is probable however that most of the ratios described will be found useful, and that those who drop any of them will substitute another ratio and not an absolute figure.

While acting on your own chapter, you should study those dealing with your colleagues' functions and also persuade them to read those chapters.

As it is anticipated, however, that most people will read only the chapters most relevant to their own function, material and ratios which are relevant to more than one function are either cross referenced between chapters or repeated in both chapters. Anyone reading this book straight through is bound to notice this and may find it irritating. It is hoped that he will forgive the repetition as it is designed to make the book of more immediate use to the manager who is short of time.

| Stage | | Chapters to read |
|---|---|---|
| 1. | Groundwork | 1, 2 and 3 |
| 2. | Select ratios | 1 and your chapter* |
| 3. | Select standard | 2 |
| 4. | Calculate your ratios and standard ratios | 3 and work sheets at end of your chapter* |
| 5. | Compare your ratios with standard | Your own chapter* |
| 6. | Consider implications | Your own chapter* |
| 7. | Decide on action | Your own chapter* plus suggestions for reading |
| 8. | Monitor results | Work sheet at end of your chapter*† |
| 9. | Get the broader view | 4, 5 and 12 and whichever of 6, 7, 8, 9, 10, 11, 13 or 14 you have not yet read |

| *Note If you are: | Your Chapter(s) is/are: |
|---|---|
| managing director | 4 and 5 |
| in marketing | 6 |
| in purchasing | 7 |
| in finance | 8 & 13 |
| in production | 9 |
| concerned with personnel | 10 |
| not in manufacturing | 11 |
| in corporate planning | 4, 5 and 12 |
| in investment analysis or stockbroking | 4, 5, 8, 12 and 13 |
| a management consultant or a management student | All (!) |
| a banker or credit controller | 8 and 13 |
| an accountant | All, but 8 and 13 in particular |
| a tax or rate payer, an MP, civil servant, local authority counsellor or employee, a consumer of the services of, or an employee of, a nationalised industry | 14 |

† *There are no work sheets for Chapter 14 or 11.4, 11.6 to 11.8*

Table 1   How to make the best use of this book

## Historical Note

Ratios have been used by managers for a long time. Foulke [*Practical Financial Statement Analysis*, R.A. Foulke, McGraw-Hill, 1968] mentions them being used in 'the last few years of the nineteenth century'.

For those interested in the history of the subject, I would recommend: J.O. Horrigan's 'A Short history of financial ratio analysis', *The Accounting Review*, April 1968.

The earliest reference I have so far come across to management ratios is in *To Coin a Phrase: A Dictionary of Origins*, E. Radford and A. Smith, Macmillan, 1981, which informed me that the origin of the phrase 'going nineteen to the dozen', usually reserved for the compulsive talker, was in fact originally a standard of efficiency for Watt's steam-powered pumps used in the Cornish mines from the 1770s on. We read, for example, 'This week Wheal Fortune hath gone nineteen to the dozen', that is, had raised 19,000 gallons for every twelve bushels of coal used.

The idea of using a simple integrated set of ratios was tried by the Du Pont company in 1919 but was not made public until 1949 (see *Du Pont Chart System for Appraising Operating Performance*, C.A. Kline, Jr, and Howard L. Hessler, N.A.C.A. Bulletin, Conference Proceedings, August 1952, pp 1595-1619). Further important developments in this sphere took place in the 1950s when H. Ingham and L. Taylor Harrington made extensive studies of the choice and use of productivity, financial and operating ratios; formulated some basic principles of ratio selection; and devised the 'QAM' or 'pyramid' method of selecting ratios (see 'Pyramid structure – a pattern for comparative performance', H. Ingham and L. Taylor Harrington, *The Manager*, September 1956, pp 657-660). On this basis, they developed detailed systems (or 'family trees') of ratios meant to give an integrated view of company performance and capable of being amended to suit the needs of different industries and levels of management. This work, allied to the results of their study of methods of interfirm comparison, formed the basis for the setting up of the Centre for Interfirm Comparison in 1959, and for the later development of integrated ratio systems for many different industries and levels of management by the Centre and others.

The author joined the Centre in 1960 and, in the course of devising sets of ratios for a large number of industries, trades and professions, developed some ratio systems of more general applicability. They include:

the set of ratios dealing with gearing (Chapter 8); alternative ways of measuring asset utilisation (Appendix 1.1); and ratios for Stockbrokers – possibly the first to be developed for a profession (Chapter 11).

Some methods of analysis described in this book were developed by the author after leaving the Centre. They include:

1    Measuring the performance of departmental managers by the ratio of departmental contribution to departmental assets
2    Integrating capacity utilisation into the system
3    The sets of ratios for the individual investor, the stock exchange, the shopfloor, the personnel department, consultants, accountants, hotels
4    The integrated analysis described in Chapter 12
5    The concept of discretionary cash flow
6    The integrated analysis of published accounts in Chapter 13
7    The suggestions for selecting and using ratios in the public sector in Chapter 14.

The subject will no doubt continue to develop.

## Feedback

The author would be interested to hear from readers who have:

1    Any problems in using the ratios advocated
2    Any experiences of the use of the ratios described that they consider might usefully be included in any later edition of this book
3    Any suggestions for additions to or deletions from the sets of ratios outlined in this book together with the arguments for the course of action advocated.

It would be helpful if such readers gave an indication of their experience and background.

# PART ONE

# Chapter 1

# Principles of ratio selection

## 1.1 Why Ratios?

Most managers are only too familiar with being asked to study figures. But these are usually absolute figures of pounds, people, tons, hours, miles, and so on. So why ratios? The answer is that *no figure is meaningful in isolation*. To give a figure meaning, whether in private, public or business life, it must be compared, consciously or subconsciously, with another figure. A ratio expresses simply in one number the result of a comparison between two figures.

It is, for example, of little value to look at an item of expenditure in isolation. It is important to know why this expenditure is being incurred, what benefits it is hoped to gain from it, and whether the benefits can be measured and quantified. A measure of the effectiveness of the expenditure is then the ratio of the measured benefits to the expenditure.

Thus, a ratio can be improved by operating on either part of it, or, of course, on both parts. (Technically, if a ratio is expressed as a fraction, the item on top is the numerator and the item on the bottom is the denominator.) The operation can be aimed at increasing sales (or output or amount of benefit that is being produced) for the same cost, or at decreasing the cost (or input or effort) incurred for the same sales.

This equal emphasis on numerator and denominator is one of the advantages of the use of ratios. It helps to avoid the pitfall, inherent in the use of absolute figures, of considering for example, costs in isolation, which rapidly leads to the feeling that all costs are bad and should therefore be cut.

Let us look at three examples which show the advantages of using ratios rather than absolute figures:

1 *Transport*. When talking about the effectiveness of transport, it can be said that it took $x$ hours to get to a place. But this is generally subconsciously related to the distance travelled, and what in fact is used is the ratio of miles per hour.

2 *Production*. Two firms in the same period produce respectively 2000 and 3000 tractors. These absolute figures of output do not indicate which firm is the more efficient. If, however, it is known that the first firm employs fifty people and the second one hundred, it is evident that the first firm has the higher productivity: its ratio of 40 tractors per employee is higher than the second firm's 30. It may not, of course, be more profitable, but that is another story.

3 *Profit*. Two firms both make a £1000 profit, but which is the more profitable? Which needed less effort to earn that profit? If firm *A* achieved its profit with £10,000 sales and firm *B* took £100,000, *A* is the more profitable, with a profit margin on sales of ten per cent against *B's* one per cent.

## 1.2 How to Select Ratios

Before any ratios can be selected for an organisation, the objective or objectives of that organisation must be defined. Only if it is known where an organisation is trying to go can one measure how far it has gone.

If an organisation has a number of objectives, they must be ranked in some order or relative importance. Then, if there is a conflict between two objectives, it is known which must yield to the other. However, it must be appreciated that this ranking is not immutable. The relative order of importance of objectives is likely to change over the course of time. As one objective is achieved, another becomes more important. Priorities will also change in response to changes in outside pressures.

It must be known, too, how the achievement of these objectives has been divided up within the organisation and what are the sub-objectives of different parts of the organisation. Each part should have a reasonably clearly defined objective to aim for and the definition should be such that the sub-objective can be achieved without prejudicing the main objective of the organisation. This leads to the ten basic principles of ratio selection:

1    If possible, a manager must be provided with a single key ratio that indicates unequivocally the degree of his success, together with subsidiary ratios explaining how this success can be improved. In choosing the subsidiary ratios, it is useful to bear in mind the next six principles.

2    Ratios should be logically interrelated. A test of this is that they are mathematically related (the converse is not, however, true – see next paragraph). The formulae linking ratios in this book are given in the diagrams. Diagram 12–9 shows how the ratios in many of the diagrams are linked to each other.

3    Pseudo ratios must be avoided. Pseudo ratios – the results of dividing items that are not logically related – may be mathematically related to real ratios but do not measure any underlying business reality. The following examples of pseudo ratios may help to clarify the point:
      (a)    Interest paid/sales (per cent). Interest paid, particularly if it is on a fixed loan such as a debenture, is not affected by the level of sales, so it should not be shown as a ratio of sales but of the amount borrowed.
      (b)    Sales per production employee (£). Many firms sell, in addition to goods of their own manufacture, goods made or largely made by other firms (factored goods). This is done to offer a wide range of products to a firm's customers. The value of the sales of these factored goods is in no way the result of the efforts of the production employees and should therefore not be included in a ratio relating to them.

4    A manager must not be given ratios which cannot lead to action by him (either as an individual or, if necessary, jointly with colleagues).

5    A ratio must measure a material factor of the business, not a trivial one.

6    The ratio of the cost of obtaining the information to the likely benefit to management of having it must always be borne in mind.

7    The number of ratios provided to any one manager must be kept to the minimum.

There is no such thing as an ideal set of ratios suitable for all firms, all industries, all managers, at all times. Hence the next three basic principles:

8    Different ratios are required for different industries and even for different firms within an industry if they are operating in different ways.

9    Within a firm, different levels of management require different ratios and so do managers with different functional responsibilities but at the same level in the hierarchy.

10   A manager's need for specific ratios changes as his problems change.

This means that selecting ratios is an exercise which must be done for each firm and manager individually. There will however be considerable similarities between the results – otherwise it would not have been possible to write this book.

It also means that from time to time (say once a year) each manager should review the ratios he receives and ruthlessly weed out those which are no longer providing information that he needs for action. There is an insidious tendency for the amount of information a manager receives to grow. The quality of the information provided is vastly improved if, as with roses, the growth is vigorously pruned.

It is important that the key ratio, or the way in which it is used and interpreted, is such that neither:

(a)    the desire to achieve a 'good' figure for it does not inhibit the undertaking of activities which would be of benefit to the organisation; nor

(b)    a 'good' figure for it may be achieved by undertaking activities which are not of benefit to the organisation.

The risk of (a) may occur, when, for example, costs are incurred in one period and the benefits do not show through until a later period. The risk of (b) may occur, particularly at the subsidiary ratio level, where an action may benefit a part of the organisation but cause greater damage to the whole, and also, for example, when expenditure (on, for example, maintenance) is deferred to a later period.

## 1.3 Difficulties with Ratios and How to Overcome Them

Like all management tools, ratios can be misused. There are some situations where ratios can appear to be misleading if care is not taken. These situations, and the steps to take to avoid being misled, are described below.

If, for example, the following information about two firms in the same industry is provided:

| Firm | A | B |
|---|---|---|
| Growth (this year's sales/last year's sales) | 10% | 30% |

Firm *A* might be criticised for its very poor growth compared with firm *B*. But one of the things affecting a firm's growth is its share of the market. It is probably easier to expand a small share than one which is already very large. So it is necessary to interpret the above ratios in the light of each firm's share of the market, which is:

| Firm | A | B |
|---|---|---|
| Share of the market (per cent) | | |
| Now | 55 | 13 |
| A year ago | 50 | 10 |

Firm *A*'s poor growth rate is put in a different perspective by its very much larger share of the market. Moreover it has increased its share by five per cent while firm *B* has only captured another three per cent. The lesson of this example is that ratios must always be interpreted *in their context*.

As a further example, if a firm's ratio of selling costs to sales is high, efforts at improvement could be directed either toward increasing sales without an increase in costs or to reducing costs without a drop in sales. The latter might be impracticable because, for example, the sales force is of the minimum size necessary to cover the country without too much time wasted on travelling. Thus, when looking at ratios it may still be necessary to consider the *magnitude of the underlying figures*. Before leaving this example it is worth adding that in such a situation a firm could consider using agents in some parts of the country instead of salesmen.

Another situation where a ratio is potentially misleading is one where there is *no cause and effect linkage* between numerator and denominator, or where the link is very indirect or tenuous. These are the pseudo ratios already mentioned in this chapter. To give another example, if a firm switches from making a part to buying it in, its ratio of output to production employees will increase because either:

1  It has reduced its production employees by those who were previously making the part, or
2  It has used them to increase its output of finished goods.

But the productivity of that firm's workers has not necessarily increased. They are doing less of the work to make the product. That is why it is often better to use value added (sales less materials and bought out parts) as a measure of output.

It is most important to see that numerator and denominator are *measured and valued* in the same terms. The ratio of sales to stock, often quoted as 'stock turnover' frequently provides examples of failure to observe this rule. If, for example the figures are taken from a firm's published accounts, sales are at selling price, while stock is at cost, and sales are for a year, while stock is a figure at the year end.

Here is an example of how misleading such a ratio can be. Firm *A* and firm *B* have the following figures in their balance sheet:

| | A | B |
|---|---|---|
| Sales for year (£) | 1200 | 1200 |
| Stock at balance sheet date (£) | 200 | 200 |
| 'Stock Turnover' therefore | six times a year for both firms | |

However the following information (which may not be published depending on the statutory format for its profit and loss account chosen by the company) shows a very different picture:

| | A | B |
|---|---|---|
| Materials used during the year (£) | 800 | 600 |
| Average value of stock during the year (£) | 100 | 400 |
| Real stock turnover (times per year) | 8 | 1½ |

The answer here is to apply the valuation and definition principles of Chapter 3 *both* to the figures of your firm *and* to the figures of any other firm with whom you are making a comparison.

### 1.4 The Effect of Volume

Few costs increase uniformly with increases in volume so that their relationship with volume would be as line OA in Diagram 1–1.

Either there is a fixed element irrespective of volume (as in line BC), or there are higher discounts at higher volumes (DEF), on higher volumes call for overtime working at higher rates (GHI) or combinations of these possibilities.

Only OA gives a constant cost to volume ratio; in all other situations volume needs to be considered as one of the factors affecting either (a) changes in the cost/volume ratio over time or (b) differences in the ratio between companies. One approach to the problem of fixed costs is discussed in section 5.3. Another approach is to graph the two items in the form of a scatter diagram (see Diagram 1–3). The relationship may then be fitted by eye or by calculating a regression equation (for methodology see any elementary statistics textbook) and deviations from the relationship investigated if sufficiently material (i.e. in the diagram beyond the cut-off line whose location is determined pragmatically by management).

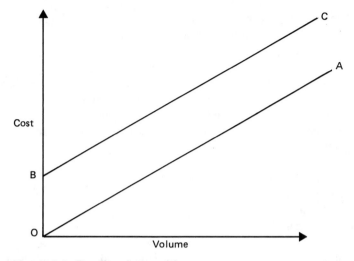

Diagram 1–1   The effect of volume (1)

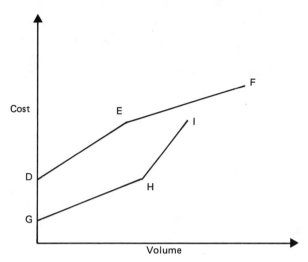

Diagram 1–2   The effect of volume (2)

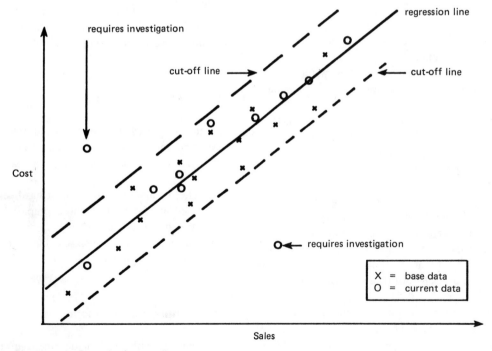

Diagram 1–3   Example of scatter diagram

5

In practice there may be several factors affecting the size of a ratio, and their relationship with the ratio may be more complex than a simple arithmetical one, or than can be dealt with by a simple diagram like 1–3. In such situations it may be desirable to use a technique called multiple regression analysis. For an example of this see Chapter 8.4 on Z scores.

## 1.5 Expressing a Ratio

All ratios are the result of dividing one number (the numerator) by another (the denominator) but there are various ways of expressing the answer to this division.

If the two numbers are measured in the same units the answer can be expressed as a ratio, as a pure number, as a percentage (%) or as a per mil (‰). For example £5 ÷ £100 can be expressed as:

1    The ratio 1:20, or
2    The pure number 0.05, or
3    The percentage 5%, or
4    The per mil 0.5‰

Method 1 is rarely used in business; however it is useful for relating more than two variables. The choice between 2, 3 or 4 is largely a matter of convention. For example, the ratio of current assets to current liabilities is usually measured by method 2 (for example 2.0 times) while the ratio of profit to sales is usually expressed as a percentage (for example 10.0%).

Ratios are often the result of dividing items measured in different units, such as money and people. In these cases none of the above methods is suitable. Indeed, care must be taken when presenting the answer to make it clear what units both numerator and denominator were measured in, such as pounds per head per year and *not* just pounds, or gallons per hour and not just gallons, and so on.

So much for labelling the ratios. An allied matter is the number of digits in the ratio. There are two points to bear in mind here: comprehension and accuracy.

Few managers (or any one else for that matter) can take in or comprehend more than about three or four digits. For most people, £153 million, or at the most £153.2 million, is just as meaningful as £153 187 529.73. In fact the former figure is probably more useful because it saves the manager the time and effort, not to mention the risk of error, in converting £153 187 529.73 in his head to £153 million.

The second point is that a ratio cannot be more accurate than the least accurate constituent of it. If £153 187 529.73 is divided by 225 000 people the answer cannot be accurate to more than two or at the most three significant figures, and should be written as:

£680 000 per head (two significant figures) or
£681 000 per head (three significant figures) *and not*
£680 833.46 per head (eight significant figures)

It is generally safe to write the result of a division as correct to one less significant figure than the less accurate of the numerator or denominator.

Just as a reminder to those who left mathematics behind them many years ago, a nought *is not* a significant figure unless it has a number other than nought on both sides of it. For example:

£500 is 1 significant figure
£0.005 is 1 significant figure
£501 is 3 significant figures
£0.105 is 3 significant figures

A final point, which I hope will not be considered pedantic. It is useful always to put a nought before a decimal point, such as £0.34 per head and not £.34. Without the nought the point can easily be overlooked by a hasty reader or disappear during photocopying or other duplicating and what was £0.34 becomes £34.

It will be seen that both our points of comprehension and accuracy lead in the same direction: fewer, rather than more, figures.

## 1.6 Asset Utilisation Ratios

The question of what ratios to use to measure asset utilisation is an important one (asset utilisation ratios occur in nearly every chapter of this book) but the answer is rather technical. It has therefore been dealt with in the following manner:

1    The discussion of the subject has been included in Appendix 1.1 which need not be read by those prepared to accept the conclusions on the strength of the author's experience.
2    The conclusions of the discussion have been incorporated in the text of the relevant chapters usually with little further reference to the discussion.

## 1.7 Presenting the Information

The frequency with which management are provided with the ratios described in this book depends on how often it is worth their taking action. This is a matter for individual management judgement. As one progresses down any management hierarchy there is a tendency for the frequency to increase.

The ratios can be presented in tables or in graphs. The latter is more expensive but it is preferable, as it has greater impact. If cost and space permits, it is useful to have a number of graphs on view simultaneously, with the graph of the key ratio for the particular manager at the top linked by suitable lines (as in the diagrams) to the graphs of the ratios measuring the factors affecting the key ratio (see Diagram 1–4).

As well as current performance, graphs can show budgeted performance, target performance, performance for 'same time last year', and competitors' behaviour (if known). It may also be possible to add limit lines to the graphs, such as, upper and lower, warning and action lines. Variations of the ratio within the upper and lower warning lines can be ignored but if the ratio crosses the warning line, and certainly if it crosses the action line, investigation and action are called for. [See M.J. Moroney, *Facts from Figures,* Chapter 11, 'Control Charts', Penguin, 1965.]

Most, if not all ratios need upper and lower warning lines because in most cases they have an optimum level. For example, too much advertising expenditure may be as harmful as too little; too fast a stock turnover may be as dangerous as too slow.

**Appendix 1.1**

**ASSET UTILISATION RATIOS**

There are at least three different ways of expressing the relationship between the value of assets and the values of sales. They are:

1    The number of times per year the asset is 'turned over' (sales divided by assets).
2    The number of days required to 'turn the asset over once' (assets divided by average daily sales).
3    The value of assets per £1000 of sales per year (assets divided by sales divided by 1000).

The advantages and disadvantages of each method will be considered in turn.

**Times per Year Method**

The first method, which is the one used by Dun & Bradstreet, the leading American firm of mercantile inquiry agents, has the advantage that the number so obtained,

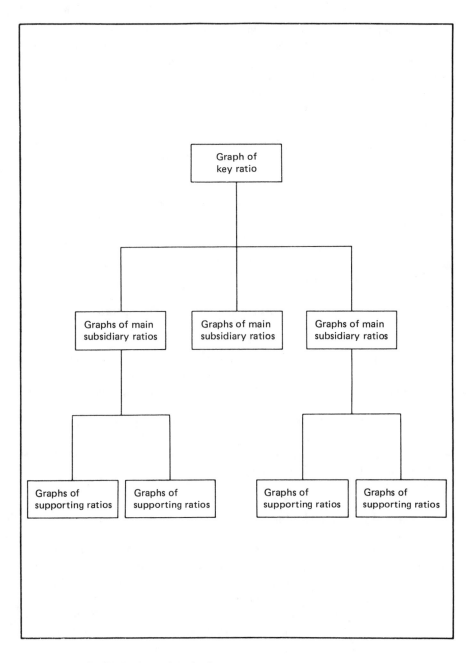

Diagram 1–4   Graphical presentation of ratios

7

when used to multiply the profit margin on sales, will give the profit on assets ratio. For example, if a firm's profit margin on sales is 10 per cent and it turns its assets over twice a year, then its profit on assets will be 20 per cent (10 per cent × 2).

However, when one is looking for the *causes* of a difference between a firm's turnover of assets and standard, the 'times per year' method is at a disadvantage in that the relationship between the turnover of the constituent parts of total assets and the turnover of total assets involves reciprocals, which most of us are not very happy about calculating in our heads. For example, if one divides assets between fixed and current, then, using the times a year method, the relationship is as follows:

> The reciprocal of the turnover of total assets is equal to the reciprocal of the turnover of current assets plus the reciprocal of the turnover of fixed assets.

Both the 'days' and the '£/£1000' methods avoid this disadvantage. If asset utilisation is measured in either of these ways, then the relationship mentioned in the previous paragraph would be as follows:

> The utilisation of total assets is equal to the utilisation of current assets plus the utilisation of fixed assets.

This is much simpler than the first relationship. This relative simplicity is illustrated by the figures in Table 1–1, which shows both the times per year method and the £/£1000 method applied to the same basic sterling figures. It is easy to see under the £/£1000 method that the £250 increase in total investment in relation to sales over the standards of £667 has resulted from the combination of £150 extra in current assets and £100 extra in fixed assets. Under the times per year method, little light is thrown on the total variance of 0.41 by the current and fixed variances of 1.35 and 0.50 – both of which are larger than the total which they are analysing.

## 'Days' Method *v.* £/£1000 Method

On the grounds that they avoid the use of reciprocals, both the 'days' method and the '£/£1000' method are equally preferable to the 'times per year' method for use in analysing causes of differences in a total asset utilisation figure. However, the 'days' method has two disadvantages when compared with the '£/£1000' method. The first is not, perhaps, a very important one; the second, however, is material. Some, with the writer, will find it bordering on the ridiculous to talk of 'turning over' such assets as land and buildings either so many times a year or in so many days. Others, perhaps with less pictorial imaginations may not, however, find this irritating.

| Method | Times per year method | | | £/£1000 method | | |
|--------|----------|--------|----------|----------|--------|----------|
| Asset | Standard | Actual | Variance | Standard | Actual | Variance |
| Total | 1.50 | 1.09 | 0.41 | 667 | 917 | 250 |
| Current | 3.75 | 2.40 | 1.35 | 267 | 417 | 150 |
| Fixed | 2.50 | 2.00 | 0.50 | 400 | 500 | 100 |

Table 1–1  Comparison of times per year method and £/£1000 method

A way of avoiding this difficulty is to use the expression 'the number of days required to turn the capital invested in an asset over once'. But this is getting very clumsy.

The second and more important disadvantage of the 'days' method arises when, and if, the analysis is continued one stage further and splits current assets into, say, raw materials stock, work in progress, finished goods and debtors. If, for its obvious analytical advantage, the arithmetical relationship is maintained whereby the figure for total current asset utilisation equals the sum of the figures for the utilisation of its constituent parts, then raw material stock turnover must be measured by dividing raw material stock (valued at cost) by average daily sales (valued at selling price). This will yield a ratio which is potentially very misleading.

Most managers, when told that their stock is turned over in so many days, will assume that on average an item stays that number of days in stock. If, however, a firm's materials-cost/sales ratio is 50 per cent (a not untypical figure for British manufacturing industry), then his assumption will be 100 per cent out. Such a situation is not likely to improve management's confidence in the reporter.

The £/£1000 method avoids both of these disadvantages of the 'days' method. (The reason why a thousandth part of sales was chosen was because it allows the smallest asset item which it is useful to measure to be expressed as a whole number and thus simplifies presentation.)

It is therefore suggested that the £/£1000 method be used in preference to the 'days' method in analysing the causes of a difference between a firm's sales/assets ratio and standard.

## 'Real' Days Method

In addition to using the £/£1000 method, with its advantage of arithmetical inter-relationships, it may be useful to present current asset turnover in terms of 'real' days (as opposed to 'days' in the 'days required to turn over once' method) because of the easily grasped significance of this everyday unit of measurement.

This may be done by dividing raw material stocks by either the value of average daily materials issued to production (the flow of materials on to the shop floor) or the value of average daily materials purchased (the flow of materials into stock); and by dividing finished stock by either average daily sales (valued in the same way as finished stock, for example at factory cost) or by the average daily value of goods entering the finished store.

Debtors may simply be divided by average daily sales, although even here allowance may have to be made for the effect of cash discounts on the value of numerator or denominator. Work in progress is probably best divided by the average of materials issued to production and completed goods entering finished store.

## Relationship Between Measurements

Diagram 1–5 illustrates the relationship between the various terms which have been used. The vertical axis measures the average value per day; the horizontal axis the average number of days. On both axes the days are 'real' days. The diagram is simplified to the extent of assuming that stock levels are not rising or falling.

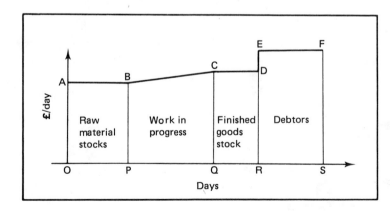

Diagram 1–5   Stock turnover ratios, flow of materials and time in stock

OA equals the average daily value of raw materials purchased, and PB equals the average daily value of raw material issued to production. OP equals the average number of days raw material stays in stock. The area OABP therefore equals the average value of raw material stock.

PQ equals the average number of days required to make a product (shop-floor time) and QC equals the average daily value of completed products. The area PBCQ represents the average value of work in progress.

QR equals the average number of days finished goods stay in stock; RD equals the average daily value of sales (at cost). The area QCDR therefore equals the average value of finished goods stock.

RS equals the average number of days' credit taken by customers, and RE equals the average daily value of sales (selling price); SF equals the average daily value of cash received from debtors. The area REFS therefore equals the average value of debtors.

The current asset utilisation ratios which are measured in terms of £s per £1000 are the areas OABP, PBCQ, QCDR and REFS divided by sales (RE × 365) divided by 1000. The ratios which are measured in terms of days are the lengths OP, PQ, QR and RS.

The fact that the vertical heights increase as one moves from left to right in the diagram emphasises that a day at a later stage in the production/sales process ties up more capital than one at an earlier stage.

The diagram illustrates incidentally the somewhat arbitrary nature of the accountant's conventional assumptions about overhead absorption and the point at which profit is made. As all the stages from O to S are necessary to earn the profit, could it not be argued that the line ABCDEF should be much smoother?

## Fixed Asset Utilisation

The measurement of fixed asset utilisation, even by such a simple method as we are using, has its problems too. One of these derives from the fact that although the value of a fixed asset declines over its useful life, it is thought to be rare for the value of the sales which it helps to produce to decline at the same rate.

The result of this is a tendency for the utilisation of a fixed asset (whichever of the three methods mentioned earlier may be used to measure this) to appear to improve as the asset gets older. However, we want an improvement in utilisation to indicate an increase in the value or number of saleable objects produced and not just an increase in age. A way out of this dilemma is to measure fixed asset utilisation in two ways: by dividing the fixed asset's depreciated value by sales and then by dividing the fixed asset's original cost by sales. If one also divides the fixed asset's depreciated value by its original cost to get its percentage unexpired life, one can complete the explanation of a difference in fixed asset utilisation in the way indicated by ratios 2, 4 and 5 in Diagram 1–6.

The analysis does not have to stop at this point. The following are *some* of the ratios used to analyse causes of differences between firms' ratio of fixed assets to sales:

| *Ratio* | *Purpose of ratio* |
|---|---|
| 1  Value of land and buildings/Sales.<br>2  Value of plant and machinery/Sales.<br>3  Value of vehicles/Sales. | To narrow down in which fixed asset there is more or less invested. |
| 4  Value of land and buildings per sq ft<br>5  Sales per sq ft | To indicate to what extent a high ratio 1 is due to using expensive property (ratio 4) or under-utilisation of floor space (ratio 5). |
| 6  Plant and machinery/Direct production employees<br>7  Output/Direct production employees | To show how much a high ratio 2 is the result of high mechanisation (ratio 6) or low 'productivity' (ratio 7). |
| 8  Picks woven/Maximum possible picks<br>9  Square yards of cloth woven per loom per year | To measure the physical (as opposed to financial) productivity of, in this case, looms. Different ratios would be used in different industries to attain the same objective. |

## Conclusion

To sum up: when presenting asset utilisation ratios to management, different methods of measurement should be used at different stages of the analysis of which these ratios form a part.

At the beginning when one is using the

$$\frac{\text{Profit}}{\text{Assets}} = \frac{\text{Profit}}{\text{Sales}} \times \frac{\text{Sales}}{\text{Assets}}$$

relationship the 'times per year' method should be used for its unique property of multiplying the profit margin on sales ratio to give the profit on assets ratio.

At the next two stages the '£/£1000' method should be used because by this method the relationship between the utilisation of total assets and the utilisation of its constituent parts is one of simple addition and because it avoids the potential confusion of the 'days' method. These two stages are the division of total assets between fixed and current, and the sub-division of these two groups into, for example, land and buildings, and plant and machinery on the one hand, and stocks and debtors on the other.

It is probably useful to present individual current asset utilisation ratios in terms of real days as well as so many £s per £1000 of sales; while fixed asset utilisation can be further analysed to extract the age factor.

The set of ratios shown in Diagram 1–6 was devised by the author while at the Centre for Interfirm Comparison and is used in many of its comparisons.

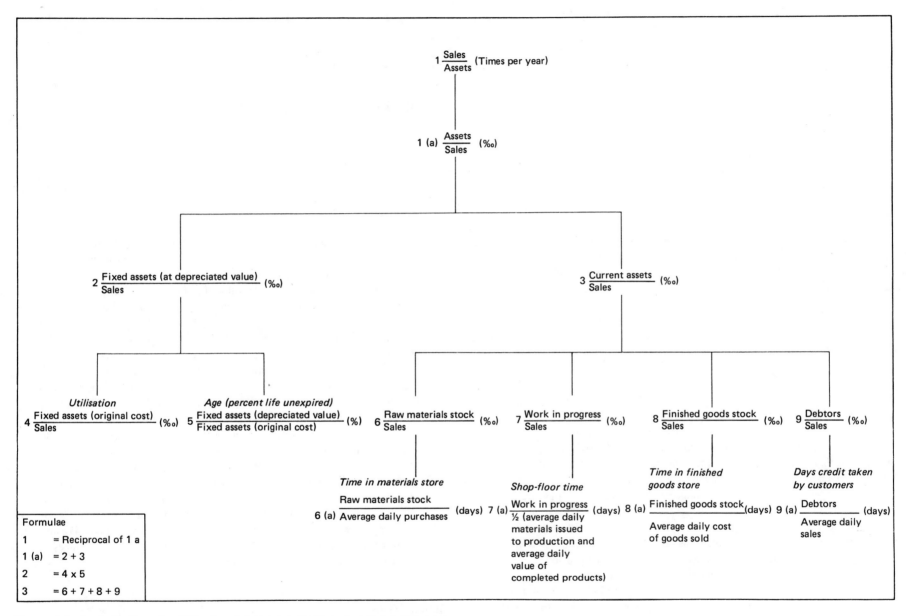

Diagram 1–6  Asset utilisation ratios. With acknowledgements to the Centre for Interfirm Comparison

11

# Chapter 2

# Standards of comparison

Just as no *figure* is meaningful in isolation, so no *ratio* is meaningful in isolation. All ratios must be compared with a standard to determine whether or not they are at a satisfactory level. This chapter deals with the relative value and availability of the standards which can be used for comparison with a firm's actual results.

## 2.1 Internal Standards

### The firm's own past

This is the most readily available and most frequently used standard. Admittedly it is not available to a new firm or to one just starting up an activity it has not previously carried on. It has the advantage of comparing 'like with like': the products and manufacturing and selling methods are the same, or similar, and the methods by which the figures have been arrived at are consistent over time.

The disadvantage of comparing performance with the same firm's past are fivefold:

1    The standards achieved in the past may have been poor and to compare with them may encourage a dangerous degree of complacency. Alternatively last year's figures may have been exceptionally good and a comparison with them may engender unnecessary gloom.
2    The level of activity in the economy as a whole, and in any part of it, is continually changing. This means that an apparent improvement may be the result more of a change in the economy than of an increase in the efficiency of any part of it. Here there is a danger of unwarranted self congratulation. Obviously the reverse can happen: a downturn in the economy can cause some ratios to get worse and it may be that there is little that management can or could do. Here the danger is unnecessary and unproductive self accusation.
3    The state of technology is continually, if not constantly, advancing. This means that a level of achievement which may have been perfectly satisfactory in the past is no longer acceptable now.
4    If a ratio has only the numerator or the denominator expressed in money terms (e.g. sales per employee) and if it relates to the past, its reliability is eroded by the effects of inflation. If both numerator and denominator are measured in money terms (e.g. profit/sales) it is possible that inflation has affected both equally and its effects will have cancelled out. If one of the parts of the ratio being considered is derived from information relating to the past (e.g. the cost of assets) while the other is not (e.g. sales) the effects of inflation are very unlikely to cancel out.
5    Methods of accounting for some items may change within a company, although if they do the company should adjust past figures on to a comparable basis. The statutory requirement to do so only covers last year's figures in the profit and loss account and balance sheet and does not cover any five or ten year summary. Care also needs to be taken if using figures from more than one document that there have not been changes in accounting policies between documents.

### Budgets/targets/forecasts

These are probably better standards of comparison than a firm's own past in that they should have taken into account:

1   Changes in the level of the economy and/or the industry concerned.
2   Changes in the state of technology.
3   Changes in the value of money.

Most budgets are however heavily influenced by what has been achieved in the past and if a firm's performance in the past has been poor the budget may set a standard which is too low. This undue reliance on the past is something which Zero Base Budgeting tries to get away from but it probably remains a relatively under-used technique (see, for example 'Accountants' role in zero base budgeting', B. Neumann, J.D. Suver and R.L. Brown, *CPA Journal,* January 1978, for a useful, brief introduction to the subject, or 'The ZBA path to improved efficiency', D. Guy and T. Bevington, *Accountancy,* May 1983, or *Zero Base Budgeting: A practical management tool for evaluating expenses,* P.A. Pyrr, Wiley, 1973 or 'Will ZBB ever catch on', B. McSweeney, *The Accountant,* 4 August 1983, p. 23).

All forecasts are of course fallible; no human being is omniscient. This introduces a potential weakness in using budgets (which must be based on forecasts) as a standard of comparison that is not present in a pure comparison with the past.

Not only are forecasts fallible but, as every manager knows, each person who helps to produce a company's budget is subject to different degrees of optimism or pessimism. This is a perfectly natural, human state of affairs, but it must not be forgotten, when using a budget as a standard of comparison, that it was compiled by ordinary, warm-blooded, fallible human beings. The fallibility of forecasts is discussed at some length in a chapter entitled 'How accurate are profit forecasts?' which I contributed to a book entitled *Profit forecasts: How they are made, reviewed and used'* which I edited for Gower (1983) and see also *Behavioural aspects of budgeting* by D. Otley, Institute of Chartered Accountants in England and Wales, 1977.

## 2.2 External Standards – Other Firms

Comparing performance with that of other firms has a number of advantages:

1   Whereas performance in the past may have been poor and therefore not a particularly good standard for comparison, if a reasonably wide and representative sample of other firms can be examined, it should be possible to perceive standards of good performance, or at least better performance than the company has so far achieved.
2   It is possible to compare results over similar periods to ensure similar economic and technological conditions.
3   Comparing performance with what other firms have achieved avoids the difficulties associated with budgets, namely their subjective elements and their (necessarily) fallible forecasts of the future.

The process of comparing the performance of a firm with that of other companies has a number of problems attached to it:

1   How similar are the other firms?
2   How can the information be obtained?
3   How reliable is the information?

### Standards of similarity

Many managers stress the importance of comparing 'like with like', but how important is it to do this? Taken to its extreme this statement would lead to comparing a firm with one which was identical in all respects – its products, its size, its location and so on – including its ratios! As ratios would be identical, nothing could be learned from the comparison. Obviously we must allow some difference, but how great a gap is permissible for the comparison to be useful? The answer is that the gap should not be so wide that it cannot be bridged by management action.

The size of a tolerable gap between activities varies with the ratio being compared. The more general a ratio the wider the range of firms it can be compared with. For example: all commercial organisations are out to make a profit from the use of their assets, so it is worth comparing this ratio with firms not only in the same industry but also in other, allied industries because this may indicate the desirability (or otherwise) of diversification. On the other hand it is only worth comparing the ratio of (say) 'shoes made per operative' with other shoe manufacturers.

The permissible width of the gap between firms compared depends on the time horizon of the management. The farther they are prepared to look ahead the wider the possible courses of action. For example, at one time Cunard would have compared itself with other *shipping* companies. With a wider horizon, management looked at other *travel* companies.

The firms with which it is worthwhile for a company to compare itself are:

1   Competitors
2   Potential competitors
3   Firms operating in fields which the company might enter (or should at least consider entering).

Obviously such comparisons must be made with thought, care and judgement; but that is what management is paid for!

In comparing like with like, most managers will want to compare themselves with a company of similar size. In all my work with ratios however I rarely found that the size of firms had any significant, measurable effect on the ratios. This view is supported by one of the conclusions in *Management policies and practices, and business performance,* Centre for Interfirm Comparison, 1977, as follows 'Size . . . was in no way related to the overall performance of firms in any of the industries studied.' (p. 153). This is perhaps not so surprising as it may seem at first sight, because size will probably affect both the numerator and the denominator of most ratios and the size effect will cancel out or be diluted. Dun and Bradstreet, on the other hand, have found that size does affect some of the ratios which they use. The difference between their experience and mine may be partly accounted for by their use of published accounts (see below). An exception to the general rule in my own experience is firms of accountants where smaller firms were less profitable to their partners than larger ones (see Chapter 11, Appendix 11.1).

Sources of information about companies

At this stage let us examine where information about companies (including your own) may be obtained.

Diagram 2–1 shows in outline the paths along which information about companies flow. It starts at the top with the events which happen inside the company (the myriad daily activities of buying, selling, making and moving; of cash coming in and going out, etc.). The next two boxes are very important for an understanding of what follows. They illustrate the fact that by no means everything that happens in a company is measured (or is indeed measurable) and recorded. What is recorded will vary from company to company and over time. Recording costs money and has to be (or at least should be) justified in terms of the value of the information generated. Marks and Spencers are famous for an exercise in cutting out unnecessary paperwork (see, for example, 'Simplification for efficiency' by M.J. Glenn, *The Manager,* June 1959).

What has been recorded will then be classified and aggregated according to the conventions and nomenclature of the company.

What this means for the information seeker is that in some cases what he wants is just not available, or if it is, is not in the format he wants. Sometimes the raw data can be reprocessed to meet his needs, but this will often be expensive and, especially with computerised systems, sometimes virtually impossible.

Once the data have been processed they become available to different users in many different ways. Each will be considered in turn; but all users need to ask: is this the information I want, is it reliable, it is comparable, is it timely, is it comprehensive, and how much does it cost?

*Management accounts* should provide their users within a company with the information they want, and on a timely basis. If not, then their accountant is not doing his job properly, or maybe they are a smaller company which has not yet realised the benefit of having a management accountant. He need not, incidentally, be a full time employee – a company's auditor should be able to provide a management accounting service, as well as the more usual tax and auditing work.

Management accounts are rarely audited and they may therefore be less reliable than audited accounts. However, they are usually far more useful and any suspected unreliability can be checked out fairly quickly by the company's own staff. Larger companies have internal auditors whose job involves, among other things, checking on the reliability of information flows.

*Accounts for shareholders* usually contain far less information than management accounts, and are prepared less frequently and more slowly. The shareholder has little or no say on their content. This is governed mainly by company law. The shareholders' accounts will, however, have been audited and should therefore be more reliable than management accounts. The shareholders' accounts should be comparable over time (or changes in reporting methodology should be highlighted in the year of change) but are less comparable between companies than many users would wish. (However see Chapter 13 on using these accounts.)

*Accounts filed with the Registrar of companies* are either the same as those sent to shareholders or an abbreviated version of them. Companies however sometimes delay filing their accounts. Their usefulness is therefore similar to, or less than, those for shareholders.

Some *Trade Associations* collect performance data from members. Such data's usefulness usually falls somewhere between those of management and shareholders' accounts. Their content will reflect a compromise between what members want to know and what they are prepared to reveal. The returns are not often audited but may be subject to some limited review. Depending on how clearly the information has been defined it should be more comparable between members than either published or management accounts. Depending on the energy of the Trade Association and the responsiveness of the members the information should be reasonably timely.

*Government departments* collect data about companies either as a by-product of some other process (e.g. tax collection, payment of unemployment benefit) or to help the management of the economy. Some of it is then published, usually in aggregate form. The data may be what you need but the influence of non-government users on their content is small. It is difficult to assess their reliability, but one must exercise some caution, as the data providers are often less than enthusiastic about filling in the questionnaires in the first place. When using such data it is most important to check how they were collected, by whom, from whom (often a sample), for what purposes (what biases may this have introduced?) and to look at a copy of the questionnaire (if there was one) to see how items were defined.

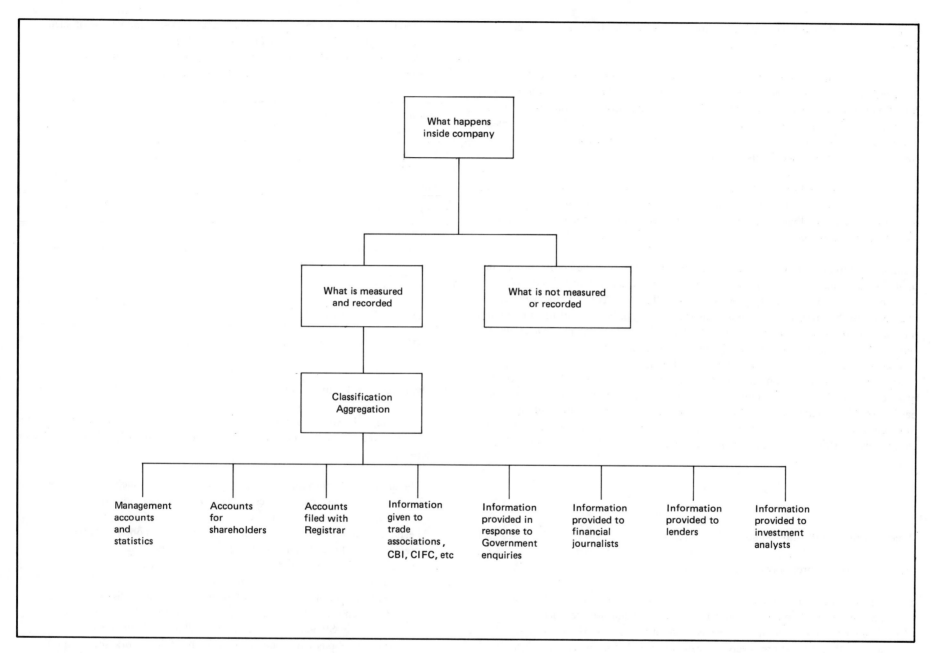

Diagram 2–1   Information about companies

The speed with which government statistics are produced varies from weeks to years.

*Journalists.* Useful information about companies can often be gleaned from the financial press (e.g. *Financial Times, Economist, Investors' Chronicle*) and trade press. It will be timely, but readers must form their own judgement on its reliability. Some journalists are very good at winkling out stories from a variety of well informed and/or indiscreet sources. Others may be more interested in an exciting story and less concerned with cross checking its reliability.

*Lenders* (e.g. Banks, Finance Companies) may, because of their strong negotiating position, be better able to ask for, and obtain, the information they want from a company than many other users. However they need to be particularly careful about its reliability and timeliness.

*Stockbrokers* and investment analysts have access not only to all the information in the public domain but, for companies in which they are particularly interested, will also have meetings with these companies and discuss their results and plans with senior managers. Both parties to such discussions should beware however of the limitations imposed by the law and rules on 'Insider Dealing' (see, for example, *Guidelines to Insider Dealing,* the Society of Investment Analysts, May 1981).

Some of these sources will now be examined in more depth.

Appendix 2.1 is a guide on how to trace company information. This was originally produced by A.L. Smyth, Commercial Librarian, Central Library, Manchester, and has been updated and revised by his successor, Alec Gallimore. I am grateful to them for permission to reproduce it here. Appendix 2.2 gives details of many sources of comparative performance data. Appendix 2.3 contains examples of the data available from some of these sources.

## Accounts filed with the Registrar of Companies

There are broadly three ways of examining these:

1    Visiting the appropriate Companies Registry (see Table 2–1) (for addresses see Chapter 13.5) and purchasing a fiche of the latest accounts. This costs £1. To read this one needs a microfiche reader. There are some at each Registry. Alternatively one can obtain a photocopy from the fiche (i.e. full size) at a cost of 10p per page.

2    Obtaining the same information via a Search Agent (addresses of such agents from Yellow Pages under Company Registration Agents).

3    Using an organisation which summarises published accounts. There are several of these which are listed (in alphabetical order) in Appendix 2.2.

| Accounts obtainable at | London | Cardiff | Edinburgh | Belfast |
|---|---|---|---|---|
| Company registered at | | | | |
| London | Y | Y | D | N |
| Cardiff | Y | Y | D | N |
| Edinburgh | D | D | Y | N |
| Belfast | N | N | N | Y |
| Key  Y = Yes<br>N = No<br>D = Yes, but with a delay of 10 days | | | | |

Table 2–1   Availability of information at Companies Registries

## Disadvantages of published accounts

Before looking at the various sources of information based on published accounts it is desirable to consider their limitations (but see also Chapter 13, 'Using published accounts'):

1    The amount of information which is published is extremely limited, but has grown over the years as a result of changes in legislation and the work of the Stock Exchange and the Accounting Standards Committee. In 1968 I estimated that only 10–20 per cent of the information obtainable from an organised interfirm comparison could have been obtained from published accounts. That percentage has grown since then to perhaps up to 40 per cent – mainly as a result of the Companies Act 1981.

2    The small amount of information which is available in published accounts has often been arrived at in different ways by different firms – although the Accounting Standards Committee is seeking to limit the variety of accounting methods (for a description of the ASC's work see Chapter 13.3).

3 Not all organisations have to publish accounts – a division of a large organisation does not. The Companies Act 1981 has paradoxically both increased and decreased the amount and comparability of information available to users of company accounts. The amount of information that must be sent to all shareholders has been substantially increased, but the amount of information that must be filed at Companies House by medium and small companies (see Chapter 13.4), and thus made available to users of accounts other than shareholders, has been reduced. However, some medium and small companies may file at Companies House the same full accounts that they send to their shareholders in order to avoid the cost of preparing a second set only for filing.

4 By the time some information is published – some Government statistics are notorious for this – they are of more use to economic historians than to practical managers.

5 Very few firms take into account the effects of inflation on their figures, and this can have a considerably distorting effect.

6 Figures shown in the balance sheet (of stock for example) may be untypical of the level carried on average over the year. It is potentially dangerous to relate stock as shown in the balance sheet to the sales figure in order to arrive at stock turnover.

As management may have to use published information in the absence of any other it is desirable to spell out in more detail some of the limitations summarised above. These limitations, and the steps taken by ASC to minimise them, are classified under the items in the accounts which are affected.

*Fixed assets* (land, buildings, plant, machinery, vehicles). As a result of the combined effects of inflation and the (relatively) long life of these assets, the figure shown for them in a firm's historical cost accounts is likely to understate their current value. As the pattern of purchases of these assets over the course of time is likely to differ between firms, the effects of inflation will also differ, rendering the figures to a large extent non-comparable. Some firms will have revalued some or all of their fixed assets while most will have not. Often firms have had different parts of their total fixed assets valued at different dates. All this introduces a further element of non-comparability.

To overcome these disadvantages valuations given in the Directors' Report or the Notes to the Accounts should be used whenever possible in preference to the historical cost figures.

Different firms adopt different rates and methods of depreciation. To some extent this will reflect differences in intensity of use, maintenance policy, and estimates of the rate of obsolescence of the assets concerned. Such differences do not make the figures non-comparable but difference due solely to different bookkeeping practices (e.g. straight-line or reducing balance methods) do. It is not possible to distinguish between the two causes from published information. This situation has been improved, but not completely remedied, by SSAP 12, *Accounting for Depreciation* which came into effect from 31 December 1978 but does not apply to 'investment properties'. At the time of writing this SSAP is under review by ASC and may be amended (see *A review of SSAP 12 – Accounting for Depreciation,* ASC, 1982, and ED 37, *Accounting for Depreciation,* ASC, 1985).

Only owned assets are shown in a firm's balance sheet; assets which are leased, rented or hired are not. Such differences may not affect the ratio of profit to assets because a firm renting some of its fixed assets will have a smaller figure for the assets, but also a smaller figure for its profit (because the rent charge will have been deducted) than the firm owning all its assets. But this difference will affect such ratios as sales to assets or assets to employees and, to a lesser extent, profit to sales, because of the likelihood that the rent charge for an asset will be higher than the depreciation of the same asset. When SSAP 21 (published August 1984) on leased assets comes into effect (latest date is years commencing on or after 1 July 1987), this situation will be improved but not totally remedied as SSAP 21 requires only 'finance leases' but not 'operating leases' to be capitalised. Finance leases are those that transfer substantially all the risks and rewards of ownership of an asset to the lessee.

The treatment of *government grants* adopted by firms affects the figure of fixed assets shown in the balance sheet. Some firms deduct the grant from the asset; other firms credit the grant to a reserve. The figure for profit should however not be affected by different treatments of government grants as a result of SSAP 4, which requires the grant to be amortised to the profit and loss account over the life of the asset if it has been credited to reserve. This has the same effect as depreciating the net of grant cost of the asset.

*Current assets* (stock, debtors, cash). Only year-end figures for these assets are shown in a firm's balance sheet whereas the level of these assets may fluctuate considerably during the year. Different firms will probably value their stocks in different ways, e.g. the amount of overheads included or the size of any writedown to net realisable value – although SSAP 9 has reduced the scope for this. These differences will affect such ratios as stocks/sales, debtors/sales, assets to sales, profits to assets, assets per employee.

The figures for debtors (and for creditors) in a related company's balance sheet (such as that of a holding or subsidiary company) may be distorted because the indebtedness of related companies as a result of intra-group trading will be shown in a separate item often described as holding/subsidiary company current account. The debtor turnover (sales/debtors) of such companies will tend therefore to be overstated.

*Profit.* Because of differences in methods of depreciation of fixed assets, valuation of stock and work-in-progress, the treatment of pension costs, extraordinary items, overseas operations, development costs, deferred taxation, goodwill, and in policies of hiring or buying assets, the figure of profit is likely to be not comparable between firms.

The profit of owner-manager firms may be depressed by the owners taking profits out of the firm in the form of directors' salaries (which are deductions from profit) rather than in dividends (which are not). However the relative attraction of salaries compared to dividends has been diminished by the March 1985 Budget's removal of the ceiling on employers' National Insurance Contributions (see *The Accountant,* 28 March 1985, p. 7; 30 May, p. 11; 24 July, p. 26; and *UK taxation of the family company,* Arthur Andersen & Co, 1986).

Transactions between related companies (holding and/or subsidiary companies) in goods and/or services may not be at 'open market' prices (an element of levy or subsidy may be present). This will affect the profits and may affect the turnover of individual companies within a group but should not affect the consolidated results of the group.

The manner in which research and development is financed within a group and the way in which finance is raised and paid for within a group may also affect the reported profits of companies within the group, but not that of the group as a whole.

*Employees.* No distinction between part-or full-time workers is required in the figures for employees given in a firm's accounts. To the extent that a firm employs people part-time its ratios of sales, assets and remuneration per employee are depressed. Nor is a distinction required between males, females, adults or juveniles. This means the ratio of average employee's remuneration may differ between firms because of a difference in the proportion of the above categories of workers employed by each firm.

If a firm uses out-workers or sub-contracts some of its work then its sales per employee will tend to be higher than of a firm which does not, as out-workers are not normally considered to be employees.

If a firm works more than one shift, then assets per employee will appear lower than for a similar firm working only one shift.

The figure of employees combines factory workers with sales and office staff. The figure of average remuneration is therefore also affected by the make-up of the total work force.

## Causes of delay in publishing information

The time that elapses between the end of a firm's financial year and the availability of its results is made up of the following elements:

1  Preparation of the accounts
2  Auditing of the accounts
3  Printing of the accounts
4  Circulating the accounts to shareholders
5  Filing the accounts at Companies House
6  Searching of these files
7  Calculations (if any) on the extracted information
8  Printing and publishing the information.

Directors receive information at the end of stages 1 and/or 2; shareholders at stage 4; those prepared to go to Companies House at stage 5; those who rely on sources such as *The Times 1000* at Stage 8. Stage 8 may be delayed by the fact that firms' year ends differ and the need to wait for the firm with the latest year end.

For information on the time allowed, and taken, by companies to file accounts see Chapter 13.4.

## Processing methods of intermediate agencies

There are at least four methods by which the published data of firms are processed by intermediate agencies for the use of interested parties.

1  The accounts for a number of past years are summarised in one document. This is the method used to produce Extel cards (see Table 2–2 in Appendix 2.3). The minimum of processing has been done but the reader is saved the laborious and time consuming search at Companies House. Cards for a company may be revised several times a year as events require.

2  Selected figures and ratios for a number of firms are tabulated in one document. This is the method of *Management Today* (Table 2–3), the NEDO league tables, Inter Company Comparisons Limited (Table 2–4), and Jordans. Firms can be tabulated in order of size (as in *The Times 1000*) (Table 2–5) or some criteria of profitability (as in the NEDO league tables) or growth (*Management Today* Growth League) or in alphabetical order (Jordans) (Table 2–6) or separately for each ratio (as in Inter Company Comparisons).

3  The figures for a number of firms are added together to produce a 'consolidated' profit and loss account and balance sheet for an industry. This is the method which is used in the *Financial Times Trend of Industrial Profits* (Table 2–7).

4    Selected ratios for individual firms are calculated and then the median and the upper and lower quartile ratios are calculated.* This is the method which I used in my book *A Study of Profitability in the Hosiery and Knitwear Industry* for the Hosiery and Knitwear Economic Development Council. Table 2–8 is an example of one of the tables from that book.

The 'League Table' approach (method 2) has two advantages over the statistical approaches of methods 3 and 4.

1    It is possible to see the combination of ratios achieved by each individual firm – to see, for example, how fast a firm with a high profitability turns its stock over.
2    Businessmen in the industry can add to the figures their own knowledge of the firm's operations and thus improve the interpretation of the ratios.

The 'consolidated' approach (method 3) has the disadvantage that all the figures will be heavily influenced by the larger firms. The 'median' approach (method 4) may overcome or circumvent some of the limitations of published data. Ratios calculated from figures in published accounts, which suffer from the limitations already discussed, tend either to be too large or too small. Use of the quartiles excludes the largest and smallest quarters of the range and may therefore exclude the most distorted figures.

## Organised interfirm comparisons

As mentioned above, comparisons of ratios which can be derived from published accounts of companies have limitations which make them less than ideal as a basis for management decisions. Only some of the comparative ratios needed by management (and recommended in this book) are available from published accounts, and even that

---

*1    Median and quartiles are calculated by listing all the figures for a ratio (such as profit/total assets) from the smallest to the largest. The median is the figure in the middle of the list, the lower quartile is one-quarter of the way up the list, the upper quartile is three-quarters of the way up.

2    The median is used, rather than the arithmetical average, as a measure of typical performance because it is less affected by extreme values which may be untypical and/or the result of the distortions arising from the use of published data.

3    The quartiles and the median divide the sample into four equal parts and give an indication of the range of results. Half the sample lies between the upper and lower quartiles (termed the interquartile range).

4    As the process of calculating the median and quartiles is repeated for each ratio, the median for each ratio is likely to be derived from a different firm.

information may not be sufficiently comparable to enable management to make firm decisions based on a study of it.

In order to enable firms to obtain better data properly organised interfirm comparisons are desirable. These involve firms in pooling their data under agreed conditions of confidentiality and comparability with some central organisation. The latter carefully checks and processes the data, then issues reports showing each participant's results anonymously under code numbers (together with medians and quartiles etc.). Ideally, the comparisons should relate to a carefully chosen set of ratios and supporting data which show each participant in a systematic and logical fashion how his performance compares with that of others and why it differs. The ratios and other yardsticks should cover every significant aspect of performance and should be supplemented by background data which enable participants to take into account the effect on comparative performance of company characteristics and practices such as size; product range; location; production, distribution and marketing methods; and other relevant factors. Ideally, too, the comparisons should provide participants not only with the tables of results, but also with a well designed guide to their use. If desired, the organiser should provide individual reports to participants and arrange to visit them to discuss the results and their meaning. The comparisons should be organised on a regular (e.g. annual) basis.

The above principles of proper interfirm comparisons were formulated during the British Institute of Management's research which preceded the setting up of the Centre for Interfirm Comparison, and have been fundamental features of the Centre's operations since its foundation in 1959 as an independent non-profit organisation. The Centre, which is regarded both nationally and internationally as a leading organisation in the field, has now prepared interfirm comparisons in over 100 industries, trades, professions and services.

Participation in a properly organised interfirm comparison involves firms in paying a fee which is, of course, higher than that payable for surveys based on published accounts. It also involves firms in the time and trouble of providing data for the comparisons – although it must be said that a well organised firm should have internal data of the kind in question fairly readily available. Fees currently quoted (1985) by the Centre for Interfirm Comparison for new projects range from about £500 to £1,500 per firm per comparison – the exact figure depends on the degree of detail of the comparisons; the amount of individual analysis; whether or not firms are visited to discuss the results; and whether the scheme is on a national or international basis.

The results of full interfirm comparisons tend to cover fewer firms than is the case with published accounts surveys – but against this (and offsetting also the cost of participation) must be put the advantages of greater relevance, depth and comparability of data which means that the results can be of real value to management in raising productivity and profitability.

For obvious reasons, the full results of these properly organised interfirm comparisons are made available only to participants. Table 2–9 is an example of the method of presenting the results of the comparison used by the Centre for Interfirm Comparison. It is a much condensed example. A full report would typically cover, say, 30–40 companies and over 100 ratios, as well as anonymous supporting data about company characteristics and practices and interpretative guidance. The figures in Table 2–9, although based on actual results, are imaginary.

## 2.3 External Standards – Work Measurement

This family of techniques provides standards for the shopfloor ratios of Diagram 9.3. The principal methods are:

1   *Time study* – recording the times (measured with a stop watch) and the rate (or pace) of working for a specified job under specified conditions, and then analysing the data so as to obtain a standard time for carrying out the job at a defined level of performance.

2   *Activity sampling* – making a large number of observations over a period of time. Each observation records what is happening at that instant and the percentage of observations recorded for a particular activity or cause of delay is a measure of the percentage of time during which that activity or cause of delay occurs.

3   *Synthesis from standard data* – building up a time for a job by, first of all, breaking the job down into elements for each of which a standard time is already available from time studies of other jobs containing these elements, and then adding up these standard times for each element of the new job.

4   *Predetermined motion time systems* (PMTS) – building up the standard time for a job from a series of times which have been established for basic human motions (grasp, crank, side step, and so on). Method Time Measurement (MTM) is one of the principal PMT systems.

5   *Estimating* – assessing the time for a job based on knowledge and experience of similar types of work but without breaking the job down into elements as is done when synthesising from standard data.

6   *Analytical estimating* – a half-way house between estimating and synthesising from standard data. The job is broken down into elements and the standard time for these is found partly from knowledge and practical experience and partly by reference to standard data from time studies of other jobs.

7   *Comparative estimating* – arriving at a time for a job by comparing the work in it with the work in a series of similar, benchmark jobs, the work content of which has been measured.

All the above methods lead to a standard time in which a job should be completed by a qualified and motivated worker using the specified method and taking the appropriate relaxation allowance.

Anyone wanting detailed information should refer to one of the many books on the subject. One which may be recommended is: *Introduction to Work Study*, International Labour Office, 3rd Edition, Geneva, 1979. Two other sources of information are the Institute of Management Services, 1 Cecil Court, London Road, Enfield, Middlesex EN2 6DD (Telephone 01-363 7452) and MTM Association Limited, 240 Manchester Road, Warrington, Lancashire WA1 3BN (Telephone 0925 32615).

## 2.4 Composite Standards – Internal plus External

There are some standards which are a mixture of internal and external, as follows.

Performance of other subsidiaries or units

If a company operates through a number of subsidiaries or divisions or units it is always possible to obtain standards of performance by organising comparisons between them. Such a comparison shares a disadvantage with the process of a firm comparing itself with its own past, because all the units may be equally bad. As this is always a possibility this method is no real substitute for an external comparison with other companies.

On the other hand such a comparison has some of the advantages of an organised interfirm comparison, namely the larger amount of data that can be obtained and the fact that it is possible to ensure that they have been arrived at in a uniform manner.

How much information can be compared depends on how similar the activities of the units are. But however dissimilar they are they should all be comparable to the extent that they are all being run to make a profit out of good use of their assets.

It is often useful to compare dissimilar subsidiaries, because the very process of asking questions as to why ratios should or should not be similar between different units leads management to reconsider assumptions about practices, processes, and so on, with the result that these may be improved or changed rather than their existence and 'rightness' remaining unchallenged. The sort of question which management should ask itself is: 'Bearing in mind our similarity/dissimilarity to unit $X$, would we expect our ratios for $A$, $B$, $C$, etc. to be higher than/lower than/the same as those of unit $X$ and why?' This question should be asked preferably before the comparative data are available. When it is, management should discuss why their predictions were or were not right (particularly bearing in mind the degree and/or trend of difference) and what action or further investigation this suggests.

## Other people

It is nearly always possible to establish some yardstick of performance within a firm by making a comparison between employees. Such a process may have the same advantages and disadvantages as a comparison between subsidiaries. For example, workers may have been operating under different conditions or salesmen in different territories. However, if they were, management should know and should ask itself whether the differences in environment were enough (or perhaps more than enough) to account for differences in performance. This should help it to set realistic targets for, and provide equitable rewards to, its employees.

## 2.5 Constraints

While considering standards against which a firm's ratio should be compared it should be recognised that the possible magnitude of a number of ratios is affected by various external constraints to which a firm's management is subject:

1   *Legal/social.* The size of some ratios is determined for a firm by the legal and social framework in which it operates. For example:

   (*a*)   The speed on roads
   (*b*)   Minimum wages (National Agreements)
   (*c*)   Maximum hours of work (Factories Act).

2   *Physical.* It is possible that the magnitude of some ratios might be limited by the physical properties of matters such as the boiling point of water, the conductivity of copper and so on.

3   *Suppliers/customers.* The specifications of machines (such as rate of operation), the prices of raw materials and the specifications of products made to customers' order are all factors which limit the size of some of the ratios which management must watch.

## 2.6 Summary

There are many standards available to management against which to measure current performance. The standards vary in their availability, reliability and applicability. Probably no one standard is best for all purposes, but if a budget is composed with due regard to a firm's performance in the past, and the performance of competitors and, to a lesser extent, fellow subsidiaries (if any), and if the budget for the appropriate ratios is based on work measurement, then such a budget will form a useful yardstick against which management can monitor its performance and control its business.

## Appendix 2.1

## HOW TO TRACE COMPANY INFORMATION

Directory Search Sequences

The following have been found to be the most effective orders in which to consult directories for particular kinds of information. The sequences are offered merely as a considered assessment of individual directories (see Diagram 2–2). Figures in parentheses indicate estimated numbers of enterprises included.

### UNITED KINGDOM
**Business enterprises – Addresses**
1   *CRO Directory of English and Welsh Companies:* (950,000, not all active) (Quarterly; cumulated weekly update. Provides registered office which is not necessarily administrative headquarters).
2   *Kelly's Manufacturers and Merchants* (80,000)
3   *Sell's Directory* (60,000)
4   *British Telecom Telex Directory* (85,000)
5   *Kompass Register* (30,000)
6   *Belfast and Northern Ireland Directory* (10,000) (includes directors and capital)

*Area known*
1   Local telephone directories
2   *Kompass Register/Kompass Management Register* (30,000)
3   Post Office. Postcodes (Section 2 – postcodes of larger users)
4   Official town guides (often include interesting background material about local firms).

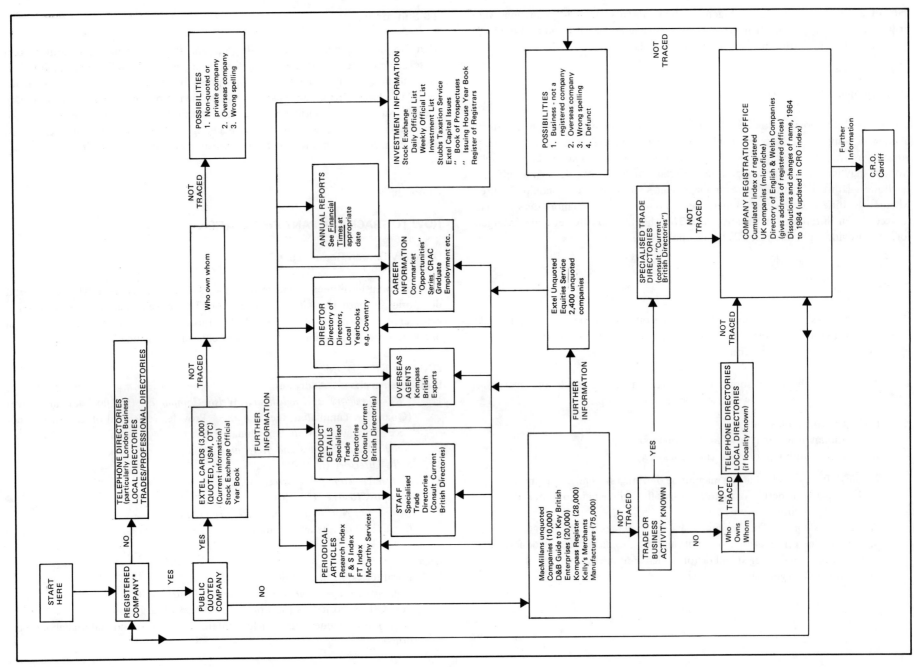

Diagram 2–2   How to trace UK company information

1    Specialised trade directories (consult index of *Current British Directories* for appropriate title).

## Company information

1    Extel Quoted (3,000), Unquoted (2400), Analyst's, USM and OTC Services.
2    McCarthy's Quoted and Unquoted Services
3    Guide to Key British Enterprises (20,000)
4    ICC Financial Surveys (35,000) (tabulated financial information on individual companies by industry)
5    *Kompass Register/Kompass Management Register* (30,000)
6    *Who Owns Whom* (90,000)
7    Britain's Top Private Companies (4000)/Top 1000 Foreign Owned Companies
8    *CRO Directory of English and Welsh Companies* (950,000)
      (Quarterly, cumulated weekly update. Address of registered office, company number, date of incorporation, accounting reference date, latest annual return and accounts filed).
9    CRO Dissolutions and Changes of Name (last 20 years)
10   *Financial Times* Index/Research Index
11   Macmillans' Unquoted Companies (10,000)
12   ICC Business Ratios (10,000) (arranged by industry)

*Activity known*

1    Specialised trade directories (the entry in *Current British Directories* indicates the kind and extent of company information available).
2    ICC Financial Surveys (35,000) (tabulated financial information on individual companies by industry).
3    ICC Business Ratios (10,000) (arranged by industry).

## Product and service information

1    Appropriate special directory if available (consult *Current British Directories* index)
2    *Kompass Register* (38,000 product headings)
3    *Kelly's Manufacturers and Merchants* (10,000 headings)
4    *Sell's Directory* (25,000 products and services indexed)
5    *Post Office Commercial Classified Telephone Directories* – London, Midlands, Northern

*Given area*

1    Telephone Yellow Pages Classified Directories
2    Chambers of Commerce Directories

USA

**Business enterprises – Addresses**

1    *Thomas Register* (130,000)
2    *Dun and Bradstreet Million Dollar Directory* (160,000)
3    *MacRae's Blue Book* (60,000)
4    *Standard and Poor's Register* (45,000)
5    *Standard Directory of Advertisers* (17,000)
6    *Sheldon's Retail* (3,100) (retail stores)
7    *Directory of Inter-Corporate Ownership* (90,000)
8    *Directory of Corporate Affiliations* (16,000)
9    Telex directories

*Area known*

1    Telephone directories
2    *Dun and Bradstreet Million Dollar Directory* (yellow pages)
3    *Directory of US importers* (25,000)

*Activity known*

1    Specialised trade directories (consult Ethridge's *Directory of Directories*)

*UK agent*

1    *Anglo-American Trade Directory* (13,000)

## Corporation information

1    *Moody's Manuals* (20,000 main and 40,000 index entries).
      Check in *Moody's Complete Corporate Index* (main entries only)
2    *Dun and Bradstreet Million Dollar Directory* (160,000)
3    *Standard and Poor's Register* (45,000)
4    *Standard Directory of Advertisers* (17,000)
5    *Sheldon's Retail* (3,100) (if appropriate)
6    *Directory of US Importers* (25,000) (if appropriate)
7    *Directory of Inter-Corporate Ownership* (90,000)
8    *Directory of Corporate Affiliations* (16,000)
9    *Thomas Register* (130,000)
10   *MacRae's Blue Book* (60,000)

*Activity known*

1    Specialised trade directories (consult Ethridge's *Directory of Directories*).

*Overseas subsidiaries*

1    *Who Owns Whom* (North American edition) (25,000)

**Product and service information**

1 Appropriate special directory if available (consult Ethridge's *Directory of Directories*)
2 *Thomas Register*
3 *MacRae's Blue Book*
4 *Dun and Bradstreet Million Dollar Directory* (blue pages – S.I.C.)
5 *Standard and Poor's Register* (S.I.C.)
6 *Standard Directory of Advertisers* (1,000 subject groups)
7 Buying Guide Issue of *Consumer Reports*
8 *Directory of US Importers* (S.I.T.C.)
9 *American Register of Exporters and Importers*

*Area known*

1 Local telephone directories yellow pages

GERMANY

**Company addresses**

1 *Kompass Register* (36,500)
2 *Das Deutsche Firmen – Alphabet* (300,000)
3 *Das Deutsche Telegrammadressbuch* (50,000)
4 *Seibt Industriekatalog* (20,000)
5 *BDI – Deutschland Liefert* (16,000)
6 *Who Owns Whom* Continental Edition (25,000)
7 *Wer Gehört zu Wem* (7,000)

*Area known*

1 *Deutsches Bundes – Adressbuch* (500,000)
2 *Kompass Register* (50,000)
3 Local telephone directories
4 *ABC Ortslexikon für Wirtschaft und Verkehr* (15,000)

*Activity known*

1 Specialised trade directories (consult *Current European Directories*)
2 *ABC Industrielle Informationen und Referenzen* (92,000)

**Company information**

1 *Handbuch der Deutschen Aktiengesellschaften* (2,600)
1a McCarthy European Service (300)
2 *Handbuch der Grossunternehmen* (22,000)
3 *Kompass Register* (50,000)

4 *Who Owns Whom* Continental Edition (25,000)
5 *Wer Gehört zu Wem* (7,000)

*Activity known*

1 Specialised trade directories (consult *Current European Directories*)
2 *ABC Industrielle Informationen und Referenzen* (92,000)

**Product and service information**

(E = English index)
1 Appropriate special directory if available
2 *Kompass Register* (E)
3 *ABC der Deutschen Wirtschaft Quellenwerk für Einkauf–Verkauf* (E) (28,000)
4 *Einkaufs der Deutschen Industrie* (E)
5 *Seibt Industriekatalog* (E)
6 *BDI – Deutschland Liefert* (E)
7 *Das Deutsche Branchen Fernsprechbuch* (has many non-industrial headings but only classification is in English).

*Area known*

1 Local telephone directories yellow pages

**Appendix 2.2**

**SOURCES OF COMPARATIVE PERFORMANCE DATA**

The Appendix is limited to information about organisations in the UK. Some of the sources listed provide data about organisations elsewhere in the world.

Wherever possible, prices have been quoted to help readers assess the likely cost involved. It should be appreciated, however, that these may become out of date and up to date prices should be obtained from the sources concerned. Relative prices may change less than absolute prices.

ORGANISATIONS WHICH SUMMARISE PUBLISHED ACCOUNTS

*Dun and Bradstreet Ltd* (26–32 Clifton Street, London EC2P 2LY, Tel: 01-247 4377) offers a customised Company Analysis and Ratio Service based on its records of 175,000 business enterprises. Using a computerised database, ratios can be produced on single or groups of companies and are tailored to meet the customer's brief. Costs are based on customer's requirements.

*Extel Statistical Services Ltd* (37–45 Paul Street, London EC2A 4PB, Tel: 01-253 3400, Telex: 262687) operates differently from the others. It produces a 'card' for each company in each of its services.

| Name/Cost | Coverage | Data provided | Updated |
|---|---|---|---|
| UK Listed Companies Service £1,750 p.a. | Most listed companies (over 3,100) | Summarised accounts share prices, yields, etc. for last ten years | Daily as news warrants |
| Analyst's Service £580 p.a. | Over 1,300 listed companies with Trustee status | Ditto | Weekly as news warrants |
| Unquoted Companies Service £1,350 p.a. | Over 2,100 unquoted companies | Ditto | Ditto |
| Unlisted Securities Market Service £500 p.a. | All companies traded in this market | Ditto | Twice weekly as news warrants |
| Over-The-Counter Service £330 p.a. | All companies traded on the O–T–C markets | Ditto | Weekly |
| Unlisted Securities Handbook £25 sub. for 2 books per year | All companies traded on Stock Exchange's Unlisted Securities Market | Company financial data, share price record, company directory and registrars | Twice yearly |
| Handbook of Market Leaders £79 sub. for 2 books per year | All companies in F.T. Actuaries Index (approx. 735) | Company details, Profit and loss record, capital employed, share record, dividend details | Twice yearly |

*Inter Company Comparisons Ltd* (28–42 Banner Street, London EC1Y 8QE, Tel: 01-253 6131) produces:

1. *ICC Business Ratio Reports* for some 150 industries. Each report covers up to 99 leading companies in the industry and provides 19 ratios and 6 growth rates, plus the figures on which these are based, for named individual companies ranked in order of most recent year's performance. Sector averages are also given. A commentary is included in each report, as are data sheets on the individual companies. The reports are published annually, provide three to four years' data, and cost £121 or £137 each.
2. *ICC Financial Surveys* on some 170 industries. Each annually published survey contains details on up to 600 companies, including two years' key financial information, principal activities and name of holding company if any. They cost £92 or £110 each.
3. *Industrial Performance Analysis*. An annual publication providing average performance statistics (using 13 key ratios) for 140 industry sectors, and covering a three year period. The 1985/6 edition costs £44.

*Jordan & Sons Ltd* (Jordan House, Brunswick Place, London N1 6EE, Tel: 01-253 3030) produces:

1. *Industrial Surveys* for some 28 industries. Each annual survey covers between 50 and 150 companies and contains key accounts information, ratios, activities, etc and a commentary by an industry expert. Data are for the past two to four years. Cost £65–£90 each.
2. *'Top' series* (e.g. Top 2000 private companies). Each annual publication gives a few key accounts figures for between 300 and 2000 companies and covers two to three years. Cost £25–£55.

*Key Note Publications Ltd* (28–42 Banner Street, London EC1Y 8QE, 01-253 3006), publishes annual Key Notes for some 130 market sectors. Each survey provides an overview of the industry's structure, market background, recent developments and future prospects. Recent major press references are listed, and a financial appraisal is given for the industry's major companies together with salient ratios. Sources of further information are identified. Individual Key Notes cost £75 each. Reductions for multiple orders.

## INFORMATION FROM GOVERNMENT SOURCES

All Government publications may be purchased from:

Government Bookshops, London

| | |
|---|---|
| 49 High Holborn, London WC1V 6HB (callers only) | 01-928 6977 |
| PO Box 276, London SW8 5DT (mail order only) | |
| PO Box 276, London SW8 5DT (telephone orders only) | 01-622 3316 |

Government Bookshops outside London (callers or mail order)

| | |
|---|---|
| 13A Castle Street, Edinburgh EH2 3AR | 031-225 6333 |
| 80 Chichester Street, Belfast BT1 4JY | Belfast 34488 |
| 258 Broad Street, Birmingham B1 2HE | 021-643 3740 |
| Southey House, Wine Street, Bristol BS1 2BQ | Bristol 24306 |
| Brazenose Street, Manchester M60 8AS | 061-834 7201 |

Enquiries about government statistics should be addressed to:
Central Statistical Office
Press and Information Service
Great George Street
London SW1P 3AQ                                              01-233 6135/6193

A very useful guide to Government (and important non-official) statistics is *Guide to Official Statistics No. 4*, CSO, HMSO, 1982.

The Business Statistics Office has a central inquiry point – Newport (STD Code 0633) 56111, ext. 2973 – whose primary function is to help people find their way through the mass of data available from the Government Statistical Service.

### Sources for specified areas of performance

Statistics on comparative performance data in the areas indicated will be found in the following publications:

*Marketing*

1    to assess market share trends in a large number of product fields; to watch size and growth of existing and potential markets (*Business Monitors* and *Overseas Trade Statistics*).

*Buying*

2    to be aware of the sales trends of materials and goods purchased (*Business Monitors;* Customs and Excise Bill of Entry Service);

3    to trace the price movements of materials (*British Business; Business Monitor MM17 Price Index Numbers for Current Cost Accounting;* The Department of Trade and Industry also constructs some price index numbers to meet specialised requirements).

*Personnel*

4    to watch trends by industry and by region in unemployment, vacancies, earnings, overtime, wage rates, hours of work, industrial disputes *(Department of Employment Gazette).*

*Overall efficiency and finance*

5    operating ratios – net output per head, stocks as a percentage of sales, wages per £ of total sales, etc. (*Census of Production*); stock/turnover ratio, gross margin, turnover per employee, etc. (*Annual Retail Inquiry Business Monitor* SDA 25);

6    labour costs (*Department of Employment Gazette* and *New Earnings Survey*);

7    company finance – aggregated balance sheet; appropriation accounts; sources and uses of funds; income, interest and dividend payments as percentage of assets; analyses by listed/unlisted companies and industry analysis; liquid assets of companies (*Business Monitor MA3 Company Finance; Financial Statistics*).

### Business Monitors

*Business Monitors* are the medium through which the Government publishes the business statistics it gathers on the manufacturing, mining, distributive and service industries.

They are a series of monthly, quarterly and yearly publications based on information collected regularly by the Business Statistics Office (BSO) from firms in the industries covered. From more than 30,000 firms in the case of the manufacturing and mining sectors alone.

There are three main series:

1    *Production Monitors* (P series).
2    *Service and Distributive Monitors* (SD series).
3    *Miscellaneous Monitors* (M series).

1    *Production Monitors*

*Quarterly Production Monitors (PQ)*
The *Quarterly Production Monitors* cover over 190 industries and can help to

assess market trends by supplying up to date information on the sales of over 3,000 individual products. In some instances, quantity detail is shown for the number of products sold as well as their total sales value. This information is supplemented by data on imports, exports, prices and employment. The PQ Monitors appear about three months after the quarter to which they relate, providing valuable short term market indicators.

For an early indication of general trends in the manufacturing sector, *Monitor PQ* 1002 provides a quarterly summary of the total sales for most manufacturing industries.

There are 175 *Quarterly Production Monitors.*

*Monthly Production Monitors (PM)*
Monthly statistics are available for a limited number of industries. The statistics include information on the sales and orders for the important engineering industries and considerable detail of production for the car and commercial vehicle industries.

There are four *Monthly Production Monitors.*

*Annual Production Monitors (PA)*
The *Annual Census of Production Monitors* deal with the manufacturing, energy, mining and construction industries. They provide comprehensive information on total purchases, capital expenditure, operating ratios, employment, wages, net output and gross value added, as well as analyses of output and costs, of establishments by size, and of net capital expenditure.

There are 118 *Annual Production Monitors,* some of which cover more than one industry.

*Occasional Production Monitors (PO)*
Three *Occasional Production Monitors* are relevant: PO 1000, *Index of commodities;* PO 1001, *Guide to short term statistics of manufacturers' sales* (a comprehensive guide to the way in which the BSO gathers and presents its statistics for the *Quarterly Production Monitors*); and PO 1007, the *Classified list of manufacturing businesses* (6 volumes).

*The index of commodities* (PO 1000) identifies the classification of individual commodities.

The *Classified list of manufacturing businesses* (PO 1007) is compiled from the BSO's *Register of Manufacturing Businesses in the UK.* Updated every three or four years, it contains the names and addresses of some 13,000 manufacturers, classified by the Standard Industrial Classification. Special geographical and alphabetical analyses in the form of computer print-outs are available for users looking for a regional or local sorting of businesses. A magnetic tape version of the list is also available. This publication can prove most useful to marketing

departments and others who require the names and addresses of UK businesses classified by industry.

2    *Service and Distributive Monitors (SD)*

*Service and Distributive Monitors* deal with aspects of the service industries and the distributive trades. They range from the dealings of finance houses and consumer credit companies to reports on the computer services industry, the motor trades, retailing, wholesaling and catering. Statistics on the retail trades are available in *Monitor* SDO 25, which includes biennial figures of types and numbers of businesses, turnover, gross margins and numbers employed.

3    *Miscellaneous Monitors (M)*

*Miscellaneous Monitors* cover subjects falling outside the scope of the other two series: new vehicle registrations, the cinema industry, overseas travel and tourism, acquisitions and mergers of companies, investment by pension fund and insurance companies, insurance business, overseas transactions, company finance, and others. They are published monthly, quarterly, annually or occasionally – except in the case of MR 15, *General trends in shipping,* which is classified as a *Repetitive Monitor* since it appears regularly at intervals of less than one year but not monthly or quarterly.

MM 17, *Price index numbers for current cost accounting (PINCCA),* is an aid to firms preparing accounts according to the Accounting Standards Committee directive, and includes indices based upon the most heavily used Government statistics. These cover plant and machinery, stocks, assets, buildings and works, the Retail Price Index and All Stocks Index.

*Cost* (Up to date prices may be obtained from HMSO or the BSO)

*Business Monitors*
*Monthly and Quarterly Business Monitors*
Available on subscription
Price: monthly issues                                                    £15.75 each set per year
                                                                                      except MM17 £16.75
Quarterly issues                                                           £8.50 each set per year
Complete sets of all monthly and quarterly
monitors in the PQ and PM Production Series     £595

## Annual and Occasional Business Monitors

Available on standing order. A standing order ensures that selected titles in the annual series are supplied automatically on publication and that all occasional monitors in the series selected are supplied as they are published. A £25 deposit will open an account. Additionally, single copies of annual and occasional monitors can be obtained from HMSO bookshops (individually priced).

## Individual and back copies

Single copies of current monthly and quarterly *Business Monitors* and back copies of all *Monitors* may be purchased by post (cash with order) from the Library, Business Statistics Office, Cardiff Road, Newport, Gwent NPT 1XG. Telephone: 0633 56111 ext. 2973, telex 497121 – answerback BSONPT G.

## Other sources

### Customs and Excise Bill of Entry Service

With a few exceptions, analyses of exports and imports under individual trade headings and with individual countries or through UK ports for particular months or cumulative periods can be obtained from the Bill of Entry Service Statistical Office, HM Customs and Excise, Portcullis House, 27 Victoria Avenue, Southend-on-Sea SS2 6AL (Southend-on-Sea 49421 ext. 310) on payment of a fee to cover the costs of the service.

*British Business* Weekly £1.25 (Annual subscription £75)
*Department of Employment Gazette* Monthly £2.95 (Annual subscription £34.50)
*Census of Production* see Business Monitors above
*Retailing Inquiry* (SDO 25) Every 2 years (latest 1982 published 1984 £12.50)
*Financial Statistics* Monthly £7.95 (Annual subscription including explanatory handbook and postage £100).

## INFORMATION FROM TRADE ASSOCIATIONS

Trade Associations are listed in *Henderson's Directory of British Associations,* CBD Research, 7th edition, 1982 and *Trade Associations and Professional Bodies of the United Kingdom,* ed P. Millard, Pergamon, 7th edition, 1984. By no means all Trade Associations produce comparative data. In a survey I conducted in 1980 roughly 1 in 5 did. The type of data varies enormously and is usually available only to members. The following associations provided comparative data in 1980. Some may of course no longer do so; others may now do so, or be willing to do so. It is well worth a call to the relevant association.

Aerosol Manufacturers Assoc. (British)
Agricultural Engineers Association
Aluminium Foil Container Manufacturers Association
Aluminium Stockholders' Association
Bicycle Association of G.B. Limited
Booksellers' Association of G.B. and Ireland
Brewers' Society
Builders' Merchants Federation
Building Material Producers (National Council of)
Caravan Council (National)
Carton Association (British)
Chartered Accountants, Institute of, in England and Wales
China Clay Association
Commercial Rabbit Association
Compressed Air Society (British)
Confederation of British Industry
Co-operative Union Limited
Covered Conductors Association
Curers' Association
Dairy Trade Federation
Dental Laboratories' Association
Door & Shutter Association
Drapers' Chamber of Trade
Dyers' and Finishers' Association
Electrical Appliances, Domestic, Association of
Electronic Components Industry, Federation
Engineering Employers' Federation
Engine Remanufacturers, Federation of
Farmers' Trading Agency (United)
Footwear Manufacturers' Federation (British)
Footwear Wholesale Distributors' Association
Freight Transport Association
Furniture, High Wycombe Manufacturers' Society
Grain Producers Limited (United)
Grit Association (British)
Hand Tool Manufacturers (Federation of British)
Heating and Ventilating Contractors' Association
Insurance Association (British)
Jute Spinners' and Manufacturers' Association
Knitting Industry, Hinckley and District Association
Leather Producers' Association

Milk Products, Scottish Association of
Motor Agents' Association
Newspaper Society
Non-Woven Manufacturers' Association, British
Pharmaceutical Association Limited (National)
Printers in Scotland Society (Master)
Printing Industries, Federation (British)
Radio Equipment Manufacturers' Association, British
Ready Mixed Concrete Association
Retail Distributors, Association of
Retread Manufacturer's Association
Savings Bank Central Board (Trustee)
Ship Repairers & Shipbuilders, Scottish East Coast Association
Silk Association
Solus Outdoor Advertising Association Limited
Stationery & Office Products Federation, British
Steel Stockholders (National Association of)
Steel Window Association
Tea Brokers' Association of London
Timber Importers' Association
Toy and Hobby Manufacturers' Association
Vodka Trade Association
Worsted Spinners' Federation Limited
Whiting Federation of Britain
Wood Wool Slab Manufacturers' Association
Yacht Charter Association
Zip Fasteners Manufacturers' Association

In the survey mentioned above, 4 out of 10 restricted the data to their members, a third restricted it to those who had contributed figures, 2 out of 10 said that they provided some or all of the results to all who requested the information.

The frequency with which comparisons are conducted varied from weekly to annually as follows:

|  | % |
|---|---|
| Weekly | 4 |
| Monthly | 40 |
| Quarterly | 22 |
| Half-yearly | 13 |
| Annually | 31 |
| Other and not given | 22 |

The percentages sum to more than 100 per cent because some associations conduct more than one information exchange.

The way in which the information was provided also varies as follows:

|  | % |
|---|---|
| Totals | 59 |
| Averages | 24 |
| Ratios | 32 |
| Individual companies shown anonymously | 18 |
| Individual companies identified | 16 |
| Other or not given | 24 |

The information provided was as follows:

|  |  | % |
|---|---|---|
| (a) | Output | 31 |
| (b) | Sales | 62 |
| (c) | Costs | 37 |
| (d) | Gross profit | 22 |
| (e) | Net profit | 22 |
| (f) | Assets employed | 21 |
| (g) | Credit given | 16 |
| (h) | Credit taken | 4 |
| (i) | Quotation success rate | 3 |
| (j) | Number of employees | 25 |
| (k) | Wages/salaries rates | 25 |
| (l) | Employee turnover | 10 |
| (m) | Prices charged to customers | 9 |
| (n) | Prices paid to suppliers | 4 |
| (o) | Share of market | 22 |
| (p) | Productivity | 21 |
| (q) | Other | 21 |

THE CENTRE FOR INTERFIRM COMPARISON

The Centre's work is described on page 19 above.

The Centre publishes a brochure about its services, which may be obtained on request from either the London office (25 Bloomsbury Square, London WC1A 2PJ, Tel: 01-637 8406), or the Colchester office (8 West Stockwell Street, Colchester CO1 1HN, Tel: 0206 562274).

The fees charged to participants vary from project to project, and are determined by such factors as:

(a) the degree of complexity of the project,
(b) frequency of reporting (e.g. once a year or four times a year),
(c) whether an individual report to a firm is provided (as well as a general report),
(d) whether a reporting visit to a firm is made,
(e) whether the comparison is within the UK or on an international basis (involving higher travel costs, translations etc.).

In 1985 fees for annual comparisons ranged from about £500 to £1,500 per participant.

Information on the current status and development of the Centre's work is given from time to time in *B.I.M. Management News*.

Most of the projects are carried out on an annual basis. For some sectors an 'Appraisal Service' is in operation, which enables a firm to send in its data at any time, and quickly receive in return a written appraisal of its performance as measured against the existing data bank for that sector.

*List of industries, trades, services and functions in which the Centre has conducted comparisons*

A Abattoirs
A Academic libraries
A Adoption services
A Aluminium Anodisers
A Aluminium home improvement systems
A Automatic vending
B Bedding manufacture
B Biscuit manufacture
B Blanket manufacture
A Book publishing
A Book publishers' distribution
A Breweries: Managed houses
A Breweries: Tenanted houses' rents
A Builders' Merchants
A Building and civil engineering
A Bulk liquid haulage contractors
B Carpet manufacture: (a) woven
                        (b) tufted
A Chemical manufacture*
B Clothing manufacture

B Cold rolled sections manufacture
B Colour makers
A Comparison of firms' performance in different geographical areas
A Computing bureaux
B Corn and agriculture merchants
B Cotton spinning
B Crane manufacture
A Credit card finance
A Decorators' merchants
A Distribution of food & consumer goods
B Domestic central heating equipment manufacture
B Drop forgers
A Electrical contractors
A Electrical/electronic manufacture
A Electrical engineering
B Engineers' tool manufacture
B English woollen and worsted industry
A Express Carriers

A Finance Houses
B Flexible package manufacture
A Food distribution
A Food manufacture
B Forgemasters
A Fork lift truck manufacture (international)
B Gauge and tool manufacture
B Glass container manufacture
B Hand tool manufacture
A Hotels
A Housing associations
A Industry in New Towns
A Invoicing and Credit Control
A Iron foundries
B Joinery manufacture
B Leather dressing
A Local authority services
A Machine tool importers
A Machine tool manufacture
B Mains cable manufacture
A Maintenance costs in manufacturing industry*
A Marketing research
A Mechanical engineering*
B Narrow fabric manufacture
A Non-ferrous foundries
B Nylon hose dyeing
A Painting and decorating contractors
A Paint manufacture: (a) UK
                      (b) Europe
B Paper manufacture
A Paper sack manufacture (international)

A Passenger transport systems
A Periodical publishers
A Pharmaceutical manufacture
B Pipework contractors
B Plastics moulding
A Public libraries
A Pump manufacture
A Radio and electronic component manufacture
A Raw material costs
B Rayon weaving
A Residential homes for the elderly
A Road haulage*
B Rubber manufacture*
A Scientific instrument manufacture
B Scottish woollen industry
A Secondary aluminium ingots
B Shirt manufacture
B Soft drinks manufacture
A Solicitors
A Steel stockholders
B Stockbrokers
A Structural steelwork
A Synthetic resin manufacture
B Tank and industrial plant manufacture
B Throwsters
A Tie manufacture
B Timber importers
B Timber merchants
A Valve manufacture (mechanical)
A Veterinary practices
A Wallcover manufacture
A Warp knitting
A Water authorities

A = project currently or recently in operation
B = project which has not been operated recently, but could be conducted again at short notice
* Covering various types and size groups

The Centre is always available to set up comparisons in new fields.

## SALARY SURVEYS

Many organisations conduct salary surveys. Income Data Services Ltd, 140 Great Portland Street, London W1 (01-580 0521) produces an annual directory to provide guidance to those seeking usable salary comparisons from the multitude of available surveys.

The directory gives details of each survey including the price, reference date, length, sample size and availability of the report. There is then a description of the format, scope and methodology and this is followed by a brief comment on the reliability of the data and any new features in the current year's directory. Forty UK surveys are included, and a further 18 are analysed in the international section.

IDS is an independent research centre that has been reporting on pay and industrial relations since 1966. It produces five different groups of publications:

1   *Incomes Data Report* gives up to date information on pay and conditions of employment. There are 24 issues per annum and the main subscription is £125 per annum (£110 first year) and £60 per annum group rate.
2   *IDS Study.* Each fortnightly IDS study provides comprehensive data and analysis on one industrial relations topic. The annual subscription is £90 per annum, group rate £65.
3   *IDS Brief* is published twice a month and keeps subscribers up to date on the legal side of industrial relations and the changes in the collective procedures used by employees and trade unions. The subscription is £105 per annum, group rate £65.
4   *IDS Focus* is about ideas and issues that stem from the actions of government, unions and organisations. It is published quarterly and the subscription is £20 per annum.
5   *IDS International* published every fortnight keeps subscribers informed of overseas developments in industrial relations, on two levels: up to date information on events in industrial countries; and through the analysis of foreign trends which have – or could have – a special relevance for labour affairs in the UK. The subscription is £60 per annum.

## SOURCES OF MARKETING INFORMATION

This section is in two parts. The first is based on a pamphlet prepared by the City of London Business Library for its users. I am very grateful to the library for permission to make this use of their pamphlet. The second gives details of various companies providing marketing data.

## Literature sources

1   Guides to existing surveys
   (*a*)   Industrial Aids Ltd – published data on European industrial markets. List of market reports freely available for purchase with guide to other sources of information on industrial markets.
   (*b*)   International directory of published market research (British Overseas Trade Board).
2   Statistics – general guides
   (*a*)   C.S.O. – *Guide to official statistics* (HMSO). Recent developments are reported in the quarterly Statistical news.
   (*b*)   NEDO publish a series of specialised guides, e.g. *Distributive trade statistics, Motor industry statistics.*
   (*c*)   *Government statistics* – a brief guide to sources is updated annually and available free.
   (*d*)   J.M. Harvey, *Sources of statistics* (Clive Bingley, 2nd edn, 1971). Lists, with brief descriptions, the principal sources of statistics in UK, USA and from main international organisations.
   (*e*)   UN, *Directory of International Statistics.* Guide to series published by the UN and other international agencies.
   (*f*)   W.F. Maunder, *Reviews of United Kingdom statistical sources* (Heinemann Education). 13 volumes so far published, each detailing sources in a given subject area.
   (*g*)   R.A. Critchley, *Quick reference guide to statistical sources in consumer marketing.*
   (*h*)   John Fletcher, *Information sources in economics* (2nd edn, Butterworth, 1984). Has helpful chapter on economic statistical sources.
   (*i*)   Bernard Edwards, *Sources of economic and business statistics* (Heinemann, 1972).
   (*j*)   C. Hull, *Principal sources of marketing information* (Times Information Marketing and Intelligence Unit).
   (*k*)   *S.I.S.C.I.S. (Subject index to sources of comparative statistics,* C.B.D. 1978). Guide to international statistical sources.
   (*l*)   *Business Statistics Index,* P. Foster, Headland Press, 1983.
3   Statistics and surveys – UK market
   (*a*)   Office of Population Census and Surveys – *Census.* Official statistics on population, occupations, socio-economic groups, etc. in England and Wales. Separate publications are available for Scotland and Northern Ireland. The OPCS also publish annual *Population estimates* and *Population trends.*

(b) Inland Revenue, *Survey of personal incomes.*
(c) Department of Employment, *Family expenditure survey.*
(d) *M.G.N. Marketing manual of the UK* (last published 1979). Survey of UK social and economic conditions with market-place data on over 90 product fields. Useful feature is citation of sources for statistics. Section C is an analysis of advertising expenditure by product, brands and media. A companion volume covers industrial marketing.
(e) *N.O.P. – Political, social, economic review.* Monthly bulletin recording reactions to controversial political and social topics, as well as surveys of individual UK markets.

4   Abstracts and indices
There are few abstracting services covering marketing information. Most services concentrate on technical aspects and contain few, if any, commercial references.
(a) *Market research abstracts.* Semi-annual publication from the Market Research Society. Concerned more with the theory of marketing, but articles on actual markets sometimes included.
(b) *Anbar Abstracts.* Series covers: accounting and data processing; marketing and distribution; personnel and training; top management; work study and O & M.
(c) *Marketing information guide.* Monthly annotated bibliography, published in the USA, of books, reports, and articles on domestic and foreign markets.
(d) *Business periodicals index.* Monthly service, cumulating annually, indexing articles by specific subject from a wide range of economic and commercial publications.
(e) *Funk & Scott indexes – Europe and International.* Monthly indexes, with quarterly and annual cumulations, of articles from major commercial journals and most non-US countries. Both product and country approaches are catered for on the blue and yellow pages respectively.

5   Advertising and readership surveys
(a) JICNARS, *National readership survey.* Readership profiles of individual newspapers, magazines and journals with detailed analysis by sex, age, social grade and geographical area.
(b) *National businessman readership survey.* Analysis of readership of newspapers and journals among different categories of businessmen.

Companies providing marketing data

*Dun & Bradstreet Ltd,* Marketing Services Division, P.O. Box 17, 26–32 Clifton Street, London EC2P 2LY. Tel: 01-377 4377.

Data available: Industrial information from computerised files for market research, product development, product promotion, direct selling, location of offices and depots, acquisition searches. Files include:

(a) *UK Market Facts File* of over 200,000 business enterprises.
(b) European file of approx. 180,000 manufacturers: head office only.
(c) Other computerised files include *Key British Enterprises, Who Owns Whom, Principal International Businesses.*

Market Research Survey services are also available.

*The Economist Intelligence Unit Ltd,* 27 St James's Place, London SW1A 1NT. Tel: 01-493 6711. Issues the following business publications:

*Retail Business* – Monthly (Annual subscription £115)
*Multinational Business* – Quarterly (Annual subscription £110)
*International Tourism Quarterly* (Annual subscription £80)
*Rubber Trends* – Quarterly (Annual subscription £135)
*Motor Business* – Quarterly (Annual subscription £155)
*Paper and Packaging Bulletin* – Quarterly (Annual subscription £135)
*Marketing in Europe* – Monthly (Annual subscription £165)
*European Trends* – Quarterly (Annual subscription £70)
*The Quarterly Economic Reviews Service* – (83 reviews) (Annual subscription £45 per review (basic) )
*Quarterly Energy Reviews* (7 reviews) (Annual subscription £75 per review (basic)
The EIU also publishes *Special Reports* and *Multi Client Studies.*

*Euromonitor Publications Limited,* 87–88 Turnmill Street, London EC1M 5QU. Tel: 01-251 8024, publishes *UK Market Reports* (prices between £95 and £180) which contain analysis and statistical data on UK consumer markets. Other publications include *Factfinders* and *Market Direction Reports* and a wide range of marketing and business information publications at prices from £18 to £225. Catalogue on request.

*Mintel Publications Ltd,* 7 Arundel St., London WC2R 3DR. Tel: 01-836 1814, publishes:

(a) *Market Intelligence* (monthly reports on 5 consumer goods markets and marketing using original research).
Annual subscription £325, single copies £55

(b) *Retail Intelligence* (quarterly journal devoted to aspects of distributive trade with original research).
Annual subscription £420, single copies £125

(c) *Leisure Intelligence* (quarterly journal reporting on leisure market/activities with original research).
Annual subscription £420, single copies £125

(d) *Personal Finance Intelligence* (a quarterly journal concentrating on developments in the area of financial services).
Annual subscription £420, single copies £125

(e) *Daily Digest* (senior management guide compiled from national press and specialist journals).
Annual subscription £450

(f) *Monthly Review* (a list of key appointments and a wide variety of market sizes).
Annual subscription £60

(g) *Monthly Digests.*
Annual subscription £100

Also provides:

(a) Mintel Information Service (for desk or original research).
Fees on request.

(b) Mintel Library (access to files and journals).
Fees on request.

(c) Mintel exclusive report service (reports tailored to client's requirements).
Fees on request.

*A.C. Nielsen Company Ltd,* Nielsen House, Headington, Oxford OX3 9RX. Tel: 0865 64851, Telex 83136, provides:

(a) Continuous national and regional measurements of consumer sales and sales influencing factors at the retail and wholesale outlet for manufacturers of packaged consumer goods.

(b) Other market and consumer research services.
(Fees on request).

*Nielsen Researcher* and *Nielsen Marketing Trends* issued periodically covering topics of general marketing interest, available from Sales Office, address as given above.

TELETEXT, VIEWDATA AND SOURCES NEEDING A COMPUTER TO ACCESS

Most of the sources listed in this appendix rely on traditional paper and print to convey their information. A growing number however are using electronic means of communication, e.g. VDUs (visual display units), television, telephone and computers.

There are three teletext and viewdata sources in the UK:

CEEFAX – broadcast by the BBC
ORACLE – broadcast by ITV
Prestel – the British Telecom viewdata service

All three services can be displayed on a normal television receiver screen. Colour television receivers to receive teletext are made by all the major UK manufacturers.

A small, hand-held control box (rather like a pocket calculator) called a keypad is also required to select and 'turn the pages'.

To use Prestel requires, in addition to a keypad and a suitable domestic TV receiver or a special Prestel receiver, a telephone plug and socket to link the receiver to the telephone. Not only simple terminals to view information on are available, but ones which, in addition, enable the user to perform calculations on the data and/or obtain a hard copy print-out of the data.

Information for CEEFAX and ORACLE is provided by the BBC and ITV respectively at no charge to the viewer. Information for Prestel is provided by 'Prestel Information Providers' who may charge the viewer.

CEEFAX and ORACLE transmit information in one direction only (to the viewer). Prestel permits the viewer, in situations selected by the Information Provider, to respond to what he sees by using the keypad and a 'response frame' to send a message to another Prestel subscriber or to order goods or services.

CEEFAX and ORACLE provide up-to-the-minute financial and company news, UK and overseas share prices, foreign exchange rates, commodity prices, etc. as well as a general service of news, information and features.

Up to date information may be obtained from:

CEEFAX, Citynews, Room 4081, BBC, Broadcasting House, London W1A 1AA. Tel: 01-927 4443, Telex: 265781 attn CIT
ORACLE, Oracle Teletext Ltd., Craven House, 25-32 Marshall Street, London W1V 1LL. Tel: 01-434 3121, Telex: 8813039
Prestel, British Telecommunications, Temple Avenue, London EC4Y 0HL. Tel: 01-583 9811.

*Cost*

The cost of Prestel is made up of:

1 A special Prestel TV set, or Prestel adaptor. At present these cost about £200 over an equivalent TV's price, or approximately £15 per month total rental.

2 Standing charge: Business £15 per quarter, Residential £5 per quarter.

3 Connection to telephone: £15 installation charge plus rental 15p per quarter.

4 Cost of telephone call at normal rates (which vary according to distance and time of day). Where Prestel exists in a region then the telephone call is at local rates.

5 Time based charge (5p per minute between 8 a.m. and 6 p.m. on week days and 8 a.m. to 1 p.m. on Saturdays, free at all other times) this money goes to pay for use of Prestel computer.

6 Cost of page (set by information provider).

*Data Stream International Ltd,* Monmouth House, 58-64 City Road, London EC1Y 2AL. Tel: 01-250 3000. Provides a service of 26,500 quoted and unquoted company, stock market and economic information relating to the UK and overseas which is stored on a central computer and is continuously updated. Users have direct access to the main data banks through their own terminal equipment or microcomputers via an ordinary telephone connection. Data Stream also provides programs for clients to use to manipulate the data on their own computers. Cost on application.

*EXSTAT and (Micro EXSTAT)* are Database services from Extel (for address see p. 25 above) which provide accounting information on 3,500 UK and overseas companies (2,000 UK companies) in a form suitable for processing and analysis by computer. The information is supplied on a standard magnetic tape (or floppy disk) with regular weekly (monthly) updates for use through an organisation's in-house computer system and/or through outside computer bureau time-sharing services. Cost on application.

*ICC*

Much of the information available from ICC as hardcopy (p. 25 above) is also available via Prestel (details and fees from ICC).

*Jordan*

Some of the information available from Jordan as hardcopy (p. 25 above) is also available via Prestel (details and fees from Jordan).

## Other Databases and banks

There is a growing number of databases and banks which are of relevance to the businessman. Databases accumulate and store information concerning the location of:

(*a*) reference to topics or companies in newspapers, magazines and journals;

(*b*) financial and economic statistics.

Databanks, in addition, contain the articles, or abstracts of them, and the numeric data.

Databases and banks can be accessed, via a suitable computer terminal, modem and telephone line, by subscribers to the database who have been trained and are experienced in the use of the relevant interrogation technique.

Readers wishing to know more about this fast developing subject should contact their company librarian (if they have one), their local public commercial library, or the Online Information Centre, Aslib, 26/27 Boswell Street, London WC1. Tel: 01-430 2671 or consult:

*The Directory of Computerised Business Information,* Douglas Tookey (ed.), Trade Research Publications, 1979.

*Directory of Online Databases,* Cuadra Associates Inc., annual with updating supplements.

*Which Data Base,* Allan Foster, Headland Press, 1981.

*Data Bases in Europe 1982,* Euronet Diane, EEC, 1982.

*UK Online Search Services,* compiled by J.B. Deunette, 2nd edition, 1982 (Aslib).

*News Databases,* Online Information Centre, 1980.

*Comparative Cost Chart for Online Files,* Hertfordshire County Library Service, £8.60 p.a.

*Which Databank,* A. Foster, Headland Press, 1983 (£18.95).

'The future for viewdata', C. Newman, *The Accountant,* 2 June 1983, p. 21.

*Online Business Sourcebook,* Headland Press, September 1985.

'Online information retrieval systems: A guide for accountants', D. Tinker, *Accountants Digest,* no. 166, ICAEW, Winter 1984/85.

## OTHER SOURCES

### Periodicals

Many periodicals and annuals contain, from time to time, comparative performance data about one or more industries or aspects of performance.

The trade journal(s) of the relevant industry should always be examined. Other journals worth looking at are e.g. *Investor's Chronicle, Economist* and *Management Today.*

## Information Services

*Aslib.* It may be worth subscribing to an information service such as that offered as one of the membership benefits of Aslib, The Association for Information Management, Information House, 26-27 Boswell Street, London WC1N 3JZ. Tel: 01-430 2671.

Aslib offers referral assistance to inquiries on any subject by advising on appropriate information sources, and will carry out online searching on request. They can also give informal advice on all aspects of information management, from the selection of equipment to the automation of a company information centre.

*Aslib Directory of Information Sources in the United Kingdom,* edited by E.M. Codlin. 2 volumes – Volume 1 Science, Technology and Commerce: 5th edition, 1982, £34 – Volume 2 Social Sciences, Medicine and the Humanities: 4th edition, 1980, £39.

*Financial Times Business Information Ltd,* Bracken House, 10 Cannon Street, London EC4. Tel: 01-248 8000.

The *Financial Times'* Business Information Service gives access to subscribers (annual fee – minimum £250) to: files covering 60,000 companies containing press cuttings, accounts and other published material; economic, industrial and biographical material; IMF & CSO Statistics; market research publications; and trade directories.

*McCarthy Information Service,* Manor House, Ash Walk, Warminster, Wilts, BA12 8PY. Tel: 0985 215151 provides a service of reprinted press cuttings which contain news and comments on companies and industries going back to about 1970. Either daily for the UK Quoted Company Service, or weekly for the other services, a subscriber receives separate information sheets for each company or industry on which an article has appeared in the press. Other services include UK Unquoted, European, Australian and North American Companies. Information is available either by regular update or on demand. Costs are relative to amount of information supplied.

*Warwick Statistics Service,* University of Warwick Library, Coventry CV4 7AL. Tel: 0203 418938 offers, for a range of subscriptions, a choice of: access to the library; an enquiry service; an alerting service; a research service; a series of occasional reviews, twice yearly seminars on sources of information, and a newsletter.

## Car running costs

Information on this subject may be obtained from:

(a) *Fleet Facts,* Telepress Limited, Strand House, Great West Road, Brentford, Middlesex TW8 9EY (01-560 4191) £35 for 12 monthly issues.

(b) *Car Fleet Management,* Business Press International Limited, Quadrant House, The Quadrant, Sutton, Surrey SM2 5AS (01-661 3338). Free to fleet managers. Bi-monthly.

(c) *Fleet Car Comparisons* is published by Interleasing (UK) Limited, Sardinia House, 52 Lincolns Inn Fields, London WC2A 3LZ (Tel: 01-404 0509) and gives overall operating costs for over 80 leased cars.

## Business names

*London Chamber of Commerce and Industry.* Since the registration of business names has ceased to be compulsory and the official registry was abolished, the London Chamber of Commerce and Industry has been running a similar, voluntary service.

For a fee of £15 the LCCI will search through its computerised files to see if there are businesses using the same or similar names registered with the LCCI, or which appear on the 'modern index' previously controlled by the Department of Trade. It will also advise as to whether the name is prohibited or requires government approval, and will provide a certificate of registration which, if correctly displayed, ensures compliance with the appropriate requirements of the 1985 Companies Act.

So far about 5,000 businesses have registered. The LCCI hopes that, as the service becomes more generally known, this figure will increase, since registration provides a valuable credential for small businesses and those trading overseas.

Further details about the registry are available from the Registrar, LCCI Business Registry, 69 Cannon Street, London, EC4N 5AB.

*Registrar of Companies.* A directory of all companies registered in England and Wales can be purchased in microfilm form from the Registrar of Companies. This provides an alphabetical index of some 800,000 companies registered in England and Wales, showing registered numbers, dates of incorporation, registered office addresses, accounting reference dates and the latest dates to which annual returns and accounts have been made up and filed with the Registrar.

New issues of the directory will be published at quarterly intervals, together with cumulative updating information at approximately weekly intervals. It is available on microfiche or roll film and a limited number may also be available on magnetic tape. Prices range from £78.00 to £216.00 for microfiche, and from £223.00 to £348.00 for roll film. Further details are available from the Registrar, Companies House, Crown Way, Maindy, Cardiff CF4 3UZ (Tel: 0222 388588, ext. 2243).

## Miscellaneous Sources

*NEDO*, Millbank Tower, Millbank, London SW1P 4QX. Tel: 01-211 5989 or 5985. Produces reports on a wide range of industries. Based on discussions between management, unions and government representatives, the reports aim to improve economic and industrial performance.

*The Institute of Administrative Management*, 205 High Street, Beckenham, Kent, BR3 1BA. Tel: 01-658 0171 publishes surveys of administrative and overhead costs (£7.50), office salaries, holidays and hours (£75), etc.

*Monopolies and Price Commissions* reports often give cost and market data not available elsewhere.

*Public libraries* with business or commercial departments are a very useful source.

*Charities Charity Statistics* is published annually by Charities Aid Foundation, 48 Pembury Road, Tonbridge, Kent TN9 2JD (0732 356323) and gives comparative statistics on individual charities, sources of income and types of expenditure.

*Independent Schools Cost Survey* by J. Garton Ash, Price £19.00, The Institute of Chartered Accountants in England and Wales, 1985.

## Guide to Sources

*Sources of British Business Comparative Performance Data*, C.A. and W.J. Westwick, Institute of Chartered Accountants in England and Wales, 1986 covers the subject in more detail than there is space for here and contains a Bibliography and a list of sources classified by industry.

## OVERSEAS SOURCES

### Europe and North America

A list of organisations which have conducted interfirm comparisons in Europe and North America will be found in *Productivity Measurement Review* No. 26 (August 1961) published by the Organisation for European Co-operation.

### French companies

Some ratio information is available for French companies from a scheme run by Bank of France (see 'Interfirm comparisons: the French banks' achievement', D.A.R. Forrester, *Management Accounting*, September 1983, pp. 28–30).

### USA

*The Almanac of Business and Industrial Financial Ratios*, Prentice Hall, 1982, (£18), gives 22 ratios for businesses in the USA classified by size and industry.

**Appendix 2.3**
**EXAMPLES OF DATA AVAILABLE FROM SOME SOURCES OF COMPARATIVE PERFORMANCE DATA**

GENERAL STORE PROPRIETORS.

Reg. 1926. Reg. No. 214436. Re-registered 1981 as a Public Limited Company under the Companies Act, 1980.
Reg. Office: Michael House, 37-67 Baker Street, London, W1A 1DN. Tel.: 01 - 935 4422. Telex: 267141.
Registrars: Ravensbourne Registration Services Ltd, Bourne House, 34 Beckenham Road, Beckenham, Kent, BR3 4TU. Tel.: 01 - 650 4866.

Co. was formed to acquire business registered in 1903.
RETAILING: Group sells clothing, foods and household goods under 'St. Michael' trade mark in its chain of stores in UK, France, Belgium and Ireland. It also sells a range of 'St. Michael' merchandise and other consumer goods through a chain of stores in Canada. 'St.Michael' merchandise is also sold for export. FINANCIAL ACTIVITIES comprise operation of Marks and Spencer Chargecard together with leasing and in-surance activities.
Co. has chain of 265 retail stores in UK, 9 in Europe and 227 in Canada.
Total square footage in operation: UK 7,216,000; Europe 266,000; Canada 2,304,000.

PRINCIPAL SUB. COS. (Wholly owned unless otherwise stated): St. Michael Financial Services Ltd and St. Michael Finance Ltd (Finance);Marks and Spencer (Nederland) BV (Holding Co; The Netherlands); Marks & Spencer Canada Inc. (Canada; 53.7% Ord. and 100% Pref.); Marks and Spen-cer (France) SA (France); Marks and Spencer (Ireland) Ltd (Ireland) and SA Marks and Spencer (Belgium) NV (Belgium) (Chain Store); M.S.In-surance Ltd (Insurance; Guernsey); St. Michael Leasing Ltd (Leasing).

**DIRECTORS: Lord Sieff of Brimpton, OBE, MA (President); The Lord Rayner (Chairman); *W.B.Howard, BA Deputy Chairman); *R.Greenbury;
N.L.Colne; A.E.Frost; J.A.Lusher; J.K.Oates, BSc (Econ), MSc, FCT; S.J.Sacher, MA; J.J.Salisse; The Hon David Sieff; C.V.Silver BSc(Econ);
A.K.P.Smith MA; P.H.Spriddell MA; D.R.Susman (South African); D.G.Trangmar.   *Joint Managing.  **See over.

SECRETARY: M.Epstein FCA.

BANKERS: Midland Bank PLC.

AUDITORS: Deloitte Haskins & Sells.

*CAPITAL

| | AUTHORISED | ISSUED | SHARES ISSUED |
|---|---|---|---|
| 7% (formerly 10% gross) Cum. Pref. shares of £1 | £350,000 | £350,000 | 350,000 |
| 4.9% (formerly 7% gross) Cum. Pref. shares of £1 | £1,000,000 | £1,000,000 | 1,000,000 |
| Ord. shares of 25p | £700,000,000 | £659,916,688 | 2,639,666,750 |

*At 31-3-85 year end. For latest capital position, see over.
In June 1978, 822,609 Ord. shares of 25p were issued under UK Profit Sharing Schemes. In Aug. 1978, Scrip issue, 649,827,807 Ord. shares of 25p (one for one; xc Aug. 7). In July 1979, 2,031,431 Ord. shares of 25p were issued under UK Profit Sharing Schemes. In June 1980, 3,236,664 Ord. shares of 25p were issued under UK Profit Sharing Schemes. Also During 1980/81, 16,000 Ord. shares of 25p were issued against options. In June 1981, 2,182,914 Ord. shares of 25p were issued under UK Profit Sharing Schemes. Also during 1981/82, 2,779,046 Ord. shares of 25p were issued against options. In June 1982, 2,555,848 Ord. shares of 25p were issued under UK Profit Sharing Schemes. Also during 1982/83, 1,478,733 Ord. shares of 25p were issued against options. In June 1983, 1,993,048 Ord.shares of 25p were issued under UK Profit Sharing Schemes. Also, during 1983/84, 606,084 Ord. shares of 25p were issued against options. In June 1984,2,072,693 Ord.shares of 25p were issued under UK Profit Sharing Schemes. In July 1984, Scrip issue, 1,318,911,755 Ord. shares of 25p (one for one; xc July 30). Also during 1984/85, 2,146,920 Ord. shares were issued against options.

SHARE SCHEMES. 2 Profit Sharing Schemes, 2 Share Option Schemes, 2 Share Option Scheme and Savings-Related Share Option Schemes are in operation under which maxi-mum total number of Ord. shares that may be issued under all Schemes is limited to 259,600,000. At 31-3-85 options were outstanding over 34,361,574 Ord. shares.

DIRECTORS' INTERESTS in shares of Co. at 7-5-85: BENEFICIAL AND FAMILY: 2,162,365 Ord. 500 4.9% Pref. 3,630,073 Options. AS TRUSTEES (in-cluding duplications): of Charitable Trusts 3,093,520 Ord.; Others 940,312 Ord.

OTHER INTERESTS: At 7-5-85 Prudential Corpn PLC and its Subs. held 178,175,734 Ord. shares (6.8%).

SHAREHOLDERS at 31-3-85 numbered: Ord. 251,657; Pref. 978.

VOTING: One vote per share or 2 Ord. shares, but Pref. only vote in certain circumstances.

CLOSE CO. (Income and Corporation Taxes Act, 1970): No.

DIVIDENDS: 7% Pref. due May and Nov. 1, 4.9% Pref. due Jan. 1 and July 1.
7% and 4.9% Pref., rank in that order for dividend and in a liquidation, for repayment of capital (at 112.5p per share in case of 4.9% Pref. shares).

ORD. DIVIDEND PAYMENT DETAILS. Year end March 31.

| | | % Payable | | Per Share | | | Tax Rate | Shares Ranking for Dividend (m) | Announced | Paid | Holders | Ex Date |
|---|---|---|---|---|---|---|---|---|---|---|---|---|
| | | Gross | Net | Gross | Net | | | | | | | |
| 1981 | Int | 8.571 | 6 | 2.143p | 1.5p | 30% | 1,305 | 16-10-80 | 16-1-81 | 14-11-80 | 27-10-80 |
| | Fin | 13.143 | 9.2 | 3.286p | 2.3p | 30% | 1,305 | 20-5-81 | 17-7-81 | 20-5-81 | 1-6-81 |
| 1982 | Int | 10 | 7 | 2.857p | 1.75p | 30% | 1,310 | 19-10-81 | 15-1-82 | 13-11-81 | 26-10-81 |
| | Fin | 16.286 | 11.4 | 4.071p | 2.85p | 30% | 1,314 | 29-4-82 | 16-7-82 | 28-5-82 | 17-5-82 |
| 1983 | Int | 10.571 | 7.4 | 2.643p | 1.85p | 30% | 1,314 | 26-10-82 | 14-1-83 | 19-11-82 | 1-11-82 |
| | Fin | 18.571 | 13 | 4.643p | 3.25p | 30% | 1,314 | 4-5-83 | 15-7-83 | 20-5-83 | 9-5-83 |
| 1984 | Int | 11.714 | 8.2 | 2.929p | 2.05p | 30% | 1,317 | 2-11-83 | 13-1-84 | 25-11-83 | 14-11-83 |
| | Fin | 24 | 16.8 | 6p | 4.2p | 30% | 1,317 | 1-5-84 | 13-7-84 | 25-5-84 | 14-5-84 |
| | Cap 100 | | | | | | | 1-5-84 | - | 30-7-84 | - |
| 1985 | Int | 6.171 | 4.32 | 1.543p | 1.08p | 30% | 2,640 | 23-10-84 | 18-1-85 | 16-11-84 | 29-10-84 |
| | Fin | 13.257 | 9.28 | 3.314p | 2.32p | 30% | 2,640 | 7-5-85 | 12-7-85 | 24-5-85 | 13-5-85 |

ORD. DIVIDENDS OF EARLIER YEARS (% net): 1976, 13.818; 1977, 15.2, Spec. 0.152; 1978, 16.977, Cap 100; 1979, 10.435; 1980, 13.6.

## PER SHARE RECORD OF 25p ORDINARY

| | | 1981 | 1982 | 1983 | 1984 | 1985 |
|---|---|---|---|---|---|---|
| Earnings | | | | | | |
| *Reported .. .. .. .. | | 7.62p | 9.22p | 10.3p | 12.6p | 6.9p |
| *Net Actual .. .. .. .. | | 7.436p | 9.207p | 10.265p | 13.419p | 6.964p |
| *Net Maximum Distribution .. | | 7.436p | 9.207p | 10.265p | 12.865p | 6.846p |
| | | | | | | |
| Shares on which earnings calculated (m) .. .. | | a 1,304.5 | a 1,308.7 | a 1,313.1 | a 1,316.0 | a 2,638.1 |
| | | | | | | |
| Net Dividend .. .. .. | | 3.8p | 4.6p | 5.1p | 6.25p | 3.4p |
| Dividend Cover – Maximum Distribution .. .. | | 2.0 | 2.0 | 2.0 | 2.1 | 2.0 |
| | | | | | | |
| **Net Asset Value .. .. | | 45.7p | 81.2p | 87.0p | 93.1p | 50.2p |

*Calculated on adjusted profit. **At Balance Sheet date. (a)Weighted average.

## PRICES OF 25p ORDINARY SHARES

| Cal.Year | 1976 | 1977 | a1978 | 1979 | 1980 | 1981 | 1982 | 1983 | 1984 | *1985 |
|---|---|---|---|---|---|---|---|---|---|---|
| Highest | 109p | 174p | 95p | 137-1/2p | 122p | 144p | 239p | 230p | 137p | 151p |
| Lowest | 68p | 93p | 66-3/4p | 75p | 75p | 101p | 122p | 185p | 98.5p | 110p |

*To May 17. (a)Adjusted for Scrip issues: 1978, Prices to July 17, 161p, 132-1/2p – Quotation Aug. 4, 155p, 175p; 1984, to July 13, 274p, 204p. Quotation July 27, 208p, 228p.

## LOAN CAPITAL.

5.5% DEB. STOCK 1985/90. Issued and Outstanding: £5,000,000. Redeemable at par on 30-6-90 or earlier on Co.'s notice on or after 30-6-85. Trustees: Prudential Corpn PLC. Issued privately June 1960 at 97.5%.
6.5% DEB. STOCK 1989/94. Issued and Outstanding: £10,000,000. Issued to Prudential Corpn PLC £5,000,000 in Oct. 1964 at 98% and £2,500,000 in June 1965 at par. Balance issued at par in June 1966.
7.25% DEB. STOCK 1993/98. Issued and Outstanding: £15,000,000. Issued to Prudential Corpn PLC £7,500,000 on 16-1-67 at 97.75% and balance on 16-1-78 also at 97.75%.
7.75% DEB. STOCK 1995/2000. Issued and Outstanding: £15,000,000. Issued to Prudential Corpn PLC £7,500,000 in Jan. 1968 at par, and balance in Jan. 1970 also at par.

OTHER LOANS. Outstanding: Sub. Cos. £4,300,000.

## *CONSOLIDATED PROFIT AND LOSS ACCOUNT

| | Mar.31 1981 £m | Mar.31 1982 £m | Mar.31 1983 £m | Mar.31 1984 £m | Mar.31 e1985 £m |
|---|---|---|---|---|---|
| TURNOVER .. .. .. | 1,872.9 | 2,198.7 | 2,505.5 | 2,854.5 | 3,213.0 |
| Cost of Sales .. .. | a 1,590.5 | 1,807.7 | 2,048.9 | 2,292.5 |
| GROSS PROFIT .. .. | a | 608.2 | 697.8 | 805.6 | 920.5 |
| Staff Costs .. .. | 31.3 | 250.8 | 291.4 | 332.9 | 382.3 |
| Other Expenses .. .. | 34.0 | 145.5 | 180.6 | 212.4 | 241.8 |
| Other Income .. .. | (24.0) | (27.9) | (35.2) | (34.7) | (12.8) |
| Interest Payable .. .. | 15.8 | 17.7 | 21.7 | 15.7 | 5.8 |
| PROFIT (LOSS) BEFORE TAX | 181.2 | 222.1 | 239.3 | 279.3 | 303.4 |
| Corporation Tax .. .. | 76.8 | 100.0 | 78.6 | 74.7 | 111.9 |
| Deferred Tax .. .. | 3.6 | 0.1 | 22.8 | c 31.5 | c 2.8 |
| Overseas Tax .. .. | 0.2 | 0.2 | 1.1 | 4.9 | 5.6 |
| Total Taxation .. .. | 80.6 | 100.3 | 102.5 | 111.1 | 120.3 |
| PROFIT (LOSS) AFTER TAX | 100.6 | 121.8 | 136.8 | 168.2 | 183.1 |
| Minority Interest .. .. | 1.1 | 1.1 | 1.6 | 1.8 | 2.0 |
| ATTRIB. TO MEMBERS .. | 99.5 | 120.7 | 135.2 | 166.4 | 181.1 |
| Preference Dividends .. | 0.1 | 0.1 | 0.1 | 0.1 | 0.1 |
| PROF. AFT. PREF. DIVS... | 99.4 | 120.6 | 135.1 | 166.3 | 181.0 |
| Ordinary Dividends .. | 49.6 | 60.2 | 67.0 | 82.3 | 89.7 |
| RETAINED PROFIT (LOSS) | 49.8 | 60.4 | 68.1 | 84.0 | 91.3 |
| Company .. .. .. | 46.5 | 56.1 | 62.6 | 73.9 | 82.7 |
| Subsidiaries .. .. | 3.3 | 4.3 | 5.5 | 10.1 | 8.6 |
| RETAINED PROFIT (LOSS) | 49.8 | 60.4 | 68.1 | 84.0 | 91.3 |
| PROFIT BEFORE TAX is after charging/(crediting) | | | | | |
| Relocation Costs .. .. | 0.3 | 0.5 | – | – | – |
| Closure Costs .. .. | 0.5 | 0.2 | – | – | – |
| FINANCIAL ACTIVITIES | | | | | |
| Profit for Year .. .. | – | – | – | – | (4.0) |
| PROFIT FOR YEAR includes | | | | | |
| d Sale of Invests .. .. | – | – | – | – | 0.3 |

| NOTES | | Mar.31 1981 £m | Mar.31 1982 £m | Mar.31 1983 £m | Mar.31 1984 £m | Mar.31 e1985 £m |
|---|---|---|---|---|---|---|
| TURNOVER includes | | | | | | |
| FINANCIAL ACTIVITIES | | | | | | |
| Bank &c Int Rcble .. | .. | – | – | – | – | 8.0 |
| Finance Leases Inc. | .. | – | – | – | – | 10.4 |
| Listed Invest Inc. | .. | – | – | – | – | 0.3 |
| | | | | | | 18.7 |
| COST OF SALES includes | | | | | | |
| FINANCIAL ACTIVITIES | | | | | | |
| Bank &c Int P'ble | .. | – | – | – | – | 13.0 |
| STAFF COSTS | | | | | | |
| Wages & Salaries .. | .. | a | 189.0 | 227.9 | 261.5 | 300.3 |
| Social Security .. | .. | a | 17.9 | 19.0 | 21.3 | 23.0 |
| Pensions .. .. | .. | 28.1 | 30.8 | 29.1 | 33.1 | 37.9 |
| Profit Sharing .. | .. | 3.2 | 4.2 | 4.6 | 5.8 | 6.5 |
| Welfare & Other .. | .. | a | 8.9 | 10.8 | 11.2 | 14.6 |
| | | 31.3 | 250.8 | 291.4 | 332.9 | 382.3 |
| Av. No. of Employees | | | | | | |
| UK – Full Time .. | .. | 17,579 | 17,610 | 18,183 | 18,754 | 19,665 |
| – Part Time .. | .. | 27,067 | 28,093 | 30,282 | 32,152 | 34,298 |
| – Total .. .. | .. | 44,646 | 45,703 | 48,465 | 50,906 | 53,963 |
| Total .. .. | .. | | 51,147 | 54,136 | 56,891 | 60,252 |
| OTHER EXPENSES | | | | | | |
| Occupancy Costs .. | .. | a | 52.4 | 63.7 | 70.0 | 79.9 |
| Auditors' Remn .. | .. | 0.2 | 0.5 | 0.3 | 0.3 | 0.3 |
| Plant Hire .. .. | .. | 0.5 | 0.9 | 1.2 | 1.2 | 2.0 |
| Centenary Expenses .. | .. | – | – | – | 3.4 | – |
| Repairs & Maintenance | .. | 14.2 | 18.2 | 21.7 | 24.7 | 29.3 |
| Depreciation .. .. | .. | 19.1 | 22.7 | 30.3 | 39.9 | 44.3 |
| Other Costs .. .. | .. | a | 51.1 | 63.4 | 72.9 | 86.0 |
| | | 34.0 | 145.5 | 180.6 | 212.4 | 241.8 |
| OTHER INCOME | | | | | | |
| Bank & Other Interest | .. | (17.1) | (12.1) | (13.0) | (7.4) | (1.2) |
| Leasing Income .. | .. | (1.7) | (1.7) | (1.7) | (11.5) | – |
| Sale of Tang. Assets | .. | (3.2) | (0.8) | (0.3) | (0.2) | (0.3) |

Table 2-2 Example of Extel card

## DIRECTORS'

| | Mar.31 1981 £m | Mar.31 1982 £m | Mar.31 1983 £m | Mar.31 1984 £m | Mar.31 e1985 £m |
|---|---|---|---|---|---|
| Emoluments | 1.2 | 1.3 | 1.8 | 1.9 | 2.1 |
| Ex-gratia Payments | - | 0.1 | - | - | 0.4 |
| Pmt to Former Dir | - | - | - | - | - |

## NOTES

| | Mar.31 1981 £m | Mar.31 1982 £m | Mar.31 1983 £m | Mar.31 1984 £m | Mar.31 e1985 £m |
|---|---|---|---|---|---|
| **INVESTMENT INCOME** | | | | | |
| Listed | 0.8 | (2.0) | (2.1) | (1.2) | (1.1) |
| Unlisted | - | (9.4) | (12.8) | (9.8) | (7.5) |
| d Sale of Investments | (1.2) | (0.7) | (1.9) | (2.0) | (0.6) |
| Miscellaneous | - | (1.2) | (2.2) | (2.6) | (2.1) |
| | (24.0) | (27.9) | (35.2) | (34.7) | (12.8) |
| **INTEREST PAYABLE** | | | | | |
| Debentures | 3.2 | 3.2 | 3.2 | 3.2 | 3.2 |
| Bank | 9.0 | 10.5 | 14.8 | 12.3 | 2.1 |
| Loans after 5 Years | 3.6 | 4.0 | 3.7 | 0.2 | 0.5 |
| Discount on Bills | - | - | - | - | - |
| | 15.8 | 17.7 | 21.7 | 15.7 | 5.8 |
| CORPORATION TAX RATE % | 52 | 52 | 52 | 50 | 45 |
| b EXPORTS | 47.6 | 58.0 | 67.9 | 84.0 | 92.7 |

*Amounts credited to profit are denoted by use of brackets. (a)Not disclosed. (b)Including shipments to overseas Sub. Cos. (c)Including £8.8m transferred from deferred tax account to reduce net book value of leased assets in 1984 and £3.0m in 1985. (d)Mainly UK Government Securities. (e)Turnover includes interest and other income attributable to financial activities (comprising operation of Marks and Spencer Chargecard together with leasing and insurance) previously shown under other income. Comparative figures for 1984, turnover £2,868.4m, other income £15.6m.

## RECORD OF ADJUSTED PROFITS

| | 1981 £m | 1982 £m | 1983 £m | 1984 £m | 1985 £m |
|---|---|---|---|---|---|
| REPORTED PROFIT (LOSS) BEFORE TAX | 181.2 | 222.1 | 239.3 | 279.3 | 303.4 |
| Profit on Sale of Tangible Assets | - 3.2 | - 0.8 | - 0.3 | - 0.2 | - 0.3 |
| Centenary Expenses | - | - | - | + 3.4 | - |
| Relocation Costs | + 0.3 | + 0.5 | - | - | - |
| Canadian Closure Costs | + 0.5 | + 0.2 | - | - | - |
| Addl Pension Fund Contribn | - | - | - | - | - |
| a ADJUSTED PROFIT (LOSS) BEFORE TAX | 178.8 | 222.0 | 239.0 | 282.5 | 303.1 |
| Reported Tax | 80.6 | 100.3 | 102.5 | 111.1 | 120.3 |
| Estimated Tax on Centenary Expenses | - | - | - | + 1.7 | - |
| Transfer from Deferred Tax | - | - | - | - | - 3.0 |
| Estimated Tax on Pension Fund | - | - | - | - 8.8 | - |
| Adjusted Tax | 80.6 | 100.3 | 102.5 | 104.0 | 117.3 |
| ADJUSTED PROFIT (LOSS) AFTER TAX | 98.2 | 121.7 | 136.5 | 178.5 | 185.8 |
| Minority Interest | 1.1 | 1.1 | 1.6 | 1.8 | 2.0 |
| ADJUSTED ATTRIB. TO MEMBERS | 97.1 | 120.6 | 134.9 | 176.7 | 183.8 |
| Preference Dividends | 0.1 | 0.1 | 0.1 | 0.1 | 0.1 |
| ADJUSTED PROFIT AFTER PREF. DIVS. | 97.0 | 120.5 | 134.8 | 176.6 | 183.7 |
| Ordinary Dividends | 49.6 | 60.2 | 67.0 | 82.3 | 89.7 |
| *ADJUSTED RETAINED PROFIT (LOSS) | 47.4 | 60.3 | 67.8 | 94.3 | 94.0 |

*Before extraordinary items. (a)To reduce net book value of leased assets.

## CONSOLIDATED PRIORITY PERCENTAGES - based on adjusted profits

| | Deb.Stks.(Net) | 7% Pref.(Net) | 4.9% Pref.(Net) | Ord.(Net) | *Retained | Total |
|---|---|---|---|---|---|---|
| 1985 | £1.8m 0-1.0% | £0.1m 1.0-1.0% | | £89.7m 1.0-50.2% | £90.9m 50.2-100.0% | £182.5m |

*Estimated (maximum distribution basis).

## ANALYSIS OF TURNOVER (£m)

| | Total | Clothing | Foods | Homeware, Footwear & Accessories | General Merchandise &c |
|---|---|---|---|---|---|
| 1982 | 2,198.7 | 1,226.0 | 774.7 | 172.4 | 25.6 |
| 1983 | 2,505.5 | 1,353.0 | 902.9 | 216.3 | 33.3 |
| 1984 | 2,854.5 | 1,493.6 | 1,060.6 | 261.8 | 38.5 |
| 1985 | 3,213.0 | 1,611.8 | 1,215.9 | 385.3 | |

## GEOGRAPHICAL ANALYSIS OF TURNOVER (£m)

| | Total | UK Stores | Overseas Stores Europe | Overseas Stores Canada | Export Europe | Export America | Export Africa | Export Far East | Financial Activities |
|---|---|---|---|---|---|---|---|---|---|
| 1981 | 1,872.9 | 1,739.2 | 33.3 | 78.1 | | 22.3 | | | |
| 1982 | 2,198.7 | 2,025.3 | 43.6 | 103.3 | 14.0 | 2.2 | 5.9 | 4.4 | |
| 1983 | 2,505.5 | 2,276.2 | 64.4 | 137.3 | 15.6 | 3.1 | 3.2 | 5.7 | |
| 1984 | 2,854.5 | 2,596.7 | 74.4 | 150.2 | 18.3 | 3.2 | 5.2 | 6.5 | |
| 1985 | 3,213.0 | 2,900.2 | 80.9 | 175.0 | 19.5 | 4.8 | 7.6 | 6.3 | 18.7 |

## GEOGRAPHICAL ANALYSIS OF PROFIT BEFORE TAX (£m)

| | Total | UK | Europe | Canada |
|---|---|---|---|---|
| 1981 | 181.2 | 176.8 | 1.9 | 2.5 |
| 1982 | 222.1 | 216.4 | 3.1 | 2.6 |
| 1983 | 239.3 | 231.0 | 3.7 | 4.6 |
| 1984 | 279.3 | 265.3 | 6.7 | 7.3 |
| 1985 | 303.4 | 288.7 | 7.1 | 7.6 |

# MAN-R 58      MARKS AND SPENCER PLC (CARD 2)      MAR

## STATEMENT OF SOURCE AND APPLICATION OF FUNDS

### Source of Funds (£m)

| Source of Funds | 1981 | 1982 | 1983 | 1984 | 1985 |
|---|---|---|---|---|---|
| Operations | 200.3 | 244.8 | 269.6 | 319.2 | 347.7 |
| Shares Issued | 2.8 | 5.0 | 5.0 | 4.8 | 6.4 |
| Asset Disposals | 4.4 | 4.6 | 2.1 | 4.5 | 2.4 |
| Other | (1.4) | 0.6 | 1.1 | 1.4 | (1.2) |
| Net Liquid Funds | | | | | |
| Cash & Deposits | (7.9) | (25.2) | 2.9 | (10.4) | (10.4) |
| Investments | 13.7 | (22.2) | 18.5 | (7.4) | (5.0) |
| Certs of Tax Deposits | (55.7) | 17.5 | (42.0) | 54.4 | (44.9) |
| Bank Loans | 19.3 | (0.8) | 59.7 | (13.6) | 54.4 |
| Bills of Exchange | 24.3 | 12.0 | (22.0) | (9.5) | – |
| Decrease (Increase) | (6.3) | (18.7) | 17.1 | 13.5 | (5.9) |
| **Total** | **199.8** | **236.3** | **294.9** | **343.4** | **349.4** |

### Application of Funds (£m)

| Application of Funds | 1981 | 1982 | 1983 | 1984 | 1985 |
|---|---|---|---|---|---|
| Dividends | 44.5 | 53.0 | 61.7 | 69.8 | 83.9 |
| Fixed Assets | 74.9 | 91.9 | 110.5 | 120.4 | 121.8 |
| Leased Assets | 2.0 | 4.9 | 35.3 | 76.8 | – |
| Taxation | 76.9 | 77.6 | 99.6 | 71.3 | 94.1 |
| Stocks | 7.5 | 27.3 | 19.6 | 30.8 | 35.6 |
| Debtors | 10.4 | 8.1 | 5.9 | (9.5) | 0.6 |
| CREDITORS | | | | | |
| Under 1 Year | (18.3) | (25.9) | (33.2) | (15.0) | (18.7) |
| Over 1 Year | 1.9 | (0.6) | (4.5) | (1.2) | 0.2 |
| Group Relief | – | – | – | – | 24.0 |
| FINANCIAL ACTIVITIES | | | | | |
| Leased Assets | – | – | – | – | 28.6 |
| Repmt on Leases | – | – | – | – | (13.9) |
| Trade Debtors | – | – | – | – | 4.2 |
| Group Relief | – | – | – | – | (24.0) |
| Bank Loans | – | – | – | – | 9.4 |
| Other Wkg Capital | – | – | – | – | 3.6 |
| *Working Capital | 1.5 | 8.9 | (12.2) | 5.1 | 49.6 |
| **Total** | **199.8** | **236.3** | **294.9** | **343.4** | **349.4** |

*Excluding net liquid funds.

## CONSOLIDATED BALANCE SHEETS (£m)

| | Mar.31 1982 | Mar.31 1983 | Mar.31 1984 | *Mar.31 1985 |
|---|---|---|---|---|
| FIXED ASSETS | | | | |
| a Tangibles | 1,132.6 | 1,252.1 | 1,386.5 | 1,362.8 |
| b Financial Activities Net Assets | – | – | – | 10.7 |
| | 1,132.6 | 1,252.1 | 1,386.5 | 1,373.5 |
| CURRENT ASSETS | | | | |
| Stocks | 143.7 | 163.3 | 194.1 | 229.7 |
| Debtors (within one year) | | | | |
| Trade | 27.5 | 17.6 | 16.0 | 17.8 |
| Other | 7.8 | 11.8 | 9.8 | 5.8 |
| Prepayments | 11.1 | 21.1 | 14.2 | 11.2 |
| Debtors (after one year) | | | | |
| ACT | 7.6 | 7.1 | 8.1 | 9.3 |
| Other | 5.3 | 16.4 | 23.8 | 25.3 |
| c Listed Investments | 34.9 | – | 38.1 | 23.3 |
| Certificates of Tax Deposit | 50.5 | 92.5 | – | 83.0 |
| Cash & Deposits | 80.7 | 77.8 | 73.6 | 83.8 |
| | 369.1 | 407.6 | 377.7 | 489.2 |
| CREDITORS (Due within one year) | | | | |
| Loans & Overdrafts | 62.9 | 122.6 | 94.4 | 91.0 |
| Trade Creditors | 61.0 | 78.6 | 82.1 | 99.1 |
| Group Relief Payable | – | – | – | 1.9 |
| Bills of Exchange | 55.5 | 33.5 | 24.0 | 16.2 |
| Taxation | 105.7 | 88.1 | 101.9 | 127.8 |
| Social Security & Other Taxes | 10.9 | 12.4 | 13.1 | 12.1 |
| Other Creditors | 30.5 | 38.2 | 48.5 | 49.6 |
| Accruals | 20.0 | 26.4 | 31.5 | 18.4 |
| Dividend | 37.3 | 42.7 | 55.3 | 61.2 |
| | 383.8 | 442.5 | 450.8 | 477.3 |
| NET CURRENT ASSETS | (14.7) | (34.9) | (73.1) | 11.9 |
| TOTAL ASSETS LESS CURT LIABS | 1,117.9 | 1,217.2 | 1,313.4 | 1,385.4 |
| CREDITORS (Due after one year) | | | | |
| Deb. Stk | 45.0 | 45.0 | 45.0 | 45.0 |
| Loans | 2.9 | 7.4 | 8.6 | 4.3 |
| PROVN FOR LIABS. AND CHARGES | | | | |
| d Deferred Tax | – | 12.9 | 24.2 | – |
| | 47.9 | 65.3 | 77.8 | 49.3 |
| | 1,070.0 | 1,151.9 | 1,235.6 | 1,336.1 |
| CAPITAL | 328.8 | 329.8 | 330.5 | 661.3 |
| SHARE PREMIUM ACCOUNT | 7.8 | 11.8 | 15.9 | 0.3 |
| REVALUATION RESERVE | 391.5 | 397.6 | 391.2 | 82.9 |
| PROFIT & LOSS ACCOUNT | 337.0 | 405.4 | 489.2 | 580.8 |
| MINORITY INTERESTS | 4.9 | 7.3 | 8.8 | 10.8 |
| | 1,070.0 | 1,151.9 | 1,235.6 | 1,336.1 |

### Fixed Asset Schedule (£m)

| | Mar.31 1982 | Mar.31 1983 | *Mar.31 1985 (1984 / 1985) | |
|---|---|---|---|---|

| | Mar.31 1982 | Mar.31 1983 | Mar.31 1984 | *Mar.31 1985 |
|---|---|---|---|---|
| a LAND AND BUILDINGS | | | | |
| At cost | 45.5 | 110.2 | 160.5 | – |
| At valuation 31-3-82 | 980.7 | 979.5 | 978.5 | – |
| | 1,026.2 | 1,089.7 | 1,139.0 | – |
| Depreciation | 4.7 | 14.0 | 23.3 | – |
| | 1,021.5 | 1,075.7 | 1,115.7 | – |
| Net book value comprises | | | | |
| Freeholds | 639.6 | 673.5 | 703.0 | – |
| Leaseholds | 381.9 | 402.2 | 412.7 | – |
| | 1,021.5 | 1,075.7 | 1,115.7 | – |
| FREEHOLD LAND AND BUILDINGS | | | | |
| At cost | – | – | – | 123.1 |
| At 31-3-82 valuation | – | – | – | 615.3 |
| | – | – | – | 738.4 |
| Depreciation | – | – | – | 14.6 |
| | – | – | – | 723.8 |
| LEASEHOLD LAND AND BUILDINGS | | | | |
| At cost | – | – | – | 113.2 |
| At 31-3-82 valuation | – | – | – | 361.1 |
| | – | – | – | 474.3 |
| Depreciation | – | – | – | 19.7 |
| | – | – | – | 454.6 |
| FIXTURES & EQUIPMENT | | | | |
| At cost | 127.3 | 163.8 | 207.7 | 261.4 |
| Depreciation | 46.5 | 57.9 | 70.8 | 94.3 |
| | 80.8 | 105.9 | 136.9 | 167.1 |
| ASSETS UNDER CONSTRUCTION | | | | |
| At cost | 19.1 | 26.2 | 33.2 | 17.3 |
| LEASED ASSETS | | | | |
| At cost | 14.1 | 49.1 | 124.6 | – |
| Depreciation | 2.9 | 4.8 | 23.9 | – |
| | 11.2 | 44.3 | 100.7 | – |
| b CURRENT ASSETS | | | | |
| Debtors (due within one year) | | | | |
| Trade | – | – | – | 3.0 |
| Finance Leases | – | – | – | 19.7 |
| Group Relief Receivable | – | – | – | 1.9 |
| Other | – | – | – | 1.8 |
| Prepayments &c | – | – | – | 0.3 |
| Debtors (due after one year) | | | | |
| Finance Leases | – | – | – | 82.2 |
| Trade | – | – | – | 2.1 |
| Listed Investments | – | – | – | 4.0 |
| Cash | – | – | – | 4.2 |
| | – | – | – | 119.2 |
| CREDITORS (due within one year) | | | | |
| Bank Loans & Overdrafts | – | – | – | 50.3 |
| Other Creditors | – | – | – | 6.6 |
| Accruals &c | – | – | – | 15.2 |
| | – | – | – | 72.1 |

Table 2-2 *continued*

| | Mar.31 1982 | Mar.31 1983 | Mar.31 1984 | *Mar.31 1985 |
|---|---|---|---|---|
| NET CURRENT ASSETS | – | – | – | 47.1 |
| CREDITORS (due after one year) | – | – | – | 2.2 |
| PROVN FOR LIABS. & CHARGES | – | – | – | 34.2 |
| | | | | 10.7 |
| e Market value | 36.1 | 17.4 | 24.4 | 25.7 |
| d After deducting ACT recoverable | – | 18.3 | 23.7 | – |
| CAPITAL COMMITMENTS | | | | |
| Properties in course of development | 63.7 | 64.9 | 73.9 | 78.6 |
| On leased Assets – | | | | |
| Contracted for | – | 17.1 | 19.5 | – |
| Other – not contracted for | 75.6 | 103.1 | 115.0 | 155.4 |
| FINANCIAL COMMITMENTS | | | | |
| Operating Leases | – | – | – | 26.4 |

*Figures reclassified to separate net assets of financial activities. Had policy applied with effect from 1-4-83 salient figures for year ended 31-3-84 would have been (£m): Tangible Fixed Assets 1,285.7; Net Assets of Financial Activities 8.0; Current Assets 387.8; Creditors (due within one year) 396.4; Creditors (due after one year) 49.5; Provision for liabilities and Charges Nil. NOTES (1985): TANGIBLE FIXED ASSETS: (i)If Co.'s land and buildings had not been valued at 31-3-82 they would have been included at: 31-3-75 valuation £362,400,000; cost £408,000,000, total £770,400,000 less £41,700,000 depreciation. Co. also valued its land and buildings in 1955 and in 1964. In opinion of Directors unreasonable expense would be incurred in obtaining original costs of assets valued in those years and in 1975.

REPORT for year ended 31-3-85.
DIRECTORATE. Lord Sieff of Brimpton will retire from Board on 30-9-85 and will become Honorary President from 1-10-85. Mr.J.Salisse will retire from Board at end of Oct.1985.
SHARE ISSUES. During period 2-4-85 to 1-6-85, 286,461 Ord. shares of 25p were issued against options.
ISSUED ORD. CAPITAL is now £659,988,303.
FUTURE DEVELOPMENTS. Group will continue to expand into new areas of merchandise where these are considered appropriate and plans to continue its physical expansion. In UK planned annual capital expenditure on new stores and extensions is now of order of £220 million. Currently they have no plans for developments in Europe but shall resume expansion when it is beneficial to do so.
Meeting, July 9.
CHAIRMAN'S STATEMENT. Profits after taxes and an allocation to UK Employees' Profit Sharing Scheme were up 8.8% on last year. Miners' strike had localised effects and some impact on profitability as stores affected incurred full operating costs, while achieving lower than expected levels of turnover. They estimate lost turnover because of strike to have been nearly £24 million, mostly in Yorkshire and Wales.
UK store sales increased by 11.7% to £2,900.2 million net of VAT, compared with £2,596.7 million last year.
CLOTHING sales increased by 7.4%. Sales of Ladies' Outerwear were disappointing and fell short of planned growth. They have taken steps to improve appeal of clothing and introduced substantially more casualwear. They anticipate that performance of this sector of business will improve in year ahead.
Men's clothing made excellent progress with market share increasing. They have set up a new department to deal with development of men's casualwear for which there is a substantial demand.
HOMEWEAR AND FOOTWEAR. Group of departments made good progress, with sales increasing by 22.4%. In year ahead, they are planning substantial expansion of existing ranges, introducing new lines for kitchen and garden.

Childrens wear Group has been re-organised. In year ahead they foresee a significant expansion of business throughout age groups.

**Compiled, Printed and Published by EXTEL STATISTICAL SERVICES LTD, 37/45 PAUL ST, LONDON EC2A 4PB**

Tel: 01-253 3400     Extra Cards 01-251 1437

C1     Please withdraw previous card     Copyright—Reproduction prohibited     No responsibility accepted for error or omission     ANA

MARKS AND SPENCER PLC

FOOD. Sales increased by 14.6% to £1,171 million compared with £1,022 million last year.
STORE DEVELOPMENT. They added 245,000 sq ft of selling space to stores last year. Major extensions were made to stores in Glasgow, Belfast, Manchester and Leeds. They converted into sales floors fallow space at Yeovil and Lincoln and opened new stores at Horsham and Bishop's Stortford. During year they carried out a number of experiments aimed at improving appearance of stores. As result they have embarked upon major programme of modernisation and introduction of new equipment.
Success of experiment at Yeovil and Lincoln stores has led them to plan extension of a further 38 stores, first of which, at Macclesfield, is already trading successfully. This approach will bring rapidly into use some 400,000 extra sq ft.
During March they opened a satellite store at York for sale of Children's wear and early results are encouraging. They have many other stores in country where they cannot expand selling area on existing sites and they are seeking satellite stores in these towns.
They announced during year first out of town development at Metro Centre near Gateshead which will open in autumn 1986. They came to an agreement with Tesco PLC to develop joint sites in edge of town locations where they can secure adequate car parking. As result of this association they expect to announce further expansion during year ahead. Cos. will trade in full competition.
Total footage development already known over next two years will add 660,000 sq ft of selling space. Total value of planned capital expenditure over next two years currently stands at £480 million.
CANADA. In financial year ended 31-1-85, Marks & Spencer Canada Inc. sales increased by 6.8% to C$295 million. D'Allaird's Division showed an increase in sales of 4.9%. Marks & Spencer Division showed only a 1.6% increase in sales, although Food section continued to expand, showing a sales increase of 11%. They have embarked upon a substantial programme of modernising Marks & Spencer stores in Canada and early results are encouraging. Peoples Division achieved an increase in sales of 12.9%. 3 Divisions will open new stores in 1985 increasing sales footage by 130,000 sq ft.
EUROPEAN ECONOMIC COMMUNITY. Stores in Europe outside UK increased sales by 8.7%.
CHARGECARD. Scheme became operational nationally on 2-4-85. Response was substantially ahead of expectations and initially they had a problem in dealing with many applications received. A new Sub. St Michael Financial Services Ltd, has been formed to operate scheme which is at present administered by North West Securities Ltd.

LATER INFORMATION WILL BE PUBLISHED ON NEWS CARD.

NEWS CARD                    EXTEL U.K. LISTED COMPANIES SERVICE                    UP-DATED TO 9-7-85.

MAN-R 58                                                                                              MAR

# MARKS AND SPENCER PLC

ISSUED EQUITY CAPITAL: £659,988,303.
SHARE PRICES. 25p ORD.: 1985, High 151p, Low 110p. To June 14.
YIELD INDICATOR based on Gross Dividend 19.429%, *Earnings 39.121% (9.78p per share).

| PRICE | p | 100 | 110 | 120 | 130 | 140 | 150 | 160 |
|---|---|---|---|---|---|---|---|---|
| DIVIDEND YIELD | % | 4.86 | 4.42 | 4.05 | 3.74 | 3.47 | 3.24 | 3.04 |
| *EARNINGS YIELD | % | 9.78 | 8.89 | 8.15 | 7.52 | 6.99 | 6.52 | 6.11 |
| **P/E RATIO | | 14.36 | 15.80 | 17.23 | 18.67 | 20.10 | 21.54 | 22.98 |

Earnings calculated on £6,595,000 weighted average capital. *On gross actual basis. **On net actual basis. **On net actual basis per share 6.964p.
LAST ACCOUNTS PUBLISHED 13-6-85.
ORD. DIVIDEND PAYMENT DETAILS. Year end March 31.

| | | Per Share | | | | | | |
|---|---|---|---|---|---|---|---|---|
| | | % Gross | Net | Tax Rate | Announced | Paid | Holders | Ex Date |
| 1983 | Int | 10,571 | 2.643p | 1.85p | 30% | 26-10-82 | 14-1-83 | 19-11-82 | 1-11-82 |
| | Fin | 18,571 | 4.643p | 3.25p | 30% | 4-5-83 | 15-7-83 | 20-5-83 | 9-5-83 |
| 1984 | Int | 11,714 | 2.929p | 2.05p | 30% | 2-11-83 | 13-1-84 | 25-11-83 | 14-11-83 |
| | Fin 24 | | 6p | 4.2p | 30% | 1-5-84 | 13-7-84 | 25-5-84 | 14-5-84 |
| | Cap 100 | | - | - | - | 1-5-84 | - | 25-5-84 | 30-7-84 |
| 1985 | Int | 6,171 | 1.543p | 1.08p | 30% | 23-10-84 | 18-1-85 | 16-11-84 | 29-10-84 |
| | Fin | 13,257 | 3.314p | 2.32p | 30% | 7-5-85 | 12-7-85 | 24-5-85 | 13-5-85 |

CONSOLIDATED INTERIM STATEMENT (unaudited) for half year to Sept. 30 approx.

| | Clothing | Homeware | Food | UK Total | | Europe | | Canada | |
|---|---|---|---|---|---|---|---|---|---|
| | Sales | &c Sales | Sales | Sales | Prof. | Sales | Prof. | Sales | Prof. |
| | £m | £m | £m | £m | £m | £m | £m | £m | £m |
| 1983 | 599.2 | 100.3 | 474.4 | 1,173.9 | 104.7 | 31.1 | 1.4 | 64.4 | L 0.5 |
| 1984 | 644.6 | 118.5 | 550.2 | 1,313.3 | 111.1 | 37.3 | 3.0 | 77.6 | L 0.7 |

| | Direct | Total Sales | Profit | | Min. | Attrib.to | | |
|---|---|---|---|---|---|---|---|---|
| | Exports | Excl. Taxes | Bef.Tax | Taxn | Int | Members | | |
| | £m | £m | £m | £m | £m | £m | | |
| 1983 | 15.7 | 1,285.1 | 105.6 | 42.2 | Cr.0.2 | 63.4 | | |
| 1984 | 18.1 | 1,446.3 | 113.4 | 46.7 | Cr.0.2 | 67.0 | | |

L-Loss.
EARNINGS PER SHARE stated by Co. for 26 weeks to 29-9-84, 2.5p (2.4p adjusted).

P.T.O.

---

Compiled, Printed and Published by **EXTEL STATISTICAL SERVICES LTD, 37/45 PAUL ST, LONDON EC2A 4PB**
Tel: 01-253 3400          Extra Cards 01-251 1437
C1    Please withdraw previous card          Copyright—Reproduction prohibited          No responsibility accepted for error or omission          ANA

---

MARKS AND SPENCER PLC

23-10-84.

INTERIM REPORT. For figures for 26 weeks to 29-9-84, see table.

9-7-85.

Chairman said that if half year results are as good as the first 3 months sales and profits are heading for a very good year.

Table 2-2 continued

EXTEL ANALYST'S SERVICE

# MARKS AND SPENCER, PLC

**MAN-R 58**

## CAPITAL EMPLOYED

| YEARS ENDED MAR.31 | BANK LOANS & OVERDRAFT £000 | LOANS £000 | DEFERRED TAX £000 | LIABILITIES OTHER £000 | MINORITY INTEREST £000 | PREFERENCE £000 | ORDINARY £000 | *NET RESERVES £000 | NET CAP. EMPLOYED £000 | INTAN-GIBLES £000 |
|---|---|---|---|---|---|---|---|---|---|---|
| 1976 | 23,322 | 45,000 | 19,852 | - | 5,183 | 1,350 | 162,251 | 189,766 | 446,724 | 8,864 |
| 1977 | 27,825 | 45,000 | 24,383 | - | 3,241 | 1,350 | 162,251 | 215,789 | 479,839 | 7,228 |
| 1978 | 64,706 | 45,000 | - | - | 2,419 | 1,350 | 162,251 | 286,300 | 562,026 | - |
| 1979 | 63,541 | 45,000 | 1,000 | - | 1,855 | 1,350 | 324,914 | 175,075 | 612,735 | - |
| 1980 | 48,577 | 45,000 | 4,700 | - | 2,371 | 1,350 | 325,422 | 222,965 | 650,385 | - |
| 1981 | 66,000 | 45,000 | 8,300 | - | 3,300 | 1,400 | 326,200 | 270,200 | 720,400 | - |
| 1982 | 65,800 | 45,000 | 8,400 | - | 4,900 | 1,400 | 327,400 | 736,300 | 1,189,200 | - |
| 1983 | 130,000 | 45,000 | 12,900 | - | 7,300 | 1,400 | 328,400 | 814,800 | 1,339,800 | - |
| 1984 | 103,000 | 45,000 | 24,200 | - | 8,800 | 1,400 | 329,100 | 896,300 | 1,407,800 | - |
| 1985 | 147,800 | 45,000 | 10,900 | - | 10,800 | 1,400 | 659,900 | 664,000 | 1,539,800 | - |

*Reserves less intangibles shown in end column.

## EMPLOYMENT OF CAPITAL

| YEARS ENDED MAR.31 | BEF.DEPN PROPERTY £000 | BEF.DEPN OTHER £000 | TOTAL AFT.DEPN £000 | INVESTS £000 | CASH & CASH EQUIVT £000 | QUICK LIABS. £000 | STOCK & W/P £000 | % | TRADE DEBTORS A £000 | TRADE CREDS. B £000 | RATIO B:A | CURRENT ASSETS C £000 | **CURRENT LIABS. D £000 | RATIO C:D | OTHER ASSETS £000 |
|---|---|---|---|---|---|---|---|---|---|---|---|---|---|---|---|
| 1976 | 429,807 b | 30,033 | 453,153 | - | 22,862 | 56,775 | 59,750 | 6.6 | 13,747 | 46,013 | 3.3 | 96,359 | 126,110 | 0.8 | - |
| 1977 | 455,049 b | 34,231 | 478,998 | - | 19,926 | 67,060 | 81,009 | 7.6 | 16,336 | 49,316 | 3.0 | 117,217 | 144,201 | 0.8 | - |
| 1978 | 484,803 b | 40,887 | 512,411 | - | 25,673 | 71,303 | 86,168 | 6.9 | 19,046 | 61,377 | 3.2 | 173,788 | 197,386 | 0.9 | 8,507 |
| 1979 | 523,338 b | 47,899 | 555,702 | - | 50,751 | 110,779 | 95,748 | 6.5 | 18,854 | 73,318 | 3.9 | 231,793 | 247,638 | 0.9 | 9,337 |
| 1980 | 568,360 b | 62,490 | 611,197 | 26,335 | 59,889 | 121,527 | 108,894 | 6.5 | 33,233 | 78,235 | 2.4 | 248,339 | 316,000 | 0.8 | 25,179 |
| 1981 | 613,100 b | 72,300 | 661,300 | 12,700 | 123,500 | 153,500 | 116,400 | 6.2 | 43,600 | 96,500 | 2.2 | 356,200 | 386,700 | 0.9 | 27,500 |
| 1982 | 1,026,200 | 141,400 | 1,113,500 | - | 167,300 | 209,400 | 143,700 | 6.5 | 27,500 | 61,000 | 2.2 | 400,500 | 449,900 | 0.9 | 40,400 |
| 1983 | 1,089,700 | 212,900 | 1,225,900 | - | 187,700 | 176,700 | 163,300 | 6.5 | 17,600 | 78,600 | 4.5 | 459,400 | 491,500 | 0.9 | 33,300 |
| 1984 | 1,139,000 | 332,300 | 1,353,300 | - | 136,100 | 194,300 | 194,100 | 6.8 | 16,000 | 82,100 | 5.1 | 459,400 | 555,900 | 0.8 | 41,300 |
| 1985 | 1,212,700 | 261,400 | 1,345,500 | - | 200,700 | 217,300 | 229,700 | 7.1 | 20,800 | 99,100 | 4.8 | 491,500 | 555,900 | 0.9 | 110,900 |

*Percentage of Turnover. **Including Bank Loans and Overdraft. (a)Property revalued. (b)After Depn.

## CAPITAL CHANGES

| DATE | | CUM PRICE | EX DATE | EX PRICE | FACTOR APPLIED |
|---|---|---|---|---|---|
| July 1975 | Cap issue of 324,502,599 25p Ord. (1 for 1) | 200p | 14-7-75 | 90p | .500 |
| June 1978 | 822,609 25p Ord. issued under UK Employees Profit Sharing Scheme | | | | |
| Aug. 1978 | Cap issue of 649,005,198 25p Ord. (1 for 1) | 165p | 7-8-78 | 85p | .500 |
| July 1979 | 2,031,431 25p Ord. issued under UK Employees Profit Sharing Scheme | | | | |
| June 1980 | 3,236,664 25p Ord. issued under UK Employees Profit Sharing Scheme | | | | |
| Mar. 1981 | 16,000 25p Ord. issued under UK Employees Profit Sharing Scheme | | | | |
| June 1981 | 2,182,914 25p Ord. issued under UK Employees' Profit Sharing Scheme | | | | |
| Mar. 1982 | 2,779,046 25p Ord. issued under UK Employees' Profit Sharing Scheme | | | | |
| 1982/83 | 4,034,581 25p Ord. issued under UK Employees' Profit Sharing Scheme | | | | |
| Nov. 1983 | 1,993,048 25p Ord. issued against options | | | | |
| 1983/84 | 606,084 25p Ord. issued against options | | | | |
| 1984 | 304,176 25p Ord. issued against options | | | | |
| 1984 | 2,072,157 25p Ord. issued under UK Employees' Profit Sharing Scheme | 218p | 30-7-84 | 113p | .500 |
| July 1984 | Cap issue of 1,318,911,755 25p Ord. (1 for 1) | | | | |
| 1984 | 1,842,744 25p Ord. issued against options | | | | |

## INCOME STATISTICS

| YEARS ENDED MAR.31 | A *NET CAP. EMPLOYED £000 | FUNDED DEBT £000 | % | B TURN-OVER £000 | RATIO B:A | NET PROFIT BEF. INT & TAX AMOUNT £000 | % ON A | % ON B | C NET PROF. BEF.TAX £000 | TAXATION CHARGED £000 | AS % OF C | NET PROF. AFT.TAX £000 | COST OF DIVS. PAID £000 | DEPN & RETD PROF. £000 | CAPITAL COMMIT-MENTS £000 |
|---|---|---|---|---|---|---|---|---|---|---|---|---|---|---|---|
| 1976 | 407,034 | 1,525 | 4 | 900,923 | 2.2 | 88,937 | 21.9 | 9.9 | 83,582 | 46,515 | 55.7 | 37,148 | 22,494 | 23,437 | 33,000 |
| 1977 | 446,724 | 1,525 | 3 | 1,064,837 | 2.5 | 114,491 | 25.6 | 10.8 | 107,820 | 56,994 | 52.9 | 52,080 | 24,982 | 37,368 | 23,250 |
| 1978 | 479,839 | 1,525 | 2 | 1,254,055 | 2.6 | 129,559 | 27.0 | 10.3 | 121,604 | 54,829 | 45.1 | 67,131 | 27,619 | 50,928 | 39,600 |
| 1979 | 562,026 | 1,525 | 2 | 1,472,954 | 2.6 | 176,233 | 31.4 | 12.0 | 166,254 | 78,129 | 47.0 | 88,395 | 33,977 | 67,751 | 65,853 |
| 1980 | 612,735 | 1,526 | 1 | 1,667,905 | 2.7 | 183,816 | 30.0 | 11.0 | 173,043 | 80,595 | 46.6 | 91,929 | 44,331 | 63,011 | 69,672 |
| 1981 | 650,385 | | | 1,872,900 | 2.9 | 191,000 | 29.4 | 10.2 | 178,800 | 80,600 | 45.1 | 97,100 | 49,700 | 66,500 | 66,900 |
| 1982 | 720,400 | | | 2,198,700 | 3.1 | 235,700 | 32.7 | 10.7 | 222,000 | 100,300 | 45.2 | 120,600 | 60,300 | 83,000 | 63,700 |
| 1983 | 1,189,200 | | | 2,505,500 | 2.1 | 257,000 | 21.6 | 10.3 | 239,000 | 102,500 | 42.9 | 134,900 | 67,100 | 98,100 | 82,000 |
| 1984 | 1,339,800 | | | 2,854,500 | 2.1 | 298,000 | 22.2 | 10.4 | 282,500 | 104,000 | 36.8 | 176,700 | 82,400 | 134,200 | 93,400 |
| 1985 | 1,407,800 | | | 3,213,000 | 2.3 | 321,900 | 22.9 | 10.0 | 303,100 | 117,300 | 38.7 | 183,800 | 89,800 | 138,300 | 78,600 |

M-Minus.

*At beginning of year.

## *PRIORITY PERCENTAGES—CONSOLIDATED EARNINGS

| YEARS ENDED MAR.31 | FUNDED DEBT £000 | % | RATIO B:A | PREFERENCE £000 | % | ORDINARY £000 | % |
|---|---|---|---|---|---|---|---|
| 1976 | 1,525 | 4 | 2.2 | 73 | 2 | 22,421 | 62 |
| 1977 | 1,525 | 3 | 2.5 | 73 | | 24,909 | 49 |
| 1978 | 1,525 | 2 | 2.6 | 73 | | 27,546 | 42 |
| 1979 | 1,525 | 2 | 2.6 | 73 | | 33,904 | 39 |
| 1980 | 1,526 | 1 | 2.7 | 73 | | 44,258 | 49 |
| 1981 | 1,500 | 2 | | 100 | 2 | 49,600 | 52 |
| 1982 | 1,500 | 1 | | 100 | 1 | 60,200 | 51 |
| 1983 | 1,500 | 1 | | 100 | 1 | 67,000 | 50 |
| 1984 | 1,600 | 1 | | 100 | 1 | 82,300 | 49 |
| 1985 | 1,800 | 1 | | 100 | 1 | 89,700 | 50 |

*Cumulative.

Marks and Spencer PLC

## ORDINARY SHARE RECORD
### NEW PENCE PER SHARE

| YEARS ENDED MAR.31 | *NET ASSET VALUE ACTUAL | ADJD | **CASH FLOW GROSS | NET | % EARNED ON ORD. GROSS ACTUAL | ADJD |
|---|---|---|---|---|---|---|
| 1976 | 54.2 | 13.5 | 1.76 | 0.90 | 35.2 | 8.8 |
| 1977 | 58.2 | 14.5 | 2.40 | 1.44 | 49.3 | 12.3 |
| 1978 | 69.1 | 17.2 | 3.02 | 1.96 | 61.9 | 15.4 |
| 1979 | 38.5 | 19.2 | 3.91 | 2.60 | 38.8 | 19.4 |
| 1980 | 42.1 | 21.0 | 4.12 | 2.42 | 40.3 | 20.1 |
| 1981 | 45.7 | 22.8 | 4.45 | 2.55 | 42.5 | 21.2 |
| 1982 | 81.2 | 40.6 | 5.47 | 3.17 | 52.6 | 26.3 |
| 1983 | 87.0 | 43.5 | 6.28 | 3.73 | 58.7 | 29.3 |
| 1984 | 93.1 | 46.5 | 8.22 | 5.10 | 73.5 | 36.7 |
| 1985 | 50.2 | 50.2 | 8.64 | 5.24 | 39.1 | 39.1 |

### DIVIDENDS PAID

| GROSS ACTUAL % | ADJD % | TIMES COVERED | EX DIV. | PAYABLE | TAX RATE % |
|---|---|---|---|---|---|
| Int 7.385 / Fin 13.874 | 5.3 | 1.7 | 3-11-75 / 3-5-76 | 16-1-76 / 16-7-76 | 35 / 35 |
| Int 8.123 / Fin 15.030 | 5.8 | 2.1 | 1-11-76 / 9-5-77 | 14-1-77 / 15-7-77 | 35 / 34 |
| Spec a 0.231 / Int 10.303 / Fin 15.19 | 6.3 | 2.4 | 31-10-77 / 31-10-77 / 15-5-78 | 13-1-78 / 13-1-78 / 14-7-78 | 34 / 34 / 33 |
| Cap 100 | | | | | |
| Int 6.866 / Fin 8.335 | 7.6 | 2.6 | 30-10-78 / 21-5-79 | 12-1-79 / 13-7-79 | 33 / 30 |
| Int 8.571 / Fin 10.857 | 9.7 | 2.1 | 22-10-79 / 12-5-80 | 11-1-80 / 18-7-80 | 30 / 30 |
| Int 8.571 / Fin 13.143 | 10.8 | 2.0 | 27-10-80 / 1-6-81 | 16-1-81 / 17-7-81 | 30 / 30 |
| Int 10 / Fin 16.286 | 13.1 | 2.0 | 26-10-81 / 17-5-82 | 15-1-82 / 16-7-82 | 30 / 30 |
| Int 10.571 / Fin 18.571 | 14.5 | 2.0 | 1-11-82 / 9-5-83 | 14-1-83 / 15-7-83 | 30 / 30 |
| Int 11.714 / Fin 24 | 17.9 | 2.1 | 14-11-83 / 14-5-84 | 13-1-84 / 13-7-84 | 30 / 30 |
| Cap 100 | | | | | |
| Int 6.171 / Fin 13.257 | 19.4 | 2.0 | 29-10-84 / 13-5-85 | 18-1-85 / 12-7-85 | 30 / 30 |

*Excluding intangibles. **Adjusted. (a)Compensating dividend due to change in tax rate.

## YIELD COMPARISONS

| YEARS ENDED | REPORT RECEIVED | PRICE | GROSS YIELD % EARNINGS A | DIVIDEND B | GROUP YIELD % EARNINGS C | DIVIDEND D | "500" YIELD % EARNINGS E | DIVIDEND F |
|---|---|---|---|---|---|---|---|---|
| 1976 | 9-6-76 | 97p | 9.07 | 5.48 | 13.14 | 5.84 | 13.99 | 5.83 |
| 1977 | 10-6-77 | 122p | 10.41 | 4.79 | 12.36 | 5.22 | 15.62 | 5.53 |
| 1978 | 25-5-78 | 150p | 10.32 | 4.25 | 11.62 | 4.48 | 16.18 | 5.39 |
| 1979 | 7-6-79 | 120p | 8.08 | 3.17 | 11.12 | 4.01 | 14.43 | 5.02 |
| 1980 | 2-6-80 | 89p | 11.32 | 5.46 | 15.35 | 6.12 | 21.72 | 7.31 |
| 1981 | 23-6-81 | 132p | 8.05 | 4.11 | 10.86 | 4.98 | 13.99 | 5.81 |
| 1982 | 9-6-82 | 171p | 7.69 | 3.84 | 10.25 | 4.84 | 12.90 | 5.51 |
| 1983 | 7-6-83 | 218p | 6.73 | 3.34 | 8.11 | 3.78 | 9.69 | 4.50 |
| 1984 | 8-6-84 | 255p | 7.21 | 3.50 | 9.04 | 3.89 | 10.84 | 4.51 |
| 1985 | 13-6-85 | 135p | 7.24 | 3.60 | 8.02 | 3.37 | 10.70 | 4.49 |

(a)Not available.

### YIELD RATIOS

| | EARNINGS A:C | A:E | DIVIDEND B:D | B:F |
|---|---|---|---|---|
| | 0.69 | 0.65 | 0.94 | 0.94 |
| | 0.84 | 0.67 | 0.92 | 0.87 |
| | 0.89 | 0.64 | 0.95 | 0.79 |
| | 0.73 | 0.56 | 0.79 | 0.63 |
| | 0.74 | 0.52 | 0.89 | 0.75 |
| | 0.75 | 0.58 | 0.83 | 0.71 |
| | 0.73 | 0.59 | 0.79 | 0.70 |
| | 0.83 | 0.69 | 0.88 | 0.74 |
| | 0.80 | 0.67 | 0.90 | 0.78 |
| | 0.90 | 0.68 | 1.07 | 0.80 |

F.T. - ACTUARIES

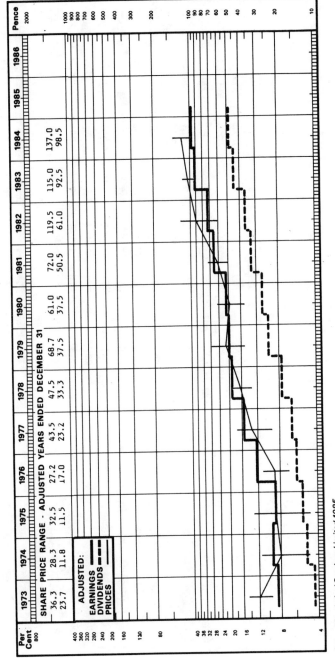

SHARE PRICE RANGE - ADJUSTED YEARS ENDED DECEMBER 31

| | 1973 | 1974 | 1975 | 1976 | 1977 | 1978 | 1979 | 1980 | 1981 | 1982 | 1983 | 1984 | 1985 | 1986 |
|---|---|---|---|---|---|---|---|---|---|---|---|---|---|---|
| | 36.3 | 28.3 | 32.5 | 27.2 | 43.5 | 47.5 | 68.7 | 61.0 | 72.0 | 119.5 | 115.0 | 137.0 | | |
| | 23.7 | 11.8 | 11.5 | 17.0 | 23.2 | 33.3 | 37.5 | 37.5 | 50.5 | 61.0 | 92.5 | 98.5 | | |

ADJUSTED:
EARNINGS ———
DIVIDENDS ■ ■ ■
PRICES ▪▪▪▪

Table 2-2 continued

45

| Rank | Company | Market value[1] £m 27.3.85 | Percentage increase 1975–1984 | | | | | Growth rating[5] |
|---|---|---|---|---|---|---|---|---|
| | | | Net capital employed[2] | Pre-tax profit | Sales | Gross cash flow[3] | % Change in share value[4] | |
| 1. | Polly Peck Int. | 222 | 3,426 | N/A | 6,899 | N/A | 26,344 | 27,646 |
| 2. | Sound Diffusion | 149 | 909 | N/A | 754 | N/A | 15,329 | 15,661 |
| 3. | Pentland Inds | 84 | 478 | 2,403 | 1,454 | 1,021 | 13,525 | 13,827 |
| 4. | MFI Furniture | 453 | 3,225 | 51,078 | 1,876 | 24,302 | 12,332 | 13,805 |
| 5. | Automated Security | 105 | 2,036 | 3,933 | 1,586 | 2,421 | H 7,818 | 8,081 |
| 6. | Flight Refuelling | 151 | 871 | 1,313 | 648 | 1,661 | 7,583 | 7,960 |
| 7. | Avana | 213 | 797 | 6,050 | 1,077 | 2,795 | 6,527 | 7,108 |
| 8. | Farnell Electronics | 217 | 570 | 1,035 | 335 | 1,075 | 6,504 | 6,810 |
| 9. | Pleasurama | 159 | 1,617 | 3,992 | 790 | 2,606 | 5,458 | 5,773 |
| 10. | Home Charm | 121 | 1,676 | 1,051 | 1,676 | 1,556 | 5,221 | 5,428 |
| 11. | Hazlewood Foods | 104 | 4,345 | 19,069 | 5,286 | 14,188 | 4,591 | 4,887 |
| 12. | Wilson (Connolly) | 82 | 544 | 1,034 | 616 | 1,268 | 4,319 | 4,633 |
| 13. | J. Bibby | 271 | 194 | 834 | 125 | 721 | 4,074 | 4,615 |
| 14. | BTR | 3,742 | 2,869 | 1,623 | 1,682 | 1,973 | 4,155 | 4,475 |
| 15. | Argyll | 537 | 5,473 | 43,161 | 6,407 | 36,833 | 3,974 | 4,258 |
| 16. | Burton | 808 | 56 | 4,125 | 209 | 1,315 | 3,670 | 3,987 |
| 17. | Dawson Int. | 260 | 420 | 4,950 | 322 | 1,887 | 3,123 | 3,770 |
| 18. | A. B. Electronic | 86 | 682 | 1,389 | 525 | 566 | 3,406 | 3,679 |
| 19. | Electrocomponents | 283 | 996 | 832 | 912 | 1,032 | 3,249 | 3,526 |
| 20. | Diploma | 108 | 354 | 733 | 407 | 838 | 3,076 | 3,476 |
| 21. | Allied Colloids | 279 | 664 | 995 | 674 | 1,050 | 2,997 | 3,165 |
| 22. | Hawley | 181 | 17,251 | N/A | 12,218 | N/A | 2,777 | 3,016 |
| 23. | AGB Research | 96 | 5,462 | 1,128 | 1,425 | 1,293 | 2,567 | 3,015 |
| 24. | Saatchi & Saatchi | 341 | F 1,696 | F 877 | F 1,347 | F 1,435 | F 2,778 | 2,941 |
| 25. | Stakis | 154 | 900 | 793 | 477 | 1,920 | 2,419 | 2,644 |
| 26. | Dixons | 598 | 844 | 376 | 483 | 615 | 2,465 | 2,625 |
| 27. | United Scientific | 90 | 3,018 | 1,315 | 1,579 | 2,379 | 2,100 | 2,559 |
| 28. | Bullough | 92 | 412 | 730 | 535 | 795 | 2,199 | 2,547 |
| 29. | John Menzies | 131 | 455 | 538 | 343 | 874 | 2,211 | 2,405 |
| 30. | UEI | 102 | 999 | 1,587 | 508 | 1,404 | 1,733 | 2,101 |
| 31. | Hillards | 79 | 809 | 975 | 539 | 1,298 | 1,834 | 2,029 |
| 32. | Wm. Morrison Supermarkets | 96 | 837 | 588 | 676 | 793 | 1,782 | 1,899 |
| 33. | Mount Charlotte Invs | 165 | 644 | N/A | 212 | N/A | 1,751 | 1,896 |
| 34. | J. Sainsbury | 2,088 | 239 | 774 | 478 | 917 | 1,730 | 1,867 |
| 35. | Savoy Hotel | 216 | 58 | N/A | 278 | 2,743 | 1,748 | 1,830 |
| 36. | Associated Dairies | 1,265 | 1,303 | 949 | 693 | 1,169 | 1,575 | 1,718 |
| 37. | M. K. Electric | 99 | 337 | 2,587 | 446 | 1,237 | 1,306 | 1,680 |
| 38. | Hanson Trust | 2,119 | 1,999 | 1,294 | 3,048 | 2,014 | 1,518 | 1,671 |
| 39. | Bejam | 203 | 955 | 875 | 748 | 1,163 | 1,447 | 1,638 |
| 40. | Christies Int. | 83 | 828 | 530 | 626 | 571 | 1,448 | 1,633 |
| 41. | De La Rue | 339 | 329 | 352 | 172 | 466 | 1,278 | 1,623 |

| Rank | Company | Market value[1] £m 27.3.85 | Percentage increase 1975–1984 | | | | % Change in share value[4] | Growth rating[5] |
|---|---|---|---|---|---|---|---|---|
| | | | Net capital employed[2] | Pre-tax profit | Sales | Gross cash flow[3] | | |
| 51. | J. Hepworth | 243 | 285 | 299 | 262 | 465 | 1,279 | 1,416 |
| 52. | Glaxo | 4,123 | 313 | 508 | 278 | 640 | 1,280 | 1,374 |
| 53. | Dee Corporation | 775 | 1,444 | 1,127 | 750 | 1,411 | 1,083 | 1,304 |
| 54. | Trusthouse Forte | 1,138 | 289 | 644 | 206 | 421 | 1,003 | 1,291 |
| 55. | Racal Electronics | 1,221 | 2,156 | 1,147 | 1,524 | 1,832 | 1,130 | 1,261 |
| 56. | Nurdin & Peacock | 104 | 597 | 458 | 402 | 638 | 1,069 | 1,237 |
| 57. | Extel | 113 | 418 | 978 | 1,101 | 647 | 1,037 | 1,216 |
| 58. | Security Services | 133 | 334 | 321 | 304 | 661 | 1,061 | 1,183 |
| 59. | Matthew Hall | 105 | 672 | 507 | 415 | 639 | 971 | 1,159 |
| 60. | Carlton Communications | 173 | D 5,802 | D 1,802 | 3,114 | D 3,633 | C 1,125 | 1,156 |
| 61. | Scapa | 154 | 309 | 246 | 312 | 288 | 953 | 1,145 |
| 62. | Fleet | 250 | B 183 | B 486 | B 47 | B 203 | B 1,088 | 1,135 |
| 63. | BPB Industries | 491 | 257 | 548 | 289 | 633 | 912 | 1,122 |
| 63. | Dowty | 443 | 409 | 349 | 324 | 376 | 939 | 1,122 |
| 63. | Lep | 88 | 176 | (31) | 136 | 32 | 986 | 1,122 |
| 66. | William Collins | 109 | 86 | 182 | 213 | 608 | 1,006 | 1,105 |
| 67. | British & Commonwealth | 495 | 131 | 148 | 137 | 103 | 982 | 1,101 |
| 68. | Northern Foods | 478 | 748 | 1,506 | 1,845 | 1,998 | 885 | 1,090 |
| 69. | Sketchley | 89 | 522 | 556 | 382 | 656 | 819 | 1,065 |
| 70. | Ibstock Johnsen | 86 | 590 | 224 | 148 | 320 | 884 | 1,058 |
| 71. | Spirax-Sarco Engineering | 129 | 385 | 485 | 256 | 573 | 878 | 1,057 |
| 72. | Vantona Viyella | 137 | 395 | 400 | 599 | 739 | 768 | 1,041 |
| 73. | Plessey | 1,435 | 170 | 521 | 282 | 480 | 857 | 1,019 |
| 74. | Arthur Bell | 189 | 334 | 734 | 214 | 635 | 777 | 994 |
| 75. | Ladbroke | 436 | 871 | 311 | 232 | 547 | 755 | 993 |
| 76. | Foster Brothers Clothing | 97 | 189 | 123 | 184 | 212 | 829 | 988 |
| 77. | Wolseley-Hughes | 145 | 499 | 572 | 611 | 745 | 753 | 969 |
| 78. | GEC | 5,087 | 298 | 306 | 241 | 374 | 845 | 966 |
| 79. | Dunhill | 133 | 584 | 105 | 374 | 207 | 870 | 958 |
| 80. | Smith & Nephew | 785 | 224 | 546 | 197 | 628 | 834 | 953 |
| 81. | Rentokil | 326 | 294 | 271 | 273 | 362 | 855 | 941 |
| 82. | Laporte Industries | 410 | 127 | 197 | 215 | 169 | 796 | 942 |
| 83. | Matthew Brown | 97 | 370 | 221 | 288 | 371 | 760 | 917 |
| 84. | Tarmac | 780 | 210 | 383 | 248 | 355 | 745 | 916 |
| 85. | BOC | 1,156 | 418 | 191 | 328 | 549 | 727 | 906 |
| 86. | Rothmans Int. | 418 | 230 | 718 | 49 | 627 | 701 | 904 |
| 87. | S. & W. Berisford | 310 | 1,817 | 733 | 853 | 1,387 | 569 | 901 |

The companies are the 250 largest publicly quoted industrial and commercial companies measured by market capitalization of equity on 27.3.85. Companies where more than 60% of the equity is owned by others in the Leagues have been excluded. Changes in capital structure made some comparisons with previous Extel calculations impossible. Figures relate to financial year 1984, or to financial years ending in 1984, or at earliest 31.12.83, when later statistics were not available at time of compilation.

1. Market capitalization of equity on date given.
2. Equals loans, deferred tax, deferred liabilities, minority interests, preference and ordinary capital plus net reserves.
3. Equals total profits available to ordinary shareholders plus depreciation.
4. Increase or decrease in share price adjusted for capital changes, from middle price of 1975 base year to market price on 14.3.84.
5. Equals percentage change in adjusted share price plus gross dividends to give total return expressed as percentage of shareholders' original capital. Statistics by Extel.

Table 2–3   Extract from British Business Growth League 1985 (*Management Today*, June 1985)

# DEPARTMENT STORES

## Table 01 Return on Capital

| | Latest Date of Accs. | Profit before Tax £000 | | | Capital Employed £000 | | | Profit / Capital Empld Percentage | | | |
|---|---|---|---|---|---|---|---|---|---|---|---|
| | | 83/84 | 82/83 | 81/82 | 83/84 | 82/83 | 81/82 | Later Ratio | 83/84 | 82/83 | 81/82 |
| COLE BROTHERS LTD | 01.84 | 2580 | 2728 | 2286 | 4479 | 4479 | 32088 | | 57.6 | 60.9 | 7.1 |
| HABITAT DESIGNS LTD | 03.84 | 8299 | 6456 | 3658 | 16709 | 9720 | 9465 | | 49.7 | 66.4 | 38.6 |
| DENNERS LTD | 01.84 | 182 | 81 | 121- | 650 | 513 | 410 | | 28.0 | 15.8 | 29.5- |
| JAMES BEATTIE PLC | 01.84 | 4189 | 3479 | 3182 | 15469 | 14031 | 12835 | | 27.1 | 24.8 | 24.8 |
| FENWICK LTD  * | 01.84 | 9814 | 8569 | 8451 | 36446 | 31452 | 26458 | | 26.9 | 27.2 | 31.9 |
| BRITISH HOME STORES PLC | 03.84 | 55193 | 48874 | 42562 | 256970 | 234326 | 213009 | | 21.5 | 20.9 | 20.0 |
| MARKS & SPENCER PLC | 03.84 | 279300 | 239300 | 222100 | 1337300 | 1235900 | 1117900 | | 20.9 | 19.4 | 19.9 |
| BAKERS HOUSEHOLD STRS (LEEDS)PLC | 10.83 | 828 | 739 | 963 | 4178 | 3742 | 3451 | | 19.8 | 19.7 | 27.9 |
| P.H.WOODWARD AND CO. LTD | 01.84 | 191 | 162 | 181 | 1079 | 986 | 841 | | 17.7 | 16.4 | 21.5 |
| W.BOYES AND CO. LTD. | 01.84 | 512 | 277 | 142 | 3028 | 2309 | 2216 | | 16.9 | 12.0 | 6.4 |
| SELFRIDGES LTD | 01.84 | 17816 | 13490 | 11335 | 110630 | 107654 | 99588 | | 16.1 | 12.5 | 11.4 |
| SCHOFIELDS (YORKSHIRE) LTD | 02.84 | 1116 | 796 | 763 | 7592 | 7468 | 7685 | | 14.7 | 10.7 | 9.9 |
| Wm. ROBB & SON LTD  * | 01.84 | 185 | 84 | 124 | 1315 | 1217 | 1173 | | 14.1 | 6.9 | 10.6 |
| BENTALLS PLC  * | 01.84 | 2606 | 2108 | 2033 | 19517 | 18712 | 18103 | | 13.4 | 11.3 | 11.2 |
| HARRODS LTD | 01.84 | 20462 | 16685 | 14282 | 159065 | 157777 | 155655 | | 12.9 | 10.6 | 9.2 |
| LIBERTY PLC | 01.84 | 1431 | 606 | 514 | 12120 | 11593 | 10145 | | 11.8 | 5.2 | 5.1 |
| PALMERS (GT.YARMOUTH) LTD. | 01.84 | 121 | 92 | 79 | 1026 | 956 | 896 | | 11.8 | 9.6 | 8.8 |
| CHADDS OF HEREFORD LTD | 01.84 | 75 | 39 | 45 | 672 | 611 | 586 | | 11.2 | 6.4 | 7.7 |
| JENNERS PRINCES ST EDINBURGH LTD | 01.84 | 945 | 732 | 687 | 8928 | 8617 | 9154 | | 10.6 | 8.5 | 7.5 |
| GOULDS(DORCHESTER) LTD | 01.84 | 82 | 114 | 55 | 807 | 546 | 481 | | 10.2 | 20.9 | 11.4 |
| S & U STORES PLC.  * | 01.84 | 725 | 767 | 670 | 7300 | 7415 | 6685 | | 9.9 | 10.3 | 10.0 |
| FORTNUM & MASON PLC | 01.84 | 522 | 189 | 269 | 5264 | 5095 | 5005 | | 9.9 | 3.7 | 5.4 |
| JOHN LEWIS PARTNERSHIP PLC      # | 01.84 | 33449 | 21755 | 20084 | 343160 | 328845 | 308642 | | 9.7 | 6.6 | 6.5 |
| JOPLINGS LTD | 01.84 | 690 | 109 | 280 | 7358 | 7029 | 6587 | | 9.4 | 1.6 | 4.3 |
| RICEMANS (HOLDINGS) LTD | 01.84 | 185 | 99 | 328 | 2114 | 2127 | 2045 | | 8.8 | 4.7 | 16.0 |
| WADES DEPARTMENTAL STORES LTD  * | 04.83 | 526 | 1070- | 471- | 6143 | 5941 | 6846 | | 8.6 | 18.0- | 6.9- |
| SELFRIDGES (OXFORD) LTD | 01.84 | 507 | 546 | 259 | 5936 | 5676 | 2618 | | 8.5 | 9.6 | 9.9 |
| DEBENHAMS PLC | 01.84 | 32657 | 19575 | 27038 | 386895 | 375131 | 351243 | | 8.4 | 5.2 | 7.7 |
| ROOMES STORES LTD  * | 01.84 | 100 | 96 | 79 | 1208 | 1124 | 1053 | | 8.3 | 8.5 | 7.5 |
| F.W.WOOLWORTH PLC | 01.84 | 38809 | 24269 | 38261 | 507970 | 600370 | 566071 | | 7.6 | 4.0 | 6.8 |
| BONDS (NORWICH) LTD | 01.84 | 121 | 312- | 350- | 1968 | 1968 | 2681 | | 6.1 | 15.9- | 13.1- |
| R.W.WEEKES LTD | 12.83 | 76 | 70 | 60 | 1254 | 1058 | 1024 | | 6.0 | 6.6 | 5.9 |
| HATCHER AND SONS LTD | 01.84 | 80 | 7- | 36 | 1413 | 1394 | 817 | | 5.7 | 0.5- | 4.4 |
| ELYS (WIMBLEDON) PLC | 01.84 | 380 | 426 | 346 | 7150 | 6954 | 6097 | | 5.3 | 6.1 | 5.7 |
| THE LITTLEWOODS ORGANISATION PLC | 12.83 | 26896 | 9786 | 12515 | 539401 | 557717 | 471445 | | 5.0 | 1.8 | 2.7 |
| OWEN OWEN PLC  * | 01.84 | 1187 | 1649- | 220- | 25768 | 26097 | 31649 | | 4.6 | 6.3- | 0.7- |
| A. GOLDBERG & SONS PLC | 03.84 | 1861 | 1717 | 1451 | 44531 | 34481 | 22105 | | 4.2 | 5.0 | 6.6 |
| PEARSONS (ENFIELD) LTD | 01.84 | 64 | 112 | 76 | 1703 | 1758 | 1285 | | 3.8 | 6.4 | 5.9 |
| WELWYN DEPARTMENT STORE LTD | 01.84 | 9 | 41 | 276 | 377 | 1551 | 8421 | | 2.3 | 2.6 | 3.3 |
| SIMPSON (PICCADILLY) LTD  * | 07.83 | 78 | 11 | 90 | 3406 | 3318 | 3354 | | 2.3 | 0.3 | 2.7 |

Table 2–4   Extract from Business Ratio Report – Department Stores – Tables 01 and 02

# DEPARTMENT STORES

## Table 02 Return on Assets

| | Latest Date of Accs. | Profit before Tax £000 | | | Total Assets £000 | | | Profit / Total Assets Percentage | | | |
|---|---|---|---|---|---|---|---|---|---|---|---|
| | | 83/84 | 82/83 | 81/82 | 83/84 | 82/83 | 81/82 | Later Ratio | 83/84 | 82/83 | 81/82 |
| HABITAT DESIGNS LTD | 03.84 | 8299 | 6456 | 3658 | 32632 | 25759 | 16837 | | 25.4 | 25.1 | 21.7 |
| FENWICK LTD  * | 01.84 | 9814 | 8569 | 8451 | 49206 | 42118 | 36763 | | 19.9 | 20.3 | 23.0 |
| JAMES BEATTIE PLC | 01.84 | 4189 | 3479 | 3182 | 21476 | 19405 | 18317 | | 19.5 | 17.9 | 17.4 |
| BRITISH HOME STORES PLC | 03.84 | 55193 | 48874 | 42562 | 336665 | 284604 | 258972 | | 16.4 | 17.2 | 16.4 |
| BAKERS HOUSEHOLD STRS (LEEDS)PLC | 10.83 | 828 | 739 | 963 | 5261 | 5449 | 5718 | | 15.7 | 13.6 | 16.8 |
| MARKS & SPENCER PLC | 03.84 | 279300 | 239300 | 222100 | 1788100 | 1678400 | 1501700 | | 15.6 | 14.3 | 14.8 |
| P.H.WOODWARD AND CO. LTD | 01.84 | 191 | 162 | 181 | 1268 | 1196 | 1034 | | 15.1 | 13.5 | 17.5 |
| DENNERS LTD | 01.84 | 182 | 81 | 121- | 1425 | 1312 | 1139 | | 12.8 | 6.2 | 10.6- |
| SELFRIDGES LTD | 01.84 | 17816 | 13490 | 11335 | 139908 | 130122 | 123187 | | 12.7 | 10.4 | 9.2 |
| HARRODS LTD | 01.84 | 20462 | 16685 | 14282 | 195706 | 189409 | 186222 | | 10.5 | 8.8 | 7.7 |
| SCHOFIELDS (YORKSHIRE) LTD | 02.84 | 1116 | 796 | 763 | 10907 | 10664 | 11255 | | 10.2 | 7.5 | 6.8 |
| W.BOYES AND CO. LTD. | 01.84 | 512 | 277 | 142 | 5306 | 4116 | 4233 | | 9.6 | 6.7 | 3.4 |
| Wm. ROBB & SON LTD  * | 01.84 | 185 | 84 | 124 | 2106 | 2040 | 2110 | | 8.8 | 4.1 | 5.9 |
| BENTALLS PLC  * | 01.84 | 2606 | 2108 | 2033 | 29684 | 28412 | 27745 | | 8.8 | 7.4 | 7.3 |
| PALMERS (GT.YARMOUTH) LTD. | 01.84 | 121 | 92 | 79 | 1389 | 1368 | 1188 | | 8.7 | 6.7 | 6.6 |
| JENNERS PRINCES ST EDINBURGH LTD | 01.84 | 945 | 732 | 687 | 10917 | 10280 | 10537 | | 8.7 | 7.1 | 6.5 |
| CHADDS OF HEREFORD LTD | 01.84 | 75 | 39 | 45 | 943 | 878 | 878 | | 8.0 | 4.4 | 5.1 |
| FORTNUM & MASON PLC | 01.84 | 522 | 189 | 269 | 7141 | 6722 | 6460 | | 7.3 | 2.8 | 4.2 |
| JOHN LEWIS PARTNERSHIP PLC       # | 01.84 | 33449 | 21755 | 20084 | 477394 | 427248 | 400187 | | 7.0 | 5.1 | 5.0 |
| COLE BROTHERS LTD | 01.84 | 2580 | 2728 | 2286 | 37634 | 35198 | 35999 | | 6.9 | 7.8 | 6.4 |
| LIBERTY PLC | 01.84 | 1431 | 606 | 514 | 21830 | 19979 | 16204 | | 6.6 | 3.0 | 3.2 |
| GOULDS(DORCHESTER) LTD | 01.84 | 82 | 114 | 55 | 1275 | 949 | 909 | | 6.4 | 12.0 | 6.1 |
| DEBENHAMS PLC | 01.84 | 32657 | 19575 | 27038 | 517596 | 486496 | 463335 | | 6.3 | 4.0 | 5.8 |
| ROOMES STORES LTD  * | 01.84 | 100 | 96 | 79 | 1640 | 1572 | 1412 | | 6.1 | 6.1 | 5.6 |
| F.W.WOOLWORTH PLC | 01.84 | 38809 | 24269 | 38261 | 688811 | 809383 | 838901 | | 5.6 | 3.0 | 4.6 |
| S & U STORES PLC.  * | 01.84 | 725 | 767 | 670 | 12983 | 11997 | 10671 | | 5.6 | 6.4 | 6.3 |
| JOPLINGS LTD | 01.84 | 690 | 109 | 280 | 13468 | 12609 | 12048 | | 5.1 | 0.9 | 2.3 |
| BONDS (NORWICH) LTD | 01.84 | 121 | 312- | 350- | 2464 | 4921 | 5002 | | 4.9 | 6.3- | 7.0- |
| ELYS (WIMBLEDON) PLC | 01.84 | 380 | 426 | 346 | 7750 | 7612 | 6635 | | 4.9 | 5.6 | 5.2 |
| SELFRIDGES (OXFORD) LTD | 01.84 | 507 | 546 | 259 | 10751 | 10529 | 7184 | | 4.7 | 5.2 | 3.6 |
| HATCHER AND SONS LTD | 01.84 | 80 | 7- | 36 | 1797 | 2295 | 1377 | | 4.5 | 0.3- | 2.6 |
| RICEMANS (HOLDINGS) LTD | 01.84 | 185 | 99 | 328 | 4340 | 4112 | 3406 | | 4.3 | 2.4 | 9.6 |
| A. GOLDBERG & SONS PLC | 03.84 | 1861 | 1717 | 1451 | 50967 | 41475 | 29394 | | 3.7 | 4.1 | 4.9 |
| THE LITTLEWOODS ORGANISATION PLC | 12.83 | 26896 | 9786 | 12515 | 780084 | 753088 | 634513 | | 3.4 | 1.3 | 2.0 |
| OWEN OWEN PLC  * | 01.84 | 1187 | 1649- | 220- | 36071 | 39218 | 52227 | | 3.3 | 4.2- | 0.4- |
| R.W.WEEKES LTD | 12.83 | 76 | 70 | 60 | 2319 | 1989 | 1922 | | 3.3 | 3.5 | 3.1 |
| PEARSONS (ENFIELD) LTD | 01.84 | 64 | 112 | 76 | 2659 | 2513 | 2096 | | 2.4 | 4.5 | 3.6 |
| SIMPSON (PICCADILLY) LTD  * | 07.83 | 78 | 11 | 90 | 4291 | 4335 | 4422 | | 1.8 | 0.3 | 2.0 |
| WADES DEPARTMENTAL STORES LTD  * | 04.83 | 526 | 1070- | 471- | 32035 | 30399 | 21822 | | 1.6 | 3.5- | 2.2- |
| E.SHEPHARD LTD  *                 # | 01.84 | 30 | 21 | 19 | 4235 | 4136 | 4061 | | 0.7 | 0.5 | 0.5 |

Table 2—4   concluded

49

# 1 The 1000 largest UK industrial companies

| Rank by turn-over | COMPANY | Main activity | Chairman and Managing Directors (in italics) §‖ | Accounting period ended |
|---|---|---|---|---|
| 1 (1) | British Petroleum Co. | Oil industry | P. I. Walters (J.M.D.) (*see page 64*) | 31–12–83 |
| 2 (2) | 'Shell' Transport & Trading[11] | Oil industry | Sir Peter Baxendell (J.M.D.) (*see page 64*) | 31–12–83 |
| 3 (3) | B.A.T Industries | Tobacco, retailing, paper, packaging, etc. | P. Sheehy | 31–12–83 |
| 4 (4) | Imperial Chemical Industries | Petrochemicals, pharmaceuticals, etc. | J. H. Harvey-Jones | 31–12–83 |
| 5 (5) | Shell U.K. | Oil industry | J. M. Raisman (C.E.) (*see page 64*) | 31–12–83 |
| 6 (6) | Esso U.K.[29] | Oil industry | A. W. Forster (C.E.) (*see page 64*) | 31–12–83 |
| 7 (7) | Unilever Plc | Food products, detergents, etc. | K. Durham | 31–12–83 |
| 8 (12) | Rio Tinto-Zinc Corporation | Mining & industrial – metals & fuel | Sir Anthony Tuke, *Sir Alistair Frame* (C.E.) | 31–12–83 |
| 9 (10) | General Electric Co. | Electrical engineers | Lord Carrington, *Lord Weinstock* | 31–03–83 |
| 10 (11) | Grand Metropolitan | Hotel props, milk prds, brewers, etc. | S. G. Grinstead (C.E.) (*see page 64*) | 30–09–83 |
| 11 (8) | Imperial Group | Tobacco, food, drink and packaging | G. C. Kent (C.E.) | 31–10–83 |
| 12 (16) | S. & W. Berisford | Merchanting & commodity trading, etc. | E. S. Margulies (M.D.) | 30–09–83 |
| 13 (—) | Phibro-Salomon | Commodity brokers, etc. | None designated | 31–12–82 |
| 14 (13) | Ford Motor Co. | Motor vehicle manufacturers | S. E. G. Toy (M.D.) | 31–12–83 |
| 15 (14) | BL | Motor vehicle manufacturers, etc. | Sir Austin Bide | 31–12–83 |
| 16 (20) | Rothmans International | Tobacco, luxury consumer products etc. | Sir David Nicolson, *V. A. Brink* (C.E.) | 31–03–83 |
| 17 (15) | George Weston Holdings | Food manufacturers & distributors | G. H. Weston | 02–04–83 |
| 18 (21) | Marks & Spencer | General store proprietors | Lord Raynor (C.E.) (*see page 64*) | 31–03–84 |
| 19 (17) | Allied Lyons | Brewers, vintners, hoteliers, etc. | Sir Derrick Holden-Brown (C.E.) | 03–03–84 |
| 20 (19) | Dalgety | International merchants | D. L. Donne, *G. T. Pryce* (C.E.) | 30–06–83 |
| 21 (22) | THORN EMI | Elec. & electronic eng., music, etc. | P. Laister (C.E.) | 31–03–83 |
| 22 (25) | Gallaher | Tobacco, optics, pumps & valves disbn. | S. G. Cameron (C.E.) | 31–12–83 |
| 23 (26) | J. Sainsbury | Retail distribution of food | Sir John Sainsbury (C.E.), *E. R. Griffiths* | 24–03–84 |
| 24 (18) | Texaco | Oil industry | J. D. Ambler, *H. M. Matthews* | 31–12–82 |
| 25 (23) | Lonrho | Mining, agric., textiles, constr., etc. | Rt. Hon. Lord Duncan-Sandys (*see page 64*) | 30–09–83 |
| 26 (28) | British Aerospace | Manufacture of aircraft, etc. | Sir Austin Pearce, *Sir Raymond Lygo* | 31–12–83 |
| 27 (29) | Tesco | Multiple retailing | Sir Leslie Porter (C.E.) | 26–02–83 |
| 28 (42) | Amalgamated Metal Corp. | Metal & ores | G. Sassmannshausen, *T. Lock* (C.E.) | 31–12–83 |
| 29 (50) | Ultramar | Petroleum exploration & development | L. Bensen (C.E.) (*C'man from 31–12–84*) | 31–12–83 |
| 30 (31) | Courtaulds | Man-made fibres, textiles, chemicals | C. A. Hogg | 31–03–84 |

NOTES: *Total tangible assets less current liabilities (other than bank loans and overdrafts and future tax). †As percentage of capital employed at beginning of year. ‡As at 2 July 1984. §Appendix on page 64 gives list of managing directors whose names cannot be fitted into the main text. ‖M.D. = Managing Director; J.M.D. = Joint Managing Director: A.C. = Acting Chairman; C.E. = Chief Executive. ¶As percentage of capital employed at end of year. N/A Not available. [1] UK only. [4] Including added value and sales taxes in overseas territories, but excluding UK VAT and including share of turnover of Assoc. Cos. [5] Including excise duties but excluding VAT. [6] Including excise duties and VAT. [9] Including duties and sales taxes. [11] Based on 40% of Royal Dutch/Shell Group. [12] Including sales taxes, excise duties and similar taxes. [29] Previous year's figures and rankings relate to Esso Petroleum Co.

Table 2–5 Extract from *The Times 1000* 1984–1985

| TURNOVER | | *CAPITAL EMPLOYED | | | NET PROFIT BEFORE INTEREST AND TAX | | | | | | No. of employees | ‡Equity market cap. £M. |
| Total £000 | Export £000 | £000 | Rank Latest year | Rank Previous year | Latest year £000 | Rank | Previous year £000 | % to turnover Latest year | †% to capital employed Latest year | †% to capital employed Previous year | | |
|---|---|---|---|---|---|---|---|---|---|---|---|---|
| 37,960,000[9] | N/A | 19,223,000 | 1 | 1 | 5,606,000 | 1 | 5,589,000 | 14·8 | 32·3 | 34·7 | 131,600 | 8,442·8 |
| 24,411,000[12] | N/A | 15,213,000 | 2 | 2 | 3,788,000 | 2 | 3,246,000 | 15·5 | 32·0 | 35·6 | N/A | 6,960·5 |
| 11,652,000[4] | 319,000 | 4,893,000 | 5 | 5 | 1,113,000 | 5 | 1,018,000 | 9·6 | 24·8 | 31·6 | 187,173 | 3,220·3 |
| 8,256,000 | 1,835,000 | 5,541,000 | 4 | 3 | 1,017,000 | 6 | 724,000 | 12·3 | 18·9 | 14·2 | 117,900 | 3,489·4 |
| 7,807,000[6] | 2,139,000 | 3,656,000 | 6 | 6 | 1,911,000 | 3 | 1,213,700 | 24·5 | 51·1 | 36·9 | 17,653 | HOL |
| 7,565,200[6] | N/A | 3,300,100 | 7 | 7 | 1,895,000 | 4 | 1,314,500 | 25·0 | ¶57·4 | 43·2 | 6,619 | USA |
| 5,355,000 | N/A | 2,519,000 | 10 | 8 | 400,000 | 11 | 412,000 | 7·5 | 16·7 | 20·8 | 127,000 | 1,391·0 |
| 4,811,000 | N/A | 5,929,100 | 3 | 4 | 749,000 | 7 | 491,900 | 15·6 | 14·1 | 13·3 | 73,844 | 1,807·0 |
| 4,625,500 | 1,142,000 | 2,862,300 | 8 | 11 | 703,300 | 8 | 621,400 | 15·2 | 27·5 | 34·9 | 178,061 | 5,217·4 |
| 4,468,800 | 133,400 | 2,723,000 | 9 | 9 | 421,000 | 10 | 366,300 | 9·4 | 17·1 | 16·1 | 102,406 | 2,313·6 |
| 4,381,500 | N/A | 1,232,600 | 23 | 21 | 220,400 | 22 | 205,500 | 5·0 | 18·6 | 18·9 | 97,539 | 1,147·5 |
| 4,325,341 | N/A | 906,967 | 39 | 41 | 126,411 | 48 | 104,883 | 2·9 | 16·1 | ¶13·4 | 9,446 | 333·1 |
| 4,036,181 | N/A | 346,015 | 115 | — | 53,469 | 105 | 0 | 1·3 | ¶15·5 | 0·0 | 754[1] | USA |
| 3,585,000 | N/A | 2,262,000 | 11 | 10 | 261,000 | 16 | 278,000 | 7·3 | 12·2 | 14·7 | 60,700 | USA |
| 3,421,000 | 917,000 | 1,528,200 | 15 | 15 | 48,100 | 114 | Loss 93,400 | 1·4 | 3·6 | 0·0 | 101,346 | 2,481·8 |
| 3,411,732 | N/A | 910,797 | 38 | 43 | 179,512 | 29 | 145,648 | 5·3 | 23·6 | 23·1 | 21,655 | 298·3 |
| 3,376,195 | N/A | 1,003,492 | 30 | 39 | 177,678 | 30 | 156,828 | 5·3 | 21·8 | 23·1 | 68,924[1] | UQ |
| 2,854,500 | 84,000 | 1,407,800 | 17 | 16 | 298,000 | 13 | 257,000 | 10·4 | 22·2 | 21·6 | 56,891 | 2,901·6 |
| 2,850,500 | 74,100 | 1,692,000 | 13 | 13 | 232,100 | 19 | 205,100 | 8·1 | 16·3 | 15·2 | 71,204 | 1,088·3 |
| 2,842,000 | N/A | 522,700 | 74 | 71 | 79,700 | 76 | 78,700 | 2·8 | 15·5 | 16·6 | 21,243 | 299·6 |
| 2,715,900 | N/A | 959,800 | 36 | 31 | 172,800 | 31 | 150,100 | 6·4 | 19·2 | 16·6 | 91,544 | 892·1 |
| 2,579,700 | N/A | 465,700 | 84 | 89 | 111,900 | 54 | 89,900 | 4·3 | 27·2 | 24·6 | 27,805 | USA |
| 2,574,800 | N/A | 566,700 | 71 | 69 | 130,300 | 46 | 102,978p.a. | 5·1 | 26·2 | 25·6p.a. | 56,636 | 1,749·4 |
| 2,379,458[5] | 133,000 | 660,010 | 60 | 42 | Loss 150,963 | 1000 | 41,778 | 0·0 | 0·0 | 6·8 | 4,928[1] | USA |
| 2,356,500 | N/A | 1,311,200 | 20 | 17 | 195,600 | 25 | 168,200 | 8·3 | 15·4 | 12·9 | 94,187 | 373·5 |
| 2,300,300 | 1,416,900 | 1,293,900 | 21 | 32 | 147,700 | 38 | 25,600 | 6·4 | 13·7 | 3·3 | 77,980 | 736·1 |
| 2,276,600 | N/A | 423,500 | 92 | 106 | 64,000 | 88 | 53,200 | 2·8 | 18·5 | 17·4 | 49,372 | 534·3 |
| 2,076,726 | N/A | 95,261 | 272 | 316 | 16,502 | 251 | 9,477 | 0·8 | 22·6 | 15·1 | 2,155 | GER |
| 2,057,100 | N/A | 1,022,600 | 29 | 26 | 166,500 | 33 | 206,300 | 8·1 | ¶16·3 | 45·6 | 3,733 | 719·3 |
| 2,038,100 | 433,000 | 764,500 | 47 | 51 | 145,100 | 39 | 98,600 | 7·1 | 20·9 | 14·4 | 73,000 | 455·2 |

The following letters in the market capitalisation column denote unquoted companies and country of control:

| | | | | | | | | | | |
|---|---|---|---|---|---|---|---|---|---|---|
| AUS | = | Australia | FRA | = | France | IT | = | Italy | MAL | = Malaysia |
| BEL | = | Belgium | GB/US | = | Gr. Britain/U.S.A. | JAP | = | Japan | NAT | = Netherlands Antilles |
| CAN | = | Canada | GER | = | Germany | JER | = | Jersey | NOR | = Norway |
| CAY | = | Cayman Islands | HOL | = | Holland | LEB | = | Lebanon | NZ | = New Zealand |
| DEN | = | Denmark | HON | = | Hong Kong | LIE | = | Liechtenstein | SAF | = South Africa |
| FIN | = | Finland | IRE | = | Ireland | LUX | = | Luxembourg | SAR | = Saudi Arabia |

SIN = Singapore
SWE = Sweden
SWZ = Switzerland
UQ = Unquoted
USA = United States of America
USSR = Union of Soviet Socialist Republics

Table 2–5   concluded

## SELECTED PROFITABILITY AND CAPITAL UTILISATION ITEMS AND RATIOS

| COMPANY NAME | No. OF MTHS | YEAR END | SALES £000 | NET TANG. ASSETS £000 | PRE-TAX PFT. £000 | INT. PD £000 | PRE-TAX PFT/NET TANG ASSETS % | PRE-TAX PFT/SALES % | FIXED ASSETS £000 | CURRENT ASSETS £000 | CURRENT LIABILITIES £000 | BANK O/D AND SHORT TERM LOANS £000 |
|---|---|---|---|---|---|---|---|---|---|---|---|---|
| Adcocks (Peterborough) Ltd. | | 12 81 | 732 | 262 | 16 | NIL | 6.11 | 2.19 | 104 | 398 | 240 | 58 |
| | | 12 80 | 626 | 246 | 31 | NIL | 12.60 | 4.95 | 99 | 347 | 200 | 10 |
| | | 12 79 | 521 | 217 | 26 | NIL | 11.98 | 4.99 | 102 | 303 | 188 | 37 |
| Alpine Soft Drinks Ltd. | | 3 84 | 17037 | 4594 | −799 | 68 | −17.39 | −4.69 | 4313 | 2765 | 2484 | 91 |
| | | 3 83 | 18209 | 6209 | 262 | 15 | 4.22 | 1.44 | 5455 | 3170 | 2416 | 85 |
| | | 3 82 | 18894 | 5624 | 1659 | 3 | 29.50 | 8.78 | 5227 | 3391 | 2994 | NIL |
| Apollo Soft Drinks Ltd. | | 9 83 | 2243 | 717 | 603 | NIL | 84.10 | 26.88 | 76 | 1766 | 1125 | 278 |
| | | 9 82 | 2008 | 716 | 535 | NIL | 74.72 | 26.64 | 84 | 1616 | 984 | 220 |
| | | 9 81 | 2146 | 717 | 574 | NIL | 80.06 | 26.75 | 124 | 1855 | 1262 | 226 |
| Aqualac (Spring Waters) Ltd. | | 4 83 | 5577 | 119 | 43 | NIL | 36.13 | 0.77 | 108 | 1628 | 1617 | 1151 |
| | | 4 82 | 4442 | 85 | 95 | NIL | 11.76 | 2.14 | 89 | 871 | 875 | 441 |
| | | 4 81 | 3221 | 91 | 152 | 1 | 167.03 | 4.72 | 85 | 790 | 784 | 357 |
| Barnett & Foster Ltd. | | 10 83 | 7080 | 2115 | 159 | 200 | 7.52 | 2.25 | 660 | 3152 | 1697 | 154 |
| | | 10 82 | 6425 | 2036 | 124 | 256 | 6.09 | 1.93 | 673 | 2999 | 1636 | 146 |
| | | 9 81 | 6173 | 1975 | −220 | 286 | −11.14 | −3.56 | 692 | 2587 | 1304 | 121 |

ADCOCKS (PETERBOROUGH) LTD.
BUSINESS: Soft drinks manufacturer and distributors of wines, spirits and foodstuffs.
Private Company

ALPINE SOFT DRINKS LTD.
BUSINESS: Sale of sugar-based sparkling drinks direct to customers at their homes and to retail shops.
Public Quoted

| MAJOR SHAREHOLDERS: | ORD 10p |
|---|---|
| M. & G. Investments Management Ltd. | 1500000 |
| C. Robinson & Co. Ltd. | 611500 |

NOTES: Active subsidiaries are Alpine Soft Drinks (Scotland) Ltd and Thompson & Pearson Ltd. The increased loss in 1983/84 was attributed to extensive sales re-development work and the effects of price reductions. Factories were closed at Rutherglen and Walthamstow and the South East area sold.

APOLLO SOFT DRINKS LTD.
BUSINESS: Manufacturing of soft drinks and factoring of crisps, cider, perry and kindred drinks and the wholesaling of these products.
IHC and UHC: Home Brewery Plc.

AQUALAC (SPRING WATERS) LTD.
BUSINESS: Importation, marketing and distribution of mineral waters.
IHC: Societe Generale de Grandes Sources Minerales (France)      UHC: Source Perrier SA. (France)

BARNETT & FOSTER LTD.
BUSINESS: Manufacturing essences and fruit juice compounds.
IHC: Borthwick Food Products Ltd.      UHC: Thomas Borthwick & Sons Plc.

NOTES: Owns 74% of capital of Barnett & Foster (Hellas) Ltd – a Greek company.

Table 2–6   Extract from Jordans British Soft Drinks Industry

# SELECTED OPERATING AND LIQUIDITY ITEMS AND RATIOS

| STK. & WK. IN PROG. £000 | % OF SALES | EXPORTS £000 | % OF SALES | Nos. EMPLOYED | TOTAL WAGE BILL £000 | DRCTS. REMUN. £000 | AV REMUN PER EMPLOYEE £ | CASH & NR CASH £000 | % OF CUR. LIABS. | TYPE | FORM OF ACCOUNTS |
|---|---|---|---|---|---|---|---|---|---|---|---|
| 160 | 21.86 | NIL | NIL | N.A | N.A | 69 | N.A | 75 | 31.25 | 1 | Co. only – no subsidiaries |
| 154 | 24.60 | NIL | NIL | N.A | N.A | 46 | N.A | 60 | 30.00 | | |
| 121 | 23.22 | NIL | NIL | N.A | N.A | 36 | N.A | 67 | 35.64 | | |
| 1005 | 5.90 | NIL | NIL | 1598 | 6626 | 108 | 4146 | 1352 | 54.43 | 3 | Consolidated |
| 1296 | 7.12 | NIL | NIL | 1724 | 6684 | 95 | 3877 | 1357 | 56.17 | | |
| 1017 | 5.38 | NIL | NIL | 1679 | 6897 | 88 | 4108 | 1847 | 61.69 | | |
| 581 | 25.90 | N.A | N.A | 35 | 215 | NIL | 6143 | 1139 | 101.24 | 5 | Co. only – no subsidiaries |
| 549 | 27.34 | 12 | 0.60 | 37 | 202 | NIL | 5459 | 1024 | 104.07 | | |
| 505 | 23.53 | 105 | 4.89 | 36 | 183 | 5 | 5083 | 1291 | 102.30 | | |
| 593 | 10.63 | NIL | NIL | N.A | N.A | NIL | NIL | 619 | 38.28 | 4 | Co. only – no subsidiaries |
| 252 | 5.67 | NIL | NIL | N.A | N.A | NIL | NIL | 171 | 19.54 | | |
| 287 | 8.91 | NIL | NIL | N.A | N.A | NIL | NIL | 162 | 20.66 | | |
| 922 | 13.02 | N.A | N.A | 171 | 1061 | 36 | 6205 | 699 | 41.19 | 5 | Subsidiaries not consolidated |
| 1120 | 17.43 | N.A | N.A | 174 | 997 | 34 | 5730 | 541 | 33.07 | | |
| 940 | 15.23 | 1014 | 16.43 | N.A | N.A | 99 | N.A | 295 | 22.62 | | |

REGISTERED OFFICE: 38 Huntley Grove, Peterborough PE1 4DJ, TEL NO: 0733 43303
CHIEF EXECUTIVE: K.A.L. Adcock (CH)

REGISTERED OFFICE: Richmond Way, Chelmsley Wood, Birmingham B37 7TT, TEL NO: 021 770 6816

| DIRECTORS: | OTHER DIRECTORSHIPS: |
|---|---|
| R.J. Wade (CH) | R.M.B.I. Services Ltd; Techpress Publishing Co. Ltd & Or. |
| S.F. Crew (M.D.) | None |
| A. English | Damerham Hot Bread Kitchens Ltd; Parkham Foods Ltd. |
| K.E. Price, M.D. Lees, P.F. McAdam | None |

REGISTERED OFFICE: Daybrook Road, Arnold, Nottinghamshire, TEL NO: 0602 268525
CHIEF EXECUTIVE: B.H. Farr (CH)

REGISTERED OFFICE: 6 Lygon Place, London SW1W 0JR, TEL NO: 01 730 0784

| DIRECTORS: | OTHER DIRECTORSHIPS: |
|---|---|
| J.M.B. Bowes (CH) | Jules Bowes Ltd; Lygon Marketing Ltd & Ors. |
| A.P. Segui (French) | None |

REGISTERED OFFICE: Priory House, St. Johns Lane, London EC1M 4BX, TEL NO: 01 253 8661

| DIRECTORS: | OTHER DIRECTORSHIPS: |
|---|---|
| R.C. Wheeler-Bennett | Thomas Borthwick & Sons Plc. & Subs. |
| A.S. Ninian (C/E) | Subs. of Thomas Borthwick & Sons Plc. |
| R.G. Hine | Thomas Borthwick & Sons Plc. & Subs. |
| D.C.P. Carey, B. Lund | As above |
| B.J.A. Weedon, Dr. J.P.V. Gracey, T.W. Ward, G.H. Ashworth, B.J. Edwards | None |

Table 2–6 *concluded*

# TREND OF INDUSTRIAL PROFITS ANALYSIS OF 99 COMPANIES

Corporate profits for 99 companies reporting annual results between July 1 and September 30 last year suggest that the recovery in the consumer sector that had been noted previously was beginning to feed through to capital goods—although the emphasis was on the short-term rather than the long. Hence the centre of growth for capital goods was in materials, electronics, metals and motors—all industries that can respond quickly to rising demand and who see additional volume coming through in profit terms. The laggards were construction, electricals and engineering where the time scale of projects and internationally poor markets plus continued shake-out were a depressing influence.

The other strong growth area seen from these figures is banking—both high street and merchant—which lifted the financial sector by one third. These figures are somewhat distorted, however, by the small number of institutions reporting in the period. Within the consumer sector there was a clear divide this time between brewing and foods (both with seriously below average growth) and stores, leisure, packaging and paper and textiles. The beer and foodmakers had less than half the sectors average growth causing it to drop behind capital goods overall.

All figures in the table are in £m with the corresponding results for the previous year in brackets.

| INDUSTRY | No. of Cos. | Turnover (1) | Profits before Int. & Tax (2) | Pre tax Profits (3) | % chnge | Tax (4) | Earned for Ordinary Dividends (5) | % chnge | Ord. dividends (6) | % chnge | Cash Flow (7) | Net Capital Employed (8) | Net Capital Return on Cap (9) | Net Current assets (10) |
|---|---|---|---|---|---|---|---|---|---|---|---|---|---|---|
| BUILDING MATERIALS | 3 | 581.8 (480.6) | 41.7 (29.2) | 37.5 (24.8) | +51.2 | 13.2 (8.3) | 24.1 (16.5) | +46.1 | 6.2 (5.0) | +24.0 | 26.6 (19.2) | 216.4 (187.3) | 19.3 (15.6) | 117.6 (91.4) |
| CONTRACTING, CONSTRUCTION | 7 | 883.8 (774.1) | 66.4 (52.8) | 55.0 (40.0) | +37.5 | 22.0 (14.1) | 32.0 (25.4) | +26.0 | 11.1 (9.1) | +22.0 | 40.2 (34.8) | 249.2 (394.8) | 15.5 (13.4) | 192.6 (165.6) |
| ELECTRICALS | 1 | 34.5 (31.1) | 2.2 (2.5) | 1.2 (1.5) | 20.0 | 0.4 (0.3) | 0.7 (1.2) | −41.7 | 0.4 (0.4) | — | 1.3 (1.8) | 21.0 (22.0) | 10.5 (11.4) | 8.8 (8.1) |
| ELECTRONICS | 6 | 273.3 (183.4) | 43.7 (23.1) | 40.3 (24.5) | +64.5 | 15.6 (11.4) | 23.9 (12.8) | +86.7 | 5.9 (4.0) | +47.5 | 25.2 (11.9) | 140.0 (79.4) | 31.2 (29.1) | 108.2 (64.7) |
| MECHANICAL ENGINEERING | 9 | 1,478.9 (1326.9) | 123.3 (118.0) | 100.3 (97.5) | +2.9 | 32.1 (31.2) | 64.4 (62.2) | +3.5 | 25.3 (22.7) | 11.5 | 80.0 (74.3) | 849.8 (803.2) | 14.5 (14.6) | 394.9 (413.0) |
| METALS AND METAL FORMING | 3 | 335.7 (342.9) | 19.3 (9.9) | 12.2 (2.3) | +430.4 | 6.6 (4.1) | 4.8 (−2.0) | +340.0 | 4.8 (4.6) | +4.4 | 9.7 (1.9) | 238.6 (245.5) | 8.1 (4.0) | 53.8 (67.3) |
| MOTORS | 6 | 2,460.3 (2,224.8) | 131.8 (90.4) | 86.6 (42.1) | +105.7 | 22.6 (16.3) | 61.4 (24.0) | +155.8 | 17.3 (13.3) | +30.1 | 110.3 (67.5) | 1,227.1 (1,162.3) | 10.7 (7.8) | 348.6 (367.9) |
| OTHER INDUSTRIAL MATERIALS | 1 | 604.2 (490.2) | 75.9 (58.2) | 63.8 (46.5) | +37.2 | 28.7 (18.5) | 35.1 (27.9) | +25.8 | 15.6 (14.2) | +9.9 | 48.1 (38.5) | 529.8 (479.9) | 14.3 (12.1) | 69.1 (56.6) |
| TOTAL CAPITAL GOODS | 36 | 6,652.5 (5,844.0) | 504.3 (384.1) | 396.9 (274.8) | +44.4 | 141.2 (104.2) | 246.4 (168.0) | +46.7 | 86.6 (73.3) | +18.1 | 341.4 (249.9) | 3,651.9 (3,374.4) | 13.8 (11.4) | 1,293.6 (1,234.6) |
| BREWERS AND DISTILLERS | 10 | 8,947.0 (2,954.1) | 860.7 (765.9) | 689.1 (589.6) | +16.9 | 222.5 (200.1) | 447.8 (375.0) | +19.4 | 137.5 (198.5) | −30.7 | 528.9 (440.1) | 5,765.7 (5,147.5) | 14.9 (14.9) | 585.0 (507.5) |
| FOOD MANUFACTURING | 4 | 8,730.5 (7,289.4) | 318.4 (287.7) | 195.5 (178.2) | +9.7 | 51.4 (35.7) | 132.8 (136.0) | −2.3 | 45.8 (40.0) | +14.5 | 152.9 (152.4) | 1,775.2 (1,864.5) | 17.9 (15.4) | 409.9 (434.0) |
| FOOD RETAILING | 2 | 795.7 (688.8) | 37.6 (31.6) | 36.9 (31.2) | +18.3 | 17.2 (14.1) | 19.7 (17.2) | +14.5 | 7.1 (6.1) | +16.4 | 18.8 (16.3) | 121.0 (106.8) | 31.1 (29.6) | −17.2 (−16.2) |
| HEALTH AND HOUSEHOLD PRODUCTS | | | | | | | | | | | | | | |
| LEISURE | 5 | 1,053.7 (858.7) | 98.1 (76.8) | 83.4 (61.5) | +35.6 | 37.2 (28.5) | 46.3 (32.6) | +42.0 | 22.5 (14.9) | +51.0 | 134.4 (104.9) | 709.6 (533.8) | 13.8 (14.4) | −111.5 (−100.6) |
| NEWSPAPERS, PUBLISHING | 2 | 480.4 (406.4) | 32.6 (26.5) | 29.0 (24.2) | +19.8 | 6.8 (7.5) | 21.0 (16.7) | +25.7 | 6.5 (5.2) | +25.0 | 30.4 (23.5) | 371.4 (180.9) | 8.8 (14.7) | 44.4 (34.5) |
| PACKAGING AND PAPER | 2 | 184.3 (121.5) | 56.6 (28.1) | 54.8 (27.1) | +102.2 | 7.5 (4.7) | 47.1 (22.5) | +109.9 | 4.0 (2.7) | +48.2 | 45.5 (21.4) | 128.0 (81.0) | 44.2 (34.7) | 37.9 (21.2) |
| STORES | 3 | 677.7 (543.4) | 77.3 (55.8) | 75.4 (53.1) | +42.0 | 30.9 (20.0) | 44.2 (32.8) | +34.8 | 15.8 (12.0) | +31.7 | 45.3 (33.7) | 453.9 (401.3) | 17.0 (13.9) | −3.6 (19.3) |

| | No. | Col. 1 | Col. 2 | Col. 3 | % | Col. 4 | % | Col. 5 | % | Col. 6 | Col. 8 | Col. 9 | Col. 10 |
|---|---|---|---|---|---|---|---|---|---|---|---|---|---|
| TEXTILES | 1 | 32.0 (26.1) | 3.9 (2.7) | 3.9 (2.7) | 1.5 (—) | 2.3 (2.7) | −14.8 | 0.7 (0.6) | +16.7 | 2.3 (2.6) | 23.9 (22.2) | 16.3 (12.2) | 20.4 (19.4) |
| TOBACCOS | | (—) | (—) | (—) | (—) | (—) | | (—) | | (—) | (—) | (—) | (—) |
| OTHER CONSUMERS | | (—) | (—) | (—) | (—) | (—) | | (—) | | (—) | (—) | (—) | (—) |
| TOTAL CONSUMER GRP ‡ | 29 | 20,901.3 (12,888.4) | 1,485.2 (1,275.1) | 1,168.0 (967.6) | +20.7 | 375.0 (310.6) | +19.8 | 239.9 (280.0) | +14.3 | 958.5 (794.9) | 9,348.7 (8,338.0) | 15.9 (15.3) | 965.3 (919.1) |
| CHEMICALS | 1 | 2,103.0 (1,701.6) | 285.4 (222.6) | 178.8 (136.8) | +30.7 | 32.1 (19.8) | +36.9 | 29.0 (24.3) | +19.3 | 247.8 (178.7) | 2,346.6 (2,042.4) | 12.2 (10.9) | 330.8 (220.2) |
| OFFICE EQUIPMENT | | (—) | (—) | (—) | (—) | (—) | | (—) | | (—) | (—) | (—) | (—) |
| SHIPPING AND TRANSPORT | | | | | | | | | | | | | |
| MISCELLANEOUS | 6 | 5,205.7 (3,756.8) | 445.3 (273.1) | 323.5 (199.8) | +61.9 | 89.6 (49.7) | +57.6 | 68.1 (46.3) | +47.1 | 270.6 (173.6) | 2,493.0 (1,594.7) | 17.9 (17.1) | 904.7 (539.6) |
| TELEPHONE NET WORKS | | (—) | (—) | (—) | (—) | (—) | | (—) | | (—) | (—) | (—) | (—) |
| TOTAL INDUSTRIAL GRP | 72 | 34,862.5 (24,190.8) | 2,720.2 (2,154.9) | 2,057.2 (1,579.0) | +30.9 | 637.9 (484.3) | +30.9 | 423.6 (423.9) | 0.1 | 1,818.3 (1,397.1) | 17,840.2 (15,349.5) | 15.3 (14.0) | 3,494.4 (2,913.5) |
| OILS | | | | | | | | | | | | | |
| BANKS | | 156.2 (102.2) | 128.1 (86.6) | +47.9 | 63.4 (14.9) | 64.1 (71.2) | −10.0 | 19.3 (16.7) | +15.6 | 63.7 (71.0) | 969.6 (977.6) | 16.1 (10.5) | 604.4 (626.9) |
| DISCOUNT HOUSES | | (—) | (—) | (—) | (—) | (—) | | (—) | | (—) | (—) | (—) | (—) |
| INSURANCE (LIFE) | | (—) | (—) | (—) | (—) | (—) | | (—) | | (—) | (—) | (—) | (—) |
| INSURANCE (COMPOSITE) | | (—) | (—) | (—) | (—) | (—) | | (—) | | (—) | (—) | (—) | (—) |
| INSURANCE BROKERS | | (—) | (—) | (—) | (—) | (—) | | (—) | | (—) | (—) | (—) | (—) |
| MERCHANT BANKS | 1 | 14.2 (6.9) | 10.0 (1.5) | +766.7 | 2.7 (1.4) | 7.1 (3.0) | +336.7 | 2.6 | | 6.3 (1.9) | *105.1 (*84.6) | 13.5 (8.2) | 13.9 (6.9) |
| PROPERTY | 5 | 110.9 (94.8) | 60.6 (53.7) | +12.9 | 23.7 (21.7) | 36.2 (31.7) | +14.2 | 24.3 (21.4) | +13.6 | 13.1 (11.2) | 1,573.0 (1,392.7) | 7.1 (6.8) | 30.3 (33.5) |
| OTHER FINANCIAL | 4 | 68.3 (65.5) | 21.5 (25.4) | +24.0 | 7.2 (10.5) | 13.9 (14.9) | 6.7 | 7.0 (5.1) | +37.3 | 12.4 (13.0) | 680.2 (503.3) | 10.0 (13.0) | 127.2 (44.0) |
| TOTAL FINANCIAL GROUP | 10 | 349.4 (269.4) | 220.2 (164.2) | +34.1 | 97.0 (48.5) | 121.3 (114.8) | +5.7 | 53.2 (43.2) | +23.2 | 95.5 (93.3) | †3,223.1 (†2,873.6) | 10.9 (9.4) | 775.8 (771.3) |
| INVESTMENT TRUSTS | 14 | 50.8 (44.7) | 40.3 (37.6) | 7.2 | 14.6 (14.1) | 25.4 (23.3) | +9.0 | 24.7 (22.3) | +10.8 | 0.9 (1.2) | 1,553.2 (1,242.1) | 3.3 (3.6) | 23.2 (−2.1) |
| MINING FINANCE | | (—) | (—) | (—) | (—) | (—) | | (—) | | (—) | (—) | (—) | (—) |
| OVERSEAS TRADERS | 3 | 2949.9 (2955.7) | 240.6 (217.5) | 144.7 (117.8) | +23.0 | 63.3 (56.3) | +50.7 | 27.1 (24.1) | +12.5 | 81.6 (62.9) | 1,619.9 (1,455.4) | 14.9 (14.9) | 64.2 (73.4) |

## NOTES ON COMPILATION OF THE TABLE

The classification is that of the Institute and Faculty of Actuaries used in the daily Financial Times Actuaries Indices.

Col. 1 gives turnover, exclusive of VAT unless otherwise indicated.

Col. 2 gives profits before interest and taxation, that is to say profits after all charges except loan and other interest but before deducting taxation provisions and minority interests.

N.B.—Certain companies, including merchant banks, discount houses, insurance and shipping companies are exempted from disclosing the full information required under the Companies Act 1948.

Col. 3 gives Pre-tax Profits, that is to say profits after all charges including debentures and loan interest but before deducting taxation provision and minority interests.

Col. 4 groups all corporation taxation including Dominion, Colonial and Foreign liability and future tax provisions but excluding adjustments relating to previous years.

Col. 5 gives the net profits accruing on equity capital after meeting—

1—Minority interests.

2—All prior charges—sinking fund payments, etc. and Preference dividends and

3—Provisions for staff and employees pensions funds where this is a standard annual charge against net revenue.

Col. 6 sets out the net cost of dividend on equity capital.

Col. 7 is the capital generated internally over a year's trading. For the purposes of comparison equity earnings plus depreciation less equity dividends is the recognised method of computing this figure.

Col. 8 constitutes the total net capital employed. This is the total of net fixed assets—excluding intangibles such as goodwill—plus current assets less current liabilities, except bank overdrafts.

*For merchant banks a more realistic figure to quote is the balance-sheet total.

Col. 9 represents the net return on capital employed. Col. 2 as a percentage of Col. 8 provides an indication of average profitability.

†Excluding merchant banks and insurance (life and composite).

Col. 10 net current assets are arrived at by the subtraction of current liabilites and provision from current assets.

‡Other Consumer Group has been absorbed into other groups.

Table 2–7   Extract from *Financial Times* 'Trend of Industrial Profits', 18 May 1985

**Profit/Total assets (percentage) ratio**

( ) indicates a loss

| | Number of firms | Lower Quartile | Median | Upper Quartile |
|---|---|---|---|---|
| **Product group** | | | | |
| A   Multi product | 48 | 4.2 | 8.0 | 12.5 |
| B   Stockings and tights | 25 | (0.6) | 3.9 | 12.6 |
| C   Half hose | 16 | 2.8 | 7.4 | 15.4 |
| D   Knitted outerwear | 52 | 1.9 | 7.5 | 11.4 |
| E   Knitted innerwear | 17 | 2.5 | 7.1 | 15.0 |
| F   Knitted fabric | 37 | 6.1 | 11.0 | 16.0 |
| H   Dyeing | 25 | 8.8 | 14.9 | 22.0 |
| **Asset size** (£ million) | | | | |
| L   Under 0.25 | 127 | 1.8 | 6.6 | 12.4 |
| M   0.25 to 0.5 | 30 | 3.6 | 9.2 | 16.1 |
| N   0.5 to 1.0 | 25 | 8.5 | 11.7 | 17.1 |
| O   1.0 to 3.0 | 19 | 5.5 | 10.8 | 14.8 |
| P/Q Over 3.0 | 19 | 7.8 | 11.4 | 13.5 |
| All firms | 220 | 3.2 | 8.9 | 13.7 |

Table 2–8   Extract from *A study of profitability in the hosiery and knitwear industry*

# A brief example of interfirm comparison – using the pyramid of ratios for general management

This example is intended to show the way in which the pyramid ratios for a comparison are presented, and how conclusions may be drawn from them. The actual figures used are hypothetical, but are typical of the results found by the Centre for Interfirm Comparison in its work in many industries. In practice a comparison normally covers more firms, and also includes more detailed data, such as those referred to in 'What the Comparison Shows: Firm 6'.

| RATIOS | FIRMS | | | | | | | | | MEDIAN* |
|---|---|---|---|---|---|---|---|---|---|---|
| | 1 | 2 | 3 | 4 | 5 | 6 | 7 | 8 | 9 | |
| 1. Operating profit/Operating assets | 20.2 | 17.9 | 14.3 | 13.3 | 11.3 | 7.9 | 7.4 | 3.9 | 3.1 | 11.3 |
| 2. Operating profit/Sales | 18.2 | 14.9 | 13.1 | 11.9 | 10.9 | 6.1 | 7.6 | 3.1 | 3.8 | 10.9 |
| 3. Sales/Operating assets (times) | 1.11 | 1.20 | 1.09 | 1.12 | 1.04 | 1.30 | 0.98 | 1.25 | 0.81 | 1.11 |
| *Departmental costs* (as a percentage of sales) | | | | | | | | | | |
| 4. Production costs | 71.3 | 77.1 | 77.4 | 79.6 | 79.4 | 84.2 | 82.5 | 89.5 | 84.3 | 79.6 |
| 5. Distribution and marketing costs | 4.9 | 3.7 | 4.1 | 2.2 | 3.3 | 2.9 | 4.4 | 3.3 | 3.6 | 3.6 |
| 6. Administrative costs | 5.6 | 4.3 | 5.4 | 6.3 | 6.4 | 6.8 | 5.7 | 4.1 | 8.3 | 5.7 |
| *Production costs* (as a percentage of sales value of production) | | | | | | | | | | |
| 7. Materials cost | 46.9 | 53.0 | 51.0 | 50.8 | 56.2 | 55.3 | 56.3 | 56.5 | 51.7 | 53.0 |
| 8. Works labour cost | 10.4 | 9.8 | 7.3 | 10.1 | 9.2 | 12.3 | 8.2 | 16.1 | 14.7 | 10.1 |
| 9. Production overheads | 14.0 | 14.3 | 19.1 | 18.7 | 14.0 | 16.6 | 18.0 | 16.9 | 17.9 | 16.9 |
| *Asset utilisation* (£'s per £1,000 of sales) | | | | | | | | | | |
| 3a. Total operating assets | 899 | 833 | 918 | 893 | 960 | 770 | 1,019 | 798 | 1,233 | 899 |
| 10. Current assets | 328 | 384 | 400 | 351 | 379 | 404 | 589 | 423 | 430 | 400 |
| 11. Fixed assets | 571 | 449 | 518 | 542 | 581 | 366 | 430 | 375 | 803 | 518 |
| *Current asset utilisation* (£'s per £1,000 of sales) | | | | | | | | | | |
| 12. Material stocks | 58 | 73 | 43 | 58 | 86 | 65 | 129 | 80 | 68 | 68 |
| 13. Work in progress | 51 | 90 | 104 | 63 | 44 | 114 | 164 | 122 | 135 | 104 |
| 14. Finished stocks | 66 | 94 | 123 | 63 | 118 | 77 | 147 | 60 | 84 | 84 |
| 15. Debtors | 153 | 127 | 130 | 167 | 131 | 148 | 149 | 161 | 143 | 148 |
| *Fixed asset utilisation* (£'s per £1,000 of sales) | | | | | | | | | | |
| 16. Land and buildings | 240 | 87 | 102 | 143 | 156 | 88 | 47 | 73 | 299 | 102 |
| 17. Plant and machinery | 316 | 343 | 407 | 389 | 413 | 267 | 363 | 289 | 486 | 363 |
| 18. Vehicles | 15 | 19 | 9 | 10 | 12 | 11 | 20 | 13 | 18 | 13 |

*The median is the middle figure for each ratio

## SUMMARY: THE SCOPE FOR IMPROVEMENT, MEASURED IN RATIOS AND ABSOLUTE FIGURES

If you were able to achieve materials and labour cost ratios equal to the medians, whilst retaining your present production overheads ratio and the same ratios for your other departmental costs, your profit to sales ratio would improve to 10.6 per cent.

In order to achieve your improved labour cost ratio, you might have to spend more on new plant. Supposing you increased your plant value (which at the moment is £267 per £1,000 of sales) by 50 per cent, then your fixed assets ratio would increase to £499. However, you should be able to improve your work in progress figure to the median, giving a lower current asset ratio (ratio 10) of £394. Your rate of turnover of operating assets (ratio 3) would then become 1.12 times. Because of your increased investment in plant and machinery, your depreciation would go up, and the effect of this would be to increase your production overheads ratio to 17.6 per cent; your profit margin on sales would then become 9.6 per cent and your return on assets 10.8 per cent – i.e. nearly three percentage points higher than it is now.

In terms of absolute figures: your present sales volume is £2 millions. At the same volume of sales, your new profit ratio would mean a profit of £192,000 – an improvement of £70,000 on your present profits.

Table 2–9   Example of interfirm comparison

## WHAT THE COMPARISON SHOWS: FIRM 6

Suppose you are the managing director of firm 6 in the table opposite, what does the comparison show you?

1. First and most important, the comparison gives you for the first time an objective yardstick of your firm's overall success – as indicated by the standing of your operating profit/operating assets ratio against that of other firms.
   The comparison of this primary ratio shows that your firm's overall success and effectiveness is *less* than that of the majority of the others, since your return on assets is only 7.9 per cent against the median of 11.3 per cent.

2. What is the cause of your low operating profit/operating assets? Comparison of ratios 2 and 3 shows that the reason is your low operating profit/sales – your figure of 6.1 per cent is the third lowest of the figures shown. On the other hand, your turnover of assets, ratio 3, is the fastest of any firm. It therefore seems that you should first of all investigate the cost ratios which determine your operating profit/sales.

3. Looking at the departmental cost ratios, you find that your production cost, ratio 4, is high; your distribution and marketing cost, ratio 5, is below-average; and your administration cost, ratio 6, is above-average.

4. The causes of your high ratio 4 are shown by ratios 7 and 8 to be your high materials and labour costs. In the actual comparison, you have access to more detailed comparative data which throws further light on these points – it shows (a) that your high materials cost is related to your high materials waste ratio, and (b) that your high works labour cost is caused, not by high wages, etc. costs per employee, but by low volume of output per employee.

5. Turning to the asset utilisation ratios you see that your fast turnover of total operating assets (ratio 3) is expressed in a different way by ratio 3a, which shows that you have the lowest figure of total operating assets per £1,000 of sales. You will see from ratio 11 that this is because you have the lowest figure of fixed assets in relation to sales. This is, in turn, mainly due to your low plant and machinery ratio (ratio 17). Incidentally, the fixed asset figures used in this comparison are based upon comparable valuations.
   The more detailed data available (not shown in this table) indicate that the average age of your plant is greater than that of most other firms; and that your value of plant and machinery per works employee is below the average. The comparison therefore suggests that your low labour productivity (a major cause of your high production costs) may be due to the fact that your plant is not sufficiently up-to-date.

6. Your current asset utilisation ratios (ratios 12 to 15) show that most of your current asset items are about average – with the exception of your work in progress, ratio 13, which is above the average. This seems to provide another indication of the need for altering your production arrangements so as to allow a faster throughput.

# Chapter 3

# Principles of ratio definition and calculation

## 3.1 General Principles

*Consistency.* It is most important that there should be consistency between the numerator and the denominator of a ratio, and between the method of calculating a ratio and the standard with which it is being compared.

For example, if income from a particular activity is included in one part of a ratio, the cost of obtaining that income, or the value of the asset employed to bring that income in, should be in the other part of the ratio.

Further, if a firm that you are comparing your results with has arrived at its profit after valuing stock and calculating depreciation in certain ways, it may be necessary to recalculate your profit in the same ways in order to make an accurate comparison. It is worth bearing in mind when making any comparison based on figures either in your own accounts or in those of other firms that *accounts are not so much facts as a number of estimates and opinions clothed in the language of money.*

*Inflation.* If comparisons are being made over time involving money values, the effects of different amounts of inflation on these values at different times should be removed (see Chapter 5 – the section on Growth). Equally important is the addition of inflation to asset and capital values of an earlier period when comparing them to sales, costs or profits of a later period. The subject of adjusting for inflation is discussed in Chapter 13.7 and an approximate method of adjusting published accounts is in Appendix 13.1.

*Averages.* When relating profits, costs or sales to assets or capital, the figure for assets or capital should be an average of its values over the period to which the profits, costs or sales relate. Similarly, the number of staff who have left in a period should be related to the average number present during the same period, not to the number at either the beginning or the end of the period.

*Time Lag.* There is always a time lag between incurring expenditure and receiving the benefit from it. Calculations of ratios that relate benefit to expenditure must take account of this lag and how a firm's accountant has dealt with it, if at all. There are two accounting devices for dealing with the problem of lag. If the expenditure has produced a physical object which has not yet been sold, the expenditure is diverted into 'stock' and only the balance is left to be related to sales. If the expenditure has not produced a physical object, it may be treated as 'expenditure in advance' and not deducted in arriving at this year's profits (but it will be deducted from a future year's profit) or it may be written off straightaway. Examples of items usually treated as expenditure in advance are rent and rates. Items usually written off when incurred are advertising and research expenditure.

It is because of differences in treatment such as the above that accounts need to be used with caution, as do any ratios calculated from them. It is desirable where there is significant lag between expenditure and benefit to correct for it, using one of the accountant's devices mentioned above, or to offset the items in time, for example by relating advertising expenditure for one period to the sales of another period ending (say) six months later.

## 3.2 Main Accounting Terms

A number of terms in general use have been given a more precise meaning in this book. For the convenience of the reader they have all been set out here. The relationship between the principal ones is shown in Diagrams 3-1 and 3-2.

*Fixed assets* include those assets which it is not the intention of the firm to trade in but to use for the purpose of producing goods or services for sale. This means that the following are normally included: land, buildings, plant, machinery and vehicles. Goodwill, patents and other intangible assets are normally excluded because, more than for the other items, they are the result of bookkeeping entries. Fixed assets should be valued, if possible, at their estimated current values taking into account the effects of age, obsolescence and inflation.

*Current assets (1)* include the firm's trading assets, that is stocks and debtors. If possible average values for these items should be used, because the value at the balance sheet date may well be untypical of the period as a whole.

*Current assets (2)* When related to current liabilities, current assets includes stocks, debtors, cash, and marketable securities (that is those that can be easily converted into cash).

*Other assets* include those assets of a firm not being used in its main operations, for example sub-let property (which would then be excluded from fixed assets) investments (which should be taken at their market value – shown in a note to the balance sheet) and cash.

*Operating assets* is the sum of the fixed assets and current assets (1).

*Total assets* is the sum of operating assets and other assets.

*Borrowed capital* includes all sources of finance other than that provided by the owners or ordinary shareholders of a company. It can be subdivided into long-and short-term borrowed capital.

*Long-term borrowed capital* includes debentures, preference shares, and long-term loans. It should also include deferred tax. For convenience minority interests in the company can be included.

*Short-term borrowed capital* includes overdrafts, trade and expense creditors, short-term loans, tax provisions.

*Equity capital* includes ordinary shares, capital and revenue reserves and undistributed profits (balance on profit and loss account plus proposed dividends on ordinary shares) plus or minus any surplus or deficit on the revaluation and/or averaging of fixed, current and other assets less the value of intangible assets. Another way of arriving at the same result is to subtract borrowed capital from total assets.

*Total capital* is the sum of borrowed capital and equity capital. By definition total capital equals total assets.

*Long-term capital* is the sum of long-term borrowed capital and equity capital.

*Operating profit* is the profit derived from the main operation of the business, that is, from the employment of operating assets. Basically it will be sales less operating costs including depreciation but excluding interest and tax.

*Other income* is the income derived from other assets. It should be gross before deduction of tax.

*Total profit* equals the sum of operating profit and other income.

*Interest paid* equals all interest and/or dividends paid to the providers of borrowed capital. The gross before-tax figure should be used. For convenience it will include the minority interest's share of profit.

*Net profit* equals total profit minus interest paid.

*Tax* includes corporation tax, capital gains tax, overseas tax, income tax deducted from dividends received, *less* double taxation relief and income tax retainable from dividends payable.

*Net profit after tax* equals net profit minus tax.

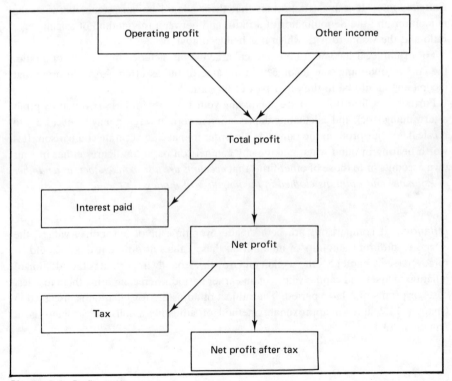

Diagram 3–1   Profits and income

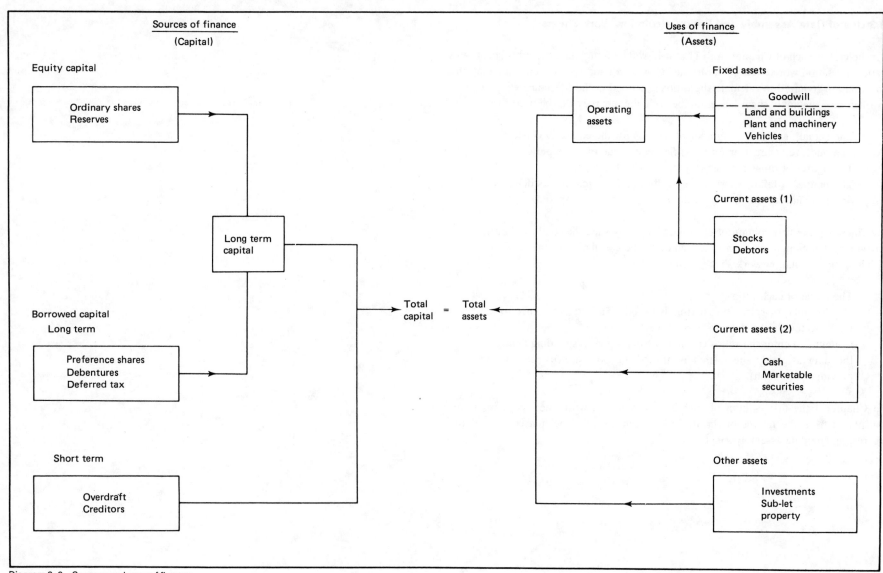

Diagram 3–2   Sources and uses of finance

*61*

## 3.3 Use of Data Assembly and Ratio Calculation Work Sheets

At the end of each of Chapters 4 to 11 and 13 will be found data assembly sheets and ratio calculation work sheets. The former provide a handy place to assemble all the information required to calculate the ratios described in the preceding chapter.

Each data assembly sheet has a number of columns; they can be used for:

1    The actual figures for a number of periods for the company concerned
2    The budgeted (target or forecast) figures for one or more periods
3    The figures of other companies (where available)
4    The figures of fellow subsidiaries or divisions or departments depending
     on the standards against which the ratios are being compared.

In Chapter 4 the first column of each data assembly sheet has had the figures of an imaginary company inserted in it as a guide to the calculation of the ratios.

The ratio calculation work sheets contain:

1    The name of each ratio
2    The formula for calculating it (this is keyed by a letter reference to the
     relevant item in the data assembly sheet)
3    Columns to enter the ratios calculated from the corresponding figures in
     the data assembly sheet (that is any of the possibilities listed in the
     previous paragraph).

In Chapter 4 the first column of each ratio calculation work sheet contains ratios calculated from the figures of the imaginary firm given in the first column of the corresponding data assembly sheet.

**PART TWO**

# Chapter 4

# Priority ratios for the chief executive

Before considering what ratios the chief executive should examine, the long-term objectives of the firm must be defined. Naturally, in the short term, there will be subsidiary objectives and it may sometimes be necessary to give a sub-objective priority in the short term. For example it may be necessary to grant a wage increase which reduces profit in the short term because not to do so would have very damaging effects on the firm's long-term profitability.

What should be the primary objective of the board of directors of a company? The philosophy of this book is founded on the belief that the answer to this question is 'the maximisation over the medium to long term of the return to the ordinary shareholder on his investment'. This means that short-term improvements in profitability must not be sought if they will be achieved at the expense of greater long-term decreases in profit. It also means that the directors are primarily concerned with the ordinary shareholder. Other providers of capital will need consideration but only to the extent that they are contributing to the profit for the ordinary shareholder. The return on the ordinary shareholder's investment is made up of dividends and capital gains. Neither should be neglected at the expense of the other.

Finally, the ordinary shareholder is concerned with the return on his investment, not just the figure of profit but the profit in relation to the money he has put into the company by initial subscription, by purchase of the shares on the market and by additional injections of capital during the life of the company.

The remainder of this chapter deals with secondary objectives, which have to be achieved if the primary one is to be met, and as the ratios will, of necessity, be looked at and action taken in the short term, it will be useful if the chief executive also considers from time to time the long-term effects of his colleagues' plans and action on the primary objective of their company.

The twenty-eight ratios that the chief executive of every company should monitor are described. This may seem a large number of ratios but they do not all need examining at the same time. While some may need to be monitored every month, others need to be looked at only once a year or every six months.

These ratios are related to the key areas which are common to nearly all businesses and with which the top man must be concerned – although in broad terms only. These key areas will fluctuate in relative importance over the course of time, and the amount of energy devoted to them and the frequency with which they are studied will correspondingly change. The order in which they are described here should not therefore be taken as in any way an order of importance.

All firms are the meeting point of a number of economic forces. It would be oversimplifying the business world to pretend that any one of these forces has priority over the others. All must be satisfied in the long-run, or at the least have their demands palliated in the short term. It is the task, by no means an easy one, of the chief executive constantly to balance the demands of one force against the needs of the others.

The areas that a chief executive must consider are the relationship between his firm and:

1    Its markets
2    The providers of its capital, both risk and loan
3    Its suppliers
4    Its employees.

He must also watch:

5    How well it is using its assets
6    How well it is providing for the future.

The ratios in this chapter are numbered as follows. The number before the decimal point refers to the key area listed above. (For example 1.1 is a marketing ratio.) The number after the decimal point is the number of the ratio within the area. (For example 1.3 is the third ratio in the marketing area.) Ratios which are alternatives are indicated by (a), (b), (c), etc.

At the end of the chapter there are data assembly sheets and ratio calculation sheets to facilitate the calculation of the ratios described.

These ratios should be graphed over time. It is even more helpful if the same graph is used to show the firm's budget or target for the ratio, and the performance of competitors' ratios (if obtainable). Needless to say, budget, target and competitors' figures must be worked out on the same basis as the firm's current, actual figures. The data assembly sheets can be used for all of the figures mentioned.

## 4.1 The Firm and its Markets

How well the market likes a firm's products is indicated by the rate of growth of its sales, which can be measured by:

1.1(a)
$$\frac{\text{Sales this year}}{\text{Sales last year}}$$

or by

1.1(b)
$$\frac{\text{Sales this month}}{\text{Sales last month}}$$

or by

1.1(c)
$$\frac{\text{Sales this month}}{\text{Sales same month last year}}$$

Ratio 1.1(b) is obviously more sensitive to changes in demand than ratio 1.1(a). In any business where demand is seasonal ratio 1.1(c) is more useful than ratio 1.1(b).

If there have been price changes during the period between last year (month) and this, it is desirable to reduce the apparent growth shown by ratios 1.1(a), 1.1(b), or 1.1(c) to growth in real terms by measuring both numerator and denominator at the same prices. This may be too time consuming to be practicable. An alternative method, if it is known that prices have on average increased by $x$ per cent, is to reduce ratios 1.1(a), (b) or (c) by that percentage.

Simple growth is usually not enough. A firm will want to increase, or at least maintain, its share of the market. If figures are available (perhaps from the firm's trade association or from government sources) as to the size of the market then the chief executive can also monitor

1.2
$$\frac{\text{Share of the market now}}{\text{Share of the market (last year/last month/same month last year)}}$$

The size of the order book is of importance to all firms. How large or how small they want it to be depends on whether they are in a heavy engineering or other long-term contracting business, or aim to provide an 'off the shelf', 'by return' service.

1.3
$$\frac{\text{Value of orders outstanding}}{\text{Average value of sales per day}}$$

It is probably a universal tendency for the range of products a firm sells to grow. Almost equally universal is the tendency for this to lead to a reduction in profitability. Every year, or thereabouts, the chief executive should have the following exercise carried out:

1    Products should be listed in descending order of their annual turnover.
2    Starting from the top of the list the turnover of each item should be added until 80 per cent of the annual turnover is reached. At this point a line should be drawn.
3    The number of items below the line should be expressed as a percentage of the total number of items (this is market ratio 1.4)
4    The ratio calculated in (3) should be compared with the same ratio calculated a year ago. If there has been an increase, then almost certainly the range has grown too wide and items below the line, starting at the bottom of the list, should be considered for removal from the range.

In this process of consideration it may be useful to use Drucker's classification* of products into:

1    Today's breadwinners
2    Tomorrow's breadwinners
3    Productive specialities
4    Development products
5    Failures
6    Yesterday's breadwinners
7    Repair jobs
8    Unnecessary specialities

---

* P.F. Drucker, *Managing for Results*, Heinemann, 1964, page 48 and following.

9    Unjustified specialities

10   Investments in managerial ego

11   Cinderellas

The last ratio to be monitored under this heading is

1.5
$$\frac{\text{Debtors} \times \text{Numbers of days in period}}{\text{Credit sales}}$$

The number of days to use for this ratio is the number of calendar days. Interest is payable on an overdraft for every day of the year! For ratio 1.3 the number of days should be the number of selling days taken to achieve the relevant sales figure. Ratio 1.3 is then the number of selling or working days required to work off the order book.

    Ratio 1.5 shows how much credit a firm's customers are taking. The more this can be reduced the more profitable will be the business; and the greater the risk that it will lose customers to competitors who are prepared to give longer credit! It is very much a matter of judgement where the line should be drawn. But no judgement can be exercised unless this and other ratios are first monitored.

    This subject is dealt with more fully in Chapters 5 and 6.

    To calculate ratios 1.1 to 1.5 use data assembly and ratio calculation sheet 4–1 at the end of this chapter.

## 4.2 The Firm and the Providers of Capital

The return that the providers of risk capital are getting is best measured by the ratio

2.1
$$\frac{\text{Net profit after tax}}{\text{Equity capital}}$$

If this ratio declines and/or remains depressed for any length of time, the chief executive, and perhaps his fellow board members, must be prepared for:

1    A move by shareholders to replace them at the next AGM

2    A takeover bid from another company whose board consider they can run the firm more profitably.

The chief executive can gauge the opinion of the stock market of his company (if it is quoted) by the size of its P/E ratio.

2.2
$$\frac{\text{Price per share}}{\text{Earnings after corporation tax per share}}$$

This ratio reflects the view of the stock exchange not only of the company, but of the industry in which it operates and of the economy as a whole. Any changes in this ratio need therefore to be looked at in the context of changes in the P/E ratios of competitors. Within this limitation the higher his firm's P/E ratio is the happier should the chief executive be, unless:

1    It has been pushed up as the result of a takeover bid or the rumours of one,

    or

2    He thinks it is unreasonably high in the light of his knowledge of any likely future growth in profits.

The ratio of

2.3
$$\frac{\text{Interest paid}}{\text{Borrowed capital}}$$

tells us how much a firm is having to pay for the finance obtained from sources other than the providers of risk capital. This ratio needs to be compared with:

1    The market rate for such finance (on debentures and overdrafts)

2    The return on risk capital (2.1 above)

3    The return being earned on the assets of the business (ratio 5.1 below).

The market rate will be particularly relevant if the firm has a debenture whose redemption date(s) is/are near or if it wants to increase its gearing (see below).

    The return on risk capital and the return on assets should obviously both be higher than ratio 2.3. If they are lower the firm is in a very unhealthy situation.

    While on this pessimistic note 'interest cover' should be looked at. This measures a firm's ability to go on paying its interest commitments.

2.4
$$\frac{\text{Total profit}}{\text{Interest paid}}$$

Gearing enables the ordinary shareholder to get a higher return on his investment than management is obtaining from the use of the firm's assets. Gearing can be measured by

2.5

$$\frac{\text{Borrowed capital}}{\text{Equity capital}}$$

This is a ratio which management has to keep in balance. The higher it is then the bigger the return to the equity shareholders, but the risk to them and the fixed interest lenders will be greater as indicated by a decline in ratio 2.4 above.

This subject is dealt with more fully in Chapter 8.

To calculate ratios 2.1 to 2.5 use data assembly and ratio calculation sheet 4–2 at the end of this chapter.

## 4.3 The Firm and its Suppliers

There are three aspects of the performance of his firm's suppliers which a chief executive should monitor: price, delivery and quality.

Changes in price are best measured by index numbers. It may be uneconomic to monitor the price of all items used but a practical compromise would be to list purchases in descending order of value and measure changes in all items that account for the top 80 per cent (say) by value, and of a sample of the rest. This price index is the buyer's first ratio:

3.1

$$\frac{\text{Suppliers' prices now}}{\text{Suppliers' prices at the base date}}$$

Increases in price of products used may require improved purchasing by the buying department, more productivity from the work force, perhaps a change in the materials used, or an increase in the price charged to customers.

Suppliers' lead times can be measured by the ratio of

3.2

$$\frac{\text{Value of orders outstanding with suppliers}}{\text{Average daily purchases}}$$

Perhaps more significant than lead times is the (un)reliability of suppliers. The ratio to use to monitor this is

3.3

$$\frac{\text{Value of orders overdue from suppliers}}{\text{Average daily purchases}}$$

Any increase in either of these two ratios means that management must decide whether to quote longer deliveries to customers, accept a lower level of service to customers, increase its stock holding, or alter its buying pattern.

The credit given by suppliers is a useful source of finance for all firms and should be used to the limit, that is, the point where the supplier threatens to stop deliveries, or the rate of discounts not obtained becomes higher than the interest paid on other available sources of finance, or than the rate of profit earned on assets.

3.4

$$\frac{\text{Creditors}}{\text{Average daily purchases}}$$

measures the length of credit the firm is taking.

It is at this point that the chief executive must consider liquidity – the ability of the business 'to pay its way'. He is best advised to use a variant of the 'acid test' ratio for this

3.5

$$\frac{\text{Cash + Debtors + Marketable securities}}{\text{Current liabilities plus an appropriate part of capital expenditure to which the firm is committed.}}$$

This should not be allowed to fall below unity.

An indication of the quality of the goods bought from suppliers is the percentage that have to be returned.

3.6

$$\frac{\text{Value of goods returned or credited}}{\text{Purchases}}$$

An increase in this ratio might indicate the need to look for new sources of supply. A decrease might indicate that the company's quality control standards were slipping. In either case changes in this ratio should lead to investigation and remedial action.

This subject is dealt with more fully in Chapter 7.

To calculate ratios 3.1 to 3.6 use data assembly and ratio calculation sheet 4–3 at the end of this chapter.

## 4.4 The Firm and its Employees

In times of full employment, if a firm does not satisfy its work force, it may have started on the road to bankruptcy. Dissatisfied employees, if they can, vote with their feet. A chief executive should therefore keep his eye on the turnover of his employees

4.1

$$\frac{\text{Number of leavers}}{\text{Average number of employees}}$$

Like many ratios this must be kept in balance. Too high a figure can obviously be disastrous. Too low a figure can indicate stagnation, so it is suggested that the chief executive should also look at

4.2
$$\frac{\text{Average age of senior staff now}}{\text{Average age of senior staff five years ago}}$$

Is arteriosclerosis setting in?

Businesses are not charitable institutions, however, and they will only want to keep employees if their output is satisfactory. This can be measured in three ways

4.3(a)           Sales per employee
or, better,

4.3(b)    Value added (sales minus materials cost) per employee
or, best,

4.3(c)           Profit per employee

It is also necessary to know how much the firm's employees are costing, so the chief executive should look at

4.4        Wages, salaries, NI, pension contributions, etc, per employee

This subject is dealt with more fully in Chapter 10.

To calculate ratios 4.1 to 4.4 use data assembly and ratio calculation sheet 4–4 at the end of this chapter.


## 4.5 Use of Assets

As well as getting the best out of its employees, and suitably rewarding them, a firm needs to use its assets profitably in order to pay its employees and the providers of its capital. There are four ratios worth examining here. The first is

5.1
$$\frac{\text{Operating profit}}{\text{Operating assets}}$$

Operating profit is arrived at after deducting depreciation but before subtracting interest payments or tax and it does not include income from sources outside the mainstream of the business, such as investments. The two main factors which influence the size of this ratio are:

1    The balance between cost and income, best measured by

5.2
$$\frac{\text{Operating profit}}{\text{Sales}}$$

2    The balance between investment in assets and the volume of business obtained, most easily measured by

5.3
$$\frac{\text{Sales}}{\text{Operating assets}}$$

This ratio is usually called a firm's 'turnover of assets' and is described as being 'so many times per year'.

If some measure of the maximum output a plant is capable of can be obtained, either in physical or financial terms, ratio 5.3 is most usefully supplemented by

5.4
$$\frac{\text{Actual output}}{\text{Maximum output}}$$

To avoid hair-splitting arguments over how much maintenance time and changeover time should be provided for and how long is the working week/year, it is a good idea to arrive at the maximum output assuming that production can be maintained twenty-four hours a day, seven days a week, 365 days a year.

To calculate ratios 5.1 to 5.4 use data assembly and ratio calculation sheet 4–5 at the end of this chapter.


## 4.6 The Future

All the ratios described so far in this chapter deal with the company as it is at the present time. Equally important is the subject of how well it is providing for the future. There are three main divisions of this subject:

1    Product innovation
2    Staff training and development
3    Asset renewal and expansion.

On product innovation the firm's record over the immediate past can be looked at by using the ratio

6.1      $\dfrac{\text{Sales of products introduced in the past five (?) years}}{\text{Total Sales}}$

The trend of this ratio over the past ten (or more) years will indicate any tendency for the firm to rest on its laurels.

Obviously it is not enough to introduce new products to the market, they must be profitable. In fact, they should be more profitable than the old ones have become, as competition has forced down margins over the course of time. The ratio

6.2   $\dfrac{\text{Profit (or contribution) from products introduced in the past five (?) years}}{\text{Sales of these products}}$

should therefore be higher than the same ratio for the rest of the firm's products.

At this stage it is useful to introduce a new concept, namely 'discretionary cash flow'. There are some items of expenditure over which management has a greater degree of choice as to how much to spend and when to spend it. A firm must buy the raw materials and pay the employees if it is to remain in business at all. How much it spends on such items as research, staff training, the purchase of new equipment, consultancy advice, advertising, etc; and the timing of such expenditure, is much more a matter for managerial discretion. Moreover the items listed have two other features in common:

1    They are for the benefit of the future rather than the present
2    They are more likely to be affected by the amount of cash available than by the volume of sales.

Discretionary cash flow (dCF to avoid confusion with DCF – discounted cash flow) is therefore the sum of:

1    Profit after tax, depreciation and interest payments.
2    Depreciation (an item of cost which does not cause an outflow of cash).
3    Dividends on ordinary shares (their size is within the absolute discretion of directors).
4    All items mentioned above which are considered to be discretionary by the management of the firm.
5    Any money received from new share issues or new loans obtained.
6    Any money received as the result of reducing the amount invested in net current assets or from selling fixed assets.

The ratios which the chief executive needs to monitor are then

6.3(a)      $\dfrac{\text{Research and development expenditure}}{\text{dCF}}$

6.3(b)      $\dfrac{\text{Training expenditure}}{\text{dCF}}$

plus ratios relating to any other item of discretionary expenditure of importance, and

6.4      $\dfrac{\text{Fixed asset expenditure}}{\text{dCF}}$

In connection with the last it is also useful to measure

6.5      $\dfrac{\text{Fixed asset expenditure}}{\text{Depreciation}}$

Because of the 'lumpiness' of fixed asset expenditure it is better to measure both numerator and denominator over a number of years (say three or more). If this ratio falls below unity then a firm is running down its fixed assets.

Two notes of caution need to be sounded in connection with this ratio:

1    If a firm depreciates its assets faster than it really believes they are going to wear out or become obsolete for reasons of prudence or accounting conservatism, this ratio can fall below unity without it meaning that the assets are being run down. If this is the case, it is suggested that, whatever the firm shows in its accounts, it makes a realistic assessment of the true figure of depreciation and uses this for management purposes.

2    Because of inflation it will nearly always cost more to replace an asset than it originally cost. But depreciation is based in virtually all firms on original cost. This ratio can then be above unity while fixed assets are being run down. What the firm should do, as a matter of sound business sense, irrespective of what it does in its accounts, is to calculate depreciation on the basis of an estimate of what the assets would cost to replace. This was written in about 1970 and still remains true. For more on this subject, see Chapter 13.7 and Appendix 13.1.

To calculate ratios 6.1 to 6.5 use data assembly and ratio calculation sheet 4–6 at the end of this chapter.

## 4.7 Summary

The priority ratios for the chief executive are summarised below:

1 *Markets*
1.1 Growth of sales
1.2 Growth of market share
1.3 Length of order book
1.4 Proportion of items in bottom 20 per cent of turnover
1.5 Debtors/Sales

2 *Providers of capital*
2.1 Net profit after tax/Equity capital
2.2 P/E ratio
2.3 Interest paid/Borrowed capital
2.4 Total profit/Interest paid
2.5 Borrowed capital/Equity capital

3 *Suppliers*
3.1 Suppliers' prices index
3.2 Suppliers' lead time
3.3 Days orders overdue
3.4 Creditors/Purchases
3.5 Cash, debtors, marketable securities/Current liabilities and capital expenditure
3.6 Value of goods returned or credited/Purchases

4 *Employees*
4.1 Number of leavers/Average numbers employed
4.2 Average age of senior staff: now/five years ago
4.3 'Output' per employee
4.4 Employment costs per employee

5 *Assets*
5.1 Operating profit/Operating assets
5.2 Operating profit/Sales
5.3 Sales/Operating assets
5.4 Actual output/Maximum output

6 *Future*
6.1 Sales of products introduced in last five years/Total sales
6.2 Profit from above sales/Sales of these products
6.3a R & D/dCF
6.3b Training/dCF, etc
6.4 Fixed asset expenditure/dCF
6.5 Fixed asset expenditure/Depreciation

## 4.8 Data Assembly and Ratio Calculation Work Sheets

In the pages that follow forms have been provided to assemble the necessary data, and to calculate and tabulate the ratios described in this chapter. Imaginary figures have been inserted in the first column of the data sheet and these have been used to calculate the ratio shown in the corresponding column of the ratio sheet. It is hoped that this will be an aid to readers in calculating their own ratios.

## Appendix 4.1

### THE WEINSTOCK YARDSTICK OF EFFICIENCY

The selection of priority ratios for the chief executive described in this chapter reflects the views and experience of the author. Readers may like to compare it with those that Arnold Weinstock uses as described in an article by Anthony Vice in *The Times* Business News of 29 November 1968, but see also Lord Weinstock's comments reproduced at the end of the article.

### The Times Article

Arnold Weinstock, now chief executive of GEC, English Electric and Associated Electrical Industries, has built an outstanding reputation as a revitaliser of companies. The basis for his takeover of AEI and for the subsequent merger with English Electric is based on the seven years since 1961 during which he has transformed GEC from the sick man of the electrical industry into one of the most efficiently run of all large companies in Britain.

Financial control lies at the heart of Weinstock's operations, and in recent conversations he set out the seven key criteria which he uses to assess possible acquisitions and, above all, to control the performance of divisions within his own group. These seven criteria form the basis of the reports which are sent every month to Weinstock at the group's headquarters in Stanhope Gate, London. It is on the basis of these reports, and what they disclose, that Weinstock bases his control of GEC-AEI-English Electric operations.

Weinstock has built up these seven criteria partly from his own experience, and partly by sending teams to examine the methods used by General Electric and Texas Instruments in the United States – two companies which Weinstock believes to be among the most efficient in his own world-wide industry. (GEC's summary accounts, interestingly, are made up so as to show the results of the seven criteria comparison.) The seven criteria, whose results are set out in the accompanying table, are as follows

**1. Profits on capital employed** – This is probably the most widely used financial criterion in the private sector of industry. In the last resort this measures the earning power of capital which is used to make electrical equipment rather than buying gilt-edged, investing abroad or going into another line of business. GEC's 23 per cent compares with a United Kingdom industrial average of about 15 per cent; ICI's low figure of 13 per cent probably understates the company's performance, as it reflects assets which are not yet fully profit-earning. But a massive group like GE of America was able to earn nearly double the United Kingdom average, and even GE's figure is after allowing for nuclear power and computer losses. (Comparative figures may be affected to some extent by companies' different treatment of loan capital.)

**2. Profit on sales** – This is another widely used test indicating profit margins, but the figure tends to vary markedly between different industries. GEC's emerges higher than GE's while English Electric's is unusually low, probably reflecting the size of their business in heavy electrical goods.

**3. Sales as a multiple of capital employed** – This shows the productivity of the company's net capital; comparisons should be made between companies of roughly comparable financial structure and similar capital intensity, for an unusually capital-intensive group like ICI will tend to show a low ratio. But overall, the ratio of sales to total capital probably represents a fair measure of a company's efficiency through its ability to generate business from a given volume of assets. GE stands out in this comparison, and a broad contrast of British and American companies illustrates, for example, the differences in trade unions' attitudes towards the use of capital equipment.

**4. Sales as a multiple of fixed assets** – This is a major subdivision of the previous criterion. The ability of fixed assets to generate sales is probably the best measure of their real worth, often one of the most difficult problems in analysing company performance. Here again, a basic guide for management is that companies in the same sort of business should tend to show a similar sale/fixed asset ratio. GEC come out well ahead of both GE and Texas Instruments.

**5. Sales as a multiple of stocks** – This is one area where both the United States companies show up much better than their British opposite numbers. One reason is the much wider use in America of computer techniques for stock and production control, allied to the higher level of general education among middle management – which means that specialist techniques can be widely employed to control the level of working capital. United States companies also tend to receive better service from their suppliers.

Even with an efficient company like GEC the ability to sustain GE's stock/sales ratio would enable it to cut inventories by some £25 000 000. For United Kingdom industry as a whole, this would imply an inventory saving of perhaps £1 750 000 000, a massive once-for-all gain for the balance of payments and bank financing. Just under a decade ago the United States achieved a substantial reduction in imports following the introduction of computer control techniques.

**6. Sales per employee** – This is the broad measure of the productivity of a work force, and should indicate the number of non-productive personnel – whose elimination has been one of the main aims of Weinstock's planning. But both the sales and profit/employee ratios emerge as secondary pieces of evidence. They are essentially a by-product of the other five Weinstock ratios; if those are showing well, then the sales and profit/employee ratios will come right. From the employee's side, this also points to the value of the product generated by each man. An international comparison of sales per employee is thus the first step towards a comparison of relative industrial wealth.

**7. Profits per employee** – This is a closer examination of the previous criterion, to which it is related by the basic profit/sales ratio. The size of profits related to work force remains, after all, the ultimate justification for workers' employment in industry while from the employees' side this sets the area of bargaining for increases in wages. For management, this figure is a fundamental tool in assessing how far, and in which areas, a work force should be expanded.

These seven rules form a basic framework for assessing a company or a self-contained division within a company. In general terms, one can only say that if all seven criteria are showing the right results, then the company will be working successfully. In general policy terms – as opposed to a specific situation – no one of the criteria is fundamental to the others. The time to apply specific judgements, in which Arnold Weinstock has been outstandingly successful, is when one of the criteria starts to show danger. The seven rules are also valuable for making comparisons between companies which are broadly similar in their operations, as in Table 4–1 which shows two American electrical companies, GE and Texas along with GEC and English Electric. A comparison with ICI, which operates in a different sector of industry, shows ICI's low ratio of sales to capital employed and its high ratio of sales to employees.

An international comparison of these figures brings out one striking contrast between Britain and American industry. While profit margins are roughly the same, British industry uses twice the amount of capital to produce a given quantity of sales or profits. In other words, a British company will tend to spend twice as much on human or real capital to reach the American level of profits – by the same logic, British firms can be said to be working only half as efficiently. This is a measure of United States industrial power, which also highlights the British problem: how to make the best use of human and material capital. Arnold Weinstock has raised GEC to the level where it can begin to compare with the most efficient in American industry; the task in Britain is for the other 100 or more major industrial companies to do the same.

**Lord Weinstock's comments**

In a private communication to the author, Lord Weinstock commented as follows:

> The ratios which we used as part of the apparatus of measuring business performance did not derive from the 'methods used by General Electric and TI' as indicated in the *Times* article. They emerged from a study of the difference between the results turned in by those, and other, companies and what we found in the British companies of which our management team acquired control. By expressing these differences in statistical terms, we could measure not only how the different parts of the business were doing, but how far their plans would take them in the direction of the standards of efficiency already achieved by others. And, of course, the use of numbers, where they can be relied upon to mean exactly what they are presumed to mean, is the simplest and most succinct way in which to present a fact of business performance. Training managers to think in those abbreviated and simplified terms should also eliminate a lot of the useless, or even misleading, verbal padding which diminishes the value of many reports.

|  | GEC | English Electric | General Electric (US) | Texas Instruments | ICI |
|---|---|---|---|---|---|
| **1.** Profits as per cent of capital employed | 23 | 14 | 29 | 17 | 12.9 |
| **2.** Profits as per cent of sales | 11 | 4.8 | 8.8 | 7.2 | 10.3 |
| **3.** Sales as a multiple of capital employed | 2.1 | 2.8 | 3.3 | 2.4 | 1.3 |
| **4.** Sales as a multiple of fixed assets | 6.1 | 4.1 | 5.2 | 4.1 | 1.0 |
| **5.** Sales as a multiple of stocks | 3.6 | 2.8 | 5.3 | 6.2 | 4.3 |
| **6.** Sales per employee (£) | 3,000 | 3,285 | 9,600 | 6,120 | 5,570 |
| **7.** Profits per employee (£) | 330 | 160 | 840 | 440 | 595 |

Table 4–1   How major companies measure up to the Weinstock yardsticks of efficiency.

So you see, the yardsticks are really a tool which has a far more general use in the process of supervisory management than might be thought superficially to be the case, and I have not tried here to go into more illustrative detail.

As to the ratios themselves, the profit to capital employed is merely the product of profit to sales and sales to capital employed. Sales to fixed assets has not proved to be valuable as an indicator of required action, and sales per employee is less useful than sales per £1 of employee emoluments and added value per £1 of emoluments.

Data assembly sheet number 4–1 (a) will be found on the following page

**Markets**

| Code letter | Item | Month or quarter to (date) | | | | | |
|---|---|---|---|---|---|---|---|
| | | 30 Sept | | | | | |
| | | £'000 | | | | | |
| A | Our sales last year | £70 | | | | | |
| B | Our sales this year | £80 | | | | | |
| C | Percentage price increase | 5% | | | | | |
| D | Total industry sales: Last year | £750 | | | | | |
| E | This year | £970 | | | | | |
| F | Value of orders from customers outstanding | £ 20 | | | | | |
| G | Debtors | £150 | | | | | |
| H | Credit sales if different from B | £ 75 | | | | | |
| K | Number of working days in period | 20 | | | | | |
| L | Number of calendar days in period | 28 | | | | | |

| Ratio | Formula for calculation of ratio | Unit of measurement | Month or quarter to (date) | | | | | |
|---|---|---|---|---|---|---|---|---|
| | | | 30 Sept | | | | | |
| 1.1 (a) Growth of sales | (B x 100 ÷ A) − 100 | % | 14.3 | | | | | |
| 1.1 (b) Growth of sales in real terms | [(B x 100 ÷ A) x 100 ÷ (100 + C)] − 100 | % | 8.8 | | | | | |
| 1.2 Change in share of market | [(B ÷ E) × 100 ÷ (A ÷ D)] − 100 | % | −11.6 | | | | | |
| 1.3 Length of order book | F ÷ (B ÷ K) | days | 5 | | | | | |
| 1.4 Length of tail of range | See sheet 4-1(b) | % | 80 | | | | | |
| 1.5 Credit taken by customers | G ÷ (H ÷ L) | days | 56 | | | | | |

**Analysis of turnover within product range**

| Item description | | Turnover(£) | Cumulative turnover(£) |
|---|---|---|---|
| 1 | A | 1,000 | 1,000 |
| 2 | B | 800 | 1,800 |
| 3 | C | 700 | 2,500 |
| 4 | D | 650 | 3,150 |
| | | | |
| 20 | T | 5 | 3,940 |
| Total turnover for period | | | 3,940 |

As £3,150 is 80% of £3,940

Ratio 4 is $\dfrac{20 \text{ minus } 4}{20}$ =80%

i.e. 80% of the range (items E to T) are producing only 20% of the turnover

Data assembly sheet number 4–2 will be found on the following page

**Providers of capital**

| Code letter | Item | Month or quarter to (date) | | | | | |
|---|---|---|---|---|---|---|---|
| | | 30 Sept | | | | | |
| A | Equity capital | £17,600,000 | | | | | |
| B | Borrowed capital | £12,400,000 | | | | | |
| C | Number of ordinary shares | 14,400,000 | | | | | |
| D | Price of ordinary shares | £1.50 | | | | | |
| E | Total profit | £3,592,000 | | | | | |
| F | Total interest paid | £704,000 | | | | | |
| G | Corporation tax | £1,288,000 | | | | | |
| H | Net profit after tax (E−F−G) | £1,600,000 | | | | | |
| K | Number of calendar days in period | 365 | | | | | |

| Ratio | Formula for calculation of ratio | Unit of measurement | Month or quarter to (date) | | | | | |
|---|---|---|---|---|---|---|---|---|
| | | | 30 Sept | | | | | |
| 2.1 *Return on equity capital*<br>Net profit after tax/Equity capital | $(H \times 365 \div K) \times 100 \div A$ | % pa | 9.1 | | | | | |
| 2.2 *P/E ratio*<br>Price per share/ Net profit after tax per share | $D \div [(H \times 365 \div K) \div C]$ | times | 13.5 | | | | | |
| 2.3 *Rate of interest paid on borrowed capital*<br>Interest paid/ Borrowed capital | $(F \times 365 \div K) \times 100 \div B$ | % pa | 5.7 | | | | | |
| 2.4 *Interest cover*<br>Total profit/ Interest paid | $E \div F$ | times | 5.10 | | | | | |
| 2.5 *Gearing*<br>Borrowed capital/ Equity capital | $B \div A$ | times | 0.71 | | | | | |

Data assembly sheet 4–3 (a)
## Suppliers

| Code letter | Item | Month or quarter to (date) | | | | | |
|---|---|---|---|---|---|---|---|
| | | 30 Sept | | | | | |
| | *Information from buying department* | | | | | | |
| A | Value of orders outstanding with suppliers | £1,136,000 | | | | | |
| B | Value of orders overdue from suppliers | £112,000 | | | | | |
| C | Purchases | £568,000 | | | | | |
| D | Value of goods returned | £11,200 | | | | | |
| | *Information from balance sheet* | | | | | | |
| E | Creditors | £4,000,000 | | | | | |
| F | Cash at bank and in hand | £352,000 | | | | | |
| G | Debtors | £3,976,000 | | | | | |
| H | Marketable securities | £1,416,000 | | | | | |
| K | Current liabilities (e.g. creditors, overdraft, etc.) | £4,800,000 | | | | | |
| L | Number of working days in period | 20 | | | | | |
| M | Number of calendar days in period | 28 | | | | | |
| N | Capital expenditure committed | £400,000 | | | | | |

## Suppliers

| Ratio | Formula for calculation of ratio | Unit of measurement | Month or quarter to (date) | | | | | |
|---|---|---|---|---|---|---|---|---|
| | | | 30 Sept | | | | | |
| 3.1 Suppliers' price index | See sheet 4-3 (b) | | 128 | | | | | |
| 3.2 Suppliers' lead time | A ÷ (C ÷ L) | days | 40 | | | | | |
| 3.3 Days orders overdue | B ÷ (C ÷ L) | days | 4 | | | | | |
| 3.4 Credit taken | E ÷ (C ÷ M) | days | 197 | | | | | |
| 3.5 Acid test (variant) | (F + G + H) ÷ (K + N) | times | 1.1 | | | | | |
| 3.6 Returns percentage | D x 100 ÷ C | % | 2 | | | | | |

Data assembly sheet and Ratio calculation sheet 4–3 (b)
## Calculating a price index for purchases

| Major products used | Quantity used | Price Date(a) | Date(b) |
|---|---|---|---|
| A | 1000 lb | £1.50 | £1.70 |
| B | 500 dozen | £2.40 | £3.60 |
| C | 1600 gallons | £1.00 | £1.25 |

Calculation of price index     Cost

| Item | Date(a) | Date(b) |
|---|---|---|
| A | 1000 x 1.50 = 1,500 | 1000 x 1.70 = 1,700 |
| B | 500 x 2.40 = 1,200 | 500 x 3.60 = 1,800 |
| C | 1600 x 1.00 = 1,600 | 1600 x 1.25 = 2,000 |
| | 4,300 | 5,500 |

$$\text{Index at date (b)} = \frac{5,500}{4,300} \times \frac{100}{1} = 128$$

(date (a) = 100)

Data assembly sheet number 4—4 (a) will be found on the following page

Data assembly sheet 4–4 (a)
## Employees

| Code letter | Item | Month or quarter to (date) | | | | | |
|---|---|---|---|---|---|---|---|
| | | 30 Sept | | | | | |
| A | Number employed at beginning | 870 | | | | | |
| B | Plus numbers joining during | 150 | | | | | |
| C | Minus numbers leaving during | 90 | | | | | |
| D | Equals numbers at end | 930 | | | | | |
| E | Average numbers employed $(A + D) \div 2$ | 900 | | | | | |
| F | Sales | £23,880,000 | | | | | |
| G | Materials cost | £10,088,000 | | | | | |
| H | Value added $(F - G)$ | £13,792,000 | | | | | |
| K | Wages and salaries | £9,240,000 | | | | | |
| L | All other costs | £1,064,000 | | | | | |
| M | Profit $(H - K - L)$ | £3,488,000 | | | | | |
| N | Number of calendar days in period | 365 | | | | | |

| Ratio | Formula for calculation of ratio | Unit of measurement | Month or quarter to (date) | | | | | |
|---|---|---|---|---|---|---|---|---|
| | | | 30 Sept | | | | | |
| 4.1 Turnover of employees | $(C \times 365 \div N) \times 100 \div E$ | % pa | 10 | | | | | |
| 4.2 Age of senior staff, change in | See sheet 4-4(b) | years | −3.9 | | | | | |
| 4.3 (a) Sales per employee | $(F \times 365 \div N) \div E$ | £ pa | 26,500 | | | | | |
| (b) Value added per employee | $(H \times 365 \div N) \div E$ | £ pa | 15,300 | | | | | |
| (c) Profit per employee | $(M \times 365 \div N) \div E$ | £ pa | 3,880 | | | | | |
| 4.4 Wages and salaries per employee | $(K \times 365 \div N) \div E$ | £ pa | 10,270 | | | | | |

Data assembly sheet and Ratio calculation sheet 4–4 (b)
## Calculation of average age of senior staff

| Senior staff* | Age | |
| --- | --- | --- |
| | Date (a) | Date (b)† |
| Able | 45 | 50 |
| Baker | 55 | — |
| Charlie (Baker's replacement) | — | 38 |
| Dog | 40 | 45 |
| Easy | 42 | — |
| Fox (Easy's replacement) | — | 40 |
| George (a new post) | — | 35 |
| TOTAL | 182 | 208 |
| Average ((a) ÷ 4; (b) ÷ 5) | 45.5 | 41.6 |
| Average age date (a) | 45.5 | |
| Average age date (b) | 41.6 | |
| Change in average age | 3.9 | |

*Can be defined as convenient. A suggestion for a small firm is MD, those who report to him, and those who report to them. †(b) is 5 years later than (a)

Data assembly sheet number 4–5 will be found on the following page

## Use of assets

| Code letter | Item | Month or quarter to (date) | | | | | |
|---|---|---|---|---|---|---|---|
| | | 30 Sept | | | | | |
| | | £000 | | | | | |
| | Fixed assets* | 21,784 | | | | | |
| | Stocks | 2,472 | | | | | |
| | Debtors | 3,976 | | | | | |
| A | Operating assets+ | 28,232 | | | | | |
| B | Sales | 23,880 | | | | | |
| | Profit as shown in accounts | | | | | | |
| | Add back | | | | | | |
| | Subtract | | | | | | |
| C | Operating profit ‡ | 3,488 | | | | | |
| D | Actual output | 6,000,000 units | | | | | |
| E | Maximum output | 9,500,000 units | | | | | |
| F | Number of calendar days in period | 365 | | | | | |

* Preferably at their current value, i.e. what they could be bought or sold for, not at their book value.

+ N.B. operating assets does *not* include goodwill, investments or cash or any other assets not used in the main business of the company, e.g. sublet property.

‡ Operating profit is defined as the profit earned from the normal operations of the business (e.g. excluding investment income) after deducting depreciation but before charging tax or interest payments. It may be necessary, therefore, to adjust the figure of profit shown in the accounts and space has been left for this in the work sheet.

| Ratio | Formula for calculation of ratio | Unit of measurement | Month or quarter to (date) | | | | | | |
|---|---|---|---|---|---|---|---|---|---|
| | | | 30 Sept | | | | | | |
| 5.1 Operating profit/ Operating assets | $C \times (F \div 365) \times 100 \div A$ | % pa | 12.4 | | | | | | |
| 5.2 Operating profit/ Sales | $C \times 100 \div B$ | % | 14.6 | | | | | | |
| 5.3 Turnover of assets Sales/Operating assets | $B \times (F \div 365) \div A$ | times per year | 0.85 | | | | | | |
| 5.4 Capacity utilis- ation Actual output/ Maximum output | $D \times 100 \div E$ | % | 63 | | | | | | |

Data assembly sheet 4–6 (a)

**The future**

| Product | Date of introduction | Within last years* | | | More than years* ago | | |
| --- | --- | --- | --- | --- | --- | --- | --- |
| | | Sales | Costs† | Profit or contribution ‡ | Sales | Costs† | Profit or contribution‡ |
| | | | | | | | |
| Total | | 1,300 | 460 | 840 | 1,685 | 801 | 884 |
| Code letter | | A | | B | C | | D |

* The number of years to use to separate new from old products must be decided by the individual firm. Five years is a suggestion.

† Costs can be either full costs from an absorption costing system or only those which would not have been incurred if the product had not been made or marketed.

‡ Profit = sales less full costs. Contribution = sales less marginal costs.

| Ratio | Formula for calculation of ratio | Unit of measurement | Year to | | | | | |
|---|---|---|---|---|---|---|---|---|
| | | | 30 Sept | | | | | |
| 6.1   Proportion of turnover from new products | A x 100 ÷ (A + C) | % | 43.5 | | | | | |
| 6.2(a)   Contribution from new products | B x 100 ÷ A | % | 64.5 | | | | | |
| (b)   Contribution from old products | D x 100 ÷ C | % | 52.5 | | | | | |
| 6.3(a)   R & D/ Discretionary cash flow | F x 100 ÷ H | % | 3.9 | | | | | |
| (b)   Training/ Discretionary cash flow | G x 100 ÷ H | % | 0.8 | | | | | |
| 6.4   Fixed asset expenditure/ Discretionary cash flow | K x 100 ÷ H | % | 15.5 | | | | | |
| 6.5(a)   Fixed asset expenditure/ Depreciation | K x 100 ÷ E | % | 75 | | | | | |
| (b)   Fixed asset expenditure/ 'True' depreciation | K x 100 ÷ (h) | % | | | | | | |

Data assembly sheet 4–6 (b)
## The future

| Code letter | Item | Year to | | | | | |
|---|---|---|---|---|---|---|---|
| | | 30 Sept | | | | | |
| | | £,000 | | | | | |
| | Profit after tax, depreciation and interest | 200 | | | | | |
| | Add back | | | | | | |
| E | Depreciation | 80 | | | | | |
| | Dividend on ordinary shares | 90 | | | | | |
| F | R & D expenditure | 15 | | | | | |
| G | Training expenditure | 3 | | | | | |
| | Consultancy expenditure | | | | | | |
| | Advertising expenditure | | | | | | |
| | New money raised | | | | | | |
| | Reduction in net current assets | | | | | | |
| | Sale of fixed assets | | | | | | |
| H | Discretionary cash flow | 388 | | | | | |
| K | Expenditure on fixed assets | 60 | | | | | |

Data assembly sheet number 4–6 (c) will be found on the following page

**Calculation of 'true depreciation'**

| Class of asset | | | | | | | Total |
|---|---|---|---|---|---|---|---|
| Fixed assets at cost or valuation (a) Less depreciation to date (b) | | | | | | | |
| Net book value (a)−(b) (c) | | | | | | | |
| Number of years company has owned asset (d) Number of years before asset wears out or becomes obsolete (e) | | | | | | | |
| Total life of asset (d)+(e) (f) | | | | | | | |
| Estimated cost to replace asset with new equivalent (g) | | | | | | | |
| 'True' depreciation for one year (g) ÷ (f) (h) to date (g) ÷ (f) x (d) (k) | | | | | | | |
| Amount needed to be set aside for asset replacement in addition to depreciation provision in balance sheet (k)−(b) (l) | | | | | | | |

# Chapter 5

# Ratios for overall control

## 5.1 Investment in Subsidiaries and/or Divisions

If the organisation is divided into a number of subsidiaries or divisions, the board will want to monitor the performance of each. The best ratio to use is

$$\frac{\text{Profit from subsidiary}}{\text{Investment in subsidiary}}$$

How the terms are defined depends on the nature of the subordinate organisation. (It may be helpful to refer back to Chapter 3 while reading the next few paragraphs.)

If the board are dealing with a subsidiary with powers to raise some of its own finance (particularly from creditors or banks), and perhaps even with minority shareholders of its own, investment is best defined as the parent company's holding in the subsidiary's equity capital. Profit is then what remains after deducting interest payments and the minority's share of profits.

If the parent company's investment is partly in the subsidiary's ordinary shares and partly by way of loans to the subsidiary, the investment must include the loan and the profit must have added back to it the loan interest. The interest cannot be ignored because it will affect the size of profit available to the minority.

If the board are dealing with an operating division the profit is the profit from its operations and the investment is the value of its operating assets.

In both cases the parent company or head office will have assets and expenses of its own. One way of dealing with these is to allocate them to the subsidiaries and divisions: the former being added to their investment and the latter being subtracted from their profit. It is preferable however not to do this because the local management has little or no control over the size of these items (though it may benefit from them). Instead, use a system of ratios as in Diagram 5–1 (which is based on operating divisions – subsidiaries would be slightly different).

Ratios A2, A3 and A4 show how much of the company's capital is invested in each division; ratio A5 the amount in head office assets. Ratios A6, A7 and A8 can be used by the board to monitor the performance of each division.

The board should control head office by requiring to be convinced that any growth in ratio A5 (Head office assets/Total capital) or in ratio A9 (Head office costs/Head office assets), will still lead to an increase in ratio A1 (Total profit/Total capital). Depending on whether group sales or total group employees are better measures of the need for head office then it will be useful to monitor also either ratios A10 (Head office costs/Group sales) and A11 (Group sales/Head office assets) or ratios A12 (Head office costs/Total group employees) and A13 (Head office assets/Total group employees).

Ratios A6, A7 and A8 are useful for monitoring the performance of divisions. The higher these ratios are the more favourably will the board regard requests for further capital. However, decisions on the allocation of capital should be taken on the basis of the rate of return of the particular project being canvassed which may be either higher or lower than the average rate of return on past projects which is measured by ratio A6, A7 and A8. No doubt the board's view of the credibility of the proposal will be influenced by the division's past performance as shown by ratios A6, A7 and A8.

How high should the rate of return on a project be for the board to authorise it? (The relevant rate of return will be the 'after-tax-discounted-cash-flow' rate of return.*) The answer depends on where the money for the project is coming from. If it is to come from new finance which has not yet been raised, the return on the project must be higher than the rate of interest on the new finance. In theory it need be only just higher; in practice a reasonable margin is needed to cover the risks and inaccuracies associated with the estimated return on the project.

---

* See, for example, A.J. Merrett & Allen Sykes, *Capital Budgeting and Company Finance,* Longmans, 2nd edn, 1973. A.M. Alfred & J.B. Evans, *Discounted Cash Flow,* Chapman & Hall, Third Edition 1971, prepared by J. Connor & R. Cooper of Courtaulds.

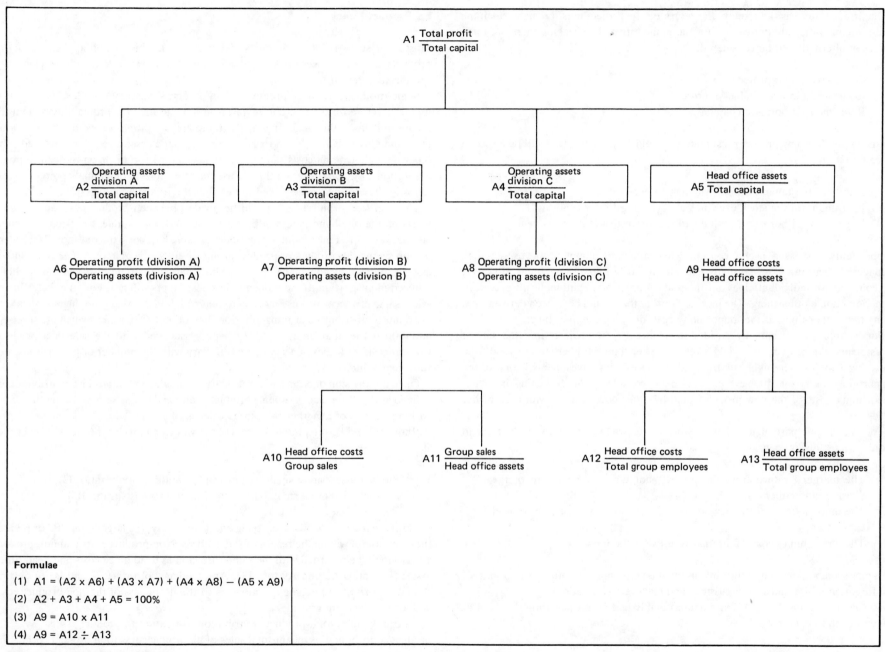

Diagram 5–1    Investment in divisions

97

If the firm already has the money, the return on the project must be higher than the return on any other alternative use for the money. Broadly speaking there are three classes of alternative to be considered:

1    Other investment projects
2    Investments in marketable securities
3    Repayment of borrowed capital

For example, if a new project is estimated to yield 10 per cent, it would take second place to:

1    Another investment proposal yielding 15 per cent
2    Investment on the stock exchange also yielding 15 per cent
3    Repayment of borrowed capital with an interest rate of 15 per cent

'Opportunity cost' is a useful concept when analysing many problems requiring managerial decision. 'Cost' normally refers to the cost of *doing* something. However, if a company (or individual) does one thing, it (or he) is often automatically precluded from doing some other thing. The income or profit that would have been derived from doing that 'other thing' is the 'opportunity cost' of doing the first thing.

For example, if a company decides to finance a new project from the sale of investments, the project must yield a return higher than the likely future yield from those investments. The likely future yield of the existing investments is one of the 'opportunity costs' of the new project to be considered in evaluating it. Other opportunity costs of the new project would be other new projects with even higher yields.

To sum up this part of the chapter: the board, when considering investment in projects, must always consider:

1    The marginal return from the project, not the average return of the division, and either
2    The marginal cost of the new money, not the average cost of borrowed capital, or
3    The 'opportunity cost' of alternative uses for the money.

This may seem a statement of the obvious but it is surprising how often these principles are forgotten in the midst of discussions and elaborate calculations.

To calculate ratios A1 to A13 use data assembly and ratio calculation sheet 5–1 at the end of this chapter.

## 5.2 Product Policy

Most firms sell a range of products and/or services. This section applies equally to products and to services, but, to avoid monotonous repetition, only products are specifically referred to.

Some products are more profitable than others; some may even lose money. It is useful therefore for the board to review from time to time the profitability of items or groups of items in the range. In doing so there are two pitfalls to avoid. One is to look at profitability only in relation to sales and ignore the asset investment involved. The other is to allocate all costs (and all assets) to specific products on the conventional absorption costing basis rather than to use the more relevant marginal approach. How to avoid these pitfalls is described in detail in the following paragraphs.

The firm's costs and assets should be divided between product costs and product assets on the one hand, and non product costs and non product assets on the other, and between different products or product groups, by asking the question: If we were to stop selling this product or product group would we be able to reduce costs and/or assets and, if so, by how much? It is probable that, while some costs and assets will be reduced in proportion to the reduction in sales, others will not. For an equal value of sales, some products may use more materials or labour, may require higher stocks, or discounts to distributors or transportation than others. One aspect which often repays attention is the number of pieces of paper associated with the sale of a product. Clerical costs and salesmen's costs tend to vary with the number of transactions, not with their value.

Once this division of costs and assets has been made, and if 'product contribution' is defined as the difference between a product's sales and its costs arrived at on the above basis, the ratios of Diagram 5–2 can be calculated.

Ratios B2 and B3 are both indicators of the value of a product profitability exercise. If

1    Product assets are a small part of total operating assets (ratio B2), or if
2    Product costs are a small part of total operating costs (ratio B3)

the exercise may not be worth carrying out. Conversely, the larger either B2 or B3 are, the more useful will be the results of the analysis. Non-product costs and non-product assets should be regarded with the same suspicion as head office costs and head office assets (see ratios A5 and A9 to A13). Any tendency of ratios B2 and B3 to decline should give rise to searching questions as to the usefulness of the non-product costs and assets which are growing.

Ratio B4 shows total product contribution in relation to product assets. By 'total product contribution' is meant total sales of all products less total product costs – the costs which are identifiable with specific product groups. Ratio B4 can be improved by:

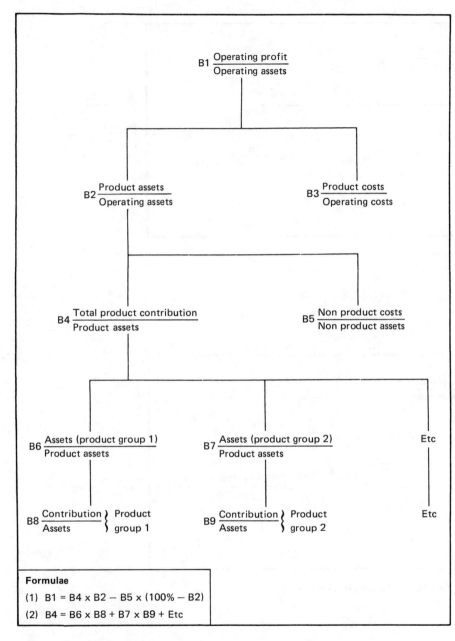

$$B1 \frac{\text{Operating profit}}{\text{Operating assets}}$$

$$B2 \frac{\text{Product assets}}{\text{Operating assets}} \qquad B3 \frac{\text{Product costs}}{\text{Operating costs}}$$

$$B4 \frac{\text{Total product contribution}}{\text{Product assets}} \qquad B5 \frac{\text{Non product costs}}{\text{Non product assets}}$$

$$B6 \frac{\text{Assets (product group 1)}}{\text{Product assets}} \qquad B7 \frac{\text{Assets (product group 2)}}{\text{Product assets}} \qquad \text{Etc}$$

$$B8 \frac{\text{Contribution}}{\text{Assets}} \Big\} \begin{array}{l}\text{Product} \\ \text{group 1}\end{array} \qquad B9 \frac{\text{Contribution}}{\text{Assets}} \Big\} \begin{array}{l}\text{Product} \\ \text{group 2}\end{array} \qquad \text{Etc}$$

**Formulae**

(1)  B1 = B4 × B2 − B5 × (100% − B2)

(2)  B4 = B6 × B8 + B7 × B9 + Etc

Diagram 5–2   Product profitability

1   Increasing the profitability of the less profitable product groups (increasing B8, B9, and so on).

2   Deploying more assets in the product groups which *are* more profitable (changing ratios B6, B7, and so on).

There are two constraints to the above process:

1   The alleged necessity of maintaining a complete range

2   The definite need to consider the likely future profitability and growth of new and less profitable ranges

To calculate ratios B1 to B9 use data assembly and ratio calculation sheet 5–2 at the end of this chapter.

**5.3 Capacity Utilisation**

The board monitors the performance of its divisions, and a smaller company measures its own performance by the ratio:

$$\frac{\text{Operating profit}}{\text{Operating assets}}$$

What ratios should be used to measure reasons for changes in this ratio?

The two main factors affecting the ratio are respectively the profit margin on sales and the rate of turnover of assets. Ratios devised by the du Pont company and by the Centre for Interfirm Comparison, measure these factors. The Centre's ratios are shown in Diagram 5–3; this analysis together with variations and developments of it has been extensively used by the Centre in recent times. Ratio C2 shows the profit margin on sales of the company. If this is too low, it indicates that there is a lack of balance between the sales of the company and the costs of achieving them. Ratio C3 shows the turnover of assets of the company. If this is too low it indicates there is a lack of balance between the size of the business and the volume of sales it is achieving.

To calculate ratios C1 to C3 use data assembly and ratio calculation sheet 5–3 at the end of this chapter.

In some companies, a better measure of the volume of its business than sales in money terms is given by some physical measure of output (such as square yards of cloth woven, pounds of bread baked, gallons of drink bottled). In these companies a variant of the basic analysis can be used (see Diagram 5–4).

To calculate ratios C1, C4 and C5 use data assembly and ratio calculation sheet 5–4 at the end of this chapter.

Another variant of the basic analysis is to use value added instead of sales. Value

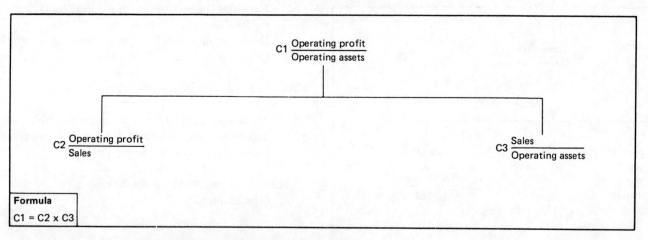

Diagram 5–3   Basic analysis of factors affecting operating profit/operating assets.
With acknowledgements to the Centre for Interfirm Comparison.

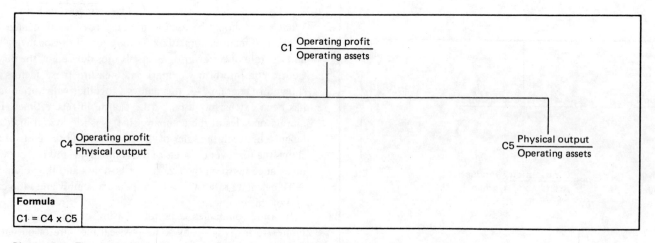

Diagram 5–4   The same analysis using the physical output variant developed at the Centre for Interfirm Comparison.

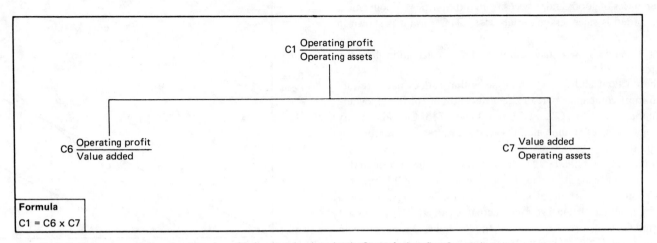

Diagram 5–5    The same analysis using the value-added variant developed at the Centre for Interfirm Comparison.

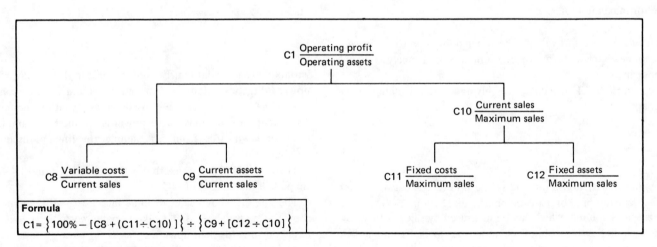

Diagram 5–6    Capacity utilisation

added is sales less all purchases of goods and services from third parties. A convenient approximation to value added is sales less materials costs. This variant is shown in Diagram 5–5.

To calculate ratios C1, C6 and C7 use data assembly and ratio calculation sheet 5–5 at the end of this chapter.

A disadvantage of the du Pont and Centre's analysis is that it does not take into account the fact that in most companies part of the costs and part of the assets are fixed. This has the result that both ratios C2 and C3 (or C4 and C5, or C6 and C7) vary as a consequence of changes in sales volume alone. This disadvantage is overcome by using the ratios in Diagram 5–6.

The denominator of ratios C10, C11 and C12 is maximum sales – the maximum that can be achieved with current capacity. The numerator of ratio C10 and the denominator of ratios C8 and C9 is current sales – the sales actually being achieved in the period currently being analysed. If sales volume fluctuates and efficiency does not change, only ratios C1 and C10 will alter – ratios C8, C9, C11 and C12 should remain unchanged. Increases in ratios C8, C9, C11 or C12 are signals of possible inefficiency, whether ratio C10 is changing or not, and pointers to the areas requiring remedial action. To be able to use these ratios a firm must be able to:

1    Divide its costs between fixed and variable
2    Divide its assets between fixed and current
3    Arrive at a figure for maximum sales.

No firm should find 2 difficult. More effort will be involved in doing 1 and 3. However, 100 per cent accuracy is not needed and the improved usefulness of the analysis should easily outweigh the labour involved.

To calculate ratios C1, and C8 to C12 use data assembly and ratio calculation sheet 5–6 at the end of this chapter.

### 5.4 Break Even Charts

The effect of differences in capacity utilisation and ot the differences between fixed and variable costs can be depicted on a break even chart (see Diagram 5–7).

The horizontal (x) axis shows volume, which can be measured by sales in £s, or by some physical measure, such as passenger miles for an airline, or bed nights for an hotel. The vertical (y) axis measures sales, costs and profit in £s.

The line AB shows fixed costs, i.e. those that do not vary with volume. What should be included in fixed costs will vary from business to business and it is to some extent a matter of judgement. In the short term more costs are fixed than in the long term. Materials costs are generally variable, but labour costs, traditionally regarded as

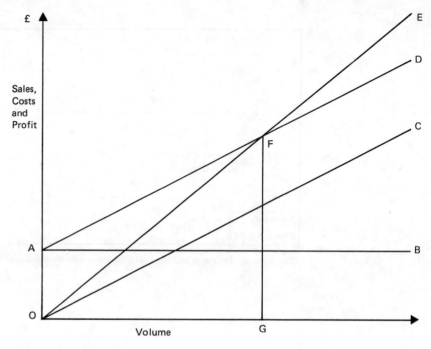

Diagram 5–7    Break even chart

variable, are nowadays fairly fixed, at least in the downward direction, but not in the upward direction. Many costs have a fixed and variable component.

The line OC shows variable costs increasing with volume. OC is shown as a straight line but in practice may curve upwards (from, for example, the effect of overtime rates) or downwards (from, for example, the effect of discounts for higher volumes of purchases).

The line AD shows costs, that is the sum of AB and OC. It must start at A and its shape will match that of OC.

The line OE shows sales revenue increasing with volume. Like variable costs it is shown as a straight line and, like variable costs, in practice it may curve, but more likely downwards than upwards.

The point (F) at which the sales line OE cuts the total cost line OD is the break even point. Below that point a loss is made; above that point a profit is made. OG is the break even volume.

A company should always know where the break even point is, and monitor actual volume against break even volume.

The nearer break even volume is to maximum capacity, the more vulnerable a company is. The wider the angle EFD the more volatile a company's profit will be to changes in sales volume. Such volatility is sometimes referred to as operational gearing in contrast to the financial gearing which results from the use of fixed interest loan capital (see Chapter 8.2).

The key information from a break even chart can be shown in a profit/volume chart (see Diagram 5–8).

OI is equal to the fixed costs (OA in Diagram 5–7). OG is the break even volume as in Diagram 5–7.

To summarise: the relevant ratios in this area are

1    *Break even position*

$$\frac{\text{Actual volume for period or year to date}}{\text{Break even volume for period or year to date}}$$

2    *Operational vulnerability*

$$\frac{\text{Break even volume}}{\text{Maximum volume}}$$

3    *Operational volatility*

$$\frac{\text{Sales} - \text{Variable costs}}{\text{Sales}}$$

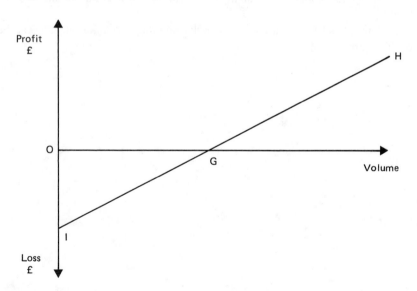

Diagram 5–8   Profit/Volume chart

## 5.5 Planning for the Future – Discretionary Cash Flow

While monitoring the present or immediate past, the board must always have an eye to the future. It is with this important aspect of a firm that the ratios in this section are concerned.

There are some items of expenditure about which management has a greater degree of choice than others. A firm must buy its raw materials and pay its work people but, within limits, it may choose how much, and when, to spend on such items as research, advertising, staff training, consultancy and the purchase of new equipment. One thing that these items have in common is that they are for the benefit of the future; they are unlikely to contribute to the sales or profits of the current period. Another thing which they have in common is that their level is likely to be influenced more by the availability of cash than by the levels of sales.

How much cash is available? What are the sources of a firm's discretionary cash flow? (This term is used because a wider field is being considered than in the traditional definition of cash flow and in order to emphasise the element of management discretion which is involved.) The sources are:

1    The firm's sales and other income less all items of cost (including taxation and interest payments) other than those which either do not involve a cash flow (such as depreciation) or management classes as discretionary. It is suggested that the following should be considered as candidates: research, advertising, staff training, consultancy, dividends on ordinary shares, directors' remuneration in owner managed companies.
2    A reduction in current assets other than cash, such as stock, debtors.
3    An increase in current liabilities.
4    New loans or other finance obtained.

The uses to which this discretionary cash flow can be put are:

1    Expenditure on revenue items for the benefit of the future (research, advertising, staff training, consultancy)
2    Expenditure on capital items for the benefit of the future (investment in buildings, equipment, and so on)
3    Build-up of stocks and debtors to increase the service to customers
4    Rewards to the risk takers and/or entrepreneurs (dividends on ordinary shares, directors' remuneration, senior staff bonuses)
5    Repayment of loans and other debts
6    Build-up of cash reserves.

The board will find it useful to express each source and each use of discretionary cash flow as a percentage of the total flow and to calculate these ratios for a number of years in order to get the trends. The questions to ask are: Has the balance between investment in the future (1, 2 and 3) and reward in the present (4) been right? Has the investment in the future paid off, and if not why not? What are the future flows likely to look like and is this what management wants?

To calculate ratios D1 to D17 use data assembly and ratio calculation sheet 5–7 at the end of this chapter.

### 5.6 Planning for the Future – Research and Development

While on the subject of payoff, it is worth considering how to decide how much to spend on research and development (R and D) and how to monitor the effectiveness of the expenditure.

R and D can be set at a certain percentage of sales and this percentage can be compared with competitors' figures, if available. This is not very satisfactory because there is no cause and effect linkage between this year's research (which it is hoped will benefit future years' sales) and this year's sales (which have benefited from the research of previous years). To allocate a certain percentage of discretionary cash inflow (item 1 only, i.e. excluding the more capital-like items 2, 3 and 4) may be more meaningful.

It is difficult to measure the effectiveness of R and D. However, two ratios are suggested:

E1  *Rate of new product innovation*

$$\frac{\text{Sales of products introduced in the past five (?) years}}{\text{Total sales}}$$

E2  *Profitability of new products*

$$\frac{\text{Profit (or contribution) from products introduced in the past five (?) years}}{\text{Total profit (or contribution)}}$$

Ratio E1 should be compared with a similar ratio for competitors if this can be obtained, deduced or guessed. Too great a divergence in either direction may be cause for concern. Although no firm wants to have a range of products which is tending to economic obsolescence, money can be equally lost by a too rapid introduction of too many new products in relation to the market's capacity to absorb them.

Ratio E2 should be compared with the profitability of the rest of the range. It is not enough to introduce new products; they must, in the early stages of their career, make more profit than the less troublesome bread and butter lines which are feeling the

effects of competitive pressure and may be on the way out. The profit/time profile of a product is well known to be of the shape shown in Diagram 5–9.

To calculate ratios E1 and E2 use data assembly and ratio calculation sheet 5–8 at the end of this chapter.

### 5.7 Growth and Stability

As well as making profit, firms want to grow. It is growth of profits that enables a firm to pay higher dividends to the ordinary shareholder. It is expectation of the growth of dividends that increases a share's price and gives its holder his capital gains. Growth is best measured by index numbers – in the case of sales by dividing each year's sales by the value of sales at some chosen base year (see ratio F2 in Diagram 5–10).

It is desirable that profit should grow faster than sales and sales faster than assets (ratios F1, F2 and F3).

Part of a firm's apparent growth is the result of inflation. The effects of inflation can be removed by applying suitable price indices derived from government statistics to the crude indices (ratios F4, F5 and F6).

As well as having its sales grow, a firm will want to increase its share of the market. This should, therefore, also be measured (ratio F7).

Most people prefer a reasonably stable rate of growth to one that fluctuates violently. Techniques to measure stability of growth are however outside the scope of this book.

To calculate ratios F1 to F7 use data assembly and ratio calculation sheet 5–9 at the end of this chapter.

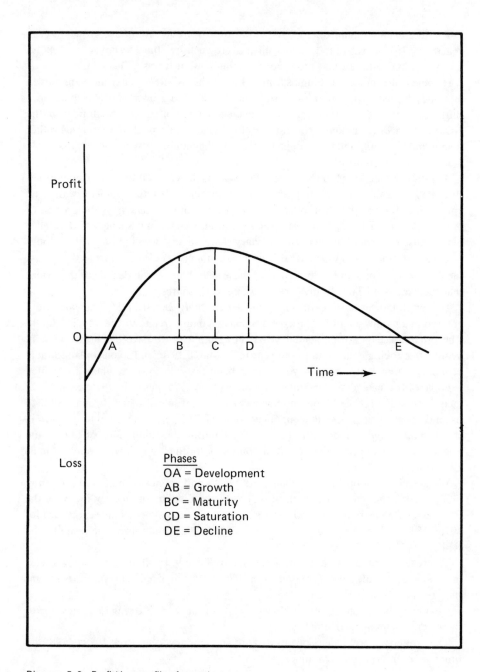

Profit

O

Loss

A    B    C    D    E

Time ⟶

Phases
OA = Development
AB = Growth
BC = Maturity
CD = Saturation
DE = Decline

Diagram 5–9   Profit/time profile of a product

**Crude Growth Indices**       **Adjusted Growth Indices**

F1 $\dfrac{\text{Profit this year}}{\text{Profit in base year}}$    $\text{F4} = \text{F1} \div \dfrac{\text{Suitable price index now}}{\text{Suitable price index in base year}}$

F2 $\dfrac{\text{Sales this year}}{\text{Sales in base year}}$    $\text{F5} = \text{F2} \div \dfrac{\text{Suitable price index now}}{\text{Suitable price index in base year}}$

F3 $\dfrac{\text{Assets this year}}{\text{Assets in base year}}$    $\text{F6} = \text{F3} \div \dfrac{\text{Suitable price index now}}{\text{Suitable price index in base year}}$

**Share of the Market**

F7 $\dfrac{\text{Our sales this year}}{\text{Our and our competitor's sales this year}}$

Diagram 5–10   Growth ratios

## Appendix 5.1

## WORKED EXAMPLE OF CALCULATION OF GROWTH INDICES

The following is a worked example of the calculation of index numbers to measure growth, both in money terms and in real terms.

It is desired to measure the growth of Marks and Spencer's turnover and profit for the last ten years (see Table 5–1).

Columns 2 and 3 were completed from Marks and Spencer's Extel card.

From the data in columns 2 and 3 it is possible to see that turnover and profit are growing. It is difficult however to form a clear impression of the rate of growth of each item, how this is changing over time, and how each item is growing in relation to the other items. Converting the absolute money figures into the type of ratio called an index number will make all of these points clearer.

The conversion is very simple. The figures for each year are divided by the figure for that item for the base year (the first year in the table – the year to 31 March 1976). For example, the 1977 index number for the growth of sales of 118.2 was arrived at by dividing sales for the year to 31 March 1977 (£1,064,837,000) by the sales for the year to 31 March 1976 (£900,923,000). In a similar manner all the figures in columns 6 and 7 were arrived at.

| Year to 31 March | Turnover £000 | Net profit after tax £000 | Index of retail prices Year | Index | Growth indices Money Turnover | Profit | Real Turnover | Profit |
|---|---|---|---|---|---|---|---|---|
| 1 | 2 | 3 | 4 | 5 | 6 | 7 | 8 | 9 |
| 1976 | 900,923 | 37,148 | 1975 | 134.8 | 100.0 | 100.0 | 100.0 | 100.0 |
| 1977 | 1,064,837 | 52,080 | 1976 | 157.1 | 118.2 | 140.2 | 101.4 | 120.3 |
| 1978 | 1,254,055 | 67,131 | 1977 | 182.0 | 139.2 | 180.7 | 103.1 | 133.8 |
| 1979 | 1,472,954 | 88,395 | 1978 | 197.1 | 163.5 | 238.0 | 111.8 | 162.8 |
| 1980 | 1,667,905 | 91,929 | 1979 | 223.5 | 185.1 | 247.5 | 111.6 | 149.3 |
| 1981 | 1,872,900 | 97,100 | 1980 | 263.7 | 207.9 | 261.4 | 106.3 | 133.6 |
| 1982 | 2,198,700 | 120,600 | 1981 | 295.0 | 244.1 | 324.6 | 111.5 | 148.3 |
| 1983 | 2,505,500 | 134,900 | 1982 | 320.4 | 278.1 | 363.1 | 117.0 | 152.8 |
| 1984 | 2,854,500 | 176,700 | 1983 | 335.1 | 316.8 | 475.7 | 127.4 | 191.4 |
| 1985 | 3,213,000 | 183,800 | 1984 | 351.8 | 356.6 | 494.8 | 136.6 | 189.6 |

Sources : Columns 1 to 3 Extel Analyst's Service Card
: Columns 4 and 5 *Monthly Digest of Statistics,* July 1985, HMSO, Table 18.1
Formulae: 6 = 2 ÷ (2 for 1976) × 100
7 = 3 ÷ (3 for 1976) × 100
8 = 6 ÷ 5 for year × 5 for 1975
9 = 7 ÷ 5 for year × 5 for 1975

Table 5–1   Calculation of index numbers to measure growth

The figures in columns 6 and 7 show that turnover and profit have grown in each year from 1977 to 1985 and that profit has grown faster than turnover. In 1984/85 turnover was 3½ times, and profit nearly 5 times, what it was in 1975/76.

However, the indices in columns 6 and 7 have a disadvantage. They measure growth in money terms; part of that growth will have been real growth (for example, more shirts will have been sold) and part will have been apparent growth resulting from the growth of prices (inflation). It is more useful to measure growth in real terms rather than in money terms and this is done by dividing the money growth index by a suitable index of price increases.

A suitable index for Marks and Spencer's sales is the General Index of Retail Prices (the RPI) because Marks and Spencer's is a retailer. Other indices would be appropriate for companies in other trades. An appropriate index for the growth of profits is also the RPI. This index is used *not* because Marks and Spencer's is a retailer but because the cost of living of the ordinary shareholders to whom the profit belongs is more easily measured by the RPI. If profits do not grow at least as fast as this index, the real income (or standard of living) of these shareholders will decline to the extent that their income comes from Marks and Spencer's shares.

The price indices were extracted from the *Monthly Digest of Statistics* and were entered in columns 4 and 5. Marks and Spencer's figures relate to years to 31 March. The price indices are for calendar years. For simplicity we have taken the calendar year 1975 as being equivalent to the year to 31 March 1976, and so on for subsequent years. For greater accuracy it would have been possible to have taken a weighted average of two calendar years' index numbers (¾ of 1975 plus ¼ of 1976) to arrive at an index number for the Marks and Spencer's year. It would also have been possible to use indices of the appropriate components of the RPI (e.g. clothing and food) (also in the *Monthly Digest*) and apply them to the appropriate subdivisions of Marks and Spencer's turnover (obtained from its accounts, or for the last four years only, from its Extel card).

We are now in a position to change the Marks and Spencer's indices of growth in money terms to indices of growth in real terms by dividing the money index by the price index for the same year (for example, by dividing the money index for sales for 1976/77 of 118.2 by the price index for 1976 of 157.1) and multiplying the result by the RPI for 1975 (134.8).

The real growth indices are shown in columns 8 and 9. It will be seen that whereas, in money terms, sales had increased from 1976 to 1985 to 356.6 per cent, in real terms the growth was *only* 136.6 per cent.

Column 9 shows that in 1980 and 1981, while profits were growing in money terms, they were declining in real terms.

The ordinary shareholder's profits had grown in money terms from 1976 to 1985 4.9 times, in real terms *only* 1.9 times.

The word *only* has been emphasised in the above sentences because these growth rates are obviously very satisfactory; the point being made is the difference between growth in money terms and in real terms.

Data assembly sheet 5–1
**Investment in divisions**

| Code letter | Item | Month or quarter to (date) | | | | | |
|---|---|---|---|---|---|---|---|
| | | | | | | | |
| A | Operating profit (division A) | | | | | | |
| B | Operating profit (division B) | | | | | | |
| C | Operating profit (division C) | | | | | | |
| D | (A + B + C) | | | | | | |
| E | Head office costs | | | | | | |
| F | Total profit (D − E) | | | | | | |
| G | Average operating assets (division A) | | | | | | |
| H | Average operating assets (division B) | | | | | | |
| K | Average operating assets (division C) | | | | | | |
| L | Average head office assets | | | | | | |
| M | Average total capital (G + H + K + L) | | | | | | |
| N | Group sales | | | | | | |
| P | Average total group employees | | | | | | |
| Q | No of working days in period | | | | | | |
| R | No of working days in year | | | | | | |

| Ratio | Formula for calculation of ratio | Unit of measurement | Month or quarter to (date) | | | | | |
|---|---|---|---|---|---|---|---|---|
| A1 Total profit/ Total capital | $(F \times 100 \div M) \times (R \div Q)$ | % pa | | | | | | |
| A2 Operating assets division A/ Total capital | $G \times 100 \div M$ | % | | | | | | |
| A3 Operating assets division B/ Total capital | $H \times 100 \div M$ | % | | | | | | |
| A4 Operating assets division C/ Total capital | $K \times 100 \div M$ | % | | | | | | |
| A5 Head office assets/ Total capital | $L \times 100 \div M$ | % | | | | | | |
| A6 Operating profit (division A)/ Operating assets (division A) | $(A \times 100 \div G) \times (R \div Q)$ | % pa | | | | | | |
| A7 Operating profit (division B)/ Operating assets (division B) | $(B \times 100 \div H) \times (R \div Q)$ | % pa | | | | | | |
| A8 Operating profit (division C)/ Operating assets (division C) | $(C \times 100 \div K) \times (R \div Q)$ | % pa | | | | | | |
| A9 Head office costs/ Head office assets | $(E \times 100 \div L) \times (R \div Q)$ | % pa | | | | | | |
| A10 Head office costs/ Group sales | $E \times 100 \div N$ | % | | | | | | |
| A11 Group sales/ Head office assets | $(N \div L) \times (R \div Q)$ | times per year | | | | | | |
| A12 Head office costs/ Total group employees | $(E \div P) \times (R \div Q)$ | £'s pa per head | | | | | | |
| A13 Head office assets/ Total group employees | $L \div P$ | £'s per head | | | | | | |

Data assembly sheet 5–2
## Product profitability

| Code letter | Item | Month or quarter to (date) | | | | | |
|---|---|---|---|---|---|---|---|
| A | Sales (product group 1) | | | | | | |
| B | Costs (product group 1) | | | | | | |
| C | Contribution (product group 1) (A − B) | | | | | | |
| D | Sales (product group 2) | | | | | | |
| E | Costs (product group 2) | | | | | | |
| F | Contribution (product group 2) (D − E) | | | | | | |
| G | Total product costs (B + E) | | | | | | |
| H | Total product contribution (C + F) | | | | | | |
| K | Non product costs | | | | | | |
| L | Operating profit (H − K) | | | | | | |
| M | Average assets (product group 1) | | | | | | |
| N | Average assets (product group 2) | | | | | | |
| P | Average product assets (M + N) | | | | | | |
| | Average non product assets | | | | | | |
| R | Average operating assets (P + Q) | | | | | | |
| S | No of working days in period | | | | | | |
| T | No of working days in year | | | | | | |

## Product profitability

| Ratio | | Formula for calculation of ratio | Unit of measurement | Month or quarter to (date) | | | | | |
|---|---|---|---|---|---|---|---|---|---|
| B1 | Operating profit/ Operating assets | $(L \times 100 \div R) \times (T \div S)$ | % pa | | | | | | |
| B2 | Product assets/ Operating assets | $P \times 100 \div R$ | % | | | | | | |
| B3 | Product costs/ Operating costs | $G \times 100 \div (G + K)$ | % | | | | | | |
| B4 | Total product contribution/ Product assets | $(H \times 100 \div P) \times (T \div S)$ | % pa | | | | | | |
| B5 | Non product costs/ Non product assets | $(K \times 100 \div Q) \times (T \div S)$ | % pa | | | | | | |
| B6 | Assets (product group 1)/ Product assets | $M \times 100 \div P$ | % | | | | | | |
| B7 | Assets (product group 2)/ Product assets | $N \times 100 \div P$ | % | | | | | | |
| B8 | Contribution (product group 1)/ Assets (product group 1) | $(C \times 100 \div M) \times (T \div S)$ | % pa | | | | | | |
| B9 | Contribution (product group 2)/ Assets (product group 2) | $(F \times 100 \div N) \times (T \div S)$ | % pa | | | | | | |

Data assembly sheet 5–3
**Basic analysis**

| Code letter | Item | Month or quarter to (date) | | | | | |
|---|---|---|---|---|---|---|---|
| A | Operating profit | | | | | | |
| B | Average operating assets | | | | | | |
| C | Sales | | | | | | |
| D | No of working days in period | | | | | | |
| E | No of working days in year | | | | | | |

| Ratio | Formula for calculation of ratio | Unit of measurement | Month or quarter to (date) | | | | | |
|---|---|---|---|---|---|---|---|---|
| C1 Operating profit/ Operating assets | $(A \times 100 \div B) \times (E \div D)$ | % pa | | | | | | |
| C2 Operating profit/ Sales | $A \times 100 \div C$ | % | | | | | | |
| C3 Sales/Operating assets | $(C \div B) \times (E \div D)$ | Times per Year | | | | | | |

Data assembly sheet 5–4
**Basic analysis in physical terms**

| Code letter | Item | Month or quarter to (date) | | | | | |
|---|---|---|---|---|---|---|---|
| A | Operating profit | | | | | | |
| B | Average operating assets | | | | | | |
| C | Physical output | | | | | | |
| D | No of working days in period | | | | | | |
| E | No of working days in year | | | | | | |

## Basic analysis in physical terms

| | Formula for calculation of ratio | Unit of measurement | Month or quarter to (date) | | | | | |
|---|---|---|---|---|---|---|---|---|
| C1 Operating profit/ Operating assets | $(A \times 100 \div B) \times (E \div D)$ | % pa | | | | | | |
| C4 Operating profit/ Physical output | $A \div C$ | £s per unit | | | | | | |
| C5 Physical output/ Operating assets | $(C \div B) \times (E \div D)$ | Units per year per £ | | | | | | |

## Basic analysis using value added

| Code letter | Item | Month or quarter to (date) | | | | | |
|---|---|---|---|---|---|---|---|
| A | Sales | | | | | | |
| B | Materials cost * | | | | | | |
| C | Value added (A – B) | | | | | | |
| D | Costs other than materials | | | | | | |
| E | Operating profit (C – D) | | | | | | |
| F | Average operating assets | | | | | | |
| G | No of working days in period | | | | | | |
| H | No of working days in year | | | | | | |

\* If stock changes are significant this should be materials cost content of sales ie purchases adjusted for changes in raw materials stock and in the materials content of work in progress and finished goods stock.

## Basic analysis using value added

| Ratio | Formula for calculation of ratio | Unit of measurement | Month or quarter to (date) | | | | | |
|---|---|---|---|---|---|---|---|---|
| C1 Operating profit/ Operating assets | $(E \times 100 \div F) \times (H \div G)$ | % pa | | | | | | |
| C6 Operating profit/ Value added | $E \times 100 \div C$ | % | | | | | | |
| C7 Value added/ Operating assets | $(C \div F) \times (H \div G)$ | times per year | | | | | | |

**Capacity utilisation**

| Code letter | Item | Month or quarter to (date) | | | | | |
|---|---|---|---|---|---|---|---|
| | | | | | | | |
| A | Maximum sales for period | | | | | | |
| B | Current sales | | | | | | |
| C | Variable costs | | | | | | |
| D | Fixed costs | | | | | | |
| E | Total costs (C + D) | | | | | | |
| F | Operating profit (B − E) | | | | | | |
| G | Average current assets | | | | | | |
| H | Average fixed assets | | | | | | |
| K | Average operating assets (G + H) | | | | | | |
| L | No of working days in period | | | | | | |
| M | No of working days in year | | | | | | |

**Capacity utilisation**

| Ratio | | Formula for calculation of ratio | Unit of measurement | Month or quarter to (date) | | | | | |
|---|---|---|---|---|---|---|---|---|---|
| C1 | Operating profit/ Operating assets | $(F \times 100 \div K) \times (M \div L)$ | % pa | | | | | | |
| C8 | Variable costs/ Current sales | $C \times 100 \div B$ | % | | | | | | |
| C9 | Current assets/ Current sales | $G \times 1000 \div (B \times M \div L)$ | ‰ pa | | | | | | |
| C10 | Current sales/ Maximum sales | $B \times 100 \div A$ | % | | | | | | |
| C11 | Fixed costs/ Maximum sales | $D \times 100 \div A$ | % | | | | | | |
| C12 | Fixed assets/ Maximum sales | $H \times 1000 \div (A \times M \div L)$ | ‰ pa | | | | | | |

**Discretionary cash flow**

| Code letter | Item | Month or quarter to (date) | | | | | |
|---|---|---|---|---|---|---|---|
| | *Sources of discretionary cash flow* | | | | | | |
| A | Profit after tax and minorities | | | | | | |
| B | Add back depreciation | | | | | | |
| C | Sub total (A + B) | | | | | | |
| D | Research | | | | | | |
| E | Advertising | | | | | | |
| F | Staff training | | | | | | |
| G | Consultancy | | | | | | |
| H | Dividend on ordinary shares | | | | | | |
| I | Directors' remuneration | | | | | | |
| J | Other 'discretionary payments' | | | | | | |
| K | Profit before depreciation and discretionary payments (the sum of items C to J) | | | | | | |
| L | Reduction in stock | | | | | | |
| M | Reduction in debtors | | | | | | |
| N | Increase in current liabilities | | | | | | |
| P | New loans obtained | | | | | | |
| Q | Total discretionary cash flow (the sum of items K to P) | | | | | | |

| Code letter | Item | Month or quarter to (date) | | | | | |
|---|---|---|---|---|---|---|---|
| | | | | | | | |
| | *Uses of discretionary cash flow* | | | | | | |
| R | Research | | | | | | |
| S | Advertising | | | | | | |
| T | Staff training | | | | | | |
| U | Consultancy | | | | | | |
| V | Dividend on ordinary shares | | | | | | |
| W | Directors' remuneration | | | | | | |
| Y | Other discretionary payments' | | | | | | |
| Z | Increase in stocks | | | | | | |
| AA | Increase in debtors | | | | | | |
| AB | Senior staff bonuses | | | | | | |
| AC | Repayment of loans | | | | | | |
| AD | Increase in cash reserves | | | | | | |
| AE | Total discretionary cash flow (the sum of items R to AE) | | | | | | |
| | | | | | | | |

NB   Item Q should equal item AE

**Discretionary cash flow**

| Ratio | Formula for calculation of ratio | Unit of measurement | Month or quarter to (date) | | | | | |
|---|---|---|---|---|---|---|---|---|
| *Sources of discretionary cash flow* | | | | | | | | |
| D1 Profit before depreciation and discretionary payments/Total discretionary cash flow | K x 100 ÷ AE | % | | | | | | |
| D2 Reduction in stock/Total discretionary cash flow | L x 100 ÷ AE | % | | | | | | |
| D3 Reduction in debtors/Total discretionary cash flow | M x 100 ÷ AE | % | | | | | | |
| D4 Increase in current liabilities/Total discretionary cash flow | N x 100 ÷ AE | % | | | | | | |
| D5 New loans obtained/Total discretionary cash flow | P x 100 ÷ AE | % | | | | | | |
| *Use of discretionary cash flow* | | | | | | | | |
| D6 Research/Total discretionary cash flow | R x 100 ÷ AE | % | | | | | | |
| D7 Advertising/Total discretionary cash flow | S x 100 ÷ AE | % | | | | | | |
| D8 Staff training/Total discretionary cash flow | T x 100 ÷ AE | % | | | | | | |

| Ratio | | Formula for calculation of ratio | Unit of measurement | Month or quarter to (date) | | | | | |
|---|---|---|---|---|---|---|---|---|---|
| D9 | Consultancy/Total discretionary cash flow | U x 100 ÷ AE | % | | | | | | |
| D10 | Dividend on ordinary shares/Total discretionary cash flow | V x 100 ÷ AE | % | | | | | | |
| D11 | Directors' remuneration/Total discretionary cash flow | W x 100 ÷ AE | % | | | | | | |
| D12 | Other 'discretionary payments'/Total discretionary cash flow | Y x 100 ÷ AE | % | | | | | | |
| D13 | Increase in stocks/ Total discretionary cash flow | Z x 100 ÷ AE | % | | | | | | |
| D14 | Increase in debtors/Total discretionary cash flow | AA x 100 ÷ AE | % | | | | | | |
| D15 | Senior staff bonuses/Total discretionary cash flow | AB x 100 ÷ AE | % | | | | | | |
| D16 | Repayment of loans/Total discretionary cash flow | AC x 100 ÷ AE | % | | | | | | |
| D17 | Increase in cash reserves/Total discretionary cash flow | AD x 100 ÷ AE | % | | | | | | |

Data assembly sheet 5–8
**Research and development**

| Code letter | Item | Month or quarter to (date) | | | | | |
|---|---|---|---|---|---|---|---|
| A | Sales of products introduced in the last 5 years | | | | | | |
| B | Total sales | | | | | | |
| C | Profit (or contribution) from products introduced in the last 5 years | | | | | | |
| D | Total profit (or contribution ) | | | | | | |

# Research and development

| Ratio | Formula for calculation of ratio | Unit of measurement | Month or quarter to (date) | | | | | |
|---|---|---|---|---|---|---|---|---|
| E1 Rate of new product innovation. Sales of products introduced in the last 5 years/ Total sales | A x 100 ÷ B | % | | | | | | |
| E2 Profitability of new products. Profit (or contribution) from products introduced in the last 5 years/ Total profit for contribution | C x 100 ÷ D | % | | | | | | |

Data assembly sheet 5–9
**Growth ratios**

| Code letter | Item | Month or quarter to (date) | | | | | |
|---|---|---|---|---|---|---|---|
| | *Base year figures* | | | | | | |
| A | Profit | | | | | | |
| B | Sales | | | | | | |
| C | Assets | | | | | | |
| D | Price index for profits | | | | | | |
| E | Price index for sales | | | | | | |
| F | Price index for assets | | | | | | |
| | *This period figures* | | | | | | |
| G | Profit | | | | | | |
| H | Sales | | | | | | |
| K | Assets | | | | | | |
| L | Price index for profits | | | | | | |
| M | Price index for sales | | | | | | |
| N | Price index for assets | | | | | | |
| P | Our competitors' sales (estimated) | | | | | | |

# Growth ratios

| Ratio | Formula for calculation of ratio | Unit of Measurement | Month or quarter to (date) | | | | | |
|---|---|---|---|---|---|---|---|---|
| *Crude growth indices* | | | | | | | | |
| F1 Profit this year/ Profit in base year | G x 100 ÷ A | % | | | | | | |
| F2 Sales this year/ Sales in base year | H x 100 ÷ B | % | | | | | | |
| F3 Assets this year/ Assets in base year | K x 100 ÷ C | % | | | | | | |
| *Adjusted growth indices* | | | | | | | | |
| F4 Growth of profit in real terms | Ratio F1 x D ÷ L | % | | | | | | |
| F5 Growth of sales in real terms | Ratio F2 x E ÷ M | % | | | | | | |
| F6 Growth of assets in real terms | Ratio F3 x F ÷ N | % | | | | | | |
| *Share of the market* | | | | | | | | |
| F7 Our sales this period/ Our and our competitors' sales this period | H x 100 ÷ (H + P) | % | | | | | | |

# Chapter 6

# Ratios for marketing management

## 6.1 Marketing Ratios in a Manufacturing Business

In Chapter 1 it was stated that it is desirable to provide each manager with a single key ratio which measures the degree of his success. Such a ratio relates the results achieved by the marketing management to the resources available.

The result that marketing management is trying to achieve is an optimum balance between:

1   Maximisation of profitable sales
2   Minimisation of marketing costs
3   Minimisation of assets used.

A ratio that measures the combined result of achieving a balance between all three of the above objectives is

$$\frac{\text{Marketing contribution}}{\text{Marketing assets}}$$

Marketing contribution is defined as sales less marketing costs less variable manufacturing costs. The reason for subtracting marketing costs is obvious; less so that for deducting variable manufacturing costs. It is as follows: no firm wants just to maximise sales; it also wants to sell proportionally more of the more profitable items and proportionally less of the less profitable ones. A useful measure of profit in this case is sales less variable manufacturing costs, that is, those costs which would not have been incurred if the product had not been made and sold.

Marketing costs will include warehousing, distribution, advertising, promotion, selling, sales office and market research costs, plus discounts given and bad debts. It is obviously up to each firm to decide which member of management should be responsible for which item of expenditure so some firms may wish to add to or subtract from this list. A few comments on some of them may be helpful.

Discounts given may be fairly obvious – there is a limit to the price reduction it is worth giving to achieve a sale – but it is surprising how many firms do not record discounts given but only net sales.

Bad debts are often on the budget of financial management because it is responsible for collecting the money from customers. In this book both marketing and financial management have bad debts as part of their responsibility because this seems better to reflect the reality of the situation. Salesmen must take some of the responsibility for selling to a customer who does not pay. The accounts department must also be alert to get money in quickly, particularly if there is a risk that a customer might go bankrupt.

Sales office cost covers all the clerical costs involved in a sale: invoices, advice and delivery notes, statements, receipts, entries in the sales ledger, sales analysis and statistics, and so on. These costs are obviously caused by the activities of marketing although some of the people may well be supervised by other managers in the organisation. Including these costs may help to emphasise the relative profitability of small and large orders.

Marketing assets will include:

1   Finished goods stock (likely to be a joint responsibility with production management)
2   Debtors (likely to be a joint responsibility with finance management)
3   Selling and distribution vehicles.

The main subsidiary ratios that marketing management should have are shown in Diagram 6–1. To improve his key ratio (G1) the marketing manager can take action in three broad fields. He can:

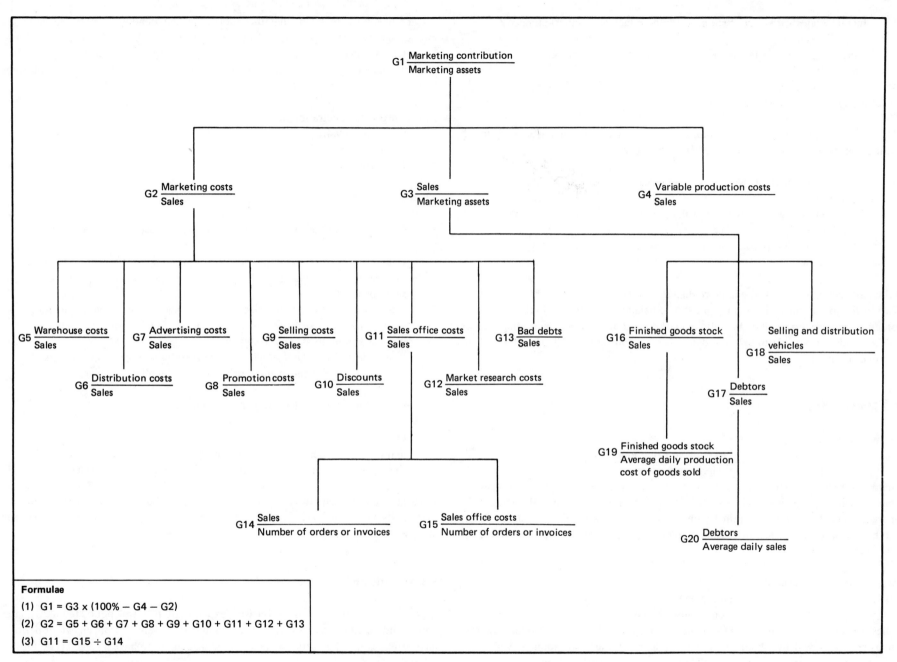

Diagram 6–1   Ratios for marketing management

1    Increase sales with a less than proportionate increase in marketing costs (ratio G2 will fall)

2    Increase sales with a less than proportionate increase in marketing assets (ratio G3 will rise)

3    Increase the proportion of sales which are of items with a higher profit margin (ratio G4 will fall).

The above tends to assume an expanding economy. If marketing management is faced with a contracting economy, the necessary action becomes:

4    To cut marketing costs with a less than proportionate drop in sales (ratio G2 will fall)

5    To cut marketing assets with a less than proportionate drop in sales (ratio G3 will rise)

6    To reduce the proportion of sales which are of items with a low profit margin (ratio G4 will fall)

Obviously action may be taken in more than one of the fields 1 to 3 or 4 to 6 at a time. Part of the job of marketing management is to balance the activities in these fields in order to optimise the result on the ratio of marketing contribution to marketing assets.

To calculate ratios G1 to G20 use data assembly and ratio calculation sheet 6–1 at the end of this chapter.

## 6.2 Market share

As well as monitoring the ratio of

$$\frac{\text{Marketing contribution}}{\text{Marketing assets}}$$

many marketing managers will also be concerned with the size of the company's market share, though it must be stressed that an increase in the size of the company's market share should not be a primary objective. The primary objective should be an increase in profitable sales; increasing market share may, or may not, contribute to that primary aim.

Market share is measured by

$$\frac{\text{Your company's sales}}{\text{Your industry's sales}}$$

Sales are usually measured in £s but may be in physical units. The figure for the industry's sales will be obtained from the relevant trade association, government statistics, an organisation like Nielsen's, or market research (see Chapter 2).

Care needs to be taken that the numerator and denominator of this ratio are measured for the same period, in the same units, and for reasonably similar products.

Kotler (*Marketing management: analysis, planning, and control,* Prentice Hall) suggests that changes or differences in market share can be analysed into the following factors:

1    Customer penetration
2    Customer loyalty
3    Customer selectivity
4    Price selectivity

where:

1    Customer penetration is the percentage of all customers who buy from your company;
2    Customer loyalty is the purchases from your company by your customers expressed as a percentage of their total purchases from all suppliers of the same products;
3    Customer selectivity is the size of the average customer purchase from your company expressed as a percentage of the average customer purchase from an average company;
4    Price selectivity is the average price charged by your company expressed as a percentage of the average price charged by all companies.

The relationship between these ratios is as follows:

| Overall market share | = | Customer penetration | × | Customer loyalty | × | Customer selectivity | × | Price selectivity |
|---|---|---|---|---|---|---|---|---|

Accurate data for such ratios may be difficult to obtain but the analytic concept may be useful. Market share may be analysed by product, type of customer, geographical area, etc.

## 6.3 Advertising

As the benefit of this period's advertising expenditure may well not be felt until a later period and as, conversely, this period's sales may be benefiting from an earlier period's advertising, it may be useful to marketing management to have a lagged ratio for this expenditure, as:

$$\frac{\text{Advertising for a previous period}}{\text{Sales for this period}}$$

It may be possible to estimate the length of the lag from past experience by graphing advertising expenditure and sales over time and measuring the time distance between successive peaks on the two lines (see Diagram 6–2).

It is very difficult to measure the effectiveness of advertising. However the following ratios are useful.

1 Cost of advertising per thousand readers or viewers (TV) analysed, if possible, into those readers/viewers most likely to purchase your product or service.
2 Percentage of readers/viewers who saw, remembered, reacted favourably to advertisement.
3 Number of enquiries from advertisement.
4 Numbers of purchases from advertisement.
5 Value of purchases from advertisement.
6 Cost per enquiry from advertisement.
7 Cost per purchase from advertisement.

It may also be worth conducting attitude surveys before, during and after an advertising campaign.

## 6.4 Sales Promotions

Sales promotions is not a term with a precise meaning but it includes such aids to marketing as:

1 Consumer promotions (e.g. coupons, 'x pence off', competitions, demonstrations, etc.).
2 Trade promotions (e.g. special discounts, sales contests, etc.).
3 Sales force promotions (e.g. special bonuses, competitions, etc.).

Measuring the effectiveness of such promotions is basically a matter of looking at the profit from any extra sales (not just the sales revenue itself) in relation to the cost of the promotion. Questions are bound to be asked however as to whether the extra sales are the result of the promotion or would have occurred anyway. Moreover care needs to be taken that the extra sales in the promotion period are not at the expense of lower sales in the post-promotion period.

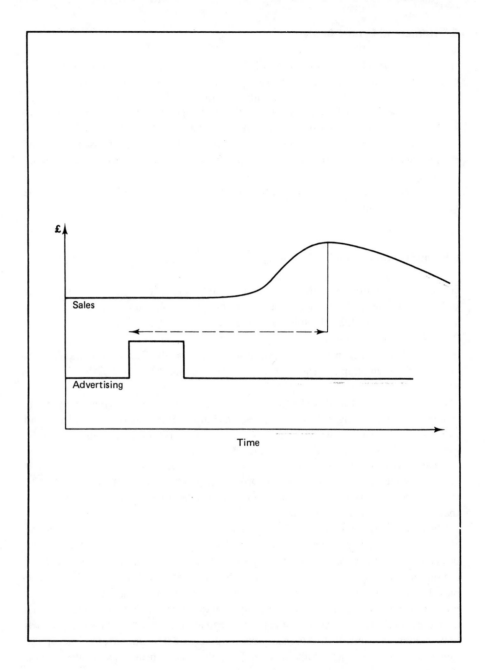

Diagram 6–2   Advertising and sales over time

## 6.5 Home and Export Analyses

If a firm does much export business and if, as is usual, its home and export selling and distribution costs are different, marketing management will probably want to have ratios H1 to H5 (Diagram 6–3), in addition to those in Diagram 6–1.

Using these ratios will quickly show whether a change in the ratios of selling costs to sales and/or distribution costs to sales is due to a change in the proportion of home to export business (ratio H1) or to a change in the costs of selling or distributing one pound's worth of home or export sales (ratios H2 to H5) and thus indicate more precisely where action is called for.

To calculate ratios H1 to H5 use data assembly and ratio calculation sheet 6–2 at the end of this chapter.

## 6.6 Three Dimensions in Marketing

It is sometimes useful for marketing management to regard its responsibilities as being in three dimensions. These are illustrated in Diagram 6–4. They are:

1    Activities, such as distributing, advertising
2    Products or product groups
3    Markets, either in the geographical sense (such as the European market) or the demographic sense (such as the teenage market).

The ratios described in this chapter so far are all activity ratios. They analyse one dimension of marketing management's responsibilities. But management will also find it useful to analyse its own key ratio of marketing contribution/marketing assets by products or by markets. The start of a product analysis is shown in Diagram 6–5.

Unallocated marketing costs and assets are those costs and assets which are not sufficiently identified with a particular product group to warrant attributing them to that group. A market analysis would be very similar to a product analysis and is therefore not separately illustrated here.

Marketing management must decide for itself how far to pursue its analysis along each of the three dimensions. Moreover, with changes in the company's fortunes, in the economic climate and so on, management may well, and indeed should, change the pattern of analysis it receives. In a small business, ratios G1 to G4 in Diagram 6–1 may be adequate for control by marketing management; a medium-sized firm's marketing management may wish to add some or all of ratios G5 to G20; a large firm's marketing management will almost certainly need all of these ratios, plus those shown in Diagrams 6–7 and 6–8. All this is giving greater detail but in only one of the dimensions in which marketing functions. Even the smaller firm will soon want to add the other two dimensions of its marketing operations.

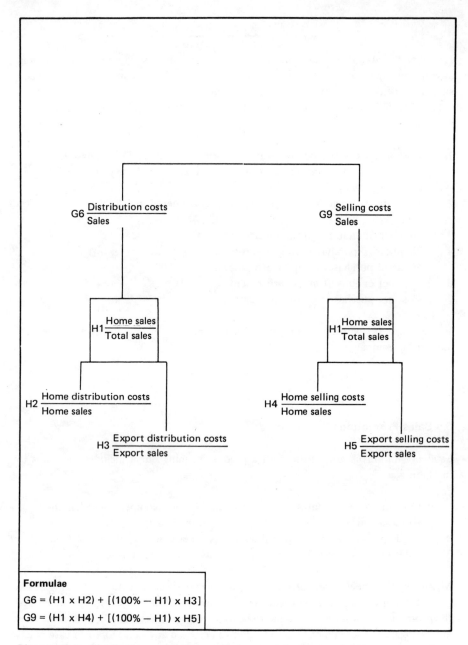

Diagram 6–3   Distribution and selling costs: home and export analyses.
Based on the scheme developed by the Centre for Interfirm Comparison.

132

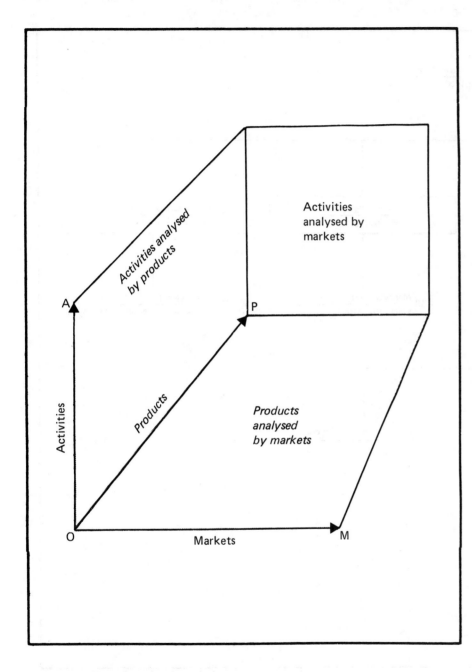

Diagram 6–4  Three dimensions in marketing

Wherever possible it is desirable that the majority of the marketing ratios of Diagrams 6–1, 6–3, 6–7 and 6–8 should be subdivided by product group and/or market. It is probably preferable to do this at the expense, if necessary, of cutting down on the number of activity ratios provided.

To calculate ratios I1 to I12 use data assembly and ratio calculation sheet 6–3 at the end of this chapter.

### 6.7 Marketing in a Business with Long-Term Contracts

The ratios in Diagram 6–1 are suitable for most manufacturing firms. If the firm manufactures on contract, however, particularly if the contracts tend to be long term, a different set of ratios is needed. In this situation marketing effort is related to obtaining orders which may not be delivered and invoiced, and hence appear in the firm's sales figure, for some months or years.

The key ratio remains the same but marketing contribution is defined as the value of orders obtained less marketing costs, less estimated variable contract costs. The set of ratios for this situation is shown in Diagram 6–6. Marketing management can improve its key ratio by:

1  Obtaining more profitable contracts; ratio J2 will then increase
2  Cutting the costs of getting an order; ratio J3 will then fall
3  Cutting the money tied up in marketing assets in relation to sales; ratio J4 will then increase
4  Increasing the volume of business being obtained now in relation to that obtained in the past; ratio J5 will increase.

The cost of getting an order (ratio J3) can be reduced by:

1  Improving the quotation success rate (ratio J5) by more effective tendering
2  Cutting the cost of making a quotation (ratio J6) by improving the efficiency of the tendering department.

Marketing assets are related to sales because there is more relationship between them and sales (the value of the work being done by the production side of the business) than between them and the orders being obtained. The investment in these assets in relation to sales volume can be reduced:

1  By prompt billing of progress claims; this will reduce ratio J8
2  By quicker debt collection; this will reduce ratio J9..

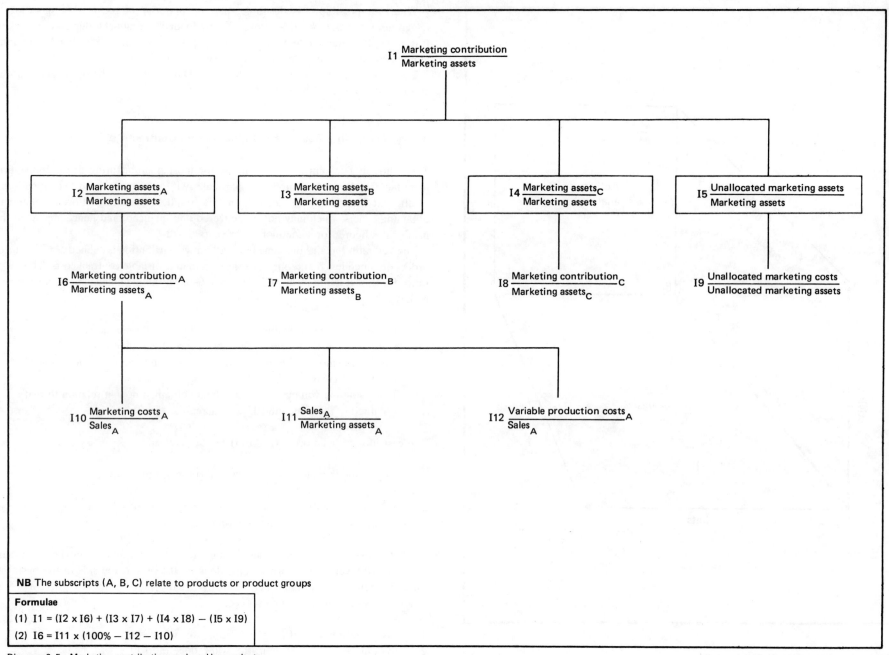

I1 $\dfrac{\text{Marketing contribution}}{\text{Marketing assets}}$

I2 $\dfrac{\text{Marketing assets}_A}{\text{Marketing assets}}$

I3 $\dfrac{\text{Marketing assets}_B}{\text{Marketing assets}}$

I4 $\dfrac{\text{Marketing assets}_C}{\text{Marketing assets}}$

I5 $\dfrac{\text{Unallocated marketing assets}}{\text{Marketing assets}}$

I6 $\dfrac{\text{Marketing contribution}_A}{\text{Marketing assets}_A}$

I7 $\dfrac{\text{Marketing contribution}_B}{\text{Marketing assets}_B}$

I8 $\dfrac{\text{Marketing contribution}_C}{\text{Marketing assets}_C}$

I9 $\dfrac{\text{Unallocated marketing costs}}{\text{Unallocated marketing assets}}$

I10 $\dfrac{\text{Marketing costs}_A}{\text{Sales}_A}$

I11 $\dfrac{\text{Sales}_A}{\text{Marketing assets}_A}$

I12 $\dfrac{\text{Variable production costs}_A}{\text{Sales}_A}$

**NB** The subscripts (A, B, C) relate to products or product groups

**Formulae**

(1) I1 = (I2 x I6) + (I3 x I7) + (I4 x I8) − (I5 x I9)

(2) I6 = I11 x (100% − I12 − I10)

Diagram 6–5   Marketing contribution analysed by products

134

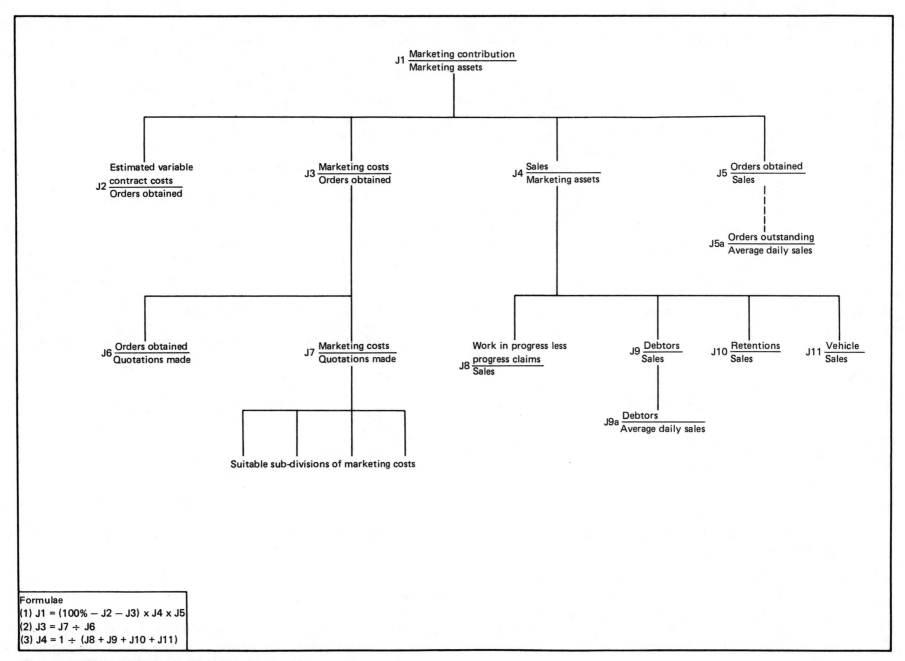

Diagram 6–6   Marketing ratios for a business with long-term contracts

*135*

Retentions are a different problem to debtors but every effort needs to be made to satisfy the client and get the retention released. Maximum use of sales and distribution vehicles will help to keep ratio J11 down.

If the marketing management is helping the business to expand, ratio J5 (orders obtained during the period/sales during the period) will be greater than 100 per cent. Unfortunately a figure for ratio J5 greater than 100 per cent is ambiguous because as well as having the favourable meaning just mentioned it could also mean that sales for the period had dropped because the production side of the business was falling down on deliveries. Such a state of affairs would be indicated by ratio J5a (orders outstanding/average daily sales) rising. This ratio measures the length of the order book in terms of the number of days' production. It also shows marketing management the average delivery date it can quote when giving rough estimates.

Ratio J5a is useful for liaison between production and sales in a contracting business. If it rises too high it may be very difficult to get orders unless and until production can be expanded. If it falls too low selling effort must be increased and/or thoughts turned to cutting back production.

What is too high or too low depends to some extent on the industry and the too high mark varies over the course of time with competitors' figures for delivery dates.

To calculate ratios J1 to J11 use data assembly and ratio calculation sheet 6–4 at the end of this chapter.

## 6.8 Selling

If the organisation is large enough it may be worth providing a further set of ratios to measure reasons for changes in ratio G9 in Diagram 6–1. This further set is shown in Diagram 6–7. It has been assumed that selling costs are partly representatives' remuneration and expenses and partly agents' commission. Agents will most probably be operating in territories where it is uneconomic to have representatives. There are three broad factors which would cause the ratio of selling costs/sales (ratio K1) to change:

1    Representatives' performance (that is the value of sales they obtain in relation to their own costs) might change, indicated by a change in ratio K5.
2    Agents' rate of commission might be altered; this would be shown up by a change in ratio K6.
3    The proportion of sales through representatives or agents might change, shown up by a movement in ratios K2 or K3. (These two ratios are complementary; if one goes down, the other must go up so that their sum is always 100 per cent.)

It will probably be worth having a separate set of ratios K1 to K6 for each major territory as an aid to controlling performance in different geographical areas. It is also worth keeping a comparative eye on the relative sizes of K5 and K6 so as to make sure that selling is being conducted by the most economical means for a territory.

It is dangerous to look at K5 and K6 in isolation, however. The growth of sales in the various representatives' and agents' territories must also be considered. Low costs may not be enough to compensate for stagnating, or worse, declining sales. Representatives' performance is affected by three factors:

1    Average cost of a call (ratio K7)
2    Call success rate (ratio K8)
3    Average value of the order obtained from successful calls (ratio K9).

The sales manager will look at these ratios not only for his force overall but for individual representatives as well. Furthermore, he may well want to sub-divide ratios K7, K8 and K9 between calls made on new customers and repeat business.

A firm may well need to have a policy on how much of its representatives' time should be spent with existing customers and how much with potential customers. Too much on either could be equally fatal. Some firms' representatives may need to make 'keeping warm' calls not so much to obtain an order as to avoid losing the next one. This fact will need to be taken into account in interpreting the size of ratio K8.

To achieve overall success a sales manager and his representatives must maintain a balance between:

1    The desire to minimise the cost of a call by making more calls per day
2    The desire to maximise the call success rate by taking small value orders in large numbers and/or only calling on easy customers
3    The desire to maximise the value of orders by neglecting the small customer.

That is why all three ratios (K7 to K9) should be used, preferably for each representative.

To calculate ratios K1 to K9 use data assembly and ratio calculation sheet 6–5 at the end of this chapter.

## 6.9 Distribution

Only in the very largest businesses or in a firm where distribution costs are a very high proportion of sales income is it necessary to provide many ratios to monitor performance in this field. Nevertheless distribution is becoming increasingly important

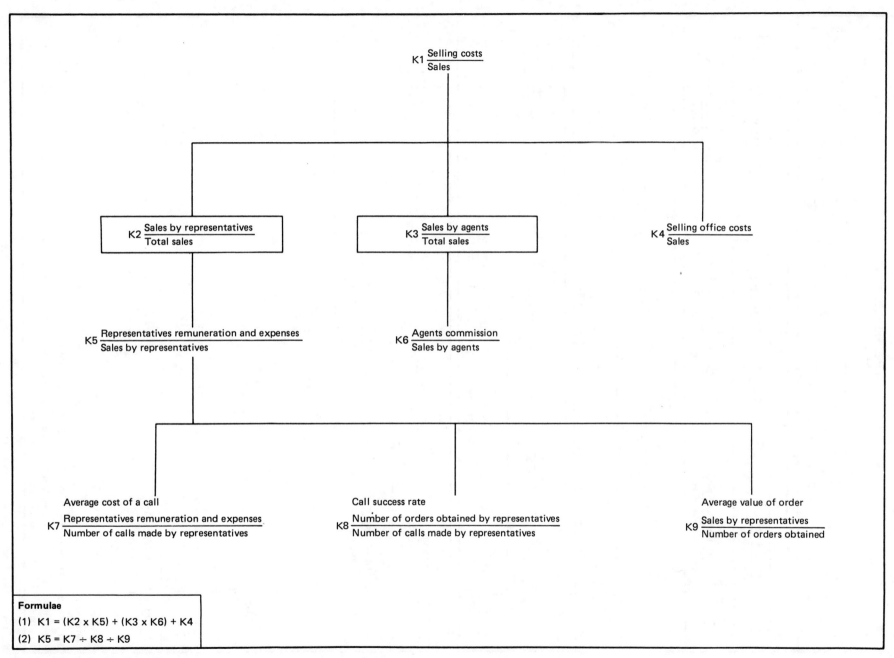

$K1 \dfrac{\text{Selling costs}}{\text{Sales}}$

$K2 \dfrac{\text{Sales by representatives}}{\text{Total sales}}$

$K3 \dfrac{\text{Sales by agents}}{\text{Total sales}}$

$K4 \dfrac{\text{Selling office costs}}{\text{Sales}}$

$K5 \dfrac{\text{Representatives remuneration and expenses}}{\text{Sales by representatives}}$

$K6 \dfrac{\text{Agents commission}}{\text{Sales by agents}}$

Average cost of a call

$K7 \dfrac{\text{Representatives remuneration and expenses}}{\text{Number of calls made by representatives}}$

Call success rate

$K8 \dfrac{\text{Number of orders obtained by representatives}}{\text{Number of calls made by representatives}}$

Average value of order

$K9 \dfrac{\text{Sales by representatives}}{\text{Number of orders obtained}}$

**Formulae**

(1)  $K1 = (K2 \times K5) + (K3 \times K6) + K4$

(2)  $K5 = K7 \div K8 \div K9$

Diagram 6–7   Ratios for sales management

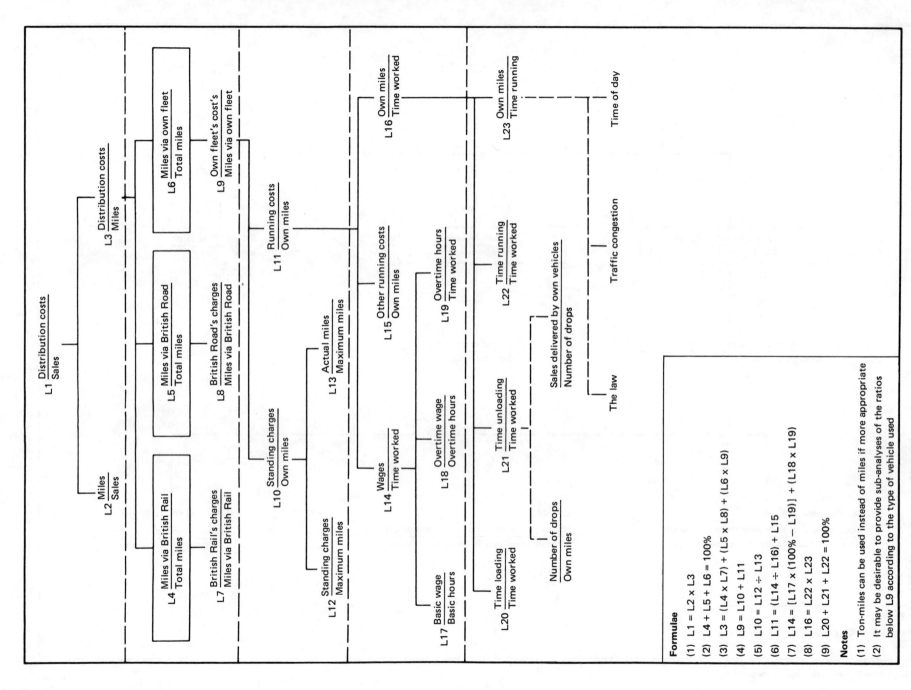

**Formulae**

(1) L1 = L2 × L3

(2) L4 + L5 + L6 = 100%

(3) L3 = (L4 × L7) + (L5 × L8) + (L6 × L9)

(4) L9 = L10 + L11

(5) L10 = L12 ÷ L13

(6) L11 = (L14 ÷ L16) + L15

(7) L14 = [L17 × (100% − L19)] + (L18 × L19)

(8) L16 = L22 × L23

(9) L20 + L21 + L22 = 100%

**Notes**

(1) Ton-miles can be used instead of miles if more appropriate

(2) It may be desirable to provide sub-analyses of the ratios below L9 according to the type of vehicle used

Diagram 6–8   Ratios for the distribution manager

and a full set of ratios has been provided in Diagram 6–8, broken up by a number of horizontal lines. Managers in this area of a firm's operations can literally 'draw the line' at one of these lines and use the ratios above it and omit those below it.

These ratios assume that the distribution manager reports to the marketing manager, who monitors his performance by the ratio of distribution costs to sales (ratio G6 in Diagram 6–1 and L1 in Diagram 6–8).

The distribution manager is providing a service related to the distance he transports the firm's goods. The first two ratios he looks at are therefore ratios L2 and L3. These show him how many miles (or ton miles) of transport he is providing for each pound of sales (ratio L2) and what his costs per mile are (ratio L3). If ratio L2 rises so, obviously, does ratio L1 which is used to monitor his performance. Yet the number of miles the firm's goods are carried is largely outside his control. It is arguable, therefore, that ratio L2 should be part of the marketing manager's set of ratios and the distribution manager's responsibility should start at ratio L3.

If the distribution manager uses a number of different types of transport (such as British Rail, British Road Services and the company's own fleet) he needs suitable switching ratios (L4, L5 and L6) to measure how much is being transported by each method. Ratios L7, L8 and L9 show the cost of the different forms of transport.

The magnitude of the ratio of standing charges to miles run (ratio L10) is affected by the ratio of these charges to the maximum number of miles the fleet could run in the year (ratio L12) – to some extent a subjective judgement – and how much the fleet's capacity was used (ratio L13).

It is useful to divide running costs between wages, which are paid largely on a time basis, and other running costs (petrol, oil) which vary largely with distance run. This gives ratios L14 and L15. Ratio L16 (average speed of vehicle) completes the picture. The average wage rate (ratio L14) depends on:

1    Basic wage rate (L17)
2    Overtime rate (L18)
3    Amount of overtime put in (L19).

The average speed of the vehicles (ratio L16) is a function of:

1    Time spent on loading (L20)
2    Time spent on unloading (L21)
3    Time spent on running (L22)
4    Speed of the vehicle when running (L23).

Loading and unloading time depends on the efficiency of both the firm's staff and of its customers' staff. It also depends on the frequency of deliveries (or drops) and the value of each drop must also be borne in mind. The running speed of the vehicle depends on the law, traffic congestion and the time of day. Only the last of these three is in the transport manager's control.

Ratios L7, L8 and L9 show average *total* cost. When deciding whether to use his own or an outside fleet the transport manager has to consider in the short run his own fleet's *marginal* cost if it is operating below capacity. This marginal cost is shown by ratio L11. The costs of the firm's own fleet can be broken down into standing charges (ratio L10) and running costs (ratio L11). The former are incurred irrespective of the miles run (licence fees, garage rent and so on), the latter vary with the distance covered.

To calculate ratios L1 to L23 use data assembly and ratio calculation sheet 6.6 at the end of this chapter.

The ratios described above draw on analysis of the distribution function carried out at the Centre for Interfirm Comparison, and readers wishing to obtain standards for these ratios are advised to consider participation in the comparison schemes run by the Centre relating to the distribution operations of manufacturers in various industries, and also relating to commercial road haulage.

## 6.10 Stock Turnover and Customers' Creditworthiness

There are two further subjects with which marketing management should be concerned. They are stock turnover and customers' creditworthiness. The former is dealt with in Chapter 7, the latter in Chapter 8.

Data assembly sheet 6-1
**Ratios for the marketing director**

| Code letter | Item | Month or quarter to (date) | | | | | |
|---|---|---|---|---|---|---|---|
| A | Warehouse costs | | | | | | |
| B | Distribution costs | | | | | | |
| C | Advertising costs | | | | | | |
| D | Promotion costs | | | | | | |
| E | Selling costs | | | | | | |
| F | Discounts | | | | | | |
| G | Sales office costs | | | | | | |
| H | Market research costs | | | | | | |
| K | Bad debts | | | | | | |
| L | Marketing costs (A + B + C + D + E + F + G + H + K) | | | | | | |
| M | Variable production costs | | | | | | |
| N | Sub total (L + M) | | | | | | |
| P | Sales | | | | | | |
| Q | Marketing contribution (P − N) | | | | | | |
| R | Finished goods stock | | | | | | |
| S | Debtors | | | | | | |
| T | Selling and distribution vehicles | | | | | | |
| W | Marketing assets (R + S + T) | | | | | | |

| Code letter | Item | Month or quarter to (date) | | | | | |
|---|---|---|---|---|---|---|---|
| Y | No of orders or invoices | | | | | | |
| Z | Production cost of goods sold | | | | | | |
| AA | No of working days in period | | | | | | |
| AB | No of working days in year | | | | | | |
| AC | No of calendar days in period | | | | | | |

**Ratios for the marketing director**

| Ratio | | Formula for calculation of ratio | Unit of measurement | Month or quarter to (date) | | | | | |
|---|---|---|---|---|---|---|---|---|---|
| G1 | Marketing contribution/ Marketing assets | $(Q \times 100 \div W) \times (AB \div AA)$ | % pa | | | | | | |
| G2 | Marketing costs/ Sales | $L \times 100 \div P$ | % | | | | | | |
| G3 | Sales/Marketing assets | $(P \div W) \times (AB \div AA)$ | times per year | | | | | | |
| G4 | Variable production costs/Sales | $M \times 100 \div P$ | % | | | | | | |
| G5 | Warehouse costs/ Sales | $A \times 100 \div P$ | % | | | | | | |
| G6 | Distribution costs/Sales | $B \times 100 \div P$ | % | | | | | | |
| G7 | Advertising costs/Sales | $C \times 100 \div P$ | % | | | | | | |
| G8 | Promotion costs/ Sales | $D \times 100 \div P$ | % | | | | | | |
| G9 | Selling costs/ Sales | $E \times 100 \div P$ | % | | | | | | |
| G10 | Discounts/ Sales | $F \times 100 \div P$ | % | | | | | | |
| G11 | Sales office costs/Sales | $G \times 100 \div P$ | % | | | | | | |
| G12 | Market research costs/Sales | $H \times 100 \div P$ | % | | | | | | |
| G13 | Bad debts/ sales | $K \times 100 \div P$ | % | | | | | | |

| Ratio | Formula for calculation of ratio | Unit of measurement | Month or quarter to (date) | | | | | |
|---|---|---|---|---|---|---|---|---|
| | | | | | | | | |
| G14 Sales/ No of orders or invoices | $P \div Y$ | £ per order or invoice | | | | | | |
| G15 Sales office costs/No of orders or invoices | $G \div Y$ | £ per order or invoice | | | | | | |
| G16 Finished goods stock/Sales | $R \times 1000 \div (P \times AB \div AA)$ | $\%_0$ pa | | | | | | |
| G17 Debtors/Sales | $S \times 1000 \div (P \times AB \div AA)$ | $\%_0$ pa | | | | | | |
| G18 Selling and distribution vehicles/ Sales | $T \times 1000 \div (P \times AB \div AA)$ | $\%_0$ pa | | | | | | |
| G19 Finished goods stock/Average daily production cost of goods sold | $R \times AB \div Z$ | days | | | | | | |
| G20 Debtors/Average daily sales | $S \times AC \div P$ | days | | | | | | |

Data assembly sheet 6–2
## Distribution and selling costs: home and export analysis

| Code letter | Item | Month or quarter to (date) | | | | | |
|---|---|---|---|---|---|---|---|
| A | Home distribution costs | | | | | | |
| B | Export distribution costs | | | | | | |
| C | Distribution costs (A + B) | | | | | | |
| D | Home selling costs | | | | | | |
| E | Export selling costs | | | | | | |
| F | Selling costs (D + E) | | | | | | |
| G | Home sales | | | | | | |
| H | Export sales | | | | | | |
| K | Sales (G + H) | | | | | | |

## Distribution and selling costs: home and export analysis

| Ratio | Formula for calculation of ratio | Unit of measurement | Month or quarter to (date) | | | | | |
|---|---|---|---|---|---|---|---|---|
| G6  Distribution costs/ Sales | C x 100 ÷ K | % | | | | | | |
| G9  Selling costs/Sales | F x 100 ÷ K | % | | | | | | |
| H1  Home sales/Total sales | G x 100 ÷ K | % | | | | | | |
| H2  Home distribution costs/Home sales | A x 100 ÷ G | % | | | | | | |
| H3  Export distribution costs/Export sales | B x 100 ÷ H | % | | | | | | |
| H4  Home selling costs/ Home sales | D x 100 ÷ G | % | | | | | | |
| H5  Export selling costs/ Export sales | E x 100 ÷ H | % | | | | | | |

Data assembly sheet 6–3
**Marketing contribution analysed by products**

| Code letter | Item | Total | Product group A | Product group B | C | Unallocated |
|---|---|---|---|---|---|---|
| | | (1) | (2) | (3) | (4) | (5) |
| A | Sales | | | | | |
| B | Variable production costs | | | | | |
| C | Marketing costs | | | | | |
| D | Subtotal (B + C) | | | | | |
| E | Marketing contribution (A − D) | | | | | |
| F | Average marketing assets | | | | | |
| G | No of working days in period | | | | | |
| H | No of working days in year | | | | | |

## Marketing contribution analysed by products

| Ratio | Formula for calculation of ratio | Unit of measurement | Month or quarter to (date) | | | | | |
|---|---|---|---|---|---|---|---|---|
| I1 Marketing contribution/Marketing assets | $(E1 \times 100 \div F1) \times (H \div G)$ | % pa | | | | | | |
| I2 Marketing assets (A)/Marketing assets | $F2 \times 100 \div F1$ | % | | | | | | |
| I3 Marketing assets (B)/Marketing assets | $F3 \times 100 \div F1$ | % | | | | | | |
| I4 Marketing assets (C)/Marketing assets | $F4 \times 100 \div F1$ | % | | | | | | |
| I5 Unallocated marketing assets/ Marketing assets | $F5 \times 100 \div F1$ | % | | | | | | |
| I6 Marketing contribution (A)/ Marketing assets (A) | $(E2 \times 100 \div F2) \times (H \div G)$ | % pa | | | | | | |
| I7 Marketing contribution (B)/Marketing assets (B) | $(E3 \times 100 \div F3) \times (H \div G)$ | % pa | | | | | | |
| I8 Marketing contribution (C)/Marketing assets (C) | $(E4 \times 100 \div F4) \times (H \div G)$ | % pa | | | | | | |
| I9 Unallocated marketing costs/ Unallocated marketing assets | $(C5 \times 100 \div F5) \times (H \div G)$ | % pa | | | | | | |
| I10 Marketing cost (A)/Sales (A) | $C2 \times 100 \div A2$ | % | | | | | | |
| I11 Sales (A)/Marketing assets (A) | $A2 \div F2 \times (H \div G)$ | times per year | | | | | | |
| I12 Variable production costs (A)/ Sales (A) | $B2 \times 100 \div A2$ | % | | | | | | |

Data assembly sheet 6–4
## Marketing ratios for a business with long-term contracts

| Code letter | Item | Month or quarter to (date) | | | | | |
|---|---|---|---|---|---|---|---|
| | | | | | | | |
| A | Orders outstanding at beginning of period | | | | | | |
| B | Orders obtained during the period | | | | | | |
| C | Sub total (A + B) | | | | | | |
| D | Sales | | | | | | |
| E | Orders outstanding at the end of the period (C − D) | | | | | | |
| F | Estimated variable contract costs | | | | | | |
| G | Marketing costs | | | | | | |
| H | Sub total (F + G) | | | | | | |
| K | Marketing contribution (B − H) | | | | | | |
| L | Work in progress | | | | | | |
| M | Progress claims | | | | | | |
| N | Work in progress less progress claims (L − M) | | | | | | |
| P | Debtors | | | | | | |
| Q | Retentions | | | | | | |
| R | Vehicles | | | | | | |
| S | Marketing assets (N + P + Q + R) | | | | | | |
| | | | | | | | |

**Marketing ratios for a business with long-term contracts**

| Code letter | Item | Month or quarter to (date) | | | | | |
|---|---|---|---|---|---|---|---|
| T | Quotations made | | | | | | |
| W | No. of working days in period | | | | | | |
| Y | No. of working days in year | | | | | | |
| Z | No. of calendar days in period | | | | | | |

## Marketing ratios for a business with long-term contracts

| Ratio | Formula for calculation of ratio | Unit of measurement | Month or quarter to (date) | | | | | |
|---|---|---|---|---|---|---|---|---|
| J1 Marketing contribution/ Marketing assets | $(K \times 100 \div S) \times (Y \div W)$ | % pa | | | | | | |
| J2 Estimated variable contract costs/Orders obtained | $F \times 100 \div B$ | % | | | | | | |
| J3 Marketing costs/ Orders obtained | $G \times 100 \div B$ | % | | | | | | |
| J4 Sales/Marketing assets | $D \div S \times (Y \div W)$ | times per year | | | | | | |
| J5 Orders obtained/ Sales | $B \times 100 \div D$ | % | | | | | | |
| J5(a) Orders outstanding/ Average daily sales | $E \times W \div D$ | days | | | | | | |
| J6 Orders obtained/ Quotations made | $B \times 100 \div T$ | % | | | | | | |
| J7 Marketing costs/ Quotations made | $G \times 100 \div T$ | % | | | | | | |
| J8 Work in progress less progress claims/Sales | $N \times 1000 \div (D \times Y \div W)$ | ‰ pa | | | | | | |
| J9 Debtors/Sales | $P \times 1000 \div (D \times Y \div W)$ | ‰ pa | | | | | | |
| J9(a) Debtors/Average daily sales | $P \times Z \div D$ | days | | | | | | |
| J10 Retentions/Sales | $Q \times 1000 \div (D \times Y \div W)$ | ‰ pa | | | | | | |
| J11 Vehicles/Sales | $R \times 1000 \div (D \times Y \div W)$ | ‰ pa | | | | | | |

Data assembly sheet number 6–5 will be found on the following page

**Ratios for the sales manager**

| Code letter | Item | Month or quarter to (date) | | | | | |
|---|---|---|---|---|---|---|---|
| | | | | | | | |
| A | Representatives remuneration and expenses | | | | | | |
| B | Agents' commission | | | | | | |
| C | Selling office costs | | | | | | |
| D | Selling costs (A + B + C) | | | | | | |
| E | Sales by representatives | | | | | | |
| F | Sales by agents | | | | | | |
| G | Total sales (E + F) | | | | | | |
| H | Number of calls made by representatives | | | | | | |
| K | Number of orders obtained by representatives | | | | | | |

# Ratios for the sales manager

| Ratio | Formula for calculation of ratio | Unit of measurement | Month or quarter to (date) | | | | | |
|---|---|---|---|---|---|---|---|---|
| K1  Selling costs/ Sales | D x 100 ÷ G | % | | | | | | |
| K2  Sales by representatives/ Total sales | E x 100 ÷ G | % | | | | | | |
| K3  Sales by agents/ Total sales | F x 100 ÷ G | % | | | | | | |
| K4  Selling office costs/ Sales | C x 100 ÷ G | % | | | | | | |
| K5  Representatives' remuneration and expenses/Sales by representatives | A x 100 ÷ E | % | | | | | | |
| K6  Agents' commission/ Sales by agents | B x 100 ÷ F | % | | | | | | |
| *Average cost of a call* | | | | | | | | |
| K7  Representatives' remuneration and expenses/No. of calls made by representatives | A ÷ H | £'s per call | | | | | | |
| *Call success rate* | | | | | | | | |
| K8  No of orders obtained by representatives/ No. of calls made by representatives | K x 100 ÷ H | % | | | | | | |
| *Average value of order* | | | | | | | | |
| K9  Sales by representatives/No. of orders obtained | E ÷ K | £'s per order | | | | | | |

## Ratios for the distribution manager

| Code letter | Item | Month or quarter to (date) | | | | | |
|---|---|---|---|---|---|---|---|
| A | Time loading | | | | | | |
| B | Time unloading | | | | | | |
| C | Time running | | | | | | |
| D | Time worked (A + B + C) | | | | | | |
| E | Basic hours | | | | | | |
| F | Overtime hours | | | | | | |
| G | Time worked (E + F) NB D should equal G | | | | | | |
| H | Basic wage | | | | | | |
| K | Overtime wage | | | | | | |
| L | Wages (H + K) | | | | | | |
| M | Other running costs | | | | | | |
| N | Running costs (L + M) | | | | | | |
| P | Standing charges | | | | | | |
| Q | Own fleet's costs (N + P) | | | | | | |
| R | British Rail's charges | | | | | | |
| S | British Road's charges | | | | | | |
| T | Distribution costs (Q + R + S) | | | | | | |

| Code letter | Item | Month or quarter to (date) | | | | | |
|---|---|---|---|---|---|---|---|
| W | Own miles | | | | | | |
| X | Miles via British Rail | | | | | | |
| Y | Miles via British Road | | | | | | |
| Z | Miles (W + X + Y) | | | | | | |
| AA | Maximum miles per period | | | | | | |
| AB | Sales | | | | | | |

**Ratios for the distribution manager**

| Ratio | Formula for calculation of ratio | Unit of measurement | Month or quarter to (date) | | | | | |
|---|---|---|---|---|---|---|---|---|
| L1  Distribution costs/ Sales | T x 100 ÷ AB | % | | | | | | |
| L2  Miles/Sales | Z ÷ AB | miles per £ | | | | | | |
| L3  Distribution costs/ Miles | T ÷ Z | £'s per mile | | | | | | |
| L4  Miles via British Rail/Total miles | X x 100 ÷ Z | % | | | | | | |
| L5  Miles via British Road/Total miles | Y x 100 ÷ Z | % | | | | | | |
| L6  Miles via own fleet/Total miles | W x 100 ÷ Z | % | | | | | | |
| L7  British Rail's charges/Miles via British Rail | R ÷ X | £'s per mile | | | | | | |
| L8  British Road's charges/Miles via British Road | S ÷ Y | £'s per mile | | | | | | |
| L9  Own fleet's costs/ Miles via own fleet | Q ÷ W | £'s per mile | | | | | | |
| L10  Standing charges/ Own miles | P ÷ W | £'s per mile | | | | | | |
| L11  Running costs/ Own miles | N ÷ W | £'s per mile | | | | | | |
| L12  Standing charges/ Maximum miles | P ÷ AA | £'s per mile | | | | | | |

| Ratio | | Formula for calculation of ratio | Unit of measurement | Month or quarter to (date) | | | | | |
|---|---|---|---|---|---|---|---|---|---|
| L13 | Actual miles/ Maximum miles | W x 100 ÷ AA | % | | | | | | |
| L14 | Wages/Time worked | L ÷ G | £'s per hour | | | | | | |
| L15 | Other running costs/ Own miles | M ÷ W | £'s per mile | | | | | | |
| L16 | Own miles/ Time worked | W ÷ G | miles per hour | | | | | | |
| L17 | Basic wage/ Basic hours | H ÷ E | £'s per hour | | | | | | |
| L18 | Overtime wage/ Overtime hours | K ÷ F | £'s per hour | | | | | | |
| L19 | Overtime hours/ Time worked | F x 100 ÷ G | % | | | | | | |
| L20 | Time loading/ Time worked | A x 100 ÷ D | % | | | | | | |
| L21 | Time unloading/ Time worked | B x 100 ÷ D | % | | | | | | |
| L22 | Time running/ Time worked | C x 100 ÷ D | % | | | | | | |
| L23 | Own miles/ Time running | W ÷ C | Miles per hour | | | | | | |

# Chapter 7

# Ratios for purchasing management

## 7.1 The Key Ratio

The key ratio which measures the success of the buyer is

$$\text{M1} \qquad \frac{\text{Buying contribution}}{\text{Buying assets}}$$

Buying assets will probably consist of stocks of raw materials, bought-in parts and components, less creditors. Buying contribution is defined as sales value of production, less purchases, less buying costs.

Calculating the buying contribution is complicated, however, by the problem of the time lag between the purchase of an item and the eventual sale of the product incorporating that item. During that time lag, the item purchased is found successively in raw materials stock, work in progress, and finished goods stock. Thus, the purchases of one period are not necessarily related to the sales of that period and a ratio of purchases/sales is unlikely to be meaningful.

As the buyer is interested in the purchasing, rather than the selling end of the operation, it is preferable to adjust the sales figures rather than the figure for purchases. Ideally, purchases would be related to the estimated selling price of the product into which they are going to be manufactured. In practice this is unlikely to be possible. The best practical compromise is likely to be:

1    To adjust purchases for changes in raw materials stock and work in progress to get materials cost content of finished production, and
2    To use sales value of production (SVOP) instead of sales. SVOP is also needed for the ratios recommended for production management, so the one figure will serve two purposes. SVOP is defined as the estimated sales

value of goods completed in a period. Details of how to calculate or to estimate it are given in Chapter 9.

## 7.2 Subsidiary Ratios

The subsidiary ratios which the buyer will want to monitor are shown in Diagram 7–1. He can improve his key ratio (ratio M1) by:

1    Obtaining lower prices from suppliers; ratio M2 will go down.
2    Reducing the cost of placing an order in relation to the value purchased; ratio M3 will go down.
3    Carrying less stock; ratio M4 will go down.
4    Obtaining longer credit from suppliers; ratio M5 will increase.

There are two ways of reducing the cost of buying in relation to the value of the items purchased (ratio M3):

1    Cut the costs of placing an order, measured by ratio M6 (but if less time is spent on shopping around a less favourable price may be paid and ratio M2 will go up)
2    Increase the amount purchased at any one time, measured by ratio M7 (but this will increase the amount of stock carried and ratio M4 will go up).

Similarly better prices may be obtained from quantity discounts and prompt payment but this will increase stock (ratio M4) and decrease credit taken (ratio M5) respectively.

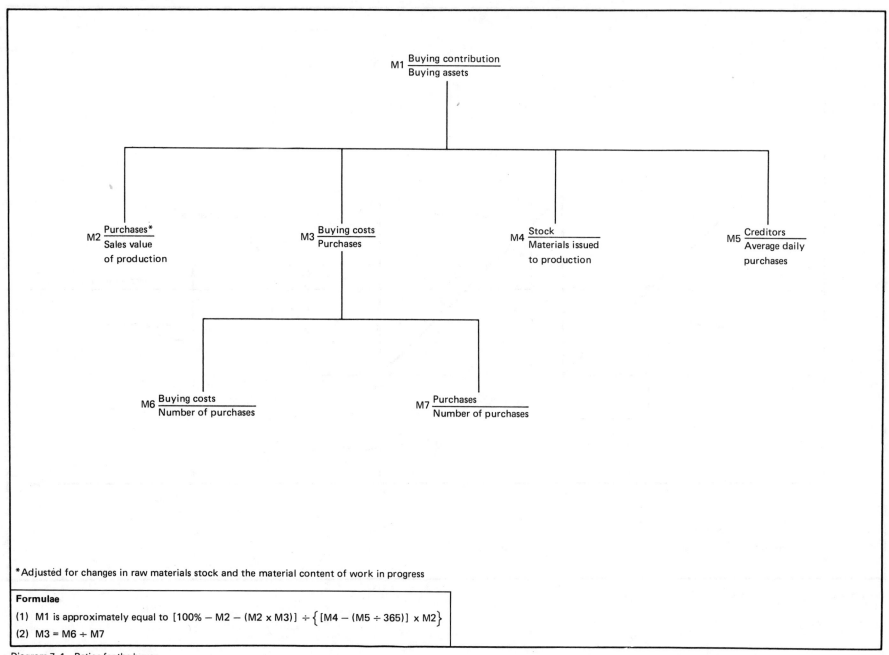

M1 $\dfrac{\text{Buying contribution}}{\text{Buying assets}}$

M2 $\dfrac{\text{Purchases*}}{\text{Sales value of production}}$

M3 $\dfrac{\text{Buying costs}}{\text{Purchases}}$

M4 $\dfrac{\text{Stock}}{\text{Materials issued to production}}$

M5 $\dfrac{\text{Creditors}}{\text{Average daily purchases}}$

M6 $\dfrac{\text{Buying costs}}{\text{Number of purchases}}$

M7 $\dfrac{\text{Purchases}}{\text{Number of purchases}}$

*Adjusted for changes in raw materials stock and the material content of work in progress

**Formulae**

(1)  M1 is approximately equal to $[100\% - \text{M2} - (\text{M2} \times \text{M3})] \div \{[\text{M4} - (\text{M5} \div 365)] \times \text{M2}\}$

(2)  M3 = M6 ÷ M7

Diagram 7–1   Ratios for the buyer

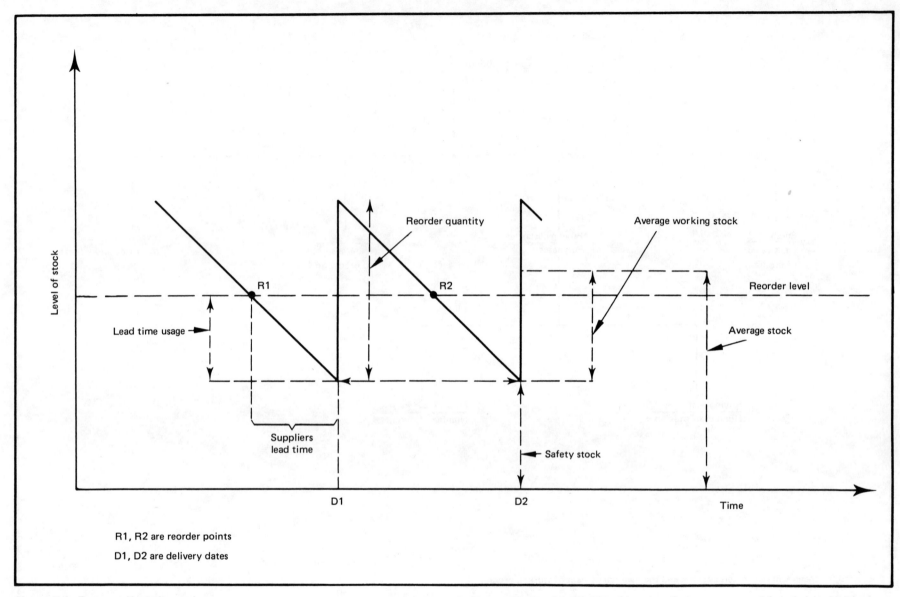

Diagram 7–2   Terms used in stock control

R1, R2 are reorder points

D1, D2 are delivery dates

The buyer must constantly weigh these pros and cons against each other. His success in doing so will be measured by his key ratio (M1) which combines the results of the various trade-offs he must make.

One item is missing, however. If the buyer cuts stock too low, production may be held up for the lack of some item and the money lost by production will outweigh any savings from lower stock. This is a difficult cost to measure – though a good system of labour cost control can quantify the cost of time waiting for materials – and even harder to attribute fairly. Did production control give the stores adequate warning? Could they, or the shopfloor superintendents, have reallocated work so that less time was lost? At this level, a quick meeting of all concerned, and a sensible prompt decision, is worth a multitude of ratios. It is suggested therefore that this cost should be left out of the system of ratio control.

To calculate ratios M1 to M7 use data assembly and ratio calculation sheet 7–1 at the end of this chapter.

### 7.3 Stock Control

It would not be appropriate to include in this book a long dissertation on stock control, but the subject is of such vital importance to most businesses, and concerns so many of the managers within a business, that it would seem desirable to include a few paragraphs on the subject and its associated ratios.

As with so many other aspects of management, stock control consists of balancing conflicting demands to arrive at the compromise which is optimum for the business as a whole. Because the demands are variable over time, as well as being conflicting, any optimum compromise will be only a temporary solution. A change in one of the factors will call for a new point of balanced compromise.

The buyer and the production manager will be concerned with the level of raw material stock. The production manager will also be involved in the amount of work in progress and finished goods stock. The sales manager is as concerned as the production manager with the level of finished stock available for delivery to the company's customers. Finally, the finance director is sure to want to keep the level of stock down as it is he who can see most clearly the problems associated with financing high levels of stock.

Diagram 7–2 shows the main terms used in stock control. The heavy black 'saw-tooth' line shows the level of stock dropping over time as it is consumed and then rising sharply as a delivery is received, only to drop again as consumption continues.

Stock is reordered at *reorder points* R1 and R2 when the level of stock falls to the *reorder level*. Between reordering and receipt of the goods is an interval of time called the *supplier's lead time* (measured by ratio N2, see page 163). Deliveries are received at D1 and D2.

*Safety stock* is held as an insurance against changes in usage, and deliveries taking longer than the expected lead time. *Average working stock* will be seen to be equal to half the *reorder quantity*. *Average stock* is equal to average working stock plus safety stock. The *reorder level* is the lead time usage plus the safety stock.

The level of safety stock is related to the 'satisfaction levels' set by management (see below), the degree of unpredictability of demand, and the degree of unreliability of suppliers (measured by ratio N3, see page 163).

Stock control starts with the sales manager's forecast of demand for the range of products which the company supplies. At this point two policy decisions need to be taken:

1   In the light of the expected demand for each item in the range is it economical to continue to keep some items in the range at all?
2   What satisfaction level (the ratio of orders fulfilled without delay to orders received) is to be aimed at for different items? In arriving at a decision on this, it is necessary to bear in mind on the one hand the profit that might be lost if the item is out of stock, and on the other the cost of stocking and ordering. It must also be remembered that the level of stock necessary to achieve different satisfaction levels rises steeply at the higher levels, Diagram 7–3 shows that it is uneconomic always to go for 100 per cent satisfaction levels.

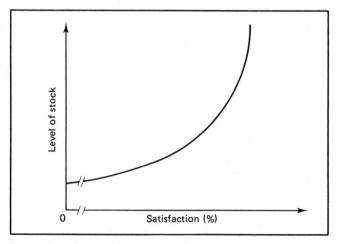

Diagram 7–3   Stock and satisfaction level

At this stage it is often useful to apply the 80/20 rule. This rule is also referred to as Pareto analysis, after the economist who invented it, and also as *ABC* analysis. It states that it is likely that 80 per cent by value of sales will be accounted for by 20 per cent of the items in the range and 80 per cent of the value of stock is likely to be accounted for by 20 per cent of the items in the stores. The *ABC* analysis is:

*A* items are those which account for the top 80 per cent by value of turnover

*B* items are those which account for the next 15 per cent by value of turnover

*C* items are those which account for the bottom 5 per cent by value of turnover.

The first practical application of the rule and analysis is that the more sophisticated stock control techniques can be applied to the relatively few *A* items whilst the *B* and *C* items are dealt with by more rudimentary methods.

The essence of stock control theory is that the larger the quantity ordered at any one time:

1    The lower the ordering cost per item
2    The higher the holding cost per item.

A typical pattern for these costs and quantities is shown in Diagram 7–4.

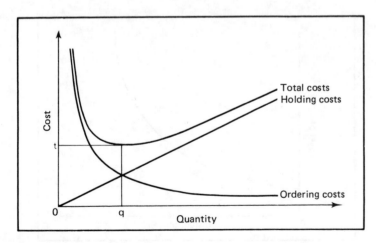

Diagram 7–4   Stock holding and ordering costs related to quantity

Holding costs rise steadily as the quantity ordered and held in stock increases. Ordering costs initially drop rapidly as quantity ordered increases but further increases in quantity cause only small decreases in cost. The total cost curve is the sum of the holding and ordering cost curves. It therefore drops rapidly to a minimum and thereafter rises gradually. The practical consequence of this cost/quantity pattern is that, whereas orders for quantities *smaller* than that which minimises total cost (the economic order quantity – see below) cause a rapid increase in costs, orders for *larger* quantities have a less deleterious effect on costs. In other words, quantities equal to or slightly above the economic order quantity will minimise costs. Diagram 7–4 shows that there is an ordering quantity *q* at which total costs *t* are at a minimum. This quantity (*q*) can be divided into annual usage to get the optimum reordering frequency *f* in times per year. The actual values of *q, t* and *f* vary from item to item, from firm to firm, and over time. Nevertheless, as a generalisation, costs can be minimised if:

1    Items of small value are ordered in bulk at long intervals
2    Items of high value are ordered in small quantities at short intervals.

Books on stock control show that the economic ordering quantity (*q* in Diagram 7–4) is given by the formula

$$q = \sqrt{\frac{2AB}{CI}}$$

where
A = quantity needed per year
B = cost per order
C = value of one unit of the item
I = inventory holding cost per year as a decimal of the value of the inventory.

The application of the formula needs modification when there are price discounts for quantity orders.

Once the economic order quantity (*q*) has been calculated, the optimum reordering frequency (*f*) can be derived by dividing *q* into the quantity needed per year (*A*). There is then a choice between using:

1    A fixed order quantity system, based on *q*, or
2    A periodic review system, based on *f*.

To pursue this very important subject further would be outside the scope of this book. (Those interested are recommended to read *Stock Control in Manufacturing Industries*, A.B. Thomas, Gower, 2nd edn, 1980). Space must be found however to mention one, relatively unsophisticated, method of stock control based on fixed order quantity, namely the 'two bin' or 'last bag' system.

This system is very suitable for the *C* items mentioned above. In it a quantity equal to the reorder level of the item is placed in a separate, second, bin or last bag, the remainder of the item being stored normally, (in the first bin etc.). Once the ordinary stock is exhausted and it is necessary to go to the second bin or last bag this is the signal to reorder the economic order quantity. When a delivery is received the second bin is topped up to the reorder level and the balance is placed in the first bin.

## 7.4 Further Subsidiary Ratios

In addition to his key ratio and the six subsidiary ratios shown in Diagram 7–1, the buyer will want some further ratio information on price, delivery, quality, the reliability and financial stability of his suppliers, and his degree of dependence on individual suppliers. The ratios which are suitable are discussed in the following paragraphs.

Changes in *price* can be measured in one or other of two ways. If a firm operates a standard costing system then the ratio to use would be

N1 $$\frac{\text{Price variance}}{\text{Budgeted purchases}}$$

the price variance being the difference between the budgeted price and the actual price, times the budgeted quantity.

If a firm does not have a standard costing system, price changes can be measured by an index number. Details of the method of calculating an index number are given in the work sheet at the end of this chapter. If a firm purchases a wide range of items, the work of calculating the index may be reduced by applying the 80/20 rule (see page 162). In this case the buyer would select the 20 per cent of the items that account for 80 per cent of the value of his purchases and measure all price changes for them and only measure the changes for a sample of the remaining 80 per cent of items which will only account for 20 per cent of the value.

A rise in prices is the signal for action on one or more of the following fronts:

1    Negotiation of price reductions/larger discounts
2    Consideration of larger purchases to get better prices
3    Consideration of alternative materials
4    Consideration of alternative suppliers
5    Improved efficiency within the firm
6    Consideration of price increases to customers.

*Suppliers' lead time* can be measured by dividing the value of orders outstanding at any one time by the average daily value of purchases.

N2 $$\frac{\text{Value of orders outstanding}}{\text{Average daily value of purchases}}$$

Any increase in this ratio will mean that:

1    The reorder level will need to be raised, and/or
2    The reorder review period will need to be shortened.

*Suppliers' reliability* can be measured by dividing the value of orders overdue at any one time by the average daily value of purchases.

N3 $$\frac{\text{Value of orders overdue}}{\text{Average daily value of purchases}}$$

Any increase in this ratio (i.e. an increase in *un*reliability) will mean that safety stock levels may need to be raised.

Increases in suppliers' lead time and/or unreliability may make it desirable:

1    To review sources of supply
2    To advise sales and production of the need to quote longer delivery dates to customers.

*Quality* can be measured by the ratio of

N4 $$\frac{\text{Value of goods returned and claims agreed}}{\text{Purchases}}$$

Any tendency for this ratio to rise is a warning to:

1    Review suppliers to find a more reliable one
2    Query prices quoted. Is poor quality a by-product of too low a price?
3    Query delivery times quoted. Are the suppliers being given too little notice of requirements?

To calculate ratios N1 to N4 use data assembly and ratio calculation sheet 7–2 at the end of this chapter.

## 7.5 Financial Stability of Supplier

No buyer wants his suppliers suddenly to go out of business leaving him to get another supplier in a hurry with resulting uncompetitive prices. The buyer must therefore be aware of any adverse trends in his suppliers' financial standing. The main ratios to examine are the trends in

N5
$$\frac{\text{Current assets}}{\text{Current liabilities}}$$

N6
$$\frac{\text{Quick assets}}{\text{Current liabilities}}$$

N7
$$\frac{\text{Net profit after tax}}{\text{Equity capital}}$$

N8
$$\frac{\text{Fixed costs}}{\text{Sales}}$$

A decline in the first three, or a rise in the last one, are all warning signs either to start looking for alternative sources of supply or to offer assistance if the nature of the relationship between your firm and your supplier makes that appropriate or necessary.

These ratios, and others relating to the financial standing of a firm, are discussed more fully in Chapter 8.

It is usually wise to have more than one source of supply for any item. This spreads and therefore diminishes the risk of the failure of a supplier. It also helps to maintain a healthy bargaining position between purchaser and seller. Conversely it is unlikely to be desirable to spread purchases so widely as to be always buying in minimum quantities. This puts up both the price and the buying costs.

A balance needs to be struck between the two extremes. A useful set of ratios to have in this connection is

N9
$$\frac{\text{Purchases from each supplier}}{\text{Total purchases}}$$

If possible this ratio should be calculated both from separate items and for purchases as a whole. Cutting down the range of items purchased and/or stocked is likely to lead to a reduction both in purchasing costs and in stock carried. These are both courses of action where the application of the 80/20 rule is helpful.

To calculate ratios N5 to N9 use data assembly and ratio calculation sheet 7–3 at the end of this chapter.

Data assembly sheet number 7–1 will be found on the following page

**Ratios for the buyer**

| Code letter | Item | Month or quarter to (date) | | | | | |
|---|---|---|---|---|---|---|---|
| A | Raw materials stock at beginning of period | | | | | | |
| B | Purchases | | | | | | |
| C | Sub total (A + B) | | | | | | |
| D | Raw materials stock at end of period | | | | | | |
| E | Materials issued to production (C−D) | | | | | | |
| F | Work in progress at beginning of period | | | | | | |
| G | Production cost (other than materials) | | | | | | |
| H | Sub total (E + F + G) | | | | | | |
| K | Work in progress at end of period | | | | | | |
| L | Production cost of goods made (H − K) | | | | | | |
| M | Finished goods stock at beginning of period | | | | | | |
| N | Sub total (L + M) | | | | | | |
| P | Finished goods stock at end of period | | | | | | |
| Q | Production cost of goods sold (N − P) | | | | | | |
| R | Sales | | | | | | |
| S | Sales value of production (L x R ÷ Q) | | | | | | |
| T | Buying costs | | | | | | |
| W | Buying contribution (S − E − T − F + K) | | | | | | |

| Code Letter | Item | Month or Quarter to (date) | | | | | |
|---|---|---|---|---|---|---|---|
| Y | Average creditors | | | | | | |
| Z | Number of purchases | | | | | | |
| AA | Average buying assets ($[(A + D) \div 2] - Y$) | | | | | | |
| AB | No. of working days in period | | | | | | |
| AC | No. of working days in year | | | | | | |
| AD | No. of calendar days in period | | | | | | |

# Ratios for the buyer

| Ratio | Formula for calculation of ratio | Unit of measurement | Month or quarter to (date) | | | | | |
|---|---|---|---|---|---|---|---|---|
| M1 Buying contribution/ Buying assets | $(W \times 100 \div AA) \times (AC \div AB)$ | % pa | | | | | | |
| M2 Purchases/ Sales value of production | $(E - F + K) \times 100 \div S$ | % | | | | | | |
| M3 Buying costs/ Purchases | $T \times 100 \div B$ | % | | | | | | |
| M4 Stock/ Materials issued to production | $[(A + D) \div 2] \div (E \div AB)$ | days | | | | | | |
| M5 Creditors/ Average daily purchases | $Y \div (B \div AD)$ | days | | | | | | |
| M6 Buying costs/ No. of purchases | $T \div Z$ | £ per order | | | | | | |
| M7 Purchases/ No. of purchases | $B \div Z$ | £ per order | | | | | | |

**Data assembly sheet number 7–2 will be found on the following page**

## Subsidiary ratios for the buyer

| Code letter | Item | Month or quarter to (date) | | | | | |
|---|---|---|---|---|---|---|---|
| A | Budgeted purchases | | | | | | |
| B | Purchases | | | | | | |
| C | Price variance | | | | | | |
| D | Value of goods returned and claims agreed | | | | | | |
| E | Value of orders outstanding | | | | | | |
| F | Value of orders overdue | | | | | | |
| G | No. of working days in period | | | | | | |

| Ratio | Formula for calculation of ratio | Unit of measurement | Month or quarter to (date) | | | | | |
|---|---|---|---|---|---|---|---|---|
| N1  Price variance/ Budgeted purchases | C x 100 ÷ A | % | | | | | | |
| N2  *Suppliers' lead time* | | | | | | | | |
| Value of orders outstanding/Average daily value of purchases | E ÷ (B ÷ G) | Days | | | | | | |
| N3  *Suppliers' reliability* Value of orders overdue/Average daily value of purchases | F ÷ (B ÷ G) | Days | | | | | | |
| N4  *Quality* Value of goods returned and claims agreed/Purchases | D x 100 ÷ B | % | | | | | | |

Data assembly sheet 7–3
**Financial stability of supplier**

| Code letter | Item | Supplier | | | | | |
|---|---|---|---|---|---|---|---|
| | | A | B | C | | | |
| A | Quick assets | | | | | | |
| B | Other current assets | | | | | | |
| C | Current assets (A + B) | | | | | | |
| D | Current liabilities | | | | | | |
| E | Equity capital | | | | | | |
| F | Sales | | | | | | |
| G | Fixed costs | | | | | | |
| H | All other costs including tax | | | | | | |
| K | Sub total (G + H) | | | | | | |
| L | Net profit after tax (F-K) | | | | | | |
| M | Purchases from each supplier | | | | | | |
| N | Total purchases | | | | | | |

# Financial stability of supplier

| Ratio | Formula for calculation of ratio | Unit of measurement | Supplier | | | | | |
|---|---|---|---|---|---|---|---|---|
| | | | A | B | | | | |
| N5  Current assets/ Current liabilities | C ÷ D | Times | | | | | | |
| N6  Quick assets/ Current liabilities | A ÷ D | Times | | | | | | |
| N7  Net profit after tax/Equity capital | L x 100 ÷ E | % | | | | | | |
| N8  Fixed costs/ Sales | G x 100 ÷ F | % | | | | | | |
| N9  Purchases from each supplier/ Total purchases | M x 100 ÷ N. | % | | | | | | |

NB  It is assumed that the figures for each supplier relate to a year. If this assumption is not correct then ratio N7 should be adjusted to put it on an annual basis.

# Chapter 8

# Ratios for financial management

The financial management of a company is generally concerned with:

1 Minimising the amount of tax the company pays
2 Raising long and short-term finance
3 Maintaining liquidity
4 Supervising investments
5 Relations between the company and the stock exchange (if the company is listed)
6 Supervising accounting and data processing activities.

The ratios that should be used to monitor and control these aspects of the company's business are described in this chapter.

## 8.1 Minimising the Rate of Tax

The subject of taxation is very complicated. Moreover it is a field where information is rendered obsolete at a very rapid rate by changes in legislation. It is proposed therefore to deal with this subject only very briefly in this book. Financial management will attempt to minimise the ratio of

01 $$\frac{\text{Taxation}}{\text{Net profit before tax}}$$

Among the things which affect the size of this ratio are: the company's status (a close company or not); its location (is it in a development area); current tax legislation; and the source of its profits (are they from overseas and have they been remitted). In pinpointing areas where action may be taken to reduce this ratio it may be useful to subdivide it according to:

1 The method of calculating the tax (income tax, corporation tax, capital gains tax and so on)
2 The geographical source of income being taxed
3 The subsidiary or division earning the income.

Detailed advice on how to improve ratio 01 should be obtainable from the firm's auditors or a consultant specialising in taxation.

## 8.2 Raising Finance

The object of raising part of a company's funds from sources other than its ordinary shareholders is to increase the rate of return on their capital. This process is known as gearing (or leverage in America). The underlying idea is very simple. A firm borrows money on which it pays $x$ per cent interest. It invests this money in assets from which it earns $y$ per cent. Provided that $y$ per cent is greater than $x$ per cent the difference is pure gain to the equity shareholder or owner of a business.

Obviously there are risks attached to such a policy. If the rate of interest paid rises and/or the rate of profit earned falls so that the former becomes greater than the latter, the difference is pure loss to the equity shareholder.

Another feature of gearing which may be considered to be a disadvantage by some people is that gearing magnifies any change in the profitability of a firm's assets so that the return on equity capital fluctuates more widely than the change in the return on assets. The following example illustrates this point:

| Year | 1 | 2 |
|------|---|---|
| *Balance Sheet* | £ | £ |
| Equity capital | 500 | 500 |
| Loan capital | 500 | 500 |
| Total capital | 1000 | 1000 |
| and total assets | | |
| *Profit and loss account* | | |
| Profit from use of assets | 150 | 100 |
| Interest on loan capital | 25 | 25 |
| Net profit | 125 | 75 |
| *Ratios* | | |
| Profit/Assets | 15% | 10% |
| Interest/Loan capital | 5% | 5% |
| Net profit/Equity capital | 25% | 15% |

A drop in the profit on assets ratio of 33½ per cent [(15 per cent − 10 per cent) ÷ 15 per cent] has caused a drop in the return on equity capital of 40 per cent [(25 per cent − 15 per cent) ÷ 25 per cent]. Two points should however be noted:

1  In both years the return to the equity shareholder is greater than it would have been if the firm had not financed part of its assets with loan capital
2  If the profit from the use of the assets in year 3 rises to the year 1 level of £150 a 50 per cent [(15 per cent − 10 per cent) ÷ 10 per cent] increase in underlying profitability will lead to a 66⅔ per cent [(25 per cent − 15 per cent) ÷ 15 per cent] increase in the return on equity capital.

Another advantage of gearing is that while profits and asset values tend to rise in a period of inflation the liability to repay the loan capital is fixed in money terms, which means that in real terms it is a decreasing liability. Anyone buying a house on a mortgage is benefiting from this aspect of gearing.

The true cost to a company of any interest payment is the nominal rate

(*a*)  less the effect of corporation tax (provided it is an allowable deduction – debenture interest is but a preference dividend is not)
(*b*)  less the effect of inflation
(*c*)  plus the effect of any issue expenses.

*For example*

A company has a 7% debenture; issue expenses were 3%; corporation tax is 40%; inflation is 4% pa.

In order to pay 7% on the nominal amount of the debentures it is necessary to earn $7\% \times 100 \div 97 = 7.21\%$ on the £97 actually obtained by the company after deducting the issue expenses from each £100 subscribed by the debenture holders. Debenture interest is an allowable deduction for corporation tax so the cost to the company is therefore

$$7.21\% \times (100-40) = 4.32\% \text{ in } money \text{ terms}$$

With inflation at 4% the cost to the company is

$$(104.32 \div 1.04) - 100\% = 0.30\% \text{ in } real \text{ terms}$$

*NB*. This rate of interest should be compared with the return on a project only after deducting both corporation tax and the effect of inflation on costs and income. As issue expenses, inflation and corporation tax effect different sources of finance in different degrees it is important to use the real cost of finance in capital budgeting decisions although for the sake of simplicity this is not done in this book.

It is worth while to monitor four main ratios in connection with gearing. They can all be plotted on the same graph. The four ratios and their relationship are shown in Diagram 8–1. The relationship expressed in this and the next two diagrams were developed by the author while at the Centre for Interfirm Comparison and are used in certain of its schemes.

The algebraic relationship between the ratios in Diagram 8–1 is as follows:

$$P1 = P2 + (P2 - P3) \times P4$$

Financial management's aim in raising finance is to maximise the difference between ratio P2 and ratio P3 over the likely range of ratio P3 in the medium term. It is because ratio P3 is likely to fluctuate in the short term (say up to three years) that the success of a firm's financial policy is best measured over the medium term (say three to six years).

To calculate ratios P1 to P4 use data assembly and ratio calculation sheet 8–1 at the end of this chapter.

Subsidiary ratios which should also be examined fall into two groups: ratios showing the constituent parts of the borrowed capital total and the rate of interest paid to each source of borrowed capital – *make-up-ratios* – and the ratios which lenders and potential lenders look at when assessing a company's financial strength – *constraint ratios*, so called because they measure the factors which act as constraints to the amount a firm can borrow.

Examining the ratios in the first sub-group shows which sources of finance have the most expensive rate of interest and which the cheapest. Management's task is to decrease the former and increase the latter – at least proportionately.

The second sub-group of ratios indicates which sources of finance are relatively untapped and from which, to increase the company's gearing, it should increase its borrowing.

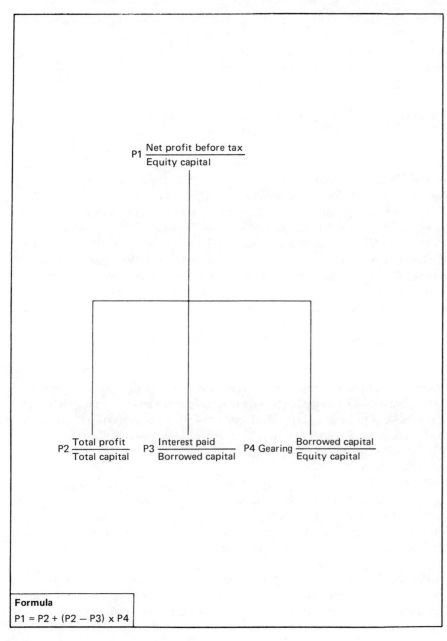

$$P1 \frac{\text{Net profit before tax}}{\text{Equity capital}}$$

$$P2 \frac{\text{Total profit}}{\text{Total capital}} \qquad P3 \frac{\text{Interest paid}}{\text{Borrowed capital}} \qquad P4 \text{ Gearing} \frac{\text{Borrowed capital}}{\text{Equity capital}}$$

**Formula**

P1 = P2 + (P2 − P3) x P4

Diagram 8–1   Gearing and return on equity.
With acknowledgements to the Centre for Interfirm Comparison.

The action outlined in the previous two paragraphs is, of course, subject to the constraint factors which, as already mentioned, potential lenders look at. These factors will be examined in a later part of this chapter.

Any action in the field of gearing needs to be considered in the context of long term movements in the rate of interest. What might appear to be a high rate of interest at the time of borrowing may be low in relation to the average rate of interest over the life of the loan. Or, of course, vice versa.

The flexibility of repayment and indeed of rates of interest is another important consideration. A debenture commits the company to paying interest for a fixed number of years but it does not have to be repaid until the end of its life (usually measured in decades). A bank overdraft does not commit a company to any particular length of time for paying interest and it can be repaid when and if it suits the company, but it will have to be repaid when the bank (or the government through the bank) wants it, which may not be at all convenient for the company. Moreover the rate of interest charged will fluctuate.

At this point it is worth examining the sources, other than the ordinary shareholder, from which a firm can raise finance. They include the following (a note has been added of the relevant interest payment):

1    Preference shares (preference dividend)
2    Debentures
3    Loans        } (debenture, loan and overdraft interest)
4    Overdrafts
5    Trade and expense creditors (cash discounts lost)
6    Corporation tax provisions
7    Deferred taxation        } (nil)
8    Capital based government grants
9    Hire purchase   } (the interest element as opposed to the
10   Leasing          } repayment element in the charge)
11   Debt factoring (the interest element as opposed to the ledger keeping and debt collection element in the charge)
12   Bill discounting (bill discount)

Traditional measures of gearing include only the first two items in borrowed capital. This restriction may stem from the fact that prior to the Companies Act 1967, information as to the amount of interest paid which had to be disclosed was limited to these two items. I prefer to include all of the items in the above list.* If any reader

---

* The arguments for this and a suggested accounting treatment for leased assets are set out in 'Towards a new measure and use of gearing'. C.A. Westwick, *Accounting & Business Research*, No. 1 Winter 1970, pp 18 to 29.

feels that this is going too far, or finds that there are difficulties in getting the necessary information, the items which are not to be included in borrowed capital and interest paid must be subtracted from assets, and profits before interest, respectively (see data assembly sheet at end of chapter).

Let us now look at the two groups of ratios already mentioned – the make-up ratios and the constraint ratios.

## Make-up ratios

This group can be divided into two sub-groups. In the first, the interest paid on each constituent part of borrowed capital is related to the relevant average amount borrowed to give the rate of interest paid on each part of borrowed capital. For example:

$$\frac{\text{Debenture interest}}{\text{Debentures}} \text{ (per cent)}$$

$$\frac{\text{Interest on overdraft}}{\text{Average overdraft}} \text{ (per cent)}$$

To calculate ratios P5-1 to P5-12 use data assembly and ratio calculation sheet 8-2 at the end of this chapter.

In the second sub-group, each constituent of borrowed capital is related to the total amount of borrowed capital to show the proportion raised from each source. For example:

$$\frac{\text{Debentures}}{\text{Total borrowed capital}} \text{ (per cent)}$$

$$\frac{\text{Average overdraft}}{\text{Total borrowed capital}} \text{ (per cent)}$$

To calculate ratios P6-1 to P6-12 use data assembly and ratio calculation sheet 8-3 at the end of this chapter.

## Constraint factors

First, there are the cover ratios:

### 1 Interest cover

$$\text{P7} \qquad \frac{\text{Total profit}}{\text{Interest paid}}$$

shows how vulnerable the lender's interest receipts are to a drop in the borrower's profit.

### 2 Asset cover

$$\text{P8} \qquad \frac{\text{Total assets}}{\text{Borrowed capital}}$$

is an indication of the safety of the lender's capital.

It is said that lenders require these two ratios to be not less than three times, but there are no doubt many exceptions to this rule of thumb in practice. Interest cover is considered the more important of the two. As Professor Paish says, a passenger is normally more interested in the speed of a ship than in the number of lifeboats.

When a company has a number of classes of loan, preference and ordinary capital, each of which has a particular place in the queue for interest or dividends the priority percentage method can be used for measuring the cover of each payment. For example, 'Five per cent debentures 0-3, preference shares 4-20, ordinary dividend 21-40, reserves 41-100' where each figure is a percentage of last year's profit after tax but before debenture interest and preference dividends.

A major constraint on borrowing is the need to maintain the company's liquidity position. The ratios to measure this are described in the next section.

## 8.3 Maintaining Liquidity

Liquidity ratios should be used not only by financial management to help maintain the firm's liquidity but by the firm's marketing and purchasing management as well. The former need to make sure that the company is selling to firms which are likely to be liquid enough to pay for their purchases. The latter wants to avoid the disruption to the company's inward flow of materials and parts which would result from a supplier going into liquidation.

### 1 The current ratio

$$\text{P9} \qquad \frac{\text{Current assets}}{\text{Current liabilities}}$$

is one test of liquidity – it looks at the assets available to pay liabilities falling due soon.

## 2    The quick ratio

P10    $$\frac{\text{Quick assets}}{\text{Current liabilities}}$$

is another, more stringent, test of liquidity in that it concentrates on those assets which can be quickly turned into cash–debtors, marketable securities and cash itself; stock is excluded.

The conventional standards for these two ratios are 2 to 1 and 1 to 1 respectively (but see below). These two ratios are what might be called first-line tests of liquidity. The interpretation which a lender puts on them will depend on the following second-line factors:

1    How quickly the borrower is turning his stock over (stock/average daily cost of sales). A fast stock turnover will excuse a lower ratio of current assets to current liabilities.

2    How quickly the borrower is getting his debts in (debtors/average daily sales). A fast debt collection will explain a low current asset/current liability ratio.

3    How much credit the borrower is taking (creditors/average daily purchases). Above average credit taken will tend to depress the ratio of current assets/current liabilities.

4    How vulnerable the borrower's profits are to a drop in turnover (fixed costs/total costs). The higher this ratio, the higher the firm's ratio of current assets to current liabilities needs to be to weather any depression. Another way of measuring this vulnerability is to calculate the 'defensive interval'. This is calculated by dividing current assets less stock by average daily cash expenditure (i.e. sales minus profit and depreciation).

5    The extent of long-term liabilities maturing in the near future.* If there are any, the current asset/current liability ratio needs to be built up in advance.

6    Proposals for capital expenditure in the future.* If there are any this will run down the current asset/current liability ratio, unless there are

7    Proposals to raise new finance soon (information on this may be found in the firm's annual report, the financial press, or in the firm's Extel card).

8    How vulnerable the company is to a squeeze on it by its creditors. This can be measured by the 'no credit interval'. This is calculated by dividing liquid assets less current liabilities by average daily cash expenditure (i.e.

---

* Information on these items must be disclosed as a result of the Companies Act.

sales less profit and depreciation). It measures how long a company could maintain its current level of operations if its creditors ceased to give it any credit.

A new liquidity ratio has been introduced recently in response to the effects of inflation on companies' liquidity. It is

$$\frac{\text{Stock} + \text{debtors} - \text{creditors}}{\text{Long-term capital}}$$

The numerator of this ratio consists of those assets (stock and debtors) which will grow in money terms as a result of inflation less the only source of finance (trade credit) which will automatically compensate for this growth. The higher this ratio is the greater will be the pressure on the company to raise new finance or to increase its dividend cover (that is, retain a higher proportion of profits) in times of inflation.

One last ratio the lender will look at is the fixed capital ratio (long term borrowed capital plus equity capital, in relation to fixed assets) to see that the assets which must remain if the business is to carry on, are financed by capital which is committed for an equally long period of time. The prudent lender prefers this ratio to be not less than unity.

All the constraint factors are summarised in Diagram 8–4

To calculate ratios P7 to P17 use data assembly and ratio calculation sheet 8-4 at the end of this chapter.

### 8.4 Z Scores

In the previous section a number of different ratios to measure liquidity were described. Some credit analysts however make use of a technique called Z scoring to combine several ratios into a single number (the Z score) the size of which gives a measure of the risk of the company getting into financial difficulty.

There are several Z score formulae but they have a common background. The various researchers took published data from groups of companies, some of which had gone bankrupt and some of which had not, and calculated many ratios for the companies in both groups.

It was then possible by statistical methods to show:

(a)    which ratios were better predictors of bankruptcy;

(b)    what weighting to give each ratio so as to combine them into a single figure (the Z score),

(The text continues on p. 181)

| P5-1 | Preference dividend/Preference shares (%) |
| P5-2 | Debenture interest/Debentures (%) |
| P5-3 | Loan interest/Loans (%) |
| P5-4 | Overdraft interest/Overdrafts (%) |
| P5-5 | Cash discounts lost/Trade and expense creditors (%) |
| P5-6 | normally there is no                       ) Corporation tax provisions |
| P5-7 | interest payable on the                  } Deferred taxation |
| P5-8 | following sources of finance            ) Investment grants |
| P5-9 | Interest element in hire purchase charge/Amount outstanding on hire purchase accounts (%) |
| P5-10 | Interest element in leasing charge/Amount outstanding on leasing accounts (%) |
| P5-11 | Interest element as opposed to the ledger keeping and debt collection element in a debt factoring charge/Debts factored (%) |
| P5-12 | Bill discount/Bills discounted (%) |

Diagram 8–2   Make-up of interest paid. With acknowledgements to the Centre for Interfirm Comparison.

| P6-1 | Preference shares/Total borrowed capital (%) |
| P6-2 | Debentures/Total borrowed capital (%) |
| P6-3 | Loans/Total borrowed capital (%) |
| P6-4 | Overdrafts/Total borrowed capital (%) |
| P6-5 | Trade and expense creditors/Total borrowed capital (%) |
| P6-6 | Corporation tax provisions/Total borrowed capital (%) |
| P6-7 | Deferred taxation/Total borrowed capital (%) |
| P6-8 | Capital based government grants/Total borrowed capital (%) |
| P6-9 | Amount outstanding on hire purchase accounts/Total borrowed capital (%) |
| P6-10 | Amount outstanding on leasing accounts/Total borrowed capital (%) |
| P6-11 | Debts factored/Total borrowed capital (%) |
| P6-12 | Bills discounted/Total borrowed capital (%) |

Diagram 8–3   Make-up of borrowed capital. With acknowledgements to the Centre for Interfirm Comparison.

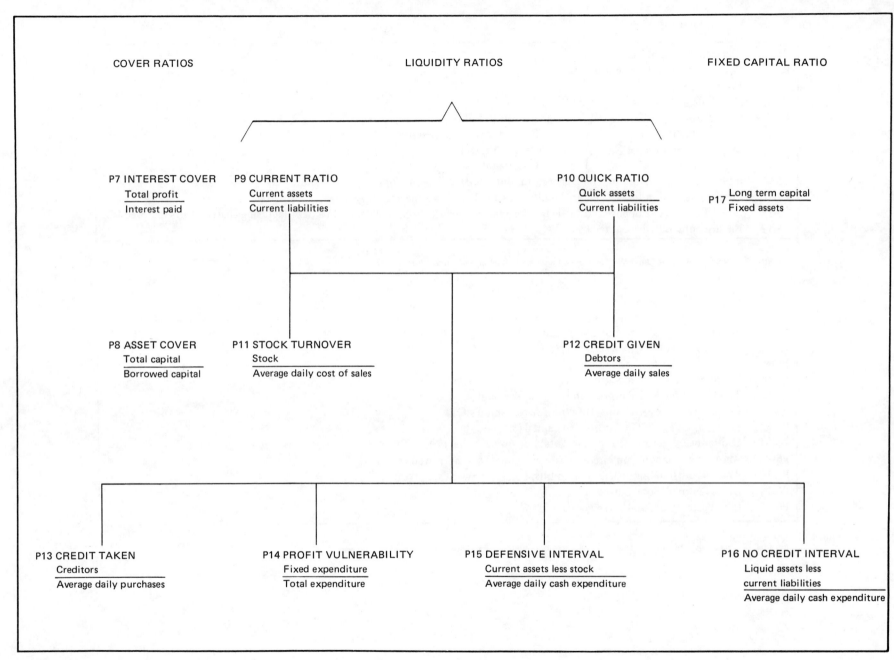

COVER RATIOS        LIQUIDITY RATIOS        FIXED CAPITAL RATIO

P7 INTEREST COVER

$$\frac{\text{Total profit}}{\text{Interest paid}}$$

P9 CURRENT RATIO

$$\frac{\text{Current assets}}{\text{Current liabilities}}$$

P10 QUICK RATIO

$$\frac{\text{Quick assets}}{\text{Current liabilities}}$$

P17 $\dfrac{\text{Long term capital}}{\text{Fixed assets}}$

P8 ASSET COVER

$$\frac{\text{Total capital}}{\text{Borrowed capital}}$$

P11 STOCK TURNOVER

$$\frac{\text{Stock}}{\text{Average daily cost of sales}}$$

P12 CREDIT GIVEN

$$\frac{\text{Debtors}}{\text{Average daily sales}}$$

P13 CREDIT TAKEN

$$\frac{\text{Creditors}}{\text{Average daily purchases}}$$

P14 PROFIT VULNERABILITY

$$\frac{\text{Fixed expenditure}}{\text{Total expenditure}}$$

P15 DEFENSIVE INTERVAL

$$\frac{\text{Current assets less stock}}{\text{Average daily cash expenditure}}$$

P16 NO CREDIT INTERVAL

$$\frac{\text{Liquid assets less current liabilities}}{\text{Average daily cash expenditure}}$$

Diagram 8–4    Constraint factors

(A 'Z score' formula is typically of the form

$$Z = C_0 + C_1 R_1 + C_2 R_2 + \ldots + C_n R_n$$

where the Cs are constants (the weights) and the $R$s are the ratios);

(c) what value for the Z scores showed:
 (i) probable bankruptcy
 (ii) probable solvency
 (iii) impossibility of prediction;

(d) how many years ahead bankruptcy could be predicted.

Some, but not all, researchers then tested their formula on a fresh batch of companies to show:

(e) the degree of confidence that could be attributed to the Z score's predictions.

Questions which analysts should ask themselves when studying the Z score literature include:

(a) Can the results obtained be transferred to a different country, and/or industry, and/or point in time?
 There is a presumption that the answer to all three questions is no, but this presumption may be rebutted by suitable evidence, but not however by mere assertion.

(b) How large is the grey area ((c) (iii) above) and how many companies fall into it? Obviously the larger the grey area the less useful the technique. But there is a trade-off between the size of the grey area and the reliability of the formula. A reduction in the size of the grey area may lead to a reduction in the reliability of the formula. Conversely an increase in the reliability of the formula may only be achievable by increasing the size of the grey area.

(c) How many years ahead can the predictions be usefully made?
 This is a difficult area because, strictly speaking, all Z score predictions should be qualified with 'provided management or others do not take some form of remedial action' and if the message of the Z score is heeded and suitable action is taken the Z score will be a self defeating prophecy. Nevertheless the size and direction of the trend of the Z score can give 2 to 3 years' warning of incipient difficulties.

(d) What was the researcher's definition of bankruptcy?

(e) Has the formula been independently validated (step (e) above)?

(f) How expensive is it
 (i) to acquire the formula and cut-off points (some are given in the literature; others have to be purchased from the researcher)

(ii) to collect the data about companies
(iii) to operate the formula?

(g) How reliable is the formula? More specifically:
 (i) how many companies in the 'safe area' went bankrupt?
 (ii) how many companies in the 'danger' area did not go bankrupt?

Along with this question there must also be considered how expensive a misclassification is likely to be. If a company in the 'safe area' goes bankrupt how much money will be lost (if it is a customer or borrower) or how much will supplies be disrupted (if the company is a supplier)? If a company in the danger area does not get into difficulties how much business and profit will have been lost by not selling to, or buying from, or investing in, the company?

(h) What (if any) other (cheaper) methods could the analyst use to arrive at the same conclusions?

Z scores may be used in a number of different situations by companies e.g.

1 As a method of credit control for new and existing customers or key suppliers.

2 In investment portfolio management:
 (a) as a prudent screen to eliminate from consideration companies with a high bankruptcy risk
 (b) for bond rating to give a risk factor to offset against the yield;

3 In turnround situations – how will proposed actions affect the company's Z score?

4 To monitor the financial viability of semi-independent subsidiaries and associates.

In addition auditors may use Z scores:

1 On audit clients to help forecast 'going concern problems' with a view to:
 (a) helping the client take suitable action in adequate time in order to avoid the danger; or
 (b) qualifying their report;

2 On some of a client's customers if debts from these customers were crucial to its continuing financial viability.

The following organisations sell Z or similar scores in the UK:

1 Datastream
2 Dun & Bradstreet

3  Performance Analysis Services

4  Credit Ratings Ltd

It is recommended that the following articles and pamphlets should be studied by the would-be user of Z scores:

D.A.J. Marais, 'A Method of Quantifying Companies' Relative Financial Strength', July 1979 (Bank of England Discussion Paper no. 4).

M. Tamari, 'Financial Ratios: analysis and prediction', Paul Elek, 1978.

E.I. Altman and T.P. McGough. 'Evaluation of a Company as a Going Concern', *Journal of Accountancy*, December 1974.

J. Argenti, 'Company Failure – long range prediction not enough', *Accountancy*, August 1977.

A. Hershman, 'How to figure who's going bankrupt', *Duns Review*, October 1975.

R. Taffler and H. Tishaw, 'Going, Going, Gone – four factors which predict', *Accountancy*, March 1977.

J. Argenti, Predicting Corporate Failure, *Accountants' Digest* no. 138, ICAEW, 1983.

## 8.5 Debtors' turnover

The control of the credit given by the company is usually part of the responsibility of the financial management although, as mentioned in Chapter 6, I believe that marketing management should also take an interest in this area too – there is not much point in selling to a customer who pays late, or even worse, never.

The most useful ratio in this area is that of Debtors to Sales. Care must be taken that such items as VAT, delivery charges, and discounts are treated in the same way in both sales and debtors. Any material cash sales should be excluded from the sales figure. There are four or five main ways to calculate this relationship. They are, in increasing order of sophistication and usefulness, as follows:

1
$$\frac{\text{Debtors at year end} \times 100}{\text{Sales for year}} \quad \text{as a percentage}$$

If the sales are for less than a year then the sales for the period should be 'annualised' by multiplying by 365 and dividing by the number of *calendar* days in the period (not the number of *selling* days) because it is the number of days' credit taken which is being measured.

2
$$\frac{\text{Debtors at end of period} \times \text{no. of days in period}}{\text{Sales for period}}$$

= no. of days credit taken by customers

Method 2 is more useful than method 1 as the resulting number can be more easily 'visualised' and related to, for example, the client's credit policy.

3  In this method the actual sales for recent weeks or months are successively subtracted from the period end debtors starting with the most recent sales and working back. This gives a more accurate measure of credit taken when sales and/or debtors are fluctuating for seasonal or other reasons.

For example:

| Sales | £000 |
|---|---|
| Jan | 50 |
| Feb | 75 |
| March | 100 |
| | £225 |

Ratio 1  Debtors/Sales =

$$\frac{£200,000 \times 100}{£225,000 \times 12 \text{ months} \div 3 \text{ months}} = 22.2\%$$

Ratio 2  Debtors/Average daily sales =

$$\frac{£200,000 \times 365 \text{ days} \times 3 \text{ months}}{£225,000 \times 12 \text{ months}} = \underline{81 \text{ days}}$$

Ratio 3

| | | |
|---|---|---|
| Debtors | £200,000 | |
| less March | 100,000 | = 31 days |
| | 100,000 | |
| less Feb | 75,000 | = 28 days |
| | 25,000 | |

£25,000 = ½ of Jan's sales of £50,000 therefore add ½ × 31 days    = 15 ½ days

74 ½ days

4    The most sophisticated approach is an age analysis, e.g.

| | |
|---|---|
| Debtors end March | £200,000 |
| relates to items invoiced in: | |

| | |
|---|---|
| March | 80,000 |
| Feb | 65,000 |
| Jan | 45,000 |
| Dec | 5,000 |
| Earlier | 5,000 |
| | £200,000 |

The results of this should be compared with the terms the company allows and with a similar analysis carried out at the end of the previous period. This approach may not be difficult if such an analysis is part of a sales ledger computer package used by the company.

5    Another approach is to analyse the debtors by customer:

| | No. of customers | Amount owed (£) |
|---|---|---|
| Owing more than £10,000 | 1 | 15,000 |
| Owing between £5,000–£10,000 | 4 | 28,000 |
| Owing between £2,000–£5,000 | 20 | 60,000 |
| Owing less than £2,000 | 75 | 97,000 |
| | 100 | £200,000 |

Both approaches 4 and 5 are useful in helping to identify the vulnerability of the company to bad debts and will help the accountant form a judgement on the adequacy of the bad debt provision. Large accounts and overdue accounts need particularly careful attention.

## 8.6 Supervision of the Firm's Investments

The investor measures the success of his investment over any period of time by the ratio of his income after taxation to the cost of the original investment (or to its value at the beginning of the period being measured). This is ratio Q1 in Diagram 8–5.

I have included in 'income' both the dividend that he has received and the capital gain over the period as this seems common sense. Some accountants may disagree with this, but so as not to bore the general reader I have included the arguments for and against this approach in an appendix to this chapter.

The size of ratio Q1 is determined by four factors (measured by ratios Q2 to Q5):

1    The size of the dividend (the ratio of the gross dividend to his original investment) – ratio Q2.
2    The capital gain (the ratio of the increase of the value of his shareholding to its original cost, that is, I am including all capital gains whether or not they have been 'realised') – ratio Q3.
3    The rate of tax on the dividend – ratio Q4.
4    The rate of tax on the capital gain – ratio Q5.

The size of a company's dividend is affected by a combination of its profitability and its directors' policy on distribution of profit (both of these subjects are dealt with later in this chapter).

The magnitude of the investor's capital gain (ratio Q3) and indeed whether it is positive or negative – is determined by changes in the view of the Stock Exchange of what is the discounted present value of the future dividends of the company. This view will be a compound of:

1    Rates of interest both present and expected
2    An assessment of the rate of growth of the company in general and of its dividends in particular
3    An assessment of the degree of risk to which the company is subjected either directly or indirectly via the industry and/or country in which it operates.

The magnitude of the investor's capital gain (ratio Q3) tends to increase if

1    Rates of interest (factor 1) decrease
2    The rate of the company's growth (factor 2) increases
3    The amount of risk to which the company is subjected (factor 3) decreases.

An investment analyst, when assessing the likely size of a company's dividends in the future (factor 2 above), will probably go through the following analytical steps:

1    What is the likely pattern of demand for the products of the industry

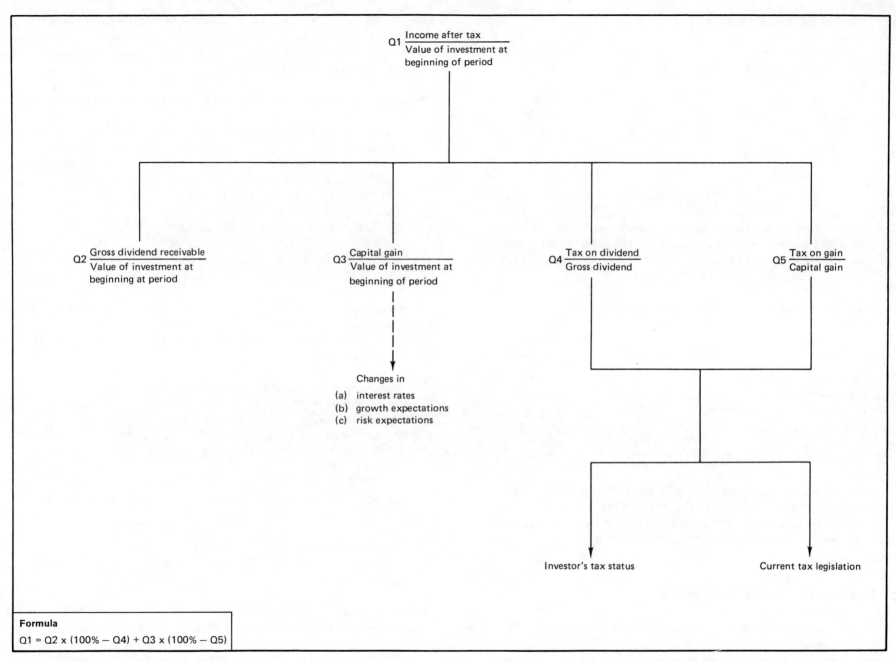

Diagram 8–5   Investor ratios

184

(or industries) in which the company operates? This will depend on the following factors among others:

(a) the point that the analyst believes to have been reached in the 'trade cycle' or 'stop-go' process and his expectations regarding the likely pattern of development of this cycle.

(b) the nature of the industry – in particular whether it is producing consumption goods such as bread, consumer durables such as cars, or capital goods such as machine tools

(c) the quantity of stocks in any pipeline between the industry and the ultimate consumer

(d) any abnormal factors affecting the industry, such as likely fall off in boom demand after introduction of new products; exceptional crops of basic raw material; foreign competition/demand for product; tariff changes; etc.

2    What is the likely share of the industry's sales which this company will get? This will depend on the following factors among others:

(a) its share in the past

(b) the success of any efforts by it or its competitors to change that share

(c) special factors (new products, production processes, selling or delivery methods, etc.)

3    Given the company's likely sales from step 2 what are its profits likely to be? This will depend on the following factors among others:

(a) the size of stocks that it is carrying or, for capital goods industries, the length of its order book, (that is, how much of these sales will need to be/can be met from current production capacity)

(b) the proportion of its costs which are fixed (that is, which are not likely to change significantly with the anticipated change in volume)

(c) any changes in price for the company's product (from the affects of competition or the lack of it)

(d) any changes in the prices of the company's inputs (such as materials and labour) from the effects of competition (or lack of it), unionism, inflation, etc.

4    Given the profit (from step 3), what are the earnings for the ordinary shareholder going to be? This will depend on

(a) prior charges (such as debenture interest and preference dividends)

(b) tax.

5    Given the earnings, what is the dividend likely to be? This will depend on

(a) the payout ratio or dividend cover (see p. 186) maintained in the past

(b) management's estimate of the permanence of any change in earn-ings (any short-lived change is less likely to affect the dividends – the cover ratio will be allowed to change instead)

(c) whether the earnings are going up or down – directors are more reluctant to cut a dividend (provided it is not 'uncovered') than to increase one

(d) the amount of cash available. Part or all of the profit may have already been invested in assets or used to repay liabilities or may be needed for new investment (either for replacement of assets or for expansion) and may not therefore be available for dividend

(e) tactical reasons. Management may wish to influence the company's share price if it is making a bid for another company, repelling a bid, or contemplating a rights issue.

The magnitude of ratio Q3 is affected by the consensus of views arrived at by reasoning similar to the above. The rate of tax paid on dividends and payable on capital gains (ratios Q4 and Q5) will depend on the combination of the investor's tax status (company or individual, basic or higher rate tax payer) and current tax legislation.

As an example, assume that X, a higher rate taxpayer, bought 100 shares at £1.25 each in Y Limited. During the year he receives a dividend of 5 per cent and at the end of the year the shares are worth £1.50 each. He pays income tax at 50 per cent and capital gains tax at 30 per cent. Indexation of the gain is ignored but could be material over a longer period.

| | |
|---|---:|
| Gross dividend (100 at 5 per cent) | £5.00 |
| Less income tax at 50 per cent | £2.50 |
| Net dividend | £2.50 |
| Capital gain – unrealised (100 × £0.25) | £25.00 |
| Less provision for capital gains tax at 30 per cent | £7.50 |
| Net gain | £17.50 |
| Total income after tax | £20.00 |

$$Q1 \quad \frac{\text{Income after tax}}{\text{Value of investment at beginning of period}}$$
$$£20 \div £125.00 = 16.0\%$$

$$Q2 \quad \frac{\text{Gross dividend receivable}}{\text{Original value of investment}}$$
$$£5.00 \div £125.00 = 4.0\%$$

$$Q3 \quad \frac{\text{Capital gain}}{\text{Original value of investment}}$$
$$£25.00 \div £125.00 = 20.0\%$$

Q4

$$\frac{\text{Tax on dividend}}{\text{Gross dividend}}$$

£2.50 ÷ £5.00 = 50.0%

Q5

$$\frac{\text{Tax on gain}}{\text{Capital gain}}$$

£7.50 ÷ £25.00 = 30.0%

To calculate ratios Q1 to Q5 use data assembly and ratio calculation sheet 8–5 at the end of this chapter.

## Risk

As part of the process of managing his investments the investor needs to consider not only the returns he is getting, or hopes to get, but the risks he is incurring in the process. Generally speaking the higher the return that is on offer then the higher the risk of loss.

Analysts talk in terms of two types of risk: market (or systematic) risk and specific (or non-market) risk. Market risk is measured by the *beta* of a company's shares. A beta of 1.2 means that for every 1 per cent that market prices move on average (measured by the FT or some other index) then that company's shares will tend to move 1.2 per cent. Beta's tend to fall within the range 0.5 to 1.5.

Specific risk relates to factors within a company such as:

(*a*)    the industry it operates within;
(*b*)    its financial gearing (see 8.2, p. 174);
(*c*)    its operating gearing (see 5.4, p. 102).

The importance of the distinction between market and specific risk is that the investor can reduce the latter by diversifying his investment but he cannot insulate himself from market risk in the same way.

## 8.7 The Company and the Stock Exchange

When considering the purchase or sale of an investment of the company, financial management will find it useful to be familiar with the ratios used by stockbrokers, investment analysts, and the financial press. Other occasions when such familiarity will be of use include: the raising of new equity capital; the making of a take-over bid for another company where part or all of the consideration is shares in the bidding company; the receipt of such a bid from another company; a merger.

The ratios have been put into a logical framework in order to bring out their inter-relationship. Financial commentators do not appear to use such a framework of analysis in a formal manner. It is possible that they might find their analysis eased by the following approach.

The first ratio in Diagram 8–6 is the dividend yield of the company. That is the most recent annual dividend per ordinary share divided by the present price of the share. The *dividend yield* is *not* the same as the *rate of dividend declared* by the company. The latter is the total gross dividend as a percentage of the nominal value of the ordinary shares. For example, if a company has a share capital of 1000 £1 shares and declares a dividend of 10 per cent it will be paying out 10 per cent of £1000, that is £100 or 10p per share.

The dividend yield is the gross (before personal tax) rate of return an investor would receive if:

1    The dividend rate is unchanged, and
2    He paid the current market price of the share.

For example, if the price of the above shares was £2, the dividend yield would be:

$$\frac{10p \times 100}{£2} = 5\%$$

It is only when the market price equals the nominal value of the share that the dividend *yield* and the dividend *rate* are equal.

The dividend rate has little meaning. The dividend yield is the actual current rate of return being earned by the shareholder on the investment. The size of ratio R1 depends on:

1    The earnings yield (profit after corporation tax, minorities and preference dividend but before ordinary dividend per share divided by the present price of the share) – ratio R2
2    The dividend cover (profit after corporation tax, minorities and preference dividends divided by the ordinary gross dividend) – ratio R3.

Ratio R1 increases if either ratio R2 increases (generally a satisfactory sign) or ratio R3 decreases (which might be an unhealthy sign, or merely a correction of ultra-conservatism in the past, or an indication that management considers the drop in ratio R2 to be a temporary phenomenon).

In recent years it has become increasingly fashionable, and it is now standard practice, to use the P/E or price/earnings ratio (ratio R2a) as a substitute for, or in

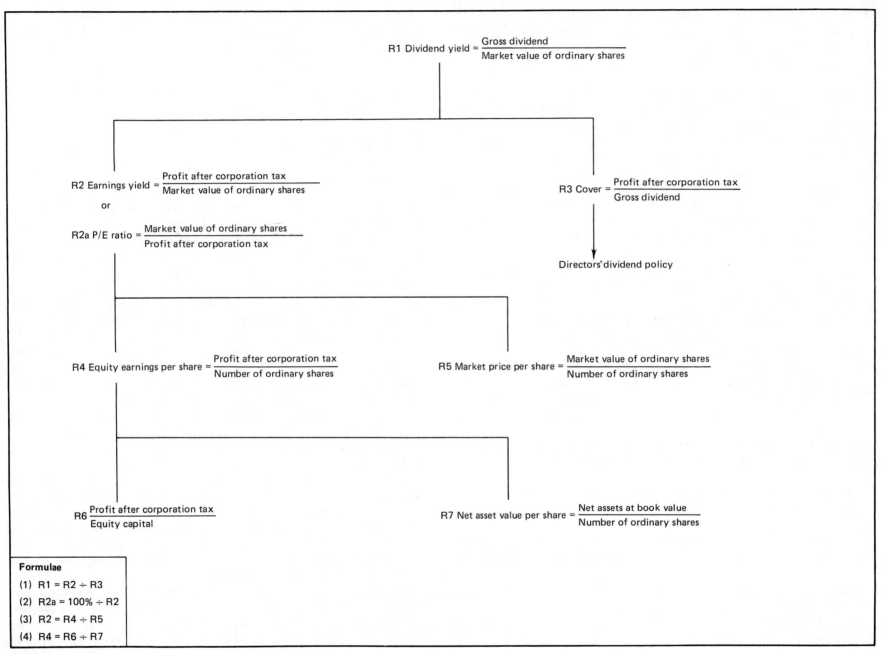

R1 Dividend yield $= \dfrac{\text{Gross dividend}}{\text{Market value of ordinary shares}}$

R2 Earnings yield $= \dfrac{\text{Profit after corporation tax}}{\text{Market value of ordinary shares}}$

or

R2a P/E ratio $= \dfrac{\text{Market value of ordinary shares}}{\text{Profit after corporation tax}}$

R3 Cover $= \dfrac{\text{Profit after corporation tax}}{\text{Gross dividend}}$

Directors' dividend policy

R4 Equity earnings per share $= \dfrac{\text{Profit after corporation tax}}{\text{Number of ordinary shares}}$

R5 Market price per share $= \dfrac{\text{Market value of ordinary shares}}{\text{Number of ordinary shares}}$

R6 $\dfrac{\text{Profit after corporation tax}}{\text{Equity capital}}$

R7 Net asset value per share $= \dfrac{\text{Net assets at book value}}{\text{Number of ordinary shares}}$

**Formulae**

(1)  R1 = R2 ÷ R3

(2)  R2a = 100% ÷ R2

(3)  R2 = R4 ÷ R5

(4)  R4 = R6 ÷ R7

Diagram 8–6   Stock Exchange ratios

addition to, the earnings yield. One is merely the reciprocal of the other. A P/E of 12.5 for example is equivalent to an earnings yield of 8.0 per cent. Thus the concept is one of the share price representing so many times or year's purchase of earnings, rather than the earnings representing a certain percentage return on the cost of the investment.

The advantage of using P/E ratios rather than earnings yields is that they facilitate international comparisons, particularly with American stocks because this is the generally accepted yardstick of share evaluation in the United States. The disadvantage is that the P/E ratio cannot be directly compared with the dividend yield to show the extent to which the dividend is covered. Nor can it be directly compared with the returns available on fixed interest or other investments.

P/E ratios are published in a number of papers, including the *Financial Times* and *The Times*. As standards of comparison they require to be used with caution however as different papers (and different stockbrokers) calculate the Earnings part of the ratio in different ways. The main areas of difference are:

1  The treatment of corporation tax (the alternatives are: to use the figure in the accounts; to substitute a 'normal' charge where the figure in the accounts is sub-or super-normal)
2  The treatment of extraordinary items in the profit and loss account
3  The treatment of convertible loan stock (some brokers calculate the P/E ratio by dividing the price per share by the earnings per share and in calculating the latter in appropriate circumstances increase earnings by the amount of interest which will be saved when the loan stock is converted to ordinary shares and increase the number of ordinary shares by the number of new ones).

The subject is discussed at length in SSAP3 on Earnings per share (see below). The size of a company's earnings yield (ratio R2) is determined by:

1  The equity earnings per share (ratio R4) and
2  The market price per share (ratio R5).

All listed companies are required by SSAP3 to show their earnings per share (EPS) at the foot of their profit and loss accounts. These may be shown on the following bases:

(*a*)  Net (undiluted)
(*b*)  Nil (undiluted)
(*c*)  Net (fully diluted)
(*d*)  Nil (fully diluted).

In the UK when a company pays a dividend the shareholder receives with it a tax credit which he can offset against his tax bill. With income tax at 30 per cent the tax credit is 3/7ths of the dividend received by the shareholder. For example:

| | | | | |
|---|---|---|---|---|
| 1 | Tax rate of investor (%) | 0 | 30 | 50 |
| 2 | Cash dividend (£) | 7 | 7 | 7 |
| 3 | Tax credit (£) | 3 | 3 | 3 |
| 4 | Tax payable on (£) | 10 | 10 | 10 |
| 5 | Tax due (line 4 × line 1) | – | 3 | 5 |
| 6 | Less tax credit (line 3) | 3 | 3 | 3 |
| 7 | Tax refund/(due) (£) | 3 | – | (2) |

However, the company has to pay an amount equal to the tax credit to the Inland Revenue as Advance Corporation Tax (ACT). This ACT can be recovered against the company's corporation tax liability. Sometimes, however, the company's corporation tax liability is less than the amount of ACT (because e.g. of overseas earnings taxed overseas, high capital allowances, tax losses). In such a situation the ACT is not recoverable and forms part of the company's UK tax charge. Because the amount of tax payable may vary with the size of dividend, companies calculate two EPS figures: net – after tax payable as a result of dividends paid and proposed; and nil – after tax payable on the assumption that *no* dividend was paid or proposed.

The advantage of the nil basis is that it produces a figure of earnings which does not depend on the level of distribution and so provides an indicator of one company's performance more closely comparable with that of another. The advantage of the net basis is that it takes account of all the relevant facts, including the additional tax liabilities inherent in the dividend policy pursued by the company for which the directors should no less be accountable to shareholders. ASC considered therefore that listed companies should report in their accounts earnings per share primarily on the net basis.

Where, however, there is a material difference between earnings per share calculated on the net basis and on the nil distribution basis, ASC regards it as most desirable that the latter also be shown.

If a company has convertible loan stock, or shares which did not rank for dividend this year but will do so in the future, or has granted options to subscribe for equity shares in the future, then the number of shares is likely to increase in the future and, all other things being equal, the EPS will decline.

Fully diluted EPS are calculated by (a) increasing the number of shares in issue by the number to be issued if the various options are exercised, (b), in the case of convertible loan stock, increasing earnings by the amount of interest to be saved on conversion (less the tax effect of not paying the interest) and (c) calculating EPS using the revised figures for shares and earnings.

Although EPS are widely quoted they do have several disadvantages:

1   Two companies could be identical in all respects except for the nominal value of their shares. This purely paper difference will make their EPS different.
2   If a company issues bonus shares its EPS will decline but there has been no decline in its profitability.
3   If, as is usual, a company retains part of its earnings and does not pay them all out as dividends, and if it earns the same return on these retained earnings as on its previous capital base, the EPS will increase even though returns on equity capital has remained stationary.

Although EPS has these disadvantages the earnings part of the ratio is useful for calculating other ratios such as the Price/Earnings ratio (see above) and Return on Equity capital (see below).

We have already described the factors affecting the market price of a share (ratio R5) in our discussion of ratio Q3 above (see pp 183 and 185). Equity earnings per share (ratio R4) are affected by the size of two ratios:

1   The net profit on the equity capital of the company (ratio R6)
2   The net asset value per share (the book value of the ordinary capital and reserves divided by the number of ordinary shares) — ratio R7.

Ratio R7 (net asset value per share) provides a necessary mathematical link between equity earnings per share (ratio R4) and net profit on equity capital (ratio R6) in that ratio R4 = ratio R6 divided by ratio R7. Some investment analysts and financial journalists endow it with a significance, particularly in relation to the market price per share (ratio R5). My own view is that any difference between market price and asset value per share is a reflection of the different approach of the stock exchange and of the company accountant. The stock exchange bases its valuations on what it can perceive in the future; the accountant bases his valuation on what has been spent in the past. Or, to express the difference more elaborately, the former is, broadly speaking, always estimating a discounted present value for a hypothetical stream of future (growing or contracting) receipts. The latter is accumulating, in accordance with generally accepted conventions, a depreciated sum of past expenditures.

The size of the asset value per share (ratio R7) does provide to some extent a lower limit for the market price (ratio R5). How far market price will fall below asset value per share in adverse circumstances depends partly on the marketability of the firm's assets and partly on takeover hopes. If the assets are very specific in their use, asset value per share provides negligible protection to the market price.

To some extent the ratio of R5 to R7 (that is of the market price to the net asset value) is a measure of the market's opinion of the management of the company. The more of a company's assets that are human as opposed to physical, the more likely are ratios R5 and R7 to diverge. Such companies are catered for in Chapter 11.3 and 11.4. A leading firm of London stockbrokers has a rule of thumb that says they need to have strong reasons for recommending a share standing at, say, more than three times its asset value. Similarly they hesitate in recommending a sale of shares whose price is, say, less than half the asset value.

In using the ratio of asset values per share it is necessary to consider the following questions:

1   Are the asset values realistic? Is property undervalued (because of, for example, the effects of inflation)? Could stock realise its book value in conditions of a forced sale?
2   How marketable are the assets? Property, quoted investments and, of course, cash are usually highly marketable; stock, plant and machinery, debtors are often much less marketable.
3   What is the company's gearing (see p. 174)? In a highly geared company a small drop in asset value could wipe the ordinary shareholders' stake out of existence. Conversely a small rise in value could make a big jump in equity assets.

An investment analyst's reactions to the size of a company's profit on equity capital ratio (ratio R6) would be as follows:

1   If profit on equity capital is high for the industry, can the company maintain it? Is it high because of good management or because of lack of competition? If the profit on equity capital is likely to drop, when will the crunch come? Have the management sufficient foresight, ability and resources to bring out a new winner as the old one fades before competition or change in demand?
2   If profit on equity capital is low for the industry what recovery potential has the company, or is it doomed to go to the wall?

Some of the main factors which affect a company's net profit after tax are shown in Diagram 8–7. These have been described earlier in this chapter.

As an example of the applications of ratios R1 to R7, assume that firm *Y* has 1 800 000 £1 ordinary shares, the market price of which is £1.50. It declared a dividend of 5 per cent on profits after tax of £200 000. Its net assets were £2 200 000.

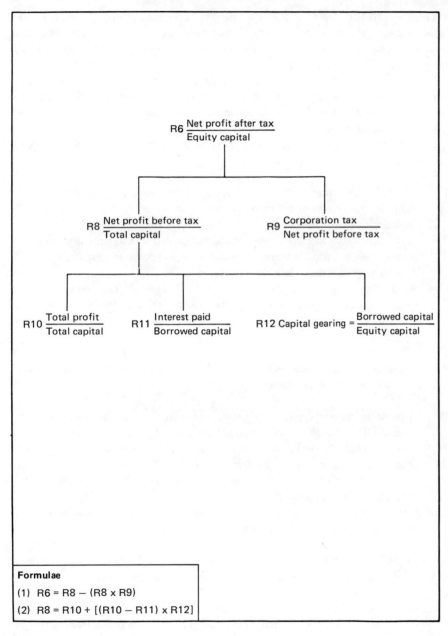

R6 $\dfrac{\text{Net profit after tax}}{\text{Equity capital}}$

R8 $\dfrac{\text{Net profit before tax}}{\text{Total capital}}$    R9 $\dfrac{\text{Corporation tax}}{\text{Net profit before tax}}$

R10 $\dfrac{\text{Total profit}}{\text{Total capital}}$    R11 $\dfrac{\text{Interest paid}}{\text{Borrowed capital}}$    R12 Capital gearing = $\dfrac{\text{Borrowed capital}}{\text{Equity capital}}$

**Formulae**

(1) R6 = R8 − (R8 × R9)

(2) R8 = R10 + [(R10 − R11) × R12]

Diagram 8–7   Overall company ratios

R1    Dividend yield    $= \dfrac{\text{Gross dividend}}{\text{Market value of ordinary shares}}$

$= \dfrac{\text{£1 800 000} \times 5\%}{\text{1 800 000} \times \text{£1.50}}$    = 3.3%

R2    Earnings yield    $= \dfrac{\text{Profit after corporation tax}}{\text{Market value of ordinary shares}}$

$= \dfrac{\text{£200 000}}{\text{1 800 000} \times \text{£1.50}}$    =7.4%

R2a    P/E ratio    $= \dfrac{\text{£2 700 000}}{\text{200 000}}$    = 13.5

R3    Cover    $= \dfrac{\text{Profit after corporation tax}}{\text{Gross dividend}}$

$= \dfrac{\text{£200 000}}{\text{£90 000}}$    = 2.2 times

R4    Equity earnings per share    $= \dfrac{\text{Profit after corporation tax}}{\text{Number of ordinary shares}}$

$= \dfrac{\text{£200 000}}{\text{1 800 000}}$    = £0.11

R5    Market price per share (given)    = £1.50

R6    Return on equity capital    $= \dfrac{\text{Profit after corporation tax}}{\text{Equity capital}}$

$= \dfrac{\text{£200 000}}{\text{£2 200 000}}$    = 9.1%

R7    Net asset value per share    $= \dfrac{\text{£2 000 000}}{\text{1 800 000}}$    = £1.22

To calculate ratios R1 to R7 use data assembly and ratio calculation sheet 8–6 at the end of this chapter.

To calculate ratios R8 to R12 use data assembly and ratio calculation sheet 8–7 at the end of this chapter.

## 8.8 Supervision of Data Processing

In supervising the firm's accounting and data processing functions financial management is concerned with how much of the firm's income is being spent on these functions. They will seek, within the constraints imposed upon them by other aspects of the company's policy, to minimise the ratio

$$\text{S1} \qquad \frac{\text{Data processing costs}}{\text{Sales}}$$

Data processing costs will include the salaries and wages of, and National Insurance and pension contributions for the relevant staff, depreciation and/or hire charges of the machinery, and may include an appropriate part of the rent, rates, heat, light, cleaning and so on of the offices used, plus software costs and data bureau costs if applicable.

The costs of data processing are caused not so much by the value of sales but by the volume of transactions. Transactions are the sum of all the items entering the system, such as all purchases, payments, sales, receipts, transfers, and so on. So financial management monitors two other ratios:

$$\text{S2} \qquad \frac{\text{Data processing costs}}{\text{Transactions}}$$

$$\text{S3} \qquad \frac{\text{Transactions}}{\text{Sales}}$$

It may be possible to reduce the first by using different methods of processing, by increasing mechanisation and employing cheaper, less skilled staff. To cut down the number of transactions in relation to the value of sales calls for the co-operation of other departments in increasing the value of orders placed or received on any one occasion, by decreasing the frequency of payments (by changing from weekly to monthly payment for employees), and so on.

To calculate ratios S1 to S3 use data assembly and ratio calculation sheet 8–8 at the end of this chapter.

The data processing department will also be producing reports. Ideally, one would have a ratio of

$$\text{S4} \qquad \frac{\text{Value (to management) of reports}}{\text{Cost of producing them}}$$

However, it is likely to be difficult to persuade management to put a monetary value on the reports they ask for and/or get. It might be a salutary exercise for all concerned if the exercise was tried though! As an alternative it would be possible to attach a note of the cost of producing a report to the document itself.

Another exercise which it would be worth carrying out periodically – particularly if the number of reports required tended, as it nearly always does, to grow – is as follows. Ask the users of reports to rank them in order of their usefulness. This ranking can be built up by means of the paired comparison technique. Each user is asked to compare each report he receives with each other report and to decide whether:

1   Report *A* is more useful than *B* (*A* is awarded 2 points)
2   Report *B* is more useful than *A* (*B* is awarded 2 points)
3   Reports *A* and *B* are of equal value – this 'decision' or lack of decision is to be discouraged (*A* and *B* are awarded 1 point each).

The data processing department assesses the marginal cost of producing the report (that is, the cost that would be saved by the data processing and other departments if the report were not produced). The points awarded to the report and its marginal cost are then graphed as in Diagram 8–8. The area of the graph can be subdivided into three bands as shown.

*Band A.* High-value low-cost reports. Almost certainly should be continued.
*Band B.* Value more or less in line with cost (that is, either high-value high-cost, or low-value low-cost, or medium-value medium-cost). The production of these reports should be given a mild degree of questioning.
*Band C.* Low-value high-cost reports. The case for dropping these is high. Arguments for retaining them must be strong.

For ratios used by the Government's Chessington Computer Centre see Chapter 14.4.15.

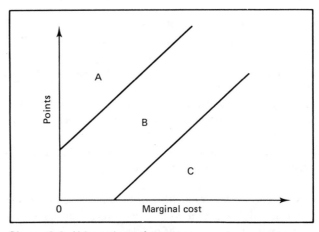

Diagram 8–8   Value and cost of reports

## 8.9 Pension Funds and Costs

One of the areas that is often part of the finance department's responsibilities is the administration of the firm's pension scheme or schemes. The finance director may or may not be a Trustee of the scheme(s), but he will often be asked to comment on the Pension Fund's report(s).

The personnel department will also be interested in this area as pensions rights are an increasingly important part of employees' terms and conditions of employment.

It must be admitted however that pension fund reports are often significantly harder to interpret than ordinary company accounts.

Part of the difficulty stems from the combination of: the very long term nature of the fund; unfamiliar terminology; and differences in actuarial and accounting practices between actuaries and funds.

However, the ASC proposed in April 1984, with the publication of an exposure draft of a non-mandatory statement of recommended practice (a SORP) on Pension Scheme Accounts, to improve the situation. The Government also proposes to issue regulations on the content, audit and filing of pension fund accounts but few details are yet available (Social Security Act 1985).

The ASC proposes that a Pension Fund's Annual Report should consist of:

1   A trustees' report
2   Accounts
3   An actuarial report
4   An investment report

The reader of such a report should look at the actuary's report to see:

(*a*)   if it is up to date – the more out of date the less valuable;
(*b*)   what it is based on – there are broadly two possible bases:

   (i)    the ability of the present funds to meet accrued benefits (i.e. on a discontinuance basis);
   (ii)   the adequacy of the present funds and future contribution levels to meet promised benefits when due (i.e. on a going concern basis).

   A deficit on basis (i) is more serious than on basis (ii). Basis (ii) is preferable as it better reflects the fund's long term nature.

(*c*)   what is the surplus or deficit on either or both of the above bases;
(*d*)   what are the actuary's recommendations for future contribution levels from the employer and employee in the light of (*c*);

(*e*)   what is the Trustees' response to (*d*).

The investment report should give some idea of the spread of investments in different sectors and the return being obtained on them (see Chapter 8.6 for suggested ratios for the management of investments). Two items which should also be looked for are:

(*a*)   any material investment by the fund in the shares of the employer – such investment puts the employees' pension as well as his job at risk if the employer experiences difficulties;
(*b*)   any undue concentration of investment in any particular sector or company.

ASC recommends the following layout for pension scheme accounts with individual items supported by more detailed disclosure

| *Revenue account* | | |
|---|---|---|
| Contributions receivable | | X |
| Investment income | | X |
| Other income | | X |
| | | X |
| Benefits payable | X | |
| Other payments | X | |
| Administrative expenses | X | |
| | | X |
| Net new money available for investment (A) | | X |

| *Net assets statement* | |
|---|---|
| Investment assets | X |
| Long term borrowings | (X) |
| Current assets and liabilities | X |
| Total value of fund (B) | X |

| *Movement of funds statement* | |
|---|---|
| Opening balance of funds employed | X |
| Net new money invested per revenue account (A) | X |
| Change in market value of investments | X |
| Closing balance of funds employed (B) | X |

Investments should be carried at market value but are often shown only at cost. Administrative costs are often borne by the employer and not charged to the fund.

The ASC has also made proposals, in a Consultative Statement of Intent on Pension Costs (November 1984), for the way in which companies should account for their pension costs in their own accounts.

Many companies currently charge in their profit and loss account the amount paid over to the pension fund. ASC proposes that the amount charged should aim to produce a substantially level percentage of current and future pensionable payroll and that this percentage should be published. ASC also proposes that the amount charged should be analysed between regular costs and variations from them arising from, for example, experience surpluses or deficiencies, changes in conditions for membership or in benefits, increases to pensions in payment or deferred pensions.

ASC is seeking views whether companies should disclose, in addition to the ratio of profit and loss actual charge/pensionable payroll (per cent), the following two ratios:

1   The standard normal rate (per cent) i.e. the contribution rate that would be required to provide a typical group of new entrants with the benefits promised by the pension scheme as it now stands.
2   The standard additional rate (per cent) i.e. that percentage of pensionable payroll which, on the assumptions made by the actuary in his valuation, would amortise any unprovided obligation over the remaining working lives of the current workforce.

If the standard normal rate and standard additional rate taken together rise above the actual percentage cost, this would suggest that an unprovided obligation has arisen during the period, and vice versa.

The standard normal rate will be some indication of the level to which the actual charge ought to tend if the standard additional rate is no longer needed in due course and if the funding level then remains steady.

ASC comments that such disclosures may entail too much detail and for this reason they are not being proposed as standard practice; however Finance Directors may well want to have them provided for their own monitoring role.

In addition to those already mentioned the following ratios may also help. They are based on suggestions by F.G. Burianek in the *Financial Executive*, January 1981, pp. 29–36, modified for use in the UK.

1   *Pension cost to adjusted operating profit*: this measures how large the pension cost is in relation to the funds available to meet it. Adjusted operating profit is profit before deducting pension costs, interest and taxes. As pension costs are deductible for tax purposes it is reasonable to relate them to the pre-tax profit. As the need to pay interest to lenders may be more pressing than the need to make payments to the pension fund, I would suggest that interest should be deducted in arriving at

adjusted operating profit.
2   *Variability ratio*: how much of the pension costs relates to amortisation of past actuarial deficiencies, etc.
3   *Pension costs after tax per ordinary share*: measures the impact of the pension scheme on earnings per share.
4   *Amount 'owed' to or by fund/size of fund*.

Pension costs, although they should be accrued in the employer's accounts, are not necessarily paid over to the fund at the same time. Moreover the fund may be in actuarial surplus or deficit. The amount of advanced funding, or the amount the company owes the fund, as a percentage of the fund or of the pension cost for the year, may indicate the company has surplus liquidity or liquidity problems depending on which way the money is 'owed'. A large amount owed to the fund makes the fund vulnerable to any difficulties experienced by the employer. A significant advanced funding may indicate lower costs to the employer in the future.

For those wanting to learn more about this subject I would recommend:

*Pensions Terminology*, The Pensions Management Institute, 1984.
*Annual Survey of Occupational Pension Schemes*, National Association of Pension Funds.
*Occupational Pension Schemes*, Survey by the Government Actuary, HMSO
*Population, Pension Costs and Pensioners' Incomes*, DHSS, HMSO, 1984
*Pension Scheme Accounts: A Discussion Paper*, ASC, 1982
*Pension Scheme Accounts*, ED34, ASC, 1984
*Disclosure of Pension Information in Company Account*, ED32, ASC, 1983
*Accounting for the cost of pensions*, C.J. Napier, ICAEW, 1983
*Accounting for Pension Costs, A consultative statement of intent*, ASC, 1984

### 8.10 The Company's Auditors

The company's financial staff are those most likely to be involved with the company's auditors. The company will expect good financial, accounting and tax advice from its auditors, in addition to a thorough but quick audit at a reasonable fee. One of the ways in which auditors, internal as well as external, can keep their costs and fees down in suitable cases is by using a technique called Analytical Review which involves the use of ratios. For more information on this technique see *Do the figures make sense?: a practical guide to analytical review*, C.A. Westwick, ICAEW, 1981, and *Analytical Review*, D.G. Smith, Canadian Institute of Chartered Accountants, 1983.

The auditors' report is dealt with in Chapter 13.6.

**Appendix 8.1**

## A NOTE ON CAPITAL GAINS

Should capital gains be included in an investor's income as well as the dividend(s) he has received? Obviously there are differences between dividends and capital gains:

1    A dividend is received in cash, whereas a capital gain is an increase in the value of the share on the market. The company will not ask for the dividend back, but a change in market sentiment may quickly reduce a capital gain.

2    Dividends and capital gains are taxed at different rates and in different ways. It is because of this that capital gains are more attractive for a higher rate tax payer than dividends.

3    Trustee and executorship law distinguishes firmly between the treatment of items deemed to be income and capital.

Against these differences need to be set such considerations as the following:

1    Dividends can be reinvested, with the result that they are no longer cash but are part of the value of the share. They then begin to look very similar to capital gains. Most building societies and unit trusts have provisions for the automatic investment of dividends. Some unit trusts have accumulator units where all income is automatically reinvested.

2    Capital gains can be realised in whole or in part. They then begin to look similar to dividends. At least one property bond has a plan for the automatic withdrawal of capital gains.

3    Some accountants appear to be worried that the capital gain has not been realised.

Yet, as one author has pointed out, it would be impossible to distinguish between $A$ who holds shares in company $X$ on which there is an unrealised capital gain, and $B$ who also holds shares in company $X$ but who has realised his capital gain and used the proceeds to reinvest in company $X$. Except, of course, that $B$ has had to pay dealing expenses and has turned his liability to capital gains tax from a contingent to an actual one.

I wonder whether accountants would have the same reservations about combining dividends and capital gains if the latter were 'losses'. I suspect that they would be happier to reduce dividend income by unrealised capital losses to show a net figure of disposable income.

When evaluating the performance of an investment, and particularly when comparing one investment with another, I consider that a more meaningful result is obtained by adding together the gross dividend(s) and the capital gain and subtracting from this sum the income tax, and capital gains tax either paid or payable. Readers who disagree with this can simplify Diagram 8–5 by the omission of ratios Q3 and Q5 and by changing the numerator of ratio Q1 to 'Net dividend'.

Data assembly sheet number 8–1 will be found on the following page

**Gearing and return on equity**

| Code letter | Item | Month or quarter to (date) | | | | | |
|---|---|---|---|---|---|---|---|
| A | Total profit | | | | | | |
| B | Interest paid | | | | | | |
| C | Net profit before tax (A − B) | | | | | | |
| D | Average borrowed capital | | | | | | |
| E | Average equity capital | | | | | | |
| F | Average total capital (D + E) | | | | | | |
| G | Number of calendar days in period | | | | | | |

| Ratio | Formula for calculation of ratio | Unit of measurement | Month or quarter to (date) | | | | | |
|---|---|---|---|---|---|---|---|---|
| P1   Net profit before tax/ Equity capital | $(C \times 100 \div E) \times (365 \div G)$ | % pa | | | | | | |
| P2   Total profit/ Total capital | $(A \times 100 \div F) \times (365 \div G)$ | % pa | | | | | | |
| P3   Interest paid/ Borrowed capital | $(B \times 100 \div D) \times (365 \div G)$ | % pa | | | | | | |
| P4   *Gearing* Borrowed capital/ Equity capital | $D \div E$ | times | | | | | | |

**Make-up of interest paid and borrowed capital**

| Code letter | Item | Month or quarter to (date) | | | | | |
|---|---|---|---|---|---|---|---|
| A | Preference dividend | | | | | | |
| B | Debenture interest | | | | | | |
| C | Loan interest | | | | | | |
| D | Overdraft interest | | | | | | |
| E | Cash discounts lost | | | | | | |
| F | Interest element in hire purchase charge | | | | | | |
| G | Interest element in leasing charge | | | | | | |
| H | Interest element in debt factoring charge | | | | | | |
| K | Bill discount | | | | | | |
| L | Interest paid (A+B+C+D+E+F+G+H+K) | | | | | | |
| M | Average preference shares | | | | | | |
| N | Average debentures | | | | | | |
| P | Average loans | | | | | | |
| Q | Average overdrafts | | | | | | |
| R | Average trade and expense creditors | | | | | | |
| S | Average corporation tax provisions | | | | | | |
| T | Average deferred taxation | | | | | | |
| W | Average capital based government grants | | | | | | |
| Y | Average amount outstanding on hire purchase accounts | | | | | | |
| Z | Average amount outstanding on leasing accounts | | | | | | |
| AA | Average debts factored | | | | | | |
| AB | Average bills discounted | | | | | | |
| AC | Average total borrowed capital (M+N+P+Q+R+S+T+W+Y+Z+AA+AB) | | | | | | |
| AD | Number of calendar days in period | | | | | | |

**Make-up of interest paid**

| Ratio | | Formula for calculation of ratio | Unit of measurement | Month or quarter to (date) | | | | | |
|---|---|---|---|---|---|---|---|---|---|
| P5-1 | Preference dividend/ Preference shares | A x 100 ÷ M x (365 ÷ AD) | % pa | | | | | | |
| P5-2 | Debenture interest/ Debentures | B x 100 ÷ N x (365 ÷ AD) | % pa | | | | | | |
| P5-3 | Loan interest/ Loans | C x 100 ÷ P x (365 ÷ AD) | % pa | | | | | | |
| P5-4 | Overdraft interest/ Overdrafts | D x 100 ÷ Q x (365 ÷ AD) | % pa | | | | | | |
| P5-5 | Cash discounts lost/Trade and expense creditors | E x 100 ÷ R x (365 ÷ AD) | % pa | | | | | | |
| P5-9 | Interest element in hire purchase charge/ Amount outstanding on hire purchase accounts | F x 100 ÷ Y x (365 ÷ AD) | % pa | | | | | | |
| P5-10 | Interest element in leasing charge/Amount outstanding on leasing accounts | G x 100 ÷ Z x (365 ÷ AD) | % pa | | | | | | |
| P5-11 | Interest element in debt factoring charge/Debts factored | H x 100 ÷ AA x (365 ÷ AD) | % pa | | | | | | |
| P5-12 | Bill discount/ Bills discounted | K x 100 ÷ AB x (365 ÷ AD) | % pa | | | | | | |

This page left blank deliberately

# Make-up of borrowed capital

| Ratio | | Formula for calculation of ratio | Unit of measurement | Month or quarter to (date) | | | | | |
|---|---|---|---|---|---|---|---|---|---|
| P6-1 | Preference shares/ Total borrowed capital | M x 100 ÷ AC | % | | | | | | |
| P6-2 | Debentures/Total borrowed capital | N x 100 ÷ AC | % | | | | | | |
| P6-3 | Loans/Total borrowed capital | P x 100 ÷ AC | % | | | | | | |
| P6-4 | Overdrafts/Total borrowed capital | Q x 100 ÷ AC | % | | | | | | |
| P6-5 | Trade and expense creditors/Total borrowed capital | R x 100 ÷ AC | % | | | | | | |
| P6-6 | Corporation tax provisions/ Total borrowed capital | S x 100 ÷ AC | % | | | | | | |
| P6-7 | Deferred taxation/Total borrowed capital | T x 100 ÷ AC | % | | | | | | |
| P6-8 | Capital based government grants/ Total borrowed capital | W x 100 ÷ AC | % | | | | | | |
| P6-9 | Amount outstanding on hire purchase accounts/Total borrowed capital | Y x 100 ÷ AC | % | | | | | | |
| P6-10 | Amount outstanding on leasing accounts/ Total borrowed capital | Z x 100 ÷ AC | % | | | | | | |
| P6-11 | Debts factored/ Total borrowed capital | AA x 100 ÷ AC | % | | | | | | |
| P6-12 | Bills discounted/ Total borrowed capital | AB x 100 ÷ AC | % | | | | | | |

Data assembly sheet 8–4
## Constraint factors

| Code letter | Item | Month or quarter to (date) | | | | | |
|---|---|---|---|---|---|---|---|
| A | Average debtors | | | | | | |
| B | Average other quick assets | | | | | | |
| C | Average quick assets (A+B) | | | | | | |
| D | Average stock | | | | | | |
| E | Average other current assets | | | | | | |
| F | Average current assets (C+D+E) | | | | | | |
| G | Average creditors | | | | | | |
| H | Average other current liabilities | | | | | | |
| K | Average current liabilities (G+H) | | | | | | |
| L | Average borrowed capital | | | | | | |
| M | Average long term capital | | | | | | |
| N | Average total capital | | | | | | |
| P | Purchases | | | | | | |
| Q | Cost of sales | | | | | | |
| R | Fixed expenditure | | | | | | |
| S | Total expenditure | | | | | | |
| T | Cash expenditure | | | | | | |
| W | Interest paid | | | | | | |
| Y | Total profit | | | | | | |
| Z | Sales | | | | | | |
| AA | Fixed assets | | | | | | |
| AB | No of working days in period | | | | | | |
| AC | No of calendar days in period | | | | | | |

# Constraint factors

| Ratio | | Formula for calculation of ratio | Unit of measurement | Month or quarter to (date) | | | | | | |
|---|---|---|---|---|---|---|---|---|---|---|
| P7 | Interest cover Total profit/ Interest paid | $Y \div W$ | times | | | | | | | |
| P8 | Asset cover Total capital/ Borrowed capital | $N \div L$ | times | | | | | | | |
| P9 | Current ratio Current assets/ Current liabilities | $F \div K$ | times | | | | | | | |
| P10 | Quick ratio Quick assets/ Current liabilities | $C \div K$ | times | | | | | | | |
| P11 | Stock turnover Stock/ Average daily cost of sales | $D \div (Q \div AB)$ | days | | | | | | | |
| P12 | Credit given Debtors/ Average daily sales | $A \div (Z \div AC)$ | days | | | | | | | |
| P13 | Credit taken Creditors/ Average daily purchases | $G \div (P \div AC)$ | days | | | | | | | |
| P14 | Profit vulnerability Fixed expenditure/ Total expenditure | $R \times 100 \div S$ | % | | | | | | | |
| P15 | Defensive interval Current assets less stock/Average daily cash expenditure | $(F - D) \div (T \div AB)$ | days | | | | | | | |
| P16 | No credit interval Liquid assets less current liabilities/ Average daily cash expenditure | $(C - K) \div (T \div AB)$ | days | | | | | | | |
| P17 | Fixed capital ratio Long term capital/ Fixed assets | $M \div AA$ | times | | | | | | | |

**Investor ratios**

| Code letter | Item | Year to (date) | | | | | |
|---|---|---|---|---|---|---|---|
| | | | | | | | |
| A | Value of investment at beginning of period | | | | | | |
| B | Value of investment at end of period | | | | | | |
| C | Capital gain (B−A) | | | | | | |
| D | Gross dividend receivable | | | | | | |
| E | Sub total (C+D) | | | | | | |
| F | Tax on dividend | | | | | | |
| G | Tax on gain | | | | | | |
| H | Sub total (F+G) | | | | | | |
| K | Income after tax (E−H) | | | | | | |

NB   As dividends usually relate to a year it is probably not worthwhile calculating these ratios for a period less than a year. They may however be calculated more frequently than annually.

| Ratio | Formula for calculation of ratio | Unit of measurement | Year to (date) | | | | | |
|---|---|---|---|---|---|---|---|---|
| | | | | | | | | |
| Q1 Income after tax/Value of investment at beginning of period | K x 100 ÷ A | % pa | | | | | | |
| Q2 Gross dividend receivable/Value of investment at beginning of period | D x 100 ÷ A | % pa | | | | | | |
| Q3 Capital gain/ Value of invest- ment at beginning of period | C x 100 ÷ A | % pa | | | | | | |
| Q4 Tax on dividend/ Gross dividend | F x 100 ÷ D | % | | | | | | |
| Q5 Tax on gain/ Capital gain | G x 100 ÷ C | % | | | | | | |

Data assembly sheet 8–6
## Stock Exchange ratios

| Code letter | Item | Year to (date) | | | | | |
|---|---|---|---|---|---|---|---|
| A | Profit after corporation tax | | | | | | |
| B | Gross dividend | | | | | | |
| C | Number of ordinary shares | | | | | | |
| D | Net assets at book value | | | | | | |
| E | Market value of ordinary shares | | | | | | |
| F | Equity capital | | | | | | |

NB   As dividends usually relate to a year it is probably not worthwhile calculating these ratios for a period less than a year. They may however be calculated more frequently than annually.

| Ratio | Formula for calculation of ratio | Unit of measurement | Year to (date) | | | | | |
|---|---|---|---|---|---|---|---|---|
| R1 *Dividend Yield* Gross dividend/ Market value of ordinary shares | B x 100 ÷ E | % pa | | | | | | |
| R2 *Earnings Yield* Profit after corporation tax/ Market value of ordinary shares | A x 100 ÷ E | % pa | | | | | | |
| R2(a) *P/E Ratio* Market value of ordinary shares/ Profit after corporation tax | E ÷ A | times | | | | | | |
| R3 *Cover* Profit after corporation tax/ Gross dividend | A ÷ B | times | | | | | | |
| R4 *Equity earnings per share* Profit after corporation tax/Number of ordinary shares | A ÷ C | £'s per share pa | | | | | | |
| R5 *Market price per share* Market value of ordinary shares/ Number of ordinary shares | E ÷ C | £'s per share | | | | | | |
| R6 Profit after corporation tax/ Equity capital | A x 100 ÷ F | % pa | | | | | | |
| R7 *Net asset value per share* Net assets at book value/ Number of ordinary shares | D ÷ C | £'s per share | | | | | | |

Data assembly sheet 8–7
**Overall company ratios**

| Code letter | Item | Month or quarter to (date) | | | | | |
|---|---|---|---|---|---|---|---|
| | | | | | | | |
| A | Total profit | | | | | | |
| B | Interest paid | | | | | | |
| C | Net profit before tax (A—B) | | | | | | |
| D | Corporation tax | | | | | | |
| E | Net profit after tax (C—D) | | | | | | |
| F | Average equity capital | | | | | | |
| G | Average borrowed capital | | | | | | |
| H | Average total capital (F+G) | | | | | | |
| K | No of calendar days in period | | | | | | |

| Ratio | Formula for calculation of ratio | Unit of measurement | Month or quarter to (date) | | | | | |
|---|---|---|---|---|---|---|---|---|
| R6    Net profit after tax/ Equity capital | E x 100 ÷ F x (365 ÷ K) | % pa | | | | | | |
| R8    Net profit before tax/ Total capital | C x 100 ÷ H x (365 ÷ K) | % pa | | | | | | |
| R9    Corporation tax/ Net profit before tax | D x 100 ÷ C | % | | | | | | |
| R10    Total profit/ Total capital | A x 100 ÷ H x (365 ÷ K) | % pa | | | | | | |
| R11    Interest paid/ Borrowed capital | B x 100 ÷ G x (365 ÷ K) | % pa | | | | | | |
| R12    *Capital gearing* Borrowed capital/ Equity capital | G ÷ F | times | | | | | | |

**Data processing**

| Code letter | Item | Month or quarter to (date) | | | | | |
|---|---|---|---|---|---|---|---|
| A | Data processing costs | | | | | | |
| B | Sales | | | | | | |
| C | Transactions | | | | | | |

| Ratio | Formula for calculation of ratio | Unit of measurement | Month or quarter to (date) | | | | | |
|---|---|---|---|---|---|---|---|---|
| S1 Data processing costs/Sales | A x 100 ÷ B | % | | | | | | |
| S2 Data processing costs/ Transactions | A ÷ C | £ per transaction | | | | | | |
| S3 Transactions per £100 of sales | C x 100 ÷ B | Numbers | | | | | | |

# Chapter 9

# Ratios for production management

In Chapter 1 it was stated that it is desirable to provide each manager with a single key ratio which measures the degree of his success. Such a ratio will relate the results achieved by production management to the resources available.

The result that production management is striving for is to reduce production costs; not to reduce them in isolation, however, but *in relation to* the sales value of what is being produced. A useful ratio is therefore

$$\frac{\text{Production costs}}{\text{Sales value of production}}$$

This ratio cannot be used as the *key* production ratio because it does not take into account the resources – the assets– used to achieve it. These production assets are: raw materials stock, work in progress, finished goods stock, factory premises, and the plant, machinery and factory vehicles such as fork lift trucks. Instead of using this ratio, therefore, it is possible to measure the same relationship by using the figure of production contribution, that is sales value of production *minus* production costs. Then the key production ratio becomes:

T1   $$\frac{\text{Production contribution}}{\text{Production assets}}$$

The subsidiary ratios that production management uses to indicate the causes of a change in the key ratio depend on whether it is possible to obtain a reliable and meaningful measure of maximum output or not. If such a measure is not obtainable, the ratios described next are used; if one is obtainable the ratios described in Section 9.2 are applicable.

## 9.1 No Measure of Maximum Output Obtainable*

The key ratio can be improved by action:

1   To reduce costs in relation to output, provided that either no increase in asset investment is called for, or the reduction in costs outweighs the increased investment.
2   To reduce asset investment in relation to output provided that such a reduction does not impair the ratio of costs to output.

From this it will be seen that the first two subsidiary ratios for production management are

T2   $$\frac{\text{Production costs}}{\text{Sales value of production}}$$

T3   $$\frac{\text{Sales value of production}}{\text{Production assets}}$$

It is useful to proceed one stage farther in the analysis of both ratios T2 and T3. Subsidiary to T2 will be the main constituents of production costs measured by their appropriate ratios, such as

T4   $$\frac{\text{Direct materials cost}}{\text{Sales value of production}}$$

---

\* Many of the ratios described in this chapter were developed when I was at the Centre for Interfirm Comparison. However, I developed the concept of bringing together all the ratios under the control of a manager and using the ratio of Production contribution to Production assets as a key ratio for the production function, and the integration of subsequent ratios beneath it, after leaving the Centre.

$$T5 \qquad \frac{\text{Direct labour cost}}{\text{Sales value of production}}$$

$$T6 \qquad \frac{\text{Production overheads}}{\text{Sales value of production}}$$

Any slowing down of the turnover of production assets (ratio T3) will have been caused by one or more of the following events. Any improvement in the turnover of production assets will have to come from action in one or more of the following fields: *Raw materials stock turnover* is slowing down, indicated by

$$T7 \qquad \frac{\text{Raw materials stock}}{\text{Average daily purchases}} \qquad \text{rising}$$

*Shopfloor time* is lengthening, or work in progress is building up, indicated by

$$T8 \qquad \frac{\text{Work in progress}}{\text{Average daily value of issues to production and products completed}} \qquad \text{rising}$$

*Finished stock* is building up, indicated by

$$T9 \qquad \frac{\text{Finished goods stock}}{\text{Average daily value of production completed}} \qquad \text{rising}$$

*Utilisation of premises* is dropping, indicated by

$$T10 \qquad \frac{\text{Value of factory premises}}{\text{Sales value of production}} \qquad \text{rising}$$

or by

$$T13 \qquad \frac{\text{Sales value of production}}{\text{Area of factory premises}} \qquad \text{falling}$$

*Value of premises* is rising, indicated by

$$T12 \qquad \frac{\text{Value of factory premises}}{\text{Area of factory premises}} \qquad \text{rising}$$

*Utilisation of plant, machinery and factory vehicles* is dropping, indicated by

$$T11 \qquad \frac{\text{Value of plant}}{\text{Sales value of production}} \qquad \text{rising}$$

*Average age of plant* is falling, as a result of old plant being replaced by new, indicated by

$$T14 \qquad \frac{\text{Plant, etc., at depreciated value}}{\text{Plant, etc., at undepreciated value}} \qquad \text{rising}$$

Changes in the sizes of ratios T10 and T11 have to be interpreted with care. There is nearly always a lag between an investment being made in a fixed asset, such as premises or plant, and the benefit of higher throughput or lower costs being obtained. This means that during such a period of lag, ratios T10 and T11 will deteriorate, although there is no real cause for alarm.

This situation can be dealt with by omitting the cost of new fixed assets from the numerators of ratios T10 and T11 until the assets are fully 'on stream'. The danger of such a course of action is that it removes from the system one of the devices that will constantly remind production management of the importance of getting the asset into profitable use. A compromise would be to have two figures for ratio T11, one including and the other excluding the value of unproductive fixed assets.

If the value of the fixed assets included in the numerators of ratios T10 and T11 is taken to be cost less depreciation, these two ratios will tend to decrease as the asset gets older. Such a change would be misleading if it was thought to indicate an improvement. This situation can be dealt with by using both the depreciated and the undepreciated values of these assets for these two ratios while still using the depreciated value for ratio T1.

This may seem inconsistent but it is not so. The depreciated value must be used for ratio T1 because as the asset gets older the profit from its use declines, either because its running costs have increased or the price that can be got for its output has declined. It is only reasonable to relate this declining profit to the decreasing value of the asset when measuring the efficiency with which it is being used. The total value of the output from the asset is likely to decline much less markedly, if at all, and for this reason it is better to relate the volume of output to an undepreciated value of the asset as is done in ratio T15. Volume of output is related to the depreciated value of the asset in ratio T11 in order to provide a link between ratio T15 and ratios T3 and T1. The average age of the assets is measured by ratio T14 in terms of the percentage of useful life remaining. (See also the discussion of this subject in Appendix 1.1.)

Over the course of the life of most fixed assets an appreciable degree of inflation will almost certainly take place. As output will be measured in terms of these inflated pounds, ratios T10 and T11 will decrease as a result of inflation as well as a result of real improvements in output. The best method of dealing with this problem is to use replacement values in place of the original cost.

Replacement values are useful for insurance purposes as well. They may be obtained from a study of the literature of machinery manufacturers and estate agents or by using suitable price indices, eg PINCCA (see p. 337).

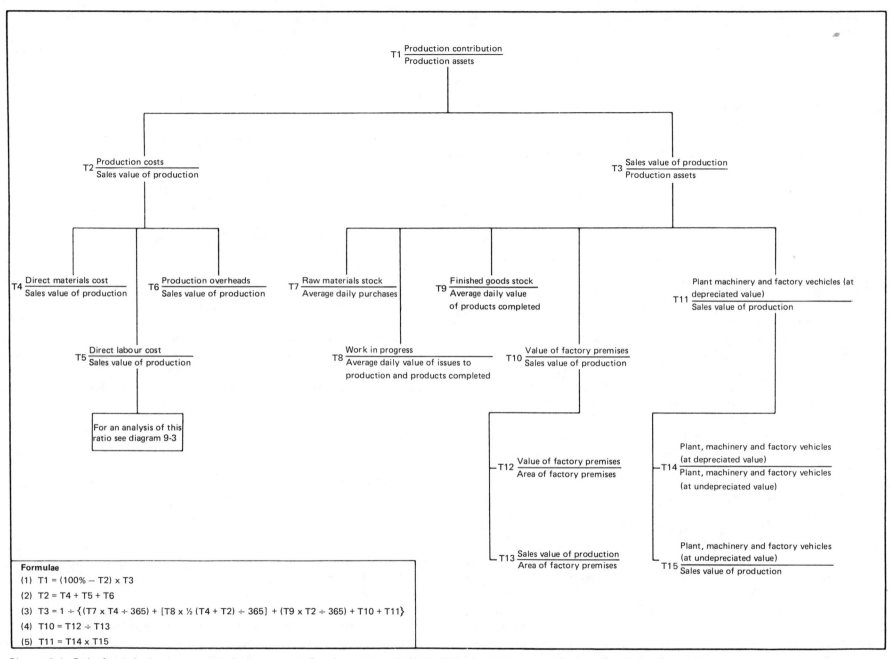

T1 $\dfrac{\text{Production contribution}}{\text{Production assets}}$

T2 $\dfrac{\text{Production costs}}{\text{Sales value of production}}$

T3 $\dfrac{\text{Sales value of production}}{\text{Production assets}}$

T4 $\dfrac{\text{Direct materials cost}}{\text{Sales value of production}}$

T6 $\dfrac{\text{Production overheads}}{\text{Sales value of production}}$

T7 $\dfrac{\text{Raw materials stock}}{\text{Average daily purchases}}$

T9 $\dfrac{\text{Finished goods stock}}{\text{Average daily value of products completed}}$

T11 $\dfrac{\text{Plant machinery and factory vechicles (at depreciated value)}}{\text{Sales value of production}}$

T5 $\dfrac{\text{Direct labour cost}}{\text{Sales value of production}}$

T8 $\dfrac{\text{Work in progress}}{\text{Average daily value of issues to production and products completed}}$

T10 $\dfrac{\text{Value of factory premises}}{\text{Sales value of production}}$

For an analysis of this ratio see diagram 9-3

T12 $\dfrac{\text{Value of factory premises}}{\text{Area of factory premises}}$

T14 $\dfrac{\text{Plant, machinery and factory vehicles (at depreciated value)}}{\text{Plant, machinery and factory vehicles (at undepreciated value)}}$

T13 $\dfrac{\text{Sales value of production}}{\text{Area of factory premises}}$

T15 $\dfrac{\text{Plant, machinery and factory vehicles (at undepreciated value)}}{\text{Sales value of production}}$

**Formulae**

(1)  T1 = (100% − T2) × T3

(2)  T2 = T4 + T5 + T6

(3)  T3 = 1 ÷ {(T7 × T4 ÷ 365) + [T8 × ½ (T4 + T2) ÷ 365] + (T9 × T2 ÷ 365) + T10 + T11}

(4)  T10 = T12 ÷ T13

(5)  T11 = T14 × T15

Diagram 9–1   Ratios for production management when no measure of maximum output obtainable. With acknowledgements to the Centre for Interfirm Comparison.

The ratios for production management to use when no measure of maximum output is obtainable are summarised in Diagram 9–1.

To calculate ratios T1 to T15 use data assembly and ratio calculation sheet 9–1 at the end of this chapter.

## 9.2 Measure of Maximum Output Obtainable

If a measure of maximum output is obtainable production management has a more sophisticated analytical tool. Performance will still be measured by the ratio of

T1      $\dfrac{\text{Production contribution}}{\text{Production assets}}$

but the factors influencing it are divided into five instead of the two used in the previous section (production costs/sales value of production and sales value of production/production assets). The five factors are the relationships between

1. Variable production costs and actual output – ratio U2
2. Variable production assets and actual output – ratio U3
3. Fixed production costs and maximum output – ratio U5
4. Fixed production assets and maximum output – ratio U6
5. Capacity utilisation (actual output as a percentage of maximum output) – ratio U4.

Variable production costs are those that tend to vary directly with the volume of output, such as the value of materials used.

Variable production assets are those whose level is likely to change as the volume of production changes, such as stocks of raw materials.

Fixed production costs are those which do not change with changes in output. An example would be the rent of a factory.

Fixed production assets are those whose value does not fluctuate with changes in sales volume, such as the value of plant.

Both fixed production costs and assets are associated with a certain level of potential output. They are incurred or exist whether that potential is realised or not. They are the consequence of being *in* business rather than of *doing* business. They increase only if there is a substantial change in the capacity of the organisation to handle a volume of business.

The disadvantage of the method of analysis outlined in the previous section is that a change in only one factor causes a number of ratios to change. This is an uneconomical use of ratios. It is like having two speedometers in a car. If the volume of output increases but all other aspects of the firm's efficiency remain unchanged then under the

method of analysis described in the previous section the following ratios change

T2      $\dfrac{\text{Production costs}}{\text{Sales value of production}}$

T3      $\dfrac{\text{Sales value of production}}{\text{Production assets}}$

T6      $\dfrac{\text{Production overheads}}{\text{Sales value of production}}$

T10      $\dfrac{\text{Value of factory premises}}{\text{Sales value of production}}$

T11      $\dfrac{\text{Value of plant}}{\text{Sales value of production}}$

Under the second method of analysis, the only ratio that changes is

U4      $\dfrac{\text{Actual output}}{\text{Maximum output}}$

The third tier of ratios is virtually the same as for the less sophisticated method of analysis. The whole set for use by production management where a measure of maximum output is obtainable is summarised in Diagram 9–2.

To calculate ratios U1 to U18 use data assembly and ratio calculation sheet 9–2 at the end of this chapter.

## 9.3 Shopfloor Ratios

Labour intensive shops

In Diagrams 9–1 and 9–2 we suggested that the production manager would look at, among other ratios, the ratio of direct labour cost to sales value of production (ratios T5 or U8). The factors affecting this ratio are, in most manufacturing businesses, so important that we are devoting the whole of this section to them.

In this section we have attempted to use British Standard terminology wherever possible. The references in brackets after some words are to BS 3138: 1979 *Glossary of Terms used in Work Study and Organisation and Methods (O & M)*, the relevant parts of which have been reproduced in Appendix 1 to this chapter.

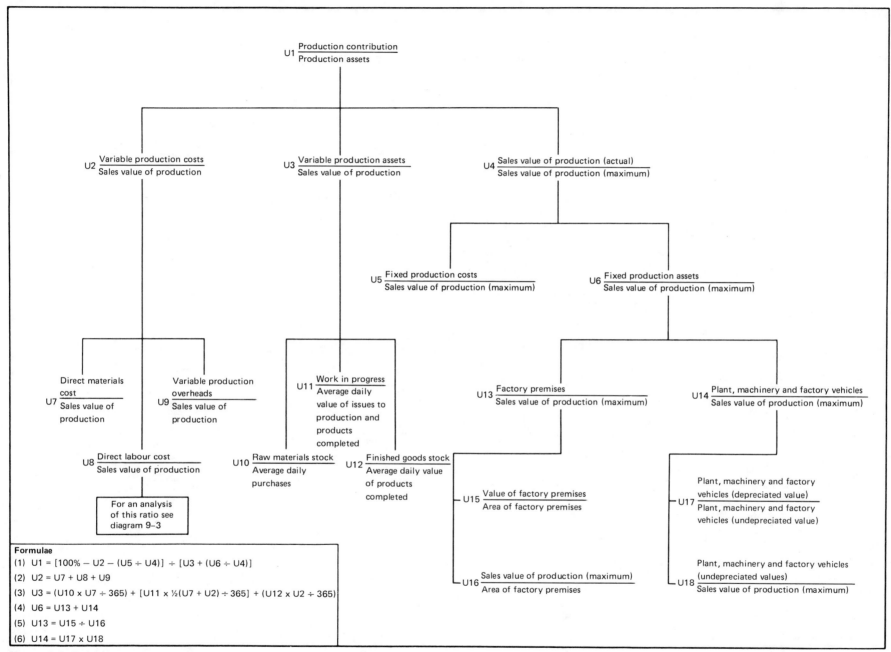

Diagram 9–2   Ratios for production management when a measure of maximum output is obtainable.

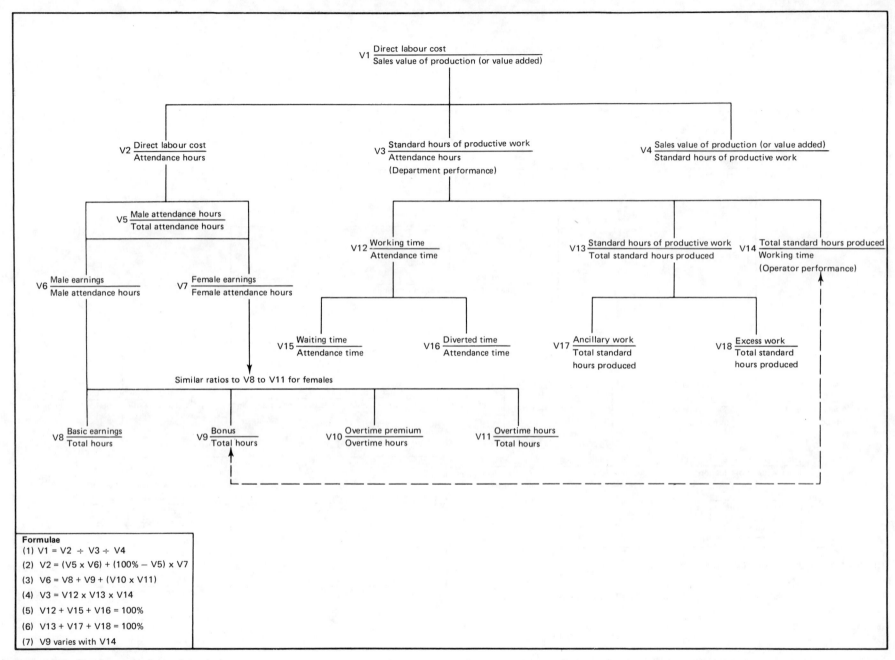

$V1 \dfrac{\text{Direct labour cost}}{\text{Sales value of production (or value added)}}$

$V2 \dfrac{\text{Direct labour cost}}{\text{Attendance hours}}$

$V3 \dfrac{\text{Standard hours of productive work}}{\text{Attendance hours}}$ (Department performance)

$V4 \dfrac{\text{Sales value of production (or value added)}}{\text{Standard hours of productive work}}$

$V5 \dfrac{\text{Male attendance hours}}{\text{Total attendance hours}}$

$V12 \dfrac{\text{Working time}}{\text{Attendance time}}$

$V13 \dfrac{\text{Standard hours of productive work}}{\text{Total standard hours produced}}$

$V14 \dfrac{\text{Total standard hours produced}}{\text{Working time}}$ (Operator performance)

$V6 \dfrac{\text{Male earnings}}{\text{Male attendance hours}}$

$V7 \dfrac{\text{Female earnings}}{\text{Female attendance hours}}$

$V15 \dfrac{\text{Waiting time}}{\text{Attendance time}}$

$V16 \dfrac{\text{Diverted time}}{\text{Attendance time}}$

$V17 \dfrac{\text{Ancillary work}}{\text{Total standard hours produced}}$

$V18 \dfrac{\text{Excess work}}{\text{Total standard hours produced}}$

Similar ratios to V8 to V11 for females

$V8 \dfrac{\text{Basic earnings}}{\text{Total hours}}$

$V9 \dfrac{\text{Bonus}}{\text{Total hours}}$

$V10 \dfrac{\text{Overtime premium}}{\text{Overtime hours}}$

$V11 \dfrac{\text{Overtime hours}}{\text{Total hours}}$

**Formulae**

(1) $V1 = V2 \div V3 \div V4$

(2) $V2 = (V5 \times V6) + (100\% - V5) \times V7$

(3) $V6 = V8 + V9 + (V10 \times V11)$

(4) $V3 = V12 \times V13 \times V14$

(5) $V12 + V15 + V16 = 100\%$

(6) $V13 + V17 + V18 = 100\%$

(7) V9 varies with V14

Diagram 9–3  Shopfloor ratios (labour intensive)

Ratio V1 in Diagram 9–3 is the same as ratio T5 in Diagram 9–1 and ratio U8 in Diagram 9–2. In some circumstances (as where light assembly work of expensive components is undertaken) it would be better to use value added in place of sales value of production. Value added being defined as sales value of production *less* direct materials cost.

The size of ratio V1 is the resultant of three forces:

1    Average earnings per clock hour (ratio V2)
2    The output of standard hours (43031) in relation to attendance time (51008) – ratio V3. (Note: This is approximately equal to Department Performance – 51035).
3    The sales value of the work produced in a standard hour (ratio V4).

The size of a firm's average earnings per clock hour (ratio V2) will depend on:

1    The proportion of hours worked by men to those worked by women (on the assumption that differences in pay will continue) – ratio V5, and
2    The average earnings of each sex (ratios V6 and V7).

An employee's average earnings is determined by:

1    The basic rate (ratio V8)
2    The bonus earned (ratio V9)
3    The overtime premium (ratio V10)
4    The proportion of overtime worked (ratio V11)

The amount of bonus (ratio V9) depends on the type of incentive scheme and the average operator performance (51034) – see ratio V14 below.
    Ratio V3 – the Department Performance – depends on:

1    The proportion of attendance time that is working time (51009) as opposed to waiting (43017) or diverted time (51010) – ratio V12.
2    The proportion of standard hours produced by the employees that are of saleable work or productive work (51013) as opposed to excess work (51014) or ancillary work (51015) – ratio V13.
3    The average operator performance (51034) – ratio V14.

Obviously production management will keep all of the above ratios under review – most particularly those that they can most directly influence, such as:

1    V11 – by keeping overtime working down
2    V12 – by organising a good flow of work on to the shopfloor and thus minimising ratio V15, and by having adequate indirect labour and thus curbing ratio V16
3    V13 – by keeping batches as long as possible (but see ratios T9 or U12 in Diagrams 9–1 and 9–2) indicated by a low ratio V17, and by making sure that the workers use the correct methods and have the right materials, machines and tools available, indicated by a low ratio V18
4    V14 – by encouragement, good employee relations, good training and a properly designed incentive scheme.

Some ratios are to some extent outside production management's control such as:

1    V4 – largely the sales department's responsibility but can be improved by value analysis which is sometimes a production responsibility, and by method improvement, an industrial engineering responsibility
2    V5 – largely determined by local supply and the personnel department, but the production engineer could devise different methods which would require cheaper (female) labour
3    V8 and V10 are the result of local supply and demand and national agreements.

To calculate ratios V1 to V18 use data assembly and ratio calculation sheet 9–3 at the end of this chapter.

### Indirect workers

There are two ways of dealing with this increasingly important group of workers who work within the factory but who are not classified as direct, such as storemen, maintenance workers, setters and foremen. The first is to add to the hours of these people the diverted time of the directs and to monitor the total indirect time by the ratio

V19    $$\frac{\text{Total indirect hours}}{\text{Direct hours (direct attendance hours less diverted time)}}$$

The second is to use the cost of both direct and indirect workers as the numerator of ratios V1 and V2 and the total attendance time of these two groups as the denominator of ratios V2 and V3 and so on down the set of V ratios. Ratio V16 will then become

$$\frac{\text{Total indirect hours}}{\text{Attendance time}}$$

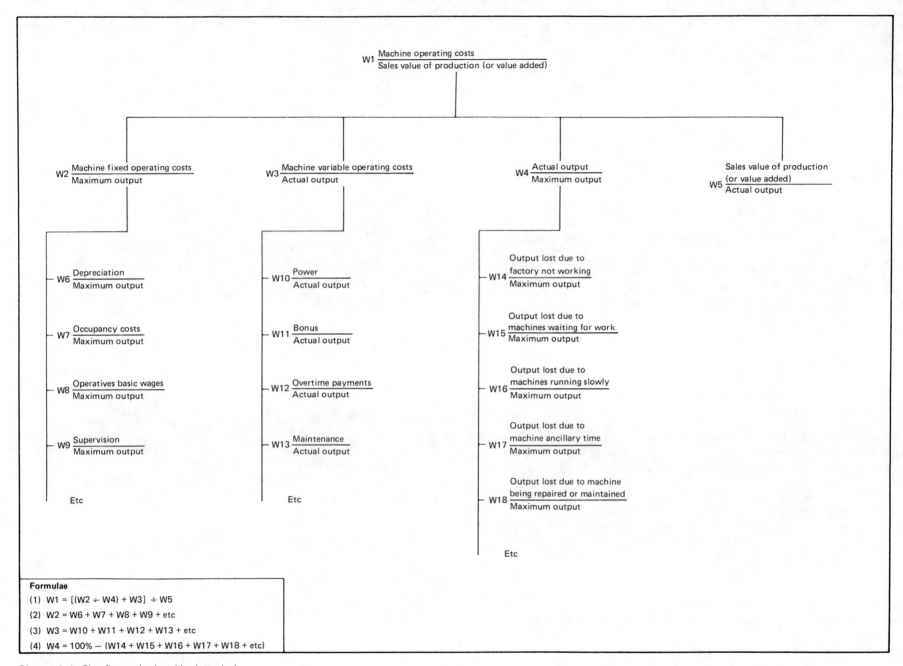

W1 $\dfrac{\text{Machine operating costs}}{\text{Sales value of production (or value added)}}$

W2 $\dfrac{\text{Machine fixed operating costs}}{\text{Maximum output}}$

W3 $\dfrac{\text{Machine variable operating costs}}{\text{Actual output}}$

W4 $\dfrac{\text{Actual output}}{\text{Maximum output}}$

W5 $\dfrac{\text{Sales value of production (or value added)}}{\text{Actual output}}$

W6 $\dfrac{\text{Depreciation}}{\text{Maximum output}}$

W7 $\dfrac{\text{Occupancy costs}}{\text{Maximum output}}$

W8 $\dfrac{\text{Operatives basic wages}}{\text{Maximum output}}$

W9 $\dfrac{\text{Supervision}}{\text{Maximum output}}$

Etc

W10 $\dfrac{\text{Power}}{\text{Actual output}}$

W11 $\dfrac{\text{Bonus}}{\text{Actual output}}$

W12 $\dfrac{\text{Overtime payments}}{\text{Actual output}}$

W13 $\dfrac{\text{Maintenance}}{\text{Actual output}}$

Etc

W14 $\dfrac{\text{Output lost due to factory not working}}{\text{Maximum output}}$

W15 $\dfrac{\text{Output lost due to machines waiting for work}}{\text{Maximum output}}$

W16 $\dfrac{\text{Output lost due to machines running slowly}}{\text{Maximum output}}$

W17 $\dfrac{\text{Output lost due to machine ancillary time}}{\text{Maximum output}}$

W18 $\dfrac{\text{Output lost due to machine being repaired or maintained}}{\text{Maximum output}}$

Etc

**Formulae**

(1)  W1 = [(W2 ÷ W4) + W3] ÷ W5

(2)  W2 = W6 + W7 + W8 + W9 + etc

(3)  W3 = W10 + W11 + W12 + W13 + etc

(4)  W4 = 100% − (W14 + W15 + W16 + W17 + W18 + etc)

Diagram 9–4   Shopfloor ratios (machine intensive)

## Machine-intensive shops

In situations where production labour cost is low in relation to production overheads, because the firm (or individual shop) is more machine than labour intensive it may not be worthwhile to use the V set of ratios. Instead one could use the W ratios of Diagram 9–4. Not surprisingly it will be seen that they have similarities to the V ratios.

The production manager's key ratio for a machine intensive shop is the machine operating costs in relation to sales value of production (or to value added) – ratio W1 in Diagram 9–4. Ratio W1 is affected by four main forces:

1    The costs of providing the shop's *capacity to produce*. These costs, described as machine fixed operating costs, do not vary significantly with the volume of actual production. They are related however to the maximum output the machinery is capable of if run twenty-four hours a day, 365 days a year (ratio W2). This output could be measured in standard hours, or gallons, or square yards, or whatever is suitable.

2    The costs of producing the shop's *actual output* – the machines' variable operating costs (ratio W3).

3    The proportion of the maximum output that is actually achieved (ratio W4).

4    The sales value of the actual output (ratio W5).

The machines' fixed operating costs will include:

1    Occupancy costs – the cost of the factory space (rent, rates, heating, lighting, cleaning, insurance)

2    The operatives' basic wages – the payment for being there as opposed to for producing output

3    The wages of supervisors, chargehands, foremen, inspectors and other people whose pay does not vary with volume of output

4    Depreciation, in so far as this is a function of time (when it would more correctly be descried as obsolescence). To the extent that depreciation is a function of use it should be included under variable costs. In most cases, in practice, it is treated however as a fixed cost.

The magnitude of these costs is largely determined by the type of machinery used and the organisation of the shop. The size of ratio W2 cannot easily be changed in the short term. This emphasises the importance of careful purchase, layout and pre-production planning.

The machines' variable operating costs will include: power, operatives' bonuses and overtime payments; maintenance; etc. Ratio W3 can be improved by attention to the design of the product, by study of the method of production, by the practice of preventive maintenance, by good production planning and a fair incentive scheme.

Ratio W4 can be improved by action on all or some of the following fronts:

1    Longer or more shifts (ratio W14)
2    Reduction of idle time due to lack of work (ratio W15)
3    Good maintenance (ratio W16)
4    Good set-up procedures (ratio W17)
5    Long batches (ratio W17)
6    Timely maintenance (ratio W18).

Ratio W5 is very similar to ratio V4 (see page 219). Improvements to this can be obtained by:

1    A better price
2    Value analysis
3    Method improvements.

To calculate ratios W1 to W18 use data assembly and ratio calculation sheet 9–4 at the end of this chapter.

## 9.4 Economic Batch Quantity (EBQ)

In order to improve its key ratio (production contribution/production assets) production management will want to optimise the level of the stocks which are its responsibility:

1    Raw materials stock (responsible jointly with the buyer)
2    Work in progress
3    Finished goods stock (responsible jointly with sales management).

The technique for determining the optimum level of raw material stocks (economic order quantity) was briefly outlined in the chapter for the buyer (see page 162); an analogous technique (economic batch quantity) is used by production management to determine the optimum level of finished goods stock.

The basis of economic batch quantity (EBQ) theory is that production costs are made up of three elements:

1    Variable production costs (which vary only with the quantity made – materials, labour, power)

2  Ancillary production costs (which vary only with the number of batches made – costs of setting up, cleaning and changing over machines from one item to the next)

3  Carrying costs (which vary with the quantity stored and the time left in store – rent of the store, insurance, wastage and so on).

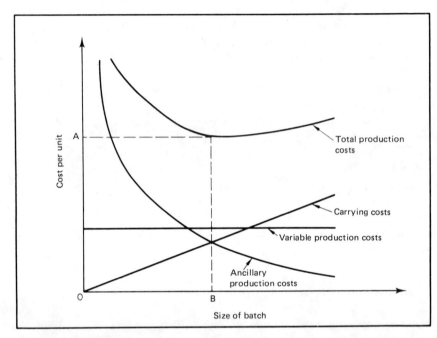

Diagram 9–5  Economic batch quantity

If these three costs are graphed, the result will be similar to Diagram 9–5, which shows tha total production costs per unit are at a minimum of £OA when the size of the batch is OB units. This is the economic batch quantity (EBQ). It is characteristic of such curves that cost rises more steeply for batches smaller than the EBQ and less steeply for batches larger than the EBQ, indicating that it is desirable to prevent batches from being smaller than the EBQ, but that it is less important if they are slightly larger than the EBQ. However each production department must construct its own graphs for its own products and circumstances and draw its own conclusions as to appropriate action.

The magnitude of (ratios T8 or U11)

$$\frac{\text{Work in progress}}{\text{Average daily value of issues to production and products completed}}$$

depends entirely on the length of time taken to complete a product. The better is production control, so that delays between production processes are minimised, and the better is production engineering, so that actual manufacturing time is minimised, then the smaller will be the amount of capital tied up in work in progress.

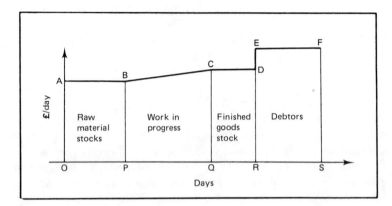

Diagram 9–6  Stock turnover ratios, flow of materials and time in stock

Diagram 9–6 illustrates the relationship between

1  The various stock turnover ratios that the production manager will monitor.

2  The flows of materials through the factory.

3  The absolute quantities of stock.

In Diagram 9–6, the vertical axis measures the average value per day; the horizontal axis the average number of days. On both axes the days are 'real' days. The diagram is simplified to the extent of assuming that stock levels are not rising or falling.

OA equals the average daily value of raw materials purchased, and PB equals the average daily value of raw material issued to production. OP equals the average number of days raw materials stays in stock. The area OABP therefore equals the average value of raw material stock.

PQ equals the average number of days required to make a product (shop-floor time) and QC equals the average daily value of completed products. The area PBCQ represents the average value of work in progress.

QR equals the average number of days finished goods stay in stock; RD equals the average daily value of sales (at cost). The area QCDR therefore equals the average value of finished goods stock.

RS equals the average number of days' credit taken by customers, and RE equals the average daily value of sales (selling price); SF equals the average daily value of cash received from debtors. The area REFS therefore equals the averages value of debtors.

The current assets utilisation ratios which are measured in terms of pounds per £1000 are the areas OABP, PBCQ, QCDR, and REFS divided by sales (RE × 365) divided by 1000. The ratios which are measured in terms of days are the lengths OP, PQ, QR, and RS.

The fact that the vertical heights increase as one moves from left to right in the diagram emphasises that a day at a later stage in the production/sales process ties up more capital than one at an earlier stage.

## Appendix 9.1

### EXTRACT FROM *GLOSSARY OF TERMS USED IN WORK STUDY AND ORGANISATION AND METHODS (O & M)*
### British Standards Institution (BS 3138: 1979)

Extracts from BS 3138: 1979 are reproduced by permission of the British Standards Institution. Complete copies can be obtained from BSI at Linford Wood, Milton Keynes, MK14 6LE. See also BS 3375: Parts 1 to 4: 1985, 1986, Work study and organisation and methods (O & M).

**43017 waiting time**
The period of time for which an operator is available for production but is prevented from working.

**43031 standard unit of work**
A unit of work consisting of basic time plus relaxation allowance and contingency allowance where appliable. In current practice, 60 or 1 standard units are produced in 1 hour when unrestricted work is carried out at standard performance.
NOTE. Standard unit of work is expressed in terms of standard minute or standard hour.

**51006 overtime**
That part of attendance time which is spent by a worker at the place or places of employment in excess of or outside the working day or week.

**51008 attendance time**
The total time spent by a worker at the place or places of employment, whether working or available for work, for which payment is made.

**51009 working time**
Time taken to do the work including authorized relaxation.

**51010 diverted time**
That part of attendance time when a worker is engaged on other than productive or ancillary work, e.g. committee work, accidents, etc.

**51013 productive work**
Work which alters the physical or chemical nature of the product or makes a necessary contribution to its completion.

**51014 excess work**
Extra work occasioned by departures from the specified method or materials.

**51015 ancillary work**
Service or any other work related to a machine or process which it is not appropriate to classify as productive.

**51034 operator performance**
An indication of the effectiveness of a worker or group of workers whilst on measured or estimated work.

NOTE. This is usually expressed in the form of an index, calculated as follows:

$$\frac{\text{total standard times for all measured and estimated work}}{\text{time on measured and estimated work excluding diverted and waiting time}} \times 100$$

**51035 department performance**
An indication of the effectiveness of a department or section.

NOTE. This is usually expressed in the form of an index, calculated as follows:

$$\frac{\text{total standard times for measured and estimated work}}{\text{time on measured and estimated work plus any waiting or diverted time for which the department is responsible}} \times 100$$

*Alternatively:*

$$\frac{\text{total standard times for measured and estimated work plus uncontrolled work at assessed performance}}{\text{total attendance time excluding time on allocated work, if any, and waiting or diverted time for which the department is not responsible}} \times 100$$

**Ratios for the production director when no measure of maximum output is obtainable**

| Code letter | Item | Month or quarter to (date) | | | | | |
|---|---|---|---|---|---|---|---|
| A | Raw materials stock at beginning of period | | | | | | |
| B | Purchases | | | | | | |
| C | Sub total (A + B) | | | | | | |
| D | Raw materials stock at end of period | | | | | | |
| E | Raw materials issued to production=direct materials cost (C − D) | | | | | | |
| F | Direct labour cost | | | | | | |
| G | Production overheads | | | | | | |
| H | Production costs (E + F + G) | | | | | | |
| K | Work in progress at beginning of period | | | | | | |
| L | Sub total (H + K) | | | | | | |
| M | Work in progress at end of period | | | | | | |
| N | Production cost of goods made (L−M) | | | | | | |
| P | Finished goods stock at beginning of period | | | | | | |
| Q | Sub total (N + P) | | | | | | |
| R | Finished goods stock at end of period | | | | | | |
| S | Production costs of goods sold (Q − R) | | | | | | |

**Ratios for the production director when no measure of maximum output is obtainable**

| Code letter | Item | Month or quarter to (date) | | | | | |
|---|---|---|---|---|---|---|---|
| T | Sales | | | | | | |
| W | Sales value of production ($N \times T \div S$) | | | | | | |
| Y | Production contribution ($W - H$) | | | | | | |
| Z | Value of factory premises | | | | | | |
| AA | Plant machinery and factory vehicles (at undepreciated value) | | | | | | |
| AB | Plant machinery and factory vehicles (at depreciated value) | | | | | | |
| AC | Production assets ($1/2[A+D+K+M+P+R] +Z+AB$) | | | | | | |
| AD | Area of factory premises | | | | | | |
| AE | No. of working days in period | | | | | | |
| AF | No. of working days in year | | | | | | |

**Ratios for the production director when no measure of maximum output is obtainable**

| Ratio | Formula for calculation of ratio | Unit of measurement | Month or quarter to (date) | | | | | |
|-------|-------|-------|-------|-------|-------|-------|-------|-------|
| T1 Production contribution/ Production assets | $(Y \times 100 \div AC)$ $\times (AF \div AE)$ | % pa | | | | | | |
| T2 Production costs/ Sales value of production | $H \times 100 \div W$ | % | | | | | | |
| T3 Sales value of production/ Production assets | $(W \div AC) \times (AF \div AE)$ | times per year | | | | | | |
| T4 Direct materials cost/Sales value of production | $E \times 100 \div W$ | % | | | | | | |
| T5 Direct labour cost/Sales value of production | $F \times 100 \div W$ | % | | | | | | |
| T6 Production overheads/ Sales value of production | $G \times 100 \div W$ | % | | | | | | |
| T7 Raw materials stock/ Average daily purchases | $\frac{1}{2}(A + D) \div (B \div AE)$ | days | | | | | | |
| T8 Work in progress/ Average daily value of issues to production and products completed | $\frac{1}{2}(K + M)$ $\div \frac{1}{2}[(B + N) \div AE]$ | days | | | | | | |
| T9 Finished goods stock/Average daily value of products completed | $\frac{1}{2}(P + R) \div (N \div AE)$ | days | | | | | | |

**Ratios for the production director when no measure of maximum output is obtainable**

| Ratio | Formula for calculation of ratio | Unit of measurement | Month or quarter to (date) | | | | | |
|---|---|---|---|---|---|---|---|---|
| T10 Value of factory premises/Sales value of production | Z x 1000 ÷ (W x AF ÷ AE) | %₀ pa | | | | | | |
| T11 Plant machinery and factory vehicles (at depreciated value)/Sales value of production | AB x 1000 ÷ (W x AF ÷ AE) | %₀ pa | | | | | | |
| T12 Value of factory premises/ Area of factory premises | Z ÷ AD | £ per sq. ft. | | | | | | |
| T13 Sales value of production/ Area of factory premises | (W x AF ÷ AE) ÷ AD | £'s per year per sq. ft. | | | | | | |
| T14 Plant machinery and factory vehicles: depreciated value/ Undepreciated value | AB x 100 ÷ AA | % | | | | | | |
| T15 Plant machinery and factory vehicles (at undepreciated value)/Sales value of production | AA x 1000 ÷ (W x AF ÷ AE) | %₀ pa | | | | | | |

Data assembly sheet 9–2
## Ratios for the production director when a measure of maximum output is obtainable

| Code letter | Item | Month or quarter to (date) | | | | | |
|---|---|---|---|---|---|---|---|
| A | Raw materials stock at beginning of period | | | | | | |
| B | Purchases | | | | | | |
| C | Sub total (A + B) | | | | | | |
| D | Raw materials stock at end of period | | | | | | |
| E | Raw materials issued to production = direct materials cost (C−D) | | | | | | |
| F | Direct labour cost | | | | | | |
| G | Variable production overheads | | | | | | |
| H | Variable production costs (E+F+G) | | | | | | |
| K | Fixed production costs | | | | | | |
| L | Total production costs (H + K) | | | | | | |
| M | Work in progress at beginning of period | | | | | | |
| N | Sub total (L + M) | | | | | | |
| P | Work in progress at end of period | | | | | | |
| Q | Production cost of goods made (N−P) | | | | | | |
| R | Finished goods stock at beginning of period | | | | | | |
| S | Sub total (Q+R) | | | | | | |
| T | Finished goods stock at end of period | | | | | | |
| U | Production cost of goods sold (S + T) | | | | | | |

# Ratios for the production director when a measure of maximum output is obtainable

| Code letter | Item | Month or quarter to (date) | | | | | |
|---|---|---|---|---|---|---|---|
| V | Sales | | | | | | |
| W | Sales value of production (actual) $(Q \times V \div U)$ | | | | | | |
| Y | Sales value of production (maximum) | | | | | | |
| Z | Production contribution $(W-L)$ | | | | | | |
| AA | Average value of factory premises | | | | | | |
| AB | Average value of plant, machinery and factory vehicles (depreciated value) | | | | | | |
| AC | Fixed production assets $(AA+AB)$ | | | | | | |
| AD | Variable production assets $\frac{1}{2}(A+D+L+N+Q+S)$ | | | | | | |
| AE | Production assets $(AC+AD)$ | | | | | | |
| AF | Area of factory premises | | | | | | |
| AG | Plant machinery and factory vehicles (undepreciated value) | | | | | | |
| AH | No. of working days in period | | | | | | |
| AK | No. of working days in year | | | | | | |

**Ratios for the production director when a measure of maximum output is obtainable**

| Ratio | | Formula for calculation of ratio | Unit of measurement | Month or quarter to (date) | | | | | |
|---|---|---|---|---|---|---|---|---|---|
| U1 | Production contribution/ Production assets | $(Z \times 100 \div AE) \times (AK \div AH)$ | % pa | | | | | | |
| U2 | Variable production costs/Sales value of production | $H \times 100 \div W$ | % | | | | | | |
| U3 | Variable production assets/Sales value of production | $AD \times 1000 \div (W \times AK \div AH)$ | ‰ pa | | | | | | |
| U4 | Sales value of production (actual)/ Sales value of production (maximum) | $W \times 100 \div Y$ | % | | | | | | |
| U5 | Fixed production costs/ Sales value of production (maximum) | $K \times 100 \div Y$ | % | | | | | | |
| U6 | Fixed production assets/ Sales value of production (maximum) | $AC \times 1000 \div (Y \times AK \div AH)$ | ‰ pa | | | | | | |
| U7 | Direct materials cost/Sales value of production | $E \times 100 \div W$ | % | | | | | | |
| U8 | Direct labour cost/Sales value of production | $F \times 100 \div W$ | % | | | | | | |
| U9 | Variable production overheads/Sales value of production | $G \times 100 \div W$ | % | | | | | | |
| U10 | Raw materials stock/ Average daily purchases | $\frac{1}{2}(A+D) \div (B \div AH)$ | days | | | | | | |

**Ratios for the production director when a measure of maximum output is obtainable**

| Ratio | | Formula for calculation of ratio | Unit of measurement | Month or quarter to (date) | | | | | |
|---|---|---|---|---|---|---|---|---|---|
| U11 | Work in progress/ Average daily value of issues to production and products completed | ½ (M+P) ÷ [ (B+Q) ÷ (AH × 2)] | days | | | | | | |
| U12 | Finished goods stock/Average daily value of products completed | ½(R+T) ÷ (Q ÷ AH) | days | | | | | | |
| U13 | Factory premises/ Sales value of production (maximum) | AA × 1000 ÷ (Y × AK ÷ AH) | ‰ pa | | | | | | |
| U14 | Plant, machinery and factory vehicles/ Sales value production (maximum) | AB × 1000 ÷ (Y × AK ÷ AH) | ‰ pa | | | | | | |
| U15 | Value of factory premises/Area of factory premises | AA ÷ AF | £ per sq. ft. | | | | | | |
| U16 | Sales of value of production (maximum)/ Area of factory premises | Y × AK ÷ AH ÷ AF | £'s pa per sq. ft. | | | | | | |
| U17 | Plant, machinery and factory vehicles: depreciated/ Undepreciated value | AB × 100 ÷ AG | % | | | | | | |
| U18 | Plant, machinery and factory vehicles (undepreciated value)/ Sales value of production (maximum) | AG × 1000 ÷ (Y × AK ÷ AH) | ‰ pa | | | | | | |

Data assembly sheet 9–3
## Shopfloor ratios (labour intensive)

| Code letter | Item | Month or quarter to (date) | | | | | |
|---|---|---|---|---|---|---|---|
| A | Male basic earnings | | | | | | |
| B | Male bonus | | | | | | |
| C | Male overtime premium | | | | | | |
| D | Male earnings (A + B + C) | | | | | | |
| E | Female basic earnings | | | | | | |
| F | Female bonus | | | | | | |
| G | Female overtime premium | | | | | | |
| H | Female earnings (E + F + G) | | | | | | |
| K | Direct labour cost (D + H) | | | | | | |
| L | Male basic hours | | | | | | |
| M | Male overtime hours | | | | | | |
| N | Male attendance hours (L + M) | | | | | | |
| P | Female basic hours | | | | | | |
| Q | Female overtime hours | | | | | | |
| R | Female attendance hours (P + Q) | | | | | | |
| S | Attendance time (N + R) | | | | | | |
| T | Waiting time | | | | | | |
| W | Diverted time | | | | | | |
| Y | Working time (S − T − W) | | | | | | |
| | | | | | | | |

| Code letter | Item | Month or quarter to (date) | | | | | |
|---|---|---|---|---|---|---|---|
| Z | Ancillary work | | | | | | |
| AA | Excess work | | | | | | |
| AB | Standard hours of productive work | | | | | | |
| AC | Total standard hours produced | | | | | | |
| AD | Sales value of production (or value added) | | | | | | |

**Shopfloor ratios (labour intensive)**

| Ratio | Formula for calculation of ratio | Unit of measurement | Month or quarter to (date) | | | | | |
|---|---|---|---|---|---|---|---|---|
| V1  Direct labour cost/sales value of production (or value added) | K x 100 ÷ AD | % | | | | | | |
| V2  Direct labour cost/ Attendance hours | K ÷ S | £ per hr | | | | | | |
| V3  Standard hours of productive work/ Attendance hours (Department performance) | AB x 100 ÷ S | % | | | | | | |
| V4  Sales value of production (or value added)/ Standard hours of productive work | AD ÷ AB | £ per st. hr | | | | | | |
| V5  Male attendance hours/ Total attendance hours | N x 100 ÷ S | % | | | | | | |
| V6  Male earnings/ Male attendance hours | D ÷ N | £ per hr | | | | | | |
| V7  Female earnings/ Female attendance hours | H ÷ R | £ per hr | | | | | | |
| V8  Basic earnings/ Total hours | A ÷ N | £ per hr | | | | | | |
| V9  Bonus/ Total hours | B ÷ N | £ per hr | | | | | | |
| V10  Overtime premium/ Overtime hours | C ÷ M | £ per hr | | | | | | |

| Ratio | | Formula for calculation of ratio | Unit of measurement | Month or quarter to (date) | | | | | | |
|---|---|---|---|---|---|---|---|---|---|---|
| V11 | Overtime hours/ Total hours | M x 100 ÷ N | % | | | | | | | |
| V12 | Working time/ Attendance time | Y x 100 ÷ S | % | | | | | | | |
| V13 | Standard hours of productive work/ Total standard hours produced | AB x 100 ÷ AC | % | | | | | | | |
| V14 | Total standard hours produced/ Working time (operator performance) | AC x 100 ÷ Y | % | | | | | | | |
| V15 | Waiting time/ Attendance time | T x 100 ÷ S | % | | | | | | | |
| V16 | Diverted time/ Attendance time | W x 100 ÷ S | % | | | | | | | |
| V17 | Ancillary work/ Total standard hours produced | Z x 100 ÷ AC | % | | | | | | | |
| V18 | Excess work/ Total standard hours produced | AA x 100 ÷ AC | % | | | | | | | |

Ratio calculation sheet number 9–4 will be found on the following page

**Shopfloor ratios (machine intensive)**

| Code letter | Item | Month or quarter to (date) | | | | | |
|---|---|---|---|---|---|---|---|
| A | Depreciation | | | | | | |
| B | Occupancy costs | | | | | | |
| C | Operatives' basic wages | | | | | | |
| D | Supervision | | | | | | |
| E | Other machine fixed operating costs | | | | | | |
| F | Machine fixed operating costs (A+B+C+D+E) | | | | | | |
| G | Power | | | | | | |
| H | Bonus | | | | | | |
| K | Overtime payments | | | | | | |
| L | Maintenance | | | | | | |
| M | Other machine variable operating costs | | | | | | |
| N | Machine variable operating costs (G+H+K+L+M) | | | | | | |
| P | Machine operating costs (F+N) | | | | | | |
| Q | Actual output | | | | | | |
| R | Output lost due to factory not working | | | | | | |
| S | Output lost due to machines waiting for work | | | | | | |
| T | Output lost due to machines running slowly | | | | | | |
| U | Output lost due to machine ancillary time | | | | | | |
| V | Output lost due to machine being repaired or maintained | | | | | | |
| W | Output lost due to other causes | | | | | | |
| Y | Maximum output (Q+R+S+T+U+V+W) | | | | | | |
| Z | Sales value of production (or value added) | | | | | | |

## Shopfloor ratios (machine intensive)

| Ratio | Formula for calculation of ratio | Unit of measurement | Month or quarter to (date) | | | | | |
|---|---|---|---|---|---|---|---|---|
| W1  Machine operating costs/ Sales value of production (or value added) | P x 100 ÷ Z | % | | | | | | |
| W2  Machine fixed operating costs/ Maximum output | F ÷ Y | £ per unit of output | | | | | | |
| W3  Machine variable operating costs/ Actual output | N ÷ Q | £ per unit of output | | | | | | |
| W4  Actual output/ Maximum output | Q x 100 ÷ Y | % | | | | | | |
| W5  Sales value of production (or value added)/ Actual output | Z ÷ Q | £ per unit of output | | | | | | |
| W6  Depreciation/ Maximum output | A ÷ Y | £ per unit of output | | | | | | |
| W7  Occupancy costs/ Maximum output | B ÷ Y | £ per unit of output | | | | | | |
| W8  Operatives basic wages/ Maximum output | C ÷ Y | £ per unit of output | | | | | | |
| W9  Supervision/ Maximum output | D ÷ Y | £ per unit of output | | | | | | |
| W10  Power/Actual output | G ÷ Q | £ per unit of output | | | | | | |
| W11  Bonus/Actual output | H ÷ Q | £ per unit of output | | | | | | |
| W12  Overtime payments/ Actual output | K ÷ Q | £ per unit of output | | | | | | |
| W13  Maintenance/ Actual output | L ÷ Q | £ per unit of output | | | | | | |
| W14  Output lost due to factory not working/ Maximim output | R x 100 ÷ Y | % | | | | | | |

## Shopfloor ratios (machine intensive)

| Ratio | Formula for calculation of ratio | Unit of measurement | Month or quarter to (date) | | | | | | |
|---|---|---|---|---|---|---|---|---|---|
| W15 Output lost due to machines waiting for work/Maximum output | S x 100 ÷ Y | % | | | | | | | |
| W16 Output lost due to machines running slowly/ Maximum output | T x 100 ÷ Y | % | | | | | | | |
| W17 Output lost due to machine ancillary time/ Maximum output | U x 100 ÷ Y | % | | | | | | | |
| W18 Output lost due to machine being repaired or maintained/ Maximum output | V x 100 ÷ Y | % | | | | | | | |

# Chapter 10

# Ratios for personnel management

What ratios should the personnel department look at? Obviously this depends on what the department is responsible for. Let us assume that its responsibilities are recruiting, training and industrial relations. In Chapter 1 it was stated that it is desirable to provide each manager with a single key ratio which measures the degree of his success. In the case of the personnel department such a ratio would probably relate the costs of the department plus the costs of poor personnel policies (this total will for convenience be called personnel costs) to the size of the total work force. Personnel costs would include:

1   Recruitment and replacement
2   Training and retraining
3   Other personnel department costs
4   Wage increases in excess of national agreement
5   Production lost through poor industrial relations.

This last cost may be hard to quantify accurately but it should include at least the value of profit lost (not the value of sales lost) as a result of strikes, go slows, workings to rule, and so on.

The size of the work force would be an average over the relevant period, part time workers being counted as an appropriate fraction. The personnel department's key ratio would then be

$$X1 \qquad \frac{\text{Personnel costs}}{\text{Average number of employees}}$$

The department would attempt to minimise this ratio over the medium term. To do this it would be necessary to balance the costs of items 1, 2, 3 and 4 above against the costs which would result from not spending enough on them (item 5).

The main subsidiary ratios which the department could use are shown in Diagram 10–1. They are discussed under the three headings of recruitment, training and industrial relations.

To calculate ratios X1 to X4 use data assembly and ratio calculation sheet 10.1 at the end of this chapter.

## 10.1 Recruitment

The costs of recruiting are fairly easily identified. They include the time of the firm's own staff, the cost of advertisements, agency fees, and candidates' expenses. The best measure of the benefits of recruiting is the number of recruits which the firm retains for a worthwhile period (say more than one year). So the ratio which would be used to monitor this aspect of the personnel department's work would be:

$$X2 \qquad \frac{\text{Recruiting costs}}{\text{Recruits retained}} \qquad \text{(See Diagram 10–2)}$$

Action that would lead to a reduction in this ratio would include:

1   Cutting the costs per recruit interviewed (ratio X5) (or increasing the cost in order to achieve 2 and 3 below)
2   Being more selective of interviewees so that a higher proportion can be offered a job (ratio X6)
3   Being more careful to whom jobs are offered so that a higher proportion accept the job (ratio X7) and, having accepted, stay for a worthwhile period (the length of this period will obviously vary from job to job) – ratio X8

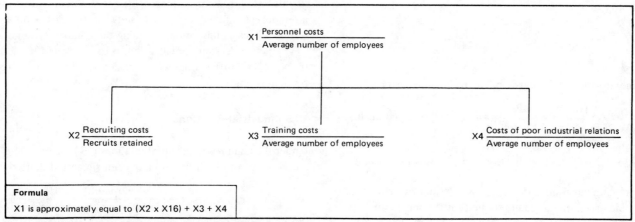

Diagram 10–1   Main subsidiary ratios for personnel department

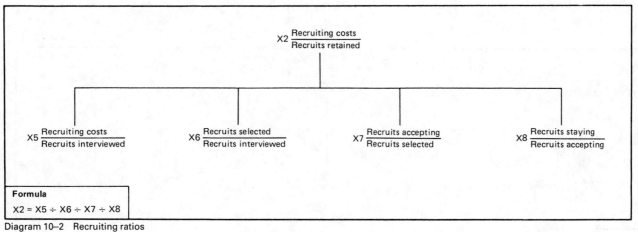

Diagram 10–2   Recruiting ratios

If the size of the personnel department's work warranted it, these ratios could be calculated separately for males and for females and for different types of jobs.

To calculate ratios X2 and X5 to X8 use data assembly and ratio calculation sheet 10–2 at the end of this chapter.

## 10.2 Training

Probably the best ratio to monitor the performance of the training department is

$$X3 \quad \frac{\text{Training costs}}{\text{Average number of employees}} \quad \text{(see Diagram 10–3)}$$

This ratio can be improved by:

1   Curbing the costs of training per trainee day (ratio X9), either by action on the cost side or by increasing the numbers trained for the same cost.
2   Reducing the number of days needed to train new recruits by improved teaching methods (ratio X10).
3   Keeping the number of recruits at a reasonable level in relation to the total number of employees (ratio X11). Too few recruits may imply stagnation; too many, either poor selection or too high a turnover of employees (or, of course, both).

To calculate ratios X3 and X9 to X11 use data assembly and ratio calculation sheet 10–3 at the end of this chapter.

If the training leads to a recognised qualification then the training department will be interested in the percentage of trainees obtaining that qualification at first, second attempt, etc. and any differences between the successful and unsuccessful trainees in terms of background prior to joining the company, training method, etc.

The personnel department will also be interested in the retention rate of qualified trainees. Training people who then leave before they have 'repaid' the cost of the training is uneconomic.

## 10.3 Industrial Relations

Under the heading of industrial relations (IR) the personnel department could look at a number of ratios. It has already been suggested that

$$X4 \quad \frac{\text{Costs of poor IR}}{\text{Average number of employees}}$$

should be monitored. In addition the two components of X4 can be shown separately:

$$X12 \quad \frac{\text{Cost of wage increases in excess of national agreements}}{\text{Average number of employees}}$$

$$X13 \quad \frac{\text{Cost of production lost through poor IR}}{\text{Average number of employees}}$$

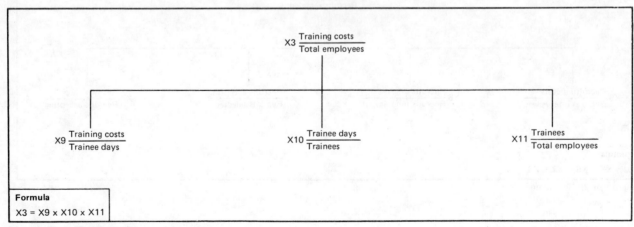

Diagram 10–3   Training ratios

particularly as there may well need to be 'horse trading' between X12 and X13 in order to minimise X4 and X1 because bad industrial relations will affect recruiting and training costs and performance as well.

If X4, X12 and X13 are not used, the following crude measure of the state of IR could be used

$$X14 \quad \frac{\text{Number of man-days lost through strikes, etc.}}{\text{Number of man-days worked}}$$

It has been suggested that absenteeism is a more sensitive measure of the state of IR, and a rise in its level may give early warning of larger trouble looming, so it would be useful to monitor

$$X15 \quad \frac{\text{Number of man-days lost through absenteeism}}{\text{Number of man-days worked}}$$

Staff turnover or employees wastage, as measured by

$$X16 \quad \frac{\text{Number of leavers}}{\text{Average number of employees}}$$

is another crude measure of the IR climate in a firm. PJ. Samuel* has suggested two better ones:

X17 The employee stability index

$$\frac{\text{Number of employees with 12 months service now}}{\text{Total employed a year ago}}$$

and

X18 The skill conservation index

$$\frac{\text{Number of employees with over 12 months service now}}{\text{Total employed now}}$$

A modification of Samuel's own example will illustrate the difference between these three indices. The data are as follows:

1   Company *A* loses during the year every person employed at the beginning of the year. As he leaves, each is replaced by someone who remains until the following year.

---

*P.J. Samuel, *Labour Turnover? Towards a Solution* – Institute of Personnel Management, 1969.

2   Company *B* loses in the course of a year half the people it employed at the beginning of that year. Their replacements also leave before the end of a year and have to be replaced.

3   Company *C* loses four people at the beginning of the year. Their jobs are filled by a succession of people, each of whom stays only a fortnight.

In addition, all three companies expand their work force by fifty people from 100 to 150, that is, the average number of employees during the year is 125. Table 10–1 shows the effect on ratios X16, X17 and X18.

| Ratio | Company | A | B | C |
|---|---|---|---|---|
| X16 | Employee wastage | $\frac{100}{125} = 80\%$ | $\frac{50+50}{125} = 80\%$ | $\frac{4 \times 25}{125} = 80\%$ |
| X17 | Employee stability | $\frac{0}{100} = 0\%$ | $\frac{50}{100} = 50\%$ | $\frac{96}{100} = 96\%$ |
| X18 | Skill conservation | $\frac{0}{150} = 0\%$ | $\frac{50}{150} = 33\%$ | $\frac{96}{150} = 64\%$ |

Table 10–1   Three methods of measuring staff turnover

Clearly there is a link between X8 (recruits staying/recruits accepting) and X11 (trainees/total employees) on the one hand and X17 and X18 (employee stability and skill conservation) on the other. Poor recruiting will lead to high training costs, low stability and poor skill conservation. It is as well therefore, that in most firms all these activities are the responsibility of a single department.

To calculate ratios X12 to X18 use data assembly and ratio calculation sheet 10–4 at the end of this chapter.

**Main subsidiary ratios for personnel department**

| Code letter | Item | Month or quarter to (date) | | | | | |
|---|---|---|---|---|---|---|---|
| A | Recruiting costs | | | | | | |
| B | Training costs | | | | | | |
| C | Costs of poor Industrial Relations | | | | | | |
| D | Other personnel department costs | | | | | | |
| E | Personnel costs (A+B+C+D) | | | | | | |
| F | Recruits retained | | | | | | |
| G | Average number of employees | | | | | | |
| H | No. of working days in period | | | | | | |
| K | No. of working days in year | | | | | | |

**Main subsidiary ratios for personnel department**

| Ratio | | Formula for calculation of ratio | Unit of measurement | Month or quarter to (date) | | | | | |
|---|---|---|---|---|---|---|---|---|---|
| X1 | Personnel costs/ Average number of employees | $(E \div G) \times (K \div H)$ | £ per head per year | | | | | | |
| X2 | Recruiting costs/ Recruits retained | $(A \div F) \times (K \div H)$ | £ per head per year | | | | | | |
| X3 | Training costs/ Average number of employees | $(B \div G) \times (K \div H)$ | £ per head per year | | | | | | |
| X4 | Costs of poor Industrial Relations/ Average number of employees | $(C \div G) \times (K \div H)$ | £ per head per year | | | | | | |

**Recruiting ratios**

| Code letter | Item | 12 months or 4 quarters to (date) | | | | | |
|---|---|---|---|---|---|---|---|
| A | Recruits interviewed | | | | | | |
| B | Recruits selected | | | | | | |
| C | Recruits accepting | | | | | | |
| D | Recruits staying (or retained) | | | | | | |
| E | Recruiting costs | | | | | | |

NB   As the process of interviewing, selection and acceptance may well take longer than a month (or even a quarter for more senior staff) and as it will not be known if a recruit is going to stay for a worthwhile period until the end of that period, it would not be sensible to calculate ratios based on items measured in the same month. One can either follow separate batches of candidates for a year (or whatever is the length of the 'worthwhile' period) and use each column of the work sheets for a separate batch, or calculate a moving annual average. The work sheets have been headed up for the second method but the first method is perhaps the more scientific.

## Recruiting ratios

| Ratio | | Formula for calculation of ratio | Unit of measurement | 12 months or 4 quarters to (date) | | | | | |
|---|---|---|---|---|---|---|---|---|---|
| X2 | Recruiting costs/ Recruits retained | E ÷ D | £'s per head | | | | | | |
| X5 | Recruiting costs/ Recruits interviewed | E ÷ A | £'s per head | | | | | | |
| X6 | Recruits selected/ Recruits interviewed | B x 100 ÷ A | % | | | | | | |
| X7 | Recruits accepting/ Recruits selected | C x 100 ÷ B | % | | | | | | |
| X8 | Recruits staying/ Recruits accepting | D x 100 ÷ C | % | | | | | | |

Data assembly sheet 10–3
**Training ratios**

| Code letter | Item | Month or quarter to (date) | | | | | |
|---|---|---|---|---|---|---|---|
| A | Training costs | | | | | | |
| B | Trainees | | | | | | |
| C | Trainee days | | | | | | |
| D | Total employees | | | | | | |
| E | Number of calendar days in period | | | | | | |

| Ratio | Formula for calculation of ratio | Unit of measurement | Month or quarter to (date) | | | | | |
|---|---|---|---|---|---|---|---|---|
| X3  Training costs/ Total employees | $(A \div D) \times (365 \div E)$ | £'s per head per annum | | | | | | |
| X9  Training costs/ Trainee days | $A \div C$ | £'s per man day | | | | | | |
| X10 Trainee days/ Trainees | $C \div B$ | Days per man | | | | | | |
| X11 Trainees/ Total employees | $B \times 100 \div D$ | % | | | | | | |

**Industrial relations ratios**

| Code letter | Item | Month or quarter to (date) | | | | | |
|---|---|---|---|---|---|---|---|
| A | Cost of wage increases in excess of national agreements | | | | | | |
| B | Cost of production lost through poor IR | | | | | | |
| C | Number of man-days lost through strikes | | | | | | |
| D | Number of man-days lost through absenteeism | | | | | | |
| E | Number of man-days worked | | | | | | |
| F | Number of leavers | | | | | | |
| G | Number of employees with 12 months' service now | | | | | | |
| H | Number of employees with over 12 months' service now | | | | | | |
| K | Total employed a year ago | | | | | | |
| L | Total employed now | | | | | | |
| M | Average number of employees | | | | | | |
| N | Number of working days in period | | | | | | |
| P | Number of working days in year | | | | | | |

| Ratio | Formula for calculation of ratio | Unit of measurement | Month or quarter to (date) | | | | | |
|---|---|---|---|---|---|---|---|---|
| X12 Cost of wage increases in excess of national agreements/ Average number of employees | (A ÷ M) x (P ÷ N) | £'s per head pa | | | | | | |
| X13 Cost of production lost through poor IR/Average number of employees | B ÷ M | £'s per head | | | | | | |
| X14 Number of man-days lost through strikes, etc./ Number of man-days worked | C x 100 ÷ E | % | | | | | | |
| X15 Number of man-days lost through absenteeism/ Number of man-days worked | D x 100 ÷ E | % | | | | | | |
| *Staff turnover* X16 Number of leavers/ Average number of employees | (F x 100 ÷ M) x (P ÷ N) | % pa | | | | | | |
| *Employee stability index* X17 Number of employees with 12 months service now/ Total employed a year ago | G x 100 ÷ K | % | | | | | | |
| *Skill conservation index* X18 Number of employees with over 12 months service now/ Total employed now | H x 100 ÷ L | % | | | | | | |

# Chapter 11

# Operating ratios for non-manufacturing organisations

Many of the ratios in this book are of general applicability, but a considerable number have related specifically to manufacturing concerns. The contents of this chapter are intended to redress this imbalance to some extent. There are separate sections for the merchant, the retailer, the professional firm, the owner-managed business, hotels, printers, newspapers and farms. The sets of ratios proposed for the first three categories of operation are based in part on schemes developed by the author while at the Centre for Interfirm Comparison.

## 11.1 Ratios for a Merchanting Organisation

A merchanting concern measures its operating success in the same way as a manufacturer, that is by the ratio of

Y1
$$\frac{\text{Operating profit}}{\text{Operating assets}}$$

The subsidiary ratios it uses are similar to those used by a manufacturing company but with a number of important differences (see Diagram 11–1). A merchant's ratio of operating profit to operating assets is affected, in the same way as a manufacturer's ratio, by:

1    The profitability of his sales (operating profit/sales – ratio Y2)
2    His turnover of assets (sales/operating assets – ratio Y3)

It is at this stage of the analysis that a difference occurs. A merchanting (as opposed to a manufacturing) concern may prefer to analyse the factors affecting its profit margin on sales (ratio Y2) between those affecting its gross margin (ratio Y4) and its

overheads (ratio Y5). Gross margin (ratio Y4) is affected by:

1    Product mix (this calls for a number of switching ratios – such as hardwood sales/total sales and softwood sales/total sales for a timber business, or food sales/total sales and clothing sales/total sales for a department store – ratios Y6, Y7)
2    Buying price for each part of the product mix – ratio Y10
3    Selling price for each part of the product mix – ratio Y11.

Overheads can be analysed between such factors as rents and rates, wages and so on. A merchant's turnover of assets is affected by

1    Stock turnover (ratio Y14)
2    Speed of debt collection (ratio Y15)
3    Utilisation of premises (ratio Y16).

To calculate ratios Y1 to Y18 use data assembly and ratio calculation sheet 11–1 at the end of this chapter.

The set of ratios in Diagram 11–1 is open to the criticism that a change in just one factor – the levels of sales – will affect more than one ratio, which is an uneconomical use of ratios. For example, ratios Y2 (operating profit/sales) and Y3 (sales/operating assets) will probably both change if the level of sales rises or falls.

An improved set depends on the ability to arrive at a figure for 'maximum sales' achievable with the present set-up. The present set-up is not a very precise concept but most managers will have a feel for the meaning in their own businesses. It is usually related to the limitations imposed by the existing premises. If maximum sales can be defined with reasonable accuracy, the set of ratios in Diagram 11–2 can be used by a merchant.

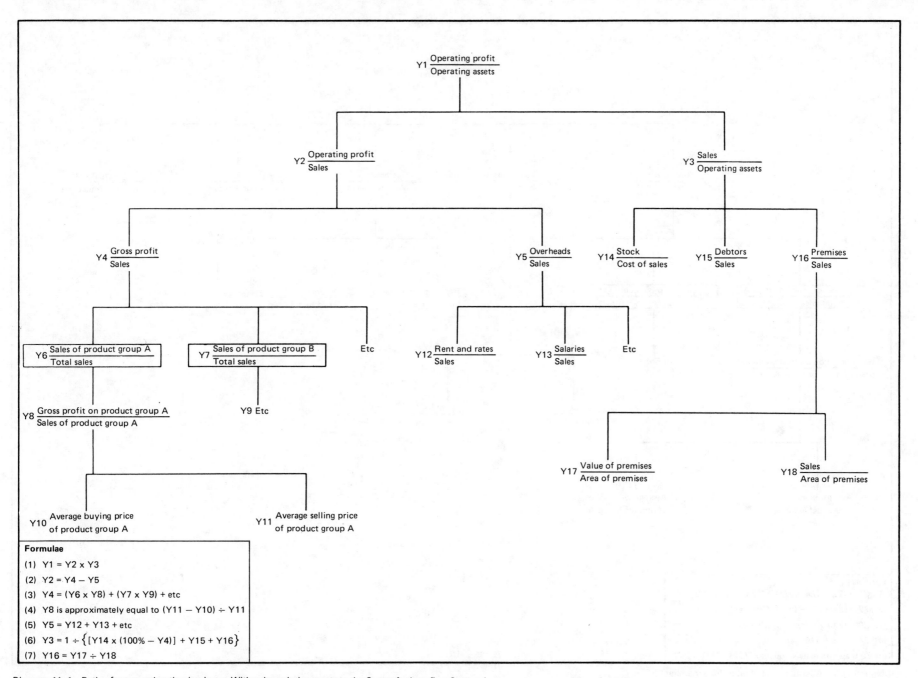

Y1 $\dfrac{\text{Operating profit}}{\text{Operating assets}}$

Y2 $\dfrac{\text{Operating profit}}{\text{Sales}}$

Y3 $\dfrac{\text{Sales}}{\text{Operating assets}}$

Y4 $\dfrac{\text{Gross profit}}{\text{Sales}}$

Y5 $\dfrac{\text{Overheads}}{\text{Sales}}$

Y14 $\dfrac{\text{Stock}}{\text{Cost of sales}}$

Y15 $\dfrac{\text{Debtors}}{\text{Sales}}$

Y16 $\dfrac{\text{Premises}}{\text{Sales}}$

Y6 $\dfrac{\text{Sales of product group A}}{\text{Total sales}}$

Y7 $\dfrac{\text{Sales of product group B}}{\text{Total sales}}$

Etc

Y12 $\dfrac{\text{Rent and rates}}{\text{Sales}}$

Y13 $\dfrac{\text{Salaries}}{\text{Sales}}$

Etc

Y8 $\dfrac{\text{Gross profit on product group A}}{\text{Sales of product group A}}$

Y9 Etc

Y17 $\dfrac{\text{Value of premises}}{\text{Area of premises}}$

Y18 $\dfrac{\text{Sales}}{\text{Area of premises}}$

Y10 Average buying price of product group A

Y11 Average selling price of product group A

**Formulae**

(1)  Y1 = Y2 x Y3

(2)  Y2 = Y4 − Y5

(3)  Y4 = (Y6 x Y8) + (Y7 x Y9) + etc

(4)  Y8 is approximately equal to (Y11 − Y10) ÷ Y11

(5)  Y5 = Y12 + Y13 + etc

(6)  Y3 = 1 ÷ {[Y14 x (100% − Y4)] + Y15 + Y16}

(7)  Y16 = Y17 ÷ Y18

Diagram 11–1   Ratios for a merchanting business. With acknowledgements to the Centre for Interfirm Comparison

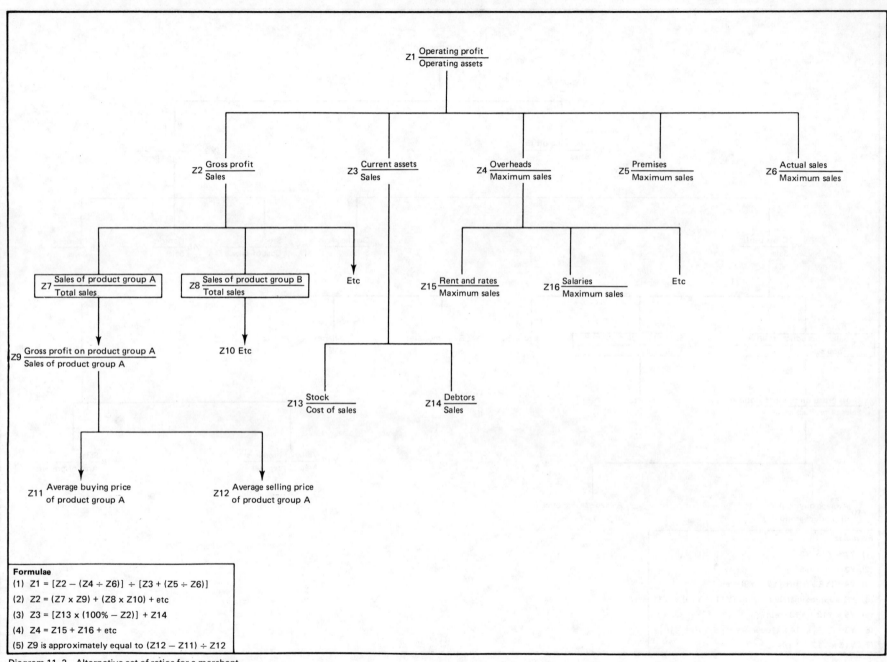

Formulae

(1)  Z1 = [Z2 − (Z4 ÷ Z6)] ÷ [Z3 + (Z5 ÷ Z6)]

(2)  Z2 = (Z7 × Z9) + (Z8 × Z10) + etc

(3)  Z3 = [Z13 × (100% − Z2)] + Z14

(4)  Z4 = Z15 + Z16 + etc

(5)  Z9 is approximately equal to (Z12 − Z11) ÷ Z12

Diagram 11–2   Alternative set of ratios for a merchant

Gross profit and current assets are most likely to vary with the level of actual sales, so they are related (in ratios Z2 and 3) to actual sales. Overheads and the value of premises are related to the size of the 'present set-up' and so are related (in ratios Z4 and 5) to maximum sales.

With this set of ratios a change in the level of sales should affect only ratio Z6 (actual sales/maximum sales). Ratios Z2 to Z5 should be unchanged.

To calculate ratios Z1 to Z16 use data assembly and ratio calculation sheet 11–2 at the end of this chapter.

## 11.2 Ratios for a Retailing Organisation

The ratios that a merchanting organisation could use (Diagrams 11–1 and 11–2) could also be used by a retailer. This part of the chapter, however, describes a set of ratios specifically for retailers.

A retailer's return on assets (ratio AA1 Diagram 11–3) depends on his profit margin on sales (AA2) and his turnover of assets (AA3). This profit margin on sales (AA2) is in turn dependent on his gross profit (AA4), his salary bill (AA5), and his other overheads (ratio AA6). He can improve his gross profit (AA4) by aiming at a higher mark up or target gross profit (AA7) and avoiding as much as possible subsequent mark downs (AA8) and shortages or stock losses (AA9)

To improve ratio AA5, a retailer needs to keep the average salary paid under review (AA10) but here he will be as much the subject of market forces as he is his own master. He can, however increase the number of transactions per employee (AA11) and the average value of each sale (AA12).

Stock and premises are the retailer's main assets. Ratios AA3 and AA3a (for an explanation of the need for ratio AA3a see Appendix 1.1) can be improved by an increase in stock turnover (AA13 and AA15) or premises utilisation (AA14). The value of the premises is fixed but AA14 can be improved by increasing the amount of selling floor or shelf space (AA16) (by putting in more shelves or by cutting down storage as opposed to selling space) and the sales per square or shelf foot (ratio AA17).

To calculate ratios AA1 to AA17 use data assembly and ratio calculation sheet 11–3 at the end of this chapter.

## 11.3 Ratios for Professional Firms

In some cases return on capital is not a suitable measure of the success with which a business is being run. Either the firm has no capital in a meaningful sense or the capital it has is not a proper measure of the resources it is using. Usually firms are partnerships of professional men (such as stockbrokers, management consultants, estate agents, consulting engineers, chartered accountants). The assets of such firms are their staff, so one could put a value on them related to their salaries but this idea does not appeal to the author as much as the following.

Most professional firms are still partnerships and from the partners' point of view a good measure of the firm's success is the profit per partner (ratio AB1 in Diagram 11–4). Profit will be after deducting such a salary as the partner would command on the open market (a nice piece of judgement that, but it can be done).

Ratio AB1 will grow;

1    If the ratio of expenses (including the partners' salaries) to revenue (ratio AB2) can be curbed,

2    If the revenue per partner (ratio AB3) can be increased.

A professional firm's staff can be divided into those responsible for:

1    Getting the business (partners and senior staff usually)

2    Doing the professional work

3    Administering the firm.

If one is going to tackle ratio AB2 it is worth looking, therefore, at the following ratios:

1    Business getting staff salaries/revenue (ratio AB4)

2    'Doing' staff salaries/revenue (ratio AB5)

3    Administrative staff salaries/revenue (ratio AB6)

4    All costs other than salaries/revenue (ratio AB7).

Ratio AB4 can be decreased by:

1    Persuading (and helping if necessary) the business getting staff to sell more (ratio AB9)

2    Employing less expensive staff on business getting if the present staff are 'over qualified' (ratio AB8)

3    Slowing down the increases given to business getting staff if their remuneration has got out of line with the market (ratio AB8)

4    Introducing a bonus scheme whereby increases in ratio AB9 are rewarded by bonuses which increase AB8 less than proportionately.

Ratio AB4 is also influenced by whether the order book is rising or falling (ratio AB10). Similar arguments apply to ratios AB5 and AB6 – see ratios AB11 and AB12, and AB13, AB14 and AB15.

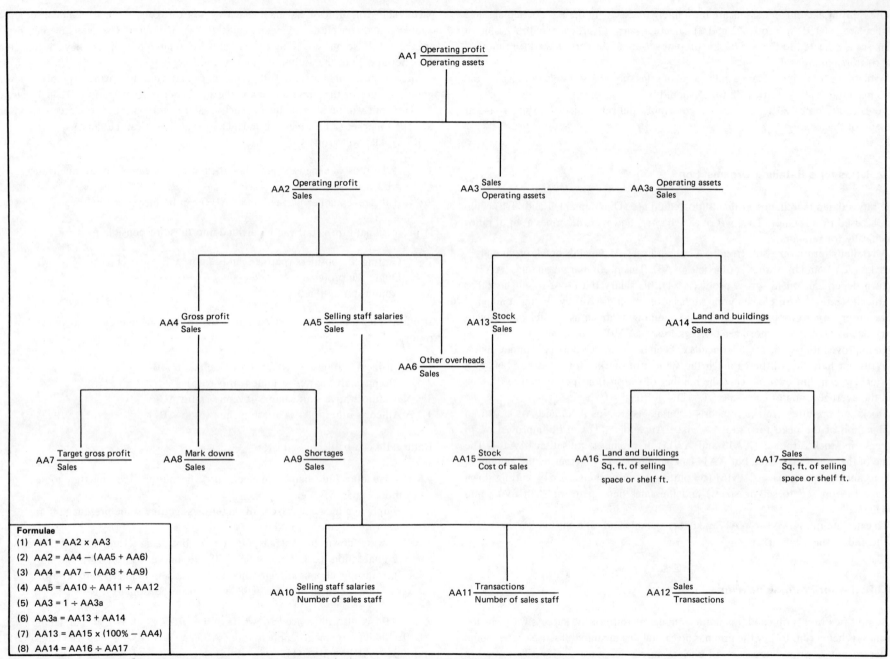

Diagram 11–3   Ratios for retailing. With acknowledgement to the Centre for Interfirm Comparison and Retail Distributors Association

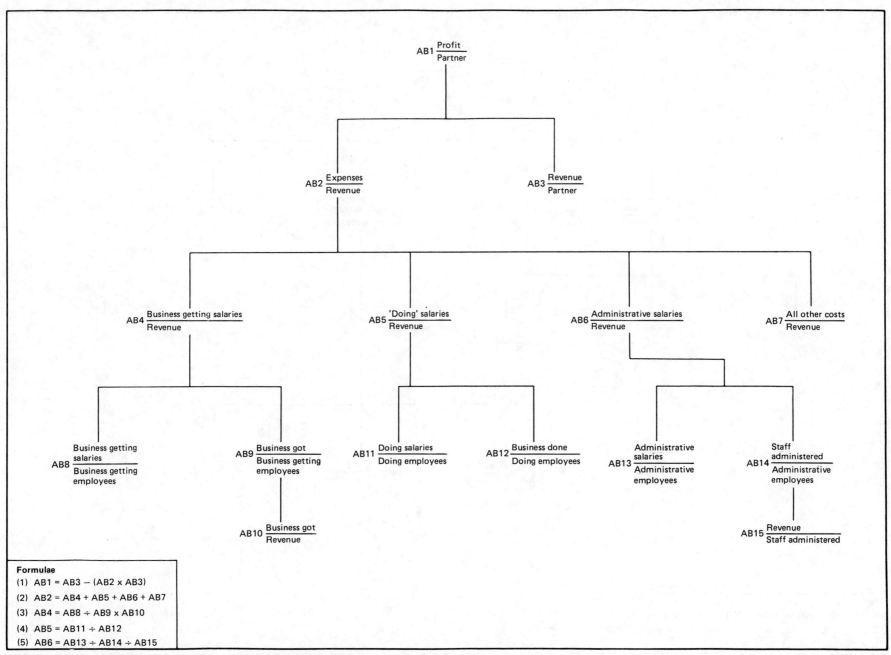

Diagram 11–4   Ratios for professional firms. With acknowledgements to the Centre for Interfirm Comparison

257

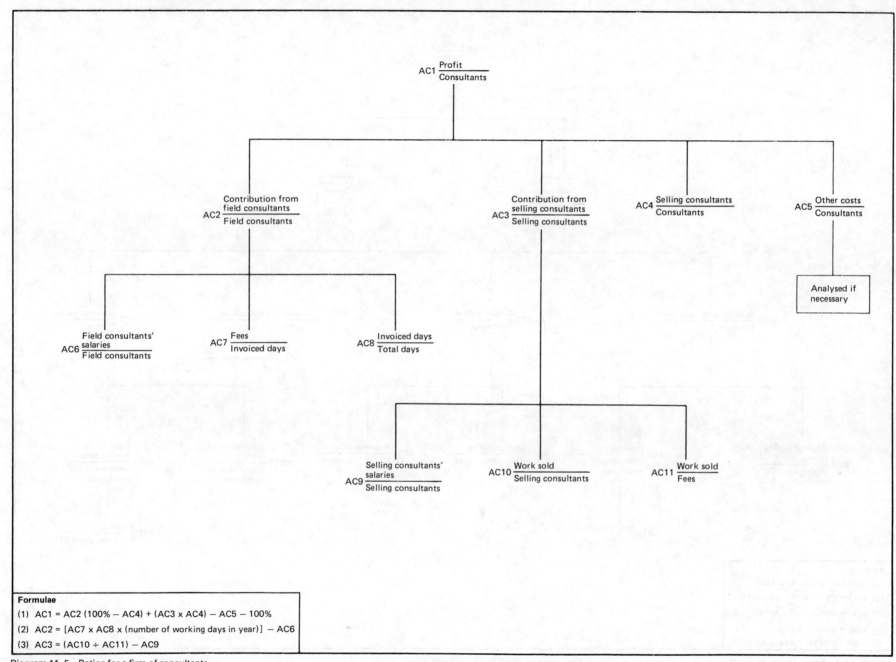

Diagram 11–5  Ratios for a firm of consultants

To calculate ratios AB1 to AB15 use data assembly and ratio calculation sheet 11–4 at the end of this chapter.

An alternative set of ratios for a professional firm is given in Diagram 11–5. It was designed with management consultants in mind but it could be used by firms in other professions.

In this set the key ratio is

AC1                                    Profit per consultant

Consultants include staff in the field doing the job and staff, however entitled, selling jobs. It does not include administrative and 'back up' staff such as librarians. This key ratio can be improved by:

1  Improving the contribution from the consultants in the field (ratio AC2) – 'contribution' is revenue from clients less the field consultants' salaries.
2  Improving the contribution from the consultants selling jobs to clients (ratio AC3) – 'contribution' is revenue from clients less the selling consultants' salaries.
3  Optimising the balance between selling consultants and field consultants (ratio AC4).
4  Minimising the overhead burden of 'other costs' (including the salaries of administrative and back up staff) without unduly diminishing the services provided to the field and sales staff by these costs (ratio AC5).

Improving the contribution of field staff (ratio AC2) depends on:

1  Optimising the salaries they receive (ratio AC6) – paying enough to attract and retain suitably qualified staff.
2  Suitable charging for jobs – indicated by the ratio of fee revenue per invoiced day (ratio AC7).
3  Maximising the utilisation of field staff on paying jobs measured by the ratio of invoiced days to total days (ratio AC8).

The sales staff's contribution can be improved by:

1  Optimising their salaries (ratio AC9) in a similar way to field staff salaries.
2  Maximising the amount of sales obtained from clients per sales consultant (ratio AC10).

If a firm of consultants is expanding (or contracting), work sold will be greater (or smaller) than fees earned. Whichever of these situations is occuring will be shown by ratio AC11 (work sold/fees) being greater or less than 100 per cent.

To calculate ratios AC1 to AC11 use data assembly and ratio calculation sheet 11.5 at the end of this chapter.

## 11.4 Ratios for the Owner Managed Business

As was indicated at the beginning of the previous section, return on capital is not usually the best measure of success for a professional firm. It is not often the best measure of success for an owner managed business either, unless modified as discussed below.

The 'profit' (sales less costs) which an owner managed business makes is partly a payment for the managerial, and maybe manual, work the owner and perhaps his family do; and partly a return on the capital he has invested and ploughed back in the business. To relate this profit to capital may give a misleadingly high rate of return. There are two alternative ways of tackling this problem:

1  Include in costs a figure equivalent to the salary, and employer's NI and pension contributions, that would have to be paid to someone outside the family to do the work done by the family (who may actually be paid nothing, or more or less than the market rate). Then calculate return on capital and other ratios as for any other business.
2  Include in costs a figure equivalent to the rate of return an outside investor would expect from the capital invested by the family (but not outsiders such as a bank) in the business (rate of interest plus an appropriate premium for risk) and then calculate the ratio of profit (after the notional cost) per member of family involved in the business.

On the whole I prefer the first alternative as it is often easier to assess market salaries for different members of a family than a suitable risk premium on the family capital in a business.

The method used to remunerate members of the family of an owner managed business is often chosen in order to minimise the amount of tax and National Insurance Contributions paid. The resulting figure of 'profit' may however be a misleading measure of performance unless adjusted as indicated above.

## 11.5 Ratios for Hotels

The Hotels and Catering EDC's *A Standard System of Hotel Accounting* (HMSO, 1969) recommends the use of the following ratios:

AF1                    $\dfrac{\text{Gross profit}}{\text{Sales}}$ (per cent)

AF2                    $\dfrac{\text{Net profit}}{\text{Sales}}$ (per cent)

$$\text{AF3} \qquad \frac{\text{Current assets}}{\text{Current liabilities}} \text{ (times)}$$

$$\text{AF4} \qquad \frac{\text{Current assets (less stock)}}{\text{Current liabilities}} \text{ (times)}$$

$$\text{AF5} \qquad \frac{\text{Stocks}}{\text{Cost of sales}} \text{ (days stock)}$$

$$\text{AF6} \qquad \frac{\text{Debtors}}{\text{Credit sales}} \text{ (days credit)}$$

$$\text{AF7} \qquad \frac{\text{Hotel net operating profit}}{\text{Capital employed in hotel operation}} \text{ (per cent)}$$

$$\text{AF8} \qquad \frac{\text{Rooms occupied}}{\text{Rooms in hotel}} \text{ (per cent)} \qquad \text{(Room occupancy)}$$

$$\text{AF9} \qquad \frac{\text{Number of guests}}{\text{Guest capacity}} \text{ (per cent)} \qquad \text{(Bed occupancy)}$$

$$\text{AF10} \qquad \frac{\text{Room sales}}{\text{Rooms occupied}} \text{ (£/room)}$$

$$\text{AF11} \qquad \frac{\text{Room sales}}{\text{Number of guests}} \text{ (£/guest)}$$

$$\text{AF12} \qquad \frac{\text{Meals served}}{\text{Restaurant seating capacity}} \text{ (per cent)}$$

$$\text{AF13} \qquad \frac{\text{Restaurant sales}}{\text{Meals served}} \text{ (£/meal)}$$

Further details of these ratios and the underlying accounting system will be found in the book quoted. Ratios 1 to 7 should be familiar to readers of this book. Ratios 8, 9 and 12 are measures of capacity utilisation. Ratios 10, 11 and 13 are measures of

average prices obtained.

The ratios listed by the EDC are obviously valuable to hotel management. It is suggested however that it would be more useful:

1   To have a key ratio to monitor overall managerial performance
2   To provide an integrated set of ratios to explain differences between the key ratio and the standard selected by management
3   To highlight the contribution to profit, and the amount of capital used in earning that profit, from each of the major departments within the hotel.

A set of ratios which is designed to meet the above objectives is shown in Diagram 11–6.

The hotel manager will measure his success by the size of ratio

$$\text{AG1} \qquad \frac{\text{Operating profit}}{\text{Operating assets}}$$

by comparison with his chosen standard.

In order to improve his key ratio (ratio AG1) he can either:

1   Improve the contribution ratios of any or all of the three main divisions of his hotel – the rooms, the restaurants and the bars – (ratios AG6, AG7 and AG8)

and/or

2   Reduce the size of his overheads (ratio AG9) or the proportion of his assets not used in any of the three main income earning divisions (ratio AG5)

and/or

3   Increase the proportion of his assets invested in the more profitable parts and reduce the proportion invested in the less profitable parts.

The hotel manager will probably be able to do 3 only in the medium to long term. Moreover he will be constrained by the need to attract customers by offering a wide range of facilities each at a competitive price.

The contribution from rooms ratio (ratio AG6) may be improved by either:

1   Raising the price per room or per guest (ratio AG10 or AG10a), and/or

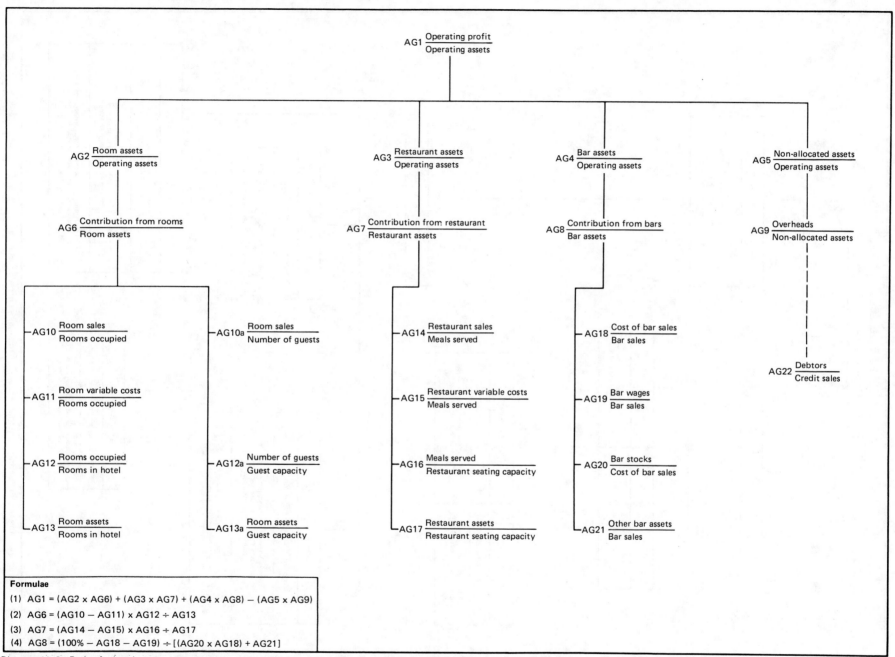

Diagram 11–6  Ratios for hotels

**Formulae**

(1)  AG1 = (AG2 x AG6) + (AG3 x AG7) + (AG4 x AG8) − (AG5 x AG9)

(2)  AG6 = (AG10 − AG11) x AG12 ÷ AG13

(3)  AG7 = (AG14 − AG15) x AG16 ÷ AG17

(4)  AG8 = (100% − AG18 − AG19) ÷ [(AG20 x AG18) + AG21]

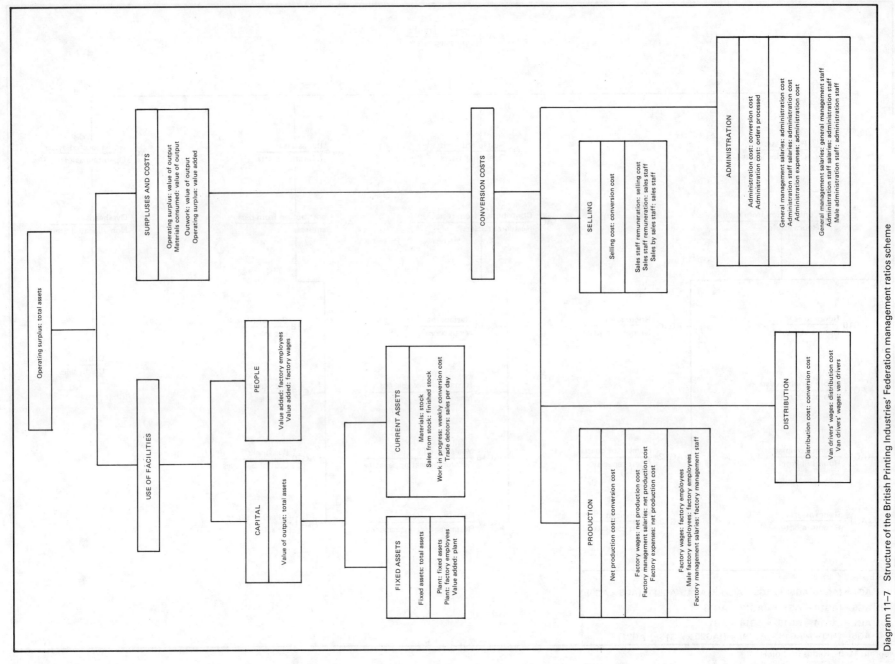

Operating surplus: total assets

**USE OF FACILITIES**

**SURPLUSES AND COSTS**

Operating surplus: value of output
Materials consumed: value of output
Outwork: value of output
Operating surplus: value added

**CONVERSION COSTS**

**CAPITAL**

Value of output: total assets

**PEOPLE**

Value added: factory employees
Value added: factory wages

**FIXED ASSETS**

Fixed assets: total assets

Plant: fixed assets
Plant: factory employees
Value added: plant

**CURRENT ASSETS**

Materials: stock
Sales from stock: finished stock
Work in progress: weekly conversion cost
Trade debtors: sales per day

**PRODUCTION**

Net production cost: conversion cost

Factory wages: net production cost
Factory management salaries: net production cost
Factory expenses: net production cost

Factory wages: factory employees
Male factory employees: factory employees
Factory management salaries: factory management staff

**SELLING**

Selling cost: conversion cost

Sales staff remuneration: selling cost
Sales staff: sales staff
Sales by sales staff: sales staff

**DISTRIBUTION**

Distribution cost: conversion cost

Van drivers' wages: distribution cost
Van drivers' wages: van drivers

**ADMINISTRATION**

Administration cost: conversion cost
Administration cost: orders processed

General management salaries: administration cost
Administration staff salaries: administration cost
Administration expenses: administration cost

General management salaries: general management staff
Administration staff salaries: administration staff
Male administration staff: administration staff

Diagram 11–7    Structure of the British Printing Industries' Federation management ratios scheme

262

2    Reducing the room variable costs (linen, cleaning, etc.) per occupied room (ratio AG11), and/or

3    Increasing the room occupancy (ratios AG12 or AG12a), and/or

4    Reducing the investment per room (again medium to long term only).

Hotel managers will realise that it may be possible to increase the room occupancy rate (ratio AG12) by *reducing* the price (ratio AG10) or even by increasing the amount of assets or service (ratios AG13 or AG11). The art of good hotel management is to balance all four ratios AG10 to AG13 over the whole year in order to maximise ratio AG6.

Similar arguments apply to the restaurant – the price of the meal (ratio AG14) must be balanced with the costs of preparing and serving it (ratio AG15) and the expenses of the restaurant and kitchens in relation to the former's seating capacity (ratio AG17) in order to get a good capacity utilisation (ratio AG16) so as to maximise the contribution ratio AG7.

In the bar it is not possible to measure capacity meaningfully. The ratios to use are:

1    The gross profit on the drinks (ratio AG18),

2    The proportion of the price paid out in wages (ratio AG19),

3    The stock turnover (ratio AG20), and

4    The investment in other bar assets in relation to sales (ratio AG21).

It is suggested that the length of credit taken by the hotel's customers should be kept under surveillance by means of ratio AG22.

It may be necessary to analyse the utilisation of other non-allocated assets and the overheads in addition.

The set of ratios in Diagram 11–6 is primarily for the day-to-day management of the hotel. In addition the hotel management will also need to use some or all of the ratios described in Chapter 8 to plan and monitor its financial affairs.

To calculate ratios AG1 to AG22 use data assembly and ratio calculation sheet 11–6 at the end of this chapter.

## 11.6 Ratios for Printers

The British Printing Industries' Federation has run a management ratio scheme for its members since 1959. The ratios currently used are shown in Table 11–1. The following is an edited version of the Federation's brief guide to interpreting the ratios. Diagram 11–7 is the Federation's own illustration of the structure of the management ratios scheme.

Ratio 1 – operating surplus/total assets – is a quick and reliable indicator for general management of the overall success of a business. A low result provides clear warning of the need for investigation of company performance and for action to improve profitability.

Ratio 1 is the product of ratio 2 (operating surplus/value of output – which shows the extent to which overall profitability is influenced by the level of costs) and ratio 10 (value of output/total assets – which shows the extent to which it is influenced by the use of capital assets). These key factor ratios are supported by groups of ratios which provide more detailed guidance.

In ratio 2 (and in ratios 3, 4 and 10) value of output is used rather than sales. This is because the difference between opening and closing work in progress values can be substantial and because it is more appropriate to relate the surplus, costs and assets values to work *produced* than to work *sold*.

If ratio 2 shows that the operating surplus is a lower than average percentage of value of output it may indicate that operating costs are too high, and ratios 3 to 9 inclusive are intended as broad pointers to which element of cost may be out of line.

### Materials and outwork costs

Ratios 3 and 4 show the percentages of value of output represented by materials consumed and by outwork. Generally, it is more important for printers to make an efficient and profitable use of men and machines than it is to process large volumes of materials or outwork; so the operating surplus is related to value added at ratio 5. Value added is value of output less the cost of materials and outwork and represents the value of the work actually done by the printer. More detailed reference to value added ratios is made later. The separation of the materials and outwork elements, however, will enable their relative importance to be determined and will indicate their likely effect on profitability.

### Conversion costs

All remaining costs of the business are attributed to the process of converting materials and outwork into the saleable product, hence they are known collectively as conversion cost (which is also equal to value added less operating surplus). Conversion cost is sub-divided into four main headings:

1    Net production cost

2    Distribution cost

3    Selling cost

4    Administration cost

Ratios 6, 7, 8 and 9 indicate whether the proportion of conversion cost represented by each of these main elements is out of line with the cost structure of similar firms. To help further in the investigation of any differences, some analyses of these groups of costs are now provided.

---

**OPERATING COSTS/SURPLUSES**

1   Operating Surplus/Total Assets (%)
2   Operating Surplus/Value of Output (%)
3   Materials Consumed/Value of Output (%)
4   Outwork/Value of Output (%)
5   Operating Surplus/Value Added (%)
6   Net Production Cost/Conversion Cost (%)
7   Distribution Cost/Conversion Cost (%)
8   Selling Cost/Conversion Cost (%)
9   Administration Cost/Conversion Cost (%)

**USE OF FACILITIES**

Capital

10   Value of Output/Total Assets (Times per Year)
11   Fixed Assets/Total Assets (%)
12   Plant/Fixed Assets (%)
13   Plant/Factory Employees (£ per cap)
14   Value Added/Plant (%)
15   Materials Consumed/Stock of Materials (Times per year)
16   Net Sales, Stock Items/Stock, Finished Goods (Times per year)
17   Work in Progress/Weekly Conversion Cost (Weeks' output)
18   Trade Debtors/Sales per Day (Days' credit)

People

19   Value Added/Factory Employees (£ per cap)
20   Value Added/Factory Wages (per £)

**NET PRODUCTION COST**

21   Factory Wages/Net Production Cost (%)
22   Factory Wages/Factory Employees (£ per cap)
23   Male Factory Employees/Factory Employees (%)
24   Factory Management Salaries/Net Production Cost (%)
25   Factory Management Salaries/Factory Management Staff (£ per cap)
26   Factory Expenses/Net Production Cost (%)

---

**DISTRIBUTION COST**

27   Van Drivers' Wages/Distribution Cost (%)
28   Van Drivers' Wages/Van Drivers (£ per cap)

**SELLING COST**

29   Sales Staff Remuneration/Selling Cost (%)
30   Sales Staff Remuneration/Sales Staff (£ per cap)
31   Sales by Sales Staff/Sales Staff (£ 000s)

**ADMINISTRATION COST**

32   General Management Salaries/Admin. Cost (%)
33   General Management Salaries/General Management Staff (£ per cap)
34   Admin. Staff Salaries/Admin. Cost (%)
35   Admin. Staff Salaries/Admin. Staff (£ per cap)
36   Male Admin. Staff/Admin. Staff (%)
37   Admin. Expenses/Admin. Cost (%)
38   Admin. Cost/Orders Processed (£ per ord)

**FACTORED/SHOP GOODS**

39   Factored/Shop Goods/Total Sales (%)
40   Factored/Shop Goods/Consumption (%)
41   Factored/Shop Goods/Stock (Times per year)
42   Sales of Shop Goods/Shop Staff (£ per cap)
43   Sales of Shop Goods/Shop Staff Wages (per £)

**DEPRECIATION**

49   Op. Surplus less Deprec./Total Assets (%)
50   Capital Expenditure/Depreciation (%)

**BALANCE SHEET**

91   Net Profit/Net Assets (%)
92   Current Assets/Current Liabilities (Times)
93   Quick Assets/Current Liabilities (Times)

**CASH FLOW**

94   Capital Expenditure/Cash Flow (%)
95   Dividends/Cash Flow (%)

Table 11-1   The British Printing Industries' Federation management ratios scheme

*Net production cost* (ratio 6) comprises (i) factory wages (ii) factory management salaries and (iii) factory expenses. Each of these is expressed as a percentage of net production cost to indicate its relative importance and to pinpoint where investigation may be needed (ratios 21, 24 and 26).

In respect of factory wages, ratio 22 shows the average amount paid per employee, and it must be borne in mind that this figure includes overtime, shift and bonus payments and the employer's share of social security contributions. The extent to which it is influenced by the proportion of men to women in the labour force is indicated by ratio 23. This latter ratio, together with ratio 13, may also provide some evidence of the extent of handwork in the factory, and if this predominates it may depress the value added per factory employee (ratio 19). Ratio 19 and ratio 20 (value added per £ of factory wages) are key ratios which show how effectively people are used. These ratios have an important influence on profitability. Factory wages ratios must be considered in conjunction with these productivity ratios, and high results for ratios 21 and 22 can usually be justified only by a high result for ratio 20.

The *per capita* payment to factory management staff is shown by ratio 25. A high figure here should be justified by good results for ratios 19 and 20 and for ratio 14 (see **Use of assets** below), but it must be recognised that low payments to these staff can lead to lack of motivation and an inefficient factory.

High factory expenses (ratio 26) need detailed investigation if unnecessary waste is to be avoided.

*Distribution cost* (ratio 7) comprises (i) van drivers' wages, which are shown as a proportion of distribution cost at ratio 27 and as a payment per capita at ratio 28, and (ii) carriage outwards and van expenses.

*Selling cost* (ratio 8) comprises (i) sales staff remuneration and (ii) selling expenses. Sales staff remuneration is expressed as a percentage of selling cost at ratio 29 and as a payment *per capita* at ratio 30. These ratios are often high in the more successful firms which recognise the importance of marketing policy and effective selling effort to the achievement of a full use of production facilities and high profitability. Ratio 30 should, however, be carefully related to ratio 31 which measures the value of sales achieved by each salesman.

*Administration cost* (ratio 9) comprises (i) general management salaries (ii) administration staff salaries and (iii) administration expenses. Each of these groups of cost is expressed as a percentage of administration cost by ratios 32, 34 and 37. The two groups of salary costs are also expressed *per capita* by ratios 33 and 35, while ratio 36 shows the proportion of male administration staff. Ratio 38 gives the administration cost per order, providing an indication of the average size of order processed. As with selling costs, the more successful firms rarely have low administration cost ratios, because the importance of efficient administration procedures and effective management information is recognised. But cost must be carefully balanced against benefits.

## Use of assets

Ratio 10 shows how many times assets have been turned into sales. Generally, with a sensible pricing policy, the faster assets can be turned over the greater is the profit accruing to the business. With a quick turnover of capital a lower than average result for ratio 2 can still provide a very satisfactory return on assets at ratio 1.

Assets should be considered in two groups – fixed and current – and ratio 11 shows whether your investment in fixed assets is greater or less than usual. If it is greater, your attention needs to be concentrated on the best possible use of fixed assets such as plant and machinery, metal and type and motor vehicles. Plant and machinery should normally be as large a proportion as possible of the total, and ratio 12 will indicate whether this is so, while the relative extent of mechanisation in your business is measured by the value of plant per employee (ratio 13). Except in certain very rare circumstances efficient use of plant facilities is an essential ingredient of success for the modern printer, and ratio 14 shows whether this is being achieved by comparing value added with plant value.

Ratios 15 to 18 are concerned with the control of investment in current assets. Of this group of ratios the first and last will be the most significant for the majority of participants. Ratio 15 measures the number of times that materials stocks are turned over, but it must be remembered that, for every firm, there is an optimum rate which keeps stock at the minimum consistent with the avoidance of production delays. Ratio 18 shows the average period of credit being extended to customers. It should be stressed that printers are sometimes rather generous in this respect – perhaps dangerously so when cash resources are subject to severe pressure. Ratio 17 measures the number of weeks' output in progress in the factory – a high result can sometimes indicate poor production control. Ratio 16 is of interest only to those firms who make for stock, and it shows how quickly stock items are turned into sales.

## Depreciation

A satisfactory uniform approach to assessment of depreciation charges is considered unattainable because of the many variable factors affecting the life expectancy of similar machines in different firms. For this reason the main structure of ratios uses operating surplus before depreciation. To show the probable approximate effect on profitability of adequate depreciation charges ratio 49 shows operating surplus less depreciation as a percentage of total assets. The depreciation charge used is calculated by the Federation using standard percentages of the estimated replacement cost of the assets concerned. Ratio 50 shows capital expenditure in the year as a percentage of this calculated depreciation figure.

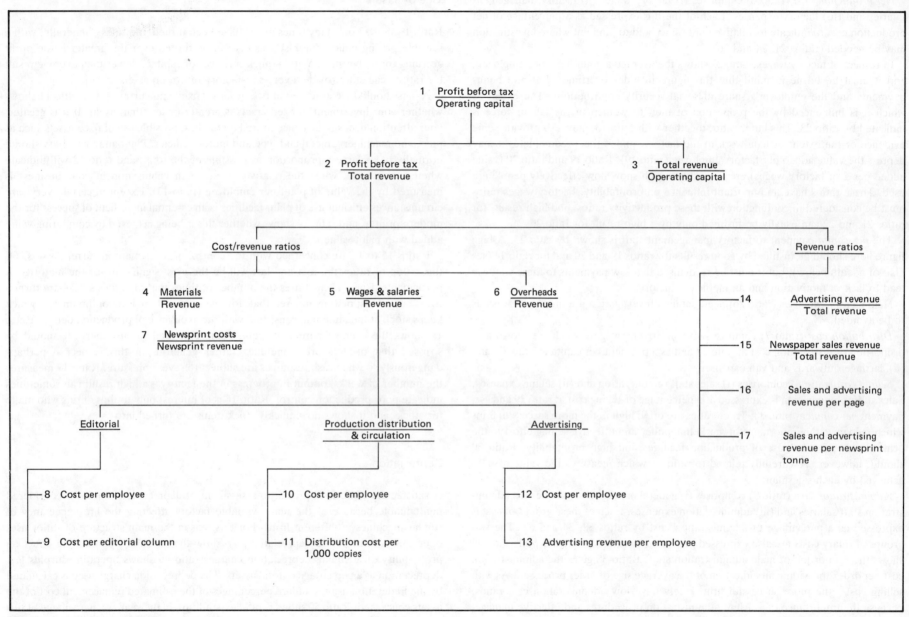

1  Profit before tax
   Operating capital

2  Profit before tax
   Total revenue

3  Total revenue
   Operating capital

Cost/revenue ratios

Revenue ratios

4  Materials
   Revenue

5  Wages & salaries
   Revenue

6  Overheads
   Revenue

7  Newsprint costs
   Newsprint revenue

14  Advertising revenue
    Total revenue

15  Newspaper sales revenue
    Total revenue

16  Sales and advertising
    revenue per page

17  Sales and advertising
    revenue per newsprint
    tonne

Editorial

Production distribution
& circulation

Advertising

8  Cost per employee

9  Cost per editorial column

10  Cost per employee

11  Distribution cost per
    1,000 copies

12  Cost per employee

13  Advertising revenue per employee

Diagram 11–8   Ratios for newspapers

266

## Balance sheet extracts

Ratios 91 to 93 are commonly used Balance Sheet Ratios which will be familiar to most printers. The ratio of net profit/net assets (ratio 91) is a popular measure of profitability which can be rather misleading to managements because of its failure to recognise the effect of inflation on fixed assets values; contrast this result with ratios 1 and 49. Ratios 92 and 93 are realistic measures of liquidity and solvency and thus of considerable importance. If either result is less than 1 the business is unable to meet its debts from its own liquid resources.

## Cash flows

Ratios 94 and 95 show how much of the net cash inflow to the business has been used for capital growth and how much has been distributed as dividends to the owners.

## 11.7 Ratios for Newspapers, etc.

The Newspaper Society calculates annually, for different groups of newspapers, several ratios, some of which are shown in Diagram 11–8. I am grateful to the Society for permission to make this use of their ratios.

These ratios could be used, with a little adaptation, for magazine and journal publication.

The key ratio is

$$1 \qquad \frac{\text{Profit before tax}}{\text{Operating capital}}$$

with fixed assets at market value.

This may be improved by:

1    increasing the profit/revenue ratio (ratio 2); and/or
2    increasing the turnover of assets (ratio 3).

Ratio 2 may be improved by:

1    reducing the materials costs in relation to revenue (ratio 4); and/or
2    reducing wages and salaries in relation to revenue (ratio 5); and/or
3    reducing overheads in relation to revenue (ratio 6).

In all cases either by cutting costs more than revenue or boosting revenue more than proportionately to costs.

Wages and salaries are then analysed under:

(*a*)    Editorial
(*b*)    Production, distribution and circulation
(*c*)    Advertising.

In all departments cost per employee is given (ratios 8, 10 and 12).

In Editorial and Distribution a measure of physical productivity is given (ratios 9 and 11). Ratio 11 is particularly important for 'giveaway' papers.

In Advertising a measure of financial productivity is given (ratio 13).

The size of ratio 2 will also be influenced by the balance between advertising and newspaper sales revenue (ratios 14 and 15) and by the amount of sales and advertising revenue per page and per newsprint tonne (ratios 16 and 17). Whilst sales and advertising are the principal sources of revenue, some newspapers also derive income from contract printing and readers' services and offers. This income is included in 'total revenue'.

## 11.8 Ratios for Farms

The ratios in this section are adapted from those produced by the University of Exeter's Agricultural Economics Unit in its *Farm Management* handbook. Not all the ratios used by Exeter are included. Some of the ratios included are not currently used by Exeter but are either being considered by Exeter or are my suggestion (e.g. ratio 1B).

I am grateful to the Unit for permission to make use of their ratios. Some other universities also produce ratios on agricultural profitability. Details are available from the Ministry of Agriculture, Fisheries & Food.

In common with many small businesses the 'profit' which the farmer and his family earn is in part payment for their manual labour, part is payable for their management expertise, and part a return on their investment in tenant's capital. Because of this two primary ratios should be calculated.

$$1A \qquad \frac{\text{Management and investment income}}{\text{Tenant's capital}} \qquad \%$$

$$1B \qquad \frac{\text{Net farm income}}{\text{Farmer (and working spouse)}} \qquad \text{£ per head}$$

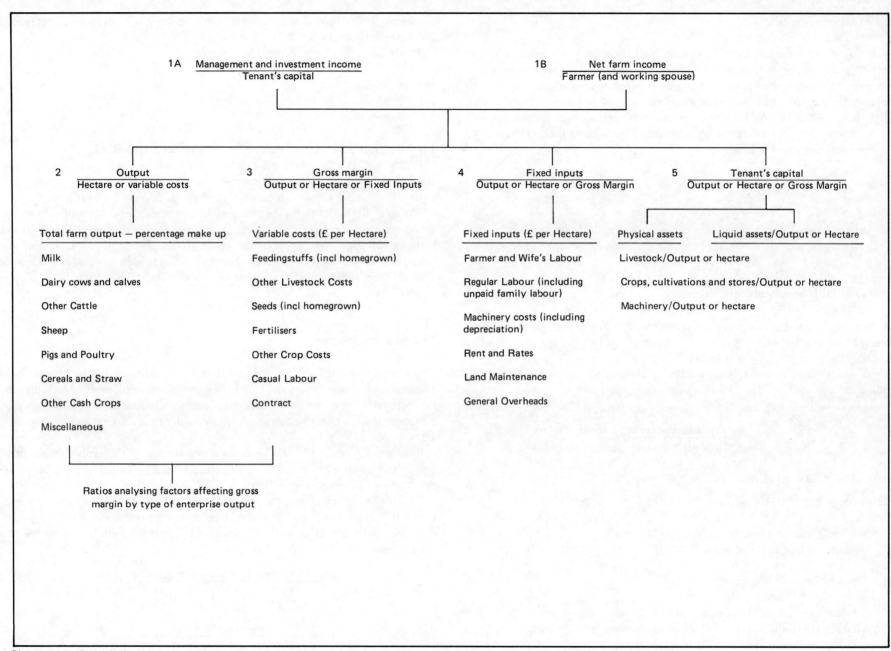

1A  Management and investment income
    Tenant's capital

1B  Net farm income
    Farmer (and working spouse)

2  Output
   Hectare or variable costs

3  Gross margin
   Output or Hectare or Fixed Inputs

4  Fixed inputs
   Output or Hectare or Gross Margin

5  Tenant's capital
   Output or Hectare or Gross Margin

Total farm output — percentage make up

Milk

Dairy cows and calves

Other Cattle

Sheep

Pigs and Poultry

Cereals and Straw

Other Cash Crops

Miscellaneous

Variable costs (£ per Hectare)

Feedingstuffs (incl homegrown)

Other Livestock Costs

Seeds (incl homegrown)

Fertilisers

Other Crop Costs

Casual Labour

Contract

Fixed inputs (£ per Hectare)

Farmer and Wife's Labour

Regular Labour (including
unpaid family labour)

Machinery costs (including
depreciation)

Rent and Rates

Land Maintenance

General Overheads

Physical assets

Livestock/Output or hectare

Crops, cultivations and stores/Output or hectare

Machinery/Output or hectare

Liquid assets/Output or Hectare

Ratios analysing factors affecting gross
margin by type of enterprise output

Diagram 11–9   Ratios for farms

In arriving at management and investment income a notional cost for the farmer's (and spouse's) manual labour is deducted from net farm income. Net farm income is the value of the farm's output less variable and fixed costs, with the latter including a rental value on owner-occupied land and a charge for family unpaid labour (excluding farmer and spouse) but interest charges are excluded.

Ratios 1A and 1B can be improved by:

1   Increasing the value of the output per hectare (ratio 2) or relative to variable and fixed inputs (ratios 2b and 2c).
2   Improving the gross margin as a percentage of output (ratio 3a) or per hectare (ratio 3b), or as a percentage of fixed inputs (ratios 3c).
3   Reducing the fixed inputs as a percentage of output (ratio 4a) or per hectare (ratio 4b) as a percentage of gross margin (ratio 4c).
4   Reducing the tenant's capital as a percentage of output (ratio 5a) or per hectare (ratio 5b) or as a percentage of gross margin (ratio 5c).

An improvement in gross margin (ratio 3) may obtained from a more efficient use of variable costs (see below ratio 3) which may include increased yields and/or prices (see below) or changing the mix of enterprises to the more profitable ones (see below ratio 2).

An improvement in the ratio of fixed costs per hectare (ratio 4) may be obtained from paying attention to the items listed below ratio 4a, including the ratios of fixed inputs to gross margin (ratio 4b and 4c).

An improvement in ratio 5 may be obtained either:

1   by reducing the physical or liquid assets per hectare or relative to output or gross margin; or
2   by increasing output or gross margin more than proportionly to any increase in physical or liquid capital.

Exeter provides typical ratios for different farms classified by type (e.g. Dairy, Crops, etc.) and size.

In addition to the ratios in Diagram 11–9 Exeter also provides ratios for each main type of enterprise output, of which the following are two examples.

*Cereals (classified by type (e.g. wheat, barley, etc.) )*
1   Yield (tonnes per hectare)
2   Price (£ per hectare)
3   Output (£ per hectare) (1 × 2)
4   Seeds (£ per hectare)
5   Fertiliser (£ per hectare)

6   Spray (£ per hectare)
7   Variable costs (£ per hectare) (4 + 5 + 6)
8   Gross margin (£ per hectare) (3 − 7)

*Dairy cows*
1   Yield (litres per cow)
2   Price (p per litre)
3   Stocking rate (cows per hectare)
4   Output (milk and calves less replacement cost) (£ per cow)
5   Concentrates (£ per cow)
6   Veterinary and medicines (£ per cow)
7   Forage (£ per cow)
8   Total variables (£ per cow) (5 + 6 + 7)
9   Gross margin per cow (£ per cow) (4 − 8)
10  Gross margin per hectare

Exeter also provides ratios on financial structures but as these are similar to those discusssed in Chapter 8.2 and 8.3 they are not included here.

**Appendix 11.1**

### THE EVOLUTION OF A SET OF RATIOS FOR FIRMS IN THE ACCOUNTANCY PROFESSION

In Chapter 1 it was stated that 'selecting ratios is an exercise which must be done by each firm and manager individually'. This appendix contains an illustration of this process in practice.

A board was set up by the Institute of Chartered Accountants in England and Wales' Technical Committee to advise on the implementation of an Interfirm Comparison for accounting firms in public practice. The author was secretary to this advisory board. Two suggestions as to the ratios which might be included in the comparison were placed before the board. One suggestion was of the set of ratios shown in Diagram 11–4; another suggestion was of the list of ratios shown in Diagram 11–10 extracted from an article entitled 'Assessing the efficiency of an Accounting Firm' by M.H. Cabourn-Smith, *Accountancy* December 1970. The board agreed with the principles (from Chapter 1) of:

1   A key ratio
2   Logical 'cause-and-effect' linkage.

It also agreed that the ratios should be easily calculated even by firms with less sophisticated management accounting systems.

The board's final choice is shown in Diagram 11–11. The following points are of interest:

1   Whereas ratio AE1 profit/number of partners, is *the* key ratio, ratios AE2 profit/fees; AE18 debtors and work in progress at selling price/fees; AE21 partners' average remuneration; AE22 growth (fees this year/fees last year); and AE23 staff turnover (number of staff leaving during the year/average number of staff during the year) are considered to be of almost equal importance.

2   Because of the number of key, or important ratios, not all ratios are wholly or partly logically linked (20 out of 23 are). There are, in fact, two sub-sets of ratios (AE1 to AE17 and AE18 to AE20) which are internally linked but are not logically connected to each other.

3   Only six of the ratios in Diagram 11–11 are in either Diagram 11–4 or 11–10 (ratios AE1, 2, 3, 5, 18 and 19). However, many of them will be found either elsewhere in this book or can be derived from ratios in Diagram 11–4 or 11–10. The thinking behind their choice is wholly consistent with the principles set out in this book.

The board's choice makes an excellent example of a workable compromise being better than the sum of its parts.

To calculate ratios AE1 to AE23 use data assembly and ratio calculation sheet 11–7 at the end of this chapter.

| | |
|---|---|
| AD1 | Productive staff cost to fees |
| AD2 | Accommodation cost to fees |
| AD3 | Administration expenses to fees |
| AD4 | Profit to fees |
| AD5 | Work in progress to fees |
| AD6 | Debtors plus work in progress at cost to fees |
| AD7 | Capital employed to fees |
| AD8 | Profit to capital employed |
| AD9 | Fees divided by total number of partners and productive staff |
| AD10 | Average size of fee |

Diagram 11–10   List of ratios for assessing the efficiency of an accounting firm (first version)

## Later developments

The previous paragraphs describe the position at the time of the first edition of this book (1973). Since then the board and I (and my successor at the Institute, Phil Shohet) have modified the scheme in the light of experience and participants' comments thereby demonstrating the practical importance of principle 10 (Chapter 1.2 above). The ratios compared in 1983 are shown in Diagram 11–12 and Table 11–2.

Nearly all the 1973 ratios have survived but considerable explanatory detail has been added for ratios relating to salary costs, charging rates, etc., for different staff grades (old AE9 and 11 – the new parts 2 and 4 ratios) and the effects of inflation on profit and growth have been incorporated (new ratios 1B and 3B).

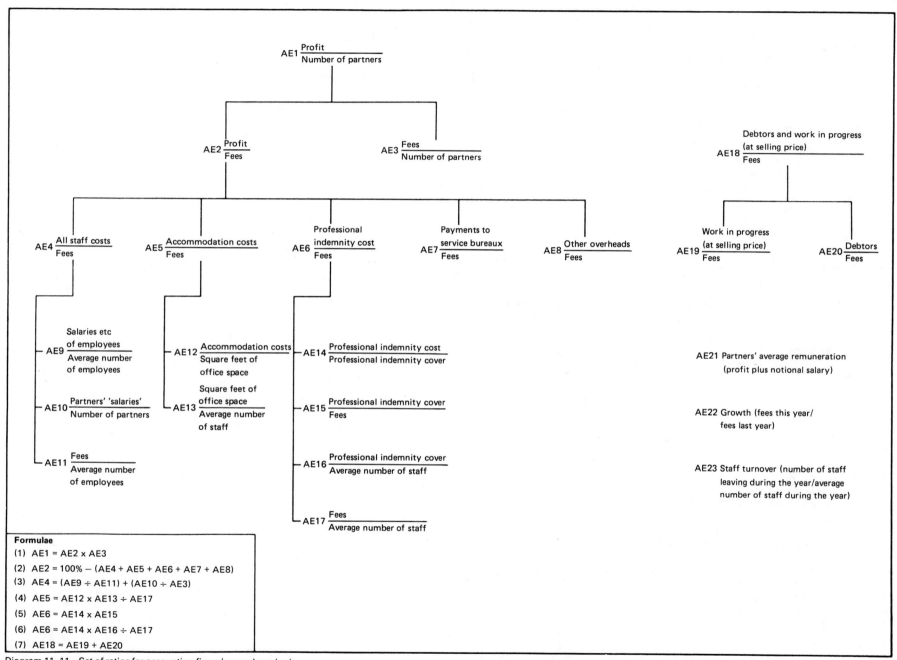

**Formulae**

(1)  AE1 = AE2 x AE3

(2)  AE2 = 100% − (AE4 + AE5 + AE6 + AE7 + AE8)

(3)  AE4 = (AE9 ÷ AE11) + (AE10 ÷ AE3)

(4)  AE5 = AE12 x AE13 ÷ AE17

(5)  AE6 = AE14 x AE15

(6)  AE6 = AE14 x AE16 ÷ AE17

(7)  AE18 = AE19 + AE20

Diagram 11–11   Set of ratios for accounting firms (second version)

## PART 2 RATIOS

A1    Average charging rate per hour (£s per hour)
A2    Salary per year (£s per year per head)
A3    Number of hours charged per year per head
A4    Percentage under or over recovery
A5    Professional staff turnover (% p.a.)
A6    Employee analysis (number of employees per partner)

## PART 3 RATIOS

*Debtors and work in progress/fees*
B1a   Debtors and work in progress (at charging rate)/fees (%)
B1b   Debtors and work in progress (at charging rate)/fees (days)
B2a   Work in progress (at charging rate)/fees (%)
B2b   Work in progress (at charging rate)/fees (days)
B3a   Debtors/fees (%)
B3b   Debtors/fees (days)
C1    Professional Indemnity Cover/fees (%)
C2    Professional Indemnity Cover/Average no. of personnel (£s per head p.a.)
C3    Fees/Number of Bills rendered (£s)
C4    Number of Bills rendered/Average no. of partners (no. per partner)

## PART 4 RATIOS

*Salaries and charging rates*
D1    Average charging rate per hour (£s per hour).
D2    Salary per year (£s per year per head).

*Note:* There are separate ratios A1, A2, A3, A6, D1 and D2 for each* of the following categories of personnel:
categories of personnel:

1     Partners
2a    Managers
2b    Others qualified – senior
2c    Other qualified – junior
2D    Qualified – other than partners (i.e. the sum of 2a, 2b and 2c)
3a    Students – senior
3b    Students – junior
3C    All students (i.e. the sum of 3a and 3b)
4a    Unqualified accounting, audit and tax staff – senior
4b    Unqualified accounting, audit and tax staff – junior
4C    All unqualified accounting, audit and tax staff (i.e. the sum of 4a and 4b)
5a    Other personnel – chargeable
5b    Other personnel – non-chargeable
5C    All other personnel (i.e. the sum of 5a and 5b)

* No ratios A2, A3 and D1 for category 5b: No ratios A6 and D2 for category 1

Table 11–2   List of ratios compared (other than those in Diagram 11–12)

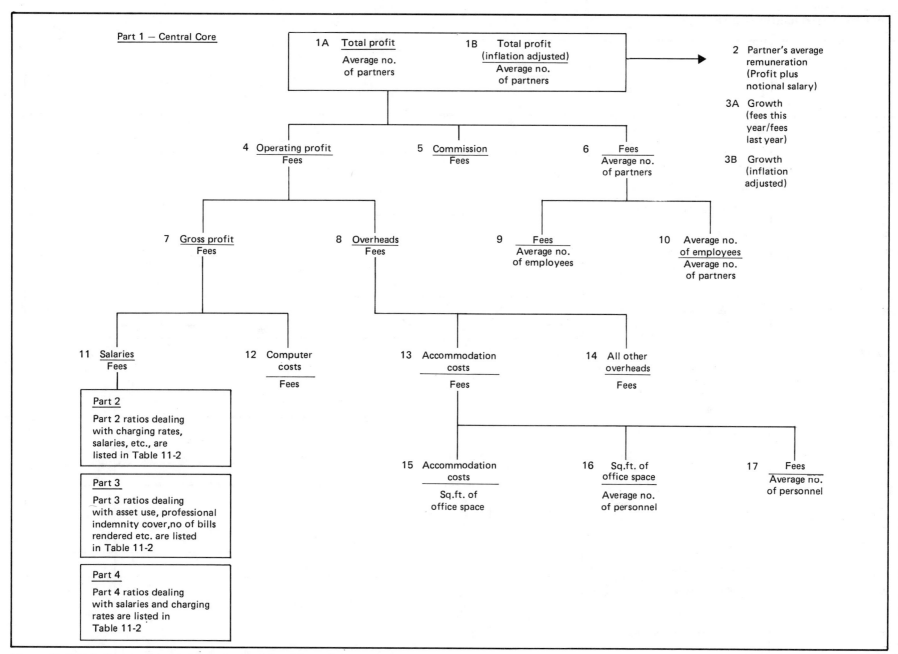

Part 1 — Central Core

1A  Total profit
$$\frac{\text{Total profit}}{\text{Average no. of partners}}$$

1B  Total profit (inflation adjusted)
$$\frac{\text{Total profit (inflation adjusted)}}{\text{Average no. of partners}}$$

2  Partner's average remuneration (Profit plus notional salary)

3A  Growth (fees this year/fees last year)

3B  Growth (inflation adjusted)

4  $$\frac{\text{Operating profit}}{\text{Fees}}$$

5  $$\frac{\text{Commission}}{\text{Fees}}$$

6  $$\frac{\text{Fees}}{\text{Average no. of partners}}$$

7  $$\frac{\text{Gross profit}}{\text{Fees}}$$

8  $$\frac{\text{Overheads}}{\text{Fees}}$$

9  $$\frac{\text{Fees}}{\text{Average no. of employees}}$$

10  $$\frac{\text{Average no. of employees}}{\text{Average no. of partners}}$$

11  $$\frac{\text{Salaries}}{\text{Fees}}$$

12  $$\frac{\text{Computer costs}}{\text{Fees}}$$

13  $$\frac{\text{Accommodation costs}}{\text{Fees}}$$

14  $$\frac{\text{All other overheads}}{\text{Fees}}$$

15  $$\frac{\text{Accommodation costs}}{\text{Sq.ft. of office space}}$$

16  $$\frac{\text{Sq.ft. of office space}}{\text{Average no. of personnel}}$$

17  $$\frac{\text{Fees}}{\text{Average no. of personnel}}$$

Part 2
Part 2 ratios dealing with charging rates, salaries, etc., are listed in Table 11-2

Part 3
Part 3 ratios dealing with asset use, professional indemnity cover, no of bills rendered etc. are listed in Table 11-2

Part 4
Part 4 ratios dealing with salaries and charging rates are listed in Table 11-2

Diagram 11–12   Interfirm comparison between accountants in public practice

273

Data assembly sheet 11–1
## Ratios for a merchanting business

| Code letter | Item | Product group A (1) | B (2) | C (3) | Total (4) | | |
|---|---|---|---|---|---|---|---|
| **Part 1** | | | | | | | |
| A | Quantity bought | | | | | | |
| B | Quantity sold | | | | | | |
| C | Purchases | | | | | | |
| D | Stock at beginning of period | | | | | | |
| E | Sub total (C + D) | | | | | | |
| F | Stock at end of period | | | | | | |
| G | Cost of sales (E − F) | | | | | | |
| H | Sales | | | | | | |
| K | Gross profit (H − G) | | | | | | |
| | | *Month or quarter to (date)* | | | | | |
| **Part 2** | | | | | | | |
| L | Rent and rates | | | | | | |
| M | Salaries | | | | | | |
| N | Other overheads | | | | | | |
| P | Total overheads (L + M + N) | | | | | | |
| Q | Gross profit (equals K4 above) | | | | | | |
| R | Operating profit (Q − P) | | | | | | |
| S | Stock (equals ½(D4 + F4 above) | | | | | | |
| T | Average value of debtors | | | | | | |
| U | Premises | | | | | | |
| V | Operating assets (S + T + U) | | | | | | |
| W | No. of working days in period | | | | | | |
| Y | No. of working days in year | | | | | | |
| Z | No. of calendar days in period | | | | | | |
| AA | Area of premises | | | | | | |

**Ratios for a merchanting business**

| Ratio | | Formula for calculation of ratio | Unit of measurement | Month or quarter to (date) | | | | | |
|---|---|---|---|---|---|---|---|---|---|
| Y1 | Operating profit/ Operating assets | R x 100 ÷ V x Y ÷ W | % pa | | | | | | |
| Y2 | Operating profit/ Sales | R x 100 ÷ H4 | % | | | | | | |
| Y3 | Sales/ Operating assets | H4 ÷ V x Y ÷ W | Times per year | | | | | | |
| Y4 | Gross profit/Sales | Q x 100 ÷ H4 | % | | | | | | |
| Y5 | Overheads/Sales | P x 100 ÷ H4 | % | | | | | | |
| Y6 | Sales of product group A/ Total sales | H1 x 100 ÷ H4 | % | | | | | | |
| Y7 | Sales of product group B/ Total sales | H2 x 100 ÷ H4 | % | | | | | | |
| Y8 | Gross profit on product group A/ Sales of product group A | K1 x 100 ÷ H1 | % | | | | | | |
| Y9 | Gross profit on product group B/ Sales of product group B | K2 x 100 ÷ H2 | % | | | | | | |
| Y10 | Average buying price of product group A | C1 ÷ A1 | £'s per unit | | | | | | |
| Y11 | Average selling price of product group A | H1 ÷ B1 | £'s per unit | | | | | | |
| Y12 | Rent and rates/ Sales | L x 100 ÷ H4 | % | | | | | | |
| Y13 | Salaries/Sales | M x 100 ÷ H4 | % | | | | | | |
| Y14 | Stock/Cost of sales | S x W ÷ G4 | days | | | | | | |
| Y15 | Debtors/Sales | T x Z ÷ H4 | days | | | | | | |
| Y16 | Premises/Sales | U x 1000 ÷ (H4 x Y ÷ W) | ‰ pa | | | | | | |
| Y17 | Value of premises/ Area of premises | U ÷ AA | £ per sq.ft. | | | | | | |
| Y18 | Sales/Area of premises | H4 x Y ÷ W ÷ AA | £ pa per sq.ft. | | | | | | |

**Alternative set of ratios for a merchant**

| Code letter | Item | Product group A (1) | B (2) | C (3) | Total (4) |
|---|---|---|---|---|---|
| **Part 1** | | | | | |
| A | Quantity bought | | | | |
| B | Quantity sold | | | | |
| C | Purchases | | | | |
| D | Stock at beginning of period | | | | |
| E | Sub total (C + D) | | | | |
| F | Stock at end of period | | | | |
| G | Cost of Sales (E − F) | | | | |
| H | Sales | | | | |
| K | Gross profit (H − G) | | | | |
| **Part 2** | | Month or quarter to (date) | | | | | |
| L | Rent and rates | | | | | | |
| M | Salaries | | | | | | |
| N | Other overheads | | | | | | |
| P | Total overheads (L + M + N) | | | | | | |
| Q | Gross profit (equals K4 above) | | | | | | |
| R | Operating profit (Q − P) | | | | | | |
| S | Stock (equals ½(D4 + F4 above)) | | | | | | |
| T | Average value of debtors | | | | | | |
| U | Current assets (S + T) | | | | | | |
| V | Premises | | | | | | |
| W | Operating assets (U + V) | | | | | | |
| Y | Maximum sales | | | | | | |
| Z | Number of working days in period | | | | | | |
| AA | Number of working days in year | | | | | | |
| AB | Number of calendar days in period | | | | | | |

**Alternative set of ratios for a merchant**

| Ratio | | Formula for calculation of ratio | Unit of measurement | Month or quarter to (date) | | | | | |
|---|---|---|---|---|---|---|---|---|---|
| Z1 | Operating profit/ Operating assets | $R \times 100 \div W \times AA \div Z$ | % pa | | | | | | |
| Z2 | Gross profit/ Sales | $Q \times 100 \div H4$ | % | | | | | | |
| Z3 | Current assets/ Sales | $U \times 1000 \div (H4 \times AA \div Z)$ | ‰ pa | | | | | | |
| Z4 | Overheads/ Maximum sales | $P \times 100 \div Y$ | % | | | | | | |
| Z5 | Premises/ Maximum sales | $V \times 1000 \div (Y \times AA \div Z)$ | ‰ pa | | | | | | |
| Z6 | Actual sales/ Maximum sales | $H4 \times 100 \div Y$ | % | | | | | | |
| Z7 | Sales of product group A/ Total sales | $H1 \times 100 \div H4$ | % | | | | | | |
| Z8 | Sales of product group B/ Total sales | $H2 \times 100 \div H4$ | % | | | | | | |
| Z9 | Gross profit on product group A/ Sales of product group A | $K1 \times 100 \div H1$ | % | | | | | | |
| Z10 | Gross profit on product group B/ Sales of product group B | $K2 \times 100 \div H2$ | % | | | | | | |
| Z11 | Average buying price of product group A | $C1 \div A1$ | £'s per unit | | | | | | |
| Z12 | Average selling price of product group A | $H1 \div B1$ | £'s per unit | | | | | | |
| Z13 | Stock/Cost of sales | $S \times Z \div G4$ | days | | | | | | |
| Z14 | Debtors/Sales | $T \times AB \div H4$ | days | | | | | | |
| Z15 | Rent and rates/ Maximum sales | $L \times 100 \div Y$ | % | | | | | | |
| Z16 | Salaries/ Maximum sales | $M \times 100 \div Y$ | % | | | | | | |

**Ratios for retailing**

| Code letter | Item | Month or quarter to (date) | | | | | |
|---|---|---|---|---|---|---|---|
| A | Target gross profit | | | | | | |
| B | Mark downs | | | | | | |
| C | Shortages | | | | | | |
| D | Gross Profit (A − B − C) | | | | | | |
| E | Selling staff salaries | | | | | | |
| F | Other overheads | | | | | | |
| G | Operating profit (D − E − F) | | | | | | |
| H | Sales | | | | | | |
| K | Number of sales staff | | | | | | |
| L | Transactions | | | | | | |
| M | Stock | | | | | | |
| N | Land and buildings | | | | | | |
| P | Operating assets (M + N) | | | | | | |
| Q | Sq. ft. of selling space or shelf ft. | | | | | | |
| R | Number of working days in period | | | | | | |
| S | Number of working days in year | | | | | | |

# Ratios for retailing

| Ratio | | Formula for calculation of ratio | Unit of measurement | Month or quarter to (date) | | | | | |
|---|---|---|---|---|---|---|---|---|---|
| AA1 | Operating profit/ Operating assets | $G \times 100 \div P \times S \div R$ | % pa | | | | | | |
| AA2 | Operating profit/ Sales | $G \times 100 \div H$ | % | | | | | | |
| AA3 | Sales/ Operating assets | $H \div P \times S \div R$ | Times per year | | | | | | |
| AA3a | Operating assets/ Sales | $P \times 1000 \div (H \times S \div R)$ | ‰ pa | | | | | | |
| AA4 | Gross profit/ Sales | $D \times 100 \div H$ | % | | | | | | |
| AA5 | Selling staff salaries/ Sales | $E \times 100 \div H$ | % | | | | | | |
| AA6 | Other overheads/ Sales | $F \times 100 \div H$ | % | | | | | | |
| AA7 | Target gross profit/ Sales | $A \times 100 \div H$ | % | | | | | | |
| AA8 | Mark downs/ Sales | $B \times 100 \div H$ | % | | | | | | |
| AA9 | Snortages/ Sales | $C \times 100 \div H$ | % | | | | | | |
| AA10 | Selling staff salaries/ Number of sales staff | $E \div K \times S \div R$ | £'s per head pa | | | | | | |
| AA11 | Transactions/ Number of sales staff | $L \div K \times S \div R$ | Transactions per head pa | | | | | | |
| AA12 | Sales/ Transactions | $H \div L$ | £'s per transactions | | | | | | |
| AA13 | Stock/ Sales | $M \times 1000 \div (H \times S \div R)$ | ‰ pa | | | | | | |
| AA14 | Land and buildings/ Sales | $N \times 1000 \div (H \times S \div R)$ | ‰ pa | | | | | | |
| AA15 | Stock/Cost of sales | $M \div (H - D) \times S \div R$ | days | | | | | | |
| AA16 | Land and buildings/ Sq. ft. of selling space or shelf ft. | $N \div Q$ | £ per sq, or shelf ft. | | | | | | |
| AA17 | Sales/ Sq. ft. or selling space or shelf ft | $H \div Q$ | £ per sq, or shelf ft. | | | | | | |

Data assembly sheet 11–4
**Ratios for professional firms**

| Code letter | Item | Month or quarter to (date) | | | | | |
|---|---|---|---|---|---|---|---|
| A | Business getting salaries | | | | | | |
| B | 'Doing' salaries | | | | | | |
| C | Administrative salaries | | | | | | |
| D | All other costs | | | | | | |
| E | Expenses (A + B + C + D) | | | | | | |
| F | Revenue (= business done) | | | | | | |
| G | Profit (F − E) | | | | | | |
| H | Business getting employees | | | | | | |
| K | Doing employees | | | | | | |
| L | Staff administered (H + K) | | | | | | |
| M | Administrative employees | | | | | | |
| N | Total employees | | | | | | |
| P | Partners | | | | | | |
| Q | Business got | | | | | | |
| R | Number of calendar days in period | | | | | | |

# Ratios for professional firms

| Ratio | Formula for calculation of ratio | Unit of measurement | Month or quarter to (date) | | | | | |
|---|---|---|---|---|---|---|---|---|
| AB1 Profit/ Partner | G ÷ P x 365 ÷ R | £'s per head pa | | | | | | |
| AB2 Expenses/ Revenue | E x 100 ÷ F | % | | | | | | |
| AB3 Revenue/ Partner | F ÷ P x 365 ÷ R | £'s per head pa | | | | | | |
| AB4 Business getting salaries/ Revenue | A x 100 ÷ F | % | | | | | | |
| AB5 'Doing' salaries/ Revenue | B x 100 ÷ F | % | | | | | | |
| AB6 Administrative salaries/ Revenue | C x 100 ÷ F | % | | | | | | |
| AB7 All other costs/ Revenue | D x 100 ÷ F | % | | | | | | |
| AB8 Business getting salaries/ Business getting employees | A ÷ H x 365 ÷ R | £'s per head pa | | | | | | |
| AB9 Business got/ Business getting employees | Q ÷ H x 365 ÷ R | £'s per head pa | | | | | | |
| AB10 Business got/ Revenue | Q x 100 ÷ F | % | | | | | | |
| AB11 Doing salaries/ Doing employees | B ÷ K x 365 ÷ R | £'s per head pa | | | | | | |
| AB12 Business done/ Doing employees | F ÷ K x 365 ÷ R | £'s per head pa | | | | | | |
| AB13 Administrative salaries/ Administrative employees | C ÷ M x 365 ÷ R | £'s per head pa | | | | | | |
| AB14 Staff administered/ Administrative employees | L ÷ M | Men per head | | | | | | |
| AB15 Revenue/ Staff administered | F ÷ L x 365 ÷ R | £'s per head pa | | | | | | |

*281*

**Ratios for a firm of consultants**

| Code letter | Item | Month or quarter to (date) | | | | | |
|---|---|---|---|---|---|---|---|
| A | Fees | | | | | | |
| B | Field consultants' salaries | | | | | | |
| C | Contribution from field consultants (A − B) | | | | | | |
| D | Selling consultants' salaries | | | | | | |
| E | Contribution from selling consultants (A − D) | | | | | | |
| F | Other costs | | | | | | |
| G | Profit (C + E − F − A) | | | | | | |
| H | Work sold | | | | | | |
| K | Field consultants | | | | | | |
| L | Selling consultants | | | | | | |
| M | Consultants (K + L) | | | | | | |
| N | Invoiced days | | | | | | |
| P | Number of calendar days in period | | | | | | |

**Ratios for a firm of consultants**

| Ratio | Formula for calculation of ratio | Unit of measurement | Month or quarter to (date) | | | | | |
|---|---|---|---|---|---|---|---|---|
| AC1 Profit/ Consultants | G ÷ M x 365 ÷ P | £'s per head pa | | | | | | |
| AC2 Contribution from field consultants/ Field consultants | C ÷ K x 365 ÷ P | £'s per head pa | | | | | | |
| AC3 Contribution from selling consultants/ Selling consultants | E ÷ L x 365 ÷ P | £'s per head pa | | | | | | |
| AC4 Selling consultants/ Consultants | L x 100 ÷ M | % | | | | | | |
| AC5 Other costs/ Consultants | F ÷ M x 365 ÷ P | £'s per head pa | | | | | | |
| AC6 Field consultants' salaries/ Field consultants | B ÷ K x 365 ÷ P | £'s per head pa | | | | | | |
| AC7 Fees/Invoiced days | A ÷ N | £'s per day | | | | | | |
| AC8 Invoiced days/ Total days | N x 100 ÷ (K x P) | % | | | | | | |
| AC9 Selling consultants' salaries/ Selling consultants | D ÷ L x 365 ÷ P | £'s per head pa | | | | | | |
| AC10 Work sold/ Selling consultants | H ÷ L x 365 ÷ P | £'s per head pa | | | | | | |
| AC11 Work sold/ Fees | H x 100 ÷ A | % | | | | | | |

**Ratios for hotels**

| Code letter | Item | Month or quarter to (date) | | | | | |
|---|---|---|---|---|---|---|---|
| A | Average room assets | | | | | | |
| B | Average restaurant assets | | | | | | |
| C | Average bar stocks | | | | | | |
| D | Average other bar assets | | | | | | |
| E | Average bar assets (C + D) | | | | | | |
| F | Average debtors | | | | | | |
| G | Average other non-allocated assets | | | | | | |
| H | Average non-allocated assets (F + G) | | | | | | |
| K | Average operating assets (A+B+E+H) | | | | | | |
| L | Room sales | | | | | | |
| M | Room variable costs | | | | | | |
| N | Contribution from rooms (L − M) | | | | | | |
| P | Restaurant sales | | | | | | |
| Q | Restaurant variable costs | | | | | | |
| R | Contribution from restaurant (P − Q) | | | | | | |
| S | Bar sales | | | | | | |
| T | Cost of bar sales | | | | | | |
| U | Bar wages | | | | | | |
| V | Contribution from bars (S − T − U) | | | | | | |
| W | Overheads | | | | | | |
| Y | Operating profit (N + R + V − W) | | | | | | |
| Z | Credit sales | | | | | | |
| AA | Rooms in hotel | | | | | | |
| AB | Rooms occupied (times no. of days occupied) | | | | | | |
| AC | Guest capacity | | | | | | |
| AD | No. of guests (times no. of days stayed) | | | | | | |
| AE | Restaurant seating capacity | | | | | | |
| AF | Meals served | | | | | | |
| AG | No. of days in period | | | | | | |

**Ratio calculation sheet number 11–6 will be found on the following page**

**Ratios for hotels**

| Ratio | | Formula for calculation of ratio | Unit of measurement | Month or quarter to (date) | | | | | |
|---|---|---|---|---|---|---|---|---|---|
| AG1 | Operating profit/ Operating assets | Y x 100 ÷ K x 365 ÷ AG | % pa | | | | | | |
| AG2 | Room assets/ Operating assets | A x 100 ÷ K | % | | | | | | |
| AG3 | Restaurant assets/ Operating assets | B x 100 ÷ K | % | | | | | | |
| AG4 | Bar assets/ Operating assets | E x 100 ÷ K | % | | | | | | |
| AG5 | Non-allocated assets/ Operating assets | H x 100 ÷ K | % | | | | | | |
| AG6 | Contribution from rooms/Room assets | N x 100 ÷ A x 365 ÷ AG | % pa | | | | | | |
| AG7 | Contribution from restaurant/ Restaurant assets | R x 100 ÷ B x 365 ÷ AG | % pa | | | | | | |
| AG8 | Contribution from bars/ Bar assets | V x 100 ÷ E x 365 ÷ AG | % pa | | | | | | |
| AG9 | Overheads/ Non-allocated assets | W x 100 ÷ H x 365 ÷ AG | % pa | | | | | | |
| AG10 | Room sales/ Rooms occupied | L ÷ AB | £ per room per day | | | | | | |
| AG10(a) | Room sales/ No. of guests | L ÷ AD | £ per guest per day | | | | | | |
| AG11 | Room variable costs/ Rooms occupied | M ÷ AB | £ per room per day | | | | | | |

286

| Ratio | | Formula for calculation of ratio | Unit of measurement | Month or quarter to (date) | | | | | |
|---|---|---|---|---|---|---|---|---|---|
| AG12 | Rooms occupied/ Rooms in hotel | AB x 100 ÷ (AA x AG) | % | | | | | | |
| AG12(a) | No. of guests/ Guest capacity | AD x 100 ÷ (AC x AG) | % | | | | | | |
| AG13 | Room assets/ Rooms in hotel | A ÷ AA | £ per room | | | | | | |
| AG13(a) | Room assets/ Guest capacity | A ÷ AC | £ per head | | | | | | |
| AG14 | Restaurant sales/ Meals served | P ÷ AF | £ per meal | | | | | | |
| AG15 | Restaurant variable costs/ Meals served | Q ÷ AF | £ per meal | | | | | | |
| AG16 | Meals served/ Restaurant seating capacity | AF x 100 ÷ (AE x AG) | % | | | | | | |
| AG17 | Restaurant assets/ Restaurant seating capacity | B ÷ AE | £ per seat | | | | | | |
| AG18 | Cost of bar sales/ Bar sales | T x 100 ÷ S | % | | | | | | |
| AG19 | Bar wages/ Bar sales | U x 100 ÷ S | % | | | | | | |
| AG20 | Bar stocks/ Cost of bar sales | C ÷ (T ÷ AG) | days | | | | | | |
| AG21 | Other bar assets/ Bar sales | D x 1000 ÷ (S x 365 ÷ AG) | $^o/_{oo}$ pa | | | | | | |
| AG22 | Debtors/ Credit sales | F ÷ (Z ÷ AG) | days | | | | | | |

NB   It is assumed that the hotel is open throughout the year. If it is not substitute the number of days it is open for 365 in all the above formulae.

**Set of ratios for accounting firms (second version)**

| Code letter | Item | Month or quarter to (date) | | | | | |
|---|---|---|---|---|---|---|---|
| A | Salaries etc. of employees | | | | | | |
| B | Partners' salaries | | | | | | |
| C | All staff costs (A + B) | | | | | | |
| D | Accommodation costs | | | | | | |
| E | Professional indemnity cost | | | | | | |
| F | Payments to service bureaux | | | | | | |
| G | Other overheads | | | | | | |
| H | Subtotal (C+D+E+F+G) | | | | | | |
| K | Fees | | | | | | |
| L | Profit (K–H) | | | | | | |
| M | Work in progress (at selling price) | | | | | | |
| N | Debtors | | | | | | |
| P | Debtors and work in progress (at selling price) (M + N) | | | | | | |
| Q | Average number of employees | | | | | | |
| R | Average number of partners | | | | | | |
| S | Average number of staff (Q+R) | | | | | | |
| T | Sq ft of office space | | | | | | |
| W | Professional indemnity cover | | | | | | |
| Y | Fees last year | | | | | | |
| Z | No. of staff leaving during the period | | | | | | |
| AA | No. of calendar days in period | | | | | | |

**Ratio calculation sheet number 11–7 will be found on the following page**

**Set of ratios for accounting firms (second version)**

| Ratio | Formula for calculation of ratio | Unit of measurement | Month or quarter to (date) | | | | | |
|---|---|---|---|---|---|---|---|---|
| AE1 Profit/ No. of partners | L x 365 ÷ AA ÷ R | £ per head pa | | | | | | |
| AE2 Profit/ Fees | L x 100 ÷ K | % | | | | | | |
| AE3 Fees/No. of partners | K x 365 ÷ AA ÷ R | £ per head pa | | | | | | |
| AE4 All staff costs/ Fees | C x 100 ÷ K | % | | | | | | |
| AE5 Accommodation costs/ Fees | D x 100 ÷ K | % | | | | | | |
| AE6 Professional indemnity cost/Fees | E x 100 ÷ K | % | | | | | | |
| AE7 Payments to service bureaux/ Fees | F x 100 ÷ K | % | | | | | | |
| AE8 Other overheads/ Fees | G x 100 ÷ K | % | | | | | | |
| AE9 Salaries etc. of employees/ Average no. of employees | A x 365 ÷ AA ÷ Q | £ per head pa | | | | | | |
| AE10 Partners' salaries/ No. of partners | B x 365 ÷ AA ÷ R | £ per head pa | | | | | | |
| AE11 Fees/ Average no employees | K x 365 ÷ AA ÷ Q | £ per head pa | | | | | | |
| AE12 Accommodation costs/ Sq ft of office space | D x 365 ÷ AA ÷ T | £ pa per sq ft | | | | | | |
| AE13 Sq ft of office space/ Average no. of staff | T ÷ S | Sq ft per head | | | | | | |

| Ratio | Formula for calculation of ratio | Unit of measurement | Month or quarter to (date) | | | | | |
|---|---|---|---|---|---|---|---|---|
| AE14 Professional indemnity cost/ Professional indemnity cover | E x 365 ÷ AA ÷ W x 100 | % pa | | | | | | |
| AE15 Professional indemnity cover/ Fees | W x 100 ÷ (K x 365 ÷ AA) | % pa | | | | | | |
| AE16 Professional indemnity cover/ Average no. of staff | W ÷ S | £ per head | | | | | | |
| AE17 Fees/ Average no. of staff | K x 365 ÷ AA ÷ S | £ per head pa | | | | | | |
| AE18 Debtors and work in progress (at selling price)/ Fees | P x 1000 ÷ (K x 365 ÷ AA) | ‰ pa | | | | | | |
| AE19 Work in progress (at selling price)/ Fees | M x 1000 ÷ (K x 365 ÷ AA) | ‰ pa | | | | | | |
| AE20 Debtors/Fees | N x 1000 ÷ (K x 365 ÷ AA) | ‰ pa | | | | | | |
| AE21 Partners' average remuneration (profit plus notional salary) | (L + B) x 365 ÷ AA ÷ R | £ per head pa | | | | | | |
| AE22 Growth (fees this year/fees last year) | K x 365 ÷ AA x 100 ÷ Y | % pa | | | | | | |
| AE23 Staff turnover (number of staff leaving during the year/Average number of staff during the year) | Z x 365 ÷ AA x 100 ÷ S | % pa | | | | | | |

# PART THREE

# Chapter 12

# Integrated control by ratios

In this chapter we shall be concentrating on *four* topics. First of all we shall be bringing together the ratios previously discussed in separate chapters to show how they form an integrated whole. Secondly we shall describe how this integrated set of ratios can be used for analysis, that is finding out what is going wrong and what is going right. Next it will be demonstrated how the same integrated set of ratios can be used by management when planning their company's future, remedying the weaknesses and capitalising on the strengths indicated by the analysis. Finally the use of integrated ratios for monitoring and controlling the implementation of these plans is described.

## 12.1 Integrated Ratios

Previous chapters have dealt with the ratios which individual managers should consider using to help monitor and control their parts of the complete business. Exceptions to this departmental approach are Chapters 4 and 5.

In this chapter we shall be concentrating on an integrated approach to the whole business in the course of which most of the ratios already described will be re-presented. Detailed descriptions of the ratios will not be repeated (back references to earlier chapters will be given); the emphasis will be on the interrelationship of the ratios within the context of the whole environment of the business.

This integrated approach will show the causal links which exist between activities on the shop floor at one end of the chain, and the income of an individual investor in the company at the other end of the chain. Diagram 12–1 shows:

1    The major blocks of ratios which have direct causal links within the company.
2    To whom information is available about each block and the degree of

interest he is likely to have about the content of each block.
3    The nature of the indirect influences of the major blocks of ratios from outside the company.

The major blocks of ratios are shown in the second column in Diagram 12–1. The double-headed arrow between them indicates that it is possible to proceed from block to block in either direction. The process of analysis is carried out by moving down the chain. The cause-and-effect linkage tends to move up the chain (changes in lower blocks of ratios are far more likely to affect upper blocks of ratios than vice versa). The planning process, as will be explained in more detail later, tends to move from initiating changes in lower blocks to their effects on higher blocks. However, if these effects are considered to be not satisfactory, questions of the type 'by how much would $x$ have to be altered to achieve $y$?' would be asked, going down the chain from $y$ in a higher block to $x$ in a lower block.

The rather peculiar shapes in the first column of Diagram 12–1 are the result of:

1    Indicating who has access to information about each block by means of a vertical line alongside the block.
2    Indicating the degree of interest by the class of person by the horizontal width of the shape alongside the block.

For example, the individual shareholder (or, more likely, his advisors – financial analysts, brokers, and so on) has information about himself, the stock market, and each company's financial policy, but no or negligible information about matters in blocks farther down the chain. His degree of interest in the information is likely to diminish as he moves down the chain from himself, via the stock market, to the company's financial policy.

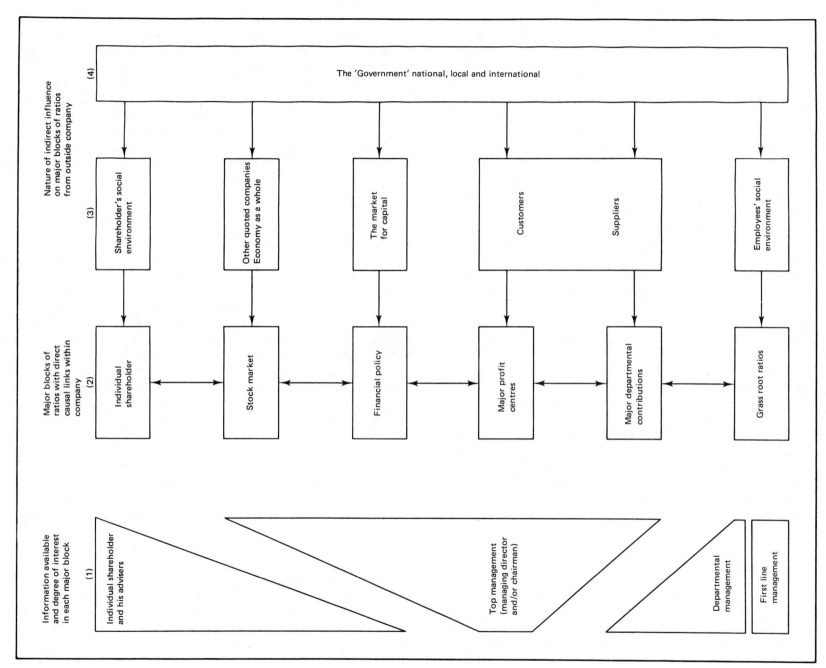

Nature of indirect influence on major blocks of ratios from outside company

(4)

The 'Government' national, local and international

(3)

Shareholder's social environment

Other quoted companies Economy as a whole

The market for capital

Customers

Suppliers

Employees' social environment

Major blocks of ratios with direct causal links within company

(2)

Individual shareholder ⟷ Stock market ⟷ Financial policy ⟷ Major profit centres ⟷ Major departmental contributions ⟷ Grass root ratios

Information available and degree of interest in each major block

(1)

Individual shareholder and his advisers

Top management (managing director and/or chairman)

Departmental management

First line management

Diagram 12–1  Interest and influences on major blocks of integrated ratios

295

As well as the 'cause-and-effect' links between blocks of ratios within a company, each block is subject to indirect influences from outside the company. These influences are outlined in the third column in Diagram 12–1. For example, the ratios which the individual shareholder is primarily interested in are directly affected by the stock market but his attitude to them, and indeed, some of the ratios themselves, are indirectly affected by his social environment (by his age, tax status etc.).

An all-pervading indirect influence on the major blocks of ratios is the government – local, national and international (including the Common Market, GATT and so on) and governmental agencies such as NEDO. This influence is represented in column 4 of Diagram 12–1.

All the 'influence' arrows move from right to left; there is of course 'feedback' from the ratios to the types of influence and this could have been shown by arrows from left to right. They were omitted however to avoid unduly cluttering the diagram.

The diagram should not be thought of as describing a static situation. The relationships it describes change continuously over time. The amount of information available to decision takers and its relative interest change. The effects of activities at the 'grass roots' levels move up the chain like electronic impulses along nerve cells. As the effects are perceived by the decision takers plans are made and action taken which in turn affect the 'grass roots'. The whole environment outside the company affects it and the company, in turn, modifies the environment. Government attempts to influence the environment while the people who make up the environment attempt to influence the government.

One should imagine the shapes and blocks in the diagram now expanding, now contracting, while pulses of information move upwards and outwards from column 2 and pulses of decisions and influences move inwards and downwards to column 2. All the parts shown in the diagram form an interrelated whole – what biologists call an ecosystem. A suitable simile for the relationships portrayed in Diagram 12–1 would not be drawn from the world of architecture – it is not a structure like a pyramid or Stonehenge – but from the sciences of living matter – it is much more like a pond on a summer's day or the nervous and muscular systems of an animal.

To continue the biological analogy for one moment longer, each major block of ratios will now be dissected in turn and the main constituents examined.

## The individual shareholder

The constituent ratios of the individual shareholder's block of ratios are shown in Diagram 12–2. It will be seen that this is very similar to Diagram 8–5.

The individual shareholder's key ratio is his income in relation to the cost of his investment or its value at the beginning of the period under review (ratio Q1). The size of this ratio is affected by his personal dividend yield (ratio Q2) his capital gain (ratio Q3) and the rates of tax he has to pay (ratios Q4 and Q5).

The government and the shareholder's social environment affect his tax rates (ratios Q4 and Q5). His capital gain (ratio Q3) is the result of changes in the stock market's expectations about a number of factors (listed on diagram) these in turn are influenced by the behaviour of other quoted companies and the economy as a whole.

The direct link with the stock market block of ratios is via ratio Q2 (gross dividend receivable/value of investment at beginning of period) but formula 2 indicates that ratio Q3 (capital gain/value of investment at beginning of period) is also involved. The constituent ratios in the individual shareholder's block are more fully described in Chapter 8. The manner in which the stock market expectations are derived is also described in Chapter 8, starting on page 183.

## The stock market

The individual ratios in the stock market block are shown in Diagram 12–3. This is a simplified and modified form of Diagram 8–6.

Dividend yield (ratio R1) provides the link with the individual shareholder's block of ratios (Diagram 12–2). It is a function of the earnings yield or P/E ratio (ratios R2 or R2a) and the dividend cover (ratio R3). It is with dividend cover that outside influences begin to have their effect (see Diagram 12.3) but it will be more convenient to discuss them at the same time as those on the market price of the share (ratio R5).

The magnitude of the P/E ratio (ratio R2a) is determined by the equity earnings per share (ratio R4) and the market price of the share (ratio R5). The size of a company's dividend cover (ratio R3) is, in practice, determined by the directors. Their actions are affected by their policy and their expectations concerning the future. These expectations are in turn affected by:

1   The government's actions or promised or threatened actions (dividend restraint, lame ducks, stop-go, and so on).
2   What other companies are doing or are thought likely to be doing (increasing or cutting their dividends, threatening or being victims of takeovers)
3   The actual and expected behaviour of the economy as a whole.

Many of the factors which affect the size of a company's dividend cover also effect its share price but instead of being channelled through the directors and their decisions they are channelled through the stock market, that is through the buy, sell, hold or abstain decisions of all actual and potential investors. These decisions are largely based on expectations; about the company's dividend policy, about other companies, the economy, and the government. In a purely logical world they would be based on

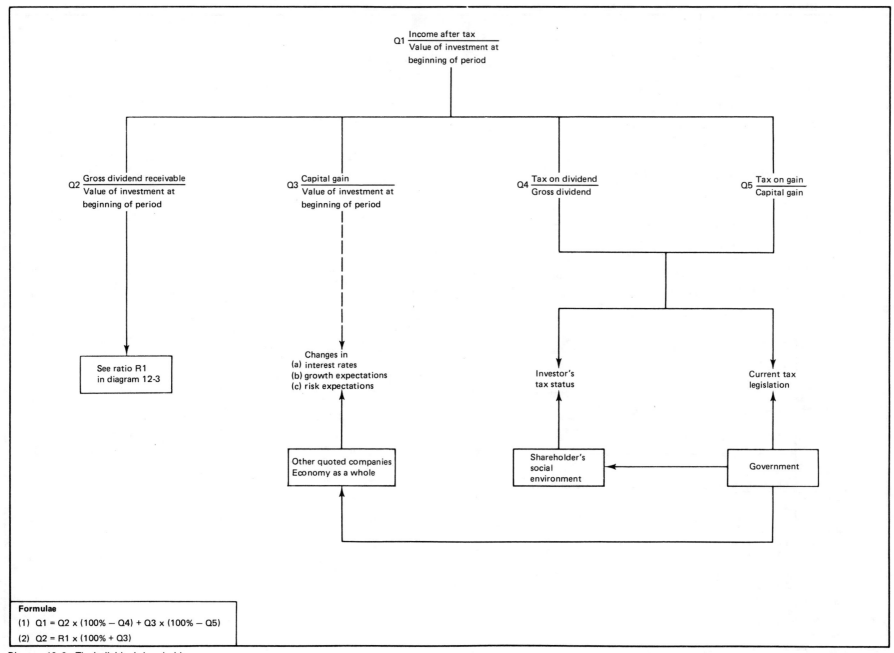

Q1 $\dfrac{\text{Income after tax}}{\text{Value of investment at beginning of period}}$

Q2 $\dfrac{\text{Gross dividend receivable}}{\text{Value of investment at beginning of period}}$

Q3 $\dfrac{\text{Capital gain}}{\text{Value of investment at beginning of period}}$

Q4 $\dfrac{\text{Tax on dividend}}{\text{Gross dividend}}$

Q5 $\dfrac{\text{Tax on gain}}{\text{Capital gain}}$

See ratio R1 in diagram 12-3

Changes in
(a) interest rates
(b) growth expectations
(c) risk expectations

Investor's tax status

Current tax legislation

Other quoted companies Economy as a whole

Shareholder's social environment

Government

**Formulae**

(1)  Q1 = Q2 x (100% − Q4) + Q3 x (100% − Q5)

(2)  Q2 = R1 x (100% + Q3)

Diagram 12–2   The individual shareholder

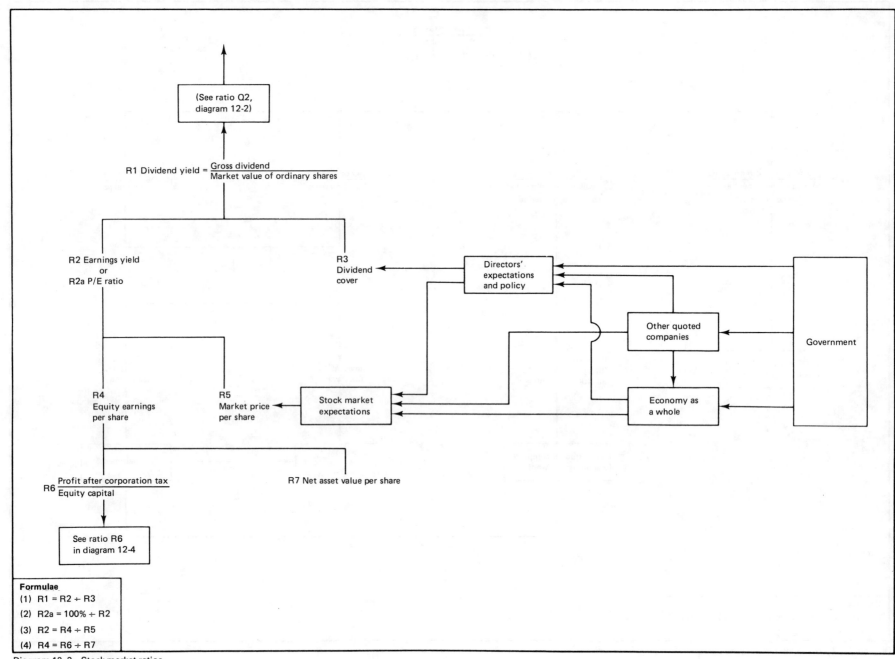

Diagram 12–3  Stock market ratios

the type of analysis described on pages 183 and 185. In practice, rumour, fear and optimism also play their part – in the short term at any rate.

The magnitude of a company's equity earnings per share (ratio R4) is determined by its post-tax return on equity capital (ratio R6) and its net asset value per share (ratio R7). Ratio R6 provides the link with the financial policy block of ratios that are described next.

All the stock market ratios are described more fully in Chapter 8, see page 186.

## Financial policy

The magnitude of a company's ratio of net profit after tax to equity capital is partly determined by a group of factors which we have labelled for convenience financial policy and partly by its operating success. Financial policy is dealt with in this section; operating success in the next three sections.

The individual ratios in the financial policy block are shown in Diagram 12–4. This is an expansion and modification of Diagram 8–7. The ratios which form part of Diagrams 12–4 and 12–5 are similar to ratios employed by the Centre for Interfirm Comparison in certain of its comprehensive schemes.

The size of a company's post-tax return on equity capital (ratio R6) is determined by its pre-tax return on equity capital (ratio R7) and its tax rate (ratio R8). Its tax rate is affected by its tax status, the actions recommended by its tax advisers and the government (see page 174).

Pre-tax return on equity capital (ratio R7) is the result of the total profitability of the business (ratio R9), which will be discussed in the next section, and the rate of interest paid (ratio R10) and the company's capital gearing (ratio R11). These last two are influenced by the 'market for capital' (see Diagram 12–4).

The market for loan capital can be considered as a group of institutions balancing part of the supply of and demand for money. It is influenced by the government's activities directly (bank rate, activities on the gilt edged market, special deposits, HP regulations) and indirectly by its actions taken to stimulate or damp down the economy or parts of it. The supply of money and demand for loan capital is affected by the actions of other companies and the state of the economy.

The institutions in the loan capital market must assess the riskiness of the investment (cover ratios are one of the tools for this) and the liquidity of the company. The ratios used are those numbered P7 to P17 and are fully described starting on page 177.

## Major profit centres

The magnitude of a company's ratio of total profit to total capital is determined by the activities within its major profit centres. For a small or simple firm there are only two such centres; its principal operations and its minor ones such as investments in securities, subletting of property. The ratios for such a situation are shown in Diagram 12–5.

For a larger firm the ratios of Diagram 12–6 are more appropriate. Diagram 12–6 is similar to Diagram 5–1 and the ratios have been fully described in Chapter 5 starting on page 96.

## Major departmental contributions

The three main departments whose contribution goes to make up a company's rate of operating profitability are purchasing, manufacturing and selling. This relationship is illustrated in Diagram 12–7, where the major influences on each department are shown to be suppliers, employees and customers.

Each of the major departments has had a chapter devoted to the ratios suitable to analyse its strengths, weaknesses, and progress. The relevant chapter is indicated in Diagram 12–7. The behaviour of employees, whichever department they work for, is crucial to the success of all companies. It is for this reason that the whole of Chapter 10 (personnel ratios) is devoted to describing suitable ratios for monitoring the behaviour of employees.

## Grass root ratios

Fundamentally the success of all companies depends on the soundness of its roots. Without sound roots no business can survive; unfortunately, to continue the analogy, even with sound roots the trunk may be so diseased that the tree is not fruitful.

Grass root ratios are those beyond which it is no longer worthwhile to conduct a formal, numerical, ratio analysis. Thus, they vary with the size and complexity of the company. The larger the company, the deeper it is profitable to delve. The smaller the company, the sooner one reaches an adequate answer.

It is a characteristic of grass root ratios that they tend to be in physical rather than abstract or financial terms – number of calls per representative, for example, rather than percentage return on capital. This is because the basis of all businesses is physical (and mental) work; only at a later stage is this translated into money terms.

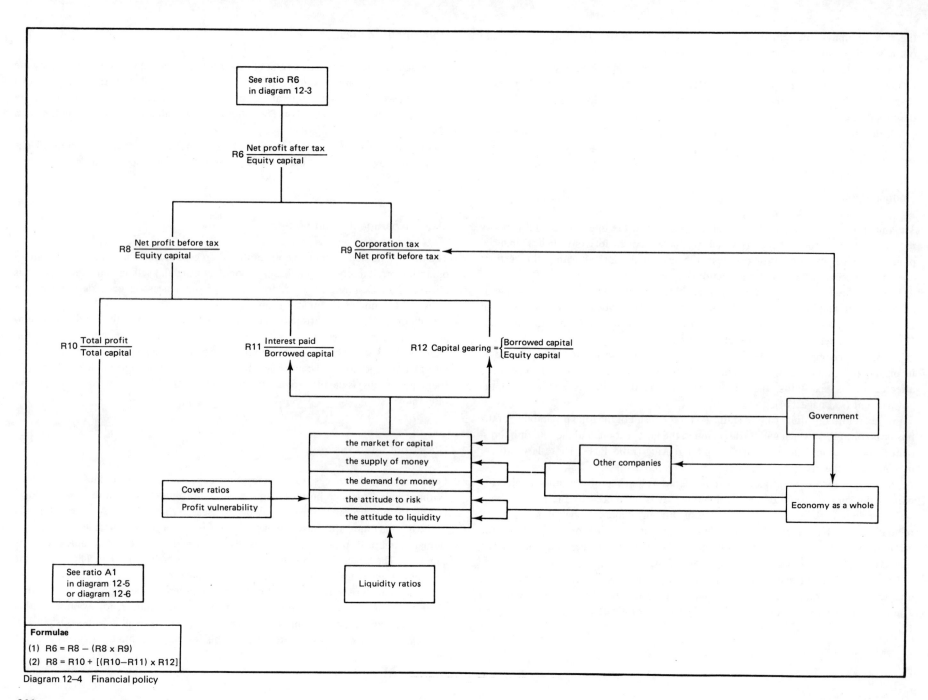

See ratio R6
in diagram 12-3

R6 $\dfrac{\text{Net profit after tax}}{\text{Equity capital}}$

R8 $\dfrac{\text{Net profit before tax}}{\text{Equity capital}}$

R9 $\dfrac{\text{Corporation tax}}{\text{Net profit before tax}}$

R10 $\dfrac{\text{Total profit}}{\text{Total capital}}$

R11 $\dfrac{\text{Interest paid}}{\text{Borrowed capital}}$

R12 Capital gearing $= \begin{cases} \text{Borrowed capital} \\ \hline \text{Equity capital} \end{cases}$

Government

the market for capital

the supply of money

the demand for money

the attitude to risk

the attitude to liquidity

Other companies

Economy as a whole

| Cover ratios |
| Profit vulnerability |

Liquidity ratios

See ratio A1
in diagram 12-5
or diagram 12-6

**Formulae**

(1)  R6 = R8 − (R8 x R9)

(2)  R8 = R10 + [(R10−R11) x R12]

Diagram 12–4   Financial policy

300

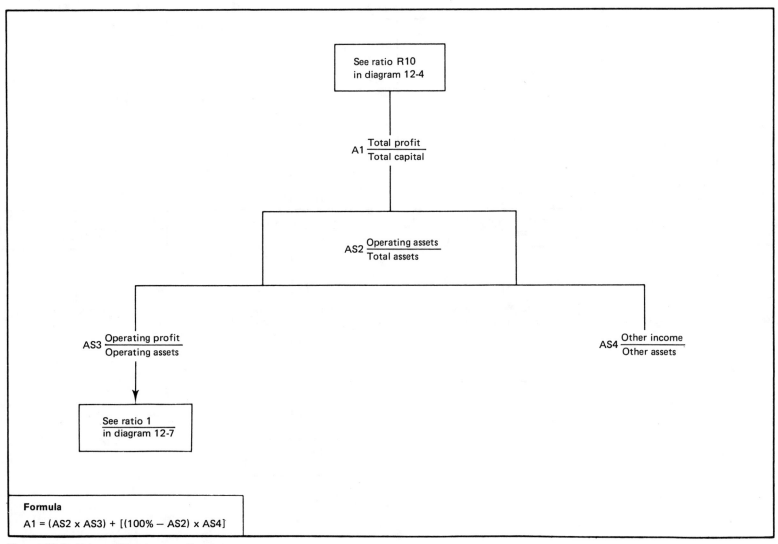

Diagram 12–5   Major profit centres – small company

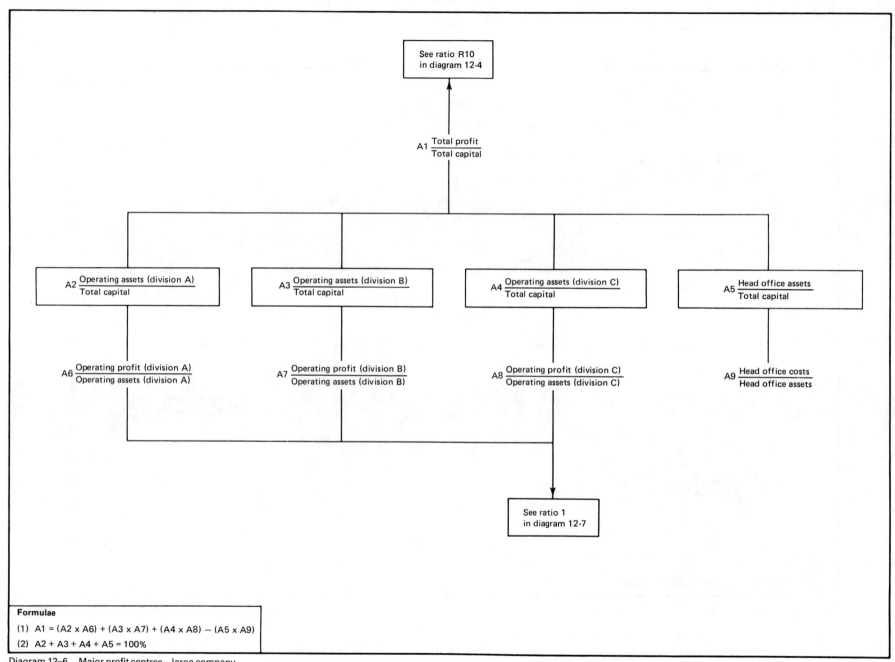

Diagram 12–6    Major profit centres – large company

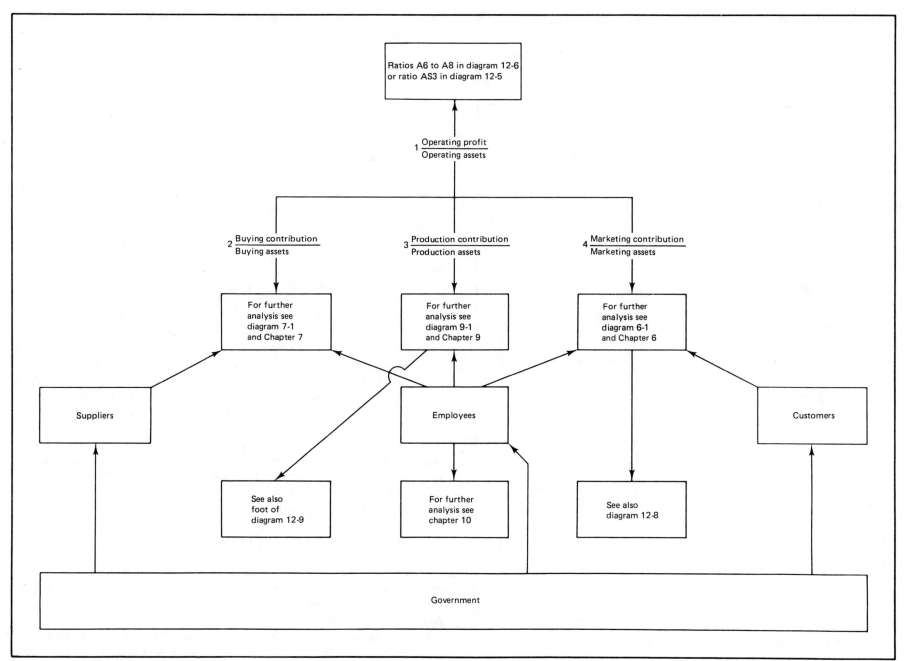

Diagram 12–7   Major departmental contributions

303

Diagram 12–8 shows some of the grass root ratios for the marketing operation and how they link with the key marketing ratio of

$$\frac{\text{Marketing contribution}}{\text{Marketing assets}}$$

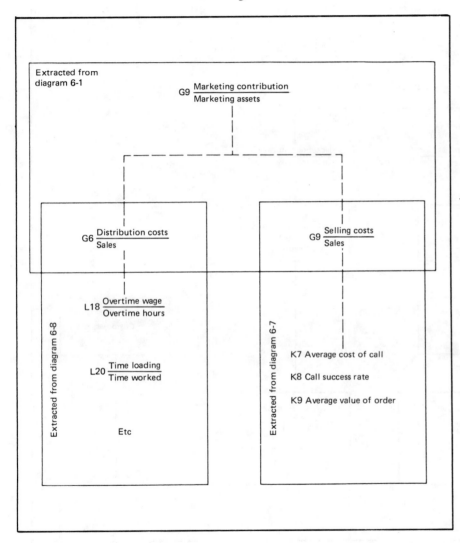

Diagram 12–8  Marketing 'grass root' ratios

The details of the linking ratios and other grass root ratios will be found in Diagrams 6–1, 6–7 and 6–8.

Other areas of the business also have grass root ratios but to avoid repetition they are not described here but at the end of the next section on the analytical pathway.

## 12.2 The Analytical Path

Diagram 12–9 illustrates the path an analyst can take when examining the factors which have caused a particular ratio to differ from his standard – whether the standard has been derived from the company's past, the company's budget, or the performance of other companies.

Analysis can commence at any point on the path; it does not have to start right at the top of the diagram. Analysis always proceed downwards.

Each rectangle in the diagram is a compressed summary of a diagram which has appeared elsewhere in this book. At the top left-hand corner is the diagram number and at the top right is the title. The location of the diagram can be found from the contents table. Not all the ratios in the original diagrams have been repeated – only those which provide the links between one diagram and another. The links and the missing ratios within the diagrams are represented by the dotted lines.

Diagram 12–9 should be used in conjunction with Diagram 12–1 which shows, as well as the major pattern of ratios, the nature of indirect outside influences as well.

Analysis can start at any point along the path and will finish when sufficient information has been obtained in order to indicate the nature of the actions required. As Diagram 12–1 shows, no one individual has access to all the information in all the diagrams. Moreover, different individuals have different degrees of interest in the ratios shown. For brevity of description in what follows, these different individuals are referred to by the generic title 'the analyst'.

If an analyst is dissatisfied with the return on his investment (ratio Q1) he will look at the ratios in Diagram 8–5. If this does not give him his answer he will move either downwards to Diagram 8–6 (Stock Exchange ratios) or sideways to Diagram 5–10 (growth ratios).

If the analyst needs to proceed further he will move to Diagram 8–7 (overall company ratios). If it seems that the cause of what he is looking for is in the field of interest paid or capital gearing (ratios R11 and R12), he may need to examine the ratios in Diagrams 8–2, 8–4, or 8–3.

However, the analyst may be more concerned with the return on the total capital of the company (ratio R10), in which case he will proceed to Diagram 5–1 (investment in divisions). Having narrowed down which division is of interest, the analyst is faced with a choice between the methods of analysis suggested in Diagram 5–2 (based on products) or one of Diagrams 5–3, 5–4 or 5–5 (based on the Du Pont analysis or variations of that) or using the ratios based on the concept of capacity utilisation, shown in Diagram 5–6 or, finally, the concept of departmental contribution on which the bulk of this book has been based.

If it turns out that it is the buyer's contribution that is of most interest, the analyst proceeds to the ratios set out in Diagram 7–1. If it is the production department's contribution that is of concern to the analyst, he has a choice between the ratios in Diagram 9–1 or in 9–2, depending on whether the company has a meaningful measure of capacity utilisation. From the ratios in these diagrams again there is a choice, depending on whether the company is labour or machine intensive. If it is the former the ratios in Diagram 9–3 require to be examined; if the latter, the ratios in Diagram 9–4 should be of interest.

If the analyst requires further information about marketing contribution he again has a choice of method. Diagram 6–1 is suitable for manufacturing industry; Diagram 6–5 approaches the problem of marketing contribution from a product analysis viewpoint. Diagram 6–6 is for firms who manufacture on long-term contracts.

In the general field of marketing, three areas have been provided with examples of more detailed analysis. Diagram 6–8 is of interest where distribution costs are a major item. Diagram 6–3 contains ratios of relevance to a firm with a substantial amount of export business. Diagram 6–7 concentrates on that aspect of marketing under the control of a sales manager – particularly one using representatives and agents.

## 12.3 Using Ratios for Planning

The integrated approach already described in the preceding section on analysis has another practical use in planning the future of the company because:

1   It can be used to demonstrate some of the major results of various courses of action under consideration.
2   It is a constant reminder that it is dangerous to consider any item in isolation.

To use the ratios for planning it is desirable to start with the activities measured by grass root ratios and to move up the analytical pathway to observe what the effect of proposed changes will be on the higher ratios which will be used to measure the success (or otherwise) of the implementation of the proposals.

It is quite likely that any proposal will affect more than one grass root ratio. The first thing to do in fact is to make a thorough check of how many ratios are indeed likely to be affected. The next step is to quantify the likely change in each of the ratios concerned. Then, using the formulae in the relevant diagrams, work out the consequential changes to the ratios higher up in the analytical path. One must continue to move upwards until one reaches the first ratio at which all the paths (along which the consequences have been flowing) converge. Only if that ratio improves is the proposed action likely to be worthwhile.

The integrated set of ratios shown in the analytical path diagram can also be used to help evaluate alternative proposals. The repercussions of each proposal are followed upwards until a ratio common to all proposals is reached. The proposal which improves that ratio by the greatest amount is, prima facie, the most attractive. Obviously for any major proposal one must also explore the likely repercussions if the proposal does not run according to plan (and how many projects do?!) It could well be that proposal A, which is prima facie the most attractive, is found to be much more sensitive to things going wrong than project B, and management could be justified in selecting the less hazardous project.

Another way of using ratios in the planning process is to tabulate for each major ratio:

1   the effect on return on capital of a 1 per cent change in the ratio;
2   the change needed to the ratio to achieve:

(a)   target return on capital
(b)   target increase in return on capital
(c)   stable return on capital – given known, or forecast, changes in costs, etc.

## 12.4 Using Ratios for Monitoring and Control

Once a plan has been agreed and action has commenced to implement it, it is highly desirable to monitor its progress. The integrated set of ratios may be used for this purpose as well as during the planning process.

Each ratio (or at least each major ratio) that is likely to be affected by the plan should be given a chart. Charts will be needed not only for ratios which it is intended should change but also for ratios which it is intended should not change as a result of the plan's implementation.

The numerical value of the ratios should be put on the vertical axis, and the horizontal axis used for the time scale extending over the estimated time required to complete the implementation of the plan. The planned change in the ratio over time can then be plotted on the chart using a dotted line. As the actual results are measured they can be marked in with a full line. Any deviation from plan can then be quickly

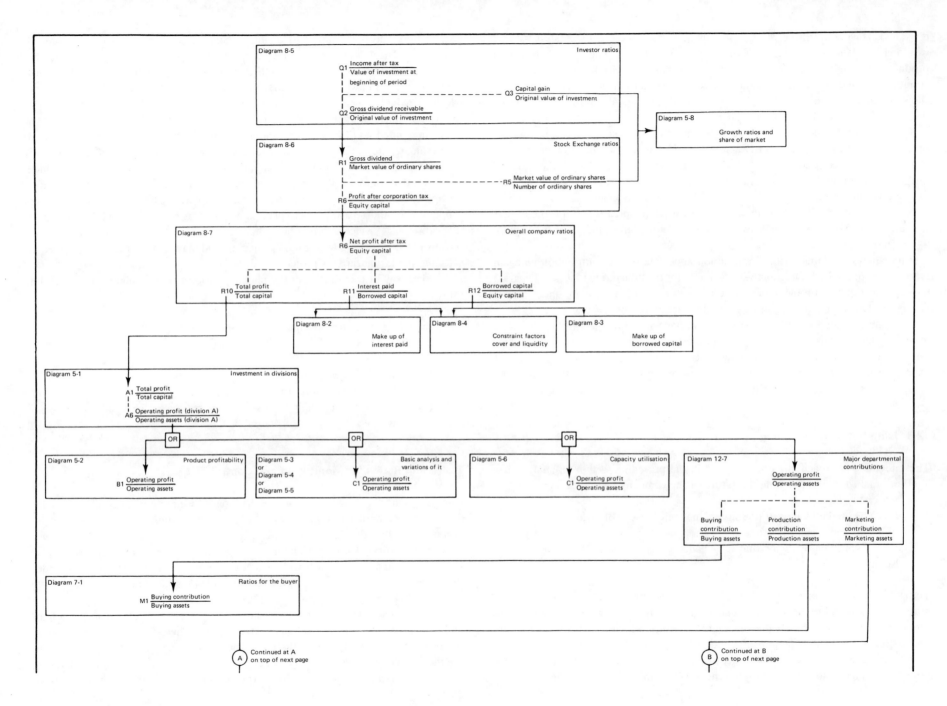

Diagram 8-5            Investor ratios

Q1 $\dfrac{\text{Income after tax}}{\text{Value of investment at beginning of period}}$

Q3 $\dfrac{\text{Capital gain}}{\text{Original value of investment}}$

Q2 $\dfrac{\text{Gross dividend receivable}}{\text{Original value of investment}}$

Diagram 5-8    Growth ratios and share of market

Diagram 8-6            Stock Exchange ratios

R1 $\dfrac{\text{Gross dividend}}{\text{Market value of ordinary shares}}$

R5 $\dfrac{\text{Market value of ordinary shares}}{\text{Number of ordinary shares}}$

R6 $\dfrac{\text{Profit after corporation tax}}{\text{Equity capital}}$

Diagram 8-7            Overall company ratios

R6 $\dfrac{\text{Net profit after tax}}{\text{Equity capital}}$

R10 $\dfrac{\text{Total profit}}{\text{Total capital}}$

R11 $\dfrac{\text{Interest paid}}{\text{Borrowed capital}}$

R12 $\dfrac{\text{Borrowed capital}}{\text{Equity capital}}$

Diagram 8-2    Make up of interest paid

Diagram 8-4    Constraint factors cover and liquidity

Diagram 8-3    Make up of borrowed capital

Diagram 5-1            Investment in divisions

A1 $\dfrac{\text{Total profit}}{\text{Total capital}}$

A6 $\dfrac{\text{Operating profit (division A)}}{\text{Operating assets (division A)}}$

OR        OR        OR

Diagram 5-2    Product profitability

B1 $\dfrac{\text{Operating profit}}{\text{Operating assets}}$

Diagram 5-3 or Diagram 5-4 or Diagram 5-5    Basic analysis and variations of it

C1 $\dfrac{\text{Operating profit}}{\text{Operating assets}}$

Diagram 5-6    Capacity utilisation

C1 $\dfrac{\text{Operating profit}}{\text{Operating assets}}$

Diagram 12-7    Major departmental contributions

$\dfrac{\text{Operating profit}}{\text{Operating assets}}$

$\dfrac{\text{Buying contribution}}{\text{Buying assets}}$    $\dfrac{\text{Production contribution}}{\text{Production assets}}$    $\dfrac{\text{Marketing contribution}}{\text{Marketing assets}}$

Diagram 7-1            Ratios for the buyer

M1 $\dfrac{\text{Buying contribution}}{\text{Buying assets}}$

(A) Continued at A on top of next page

(B) Continued at B on top of next page

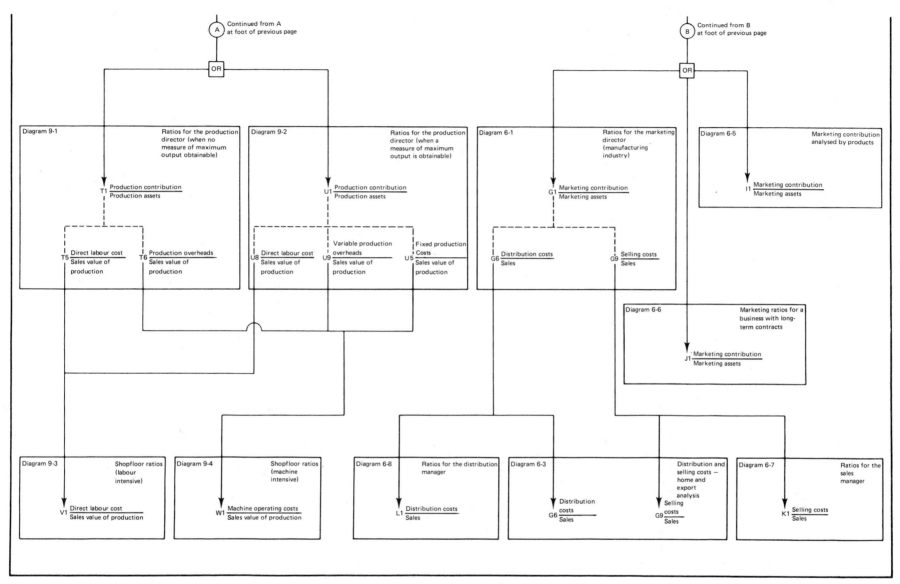

Diagram 12–9  The analytical path

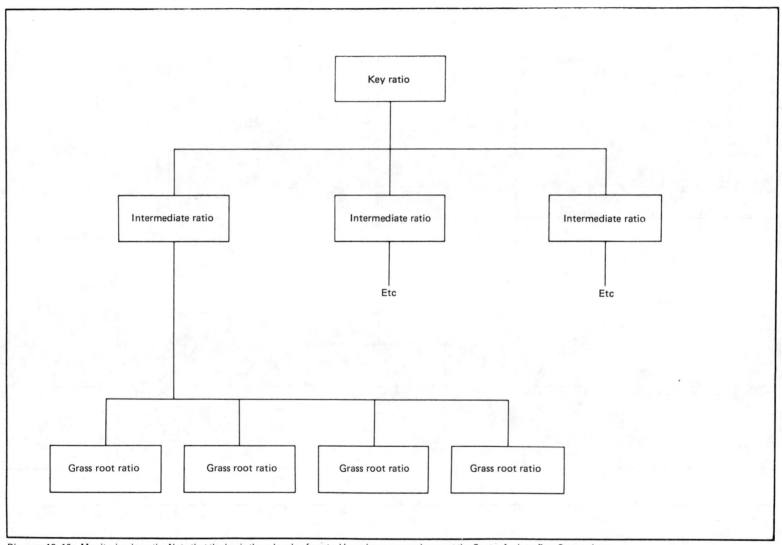

Diagram 12–10   Monitoring by ratio. Note that the basic three levels of control have been proven in use at the Centre for Interfirm Comparison

seen and management is alerted to the need for action.

It is useful to arrange the charts for each ratio in a similar manner to Diagram 12–10. The key ratio at the top is the ratio described earlier in this chapter at the point of intersection of the analytical paths from all the grass root ratios affected by the particular plan. The key ratio may therefore be different for different plans. An intermediate ratio is one where a number of analytical paths from some grass root ratios converge but is not the point at which all converge.

With this arrangement of charts senior management would look first at the key ratio. If the actual for this was on plan, there would be no need to look further. If it was deviating from plan they would look to see which intermediate ratio was off course and then look only at the grass root ratios under that particular intermediate ratio. This arrangement of charts and the use of them just described is, of course, just another application of the principle of management by exception, in this case in a graphic or pictorial form.

At this stage management will initiate corrective action and/or modify the plan. If the latter course is taken the new plan should be added to the original chart by means of another dotted line distinguished from the original plan by a different pattern of dots.

# PART FOUR

# Chapter 13

# Using published accounts

## 13.1 Introduction

When the first edition of this book was published in 1973 it was not possible to derive much useful information from the published accounts of many companies with which to compare their efficiency or profitability. Information on their solvency and liquidity was more available however (see Chapter 8.3 for the use of such data). This lack of usefulness reflected the lack of information which companies were required to publish, and the different ways in which different companies arrived at their figures for many items. Moreover it was often not possible to ascertain how some figures had been calculated.

Whilst the situation nowadays is by no means ideal it has improved sufficiently to warrant a chapter on how to use the information in published accounts in order to compare efficiency over time or between companies.

## 13.2 Structure of this Chapter

This section is intended as a guide to the structure of this chapter in order to help the busy reader decide what to read and what to skim or leave out.

Section 13.3 describes the various organisations that have contributed to an improvement in companies' accounts and outlines the changes they have introduced and are planning.

Section 13.4 sets out what different classes of companies have to publish and in what timescale.

Section 13.5 describes from where a company's accounts may be obtained.

Section 13.6 describes what is likely to be found in a company's annual report and how to make systematic use of the different parts of the report before looking at the figures.

We then turn to the accounts and start by listing in Section 13.7 the disadvantages that traditional (historical cost) accounts have in, and after, a period of inflation.

It is unlikely that you will have current cost accounts or information which attempts to remedy these defects. You therefore have a choice of:

(a) estimating what they would have been (Appendix 13–1) and then using Section 13.8 to analyse them; or

(b) using the traditional (historical cost) accounts by means of the analysis in Section 13.8.

Use of the Statement of Source and Application of Funds is dealt with in Section 13.9.

Before reading this chapter it is desirable to read:

1    Chapter 1 'Principles of ratio selection'
2    Chapter 2 'Standards of comparison' – especially the section entitled 'Disadvantages of published accounts'
3    Chapter 3.2 'Main accounting terms'

The subject of using accounts to help determine a company's credit worthiness is dealt with in Chapter 8.3 and 8.4.

To study the subject in more depth see the suggestions for further reading for this chapter and for Chapter 3.

## 13.3 Sources of Improvement

Company accounts have improved because of changes in company law, the activities of the Stock Exchange, the pronouncements of the Accounting Standards Committee, pressure for improved disclosures from investment analysts, and last, but by no means least, the desire of many companies to improve their standing in the financial community by improved annual reports.

### Company Law

The principal source of requirements for the contents of companies' annual reports is the various Companies Acts from 1948 to 1981. These were consolidated into one Act in 1985.

The principal Act until 1985 was the Companies Act 1948 but this had been amended and enlarged by several subsequent Acts and statutory instruments. The following highlights only those changes which affect the accounts.

The Companies Act 1967 required various items to be disclosed in the accounts which had not been disclosed previously. The most important item was perhaps turnover, although this disclosure was subject to certain exemptions.

The Companies Act 1976 tightened up on the requirements of companies to publish accounts within a reasonable period, and strengthened the position of auditors.

The main impact of the Companies Act 1980 was to introduce new rules for classifying companies between private and public and to introduce rules restricting the distribution of profit and assets.

Undoubtedly the major impact on the content of companies accounts was caused by the Companies Act 1981. This Act resulted from the EEC's Fourth Directive on company law. It laid down in greater detail than hitherto not only what items were to be shown in the accounts but also the lay-out of these accounts (the so-called statutory formats). Moreover it specified in detail how various items were to be calculated.

From the point of view of the user of accounts, however, the Companies Act 1981 was paradoxical. On the one hand it significantly increased the quantity, and to some extent the comparability, of information to be included in accounts for shareholders, but on the other hand it enabled the directors of small and medium sized companies to file with the Registrar of Companies accounts containing significantly less information than they had been required to include hitherto. So, while the position of the shareholder has been improved, the position of the non-shareholder analyst has, for these companies, been significantly impaired. The improvement in comparability has been restricted by the number of options allowed to companies by the Act (as permitted by the Fourth Directive) on valuation and presentation.

### Stock Exchange

Companies which have shares or loan stock quoted on the Stock Exchange (listed companies) are subject to a listing agreement, now referred to as the 'continuing obligations', details of which are set out in the so-called Yellow Book. This specifies among other things disclosure of information not required by the Companies Act. Before the enactment of the Companies Act 1981 some of the Stock Exchange requirements were in advance of those required by company law. The difference then became narrower but has started to grow again. Broadly speaking the disclosure requirements are the same for companies traded on the Unlisted Securities Market (USM) as for listed companies.

### Accounting Standards Committee

The Accounting Standards Committee was set up in 1970 by the accounting profession in response to criticisms of it at the time. The criticisms centred on the possibility that, given the same set of underlying facts, two companies, and their auditors, might legally present significantly different sets of accounts. The aims of ASC are therefore 'to narrow the areas of difference and variety in accounting practice'. ASC issues Statements of Standard Accounting Practice (SSAPs) which apply with a few exceptions to all companies' accounts. Accountants who are members of one of the bodies collectively known as the Consultative Committee of Accounting Bodies are expected to follow accounting standards. If they do not, they may have to justify their departure from the standard to their professional body. In general, most companies follow most standards most of the time. Even if they do not, provided that they disclose their departure from the standard, as is required, then the existence of the standards is a material help to the outside analyst of a company. The Stock Exchange requires listed and USM companies to explain why they have departed from a SSAP if such is the case.

Standards are produced as the culmination of a long development and consultative process. This includes:

(*a*)  research into existing theories and practices (some of this research has been published);

(*b*)  a draft standard is then produced by a sub-committee of the ASC;

(*c*)  this draft is discussed with interested parties;

(*d*)  an Exposure Draft is then published for general comment;

(*e*)  the comments are then evaluated and the Draft is amended if necessary;

(*f*)  if the changes are material and possibly contentious a new Exposure Draft is published;

(g)    otherwise a definitive Statement of Standard Accounting Practice is published;

(h)    SSAPs are kept under review and in some cases have been amended, updated, or even withdrawn and replaced.

ASC has recently announced that it intends in future to issue SORPs (Statements of Recommended Practice) for less important subjects. A list of topics on which ASC has pronounced or is working is provided in Appendix 13–2.

## Good Practice

Improvements in practice usually first come from the efforts of individual accountants, auditors, and companies. Only later is such practice encapsulated in Accounting Standards, Stock Exchange requirements, or finally the law.

A survey of good, or at least generally acceptable, practice is to be found in an annual publication of the Institute of Chartered Accountants in England and Wales entitled *Financial Reporting*. This sets out in analytical detail the practices followed by large listed, medium listed and large unlisted UK companies in various subject areas.

Another useful source document in this area is *Current Accounting Law and Practice,* by Robert Willott, published annually by Quinta Publishing.

The development of good practice is fostered by, amongst other things, the annual awards made by *The Accountant* magazine and the Stock Exchange for the best annual accounts in two categories, large and smaller companies. Most recently the Society of Investment Analysts has also started to make awards for good accounting presentation.

## 13.4 Publication Requirements

### Distinctions introduced by the Companies Act 1981

The category of exempt private company which did not have to file accounts was abolished by the 1967 Act.

The Companies Act 1981 however introduced into UK law a new distinction between the accounts sent to shareholders and the accounts which are filed with the Registrar of Companies. Before the 1981 Act the Registrar of Companies received the same accounts as were sent to the shareholders. Under the 1981 Act if a company meets certain criteria, it may omit specific information from its published accounts, although a second set of accounts must always be prepared for shareholders which contains all the statutory information.

The content, audit and filing requirements of small companies accounts is under

review, see *Burdens on Business*, DTI, HMSO, March 1985, and *Accounting and Audit Requirements for Small Firms: A consultative document,* DTI, June 1985.

Exemptions depend on the company's (or group's) size. The criteria are:

| Category | Turnover | Balance Sheet Total | Average employees per week |
|---|---|---|---|
| Large company or group | Over £5.75m | Over £2.8m | Over 250 |
| Medium company or group | Up to £5.75m | Up to £2.8m | Up to 250 |
| Small company or group | Up to £1.4m | Up to £0.7m | Up to 50 |

To qualify for 'small' or 'medium' status a company or group must satisfy (i.e. not exceed) at least two of the criteria for both the current and the previous year. 'Balance sheet total' means total gross assets. Where a financial year is not in fact twelve months long the criteria concerning turnover must be adjusted proportionately.

### Ineligible companies

Companies will not be eligible for small or medium status (and relief from disclosure) if at any time during the year they were public, or banking, insurance or shipping companies of members of a group containing such companies. Banking, insurance, and shipping companies however are permitted to prepare accounts under the pre-1981 Act rules applicable to them.

### Small companies

Eligible small companies or groups may file with the Registrar of Companies accounts containing only the following:

1    Balance sheet containing only those items preceded by letters or Roman numbers in the Statutory Formats (see Appendix 13–3). Debtors and creditors must be split between amounts due within and after one year.

2    Notes on the following: accounting policies, share capital, substantial shareholdings, allotments, debt particulars, foreign currency translation, corresponding amounts. Additional information required by earlier Acts will still have to be given, if applicable, as follows: transactions in which directors have a material interest, loans to directors and non-director officers, ultimate parent company.

3    No information on directors' emoluments or highly paid staff.

4    No directors' report.
5    No profit and loss account.
6    Special reports by directors and auditors regarding the exemptions.
7    It is thought that modified accounts would not include a statement of source and application of funds (under SSAP 10) since modified accounts would probably not be sufficient to give a true and fair view. SSAP 10 only applies to accounts which do give such a view. Modified accounts would, of course, be based on the full shareholder accounts and these would have been prepared taking into account all relevant SSAPs.

## Medium size companies

Medium size companies or groups may file accounts comprising only the following:

1    No disclosure or analysis of turnover.
2    No details of gross margin. In this case the profit and loss account begins with the figure of gross profit (rather than starting with turnover and giving the intervening figures). All other profit and loss account items and notes are required.
3    Full balance sheet and supporting notes.
4    Special reports by directors and auditors regarding the exemptions.
5    Directors' report.
6    As mentioned above, probably no statement of source and application of funds.

## Time allowed

Under the Companies Act 1985, companies are allowed several months after their year end before they have to file their accounts with the Registrar of Companies. The permitted period is seven months for a public company, and ten months for a private company. A company may apply to the Department of Trade and Industry for a three-month extension of the filing deadline where it trades, or has interests, outside the UK.

At one time some companies were very tardy in filing their accounts. But more recently the Registrar has been tightening up on the laggards (the Companies Act 1976 prescribed penalties (including, on conviction by a Magistrates' Court, disqualification from acting as a director of any company for a period of up to five years) on directors for failing to file accounts) and this has led to an improvement. However, it was reported in *The Accountant* (7 October 1982) that over half the 846,000 companies on the register had failed to file their accounts for their last year by April of the following year and that some 150,000 companies had filed no accounts for three years. There were suggestions (*The Guardian*, 22 March 1983) that private firms might take over the running of the registry and might be better at chasing defaulters and providing searchers with what they want. However so far these have come to nothing (*The Accountant*, 4 August 1983) because the EEC First Directive forbids the sale of copies of company records at a price above cost. Most recently, after criticism by MPs and the Public Accounts Committee, the Registrar has taken on 100 more staff and announced a blitz on defaulters (*The Accountant*, 28 June 1984).

Listed companies, and companies traded on the Unlisted Securities Market, are required by the Stock Exchange to issue their annual report and accounts within six months from the end of the financial period to which they relate.

In practice, the majority of larger companies tend to circulate their annual accounts within three months of the end of the year to which they relate (see Table 13–1 from *Financial Reporting* 1982/83).

|  | 1981–82 | | 1980–81 | |
|---|---|---|---|---|
|  | Number of companies | Cumulative percentage | Number of companies | Cumulative percentage |
| 60 days or less | 2 | 1 | 1 | – |
| 61–80 days | 19 | 7 | 18 | 6 |
| 81–100 days | 62 | 28 | 63 | 27 |
| 101–120 days | 94 | 59 | 87 | 56 |
| 121–140 days | 73 | 83 | 76 | 82 |
| 141–160 days | 25 | 92 | 32 | 92 |
| 161–180 days | 8 | 94 | 9 | 95 |
| 181 days or more | 3 | 95 | 7 | 98 |
| Information not available | 14 | 100 | 7 | 100 |
|  | 300 | | 300 | |

|  | 1981–82 | 1980–81 | 1979–80 |
|---|---|---|---|
|  | Days | Days | Days |
| Shortest interval | 59 | 60 | 41 |
| Median interval | 114 | 115 | 116 |
| Longest interval | 213 | 242 | 219 |

Table 13–1  Circulation of accounts to shareholders

## 13.5 How to Obtain Accounts

Possibly the simplest way to obtain accounts is to ask for a copy from the Secretary or Registrar of the company. He is however under no obligation to provide them to non-shareholders.

Accounts which have been filed with the Registrar of Companies may be inspected by anyone on the payment of a fee at the appropriate Companies Registry. The addresses are as follows:

Companies Registration Office
Companies House
Crown Way
Maindy
Cardiff
Wales
Telephone: 0222-388588

Companies Registration Office
Companies House
55–71 City Road
London EC2
Telephone: 01-253 9393

Registrar of Companies for Scotland
102 George Street
Edinburgh 2
Telephone: 031-225 5774

If a visit to the Companies Registry is inconvenient, there are several agencies which will obtain accounts for you for a fee and, as described more fully in Appendix 2–2 'Sources of Comparative Performance Data', several companies prepare abstracts and summaries of published accounts for larger companies or companies in selected industries.

## 13.6 Reading Annual Reports

### Main constituents

Most annual reports contain the following: the Chairman's Statement; the Directors' Report; a Profit and Loss Account; a Balance Sheet; a Funds Statement; Historical Summaries; Notes to the Accounts; the Auditors' Report.

The Directors' Report, the Profit and Loss Account and Balance Sheet, the Notes to the Accounts and the Auditors' Report are all required by law. The Chairman's Statement is not a legal requirement and is not always provided. The Funds Statement is required only from companies over a size specified by the relevant Statement of Standard Accounting Practice. Historical Summaries are not required of companies but this information was requested of listed companies by the Chairman of the Stock Exchange in 1964 and in practice the vast majority of large companies provide them.

*The Chairman's Statement* tends to be in general terms and not to contain many figures. It is usually a general review of the progress of the company and its business environment over the past year together with some indications of the direction in which it is hoped the company will move in the next year. It is very rare for these remarks to be in such terms as to enable the reader to convert them into a forecast of the results of the company for the next year since if they were, and the company was to be involved in a takeover bid, then the directors would have to have the 'forecast' reported on by accountants and a merchant bank or to withdraw it. The Chairman's Statement is not covered by the auditors' report.

By contrast, the content of the Directors' Report is laid down by statute and, to a smaller extent, by the requirements of the Stock Exchange for listed companies. Moreover the auditor is now required to comment in his report if any information given in the directors' report is not, in his opinion, consistent with the company's accounts.

*The Directors' Report* describes the principal activities of the business and must now include a fair review of the development of the business during the year and its position at the end of the year together with an indication of likely future developments. Particulars should be given of any important events affecting the group since the year end. It should also contain a statement of the directors' interest in the shares of the company, in the case of a listed company the identity of anyone owning more than 5 per cent of the company, and if the company has acquired any of its own shares. Information is also required on charitable and political contributions, research and development, disabled employees and employee consultation (if more than 250 employees).

*The profit and loss account* shows what profit the company has earned during the year and gives the main items of income and expenditure which have led to that profit. *The balance sheet* lists the company's assets and liabilities at the end of the year. *The Funds Statement* complements the Profit and Loss Account and Balance Sheet by showing where the company has obtained money from during the year (e.g. profit, raising new capital, etc.) and what it has used the money for (e.g. buying new plant or increasing the quantity of stock carried). It is usual for the profit and loss account and balance sheet to contain only the most important items and major totals. Many of the items are then explained in fuller detail in the notes to the accounts.

*Historical summaries* contain selected figures from the accounts of the past years. The usual period covered is about five years but many companies go back as many as ten years. The more usual items included are:

> Turnover
> Profit
> Dividends
> Capital employed
> Various ratios such as earnings per share, return on capital, profit on turnover and assets per share.

*Audit Report.* When using an annual report it is probably best to start with the auditors' report. Normally this is a 'clean' report and the reader can pass rapidly on. However, occasionally it is qualified and this will alert the reader at an early stage for possible difficulties in interpretation.

A clean audit report will look similar to the following:

*Auditors' Report*
To the members of [name of company]

We have audited the accounts set out on pages . . . to . . . in accordance with approved Auditing Standards.

In our opinion, the accounts, which have been prepared under the historical cost convention [as modified by the revaluation of land and buildings] give a true and fair view of the state of affairs of the company and of the group at . . . . . . 19. . and of the group profit and source and application of funds for the year then ended, and comply with the Companies Act 1985.

[Name and address of auditors, and date]

Where relevant the auditor must also state that:

(a) proper returns have not been received from branches he has not visited;
(b) proper accounting records have not been kept;
(c) the accounts are not in agreement with the underlying records and returns;
(d) he has not obtained all the information and explanations he thought necessary.

It should be noted that the auditor's report uses the phrase *a* true and fair view. This indicates that the accounting policies and presentation used by the directors are acceptable, although another company in the same financial position could, by adopting different policies, which would also be acceptable, show a different profit.

The approved Auditing Standards referred to in the Auditors' Report are produced by the Auditing Practices Committee of the bodies of accountants entitled to audit limited companies' accounts. They prescribe the basic principles and practices which members are expected to follow in the conduct of an audit. They are supported by Auditing Guidelines. An indication of the subjects covered is given in Diagram 13.1.

*Qualified Audit Reports.* There are, broadly speaking, four groups of situations in which an auditor will qualify his report. They are as follows:

(a) where there is an uncertainty which prevents the auditor from forming an opinion on a matter, or
(b) where the auditor is able to form an opinion on the matter giving rise to the qualification but this conflicts with the view given by the financial statements.

Depending on whether the subject matter is:

(a) material but not fundamental; or
(b) fundamental

the auditor will use the wording indicated below.

| Nature of circumstances | Material but not fundamental | Fundamental |
| --- | --- | --- |
| Uncertainty | 'Subject to' opinion | Disclaimer of opinion |
| Disagreement | 'Except' opinion | Adverse opinion |

1 In a disclaimer of opinion the auditor states that he is unable to form an opinion as to whether the financial statements give a true and fair view.
2 In an adverse opinion the auditor states that in his opinion the financial statements do not give a true and fair view.
3 In a 'subject to' opinion the auditor effectively disclaims an opinion on a particular matter which is not considered fundamental.
4 In an 'except' opinion the auditor expresses an adverse opinion on a particular matter which is not considered fundamental.

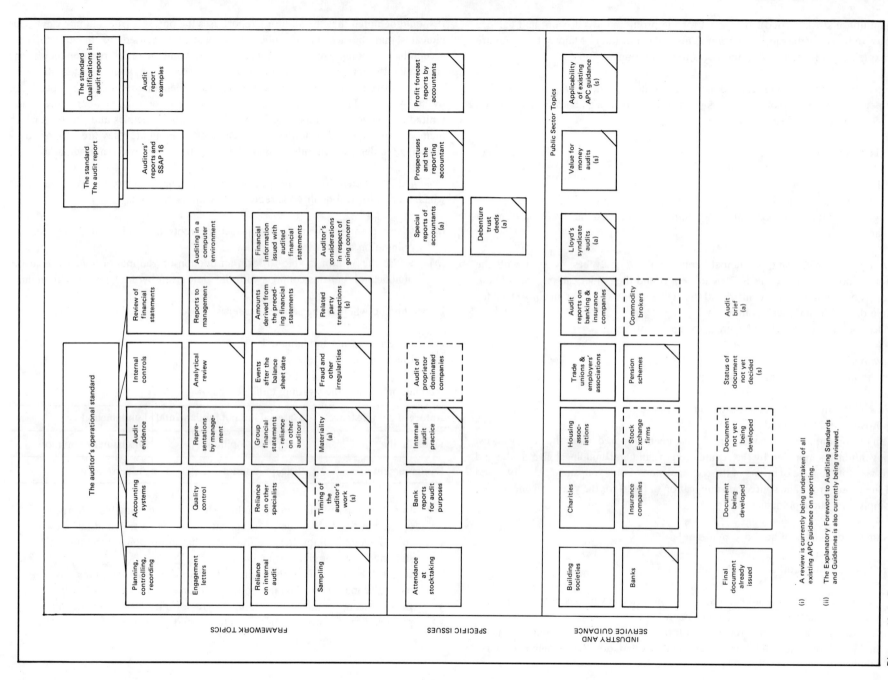

Diagram 13–1   Present and prospective auditing standards, guidelines and briefs

318

The auditor must comment where the directors' report is inconsistent with the accounts concerning information relating to the financial year.

Silence on these matters may be taken to imply that the auditor is satisfied.

Where the auditor's report is qualified, the auditor must state in his report whether any audit qualification is material in deciding whether proposed dividends are lawful.

## Misconceptions about auditors' reports

There is a widespread, popular view that an unqualified audit report is in some way a clean bill of health, guaranteeing that a company will not go out of business for at least another year. This view is, however, a misconception of the role of the audit report which is no more than that the accounts present *a* true and fair view. It is up to the reader to decide whether that view encourages him to believe in the company's continuing existence or to have doubts about its viability.

If the author concludes that there is strong evidence that a company will not remain a going concern, either in any event, or unless certain major uncertainties are favourably resolved (e.g. the continuing support of the company's bank is assured), then he should qualify his report. Auditors are understandably reluctant to do this in case the qualification becomes a self-fulfilling prophecy in the sense that it precipitates an event which makes the company no longer a going concern and which would not have happened but for the audit qualification.

An auditor does not guarantee that there has been no fraud within a company. The responsibility for the prevention and detection of irregularities and fraud rests with the management. The auditor's duties do not require him specifically to search for fraud. However, he should recognise the possibility of material irregularities or fraud and should plan his audit so that he has a reasonable expectation of detecting material mis-statements in the financial statements resulting from irregularities or fraud.

The auditor's role in relation to the prevention and detection of fraud is under review: see exposure draft of an Auditing Guideline, 'Fraud and other irregularities', APC, May 1985, and 'Report of the working party on fraud', Chairman Ian Hay Davison, ICAEW, August 1985.

## Status of auditors

In theory an auditor is employed by the shareholders and reports to them. In practice the auditor is appointed by the directors. There is therefore a potential (and sometimes actual) conflict between an auditor's professional responsibilities to report on the accounts' truth and fairness (which may involve revealing things the directors would prefer not to be disclosed) and his business desires to keep the audit by agreeing to the directors' wishes.

Auditors are human (despite widely held views to the contrary) and some are better able to resist pressures from directors than others. The user of accounts must, particularly if there is much at stake, therefore consider who the auditors are and how independent they are. Three questions are worth asking:

1   How large is the company relative to the size of the audit firm? A large company can exert more pressure on a small firm than on a large firm by threatening to take away the audit.
2   Has the company changed auditors recently or frequently? Have the last auditors resigned? Changes in auditors may be perfectly justified but they may suggest a desire by a company to find more compliant auditors.
3   Is the group audited by several or many firms? The risk of undetected malpractice is greater if there are too many fingers in the pie.

## Accounting policies

After reading the auditors' report the next item to look at is the 'Statement of Accounting Policies'. The provision of this Statement is a requirement both of company law and Statements of Standard Accounting Practice. The Statement is usually the first of the notes to the accounts. Sometimes, however, accounting policies are dealt with under the notes relating to the particular items. If you are comparing the accounts of two companies it is most important to study their accounting policies to make sure, if possible, that they have used the same accounting policies to deal with the item or items in question. If they have not, it may be possible to convert the accounts of one company to the basis used by the other. However, this is often not possible and some subjective allowance will have to be made.

There are four accounting principles which it may be assumed that all companies have followed unless they specifically state that they have not. They are:

(*a*)   The going concern principle (there is evidence to support the view that the company will continue in business for the foreseeable future and that the cost of the assets in the balance sheet will be recovered against revenue as a result of normal trading and will not have to be recovered as a result of a forced sale in a liquidation).
(*b*)   The prudence principle (only realised profits are credited to the profit and loss account and all losses anticipated at the year end are recognised even though they may not yet have occurred).

(c) Accounting principles are applied consistently from one year to the next (if there is a change in accounting policy this should be explicitly reported in the accounting policies note and the financial effects of the change should be disclosed).

(d) The accrual's basis (all income and expenses relevant to the year are accounted for regardless of the actual date of receipt or payment).

## Extracting data

Many commercial organisations are nowadays organised in the form of a parent or holding company with one or more subsidiaries. Sometimes the subsidiaries themselves have sub-subsidiaries. Each of these subsidiaries is required to produce its own accounts and, if a UK company, to file them with the Registrar of Companies. The parent company usually produces two sets of accounts contained within the one annual report:

(a) its own accounts in which the subsidiaries will be shown in the balance sheet as an investment and the dividends received from them will be shown in the profit and loss account; and

(b) its group or consolidated accounts. These show the income and expenditure, assets and liabilities of all the companies as a single economic whole and therefore usually give a much clearer and fuller picture.

A company publishing group accounts need not publish its own profit and loss account but must show how much of the group's profit is dealt with in the parent's profit and loss account.

The parent company's accounts have an important legal role. It is these accounts which are the basis for calculating the amount which the parent is legally entitled to pay in a dividend to its shareholders. Moreover a creditor should look at the accounts of the company (parent or individual subsidiary) of which he is a creditor, as it is only the assets of that company that provide him with any security and not the assets of the group, unless there are intra-group guarantees. The existence of such guarantees is disclosed in the accounts of the giver of the guarantee but not necessarily in the accounts of the beneficiary of the guarantee.

For our purposes, in this chapter, we will almost always use the group accounts. However, for a detailed analysis of a group it may be desirable to analyse the accounts of the group's major subsidiaries as well as the group accounts.

It is a statutory requirement to provide comparative information (i.e. figures for last year or at the last balance sheet date) for virtually all the items in the annual accounts. Among the very few exceptions to this general rule are certain information on

investments, loans to directors and employees, movements on fixed assets and movements on provisions and reserves.

## 13.7 Weaknesses of Historical Cost Accounts

For centuries almost all accounts have been prepared under the 'historical cost' convention under which income, expenditure, assets and liabilities are measured at the prices ruling at the time of the original transaction.

In most recent years traditional historical cost accounts have been distorted because they did not reflect the impact of inflation. Even if price rises abate the effects of past inflation they will still cause distortions to fixed asset values and depreciation.

In historical cost accounts:

1. Asset valuations are often too low, misleading some users of accounts as to the worth of the business (accountants are aware that accounts do not show the worth of assets but non-accountants should not be assumed to know of this significant limitation);

2. Depreciation is therefore inadequate to retain sufficient finance to replace assets at the end of their lives, leading to businesses being run down or to calls for 'new money' merely to keep going at existing levels;

3. 'Stock profits' (the difference between the cost of stock purchased and its replacement cost at the date of sale) are included in profit but need to be retained in order to finance the higher cost of replacing the stock consumed;

4. The losses in purchasing power resulting from holding cash and other monetary assets (e.g. debtors) are not disclosed;

5. Conversely, the gains as a result of borrowings are also not disclosed;

6. As a result of the above, profit is often overstated. Moreover, no provision is made to maintain the purchasing power of shareholders' capital;

7. Growth in turnover or profits is often exaggerated because no allowance is made for the fall in the value of money in which they have been measured.

Because of these deficiencies the accounting profession in the UK has laboured for many years to produce a method for compensating for these defects in published accounts that is acceptable to analysts, businessmen, accountants, auditors and government.

In January 1973 the ASSC (as it then was) issued ED8 'Accounting for changes in the purchasing power of money'. ED8 proposed that quoted companies should include in their financial statements a supplementary statement showing the financial position and results for the year in terms of current purchasing power (CPP).

In July 1973 the then Secretary of State for Trade and Industry announced that an independent Committee of Enquiry (the Sandilands Committee) was to be set up to consider which, if any, of the various methods should be used to adjust company accounts for changes in costs and prices. Since it would obviously be some time before the Sandilands Committee could report and before its recommendations could be considered by government, the ASSC prepared a Provisional Standard (PSSAP7) based on ED8, which was approved by its governing bodies and issued in May 1974.

The Sandilands Report was published in September 1975 with the principal recommendation that 'a system to be known as Current Cost Accounting (CCA) should be developed'. In January 1976, at Sandilands' recommendation, a Steering Group was set up by the accounting profession to prepare an exposure draft based on the Sandilands proposals. This led to the issue by the ASC of ED18 in November of that year.

In the light of the comments on ED18 and a resolution passed at a special meeting of the English Institute in July 1977 'that the members of the ICAEW do not wish any system of Current Cost Accounting to be made compulsory' the ASC was forced to reconsider its position. An interim solution, the 'Hyde guidelines', was issued in November 1977. A longer term solution appeared in April 1979 in the form of ED24, which formed the basis for SSAP16 in March 1980.

For a history of part of this period see 'The lessons to be learnt from the development of inflation accounting in the UK', C.A. Westwick, *Accounting and Business Research*, Autumn 1980.

SSAP 16 required larger and listed companies to supplement their basic historical cost accounts with summarised current cost accounts (CCA) which made allowance for the impact of inflation. The accounts comprised:

1 A balance sheet with assets at current cost (i.e. in most cases depreciated replacement cost).
2 A profit and loss account starting with historical cost profit but subtracting:

(a) a depreciation adjustment (i.e. additional depreciation based on the replacement cost of fixed assets);
(b) a cost of sales adjustment (to allow for the effect of higher replacement costs of stocks consumed);
(c) a monetary working capital adjustment (to allow for the impact of rising prices on the amount required to fund monetary working capital (mainly trade debtors less trade creditors) );

to arrive at current cost operating profit, and adding back,

(d) a gearing adjustment to allow for the 'fact' (disputed by some) that part of (a) (b) and (c) above would or could be financed by borrowing

to arrive at 'current cost profit attributable to shareholders'.

In July 1982 a motion put to another Special General Meeting of the ICAEW 'that members of the ICAEW deplore the introduction of SSAP16 and call for its immediate withdrawal' was narrowly defeated. Many of those voting against the resolution did so on the grounds that SSAP16 should be allowed to run unamended for a three-year period as envisaged when the standard was issued. During this period the implementation of SSAP16 was investigated for the ASC by the CCA Monitoring Working Party.

Current cost accounts were not without their critics however. They claimed that the figures were:

1 subjective;
2 costly to prepare;
3 not used for tax purposes;
4 not used by many investment analysts (a small minority however made extensive and apparently profitable use of the data);
5 not the only or best way of adjusting management accounts for changing prices (alternatives are LIFO* and supplementary depreciation);
6 not relevant to certain industries (e.g. shipping, commodity trading and plantation owners).

As a result of a comprehensive review of SSAP16, which included the work of the CCA Monitoring Working Party, the Inflation Accounting Sub-Committee of the ASC, and numerous research studies, the ASC issued ED35 'Accounting for the effects of changes prices' in July 1984 as a proposed successor to SSAP16. ED35 was withdrawn in March 1985 because it was apparent from the comments received that it was not regarded as an acceptable basis for an accounting standard.

---

* LIFO stands for Last In First Out. It is a method of stock valuation which, broadly speaking, charges the profit and loss account with stock consumed at the latest price paid for it. LIFO is often used in the USA because it is allowed for tax purposes. The more usual method of stock valuation is FIFO (First In First Out), which charges stock used at the oldest price paid for it.

| | | £ |
|---|---|---|
| P1 | Turnover | ................ |
| P2 | Cost of sales | ———— |
| P3 | Gross profit | ................ |
| P4 | Other operating expenses (net) | ———— |
| P5 | Operating profit | ................ |
| P6 | Investment income | ................ |
| P7 | Amounts written off investments | ................ |
| P8 | Interest payable and similar charges | ———— |
| P9 | Profit on ordinary activities before taxation | ................ |
| P10 | Tax on profit on ordinary activities | ———— |
| P11 | Profit on ordinary activities after taxation | ................ |
| P12 | Minority interests | ———— |
| P13 | Profit before extraordinary items | ................ |
| P14 | Extraordinary items less taxation & minority interests | ———— |
| P15 | Profit for the financial year | ................ |
| P16 | Dividends paid and proposed | ———— |
| P17 | Retained profit for the year | ════ |

Table 13–2   Consolidated Profit and Loss Account (format 1)

The number of companies complying with SSAP16 declined, and in June 1985 the CCAB bodies agreed to the suspension of the mandatory status of SSAP16 because it became clear that it would take some time before a new standard could be developed, exposed for comment, and issued as a replacement.

Because the rate of inflation has fallen in the UK in recent years some commentators have suggested that CCA is no longer relevant. Obviously if the CCA figures are not materially different from the HCA ones then their importance will have diminished, but past inflation will continue to affect the figures for fixed assets bought when prices were lower, and the depreciation on them, until the relevant assets are sold or wear out. Moreover companies with significant overseas operations will be affected by overseas inflation rates which may be higher than those in the UK.

Despite the criticism listed above, wherever possible the analyst of company accounts should use current cost figures for a realistic picture of how the company has performed. If such figures are not available from the company:

1   he should estimate what the current cost inflation adjusted figures would have been (see Appendix 13–1); or

2   he should fall back on the less than adequate, albeit voluminous, historical cost accounts.

| | | £ |
|---|---|---|
| | *Fixed Assets* | |
| B1 | Intangible assets | ................ |
| B2 | Tangible assets | ................ |
| B3 | Investments | ———— |
| | | ———— |
| | *Current assets* | |
| B4 | Stocks | ................ |
| B5 | Debtors | ................ |
| B6 | Investments | ................ |
| B7 | Cash at bank and in hand | ———— |
| | | ................ |
| B8 | *Creditors:* amounts falling due within one year | ———— |
| B9 | *Net current assets* | ———— |
| B10 | *Total assets less current liabilities* | ................ |
| B11 | *Creditors:* amounts falling due after more than one year | ................ |
| B12 | *Provisions for liabilities and charges* | ———— |
| B13 | *Net assets* | ════ |
| | *Capital and reserves* | |
| | Called-up share capital | ................ |
| | Share premium account | ................ |
| | Revaluation reserve | ................ |
| | Other reserves | ................ |
| | Profit and loss account | ———— |
| B14 | Shareholders' funds | ................ |
| B15 | Minority interests | ———— |
| B16 | *Total capital employed* | ════ |

Table 13–3   Consolidated Balance Sheet

### 13.8 Ratios to Analyse the Historical Cost Accounts

Using Historical Cost Accounts

The main aim of the analysis which follows is to enable you to discover in a systematic way whether the company you are looking at has done better (or worse) than last year; or by comparison with other, similar, companies. The analysis will indicate which factors have contributed how much to this success or failure. You should also consider, from the information available from the annual report and elsewhere, whether the company will maintain its strengths or remedy its weaknesses in the next year or so.

|  | | £ |
|---|---|---|
| P1 | Turnover | |
| F1 | Change in stocks of finished goods and in work in progress | |
| F2 | Own work capitalised | |
| F3 | Other operating income | |
| F4 | Raw materials and consumables | |
| F5 | Other external charges | |
| F6 | Staff costs | |
| F7 | Depreciation | |
| F8 | Other operating charges | |
| P5 | Operating profit | |
| P6 | Investment income | |
| P7 | Amounts written off investments | |
| P8 | Interests payable and similar charges | |
| P9 | Profit on ordinary activities before taxation | |
| P10 | Tax on profit on ordinary activities | |
| P11 | Profit on ordinary activities after taxation | |
| P12 | Minority interests | |
| P13 | Profit before extraordinary items | |
| P14 | Extraordinary items less taxation & minority interests | |
| P15 | Profit for the financial year | |
| P16 | Dividends paid and proposed | |
| P17 | Retained profit for the year | |

*Note:* The items which appear in both formats 1 and 2 are preceded by a P; those which appear only in format 2 are preceded by an F.

Table 13–4  Consolidated Profit and Loss Account (format 2)

What you then do will depend on your relationship with, and degree of influence on, the company, e.g. an investor with a small holding in a listed company which can be easily sold or increased, an investor with a large holding in an unlisted company, a bank manager, a debenture trustee, etc.

Possible courses of action by management are described in the relevant chapters of this book.

The historical cost accounts of a company will probably look similar to the accounts in Tables 13–2 and 13–3 which have been drawn up to comply with the Companies Act 1985. They will of course be supported by voluminous notes which have not been reproduced here. The accounts comply with formats 1 for the profit and loss account and balance sheet because these are the ones most likely to be used. If format 2 has been used for the profit and loss account (Table 13–4) then there will be several differences which the analyst will need to take into account but only at a later stage in the analysis (see 'Analysing a format 2 profit and loss account') below).

| | Item | £ | Source |
|---|---|---|---|
| W1 | Raw Material Stock | | Note to item B4 |
| 2 | Work in progress | | Note to item B4 |
| 3 | Finished goods stock | | Note to item B4 |
| 4 | Debtors[+] | | B5 |
| 5 | Current Assets* | | (W1 + W2 + W3 + W4) |
| 6 | Land and Buildings | | Note to item B2 |
| 7 | Plant and Machinery | | Note to item B2 |
| 8 | Other Fixed Assets | | Note to item B2 |
| 9 | Fixed Assets* | | (W6 + W7 + W8) |
| 10 | Operating Assets | | (W5 + W9) |
| 11 | Investments | | B3 + B6 + B7 |
| 12 | Total Capital Employed* | | (W10 + W11) |
| 13 | Borrowings | | B8 + B11 + B12 |
| 14 | Equity Capital | | (W12 − W13) |
| 15 | Minority Interests | | B15 |
| 16 | Shareholders' funds* | | (W14 − W15) |

*Note:* Check that W16 = B16 − B1
[+] This item may contain debtors other than trade debtors. If these other debtors are material they could be removed from this item and included under another heading, e.g. W11 Investments
* NB These terms have slightly different meanings from those used in the published balance sheet itself

Table 13–5  Balance sheet worksheet

The first step is to rearrange some of the items in the balance sheet using the work sheet in Table 13–5. It will be seen that some items can be taken straight from the balance sheet whereas other items (e.g. raw materials stock) will be found in the notes to a particular item on the face of the balance sheet. Other items in the worksheet are the result of adding together amounts from different places within the published balance sheet (e.g. investments and borrowings). All items in the published balance sheet should however be included in one or another of the items in the work sheet; this means that Item 16 in the work sheet (shareholders' funds) should equal Item 14 in the published balance sheet (shareholders' funds) less Item 1 in the published balance sheet (intangible assets). If it does not then check to see what has been omitted or included twice and make appropriate adjustments.

Intangible assets have been excluded because of the difficulty of valuing them and the widely different ways of accounting for them used by different companies. If they are material they should be included with fixed assets but in a separate category.

The relationship between the items in the profit and loss account (Table 13–2) and balance sheet worksheet (Table 13–5) are illustrated in Diagrams 13–2 and 13–3 respectively.

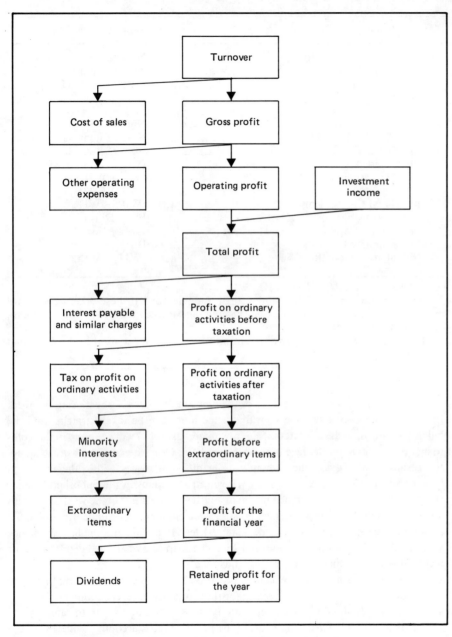

Diagram 13–2   A group's flow of income, expenditure, dividends and retentions
(the profit and loss account)

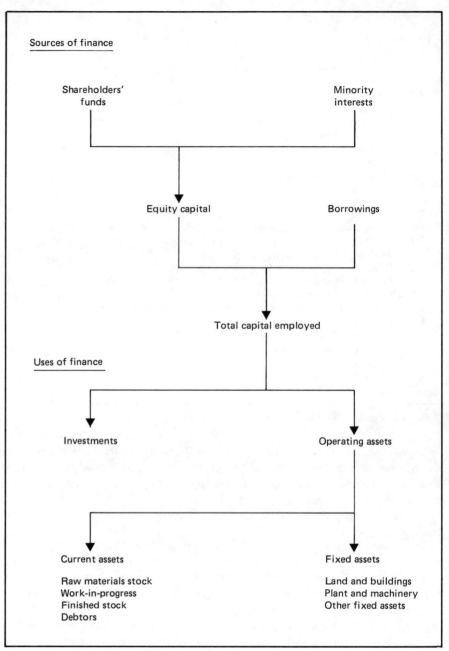

Diagram 13–3   A group's sources and uses of finance (the balance sheet)

Even though we are using the historical cost accounts it would be desirable to make use of any information on up-to-date values that is available from the annual report and substitute it for the corresponding historical cost figures.

The information that may be available is as follows:

1. A current value of property (in the Directors' report);
2. Market value of listed investments (in the notes to the accounts);
3. Replacement cost of stock (in the notes to the accounts).

It is desirable that the average figures for assets and capital employed should be used rather than those at either the beginning, or end of the year. Two Balance Sheet Worksheets should desirably therefore be completed (one for the end of the year under review, and one for the previous year from the comparative figures in this year's accounts) and the results averaged. If the two Balance Sheets do not differ materially or if the analyst is pressed for time, then the figures from only one Balance Sheet (this year) can be used.

## Dividend yield

It is suggested that the starting point for an analysis of a company's performance, as shown by its published accounts, should be a divided yield ratio. For other ratios which the investor should use see Chapter 8.6 and 8.7.

Diagram 13–4 shows some of the ratios which may be used to analyse reasons for a low dividend yield on shareholders' funds (ratio 1). The letters and numbers in brackets after the numerator and denominator of each ratio refer to the location of the item in the historical cost accounts and worksheet above.

## Dividend cover

If Ratio 1 is lower this may be due to:

(a) a low ratio of profit on shareholders' funds (ratio 2); and/or
(b) a high dividend cover (ratio 3).

Dividend cover is a rough measure of how far profit could fall before the dividend would need to be cut.

## Extraordinary items

If a company's ratio of profit on shareholders' funds (ratio 2) is low then this may be due to:

(a) the profit before extraordinary items (ratio 4) being low; and/or
(b) the extraordinary items (ratio 5) being either (i) high and a deduction or (ii) low and a credit.

'Extraordinary items' is a term of art used by accountants to mean items which result from events or transactions outside the ordinary activities of the business which are not expected to recur frequently. An example would be a profit or loss arising from closing a significant part of the business or the nationalisation of some of the company's assets. There is always a temptation for directors to include unusual costs in extraordinary items because the figure usually quoted in the financial press for earnings per share is calculated before extraordinary items. Because of this the analyst of company accounts needs always to pay particular attention to the nature of the items classified as extraordinary and to form a judgement as to whether he agrees with the directors' classification. It will have been seen that extraordinary items are shown net of the related taxation.

Extraordinary items are the subject of SSAP 6 (see Appendix 13–2).

## Minorities

If the cause of a low ratio 2 is a low ratio 4 then this may be due to the effect of minority shareholders on the profit available to the majority shareholders. Minorities arise in group accounts where the parent company does not own all the shares in some or all of its subsidiaries. The minority's figure in the profit and loss account is the sum of the shares of the profits in the relevant subsidiaries earned by the minority shareholders. Similarly, the minority interests shown in the consolidated balance sheet is the sum of the share capital and reserves 'owned' by the minority shareholders.

Ratio 8 shows how important minority interests are in relation to shareholders funds (see Diagram 13–3). Ratio 7 shows what rate of profit or loss they have earned on the capital which they have provided and ratio 6 shows what rate of profit has been earned on the total equity capital of the group (irrespective of whether it has been provided by majority or minority shareholders).

If either ratios 7 or 8 are substantial it may be worth while examining the account(s) of the relevant subsidiary(ies) whose identity should be ascertainable from the note on fixed asset investments or elsewhere in the annual report of the parent company.

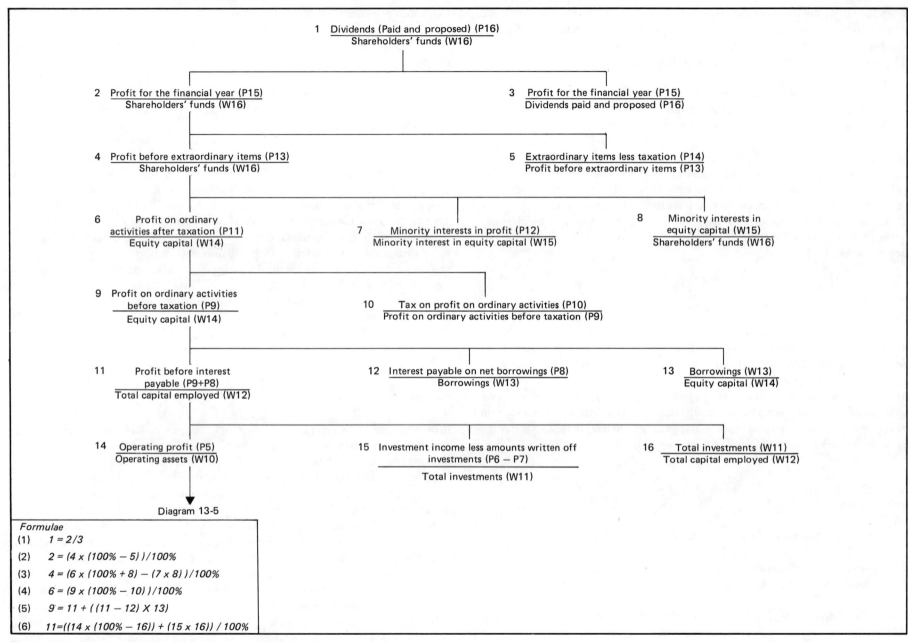

1  Dividends (Paid and proposed) (P16)
   Shareholders' funds (W16)

2  Profit for the financial year (P15)
   Shareholders' funds (W16)

3  Profit for the financial year (P15)
   Dividends paid and proposed (P16)

4  Profit before extraordinary items (P13)
   Shareholders' funds (W16)

5  Extraordinary items less taxation (P14)
   Profit before extraordinary items (P13)

6  Profit on ordinary
   activities after taxation (P11)
   Equity capital (W14)

7  Minority interests in profit (P12)
   Minority interest in equity capital (W15)

8  Minority interests in
   equity capital (W15)
   Shareholders' funds (W16)

9  Profit on ordinary activities
   before taxation (P9)
   Equity capital (W14)

10  Tax on profit on ordinary activities (P10)
    Profit on ordinary activities before taxation (P9)

11  Profit before interest
    payable (P9+P8)
    Total capital employed (W12)

12  Interest payable on net borrowings (P8)
    Borrowings (W13)

13  Borrowings (W13)
    Equity capital (W14)

14  Operating profit (P5)
    Operating assets (W10)

15  Investment income less amounts written off
    investments (P6 − P7)
    Total investments (W11)

16  Total investments (W11)
    Total capital employed (W12)

Diagram 13-5

Formulae
(1)    1 = 2/3
(2)    2 = (4 x (100% − 5) )/100%
(3)    4 = (6 x (100% + 8) − (7 x 8) )/100%
(4)    6 = (9 x (100% − 10) )/100%
(5)    9 = 11 + ( (11 − 12) X 13)
(6)    11=((14 x (100% − 16)) + (15 x 16)) / 100%

Diagram 13–4   Ratios to analyse historical cost accounts (part 1)

## Taxation

If ratio 6 is low then this may be due to:

(a)  the pre-tax return on equity capital (ratio 9) being low; and/or

(b)  the ratio of tax payable by the company (ratio 10) being high.

The size of ratio 10 will be the result of a number of factors which are to a greater or lesser extent within the control of management. They include:

(a)  the rate of tax payable on the profits earned in the country or countries in which the group operates;

(b)  the extent to which the company has been able to take advantage of the legitimate fiscal opportunities to minimise its tax rate (see next paragraph);

(c)  the extent to which it has not been able to offset overseas taxation against its UK tax liability;

(d)  the extent to which it has suffered taxation as a result of paying dividends (see under ACT below).

Whilst a company's tax bill in the UK is *based* on its historical cost profit, there are certain major adjustments to that profit made by the Inland Revenue, the most important of which is that the depreciation charge in the company's accounts is not allowed for taxation purposes but the Inland Revenue allows the company to deduct instead an allowance calculated according to tax rules.

Before the March 1984 Budget (see below) the Inland Revenue also allowed companies to deduct a figure of 'stock relief' which was based on the value of stock held at the beginning of the year times the increase in the 'all stocks index' during the year.

The tax figure in the accounts is the sum of the tax actually paid, plus amounts assessed but not yet paid, plus or minus a third figure called deferred tax. Deferred tax arises mainly because the Revenue's treatment of depreciation differs from that used by most companies. In simple terms a company will usually charge the cost of an asset evenly over its useful life but the Revenue usually allows the bulk of the cost to be written off in the early years of the asset's life.

Before March 1984 the Revenue allowed the whole cost of an asset to be written off in the year of acquisition. In the Budget of that year the Chancellor proposed to reduce this to 75 per cent for the period from 14 March 1984 to 31 March 1985, to 50 per cent from 1 April 1985 to 31 March 1986 and to nil from 1 April 1986.

In the years after the year in which a first year allowance is claimed the Revenue allows 25 per cent of the reducing balance of the cost of the asset.

The net effect is that in the early years of an asset's life tax allowances are usually greater than the company's depreciation and in later years vice versa.

In order to match the tax charge against the company's reported income the benefit of the higher tax allowances in the early years is spread (deferred) over the whole life of the asset, thereby giving an even tax charge rather than a low one in the first year(s) and higher ones thereafter. See Appendix 13–4 for an illustration.

If however a company keeps on buying plant (especially if it is at increasing prices because of inflation) giving rise to new early years' allowances, then these may outweigh some or all of the reversal of the previous years' deferred tax, so that in effect it is never actually paid. To prevent the accumulation of unnecessarily large tax provisions the accounting rules (SSAP 15 (revised) ) allow only the deferred tax that is probably going to be paid to be provided. Such estimates are necessarily subjective and the user of accounts needs to bear this in mind when interpreting the size of the tax charge. Has the company taken a conservative or optimistic view of its future tax liabilities? The size of the deferred tax balance in the balance sheet in relation to the charge in the profit and loss account may provide some clue. The company also should disclose its full potential liability in the notes.

When a company pays a dividend it has to pay to the Revenue tax (Advanced Corporation Tax – ACT) equal to the tax credit given to the shareholder. This is at the standard rate of income tax on the gross dividend (i.e. the amount paid plus the tax credit). ACT can be offset against the company's corporation tax bill but if this is not large enough then the ACT is not recoverable and will from part of the tax charge in the company's accounts.

Some analysts attempt to avoid the problems associated with the subjectivity of deferred tax and unrecoverable ACT by substituting for the company's tax charge a figure calculated by applying the rate of corporation tax to the company's figure for pre-tax profit and leaving a notional post-tax profit figure (called Fully Taxed Earnings). Analysts have also used earnings figures based on the assumption of no dividends (the nil basis) or the basis of the dividend actually proposed or paid (the net basis). It seems to me that the gain in certainty achieved by these methods is outweighed by the loss of realism, and I suggest using the actual tax charge but interpreting it in the light of what is ascertainable (from the notes to the accounts) about its make-up.

## Borrowing

If the reason for a low ratio 6 is a low ratio 9 then this in turn may be the result of the impact of the firm's borrowing policy. The effect of this is reflected in ratios 12 and 13. Ratio 13 measures the group's financial gearing by the ratio of borrowed capital to equity capital. Ratio 12 is the average rate of interest paid on this borrowing.

At present not all sources of finance are shown on the balance sheet. The most common source of 'off balance sheet finance' is leased assets. SSAP21 proposes that finance leased assets be capitalised and included in fixed assets and the 'loan' from the lessor shown among creditors. However, SSAP21 is due to come into effect on a phased basis and some lessees may not follow it until the last date of implementation (years beginning on or after 1 July 1987).

Meanwhile an indication of the extent of this source of finance may be obtained from the ratio of

$$\frac{\text{Hire charges}}{\text{Depreciation}}$$

(both of the constituents of this ratio should be in the notes to the profit and loss account) and from disclosures on Commitments.

If either the group's gearing (ratio 13), or rate of interest paid (ratio 12), is high then the group needs to look for ways of reducing borrowing, or borrowing from cheaper sources (see Chapter 8.2 and 8.3 and also Chapter 13.9).

### Investment

The final group of ratios in Diagram 13–4 shows what the impact of investment income has been on the group's results (as measured by ratio 11). Ratio 16 shows how much of the total capital employed has been invested in external investments as opposed to operating assets. Ratio 15 shows the return earned on those investments. Ratio 14 shows the rate of return earned from the main operations of the business.

If the amount invested externally (ratio 16) is substantial, and the rate of return on it (ratio 15) is particularly high or low then the reasons should be investigated (see Chapter 8.4 and 8.5).

For analysis of the factors affecting ratio 14 we must turn to a new diagram (Diagram 13–5).

### Return on operating assets

There are, broadly speaking, two main reasons why a firm may be showing a low return on its operating assets as measured by the ratio of operating profit to operating assets (ratio 1):

(a)   it may be making a low profit margin on its turnover (operating profit/turnover) (ratio 2); or

(b)   it may be turning its assets over slowly (turnover/operating assets) (ratio 3).

Or, of course, both ratios 2 and 3 may be low.

### Profit margin on sales

The analysis of the causes of a low operating profit/turnover ratio (ratio 2) will depend on the information provided by companies. The Companies Act 1985 gives companies a choice between analysing their costs by function (e.g. production, distribution, etc.) or by type (e.g. materials, staff costs, depreciation, etc.). As most large companies have chosen the functional classification, and as it is more useful, Diagram 13–5 is based on it. Diagram 13–6 is based on analysis of cost by type. From Diagram 13–5 it will be seen that the possible causes of a low profit margin on turnover are: a low gross profit margin or high distribution, research or administrative costs in relation to turnover.

The Companies Act's profit and loss account formats 1 and 3 require disclosure of only distribution costs and administrative expenses. Moreover, it needs to be stressed that none of these items (except turnover) are defined by the Companies Act and, as a consequence, different companies may well include similar costs under different headings. However, a company's practice should be consistent from one year to the next.

If the size of the gross profit (ratio 4) is of concern then look at Chapters 7 (purchasing management), 9 (production management), or 11 (if the group is not a manufacturer).

If the size of the distribution cost ratio (ratio 5) causes concern see Chapter 6.8.

If the size of the administrative cost ratio (ratio 7) causes concern see Chapter 8.8.

If the size of the research ratio (ratio 6) causes concern see Chapter 5.6.

If you are able to calculate any other overhead ratios (e.g. marketing costs/turnover) and their size warrants further investigation see the relevant part of Chapters 6, 8 or 10.

In all cases the classified suggestions for further reading at the end of this book should be helpful.

### Analysing a format 2 profit and loss account

The analysis of a format 2 profit and loss account is the same as for a format 1 profit and loss account as far as ratios 2 and 3 in Diagram 13–5. At that point turn to Diagram 13–6.

One of the problems is that part of the costs (items F4 to F8 in Table 13–4) will have been incurred in generating turnover (item P1) but part may have lead to an increase in stocks (item F1) or been capitalised (item F2) or generated other operating income (item F3). In general it would be expected than items F1, 2 and 3 would be relatively small. The analyst has three alternatives open to him:

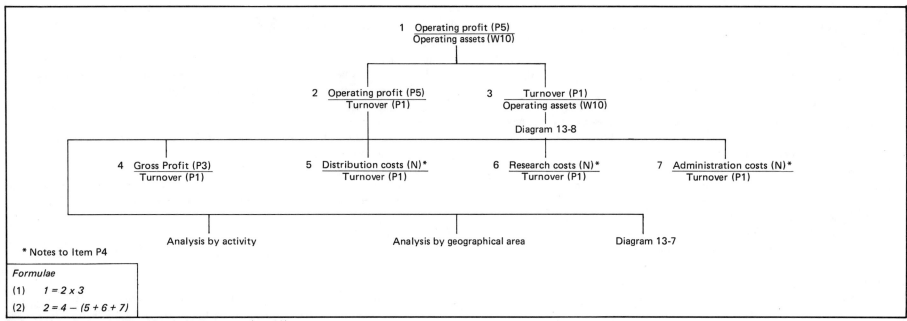

Diagram 13–5   Ratios to analyse historical cost accounts (part 2A)

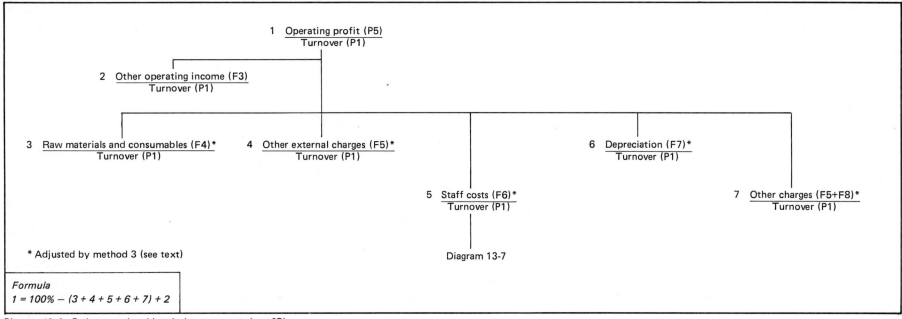

Diagram 13–6   Ratios to analyse historical cost accounts (part 2B)

1 Express each of items F1 and F8 as a percentage of turnover (P1) in order to explain differences in operating profit to turnover. This is simple, and, if items F1, 2 and 3 are small, acceptable, but ratios of items F1, 2 and 3 to turnover seem to be verging on being pseudo ratios (see Basic principle 3 in Chapter 1.2).

2 Add items F1, 2 and 3 to turnover (P1) to give a new turnover figure to which to relate items F4 to F8. Whilst F3, and to a lesser extent F2, have some of the characteristics of turnover (i.e. a saleable product if not one actually sold) item F1 does not.

3 If stock has been building up then reduce items F4 to F8 by the ratio $(F1 + F2)/(F4 + F5 + F6 + F7 + F8)$ and relate the reduced items to turnover. Show F2 as a percentage of P5. If stock had been run down items F4 to F8 would need to be increased by the ratio $(F1 - F2)/(F4 + F5 + F6 + F7 + F8)$. Whilst this method is the most complex it is probably the best. None of the methods are however totally satisfactory.

Diagram 13–6 is based on method 3. From this diagram it will be seen that the possible causes of a lower profit margin on turnover (ratio 1) are:

(a) a high cost of raw materials and other consumables (ratio 3); or
(b) high external charges (e.g. rent, rates, fuel, etc.) (ratio 4); or
(c) high staff costs (ratio 5); or
(d) high depreciation (ratio 6); or
(e) high other charges (ratio 7); or
(f) low other operating income (ratio 2)

all in relation to turnover.

## Operational gearing

Two of the factors influencing the size of the profit margin on turnover will be the proportion of a company's costs which are fixed; and whereabouts its turnover is in relation to its break-even point.

It is unlikely that the size of a company's fixed operating costs can be identified from its published accounts. However, it may be worth preparing a profit/volume chart for recent years to see how sensitive a company's profits are to changes in volume (see Chapter 5.4 for an example).

Unfortunately, because of the effects of inflation, neither profit nor sales figures will be comparable between years. Moreover, many businesses will change their methods of operation, and therefore the balance between their fixed and variable costs, over time.

## Activity and geographical analyses

The Companies Act 1985 also requires companies to give details of their 'profit on ordinary activities before taxation' analysed by activity and by geographical areas, and of their turnover analysed by geographical area. What constitutes a different activity or a different geographical area is left to the directors to decide. Such analyses can however be very useful in determining where the company's main sources of profit (or loss) are, and may enable some comparisons to be made between similar segments of otherwise different companies. Care needs to be taken to see how unallocated overheads have been dealt with in such an analysis.

Differences between companies in the calculation of profit, valuation of assets and calculation of transfer prices may also reduce the comparability between them of ratios based on segmental data.

## Staff costs

The Companies Act also requires information to be given about staff costs and numbers of employees. Diagram 13–7 shows the ratios which can be used to analyse the impact of staff costs on the ratio of operating profit to turnover.

One of the possible causes of a low ratio of operating profit to turnover (ratio 2 in Diagram 13–5) would be a high ratio of staff costs to turnover (ratio 1 in Diagram 13–7). Such a high ratio might in turn be due to:

(a) a high ratio of staff costs per employee (ratio 2); and/or
(b) a low ratio of turnover per employee (ratio 3).

The Companies Act 1985 requires companies to analyse staff numbers by category 'having regard to the manner in which the company's activities are organised'. It is to be hoped that companies will use a similar analysis to that used for costs in the profit and loss account and/or for activities and geographical area. Analysts will however have to make the best use of the information actually provided.

One of the possible reasons for a low turnover per employee (ratio 3) is that the company is providing him with too low an investment in supportive assets. It is for this reason that the ratio of assets per employee (ratio 4) is suggested. The assets included in this ratio could be either all fixed assets, or restricted to only plant and machinery. Alternatively, assets could be increased to fixed and current assets, if that is thought more appropriate, as it could well be for a retailing business – obviously an employee can sell more easily from a well stocked company than from one where the range is limited or items are frequently out of stock.

Two other ratios worth considering are

$$5 \qquad \frac{\text{Operating profit}}{\text{Staff costs}}$$

$$6 \qquad \frac{\text{Operating profit}}{\text{Number of employees}}$$

These indicate the vulnerability of the company's profit to wage increases. For example: if ratio 5 was 10 per cent then a 10 per cent increase in wages and related costs would eliminate the operating profit; if ratio 6 was £100 then a £100 per head per year increase in pay and related costs on average to all employees would also eliminate operating profit. This is provided, of course, in both cases no compensating action to reduce costs, increase output or prices were taken.

The subject of ratios for personnel management is discussed in Chapter 10.

## Turnover of assets

Returning to Diagram 13–5 it will be remembered that one of the possible reasons for a low ratio of operating profit to operating assets was a slow turnover of assets (turnover/operating assets). The possible reasons for such a low ratio are explored in Diagram 13–8.

A slow turnover of assets (ratio 1) can also be expressed more conveniently as a high investment in operating assets in relation to turnover (ratio 2) (see Appendix 1.1 for a discussion of this). Such a high ratio could be the result of either:

(a)  a high investment in fixed assets in relation to sales (ratio 3); and/or
(b)  a high investment in current assets in relation to sales (ratio 4).

## Fixed asset utilisation

If it is the former, then an examination of ratios 5, 6 and 7 will indicate whether the high investment is in land and buildings, plant and machinery, or other fixed assets (e.g. motor vehicles) in relation to the volume of business.

If any of ratios 5, 6 and 7 are poor (i.e. high) then the analyst should consider whether they are likely to improve in the next few years:

1    Has management any plans

(a)  to boost sales without extra investment?
(b)  to sell any fixed assets without a proportionate drop in turnover?

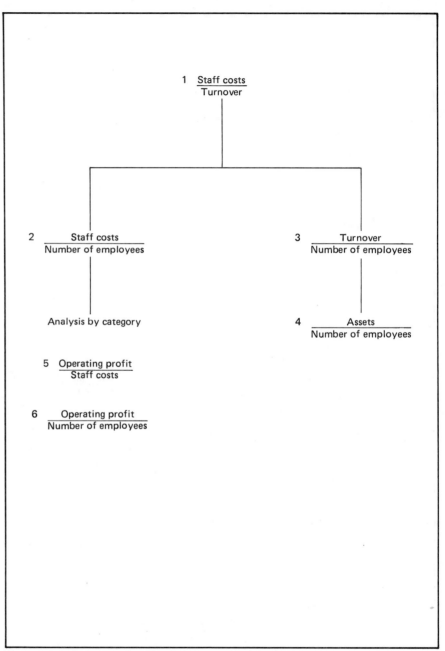

Diagram 13–7    Ratios to analyse historical cost accounts (part 3)

*331*

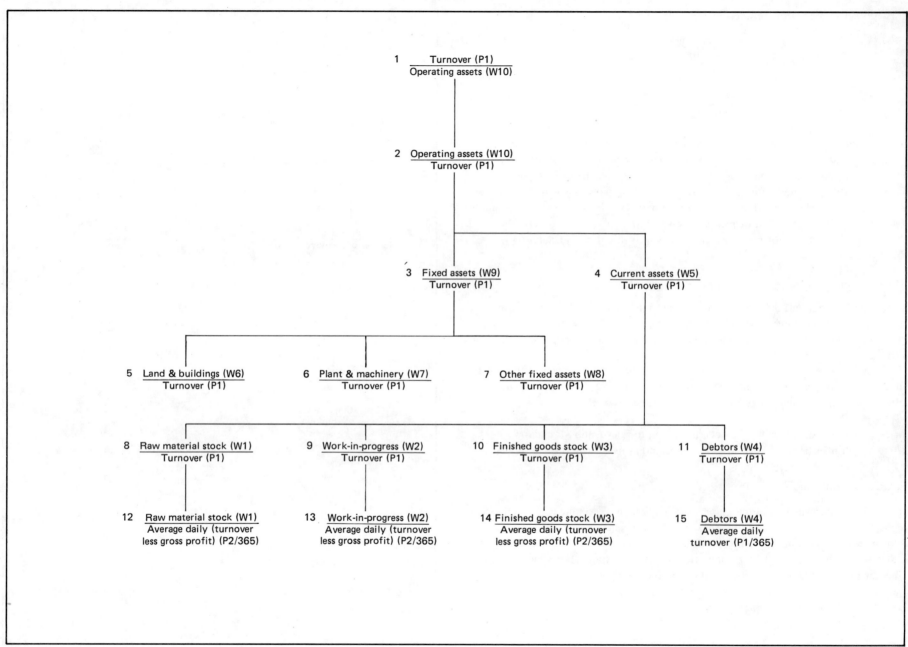

Diagram 13–8   Ratios to analyse historical cost accounts (part 4)

2    Is the business cycle at a low point so that when it picks up these ratios should improve?

Some more detailed ratios on fixed asset utilisation will be found in Chapter 9.1 and 9.2.

## Current asset turnover

If there is a high investment in current assets in relation to sales then ratios 8 to 11 will indicate whether this is the result of a high investment in, or slow turnover of: raw material stock; work-in-progress; finished goods stocks; or debtors; respectively.

Ratios 12 to 15 provide different measures of the amount of capital tied up in current assets, by relating stock figures to average daily (turnover less gross profit), and the debtors figures to average daily turnover. These ratios provide an approximate indication of the number of days' stock carried in each of the three categories, and of the number of days' credit taken by the company's customers.

The subject of stock control is discussed in Chapter 7.3.

Work-in-progress control is covered in Chapter 9.4.

Debtors control ratios are in Chapter 8.5.

## Contingencies and commitments

Companies are required to disclose in the notes to the accounts significant contingencies and commitments.

Contingencies could include such things as:

(*a*)    guarantees and indemnities;
(*b*)    pending or contested legal claims;
(*c*)    bills of exchange discounted with recourse;
(*d*)    forward purchases of currency.

Commitments could include:

(*a*)    commitments to a construction company to build a new factory;
(*b*)    commitments to lease plant and machinery or charter ships;
(*c*)    commitments to a pension fund to provide adequate finance to match its liabilities to members.

The analyst should take into account the likelihood of the contingencies crystallising and their impact on the company's balance sheet and profit and loss account in the future. Similarly the impact of commitments on future cash flow and profitability needs to be assessed.

## Movements on reserves

Whilst the most important source of information about the income of a company is its profit and loss account, the note(s) on the movements of reserves should not be neglected. This statement shows changes in the shareholders' stake in the company that have not been reflected in the profit and loss account. The most likely items are:

(*a*)    A revaluation reserve – used to reflect changes in the value of a company's assets – usually only land and buildings are revalued and revaluations tend to be carried out at varying time intervals and not necessarily for all property at the same time.

(*b*)    A foreign currency investment translation reserve (or some other title with a similar meaning). If a company has overseas subsidiaries and the rate of exchange changes between the beginning and end of the financial year then the change in the sterling 'value' of the investment is added to, or subtracted from, reserves, whilst the profits of the overseas subsidiaries are translated into sterling and included in the group's profit and loss account. A company may also offset in reserves gains or losses caused by movements in exchange rates on borrowings denominated in a foreign currency against losses or gains similarly caused on overseas investments financed by that borrowing.

(*c*)    A write-off of consolidation goodwill on the acquisition of a new subsidiary. Goodwill is the difference between the value of what was paid for a subsidiary and the value of its tangible assets (e.g. land, buildings, stock, debtors, cash, etc.) and identifiable intangibles (e.g. patents). Goodwill represents the purchaser's view that the subsidiary will earn an above average profit on these tangible and identifiable intangible assets. Writing off goodwill does not mean that it is worthless but is more a matter of accounting prudence not to include in the group balance sheet an asset whose value is so subjective.

The interpretation of reserve movements is difficult:

(*a*)    Because director's can choose whether or not and when to revalue property, any increase in values is as much a function of directors' desires to 'strengthen the balance sheet' (perhaps with a view to increasing borrowing or raising fresh capital) as of changes in values.

(*b*)    Movements on the value of overseas investments is not a matter of directors' choice but equally it is not a matter over which they have much control either. An increase in the value of overseas investments may presage an increase in the sterling worth of their profits and of course vice versa.

(c) As already indicated a write-off of consolidation goodwill does not mean that it is worthless. However, unless such goodwill write-offs are matched by above average rates of return from the relevant subsidiaries in later years then doubts will have been cast on the wisdom of the purchase or on its subsequent management.

## 13.9 Funds Statement

All companies with a turnover in excess of £25,000 per annum are required by SSAP10 to produce a statement of source and application of funds. It should look similar to Table 13–6. It is useful for seeing where the company's money has come from and gone to.

A funds statement provides a link between the balance sheets at the end of the current and previous year, but may provide additional information. Whilst the profit and loss account is about revenues, costs and profits, the funds statement emphasises movements of cash, current assets and other sources and uses of money. In the funds statement profit (from the profit and loss account) is shown as the first source of funds.

The first part of the funds statement shows where the money has come from, (sources of funds), e.g. profits, the issue of shares or the sale of assets. The second part shows where the money has gone (application of funds), e.g. dividends or the purchase of assets. The third part shows the net effect of the sources and applications on the amount of working capital.

In the first part the profit shown in the profit and loss account is adjusted for items which did not involve a movement of funds. The principal such item is depreciation. Funds move out when the fixed asset is bought; no further funds are involved when this cost is allocated, by means of the depreciation charge, to the years which benefit from the use of the asset.

The first step in analysing a funds statement could be to express each item as a percentage of total sources. This enables the relative importance of each item to be more readily seen. This calculation should be done separately for this year and last year.

Another approach is to subtract last year's figure from this year's for each item and express the difference as a percentage of last year's figure in order to see more easily any significant areas of growth or decline.

A third approach is to relate items from different parts of the statement as explained below.

The ratios of

$$1 \quad \frac{\text{Dividends paid}}{\text{Total generated from operations}}$$

$$2 \quad \frac{\text{Tax paid}}{\text{Total generated from operations}}$$

will show how much of the company's cash surplus has gone to shareholders and the Inland Revenue.

The ratio of

$$3 \quad \frac{\text{Purchases of fixed assets}}{\text{Depreciation}}$$

especially if calculated for several years, would show, if less than unity, if assets are being run down, but for the effects of inflation. As depreciation will probably be based on the old cost and the purchase is at the new price, then a greater than one figure for this ratio may merely reflect inflation. If the current cost figure for depreciation (i.e. the historical cost depreciation plus the current cost depreciation adjustment) has been calculated (see Appendix 13–1) then use this.

Expenditure on fixed assets should be financed from long-term sources, so the ratio of

$$4 \quad \frac{\text{Purchase of fixed assets}}{\text{Profit before tax} + \text{Depreciation} - \text{Dividends and tax paid} + \text{Issue of shares for cash} + \text{New long-term loans}}$$

should be not greater than one.

Similarly, increases in current liabilities should only be used to finance investment in current assets so the ratio of

$$5 \quad \frac{\text{Increase in creditors and overdraft}}{\text{Increase in debtors and stock}}$$

should desirably not be greater than one.

The funds statement will show, if long-term loans have been repaid, where the cash has come from – desirably from further long-term borrowing (provided the rate of interest is reasonable) or from new shares issued for cash or from profits previously set aside for the purpose.

| | This Year | | Last Year | |
|---|---|---|---|---|
| | £'000 | £'000 | £'000 | £'000 |
| **SOURCE OF FUNDS** | | | | |
| Profit before tax and extraordinary items, less minority interests | | 2,025 | | 2,610 |
| Extraordinary items | | 450 | | (170) |
| | | 2,475 | | 2,440 |
| *Adjustments for items not involving the movement of funds:* | | | | |
| Minority interests in the retained profits of the year | | 25 | | 30 |
| Depreciation | | 345 | | 295 |
| Profits retained in associated companies | | (40) | | – |
| *Total generated from operations* | | 2,805 | | 2,765 |
| *Funds from other sources* | | | | |
| Shares issued in part consideration of the acquisition of subsidiary* | | 290 | | – |
| Capital raised under executive option scheme | | 100 | | 80 |
| *Total sources* | | 3,195 | | 2,845 |
| **APPLICATION OF FUNDS** | | | | |
| Dividends paid | (650) | | (650) | |
| Tax paid | (770) | | (970) | |
| Purchase of fixed assets | (370) | | (736) | |
| Purchase of Subsidiary Ltd* | (350) | | – | |
| Debentures redeemed | (890) | | – | |
| | | (3,030) | | (2,356) |
| | | 165 | | 489 |

| | This Year | | Last Year | |
|---|---|---|---|---|
| | £'000 | £'000 | £'000 | £'000 |
| **INCREASE/DECREASE IN WORKING CAPITAL** | | | | |
| Increase in stocks | | 80 | | 166 |
| Increase in debtors | | 70 | | 122 |
| Decrease in creditors – excluding taxation and proposed dividends | | 155 | | 17 |
| Movement in net liquid funds: | | | | |
| Increase (decrease) in cash balance* | (35) | | 10 | |
| Increase (decrease) in short-term investments | (65) | | 174 | |
| | | (100) | | 184 |
| | | 165 | | 489 |

* Analysis of the acquisition of Subsidiary Limited

| | £'000 |
|---|---|
| *Net assets required* | |
| Fixed assets | 290 |
| Goodwill | 30 |
| Stocks | 40 |
| Debtors | 30 |
| Creditors | (40) |
| | 350 |
| *Discharged by* | |
| Shares issued | 290 |
| Cash paid | 60 |
| | 350 |

Table 13–6   Groups Limited – Statement of source and application of funds
(based on the accounts of the group and showing acquisition of a subsidiary as a separate item)

It may be worth while for the outside analyst to prepare a forecast funds statement for next year. (The company's own management certainly should.) Many of the figures will have to be guesstimates based on, e.g. this year's figures; notes in the accounts on e.g. capital expenditure that has been contracted for, and that has been approved by the directors but not yet put out to contract; remarks in the chairman's statement; the analyst's knowledge of the company's industry; expected rates of inflation; etc.

Specific points to look out for are:

1    any loans due to be repaid next year;
2    any purchases of fixed assets in the pipeline;
3    any increases in working capital as a result of inflation or projected growth.

If the forecast shows a decrease in cash balances the analyst should ask what plans, or scope, has the company to get the necessary funds: a rights issue; more long-term borrowing; increase overdraft; acquisition of cash rich company for shares; sell fixed assets; sell and lease back fixed assets; reduce capital expenditure; reducing working capital; reduce dividend, etc? What would the impact of any of these options be on costs, profitability, the share price, etc?

See also Chapter 5.5, 8.2, 8.3 and 8.4.


## Appendix 13.1

### INFLATION ACCOUNTING

#### Objectives

The objectives of inflation accounting are to remedy the defects of historical cost accounting identified in Chapter 13.7 namely that:

1    asset valuations are often too low;
2    depreciation is therefore inadequate to retain sufficient finance to replace assets at the end of their lives;
3    'stock profits' (the difference between the cost of stock purchased and its replacement cost at the date of sale) are included in profit but need to be retained in order to finance the higher cost of replacing the stock consumed;
4    the losses in purchasing power resulting from holding cash and other monetary assets (e.g. debtors) are not disclosed;
5    conversely, the gains as a result of borrowings are also not disclosed;
6    as a result of the above, profit is often overstated;

7    growth in turnover or profits is often exaggerated because no allowance is made for the fall in the value of money in which they have been measured.

Unfortunately despite many years of debate and experiment the accounting profession and the business community have so far failed to agree on a requirement to remedy these defects in published accounts.

Nevertheless it is possible (and desirable in, and for some time after, periods of high inflation) to make some approximate corrections to historical cost figures for the worst distortions of changing prices. This appendix describes how to make these approximate corrections.

The ratios to analyse these corrected figures are the same as for the historical cost accounts, but some of the numbers used to calculate these ratios, and the size of some of the ratios themselves are likely to be significantly different if inflation has had a material impact.

Factors suggesting that inflation would have had a material effect include:

1    low rate of historical cost profit to turnover or capital;
2    high rate of inflation in countries in which company operates;
3    high rate of price increases (i.e. more than 5 per cent or 10 per cent p.a.) in last year or so in the company's raw materials and/or stock in trade (especially if stock turnover is slow);
4    past relevant price increases high during lifetime of plant, machinery and other fixed assets still in use (often at least 10 years), and depreciation material in relation to profit (say more than 10 per cent);
5    high current inflation and either:
     (a)    high cash balances in relation to profit or turnover, or
     (b)    slow debtors and/or creditors turnover, or
     (c)    high borrowing in relation to equity capital.

#### Outline of method

1    Wherever possible calculate current values for assets in the balance sheet and substitute these for the historical cost figures. Any increase should be added to 'Total capital employed'. (This deals with defect 1.)
2    Recalculate depreciation (defect 2) and cost of sales (defect 3) using replacement costs.
3    Allow for the effect of inflation on net borrowings or monetary assets (defects 4 and 5).

Note: For a method of removing the effects of inflation from trend data (defect 7 above) see Appendix 5–1.

## Use of data assembly sheets

It is suggested that you initially enter the historical cost figures into a column in data assembly sheets 13–1 (or 13–3) and 13–2. Then, in the next column enter, where necessary, the inflation adjusted figures for the relevant items. Next, copy any figures which are not being adjusted for inflation from the historical cost to the inflation adjusted column. Then, in the balance sheet, add the sum of all increases in asset values to the revaluation reserve. Finally add up (or subtract where appropriate) the new figures to get new totals and subtotals.

## Revaluation of assets

### 1  Land and buildings

You may find that the directors have given an up-to-date valuation of these in the directors' report. If they have, use this. If the directors have not provided such a figure then it will be necessary to use the following procedure:

1  Calculate average age

$$\frac{\text{Accumulated depreciation}}{\text{This year's depreciation}} = \text{A years}$$

2  Revalue assets

Let

| | |
|---|---|
| Historical cost net book value | = H |
| Index at acquisition (i.e. A years ago) | = Ia |
| Index at year-end (balance sheet date) | = Ie |
| Current cost net book value | = C |

Then

$$C = H \times (Ie / Ia)$$

In step 1 of this procedure we calculate the average age of the fixed assets by dividing the accumulated depreciation by the figure for this year's depreciation. The result of this calculation is an approximation to the average age of the asset – measured in years.

We then calculate the current cost net book value of the asset by multiplying the historical cost net book value by a suitable index number at the end of the year (i.e. at the balance sheet date) and dividing by the figure for the same index at the average date of acquisition, (i.e. A years ago where A is the average age calculated in the previous step).

Suitable index numbers to use in these calculations will be found in a Government publication entitled, 'Price Index Numbers for Current Cost Accounting' (PINCCA) summary volume 1974–1982, *Business Monitor* MO18. Monthly updates are produced as *Business Monitor* MM17 (HMSO). Enquiries about these indices should be addressed to the Business Statistics Office (Newport (0633) 56111 Extension 2173).

### 2  Plant and machinery

The calculation of the current cost of plant and machinery is similar to the index method of calculating the current cost of land and buildings. Appropriate indexes will be found in PINCCA.

### 3  Investments

You will find in the notes to the accounts that investment can be sub-divided into:

Listed investments
Other investments
Loans
Related companies.

Companies are required to give the market value of listed investments and this should be substituted for their cost.

Directors may give a value for their unlisted investments. If they have done so, then substitute this for cost. If they have not done so, then you will probably have to use the cost figure.

The current cost value of loans may be assumed to be the same as the historical cost.

If related companies are very material it may be possible to obtain current cost information from their own accounts and to use that.

### 4  Stocks

Stocks may be revalued as follows. The desirability of so doing will depend on their size and age – the larger and/or older are stocks the more desirable is it to revalue them. Again, suitable index numbers will be found in PINCCA.

1  Calculate average age

$$\frac{\text{Cost of stocks (from Balance Sheet)}}{(\text{Turnover} - \text{Gross Profit}) / 12} = \text{A months}$$

## 2 Revalue stock

Let

| | |
|---|---|
| Historical cost of stock | = H |
| Index at acquisition (i.e. | |
| A months ago) | = Ia |
| Index at year-end | = Ie |
| Current cost net book value | = C |

Then

$$C = H \times (Ie / Ia)$$

As with fixed assets we first calculate the average age of the stocks, but this time by dividing the cost of stocks by the average monthly cost of sales (calculated by subtracting gross profit from turnover, and dividing the result by 12 to give an average age in months) as opposed to years in the case of fixed assets. The rest of the calculations are similar to those for fixed assets.

## 5 Total capital employed

The total of all increases to assets should be added to the revaluation reserve (part of item B14 in Data assembly sheet 13–2) or, if minority interests are material, the total increase should be shared between revaluation reserve and minority interests in the proportion of B14 and B15 in the historical cost accounts.

## Profit adjustments

### 1 Depreciation adjustment

The first of the profit adjustments to calculate is the depreciation adjustment. This is calculated as follows:

Let

| | |
|---|---|
| Historical cost depreciation | = HD |
| Historical cost net book value of asset | = H |
| Current cost net book value of asset | = C |
| Current cost depreciation | = CD |

Then

$$CD = HD \times (C / H)$$

The Depreciation adjustment $= CD - HD$

The figure or historical cost depreciation will be found in the historical cost profit and loss account or, more likely, in the notes to that account.

The historical cost net book value of the asset and the current cost net book value of the asset are the same as the figures used in, and calculated in, the stage above entitled 'Revaluation of assets'. It may be worth calculating the depreciation adjustment separately for different categories of assets (e.g. land and buildings and plant and machinery) if the rates of depreciation are substantially different.

The depreciation adjustment is the amount of money the company needs to retain in addition to historical cost depreciation to finance the replacement of fixed assets at higher prices than when they were originally bought.

### 2 Working capital adjustment (WCA)

This is calculated as follows:

Let

| | |
|---|---|
| Historical cost of stocks plus trade debtors less trade creditors (working capital) at end of year | = HSE |
| Historical cost of stocks plus trade debtors less trade creditors (working capital) at beginning of year | = HSB |
| Index at date of acquisition of working capital at | |
| end of year | = Iae |
| beginning of year | = Iab |
| Average index for the year | = Iav |

Then

$$WCA = (HSE - HSB) - \left[ \left( HSE \times \frac{Iav}{Iae} \right) - \left( HSB \times \frac{Iav}{Iab} \right) \right]$$

The WCA will be used to convert cost of sales from an historical cost basis to a current cost basis. Broadly speaking it is the amount of the historical cost profit which the business needs to retain in order to be able to finance the same volume of working capital at higher prices. It allows for the fact that in times of rising prices it costs more to replace goods than it did originally to buy them. Unless this increase is treated as a cost a company will find it does not have enough cash to replace stocks and maintain its existing level of business.

It also allows for the fact that most companies usually buy and sell their goods on credit. During a period of rising prices both creditors and debtors will rise even if there is no real increase in the volume of business. If creditors exceed debtors (as they do for some retail shops) then part of the increased cost of replacing stocks will be financed by creditors. If on the other hand debtors exceed creditors (as they do with most manufacturing companies) then companies need to provide out of historical cost profits the money to finance this growth in net debtors.

The historical cost of stocks, trade debtors and creditors at the end of the year is obtained from this year balance sheet.

The historical cost of these items at the beginning of the year will be found in the comparative figures in the balance sheet for this year.

To arrive at the date of acquisition of working capital one needs to calculate its 'age' and subtract this from the date of the end or beginning of the year as appropriate.

The 'age' of the working capital in months may be arrived at approximately by dividing the net total of stock plus debtors minus creditors by [(turnover minus gross profit) divided by 12].

As before suitable index numbers will be found in PINCCA.

Short cuts may be used for the working capital adjustment by ignoring the age of the working capital, and dividing by the index number at the beginning or end of the year, instead of the index number when the stock etc. was acquired. There may be some loss in accuracy but this may not be material.

### 3   *Borrowing*

Add up all the borrowing in the balance sheet (items B8, B11 and B12) less trade creditors used in the WCA. Take away any monetary assets (items B5 and B7) less trade debtors used in the WCA. Multipy the net figure by the percentage increase in the RPI for the year. The result of this calculation is either (a) the gain in purchasing power the company has made at the expense of its lenders as a result of the effect of inflation on the value of their loans, or (b) the loss in purchasing power the company has suffered as a result of holding cash and other monetary assets in a period of rising prices, depending on whether the company is (a) a net borrower or (b) a holder of net monetary assets.

### 4   *Adjusting the profit and loss account*

Format 1 – Data assembly sheet 13–1

1    Add the depreciation and working capital adjustments to P2 Cost of sales.
2    If the company has net borrowing subtract the borrowing adjustment from P8 Interest payable and similar charges.
3    If the company has net monetary assets subtract the borrowing adjustment from P6 Investment income.
4    Recalculate subtotals P3, P5, P9 and P11.
5    If minority interests are significant reduce P12 by the same percentage as P11 has decreased.
6    Recalculate subtotals P13, P15 and P17.

Format 2 – Data assembly sheet 13–3

1    Add the depreciation adjustment to F7 Depreciation
2    Add the working capital adjustment to F4
3    = step 2 for format 1
4    = step 3 for format 1
5    = step 4 for format 1 (except that there is no P3)
6    = step 5 for format 1
7    = step 6 for format 1

### Additional ratios

Once the current cost figures have been calculated they should be used to calculate the same ratios as are used to analyse historical cost figures. However, it may be desirable to calculate the borrowing adjustment either (a) as a separate component of ratio 12 (Interest payable/Borrowing) in Diagram 13–4 if the company has net borrowing or (b) of ratio 15 (Investment income/Total investment) if the company has net monetary assets.

Similarly the depreciation and working capital adjustment should be shown as a separate component of ratio 4 (Gross profit/Turnover) in Diagram 13–5, or ratios 6 and 3 (Depreciation/Turnover and Raw materials/Turnover) in Diagram 13–6.

**Appendix 13.2**

**ACCOUNTING STANDARDS COMMITTEE – STATUS OF TOPICS (March 1986)**

### Acquisitions and mergers

A standard, SSAP 23, *Accounting for Acquisitions and Mergers*, was published in April 1985. The SSAP applies only to group accounts. A merger is defined as a combination in which not more than 10 per cent of the consideration is in cash; all other combinations are acquisitions. In merger accounting the shares issued by the mergor may be valued at their nominal value and the assets of the mergee at their book value; pre-combination profits of the mergee are added to those of the mergor. In acquisition accounting both the shares issued and the assets acquired should be fair valued; pre-combination profits of the mergee are not included in the new group's profit and loss account.

## Added value

A study prepared for ASC entitled, *Added Value in External Financial Reporting* by Michael Renshall and others was published by the ICAEW in 1979. Another study by M.F. Morley entitled, *The Value Added Statement,* was published by Gee and the Scottish Institute in 1978.

ASC has no plans to publish anything further on this subject at present.

## Analysed reporting – see Diversified operations

## Associated companies

A standard, SSAP 1, *Accounting for Associated Companies,* was issued in January 1971, amended in August 1974 and revised in April 1982. An associated company is one where the investor's interest is for the long term and it is in a position to exert significant influence on the investee because it owns more than 20 per cent but less than 50 per cent of the investee's equity capital. The investor should include in its group profit and loss account its share of its associates' profits (or losses) and in its group balance sheet associates should be valued at the investor's share of their net assets (preferably fair valued).

In the investor's own accounts its investment in the associate may be shown at cost or at valuation but only dividends received and receivable should be included in the investor's profit and loss account.

## Charities

An exposure draft, ED 38, *Accounting for Charities,* was published in November 1985.

## Contingencies

A standard, SSAP 18, *Accounting for Contingencies,* was published by ASC in August 1980. Contingent losses, if probable, should be accrued. Other contingent losses should be disclosed. Contingent profits should be disclosed only if probable.

## Current cost accounting

A standard, SSAP 16, *Current Cost Accounting,* was published in March 1980. A booklet entitled *Guidance Notes on SSAP 16* was also published. An ED of a SSAP to replace SSAP 16 (ED 35) was published in August 1984 but later withdrawn. Compliance with SSAP 16 has fallen to a very low level and is no longer required.

SSAP 16 requires listed, and large non-listed companies with some exceptions, to supplement their historical cost accounts with a profit and loss account and balance sheet drawn up on current cost principles. Assets are to be shown at their value to the business – usually (depreciated) replacement cost. The profit and loss account is charged with the consumption of assets at their current cost.

## Deferred Taxation (See Taxation – Deferred taxation)

## Depreciation

A standard, SSAP 12, *Accounting for Depreciation,* was issued in December 1977 and revised in November 1981. ASC published a discussion paper *A review of SSAP 12 – Accounting for Depreciation* in December 1982, a Statement of Intent on revising SSAP 12 in October 1984, and an Exposure Draft (ED37) on the subject in March 1985. SSAP 12 requires the cost (or revalued amount) of all fixed assets (except investment properties) to be depreciated over the asset's expected useful life.

## Depreciation – Investment properties

A standard, SSAP 19, *Accounting for Investment Properties,* was published in November 1981. Investment properties need not be depreciated but should be revalued annually at open market value.

## Disclosure of accounting policies

A standard, SSAP 2, *Disclosure of Accounting Policies,* was issued in November 1971. SSAP 2 requires a clear explanation of all important accounting policies. It provides that unless expressly stated to the contrary accounts are to be presumed to be drawn up in accordance with the four fundamental accounting concepts: the going concern concept (the company will continue in existence for the foreseeable future); the accruals concept (revenues and costs are recognised as they occur; not when cash passes); consistency (the same accounting treatment is used for similar items from one year to the next); prudence (profits are not anticipated but are recognised only when realised; provision is made for all known liabilities).

## Diversified operations

Two studies have been prepared for ASC; one by ICI has not been published, the other, by Coopers & Lybrand entitled *Analysed Reporting* was published by the ICAEW in 1977.

## Earnings per share

A standard, SSAP 3, *Earnings per share,* was issued in February, 1972 and revised in August, 1974. Earnings are defined as being after tax, minorities and preference dividends but before extraordinary items.

## Employment Report

A study prepared for ASC entitled, *The Employment Statement in Company Reports,* by E.R. Thompson and Ann Knell was published in 1979 by the ICAEW. ASC has no plans for any further publications in this area at present.

## Extraordinary items and prior year adjustments

A standard, SSAP 6 *Extraordinary Items and Prior Year Adjustments,* was published in April 1974. A discussion paper *A review of SSAP 6 – Extraordinary Items and Prior Year Adjustments* was published in January 1983 and an Exposure Draft (ED36) of proposed modifications to SSAP 6 in January 1985..An extraordinary item is one which is derived from events outside the ordinary activities of the business, is material, and is unlikely to recur. Prior year adjustments relate either to a change in accounting policies or the correction of a fundamental error. Their significance is that they both have defined locations in the profit and loss account below the figure on which earnings per share (q.v.) is normally calculated.

## Foreign currency

A standard, SSAP 20, *Foreign Currency Translation,* was published in April 1983. SSAP 20 requires all foreign currency denominated items to be recorded initially in a company's own accounts at the rate of exchange at the date of the transaction. Non-monetary items (e.g. fixed assets and stock) remain at that figure. Monetary items (e.g. cash, debtors) are retranslated at the closing (balance sheet date) rate. Any resulting gains or losses are included in the profit and loss account. In consolidated accounts the closing rate/net investment method is normally to be used: all subsidiaries' assets are to be translated at the closing rate; any gains or losses as a result of exchange rate movements on the parent's net investment in the subsidiary are to be included in movements on reserves and not in the profit and loss account; subsidiaries' profit and loss accounts are to be translated at the average or closing rate for inclusion in the consolidated profit and loss account.

## Funds (see Source and application of funds)

## Goodwill

A standard, SSAP 22, *Accounting for Goodwill,* was published in December 1984. Goodwill is the difference between the fair value of the consideration given for a business and the fair value of the assets acquired. Normally goodwill should be written off on acquisition to reserves but may be amortised to the profit and loss account over its useful economic life.

## Government grants

A standard, SSAP 4, *The Accounting Treatment of Government Grants* was published in April 1974. Grants relating to fixed assets should be shown in the balance sheet either as a reduction of the cost of the asset or as a deferred credit. In both cases the benefit of the grant is to be credited to the profit and loss account over the life of the asset and not when the grant is received.

## Group accounts

A standard, SSAP 14, *Group Accounts,* was published in September 1978.

## Leases

A standard, SSAP 21, *Accounting for Leases and Hire Purchase Contracts,* together with guidance notes, was published in August 1984. Its main requirement is for lessees to capitalise finance leases (those which transfer substantially all the risks and rewards of ownership of an asset to the lessee). It also regulates income recognition by lessors, and requires detailed disclosures of leased assets and commitments by lessees and lessors. It is due to come into phased effect for accounting periods beginning between 1 July 1984 and 1 July 1987. Some figures will therefore not be available until 1989.

## Mergers (see Acquisitions and mergers)

## Pension Costs

An exposure draft, ED 32, *Disclosure of Pension Information in Company Accounts* was published in May 1983. ASC published a consultative Statement of Intent in November 1984. It proposes that pension costs should be charged so as to produce a substantially level percentage of the current and future pensionable payroll.

## Post balance sheet events

A standard, SSAP 17, *Accounting for Post Balance Sheet Events,* was published in August 1980. Post balance sheet events are those between the balance sheet date and the date of signing the accounts. SSAP 17 requires such events to lead either to the accounts being adjusted or to disclosure of them.

## Prior year adjustments (see Extraordinary items and prior year adjustments)

## Properties (see Depreciation – Investment properties)

## Related party transactions

ASC has this subject under consideration jointly with the Auditing Practices Committee.

## Research and development

A standard, SSAP 13, *Accounting for Research and Development* was published in December 1977. This standard is under review by ASC. Research costs must be written off immediately. Development costs may only be capitalised if there is a viable product; otherwise they too must be written off.

## Segmental Reporting (see Diversified operations)

## Source and application of funds

A standard, SSAP 10, *Statements of Source and Application of Funds,* was issued in July 1975. SSAP 10 requires all companies with a turnover of more than £25,000 p.a. to publish a funds statement.

## Stocks and work-in-progress

A standard, SSAP 9, *Stocks and Work-in-Progress,* was published in May 1975. This standard is under review by ASC. SSAP 9's main requirements are for stock values to include an appropriate share of overheads and for long-term contract work in progress to include any profit earned to date. SSAP 9 is being reviewed in the light of its apparent conflict with the Companies Act.

## Taxation – Deferred taxation

A standard, SSAP 15, *Accounting for Deferred Taxation,* was issued in October 1978 and revised in May 1985. Deferred tax is to be provided to the extent that it is probable that a liability will crystallise. Disclosure of the full amount of deferred tax is required.

## Taxation – Imputation system

A standard, SSAP 8, *The Treatment of Taxation Under the Imputation System in the Accounts of Companies,* was issued in August 1974 and revised in December 1977.

## Taxation – Value added tax

A standard, SSAP 5, *Accounting for Value Added Tax,* was issued in April 1974.

*Note:* The Institute of Chartered Accountants in England and Wales (referred to above as the ICAEW) publishes an annual volume *Accounting Standards* which contains full texts of all UK exposure drafts and accounting standards extant at the date of publication. The ICAEW's address is:

P.O. Box 433,
Moorgate Place,
London EC2P 2BJ.

See also *UK Financial Accounting Standards: a descriptive and analytical approach*, R.K. Ashton, Woodhead Faulkner, 1983, *Comparative International Accounting* edited by C.W. Nobes and R.H. Parker, Philip Allen, 1981, and *Selected Accounting Standards – Interpretation Problems Explained*, ICAEW, 1984.

## Appendix 13.3

## STATUTORY FORMATS

---

### Balance sheet formats

---

#### Format 1

---

A    Called up share capital not paid (*1*)
B    Fixed assets
    I     Intangible assets
       1     Development costs
       2     Concessions, patents, licences, trade marks and similar rights and assets (*2*)
       3     Goodwill (*3*)
       4     Payments on account
    II    Tangible assets
       1     Land and buildings
       2     Plant and machinery
       3     Fixtures, fittings, tools and equipment
       4     Payments on account and assets in course of construction
    III   Investments
       1     Shares in group companies
       2     Loans to group companies
       3     Shares in related companies
       4     Loans to related companies
       5     Other investments other than loans
       6     Other loans
       7     Own shares (*4*)

C    Current assets
    I     Stocks
       1     Raw materials and consumables
       2     Work in progress
       3     Finished goods and goods for resale
       4     Payments on account
    II    Debtors (*5*)
       1     Trade debtors
       2     Amounts owed by group companies
       3     Amounts owed by related companies
       4     Other debtors
       5     Called up share capital not paid (*1*)
       6     Prepayments and accrued income (*6*)
    III   Investments
       1     Shares in group companies
       2     Own shares (*4*)
       3     Other investments
    IV   Cash at bank and in hand
D    Prepayments and accrued income (*6*)
E    Creditors: amounts falling due within one year
       1     Debenture loans (*7*)
       2     Bank loans and overdrafts
       3     Payments received on account (*8*)
       4     Trade creditors
       5     Bills of exchange payable
       6     Amounts owed to group companies
       7     Amounts owed to related companies
       8     Other creditors including taxation and social security (*9*)
       9     Accruals and deferred income (*10*)
F    Net current assets (liabilities) (*11*)
G    Total assets less current liabilities
H    Creditors: amounts falling due after more than one year
       1     Debenture loans (*7*)
       2     Bank loans and overdrafts
       3     Payments received on account (*8*)
       4     Trade creditors
       5     Bills of exchange payable
       6     Amounts owed to group companies
       7     Amounts owed to related companies
       8     Other creditors including taxation and social security (*9*)
       9     Accruals and deferred income (*10*)

I    Provisions for liabilities and charges
- 1    Pensions and similar obligations
- 2    Taxation, including deferred taxation
- 3    Other provisions

J    Accruals and deferred income (10)

K    Capital and reserves

    I    Called up share capital (12)

    II    Share premium account

    III    Revaluation reserve

    IV    Other reserves
- 1    Capital redemption reserve
- 2    Reserve for own shares
- 3    Reserves provided for by the articles of association
- 4    Other reserves

    V    Profit and loss account

---

**Balance sheet formats**

---

*Format 2*

## ASSETS

A    Called up share capital not paid (1)

B    Fixed assets

    I    Intangible assets
- 1    Development costs
- 2    Concessions, patents, licences, trade marks and similar rights and assets (2)
- 3    Goodwill (3)
- 4    Payments on account

    II    Tangible assets
- 1    Land and buildings
- 2    Plant and machinery
- 3    Fixtures, fittings, tools and equipment
- 4    Payments on account and assets in course of construction

    III    Investments
- 1    Shares in group companies
- 2    Loans to group companies
- 3    Shares in related companies
- 4    Loans to related companies

    5    Other investments other than loans

    6    Other loans

    7    Own shares (4)

C    Current assets

    I    Stocks
- 1    Raw materials and consumables
- 2    Work in progress
- 3    Finished goods and goods for resale
- 4    Payments on account

    II    Debtors (5)
- 1    Trade debtors
- 2    Amounts owed by group companies
- 3    Amounts owed by related companies
- 4    Other debtors
- 5    Called up share capital not paid (1)
- 6    Prepayments and accrued income (6)

    III    Investments
- 1    Shares in group companies
- 2    Own shares (4)
- 3    Other investments

    IV    Cash at bank and in hand

D    Prepayments and accrued income (6)

## LIABILITIES

A    Capital and reserves

    I    Called up share capital (12)

    II    Share premium account

    III    Revaluation reserve

    IV    Other reserves
- 1    Capital redemption reserve
- 2    Reserve for own shares
- 3    Reserves provided for by the articles of association
- 4    Other reserves

    V    Profit and loss account

B    Provisions for liabilities and charges
- 1    Pensions and similar obligations
- 2    Taxation including deferred taxation
- 3    Other provisions

C    Creditors (*13*)

    1    Debenture loans (*7*)

    2    Bank loans and overdrafts

    3    Payments received on account (*8*)

    4    Trade creditors

    5    Bills of exchange payable

    6    Amounts owed to group companies

    7    Amounts owed to related companies

    8    Other creditors including taxation and social security (*9*)

    9    Accruals and deferred income (*10*)

D    Accruals and deferred income (*10*)

---

### Notes on the balance sheet formats

(*1*)    *Called up share capital not paid*

    (Formats 1 and 2, items A and CII5)

        This item may be shown in either of the two positions given in Formats 1 and 2.

(*2*)    *Concessions, patents, licences, trade marks and similar rights and assets*

    (Formats 1 and 2, items BI2)

        Amounts in respect of assets shall only be included in a company's balance sheet under this item if either:

        (*a*)    the assets were acquired for valuable consideration and are not required to be shown under goodwill; or

        (*b*)    the assets in question were created by the company itself.

(*3*)    *Goodwill*

    (Formats 1 and 2, items BI3)

        Amounts representing goodwill shall only be included to the extent that the goodwill was acquired for valuable consideration.

(*4*)    *Own shares*

    (Formats 1 and 2, items BIII7 and CIII2)

        The nominal value of the shares held shall be shown separately.

(*5*)    *Debtors*

    (Formats 1 and 2, items CII1 to 6)

        The amount falling due after more than one year shall be shown separately for each item included under debtors.

(*6*)    *Prepayments and accrued income*

    (Formats 1 and 2, items CII6 and D)

        This item may be shown in either of the two positions given in Formats 1 and 2.

(*7*)    *Debenture loans*

    (Formats 1, items E1 and H1 and Format 2, item C1)

        The amount of any convertible loans shall be shown separately.

(*8*)    *Payments received on account*

    (Formats 1, items E3 and H3 and Format 2, item C3)

        Payments received on account of orders shall be shown for each of these items in so far as they are not shown as deductions from stocks.

(*9*)    *Other creditors including taxation and social security*

    (Format 1, items E8 and H8 and Format 2, item C8)

        The amount for creditors in respect of taxation and social security shall be shown separately from the amount for other creditors.

(*10*)    *Accruals and deferred income*

    (Format 1, items E9 and H9 and J and Format 2, items C9 and D)

        The two positions given for this item in Format 1 at E9 and H9 are an alternative to the position at J, but if the item is not shown in a position corresponding to that at J it may be shown in either or both of the other two positions (as the case may require).

        The two positions given for this item in Format 2 are alternatives.

(*11*)    *Net current assets (liabilities)*

    (Format 1, item F)

        In determining the amount to be shown for this item any amounts shown under 'prepayments and accrued income' shall be taken into account wherever shown.

(*12*)    *Called up share capital*

    (Format 1, item KI and Format 2, item AI)

        The amount of allotted share capital and the amount of called up share capital which has been paid up shall be shown separately.

(*13*)    *Creditors*

    (Format 2, items C1 to 9)

        Amounts falling due within one year and after one year shall be shown separately for each of these items and their aggregate shall be shown separately for all of these items.

## Format 1
### (see note (17) below)

1    Turnover
2    Cost of sales (14)
3    Gross profit or loss
4    Distribution costs (14)
5    Administrative expenses (14)
6    Other operating income
7    Income from shares in group companies
8    Income from shares in related companies
9    Income from other fixed asset investments (15)
10    Other interest receivable and similar income (15)
11    Amounts written off investments
12    Interest payable and similar charges (16)
13    Tax on profit or loss on ordinary activities
14    Profit or loss on ordinary activities after taxation
15    Extraordinary income
16    Extraordinary charges
17    Extraordinary profit or loss
18    Tax on extraordinary profit or loss
19    Other taxes not shown under the above items
20    Profit or loss for the financial year

### Notes on the profit and loss account formats

(14)    *Cost of sales: distribution costs: administrative expenses*
      (Format 1, items 2, 4 and 5 and Format 3, items A1, 2 and 3)
         These items shall be stated after taking into account any necessary provisions for depreciation or diminution in value of assets.

(15)    *Income from other fixed asset investments: other interest receivable and similar income*
      (Format 1, items 9 and 10: Format 2, items 11 and 12: Format 3, items B5 and 6: Format 4, items B7 and 8)
         Income and interest derived from group companies shall be shown separately from income and interest derived from other sources.

## Format 2

1    Turnover
2    Change in stocks of finished goods and in work in progress
3    Own work capitalised
4    Other operating income
5    (a)    Raw materials and consumables
     (b)    Other external charges
6    Staff costs:
     (a)    wages and salaries
     (b)    social security costs
     (c)    other pension costs
7    (a)    Depreciation and other amounts written off tangible and intangible fixed assets
     (b)    Exceptional amounts written off current assets
8    Other operating charges
9    Income from shares in group companies
10    Income from shares in related companies
11    Income from other fixed asset investments (15)
12    Other interest receivable and similar income (15)
13    Amounts written off investments
14    Interest payable and similar charges (16)
15    Tax on profit or loss on ordinary activities
16    Profit or loss on ordinary activities after taxation
17    Extraordinary income
18    Extraordinary charges
19    Extraordinary profit or loss
20    Tax on extraordinary profit or loss
21    Other taxes not shown under the above items
22    Profit or loss for the financial year

*Format 3*
(see note (*17*) below)

A   Charges
  1   Cost of sales (*14*)
  2   Distribution costs (*14*)
  3   Administrative expenses (*14*)
  4   Amounts written off investments
  5   Interest payable and similar charges (*16*)
  6   Tax on profit or loss on ordinary activities
  7   Profit or loss on ordinary activities after taxation
  8   Extraordinary charges
  9   Tax on extraordinary profit or loss
  10   Other taxes not shown under the above items
  11   Profit or loss for the financial year
B   Income
  1   Turnover
  2   Other operating income
  3   Income from shares in group companies
  4   Income from shares in related companies
  5   Income from other fixed asset investments (*15*)
  6   Other interest receivable and similar income (*15*)
  7   Profit or loss on ordinary activities after taxation
  8   Extraordinary income
  9   Profit or loss for the financial year

(*16*)   *Interest payable and similar charges*
     (Format 1, item 12: Format 2, item 14: Format 3, item A5: Format 4, item A7)
     The amount payable to group companies shall be shown separately.

(*17*)   *Formats 1 and 3*
     The amount of any provisions for depreciation and diminution in value of tangible and intangible fixed assets falling to be shown under items 7(*a*) and A4(*a*) respectively in Formats 2 and 4 shall be disclosed in a note to the accounts in any case where the profit and loss account is prepared by reference to Format 1 or Format 3.

**Profit and loss account formats**

*Format 4*

A   Charges
  1   Reduction in stocks of finished goods and in work in progress
  2   (*a*)   Raw materials and consumables
       (*b*)   Other external charges
  3   Staff costs:
       (*a*)   wages and salaries
       (*b*)   social security costs
       (*c*)   other pension costs
  4   (*a*)   Depreciation and other amounts written off tangible and intangible fixed assets
       (*b*)   Exceptional amounts written off current assets
  5   Other operating charges
  6   Amounts written off investments
  7   Interest payable and similar charges (*16*)
  8   Tax on profit or loss on ordinary activities
  9   Profit or loss on ordinary activities after taxation
  10   Extraordinary charges
  11   Tax on extraordinary profit or loss
  12   Other taxes not shown under the above items
  13   Profit or loss for the financial year
B   Income
  1   Turnover
  2   Increase in stocks of finished goods and in work in progress
  3   Own work capitalised
  4   Other operating income
  5   Income from shares in group companies
  6   Income from shares in related companies
  7   Income from other fixed asset investments (*15*)
  8   Other interest receivable and similar income (*15*)
  9   Profit or loss on ordinary activities after taxation
  10   Extraordinary income
  11   Profit or loss for the financial year

**Appendix 13.4**

## EXAMPLE OF DEFERRED TAX

A company makes £1,000 profit before depreciation per year (line 1) and buys an asset for £1,000 at the beginning of year 1 which will last five years. The company therefore depreciates the asset at 20 per cent p.a. straight line (line 2) leaving a profit after depreciation of £800 per year (line 3). Tax allowance (line 4) is 25 per cent of the reducing balance of the cost (line 5) for the previous year. Taxable profit (line 6) is the profit *before* depreciation (line 1) minus the tax allowance (line 4). Tax payable (line 7) is 35 per cent (the corporation tax rate) of the taxable profit (line 6). Tax rate in line 8 is the tax payable (line 7) divided by profit after depreciation (line 3). It will be seen that this rate starts below the corporation tax rate and then climbs above it.

The deferred tax transfer is calculated in line 9. It is the difference between the company's depreciation (line 2) and the tax allowance (line 4) multiplied by the corporation tax rate (35 per cent). In year 1 this is an addition to the tax payable; in subsequent years it is a subtraction.

Line 10 shows the total tax charge, i.e. the tax payable (line 7) plus or minus the deferred tax transfer (line 9).

The tax rate based on the total tax charge (line 10) divided by the profit after depreciation (line 3) is shown in line 11. It will be seen that this is a steady 35 per cent compared to the fluctuating rate of line 7.

At the end of year 5 the company has written the asset down to nil (£1,000 − [5 × £200]); the tax authorities have written it down to only £238 (line 5). This will be allowed over future years still on the 25 per cent p.a. reducing balance basis.

The deferred tax transfers are cumulated (line 12) and shown in the company's balance sheet – as a liability (if tax allowances are greater than the company's depreciation) or an asset (if *vice versa*). In practice, the actual size of the balance will depend on the probability of payment or recovery. However this important refinement has not been covered in this example. For a discussion of the likely pattern of deferred tax balances over future years based on a computerised model see 'Deferred tax: how much to provide now', C.A. Westwick, *Accountancy*, December 1984, pp. 156–160.

This example is based on tax law in 1985. In March 1985 the Chancellor proposed amendments for assets with lives of five years or less as follows. Apart from this proposed change the principals in this example will however remain generally valid.

Where a taxpayer expects to dispose of an item of machinery or plant, acquired on or after 1 April 1986, within five years of acquisition, an election may be made to calculate separately from the main pool the writing-down allowances due on that machinery or plant. The election is to be made within two years of the year of acquisition. If an election is made, a separate calculation of any balancing adjustment will apply where the machinery or plant is sold or scrapped within five years of acquisition. If not disposed of within five years, the residual tax written-down value of the asset will be transferred to the main pool.

| Line | Year | 1 | 2 | 3 | 4 | 5 |
|---|---|---|---|---|---|---|
| 1 | Profit before depreciation | 1,000 | 1,000 | 1,000 | 1,000 | 1,000 |
| 2 | Depreciation (20% straight line) | 200 | 200 | 200 | 200 | 200 |
| 3 | Profit after depreciation (1–2) | 800 | 800 | 800 | 800 | 800 |
| 4 | Tax allowance (25% reducing balance) | 250 | 187 | 140 | 105 | 80 |
| 5 | Tax WDV at end of year | 750 | 563 | 423 | 318 | 238 |
| 6 | Taxable profit (1–4) | 750 | 813 | 860 | 895 | 920 |
| 7 | Tax payable (at 35% of 6) | 262 | 285 | 301 | 313 | 322 |
| 8 | Tax rate (%) (7/3) | 32.8 | 35.6 | 37.6 | 39.1 | 40.3 |
| 9 | Deferred tax transfer (4–2) at 35% | +18 | −5 | −21 | −33 | −42 |
| 10 | Total tax (7 + 9) | 280 | 280 | 280 | 280 | 280 |
| 11 | Tax rate (%) 10/3 | 35 | 35 | 35 | 35 | 35 |
| 12 | Deferred tax balance (sum of line 9 to date, + = liability − = asset) | +18 | +13 | −8 | −41 | −83 |

# Consolidated profit and loss account (format 1)

| Code letter | Item | Year to (date) | | | | | |
|---|---|---|---|---|---|---|---|
| P1 | Turnover | | | | | | |
| P2 | Cost of sales | | | | | | |
| P3 | Gross profit (P1 - P2) | | | | | | |
| P4 | Other operating expenses (net) | | | | | | |
| P5 | Operating profit (P3 - P4) | | | | | | |
| P6 | Investment income | | | | | | |
| P7 | Amounts written off investments | | | | | | |
| P8 | Interest payable and similar charges | | | | | | |
| P9 | Profit on ordinary activities before taxation (P5 + P6 - P7 - P8) | | | | | | |
| P10 | Tax on profit on ordinary activities | | | | | | |
| P11 | Profit on ordinary activities after taxation (P9 - P10) | | | | | | |
| P12 | Minority interests | | | | | | |
| P13 | Profit before extraordinary items (P11 - P12) | | | | | | |
| P14 | Extraordinary items less taxation & minority interests | | | | | | |
| P15 | Profit for the financial year (P13 - P14) | | | | | | |
| P16 | Dividends paid and proposed | | | | | | |
| P17 | Retained profit for the year (P15 - P16) | | | | | | |

NB   As dividends usually relate to a year it is probably not worthwhile calculating these ratios for a period less than a year. They may however be calculated more frequently than annually.

## Consolidated balance sheet

| Code letter | Item | Year to (date) | | | | | |
|---|---|---|---|---|---|---|---|
| | | | | | | | |
| | *Fixed Assets* | | | | | | |
| B1 | Intangible assets | | | | | | |
| B2 | Tangible assets | | | | | | |
| B3 | Investments | | | | | | |
| | *Current Assets* | | | | | | |
| B4 | Stocks | | | | | | |
| B5 | Debtors | | | | | | |
| B6 | Investments | | | | | | |
| B7 | Cash at bank and in hand | | | | | | |
| B8 | *Creditors:* amounts falling due within one year | | | | | | |
| B9 | *Net current assets* | | | | | | |
| B10 | *Total assets less current liabilities* | | | | | | |
| B11 | *Creditors:* amounts falling due after more than one year | | | | | | |
| B12 | *Provisions for liabilities and charges* | | | | | | |
| B13 | *Net assets* | | | | | | |
| | *Capital and reserves* | | | | | | |
| | Called-up share capital | | | | | | |
| | Share premium account | | | | | | |
| | Revaluation reserve | | | | | | |
| | Other reserves | | | | | | |
| | Profit and loss account | | | | | | |
| B14 | Shareholders' funds | | | | | | |
| B15 | Minority interests | | | | | | |
| B16 | *Total capital employed* | | | | | | |

NB   As dividends usually relate to a year it is probably not worth while calculating these ratios for a period less than a year. They may however be calculated more  frequently than annually.

## Consolidated profit and loss account (format 2)

| Code letter | Item | Year to (date) | | | | | |
|---|---|---|---|---|---|---|---|
| | | | | | | | |
| P1 | Turnover | | | | | | |
| F1 | Change in stocks of finished goods and in work-in-progress | | | | | | |
| F2 | Own work capitalised | | | | | | |
| F3 | Other operating income | | | | | | |
| F4 | Raw materials and consumables | | | | | | |
| F5 | Other external charges | | | | | | |
| F6 | Staff costs | | | | | | |
| F7 | Depreciation | | | | | | |
| F8 | Other operating charges | | | | | | |
| P5 | Operating profit (P1−(F1 + F2 .... F8)) | | | | | | |
| P6 | Investment income | | | | | | |
| P7 | Amounts written off investments | | | | | | |
| P8 | Interest payable and similar charges | | | | | | |
| P9 | Profit on ordinary activities before taxation (P5 + P6 − P7 − P8) | | | | | | |
| P10 | Tax on profit on ordinary activities | | | | | | |
| P11 | Profit on ordinary activities after taxation (P9 − P10) | | | | | | |
| P12 | Minority interests | | | | | | |
| P13 | Profit before extraordinary items (P11− P12) | | | | | | |

**Consolidated profit and loss account (format 2)**

| Code letter | Item | Year to (date) | | | | | |
|---|---|---|---|---|---|---|---|
| | | | | | | | |
| P13 | Profit before extraordinary items (P11 − P12) | | | | | | |
| P14 | Extraordinary items less taxation & minority interests | | | | | | |
| P15 | Profit for the financial year (P13 − P14) | | | | | | |
| P16 | Dividends paid and proposed | | | | | | |
| P17 | Retained profit for the year (P15 − P16) | | | | | | |

NB 1  The items which appear in Formats 1 and 2 are preceded by a P; those which appear only in Format 2 are preceded by an F.

NB 2  As dividends usually relate to a year it is probably not worth while calculating these ratios for a period less than a year. They may however be calculated more frequently than annually.

| Code letter | Item | Source | Year to (date) | | | | | |
|---|---|---|---|---|---|---|---|---|
| W1 | Raw material stock | Note to item B4 | | | | | | |
| W2 | Work-in-progress | Note to item B4 | | | | | | |
| W3 | Finished goods stock | Note to item B4 | | | | | | |
| W4 | Debtors + | B5 | | | | | | |
| W5 | Current assets* | (W1 + W2 + W3 + W4) | | | | | | |
| W6 | Land and buildings | Note to item B2 | | | | | | |
| W7 | Plant and machinery | Note to item B2 | | | | | | |
| W8 | Other fixed assets | Note to item B2 | | | | | | |
| W9 | Fixed assets* | (W6 + W7 + W8) | | | | | | |
| W10 | Operating assets | (W5 + W9) | | | | | | |
| W11 | Investments | B3 + B6 + B7 | | | | | | |
| W12 | Total capital employed* | (W10 + W11) | | | | | | |
| W13 | Borrowings | B8 + B11 + B12 | | | | | | |
| W14 | Equity capital | (W12 − W13) | | | | | | |
| W15 | Minority interests | B15 | | | | | | |
| W16 | Shareholders' funds* | (W14 − W15) | | | | | | |

Check that W16 = B16 − B1

+  NB  This item may contain debtors other than trade debtors. If these other debtors are material they could be removed from this item and included under another heading, e.g. W11 Investments.

*  NB  These terms have slightly different meanings from those used in the published balance sheet itself.

NB  As dividends usually relate to a year it is probably not worth while calculating these ratios for a period less than a year. They may however be calculated more frequently than annually.

Data assembly sheet 13–5
## Format 2 worksheet

| Code letter | Item | Year to (date) | | | | | |
|---|---|---|---|---|---|---|---|
| | | Unadjusted | Adjusted | Unadjusted | Adjusted | Unadjusted | Adjusted |
| A | Raw materials and consumables (F4) | | | | | | |
| B | Other external charges (F5) | | | | | | |
| C | Staff costs (F6) | | | | | | |
| D | Depreciation (F7) | | | | | | |
| E | Other charges (F8) | | | | | | |
| F | Total (F4 +...........+ F8) | | | | | | |
| G | Change in stock (F1) | | | | | | |
| H | Own work capitalised (F2) | | | | | | |
| I | Total (F1 $\pm$ F2) | | | | | | |
| J | Ratio (I/F) | | | | | | |
| | For use of this worksheet see text | | | | | | |

NB   As dividends usually relate to a year it is probably not worth while calculating these ratios for a period less than a year. They may however be calculated more frequently than annually.

| Code letter | Item | Year to (date) | | | | | |
|---|---|---|---|---|---|---|---|
| | | | | | | | |
| N1 | Distribution costs | | | | | | |
| N2 | Research costs | | | | | | |
| N3 | Administration costs | | | | | | |
| N4 | Staff costs | | | | | | |
| N5 | Number of employees | | | | | | |

NB 1   Check that items N1 + N2 + N3 (or their equivalent) = P4 in data assembly sheet 13–1.

NB 2   Check that item N4 = item C from data assembly sheet 13–5 if format 2 worksheet used.

**Ratios to analyse historical cost accounts 'top' financial ratios**

| | Ratio | Formula for calculating ratio | Unit of measurment | Year to (date) | | | | | |
|---|---|---|---|---|---|---|---|---|---|
| 1 | Dividends (paid and proposed)/ Shareholders' funds | P16 x 100 ÷ W16 | % | | | | | | |
| 2 | Profit for the financial year/ Shareholders' funds | P15 x 100 ÷ W16 | % | | | | | | |
| 3 | Profit for the financial year/ Dividends paid and proposed | P15 ÷ P16 | number | | | | | | |
| 4 | Profit before extraordinary items/ Shareholders' funds | P13 x 100 ÷ W16 | % | | | | | | |
| 5 | Extraordinary items less taxation/ Profit before extraordinary items | P14 x 100 ÷ P13 | % | | | | | | |
| 6 | Profit on ordinary activities after taxation/Equity capital | P11 x 100 ÷ W14 | % | | | | | | |
| 7 | Minority interests in profit/ Minority interest in Equity capital | P12 x 100 ÷ W15 | % | | | | | | |
| 8 | Minority interests in capital employed/ Shareholders' funds | W15 x 100 ÷ W16 | % | | | | | | |
| 9 | Profit on ordinary activities before taxation/Equity capital | P9 x 100 ÷ W14 | % | | | | | | |
| 10 | Tax on profit on ordinary activities/ Profit on ordinary activities before taxation | P10 x 100 ÷ P9 | % | | | | | | |
| 11 | Profit before interest payable/ Total capital employed | (P9 + P8) x 100 ÷ W12 | % | | | | | | |
| 12 | Interest payable on net borrowings/ Borrowings | P8 x 100 ÷ W13 | % | | | | | | |
| 13 | Borrowings/ Equity capital | W13 ÷ W14 | number | | | | | | |

**Ratios to analyse historical cost accounts 'top' financial ratios**

| | Ratio | Formula for calculating ratio | Unit of measurement | Year to (date) | | | | | |
|---|---|---|---|---|---|---|---|---|---|
| 14 | Operating profit/ Operating assets | P5 x 100 ÷ W10 | % | | | | | | |
| 15 | Investment income less amounts written off investments/Total investments | (P6 — P7) x 100 ÷ W11 | % | | | | | | |
| 16 | Total investments/ Total capital employed | W11 x 100 ÷ W12 | % | | | | | | |
| | | | | | | | | | |

**Ratio to analyse historical cost accounts (Part 2A)**

| Ratio | Formula for calculating ratio | Unit of measurement | Year to (date) | | | | | |
|---|---|---|---|---|---|---|---|---|
| 1  Operating profit/ Operating assets | P5 x 100 ÷ W10 | % | | | | | | |
| 2  Operating profit/ Turnover | P5 x 100 ÷ P1 | % | | | | | | |
| 3  Turnover/ Operating assets | P1 ÷ W10 | times per year | | | | | | |
| 4  Gross profit/ Turnover | P3 x 100 ÷ P1 | % | | | | | | |
| 5  Distribution costs/ Turnover | N1 x 100 ÷ P1 | % | | | | | | |
| 6  Research costs/ Turnover | N2 x 100 ÷ P1 | % | | | | | | |
| 7  Administration costs/ Turnover | N3 x 100 ÷ P1 | % | | | | | | |

| Ratio | Formula for calculating ratio | Unit of measurement | Year to (date) | | | | | |
|---|---|---|---|---|---|---|---|---|
| | | | | | | | | |
| | | | | | | | | |
| 1  Staff costs/ Turnover | N4 x 100 ÷ P1 | % | | | | | | |
| 2  Staff costs/ Number of employees | N4 ÷ N5 | £ per head | | | | | | |
| 3  Turnover/ Number of employees | P1 ÷ N5 | £ per head | | | | | | |
| 4  Operating assets/ Number of employees | W10 ÷ N5 | £ per head | | | | | | |
| 5  Operating profit/ Staff costs | P5 x 100 ÷ N4 | % | | | | | | |
| 6  Operating profit/ Number of employees | P5 ÷ N5 | £ per head | | | | | | |
| | | | | | | | | |

Ratio calculation sheet 13–4
## Asset utilisation ratios

| Ratio | Formula for calculating ratio | Unit of measurement | Year to (date) | | | | | |
|---|---|---|---|---|---|---|---|---|
| | | | | | | | | |
| 1 Turnover/ Operating assets | P1 ÷ W10 | times per year | | | | | | |
| 2 Operating assets/ Turnover | W10 x 1000 ÷ P1 | £/£1,000 | | | | | | |
| 3 Fixed assets/ Turnover | W9 x 1000 ÷ P1 | £/£1,000 | | | | | | |
| 4 Current assets/ Turnover | W5 x 1000 ÷ P1 | £/£1,000 | | | | | | |
| 5 Land & buildings/ Turnover | W6 x 1000 ÷ P1 | £/£1,000 | | | | | | |
| 6 Plant and machinery/ Turnover | W7 x 1000 ÷ P1 | £/£1,000 | | | | | | |
| 7 Other fixed assets/ Turnover | W8 x 1000 ÷ P1 | £/£1,000 | | | | | | |
| 8 Raw material stock/ Turnover | W1 x 1000 ÷ P1 | £/£1,000 | | | | | | |
| 9 Work-in-progress/ Turnover | W2 x 1000 ÷ P1 | £/£1,000 | | | | | | |
| 10 Finished goods stock/ Turnover | W3 x 1000 ÷ P1 | £/£1,000 | | | | | | |
| 11 Debtors/ Turnover | W4 x 1000 ÷ P1 | £/£1,000 | | | | | | |

| Ratio | Formula for calculating ratio | Unit of measurement | Year to (date) | | | | | |
|---|---|---|---|---|---|---|---|---|
| 12  Raw material stock/ Average daily (turnover less gross profit) | W1 ÷ (P2 ÷ 365) | days | | | | | | |
| 13  Work-in-progress/ Average daily (turnover less gross profit) | W2 ÷ (P2 ÷ 365) | days | | | | | | |
| 14  Finished goods stock/ Average daily (turnover less gross profit) | W3 ÷ (P2 ÷ 365) | days | | | | | | |
| 15  Debtors/ Average daily turnover | W4 ÷ (P1 ÷ 365) | days | | | | | | |

## Format 2 profit and loss account ratios

| | Ratio | Formula for calculating ratio | Unit of measurement | Year to (date) | | | | | |
|---|---|---|---|---|---|---|---|---|---|
| | | | | | | | | | |
| 1 | Operating profit/Turnover | P5 x 100 ÷ P1 | % | | | | | | |
| 2 | Other operating income/Turnover | F3 x 100 ÷ P1 | % | | | | | | |
| 3 | Raw materials/Turnover | A* x 100 ÷ P1 | % | | | | | | |
| 4 | Other external charges/Turnover | B* x 100 ÷ P1 | % | | | | | | |
| 5 | Staff costs/Turnover | C* x 100 ÷ P1 | % | | | | | | |
| 6 | Depreciation/Turnover | D* x 100 ÷ P1 | % | | | | | | |
| 7 | Other charges/Turnover | E* x 100 ÷ P1 | % | | | | | | |

* From adjusted column in data assembly sheet 13–5.

# PART FIVE

# Chapter 14

# Ratios in the public sector

This chapter is in four parts:

1    General
2    Nationalised industries and similar bodies
3    Local government
4    Central government

## 14.1 General

### 14.1.1 Introduction

The reasons for including this chapter are as follows:

1    the public sector is a significant part of the country's economy;
2    measuring 'efficiency' (however defined) in the public sector poses some interesting problems;
3    it is hoped that the material in this chapter will be of use to those in the public sector concerned with improving its efficiency;
4    while the public sector may be able to learn from the private sector, there are also areas where those in the private sector can learn from the public sector;
5    most readers of this book will be interested in the workings of the public sector as tax and rate payers and consumers of the services the sector provides, and will be concerned at how efficiently and equitably the sector operates.

### 14.1.2 Definition and size of the public sector

In the middle of 1982 roughly three out of every ten employees worked in the public sector. The breakdown is shown in Table 14–1.

|  | Numbers ('000) | % |
|---|---|---|
| *Central government* | | |
| HM Forces | 324 | 1.4 |
| National Health Service | 1,287 | 5.5 |
| Other central government | 735 | 3.1 |
| Total central government | 2,346 | 10.0 |
| *Local authorities* | | |
| Education | 1,483 | 6.3 |
| Health and social services | 352 | 1.5 |
| Police | 201 | 0.9 |
| Other local authorities | 895 | 3.8 |
| Total local authorities | 2,931 | 12.5 |
| *Public corporations* | 1,759 | 7.5 |
| Total public sector | 7,036 | 29.9 |
| Total private sector | 16,472 | 70.1 |
| *Total* | 23,508 | 100.0 |

Source: 'Employment in the public and private sectors 1976 to 1982', H. Morrison, *Economic Trends*, CSO, February 1983.

Table 14–1   Employees in the public sector

A similar picture is provided by an analysis of the Gross Domestic Product (GDP) for 1983 (see Table 14–2).

| | £ million | % |
|---|---|---|
| *Private sector* | | |
| Personal sector | 49,497 | 19.0 |
| Industrial & commercial companies | 129,915 | 50.0 |
| Financial companies | 6,219 | 2.4 |
| Total | 185,631 | 71.4 |
| *Public sector* | | |
| Public corporations | 27,729 | 10.7 |
| Central government | 20,724 | 8.0 |
| Local authorities | 25,747 | 9.9 |
| Total | 74,200 | 28.6 |
| *GDP at factor cost* | 259,831 | 100.0 |

Source: *United Kingdom National Accounts, 1984*, HMSO, 1984, Table 1.14.

Table 14–2   Analysis of GDP

### 14.1.3 The special problems of the public sector

It appears to have become generally accepted that achievement in the public sector should be measured by the '3Es':

1   *Effectiveness* – the extent to which objectives have been achieved;
2   *Efficiency* – the extent to which outputs have been maximised in relation to inputs;
3   *Economy* – the extent to which inputs have been minimised.

These are the normal definitions but are not the only ones. I believe that the underlying concepts would be more usefully expressed if they could be measured by ratios. See 'Some suggestions' (14.1.4, below).

Unfortunately when government sets policies it rarely seems to give adequate consideration as to how the achievement of that policy is to be established. Moreover there are often difficulties in measuring both the inputs and the outputs from government activities. There are several reasons for this:

1   Sometimes, a long time will necessarily elapse between expenditure and ultimate benefit (e.g. expenditure on child health may lead to benefit in later life as well as in childhood).

2   Outputs may be difficult to define (e.g. the objective of the education service is an educated population; the objective of the health service in a healthy population; can these objectives be adequately defined?)

3   Outputs may be difficult to measure in money or other units (e.g. how would one ascribe a money or other value to the peace-keeping role of the Forces in preventing war) but this does *not* mean that different outputs or outcomes cannot be rated in order of relative value (e.g. supporting the elderly in their own homes is more personally valuable to many of them than institutional care).

4   Costs caused by government action may be borne by others (e.g. the recent shift of the administrative costs of paying sickness benefit to the employer, and of administering mortgage interest relief to Building Societies).

5   Benefits of governmental action may be hard to distinguish from changes which may have occurred for other reasons (e.g. job creation subsidies).

6   One activity may have several benefits (e.g. enforcement of vehicle road regulations both improves safety and reduces road damage).

7   Several activities may contribute to one objective.

8   Political objectives may override other considerations and may change during the implementation of a policy (see, for example, 'Why Whitehall reform takes the same old road,' Sir Kenneth Clucas, *The Guardian*, 22 August 1983).

However these problems are not unique to the public sector. For example, in the private sector:

1   A manager often has to balance relatively known costs against such intangible benefits as level of customer service, speed and quantity of information, etc.

2   Profit is not the only measure of business success (see Chapter 4) – growth, survival, reputation, may all take precedence over profit at some stage or other.

3   The impact on profitability of many decisions by managers cannot be directly measured (e.g. some of those taken by the personnel or finance director).

4   Sometimes profit or loss comes from factors totally or largely outside the business's control.

Despite these problems it will be seen from the rest of this chapter that much progress has been made in the public sector in developing performance indicators. Because they must often, perforce, measure sub-objectives, care must be taken not to forget that they are only sub-objectives and should not be pursued at the expense of the other less easily quantified objectives.

### 14.1.4 Some suggestions

As a result of some of our discussions and work in the public sector, a colleague at Arthur Andersen & Co., David Kaye and I would like to suggest that in tackling the problem of selecting and using ratios in the public sector the principles of ratio selection (Chapter 1.2) are equally valid. Before selecting ratios however the following preliminary questions may be found useful.

1    What are objectives of scheme/policy?
2    What is their relative importance?
3    Which are final/intermediate?
4    How can we know/measure if objectives met?
5    What are costs both direct and indirect and who bears them?
6    Are costs relatable to objectives?
7    Who controls costs/achievements?

In the light of the answers to these questions one more may need to be asked:

8    Is scheme etc. in need of revision in order better to achieve overall objectives and the need for monitoring and control of performance?

Ratios in the public sector should if possible be logically linked. Diagram 14–1 is an outline of such a framework.

It may not be possible to calculate ratio 1 because of the difficulty and/or political judgement required to value impact. Ratio 2 is however much more likely to be practicable.

Success in improving ratio 2 may come in the areas of 'economy' (ratio 3), 'efficiency' (ratio 4) and 'effectiveness' (ratio 5). Note that our definition of these terms is slightly non-standard and refers to 'processing capability'. This is because in many cases it is useful to separate the costs of the capacity to provide a service (e.g. a hospital bed or an advisory service) from the costs and outputs of using that capacity.

'Economy' can be subdivided between 'price' and 'quantity' as in Diagram 14–2.

It may also be useful to separate programme costs (e.g. amounts paid to the unemployed) from administrative costs and devise separate sets of ratios to monitor the effectiveness of the former and the efficiency of the latter (see Diagram 14-3).

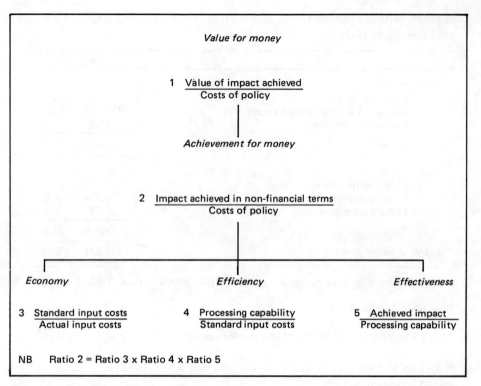

Diagram 14–1   Overall ratios for the public sector

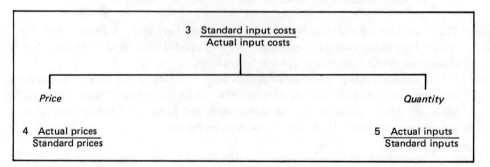

Diagram 14–2   Economy, price and quantity

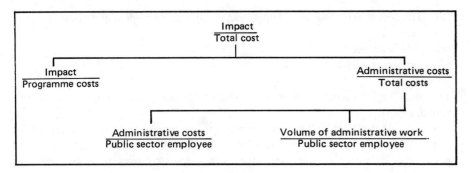

Diagram 14–3   Programme and administrative costs

An interesting discussion of the problems of measuring performance by central government departments, including several case studies, will be found in *Policy work and the FMI: Report by the Cabinet Office (MPO)/Treasury Financial Management Unit,* HM Treasury, June 1985. It suggests that, in assessing performance, information is needed on:

(*a*)   the changing external conditions, including not only hard data but also judgements, for example about changes in attitudes and behaviour which affect the policy assumptions underlying the programme (the *environment*);

(*b*)   progress made towards objectives (the *achievements*) and, insofar as progress has been made, the extent to which achievements resulted directly from the programme (the *effects*) and the expenditure involved (cost effectiveness); and

(*c*)   the administrative *efficiency* with which the programme is delivered.

The report also makes two proposals to help to improve practice in this area:

(*a*)   terms of reference of policy reviews (whether conducted within government, by external Committees of Enquiry, or however initiated) should include a requirement to state how the performance of the programme should be evaluated in the future. A recent review for the Lord Chancellor's Department of the administration of legal aid (conducted by external advisers) produced recommendations on future arrangements for performance assessment.

(*b*)   when departments bring forward policy submissions with financial and manpower implications they should not only, as now, state the resource implications, but also indicate the basis and arrangements for subsequent assessment of performance. A number of departments have been moving in this direction. For example, DES has introduced a checklist for new directly funded initiatives (details attached in Annex B to the Report).

## 14.2 Nationalised Industries and Similar Bodies

### 14.2.1 Introduction

Some of the main nationalised industries, state holding companies and similar bodies, and their size, are shown in Table 14–3.

| Rank | Name | Turnover £000 | Capital employed* £000 | Employees |
|---|---|---|---|---|
| 1 | Electricity Council (1) | 9,128,400 | 33,830,500 | 141,385 |
| 2 | British National Oil Corp. | 7,909,800 | 30,885 | 128 |
| 3 | British Telecom | 6,377,000 | 9,288,000 | 248,812 |
| 4 | British Gas Corporation (1) | 5,930,300 | 12,375,100 | 103,300 |
| 5 | National Coal Board | 4,932,000 | 3,223,000 | 268,000 |
| 6 | British Steel Corporation | 3,231,000 | 2,826,000 | 94,800 |
| 7 | British Railways Board | 3,188,800 | 1,440,100 | 200,789 |
| 8 | The Post Office (1) | 2,714,400 | 1,471,300 | 203,156 |
| 9 | British Airways | 2,513,700 | 1,025,700 | 36,096 |
| 10 | British Shipbuilders | 1,092,537 | 238,288 | 64,444 |
| 11 | British Broadcasting Corp. | 834,600 | 323,000 | 29,147 |
| 12 | South of Scotland Electricity Board | 782,456 | 1,779,305 | 12,307 |
| 13 | National Bus Company | 709,690 | 256,299 | 51,015 |
| 14 | London Transport Executive | 578,100 | 1,893,600 | 57,400 |
| 15 | British Nuclear Fuels | 457,500 | 938,900 | 16,105 |
| 16 | British Airports Authority (1) | 283,673 | 925,309 | 7,191 |
| 17 | North of Scotland Hydro-Electric Board | 275,966 | 648,816 | 3,840 |
| 18 | Scottish Transport Board | 167,541 | 164,720 | 10,364 |
| 19 | National Enterprise Board | 145,400 | 176,600 | 4,271 |
| 20 | Port of London Authority | 83,211 | 86,322 | 4,405 |
| 21 | Independent Broadcasting Authority (2) | 53,769 | 108,034 | 1,495 |

*Notes:* *Total tangible assets less current liabilities (other than bank loans and overdrafts).   (1)   Figures on Current Cost Basis   (2)   Excluding Channel Four

*Source: The Times 1,000 1984–1985,* Times Books Limited, 1984 Table 3.

Table 14–3   Size of nationalised industries

In addition to those listed by *The Times* there are also the Water Authorities.

## 14.2.2 Special characteristics of nationalised industries

It was suggested in Chapter 4 that most businesses have several objectives, the relative importance of which varies from time to time. Nationalised industries, unlike most companies in the private sector, have some, but not all, of these objectives publicly spelt out. The objectives should be set, and varied, by the government through the Minister of the sponsoring department.

In general nationalised industries' accounts are produced in accordance with 'best accounting practice', and are audited, but the sponsoring Minister approves the form in which they appear. The main differences between nationalised industries' reports and accounts and those in the private sector are:

(a)  virtually all nationalised industries' capital comes from government (directly or indirectly) and not from private investors;

(b)  as a consequence of (a) interest payments are a larger proportion of costs in a nationalised industry than in a private sector company and roughly equate with dividends;

(c)  some nationalised industries (e.g. British Rail) receive substantial grants from government to cover the cost of socially desirable but uneconomic services;

(d)  because of (a) (b) and (c) the figures of nationalised industry 'profit' and 'turnover' are not comparable, without adjustment, to private sector figures for the same items – a common source of confusion and misunderstanding – or indeed between nationalised industries, because of differences in, *inter alia* (i) the proportions of capital provided by loans and retained profits, (ii) the rates of interest payable, (iii) the amounts of grants made, (iv) the treatment of the effects of inflation, especially on depreciation, (v) other differences in accounting policies;

(e)  generally nationalised industry accounts contain more information than those in the private sector.

## 14.2.3 Financial targets

The financial targets set for a nationalised industry by the government are usually in terms of one or more of the following:

(a)  return on net assets

(b)  profit margin on sales

(c)  return on equity

(d)  (for loss-making industries) operating within a given level of grant or minimising losses

(e)  self-financing ratio

(f)  operating within a cash limit.

The target, and the actual performance, should be set out in the nationalised industry's annual report.

Readers of this book will be familiar with the advantages and disadvantages of (a) and (b) and no further comment is required other than to repeat the need to be alert to possible differences in how they have been calculated over time and between nationalised industry.

(c) is rarely used and is only appropriate where the nationalised industry is substantially financed by Public Dividend Capital (PDC) as opposed to loans (e.g. National Giro Bank).

(d) is reasonably self explanatory – even if the concept may be controversial. (e) and (f), however, call for comment.

Nationalised industries regard the self-financing ratio as an important measure of their ability to be independent. The ratio may be calculated either as

$$\frac{\text{Capital expenditure for year}}{\text{Retained profit plus depreciation}}$$

or

$$\frac{\text{Capital expenditure plus increase in working capital}}{\text{Retained profit plus depreciation}}$$

The then government's view was however that 'although forecasts of these ratios are very important in estimating the industries' requirements for Government finance they are not a suitable basis for financial targets'. (*The Nationalised Industries*, Cmnd 7131, HMSO, 1978, p. 26.)

Whilst it would not be unreasonable to expect that that part of capital expenditure which relates to the replacement of existing assets should be financed out of either historical cost depreciation and retained profits or current cost depreciation, to expect expenditure on new equipment and thus growth to be so financed would mean that this year's consumers would be paying for benefits to be reaped, if at all, by future generations.

The cash limit is strictly speaking not a ratio but is obviously linked to the self-financing ratio and is also regarded by the nationalised industries themselves as important. It is the maximum amount of cash the government will permit the industry to raise as external finance whether from the government or from other sources. It may be seen as a constraint (desirable or otherwise) on an industry's operations rather than as a target or objective.

### 14.2.4 Non-financial targets

In addition to financial targets, most nationalised industries have non-financial objectives set them. The 1978 White Paper (*The Nationalised Industries,* Cmnd 7131) stipulated that each industry should publish non-financial indicators of performance and service standards. The relevant passage reads:

> The government has . . . asked each industry, in consultation with its sponsoring department, to select a number of key performance indicators, including valid international comparisons, and to publish them prominently in their annual reports. They would be supported by an explanation of why they had been chosen and of significant trends . . .
>
> . . . There will probably be some indicators common to most including, for example, labour productivity and standards of service where these are readily measurable.

The purpose of asking the industries to do this is explained by the White Paper in terms of the need to ensure that an industry should not be able to improve its financial performance simply by increasing prices or lowering standards of service.

Andrew Likierman suggested (*Accountancy,* May 1979, p. 117) that in looking at Nationalised Industries' performance indicators the reader should ask the following questions:

1  Is it clear that these *are* performance indicators? Is the reason for putting them in shown?
2  Have international comparisons been provided?
3  Is there an explanation of why these indicators (rather than any others) were chosen? (I would suggest that this may not always be necessary as the reasons for some indicators will be self-evident to most general readers.)
4  Are trends over time given to show a historic series?
5  Are labour productivity measures included?
6  Are standards of service shown? Is it clear why these were chosen? Standards of service of course mean different things for different industries and it is difficult for anyone who is not expert in the affairs of that particular industry to know what to look for.

To which I would add:

7  Has information on prices charged been provided? Have trends in prices been related to inflation, to competitive products (if any), to costs, to other countries?
8  Is there a commentary on what the changes in the indicators over time or between countries show?

Let us now look at the performance indicators of some of the major nationalised industries in the light of this list of questions. I will concentrate mainly on the non-financial performance indicators as the financial indicators have already been dealt with elsewhere in this book, and it is in the area of non-financial ratios that most may be learnt from the nationalised industries.

The information provided varies from year to year in some cases – sometimes improving, but othertimes the amount of information provided diminishes – so Table 14–4 should be taken as no more than a snapshot at a particular point in time.

| Industry | Gas | Electricity | Rail | Bus | Coal | Telephone | Post Office |
|---|---|---|---|---|---|---|---|
| **Criterion** | | | | | | | |
| 1  Is it clear that these are performance indicators? | Y | Y | Y | Y | Y | Y | Y |
| 2  International comparisons | N | N | Y | N | N | N | P |
| 3  Explanations | P | P | N | N | N | N | N |
| 4  Trends | 10 | 5 | 5 | 5 | 10–36 | 2 | 6–10 |
| 5  Labour productivity | Y | Y | Y | Y | Y | N | Y |
| 6  Standards of service | N | P | P | N | N | Y | Y |
| 7  Price | P | P | P | Y | N | N | P |
| 8  Commentary | P | Y | P | P | P | P | Y |

*Notes*
N = No
P = Partial
Y = Yes
The number in line 4 is the number of years for which trends are shown.

Table 14–4  How satisfactory are nationalised industries' performance indicators?

## 14.2.5 British Gas Corporation

The corporation states that there are three formal targets set it by the government:

1    A financial target (an average annual return of 3.5 per cent measured by current cost operating profit/average net assets at current cost).
2    An external financial limit (measured by target borrowings or repayments).
3    A performance target (a reduction in unit net trading costs per therm of gas sold measured at constant prices).

Their 1983–84 report compares performance with these targets and also provides the performance ratios for each of the last ten years as shown in Table 14–5.

| | |
|---|---|
| *Financial performance ratios* | |
| | |
| Return on average net assets employed | |
| at current cost | |
| – Operating profit | % |
| – Profit retained | % |
| Profit as a percentage of turnover | |
| – Operating profit | % |
| – Profit retained | % |
| Self-financing ratio | % |
| Working capital as a percentage of turnover | % |
| Return on net assets employed | |
| – historical cost basis | % |
| | |
| *Ratios based on therms sold* | |
| Prime materials | |
| Natural gas and feedstocks | pence per therm |
| Gas levy | pence per therm |
| | |
| Total prime materials | pence per therm |
| | |
| Operating costs | |
| Salaries, wages and associated costs | pence per therm |
| Replacement expenditure | pence per therm |
| Other trading costs | pence per therm |
| Conversion costs and displaced plant | |
| written off | pence per therm |
| Depreciation | pence per therm |
| Monetary working capital and cost of sales | |
| adjustments | pence per therm |
| | |
| Total operating costs | pence per therm |

| | | |
|---|---|---|
| Total operating costs per therm as an index | (1974/75 = 100) | |
| | | |
| Retail price index | (1974/75 = 100) | |
| | | |
| *Ratios based on employees* | | |
| Net assets employed (at current cost) | | |
| per direct employee | £000 | |
| | | |
| Therms sold per direct employee | thousand therms | |
| | | |
| Therms sold per employee | | |
| (direct and contractor) | thousand therms | |
| | | |
| Customers per direct employee: | | |
| General engineering, production, | | |
| transmission and distribution | | |
| Marketing and sales | | |
| Customer service | | |
| Customer accounting | | |
| Administration and general services | | |
| | | |
| Total | | |
| | | |
| Total (including contractors) | | |
| | | |
| *Ratios based on domestic tariffs* | | |
| Gas costs as a proportion of: | | |
| Single person's pension | Note 1 | % |
| Couple's pension | Note 1 | % |
| National average manual worker's earnings | Note 1 | % |

*Notes*

1    Based on constant consumptions of 330 therms p.a. for pensioners and 400 therms p.a. for manual workers and on incomes and tariffs as at December in each year.

Table 14–5   British Gas performance ratios

The financial performance ratios have already been described elsewhere in the book and need no further comment.

The various costs per therm are interesting but it would have been helpful to have had sales revenue per therm (i.e. average price) as well. Similarly, a comparison of costs with the RPI is interesting but a comparison of price would have been more so. Also missing is a comparison with the price of other fuels.

However the ratios of gas costs as a proportion of pensions and earnings is a good indicator of their relative burden on such customers.

The ratios of therms sold per direct employee is a crude measure of productivity, because in a capital intensive industry such as gas, the numbers of therms sold could vary fairly widely without a marked change in the number of direct employees. Hence the importance of the ratio of net assets per employee because this gives an indication of one of the major factors contributing to productivity.

The ratios of customers per employee are perhaps better indicators of productivity but, without an indicator of the level of service provided, give only part of the story.

## 14.2.6 The Central Electricity Generating Board

The CEGB's report for the year to 31 March 1984 contains in Appendix 2 a Table of some 39 performance indicators, several of which are shown as graphs as well as ratios for the past five years. Most interestingly, the relationship between the performance indicators is shown in a diagram very similar in concept to those advocated elsewhere in this book although obviously and rightly differing in the detail of its 'grass roots' ratios (see Diagram 14–4). A definition of each ratio is provided.

Elsewhere in the report prices charged are compared to fuel cost and the RPI over a five-year period.

In a previous report (1978–79) thermal efficiency was compared with that in four other countries. It is a pity that this comparison has not been repeated and that other items which are not dependent on £ as a unit of measurement have also not been compared with those of other countries.

Overall this is an interesting report though some of the terms used would be difficult for a layman to follow.

## 14.2.7 British Rail

BR, in its annual report for 1983, published in 1984, provides a two-page graphical review of the following key performance indicators, expressed as an index number (1979 = 100), over the last five years, together with a brief comment on their significance.

| | |
|---|---|
| 1 | Total staff productivity |
| | Train miles per member of staff |
| 2 | Freight vehicle utilisation |
| | Train miles per wagon (wagon utilisation) |
| 3 | Traction, coaching stock and track utilisation |
| | Train miles per locomotive/HST set (traction unit utilisation) |
| | Loaded train miles per passenger vehicle (passenger vehicle utilisation) |
| | Train miles per single track mile (track utilisation) |
| 4 | Passenger train loads and earnings |
| | Receipts per loaded train mile (train earnings) |
| | Passenger miles per loaded train mile (average train load) |
| 5 | Freight train loads and earnings |
| | Receipts per train mile (train earnings) |
| | Net tonne miles per loaded train mile (average train load) |
| 6 | Unit costs |
| | Direct costs per train mile (train operating, maintenance and terminal expenditure) |
| | Indirect cost per train mile (infrastructure and administration) |
| | Total costs per train mile. |

Table 14–6   BR key performance indicators

In addition it provides in an appendix the 38 performance indicators shown in Table 14–7 for each of the last four years (and in most cases five years) in the order shown.

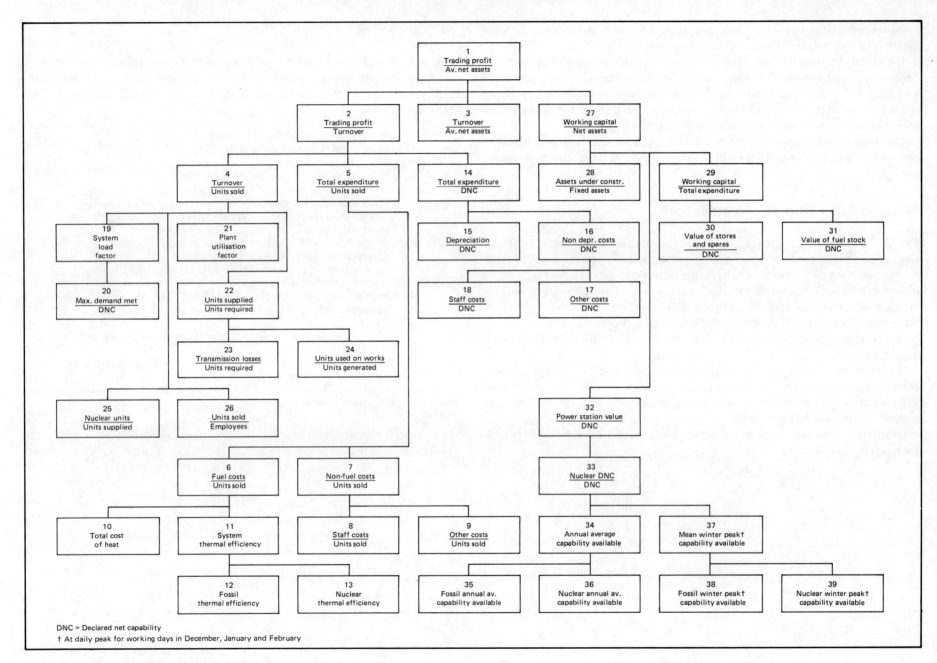

DNC = Declared net capability

† At daily peak for working days in December, January and February

Diagram 14–4   CEGB – interrelated hierarchy of performance indicators

*Total rail business*

| | | |
|---|---|---|
| 1 | Total receipts per train mile | £ |
| 2 | Train service (operating) expenses per train mile | £ |
| 3 | Train service (maintenance) expenses per train mile | £ |
| 4 | Terminal expenses per train mile | £ |
| 5 | Infrastructure expenses per train mile | £ |
| 6 | Administration costs per train mile | £ |
| 7 | Train miles per member of staff (Total staff productivity) | no. |
| 8 | Revenue per £1,000 gross paybill costs | £ |
| 9 | Train miles per train crew member (Train crew productivity) | no. |
| 10 | Track maintenance costs per single track mile | £ |
| 11 | Signal renewal and maintenance costs per single track mile | £ |
| 12 | Signal operating costs per single track mile | £ |
| 13 | Train miles per single track mile | 000s |
| 14 | Train miles per locomotive/HST set | 000s |

*Passenger business*

| | | |
|---|---|---|
| 15 | PSO grants per passenger mile | pence |
| 16 | PSO grants as a percentage of other receipts | % |
| 17 | Receipts per loaded train mile | £ |
| 18 | Receipts per passenger mile | pence |
| 19 | Passenger miles per loaded train mile (average train load) | no. |
| 20 | Train service (operating) expenses per train mile | index |
| 21 | Train service (maintenance) expenses per train mile | index |
| 22 | Terminal expenses per train mile | index |
| 23 | Loaded train miles per passenger vehicle | miles |
| 24 | Percentage of trains arriving within 5 mins of booked time | % |
| 25 | Percentage of trains cancelled | % |
| 26 | Percentage of train catering services cancelled | % |

*Freight business*

| | | |
|---|---|---|
| 27 | Operating surplus as percentage of receipts | % |
| 28 | Receipts per train mile | index |
| 29 | Receipts per net tonne mile | index |
| 30 | Tonne miles per loaded train mile (average train load) | tonnes |
| 31 | Train service (operating) expenses per train mile | index |
| 32 | Train service (maintenance) expenses per train mile | index |
| 33 | Terminal expenses per train mile | index |
| 34 | Train miles per wagon | miles |

*Parcels business*

| | | |
|---|---|---|
| 35 | Operating surplus as percentage of receipts | % |
| 36 | Train service (operating) expenses per train mile | index |
| 37 | Train service (maintenance) expenses per train mile | index |
| 38 | Terminal expenses per train mile | index |

*Notes to Table 14–7*

1   Monetary items have been converted to 1983 price levels using GDP deflator, (1979 = 67.5, 1980 = 80.4, 1981 = 88.6, 1982 = 94.3, 1983 = 100).

2   Receipts include miscellaneous receipts but exclude PSO grants.

3   Indicators 7 and 8 – staff numbers and paybill costs exclude British Rail Engineering Limited.

4   Indicator 9 includes train miles for the Board's internal use. It does not represent the average mileage per driver, since most trains have a minimum crew of two.

5   Indicator 11 includes expenditure of a capital nature chargeable to revenue account.

6   Indicators 15 and 16 include both payments made by Passport Transport Executives and the Special Replacement Allowance.

7   Indicators 23 and 34 are indirect measures of vehicle utilisation which underestimate actual utilisation by a factor equal to average train length and also do not reflect any changes in average train length.

8   Indicators 29 and 30 – net tonne mileage is the tonnage of goods carried multiplied by journey distance.

9   Indicator 34 – wagons include privately owned vehicles.

Table 14–7   BR performance indicators

It also compares the following ratios with the average of eight European Railways (Austria, Belgium, France, Great Britain, Italy, Netherlands, Switzerland and West Germany), for this and last year:

1 Train kilometres (loaded and empty) per member of staff employed
2 Average train loading (passenger kms, divided by passenger train kms, loaded and empty)
3 Average train loading (freight tonnes kms, divided by freight train kms, loaded and empty)
4 Support from public funds as proportion of Gross Domestic Product (%)

British Rail also provides the performance indicators in Table 14–8 for the last five years for its other activities.

| *Freightliners Ltd* | |
|---|---|
| 1 Operating margin | % |
| 2 Average receipts per container (TEU) | *£ |
| 3 Gross receipts per employee | *£000s |

| *British Rail Engineering Ltd* | |
|---|---|
| 4 External sales to total sales | % |
| 5 Export sales to external sales | % |
| 6 Total sales to capital employed | % |
| 7 Sales of new rolling stock per employee | *£000s |
| 8 Sales for repair and overhaul of traction and rolling stock per employee | *£000s |
| 9 Sales per £ staff costs (external sales) | £ |
| 10 Capital employed to staff costs | % |

| *Travellers Fare* | |
|---|---|
| 11 Operating margin | % |
| 12 Sales per employee | *£000s |

| *Operational and Non-operational Property* | |
|---|---|
| 13 Property income | |
| – Operational | £000s |
| – Non-operational | £000s |

| 14 Operating margin | |
|---|---|
| – Operational | % |
| – Non-operational | % |
| 15 Management expenses as a percentage of property income | % |
| 16 Growth in annual rental income | index |
| 17 Net income per employee | £000s |
| 18 Net property income per £ staff costs | £ |

| *Transmark Ltd* | |
|---|---|
| 19 Operating margin | % |
| 20 Sales per employee | *£000s |

| *Sealink UK Ltd* | |
|---|---|
| 21 Financial target performance | % |
| 22 Operating margin | % |
| 23 Return on capital employed | % |
| 24 Average receipts per passenger | *£ |
| 25 Average receipts per accompanied car | £ |
| 26 Gross receipts per employee | £000s |
| 27 Number of complaints per 1,000 passengers carried | no. |

*Notes to Table 14–8*

1 Monetary indicators marked * have been converted to 1983 price levels using the GDP deflator.
2 Indicators 1, 11, 19, and 22 are net surplus (loss) before interest as a percentage of gross income.
3 Indicator 2, TEU = 20ft equivalent unit.
4 Indicator 13 – gross income after deduction of rents payable and rates.
5 Indicator 14 – operating surplus (before development land tax) as a percentage of property income.
6 Indicator 16 – rent roll value as at 31 December indexed from 1 January 1978 (100).
7 Indicator 17 – operating surplus (before development land tax) per employee engaged on letting activities.
8 Indicator 18 – net property income related to costs of employees engaged on letting activities.
9 Indicator 21 – return before interest and tax but after adjusting for inflation on the value of net fixed assets at the year end.

Table 14–8  BR other activities performance indicators

The railway passenger or freight customer is interested in price, frequency and reliability of service. The tax payer will be concerned with how much British Rail is costing him. It is regrettable that none of these topics is addressed in the key performance indicators section of the report.

Price is the subject of ratios 18 (receipts per passenger mile) and 29 (receipts per net tonne mile) and is also covered in two further appendices which give the average fare per mile for different types of ticket and the average receipt per tonne and per wagon for different types of freight.

The price ratios have been adjusted for inflation. It would be useful to have them unadjusted as well and compared with private car costs per passenger mile and some measure of road haulage costs per mile.

Reliability is the subject of a paragraph in the main report and of ratios 24 to 26.

The cost to the tax payer is the subject of ratios 15 and 16 (PSO – Public Service Obligation – grants per passenger mile and PSO grants as a percentage of other receipts). It is also the subject of a section in the main report.

It would seem that those interested in BR's efficiency are not short of information on trends; indeed they might well complain of being overloaded. The usefulness of the ratios could be improved if they were put in a more logically structured order, and if management, and the Minister, provided substantially more commentary on their meaning and the significance of changes in the ratios over time. For a very interesting discussion of the usefulness of some of these ratios to measure and regulate BR's performance, see 'Financial Objectives, Productive Efficiency and the Regulation of a Subsidised State Monopoly', I. Lapsley, *Accounting and Business Research*, Summer 1984, pp. 217–227.

### 14.2.8 The National Bus Company

The NBC, in its 1983 report published in 1984, provides for each of its operating subsidiaries (i.e. the bus companies operating in a defined geographical area such as Bristol or the Thames Valley) absolute figures for:

1   Net revenue after interest and taxation on an historical and current cost basis.
2   Support payments.
3   Turnover.
4   Passenger journeys.
5   Vehicle mileage.
6   Traffic vehicles.
7   Net assets employed.

These are not converted into ratios – although the reader could do this for himself. I would have thought that each of 1, 2, and 3 expressed in relation to 4, 5, 6 and 7 separately; 4 as a ratio of 5, and 5 as a ratio of 6 would have been illuminating.

The company cautions that 'it should be remembered when examining these results that they include the costs of servicing capital. In a normally geared undertaking these costs would be appropriations of, rather than charges against, profits. The total sum involved is £11.5 million'.

Figures are also given for the group as a whole for the last five years for

1   Passenger journeys
2   Vehicle miles
3   Vehicles
5   Employees

The statistical indicators in Table 14–9 are given for the last five years:

| | |
|---|---|
| Working expenses per vehicle mile | (pence) |
|   Outturn | |
|   Real terms | |
| Vehicle miles per employee | (000's) |
|   Platform staff | |
|   Non-platform staff | |
|   All staff | |
| Vehicle miles per vehicle | (000's) |
| Stage carriage passenger journeys | (000's) |
|   Per employee | |
|   Per vehicle | |
| Passenger receipts as a percentage of turnover | % |
| Local authority revenue support as a percentage of turnover | % |
| Average fare per passenger journey | (pence) |
|   Outturn | |
|   Real terms | |
| Lost mileage as a percentage of total mileage | % |

Table 14–9   National Bus Company statistical indicators

The above information closely follows that recommended in the Department of Transport code of practice *Publication of Information by Bus Operators*.

## 14.2.9 The National Coal Board

The NCB, in its 1983/84 report, provides the following performance indicators in its 'Summary of the year':

Coalface output per manshift, tonnes
Overall output per manshift, tonnes
Output per man-year, tonnes
Colliery costs per tonne, £

Casualties per 100,000 manshifts
    Fatal accidents
    Total accidents

It also provides the statistics in Table 14–10 for the past ten years (plus figures at five-yearly intervals from 1947).

Output per man-year, tonnes
Output per manshift, tonnes
    Production
    All underground
    Surface
    Overall

Number of accidents per 100,000 manshifts
    Fatal
    Major injury

Disputes tonnage lost, million tonnes

Cash earnings per week, £
Value of allowances in kind per week, £

Table 14–10   National Coal Board statistics

The manpower figures given would enable employee turnover to be calculated. Their average age *is* provided.

Stock turnover could also be calculated from the absolute figures provided.

Overall this is an interesting range of indicators but the cost and earnings figures would be improved by a comparison with the RPI.

## 14.2.10 British Telecom

BT, in its 1983–84 report, provides separate measures of the quality of the telephone service for inland and international calls as shown in Table 14–11.

Local automatic telephone service
    Calls that fail due to British Telecom    %
    Calls that fail due to the customer    %
    Calls which obtain 'engaged' or 'no reply'    %
    Calls connected successfully    %

Trunk automatic telephone service
    Calls that fail due to British Telecom    %
    Calls that fail due to the customer    %
    Calls which obtain 'engaged' or 'no reply'    %
    Calls connected successfully    %

Repair service
    Yearly fault reports per telephone    %
    Fault reports cleared by end of the next working day    %

International automatic telephone service (IDD)
    Calls that fail in the international automatic exchange    %
    Calls that fail due to other causes    %
    Calls connected successfully    %

International telephone operator service
    Calls answered within 15 seconds    %

Table 14–11   Quality of telephone service

In reports for early years productivity was measured by telephones per employee, average telephone bills (both residential and business) were compared with those in nine other countries, and two indexes of prices charged (unadjusted and adjusted for inflation) were provided.

It is regrettable that these comparisons have not been provided in 1983–84. However the time taken to execute customers orders is mentioned.

### 14.2.11 The Post Office

The Post Office, in its 1983/84 report, measured its performance for the last six years (under the heading 'Performance Indicators') by:

*Quality of service*

1 % 1st class letters delivered on day after posting.
2 % 2nd class letters delivered by third day after posting.

*Productivity*

3 Volume of mails traffic index.
4 Mails operating hours.
5 A mails man hour productivity index (item 3 divided by item 4).

*Other*

6 Postman turnover.

*Price*
Elsewhere (under 10 year operational summary) it also produces a tariff index, adjusted for inflation.

*International comparisons*
In the text of the report there are comparisons with several other European countries and the USA of:

(*a*) the number of Post Offices per 20,000 of population;
(*b*) the cost of an inland letter.

Overall the Post Office presents a good range of non-financial performance indicators.

### 14.2.12 Her Majesty's Stationery Office

HMSO operates as a trading fund, i.e. it has to cover its costs from its revenue and achieve a target return on assets set by the Treasury. Its annual accounts include several pages devoted to performance indicators. These include:

1 *Price comparisons* between HMSO and suppliers in the private and public sectors both for materials purchased and items sold expressed as index numbers over a span of years.
2 *Customer service* measured by percentage of orders filled within various specified ranges of numbers of weeks. These were compared with similar figures published by *The Bookseller* for private sector publishers when available.
3 *Productivity* measured by number of items (and tonnes) issued per warehouse employee per year.
4 *Quality control* measured by two percentages: (a) of deliveries received by HMSO, and (b) deliveries made by HMSO to customers, which are found to be faulty.

Apart from these performance indicators which are published, there are a number of other measures, mainly financial ratios, which are used for internal management purposes. These include:

(*a*) Profit as a multiple of long-term interest.
(*b*) CCA return on capital employed.
(*c*) Long-term debt as a proportion of capital employed.
(*d*) Resource costs to turnover.
(*e*) Debtor weeks.
(*f*) Asset turnover rates.
(*g*) Sales per employee.

### 14.2.13 Water Authorities

The National Water Council produces an annual report which contains several performance ratios for each water authority in England and Wales. The report for 1982/83 contains the ratios listed in Table 14–12 for each of the last five years, together with three price indices (the Retail Prices Index, Index of Average Earnings, Capital Expenditure) it helps evaluate movement in the water industry's costs over the five-year period. The Council says 'caution should be exercised in interpreting the ratios shown since they largely reflect differences in the physical environment within which individual water authorities carry out their statutory responsibilities. It should also be noted that the data used in the calculation of the ratios has in some cases been estimated.'

B. Carsberg and S. Lumby in *The Evaluation of Financial Performance in the Water Industry – the role of current cost accounting*, CIPFA, 1983, commend the introduction of these performance indicators but suggest that:

1 costs ratios should be reported in real terms (i.e. after adjustment for changes in, e.g. the RPI);

2 the various items making up the figure for 'equivalent population' need to be monitored separately;

3 depreciation, because it is a major fixed cost, should be shown separately from other operating costs;

4 the ultimate indicator might be 'charges to consumers per head of population' in real terms but that this is not currently included in the ratios published.

*Water supply*
1 Operational expenditure per head of equivalent population
Percentage of water put into supply
2 Ground sources
3 Surface sources
Water supplied
4 Metered potable
5 Metered non-potable
6 Unmetered
7 Population on supply as a percentage of resident population

*Sewerage*
8 Operational expenditure per head of equivalent population connected to sewer
9 Percentage of resident population connected to the sewer

*Sewage treatment and disposal*
10 Operational expenditure per head of equivalent population
11 Pollution load removed per head of equivalent population
12 Average size of treatment works equivalent population – No. of works

Classified river length
13 Total length of classified rivers
14 Length of Class III and Class IV rivers

*Environmental services*
15 Revenue expenditure per head of equivalent population

*General*
Manpower numbers per 1000 head of equivalent population
16 Water
17 Sewerage
18 Sewage treatment and disposal
19 Land drainage

Capital expenditure per head of equivalent population
20 Water supply
21 Sewerage
22 Sewage treatment and disposal
23 Land drainage

*Notes:*

*Equivalent population*
The total equivalent population for each service comprises the estimated total resident population who receive the service, plus an allowance for holiday visitors and, where appropriate, an equivalent population for the service provided to industry and commerce.

*River classification*
The classification of rivers, including canals, follows that set out in the Council's report *River Water Quality – the next stage – Review of discharge consent conditions,* published in April 1978. Class III rivers are those which are polluted to such an extent that fish are absent or only sporadically present. Such rivers may be used for low grade industrial abstraction purposes. Class IV rivers are those which are grossly polluted and which are likely to cause nuisance.

Table 14–12  Water Authorities' performance ratios

## 14.3 Local Authorities

### 14.3.1 Introduction

In the UK there is a range of different types of local authority (e.g. metropolitan counties, London boroughs, etc.) and they have different responsibilities. Between them their main responsibilities are:

Education
Environmental health
Housing
Leisure
Planning
Police and Fire
Social services
Transport

As a consequence of the Local Government, Planning and Land Act of 1980, local authorites are being encouraged to produce an Annual Report with the aims:

1  to give ratepayers clear information about local government's activities;
2  to make it easier for electors, ratepayers and other interested parties to make comparisons of and judgements on the performance of their authorities;
3  to help councillors form judgements about the performance of their own authority.

The Department of the Environment (DoE) has issued a code of practice on the content of these Annual Reports (*Local Authority Annual Reports,* DoE, HMSO, 1981).

One important feature of the Code is its recommendation that certain key statistics and indicators should be compiled and published on a standard basis so as to enable meaningful comparisons to be made both between authorities and over a period of years. Such comparisons must be drawn with care paying due regard to the many factors that may affect any one statistic for a particular authority. Nevertheless comparisons of such indicators may often provide a useful starting point for analysis of relative performance.

The code lists the performance statistics that it would be expected each report to contain, as a minimum (see Table 14–13).

This list was selected with a view to minimising the extra work for local authorities and it builds on work done in this area by CIPFA for many years (see below).

The Chartered Institute of Public Finance and Accountancy (CIPFA), 3 Robert Street, London, WC2 (01 930 3456) has reservations, which I share, about the use of ratios expressed per 1,000 population. Particular client groups may form varying proportions of each authority's total population or even include groups from outside the authority's area, e.g. London Transport does not cater solely for GLC residents, and it is the size of the client group rather than the total population which therefore forms a better denominator for cost ratios.

Differences in ratios may reflect

(*a*)  different levels of service, and/or
(*b*)  different levels of efficiency

and it is often difficult to measure the level of service and therefore separate (*a*) from (*b*).

CIPFA warns users of the many other causes underlying the variations between authorities. These may include:

1  different social or economic characteristics, e.g. the proportion of population in a certain age group;
2  different divisions of functions, e.g. planning, which is undertaken to varying extent by each tier of local government;
3  different range of functions adopted, e.g. a municipal airport or bus undertaking;
4  different use of in-house resources, e.g. the existence of direct labour organisations affects manpower statistics;
5  different methods of financing capital investment, e.g. leasing, purchasing outright or financing from loan;
6  different prices faced by authorities, e.g. regional variations in the cost of provisions;
7  different methods of calculating and allocating overheads, e.g. central administration;
8  different committee or administrative structures;
9  different classification of certain activities, e.g. street cleansing;
10  different price base of financial estimates.

At the present state of the art it is not usually possible to eliminate the differences arising from these factors on the basis of one or two indicators only.

Figures for most of the ratios set out in the DoE list for all local authorities are summarised in *Local Government Comparative Statistics,* CIPFA, annually.

The local authorities' annual report and the CIPFA publications described below will form an invaluable source of information to ratepayers, elected representatives, consumers of the authorities services and local government employees.

### 14.3.2 CIPFA's Statistical Information Service

CIPFA has for many years provided an impressive range of comparative statistics on budgeted and actual expenditure, on all the major services provided by each local authority in England and Wales. The cost of these SIS booklets (there are over 30 of them) ranges from £9 to £17 each.

They provide all those concerned with local authority expenditure with an invaluable series of source documents to enable them to compare not only expenditure but, in some case, 'output' (e.g. number of pupils, or tonnes of rubbish collected), and some of the factors causing differences in expenditure. The layout of the tables on an authority-by-authority basis enables each authority to compare its performance with other authorities it deems similar.

CIPFA, in conjunction with the Society of Local Authority Chief Executives (SOLACE) and The Local Authorities Management Services and Computer Committee (LAMSACC), also publishes a looseleaf *Local Government Value for Money Handbook,* 2nd edition, 1984, price £35, which contains the results of over 35 value for

**PRIMARY EDUCATION**
pupil/teacher ratio
(gross) cost per pupil

**SECONDARY EDUCATION**
pupil/teacher ratio
(gross) cost per pupil

**FURTHER EDUCATION** (non advanced)
net cost per 1000 population

**SCHOOL MEALS**
revenue/cost ratio
pupils receiving free meals as a proportion of the school roll

**PERSONAL SOCIAL SERVICES**
CHILDREN IN CARE: children in care as proportion of the population under 18
(gross) cost per child in care

**CARE OF THE ELDERLY**
supported residents aged 75+ in residential homes as a proportion of the population aged 75+
(gross) cost per resident week in local authority homes for the elderly

**FIELDWORK**
social work staff per 1000 population

**HOME HELPS**
contact hours per 1000 population aged 65+

**PERSONAL SOCIAL SERVICES (TOTAL)**
net cost per 1000 population

**POLICE**
population per police officer (or force per 1000 population)
*serious offences per 1000 population

**FIRE SERVICE**
(net) cost per 1000 population
proportion of area in high fire risk categories

**PUBLIC PASSENGER TRANSPORT**
revenue support per 1000 population

passenger journeys per week per 1000 population (county council only)

**HIGHWAYS**
maintenance cost per kilometre: principal roads
maintenance cost per kilometre: non-principal roads

**HOUSING – HRA**
gross rents as a proportion of total costs
management and maintenance: cost per dwelling per week (excluding special management)
rent arrears as a percentage of rent collectable for the year

**HOUSING CONSTRUCTION**
construction cost per dwelling completed

**LIBRARIES**
(net) cost per 1000 population

**TOWN & COUNTRY PLANNING**
(net) cost per 1000 population

**RECREATION**
(net) cost per 1000 population

**REFUSE COLLECTION**
(net) cost per 1000 population

**REFUSE DISPOSAL**
(net) cost per 1000 population

**SPECIFIED TRADING SERVICES**
*revenue/gross cost ratio

**GENERAL ADMINISTRATION**
*change in numbers of support staff over previous year

---

* authorities should only publish comparisons with other authorities or with averages where they consider it relevant to do so.

---

Table 14–13   List of indicators specified in the Code of Practice

money studies carried out by local authorities, together with details of work in this area by the District auditor.

Some idea of what is contained in the SIS booklets is given in the following sections. In general the tables concentrate on providing absolute figures, but a certain number of ratios measuring 'performance' in the selected areas are also provided.

Users of the booklets may, however, use the figures provided to calculate ratios of their own choice as well, in an endeavour to start an analysis of how well an authority is doing and where and how it may make improvements. It will of course be important to bear in mind the cautionary notes sounded earlier in this chapter.

## 14.3.3 Local Government Comparative Statistics

This is the summary volume in the series and contains individual figures and averages for all relevant local authorities for over 60 ratios measuring their 'performance' together with a few key absolute figures. Because they are of such interest they are listed here. Most figures are given for both last year's actuals and this year's estimates. A few (indicated by numbers higher than 63) are given only for this year's estimates, and a few (marked with an asterisk) are not given for this year's estimates.

| GENERAL STATISTICS | | |
|---|---|---|
| 1 | Population | '000 |
| *2 | Area | ha |
| *3 | Net cost of all services | £'000 |
| 4 | Net cost of all services per capita | £ |
| *5 | Full time manpower per 1,000 population | |
| *6 | Part time manpower per 1,000 population | |
| 65 | Local rate/precept | p |
| 66 | Total rate | p |

### EDUCATION

*Primary and Nursery*

| | | |
|---|---|---|
| *7 | Percent of 3 and 4 years olds in nursery education | % |
| 8 | Pupil teacher ratio | |
| 9 | Gross cost per pupil | £ |
| 10 | Teaching staff cost per pupil | £ |
| 11 | Other staff cost per pupil | £ |
| 72 | Net cost per head of total population | £ |

*Secondary*

| | | |
|---|---|---|
| 12 | Pupil teacher ratio | |
| 13 | Gross cost per pupil | £ |
| 14 | Teaching staff cost per pupil | £ |
| 15 | Other staff cost per pupil | £ |
| 77 | Net cost per head of total population | £ |

*Miscellaneous*

| | | |
|---|---|---|
| 16 | Further Educn. (non adv.) cost per capita | £ |
| 17 | School meals revenue cost ratio | % |
| 18 | Free meals as a percent of school roll | % |
| 19 | All Education net cost per capita | £ |

### ENVIRONMENTAL HEALTH

| | | |
|---|---|---|
| 20 | Net cost per capita | £ |

### FIRE

| | | |
|---|---|---|
| *21 | Percent of area in 'high risk' category | % |
| 22 | Full time uniformed officers per 1000 population | |
| 23 | Part time uniformed officers per 1000 population | |
| 24 | Control room staff per 1000 population | |
| 25 | Net cost per capita | £ |

### HIGHWAYS AND TRANSPORTATION

*Maintenance cost per kilometre*

| | | |
|---|---|---|
| 26 | Principal roads | £ |
| 27 | Non-principal roads | £ |
| 28 | Net cost of revenue expenditure per capita | £ |

### HOUSING

| | | |
|---|---|---|
| 29 | Management and maintenance cost per dwelling week | £ |
| *30 | Number of dwellings per manager | |
| *31 | Arrears as a percent of rent collectable | % |
| 32 | Gross rents as a percent of total costs | % |
| 33 | Subsidy as a percent of total costs | % |
| 34 | Mandatory RFC as a percent of total costs | % |
| 35 | Discretionary RFC as a percent of total costs | % |
| *36 | Construction cost per dwelling completed | £ |

### LIBRARIES

| | | |
|---|---|---|
| 37 | Staff per 1000 population | |
| 38 | Net cost per capita | £ |

### POLICE

| | | |
|---|---|---|
| *39 | Serious offences per 1000 population | |
| 40 | Officers per 1000 population | |
| 41 | Civilians per 1000 population | |
| 42 | Net cost per capita | £ |

### PUBLIC PASSENGER TRANSPORT

| | | |
|---|---|---|
| 43 | Revenue support per capita | £ |
| 44 | Concessionary fares per capita | £ |

### RECREATION

| | | |
|---|---|---|
| 45 | Revenue cost ratio – sports halls | % |
| 46 | Net cost per capita | £ |
| 103 | Recreation staff per 1000 population – sports halls etc. | |

Table 14–14  Local Government Comparative Statistics

REFUSE COLLECTION
*47  Staff per 1000 population
48   Net cost per capita                                                 £

REFUSE DISPOSAL
49   Staff per 1000 population
50   Net cost per capita                                                 £

SOCIAL SERVICES
51   Children in care as a percent of those under 18                     %
52   Gross cost per child in care                                        £
*53  Supported residents aged 75+ in residential homes as a percent
     of those over 75+                                                   %
54   Cost per resident week in homes for the elderly                     £
55   Home helps contact hrs per 1000 population 65+
56   Fieldwork staff per 1000 population
57   Administrative staff per 1000 population
58   Total net cost (ex. concessionary fares) per capita                 £

TOWN AND COUNTRY PLANNING
59   Cost (ex. development) per capita                                   £
60   Net cost all planning per capita                                    £
116  Staff (ex development) per 1000 population
118  All staff per 1000 population

TRADING SERVICES
*61  Revenue cost ratio civic halls                                      %
*62  Revenue cost ratio trading and industrial estates                   %
*63  Revenue cost ratio all services                                     %

Table 14–14 concluded

In addition to the summary volume there are volumes dealing with selected areas of local authority responsibility in greater depth. They are as in Table 14–15. Some are published in two parts: one based on estimates; the second on actuals. A few of these will now be described in greater detail.

GENERAL
Local Government Comparative Statistics
Local Government Trends
Finance and General Statistics – Estimates
Capital Expenditure and Debt Financing – Actuals
Rate Collection – Actuals
Direct Labour Organisations – Actuals

EDUCATION
Education – Estimates
Education – Actuals

ENVIRONMENTAL HEALTH
Waste Disposal – Estimates
Waste Disposal – Actuals
Waste Collection – Actuals
Cemeteries and Crematoria – Actuals

HOUSING
Housing Revenue Account Statistics – Estimates
Housing Revenue Account Statistics – Actuals
Housing Rents
Housing Management and Maintenance Statistics – Actuals
Homelessness Statistics – Actuals

LEISURE
Leisure and Recreation – Estimates
Leisure Charges – Sample Survey
Public Libraries – Actuals
Public Libraries – Estimates

PLANNING
Planning and Development – Estimates
Planning and Development – Actuals

PUBLIC PROTECTION
Administration of Justice – Estimates
Fire – Estimates
Police – Estimates
Probation – Estimates
Fire – Actuals
Police – Actuals
Probation – Actuals

SOCIAL SERVICES
Personal Social Services – Estimates
Personal Social Services – Actuals

TRANSPORT
Airports – Estimates
Airports – Actuals
Highways and Transportation – Estimates
Highways and Transportation – Actuals

WATER
Water service charges statistics

Table 14–15  CIPFA Statistical Information Service (SIS) Publications

### 14.3.4 Education

A wealth of information is to be found in *Education Statistics,* CIPFA. Figures are provided for every Local Education Authority in England and Wales. The main absolute figures are for population, area, number of schools (classified by primary, middle, secondary, and by number of pupils), number of further education establishments, number of pupils, number of teachers and the costs of different categories of school analysed by category of expenditure.

Relatively little space is given to ratios, as opposed to absolute figures, but the latter provide the opportunity for calculating more ratios if desired. The ratios which are calculated are: pupil/teacher ratios and 'unit cost statistics', i.e. costs per pupil analysed by authority, type of school, and category of expenditure.

These ratios should enable those concerned (local authority officers, elected representatives, school governors, teachers, parents and ratepayers) to get some idea of relative efficiency between similar authorities. Differences between the ratios may of course indicate differences in levels of service as well as differences in efficiency.

I have extracted a few (Table 14–16) to whet readers' appetites, but would urge those interested to consult the CIPFA book (annual) itself.

|  | London | Met. Districts | Non-met. Districts | Average | High | Low |
|---|---|---|---|---|---|---|
| Teaching staff | 567 | 483 | 465 | 481 | 700 | 425 |
| Educational support staff | 46 | 33 | 19 | 26 | 108 | 3 |
| Premises related staff | 72 | 44 | 39 | 44 | 107 | 27 |
| Administrative and clerical staff | 20 | 10 | 11 | 12 | 29 | 2 |
| Premises | 130 | 98 | 93 | 99 | 178 | 65 |
| Books, etc. | 29 | 20 | 21 | 22 | 39 | 9 |
| Other | 6 | 2 | 2 | 2 | 14 | 1 |
| *Pupil/teacher ratios* |  |  |  |  |  |  |
| Qualified staff only | 19.7 | 21.3 | 22.5 | 21.8 | 25.7 | 17.2 |

Table 14–16   Primary schools – costs per pupil (£/head/year) (1983/84 estimates)

The costs relate only to what one might call the intermediate output – the number of pupils. They do not relate to the final output – the extent and depth of the education received by the pupil. It is difficult, if not impossible, to measure 'education' but it is possible to measure examination results as one part of education. As a result of the

1980 Education Act schools are now required to make information available about their exam results. These annual reports are a very valuable source – particularly if several years are studied.

Some research based on these reports has been published and, no doubt, more will come. See, for example, *Standards in English Schools,* J. Marks, C. Cox, M. Pomian – Srzednicki, National Council for Educational Standards, 1983; *School standards and spending: statistical analysis,* Department of Education and Science, December 1983; and *Value for money in education,* R. Lord, CIPFA, 1984.

### 14.3.5 Housing

CIPFA provides much detailed information for this area of local authority responsibility in *Housing Revenue Account Statistics* (Table 14–17).

|  | 1982/83 Est | |
|---|---|---|
|  | £'000 | % |
| *Expenditure* |  |  |
| Loan charges |  |  |
| interest | 2,921,517 | 54 |
| principal | 321,486 | 6 |
| Repairs and maintenance | 1,120,990 | 21 |
| Supervision and management | 779,387 | 15 |
| Other | 215,053 | 4 |
| Total | 5,378,433 | 100 |
| *Income* | £'000 | % |
| Net rent income | 2,965,036 | 55 |
| Government subsidies | 1,086,699 | 20 |
| Contributions from the local authority (including the administration of rebates) | 537,470 | 10 |
| Interest on Council House Sales | 455,264 | 9 |
| Other income | 302,992 | 6 |
|  | 5,347,461 | 100 |

Table 14–17   Housing Revenue Account Statistics

The difference between income and expenditure is transferred to or from the Housing Revenue working balances which are carried forward to the next year.

These figures and the number of dwellings are given for each housing authority in England and Wales.

The ratios provided are the management and maintenance costs per dwelling per week, and the following items of income as a proportion of total costs: gross rents, government subsidy, mandatory rate fund contributions (RFC), and discretionary rate fund contributions.

Local authorities generally prefer to compare gross rents as these are determined by individual authorities, whereas net rents are largely determined by the entitlement of their tenants to rent rebates.

Table 14–18 will be of interest to rate and taxpayers and local authority tenants.

| Authority type | Loan charges | Repairs and main-tenance | Super-vision and manage-ment | Other costs | Total expend-iture |
|---|---|---|---|---|---|
| | £-p | £-p | £-p | £-p | £-p |
| London Boroughs | 21.09 | 5.78 | 6.03 | 1.06 | 33.96 |
| Met. Districts | 10.51 | 3.56 | 2.30 | 0.31 | 16.68 |
| Non-met. Districts | | | | | |
| England | 10.46 | 4.06 | 2.50 | 0.55 | 17.57 |
| Wales | 10.65 | 4.68 | 2.23 | 0.53 | 18.09 |
| All authorities | 12.33 | 4.26 | 3.04 | 0.57 | 20.20 |

| | Gross Rent Income | As % of HRA Expenditure |
|---|---|---|
| | £-p | % |
| London Boroughs | 14.87 | 47.6 |
| GLC | 16.41 | 37.8 |
| Met. Districts | 12.30 | 75.6 |
| Non-met. Districts | | |
| England | 13.31 | 77.8 |
| Wales | 13.80 | 78.0 |
| All authorities | 13.31 | 68.4 |

Table 14–18   HRA expenditure per dwelling per week during 1982–83

The first part of the table illustrates clearly the high cost of London housing. (A more detailed analysis of management and maintenance statistics can be found in the CIPFA SIS Publication of the same name.) It is also important to bear in mind the additional special reasons for the exceptionally high costs borne by the GLC. The GLC has transferred a substantial number of dwellings to other authorities but under the terms of the Transfer Order is liable to bear the 'notional deficits' incurred by those other authorities on their Housing Revenue Accounts in respect of those transferred dwellings. The 1982/83 estimates payment in respect of this notional deficit amounting to £64,850,000. For this reason the GLC's figures, which would be based upon a false premise, are omitted from the first part of the table.

### 14.3.6 Waste collection

The CIPFA publication *Waste collection statistics* gives absolute figures for population, area, buildings, employees, weight of waste collected, vehicles used, expenditure and income (both analysed) for each local authority, in England and Wales.

Details are also given on the extent of use of outside contractors, the method of collecting waste, and the type of waste collecting system. Ratios used to measure 'efficiency' and given in the tables are shown in Table 14–19.

| Class of Authority | Gross cost per tonne | Net cost per tonne | Net cost per domestic hereditament | Waste collection (kg per head of population) |
|---|---|---|---|---|
| | £ | £ | £ | |
| London | 30 | 28 | 24 | 336 |
| Metropolitan | 26 | 24 | 20 | 307 |
| Non-metropolitan | | | | |
| England | 22 | 20 | 19 | 313 |
| Wales | 16 | 16 | 18 | 437 |
| All | 24 | 22 | 22 | 322 |

Table 14–19   Costs of collection of waste 1979/80

Other ratios may be derived from the data (see Table 14–20).

In the commentary it is stated that

> The costs which are given are a starting point for making inter-authority comparisons. However, the wide variety of differing local conditions renders it, in practice, impossible to isolate any single indicator of performance of efficiency, and users should bear this in mind when using the data. Users should bear in mind also the problems associated with the estimation of quantities of

| Class of authority | Tonnes collected per vehicle | Tonnes collected per operative | Operatives per vehicle | Ratio of vehicles to vehicle maintenance staff | Ratio of operatives to technical and admin staff |
|---|---|---|---|---|---|
| London | 1305 | 430 | 3.0 | 6.1 | 14.7 |
| Metropolitan | 1362 | 405 | 3.4 | 5.9 | 14.7 |
| Non-Metropolitan | | | | | |
| England | 1545 | 501 | 3.1 | 6.4 | 16.4 |
| Wales | 1821 | 694 | 2.6 | 6.1 | 12.4 |
| All | 1473 | 472 | 3.1 | 6.2 | 15.4 |

Table 14–20   Waste collection 1981/82 actuals

waste collected and the differences in accounting practice as regards expenditure allocations, costing systems and methods of financing acquisition of assets.

and later on

Mention has been made already of the difficulty of making inter-authority comparisons of performance of efficiency. It is perhaps worth emphasising that no simple single statistic will in fact give this measure. This reflects the complexity of the waste collection service which, although it is fairly standard throughout the country, is subject to wide local variations. In particular the standard of the service varies considerably between different localities in terms of the frequency of collection and also the quality of the service varies in that domestic refuse may be collected by a variety of different methods. The cheapest method in terms of the collection point, will always be collection from the kerbside where the householder himself moves the refuse container from the backdoor to the kerbside. It may be felt in many local authorities that such methods are not acceptable to the majority of householders. Similarly the methods and organisation of containment of waste will affect costs. Most people will be abundantly aware of the change-over from metal dustbins to plastic sacks for refuse, and this of course is accompanied by a change in cost. Again we can say that the cheapest method of collection will be the use of a transferable bin method, but again this may be unacceptable to householders.

An article by Barry Lynch in the *CES Review* of April 1980 examined the use of unit cost measures for inter-authority comparisons of the waste collection service. A number of factors which could influence costs were identified, as follows: population density; the type of rateable property to be found in an authority; income; the frequency of service provided; regional labour cost; and the relationships between capital, labour and output. The article suggested that population density, for example, could affect average cost in two ways. If the same amount of waste could be collected in densely populated areas in less time because of the proximity of pick-up points, then costs would fall. But if higher density also entails greater traffic congestion, the costs would rise because the time between pick-ups would increase. Perhaps the most significant aspect of the research was that it highlighted the extreme difficulty of comparing efficiency between local authorities – even though waste collection is one of the best documented local authority services.

### 14.3.7 Personal social services

The CIPFA booklet for this area gives figures for almost all social service authorities in England for population, area, population analysed by age band, number of handicapped people (blind, deaf, and other handicaps), and gross expenditure analysed by type of service (e.g. fieldwork, residential care, support services, and administration).

For child care the percentages looked after in different ways (e.g. community homes, boarded out, etc.) are provided. For residential child care, percent occupancy and cost per child week are given.

Separate figures are provided for residential care for the elderly, physically and mentally handicapped, for percent occupancy, income and cost per resident week.

Other data and ratios include:

Day care – sheltered employment – cost per employee day
Home helps – cost per hour of service
Meals on wheels – cost and income per meal

### 14.3.8 Systematic analysis of local authority ratios

As will have been seen there is a wealth of ratios available for local authorities. It is desirable that they be examined in a systematic manner. I am grateful to Richard Williams of Haringey for the following suggested approach. This applies to a London Borough and would need modification for other local authorities.

The diagram (Diagram 14–5) starts from the rate in the £, and explains the main factors accounting for differences in the ratios between authorities. Part of the rate is

385

raised by the authority as agent for other bodies (the GLC and Metropolitan Police) and this is much the same for all London boroughs, the major variation being in the rate in the £ for the borough's own services. An authority can to some extent draw on its balances (i.e. accumulated surplus from earlier years) and add to balances, so the net expenditure, expressed as a rate in the £ may differ from the actual rate in the £ levied.

The net expenditure as a rate in the £ is affected by both the rateable value of the authority and the net expenditure. In order to provide a common basis for comparing different sized authorities (since population varies from under 200,000 to over 300,000) both these factors are expressed on a *per capita* basis. One of the important differences between authorities is in the composition of their rateable value. Other things being equal, the higher the proportion of 'other' (i.e. non-domestic) rateable value, the lower the rate they will need to levy to cover their costs.

A high proportion of the expenditure of authorities is met by grants etc., but the amount of grants and similar assistance varies widely. Because of lack of information the figures do not show the situation quite as it is – the lower figure of government grants for some boroughs is due to part of their grant being paid to the Inner London Education Authority. The object of the ILEA (which covers the Inner Boroughs) is to give a considerable subsidy to the poorer authorities, and this is shown as Inner London Equalisation. By comparison the official equalisation scheme which is supposed to redistribute between rich and poor authorities has much less effect, particularly in the case of the outer boroughs (of which Haringey is one!).

The remaining ratios show the analysis of government grants, and the expenditure on various types of services. Most of the government grant is in the form of the Rate Support Grant which is supposed to be determined by the circumstance of the individual authority. In practice most of it is based on population which explains why the amount *per capita* is very much the same for all authorities.

## 14.4 Central Government

### 14.4.1 Introduction

There are over 60 departments in the Civil Service. The main ones, in terms of numbers employed at 1 April 1984, are given in Table 14–21.

Another indication of the relative importance of central government departments is given by their estimated expenditure in 1984/85 (see Table 14–22).

|    |                                        | Numbers | %     |
|----|----------------------------------------|---------|-------|
| 1  | Defence                                | 181,183 | 29.0  |
| 2  | Health and Social Security             | 90,474  | 14.5  |
| 3  | Inland Revenue                         | 69,833  | 11.2  |
| 4  | Employment                             | 56,381  | 9.0   |
| 5  | Home Office                            | 36,446  | 5.8   |
| 6  | Environment, including Property Services Agency | 33,836  | 5.4   |
| 7  | Customs and Excise                     | 25,142  | 4.0   |
| 8  | Royal Ordnance Factories               | 17,961  | 2.9   |
| 9  | Transport                              | 14,151  | 2.3   |
| 10 | Scottish Departments                   | 12,754  | 2.0   |
| 11 | Trade and Industry                     | 12,582  | 2.0   |
| 12 | Agriculture, Fisheries and Food        | 11,476  | 1.8   |
| 13 | Foreign and Commonwealth               | 10,031  | 1.6   |
| 14 | Lord Chancellor's Department           | 10,026  | 1.6   |
| 15 | National Savings                       | 8,038   | 1.3   |
| 16 | Other                                  | 33,658  | 5.4   |
|    |                                        | 623,972 | 100.0 |

*Source: Civil Service Statistics, 1984*, HMSO, 1984, Table 1.

Table 14–21  Numbers of Civil Servants

### 14.4.2 The financial management initiative

A significant milestone in improving the efficiency of central government was the acceptance by the government of most of the recommendations of the Treasury and Civil Service Committee on 'Efficiency and Effectiveness in the Civil Service'.

In the White Paper announcing its acceptance (Cmnd 8616, September 1982) reference is made to the 'financial management initiative', the aim of which 'is to promote in each department an organisation and system in which managers at all levels have:

a.  a clear view of their objectives and means to assess and, wherever possible, measure outputs or performance in relation to those objectives;. . .'

It is expected that every department's plans will include the following points:

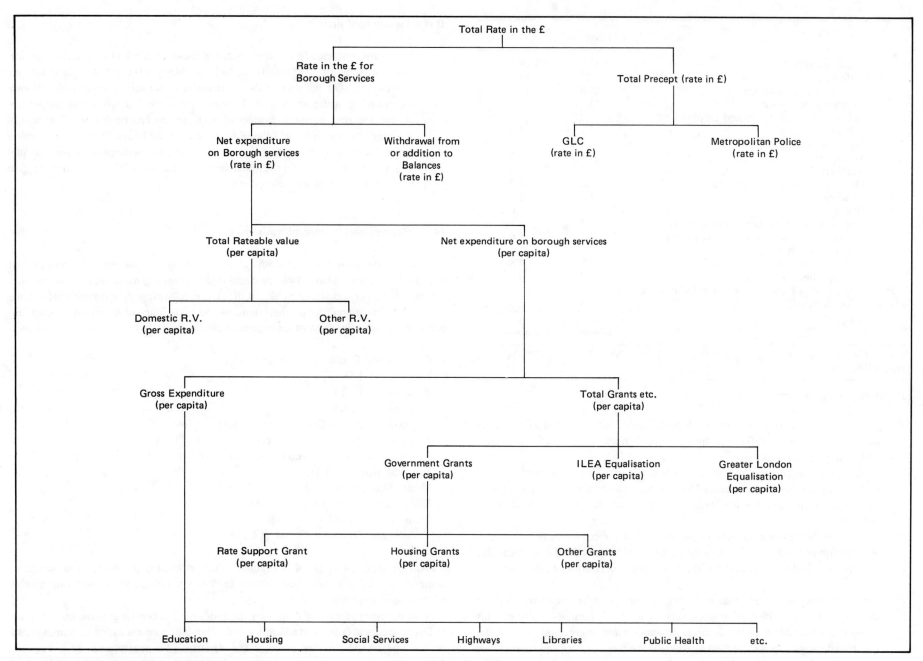

Diagram 14–5   Systematic analysis of local authority ratios

*387*

| | | £ billion cash | % |
|---|---|---|---|
| 1 | Social security | 37.9 | 29.6 |
| 2 | Defence | 17.2 | 13.4 |
| 3 | Health and personal social services | 15.8 | 12.3 |
| 4 | Education and science | 13.7 | 10.7 |
| 5 | Industry, energy, trade and employment | 7.2 | 5.6 |
| 6 | Scotland | 7.1 | 5.5 |
| 7 | Law, order and protective services | 5.1 | 4.0 |
| 8 | Transport | 4.8 | 3.7 |
| 9 | Northern Ireland | 4.1 | 3.2 |
| 10 | Other environmental services | 3.8 | 3.0 |
| 11 | Housing | 3.1 | 2.4 |
| 12 | Wales | 2.6 | 2.0 |
| 13 | Overseas aid and other overseas services | 2.5 | 2.0 |
| 14 | Agriculture, fisheries, food and forestry | 2.1 | 1.6 |
| 15 | Other public services | 1.9 | 1.5 |
| 16 | Common services | 1.0 | 0.8 |
| 17 | Arts and libraries | 0.7 | 0.5 |
| 18 | Special sale of assets and general allowance for short fall | −2.5 | −2.0 |
| | Total | 128.1 | 100.0 |

Source: *The Government's Expenditure Plans 1985-86 to 1987-88*, Cmnd 9428, HMSO, 1985, Table 1.6.

Table 14–22   Central government expenditure

(a) there will be an outline plan of development which will cover the whole of the department's activities. The assembly of each plan may proceed in stages, including pilot projects;

(b) there will be an information system that not only provides higher management with aggregated information needed for estimating and control, but managers at successive levels down the line with the information they need to do their job properly;

(c) the responsibilities of managers for the control of the resources they consume and, wherever feasible, the results they achieve will be specified systematically;

(d) the plan will include a system for the budgeting and control of administrative costs;

(e) where practicable, performance indicators and output measures will be developed which can be used to assess success in achievement of objectives. This is not less important than the accurate attribution and monitoring of costs; the question departments will address is 'where is the money going and what are we getting for it?'.

It is acknowledged that:

There are obstacles to the application of these principles in the public service. The yardstick of profitability is lacking. Many government objectives are generalised, and the test of their success is often acceptability rather than a quantified measure of output. In some areas, final measures of output are elusive and only partial indicators of performance can be devised. The task of applying the principles will therefore take time, and complete success in every particular is not to be looked for. Nevertheless, the principles are fundamental to good management and the effective use of resources. They should be applied to the maximum practicable extent.

### 14.4.3 Ratios used in central government

By comparison with local government and nationalised industries it has proved difficult to ascertain what ratios are calculated in central government departments. I am therefore very grateful to the staff in the following department's who have provided me with material on their departments experience of measuring output and performance and their use of management ratios:

Customs and Excise (14.4.4)
Defence (14.4.5)
Education (14.4.6)
Employment (14.4.7)
Manpower Services Commission (14.4.8)
Transport-Driver & Vehicle Licensing Centre (14.4.9)
Export Credits Guarantee Department (14.4.10)
Social Security (14.4.11)
Health Service (14.4.12)
Home Office – The Police (14.4.13)
Inland Revenue (14.4.14)
Chessington Computer Centre (14.4.15)

As will be seen the stage of development varied from department to department. Some are considering how best to measure output. Others are considering how to relate output to inputs.

From the point of view of describing the ratios used in central government the work of Departments may be conveniently sub-divided into administrative or running costs on the one hand, and the costs of the department's programmes (e.g. regional development grants, or unemployment benefit paid, or the costs of providing and staffing hospitals) on the other. Running cost ratios appear to be more developed than programme cost ratios.

### 14.4.4 Customs and Excise

*The Annual Report of the Commissioners of Her Majesty's Customs & Excise* (HMSO, 1984, Cmnd 9391) shows that they measure the cost of administering each of the main taxes and duties (e.g. VAT, tobacco, etc.) as a percentage of the revenue collected. The ratios ranged in 1983/84 from 0.1 per cent for tobacco to 10.5 per cent for customs duties and associated work with an average of 1.2 per cent. Very little comment is made on the figures.

The FMI project team in HM Customs and Excise are currently (1985) tackling the problem of tailoring output and performance information to meet the different needs of different levels of management. The following is an example of their work in the area of VAT control.

Control visits take place on traders premises when a LVO official calls to see the trader, the trader's activities, and the business records and accounts to check from all available evidence that the tax has been properly accounted for.

Computers are used to assist the planning of visits by listing those traders due for a control visit. In drawing up these lists priorities are based mainly on revenue risk as identified by factors such as type of trade, the turnover, complexity and compliance of the individual traders business. Final decisions about visits to traders are, however, taken by LVO management.

Significant decision areas and related management concerns therefore include:

(a) organisation of control work: management is concerned that demand-led functions are accomplished with greater effectiveness and that time spent at the LVO and travelling is reduced so as to increase the resources devoted to revenue yielding work;

(b) selection of visits: management is concerned that traders are visited with proper regard for revenue risk, to improve cost effectiveness and to preserve preventive effects;

(c) performance on visits: management is concerned to maximise additional revenue gained from discovered misdeclarations, to improve the identification of risk factors, to minimise abortive visits, to increase expertise and motivation of staff and to preserve the acceptability of the tax.

(This list is not exhaustive.)

The primary output measures include:

(a) number of control visit sessions (i.e. 1/2 days);
(b) number of control visits;
(c) number of under and over declarations of tax identified;
(d) value of under and over declarations of tax discovered.

The primary inputs are:

(a) man-days on VAT control;
(b) man-days on VAT.

Effectiveness ratios can be constructed relating actual outputs to target outputs. For example:

$$\frac{\text{actual number of control visit sessions}}{\text{target number of control visit sessions}}$$

Other output ratios that are needed for measurement of achievement are the incidence of underdeclarations and the mean value of underdeclaration per session:

$$\frac{\text{number of under-declarations}}{\text{number of control visit sessions}}$$

$$\frac{\text{value of under-declarations}}{\text{number of control visit sessions}}$$

Economy ratios can be constructed by relating actual inputs to target inputs. For example:

$$\frac{\text{actual man-days on VAT control}}{\text{target man-days on VAT control}}$$

Indicators of efficiency can be constructed by relating outputs to inputs. For example:

$$\frac{\text{value of under-declarations}}{\text{man-days on VAT control}}$$

$$\frac{\text{value of under-declarations}}{\text{man-days on all VAT work}}$$

All these items of information and ratios are needed by managers at all levels (aggregated where appropriate) and will be included in a core system of management information.

There are some types of information (collected on an on-going basis or by sampling exercises), that would be suitable for inclusion only at a local level. Examples include the number of abortive visits per man-day and the number and duration of telephone enquiries at an LVO. This information is important at the local level of management but is not needed centrally except to answer an ad hoc query. In this case a sample of local data would probably be sufficient.

The examples given illustrate that any one decision area needs a number of measures of achievement to adequately describe performance. Conversely any one measure of achievement can contribute to more than one decision area.

### 14.4.5 Defence

*Defence expenditure and weapon procurement.* There is a fundamental difficulty in measuring the final output of defence expenditure. The 'product' of deterrence cannot be measured objectively. Intermediate or surrogate outputs have to be employed, and applied as appropriate.

Intermediate outputs tend to be measures of inputs and are therefore of limited use.

Some intermediate measures of output can be derived from operational analysis (OA) studies. These consider the effectiveness of alternative weapon systems and of alternative force mixes under a number of agreed scenarios.

*Support services.* This large area encompasses the wide range of activities that maintain the operational capabilities of the front line. They range from the acquisition, storage, issue, transport, maintenance and repair of material and equipment to the recruitment, training, accommodation, welfare and medical treatment of service personnel. The work of the research and development establishments also falls into the category.

Due to the diverse nature of these activities and the different requirements, and hence approaches, of the three armed services there is a wide variation in the availability and use made of output and performance measures (OPM). Appendix 14–1 gives examples of the sort of OPM available or being developed in a cross-section of MOD support services.

Volume 2 of the *Statement on the Defence Estimates* (Cmnd 9227 – II) gives a good idea of the sort of information available on activities in the support area, although it is usually available to line managers on a more extensive basis and in a less aggregated form than it appears there.

In, for example, the RAF Medical Service statistics are collected and made available to management on sickness absence, diagnosis and diagnostic groups, sickness in occupational groups, injuries, medical discharges and deaths of service personnel, and on RAF hospitals. Some of these are used as indicators of the output of the Medical Service; for example, the sickness rate is an (inverse) indicator of its contribution to maximising the effectiveness of the total RAF and WRAF population. Trends in sickness absence broken down by diagnoses are used by management to identify issues worthy of further investigation. In recent years such exercises have led to initiatives being taken to reduce the incidence of sickness absence arising from injuries sustained in certain types of activity. In the case of RAF hospitals, statistics on patient throughput (an indicator of their output), length of stay (by category and speciality) and bed occupancy rate are collected and themselves provide performance indicators; they are also related to costing information from the management accounts to provide efficiency indicators such as cost per in-patient day/out-patient attendance.

### 14.4.6 Education

*Higher education.* Quantitative measures are being used by the Department of Education and Science (DES) and by the National Advisory Body for Public Sector Higher Education (NAB) in planning the provision for higher education in England.

Measures which could be used to reflect the output of higher education include

(*a*)   numbers of students and of successful graduates;
(*b*)   social rates of return to a first degree;
(*c*)   percentage of graduates obtaining a 'good' degree;
(*d*)   percentage of students failing or dropping out of their course;
(*e*)   unemployment rates and first destinations of graduates by degree subject area;
(*f*)   average starting salary of university graduates by main subject area.

In developing a national strategy, including e.g. advice on priorities for course development and on criteria for distribution of the 'pool' of expenditure, so as to encourage efficiency, it is necessary to consider such factors as:

(*a*)   national and regional balance:
    (i)     mode of attendance (full-time/sandwich/part-time/evening)
    (ii)    level of study
    (iii)   programme (subject grouping) of study
    (iv)    regional distribution of courses and students
    (v)     ease of access to suitable courses
    (vi)    need of industry and commerce for particular types of training
    (vii)   demand for places;

(*b*) organisation of faculty groups and programmes:
    (i)    student-staff ratios (SSRs) and component performance indicators (i.e. average class size, lecturer contact hours and student taught hours)
    (ii)   concentration of expertise in particular subjects in particular colleges
    (iii)  interdependence of provision in different subject areas and at different levels
    (iv)  number and quality of support staff and services;
(*c*) unit costs of different subject areas, institutions and modes of attendance.

These criteria are being used to set up targets for restructuring the provision of higher education by local authorities. For instance, the NAB has been identifying SSRs for each group of subjects which are in line with the most economical current best practice; and is considering the implications in terms of fewer teachers or more students of moving towards them. Beyond a certain point improvements in the efficiency of colleges through increasing student numbers for the same total cost could have an unacceptable impact on academic standards.

Measures such as current and projected age-participation rates, qualified participation rates and mature entry rates are used by the DES, together with demographic projections taking account of the variation in births by social class, to produce long term projections of the total future demand for higher education. Their planning can then be based on these demand projections and a forecast of the availability of places consistent with expenditure prospects.

Such data on student numbers, together with output data on degree quality, wastage rates, subsequent employment etc., are aspects of the value added and social rates of return on higher education. One view is that if they could be determined accurately they could be combined to provide a useful summary measure of value for money. However, in an area as complex as this is a single combined measure could never completely displace disaggregated measures for planning purposes.

The most recent development in this field will be found in Annex B to *The development of higher education into the 1990s,* DES, HMSO, 1985, Cmnd 9524. As well as a discussion of the issues, this contains figures for the following ratios:

1    recurrent costs per student in real terms;
2    cost per student and per graduate (analysed by subject);
3    recurrent costs per student in polytechnics (analysed by subject);
4    drop-out rates (analysed by subject and year of course);
5    labour market success rate (analysed by subject) – measured by percentage unemployed at the December after graduation;
6    social rate of return (per cent) (higher earnings attributable to education as a percentage of cost of education).

See also sub-section 14.3.4 on education.

## 14.4.7 Employment (see also 14.4.8)

The Department of Employment has published two reports *Financial Management Initiative: Implementation in the DoE* covering 1983 and 1984, which are very clearly laid out. For each division and branch it shows, inter alia, objectives, organisation, manpower and what output and performance indicators are used, if any. Not all of these are ratios, but of those that are in the 1984 report the following are of interest.

*Unemployment benefit service*
    Cost per payment
    Ratio of live register to staff

The Command is also developing indicators of quality of service.

*Employment measures*
    Net Exchequer cost per person off the count
    Backlog (moving average)
    Throughput per clerical unit
    Unit cost of clerical staff processing an application or claim
    Staff in post compared with the complement calculated on the basis of throughput
    Costs and savings arising from visits to employers
    Rejection or return rate of applications and claims

*Redundancy and maternity payments*
    Cost of administration as percentage of payment from Redundancy/Maternity Pay Fund

*The Survey Unit/Forms Design Unit* (part of Personnel and Management Services Division concerned with examining organisational structure, functions, procedures and posts, to see that work is performed economically and efficiently and that staff number and grading are correctly related to the needs of the work).

    Rate at which survey recommendations are implemented.
    Ratios of savings to survey costs.
    Number of forms designed per member of staff.

*Common services (Personnel and Management Services Division)*
    Output per staff unit. Output is measured by Treasury Typing Units or number of copies (photocopying) or files opened or files scrutinised.
    Per cent change in output per staff unit over previous year

*Central Pay Office (Finance Division)*

Staff paid per central pay office staff unit

Error rate in payments

## 14.4.8 Manpower Services Commission

The Manpower Services Commission (MSC) published the main information which MSC divisions supplied for their 1984 Corporate Management Information System (COMIS) reviews. From this impressive 200-page booklet it will be seen that for many of the MSC programs two key management ratios are used:

Real cost per unit output

Output per unit staff

Output is measured by such things as: vacancies notified; placings; trainees; TOPS applications forwarded; number of employers contacted; number of individuals helped; monitoring visits; etc.

In addition for some activities Administrative cost/Total cost (per cent) is measured. The percentage of costs recovered is measured for Professional and Executive Recruitment.

All the figures are supported by brief verbal commentaries.

## 14.4.9 Transport

The Driver and Vehicle Licensing Centre measures its performance primarily in terms of turn-round time. Current targets are that 90 per cent of transactions handled at Swansea should be cleared within 10 days.

The DVLC management information control system unit (MICSU) forecasts monthly receipts of each major category of work. It takes into account annual trends, seasonal factors and the estimated effects of changes in legislation and procedures. Actual receipts are monitored regularly against these forecasts which are modified accordingly. Operational areas are complemented by applying a staffing formula to projected workloads. Temporary staff are employed to deal with projected variations in workload which cannot be covered by redeployment.

MICSU prepares monthly reports and graphs for senior management which bring together data on receipts, staff availability and throughput. Productivity is calculated as the ratio of the staff hours theoretically required for the observed throughput using work measurement timings to the actual number of man-hours available. Backlogs are expressed in terms of the number of days' work required to clear the queue. The reports highlights reasons for significant deviations from planned performance in any particular area of work. Unexpected variations are investigated.

The number of transactions rejected because of errors by applicants or in DVLC can have a significant effect on workload. Separate figures are given in the reports for percentage error rates by type of application and the stage at which it failed. Where the error is discovered by the computer, details of the transaction are held until the error is resolved. Some may be due to clerical errors in coding or keying forms. Data on the percentages of rejections cleared within certain numbers of days are included in the monthly reports.

The enquiry units for the driver and vehicles systems prepare monthly reports showing the number of postal and telephone enquiries received and their nature together with the numbers cleared and in hand. In addition the number of occasions on which callers ring off whilst waiting to be connected are logged by the automatic exchange. Analyses are regularly prepared of numbers of enquiries received in each month against the assessed turn-round. There is a marked increase in enquiries and complaints when performance falls. These analyses are used to assess the public acceptability of different standards of service.

DVLC is also responsible for enforcement of vehicle licensing. At present targets are based on a yield/cost ratio of better than 2.6:1, i.e. revenue generated from mitigated penalties and arrears of duty recovered compared with the cost of enforcement; and planned increases in the number of successfully completed cases each year.

## 14.4.10 Export Credits Guarantee Department

The ECGD uses six management ratios, which are published yearly in its Accounts, as follows

1 $$\frac{\text{Cumulative reserves and trading surpluses}}{\text{Amounts at risk}}$$

2 $$\frac{\text{Cumulative reserves and trading surpluses}}{\text{Amounts at risk in C \& D markets}}$$

$$3 \qquad \frac{\text{Cumulative reserves and trading surpluses}}{\text{Recoverable political claims}}$$

$$4 \qquad \frac{\text{Business declared at constant prices}}{\text{Staff numbers}}$$

$$5 \qquad \frac{\text{Administration expenses}}{\text{Business declared}}$$

$$6 \qquad \frac{\text{Administration expenses}}{\text{Premium income} + \text{claims paid} + \text{claims recovered}}$$

In addition, for the Short Term Underwriting Branch, with a high throughput of relatively homogeneous cases, the ratios are based on caseload and reflect the aim of a speedy and accurate service. They are:

(a) applications processed per £1,000 costs;
(b) percentage of cases completed within 5, 10 and 15 working days;
(c) percentage error rates (per cent cases completed containing 'serious' errors of fact, i.e. errors with financial consequences).

## 14.4.11 Social Security

In DHSS higher management uses a series of performance indicators to monitor and assess the 500 social security local offices in the more significant aspects of their work.

Two performance indicators are in use. The first shows the amount of work cleared as a percentage of the amount of work (i.e. number of cases) available (i.e. received but not yet completely processed) in a period. It is applied to 12 key areas of work. The same information may be expressed as the number of days' clearance time.

The other type of PI measures accuracy, describing the proportion of payments that was found to be incorrect. It is applied to contributory and supplementary benefit payments. The error rates are derived from managerial checks of a sample of payments made. Random selection techniques are used to ensure that results of the checks are statistically reliable.

Quality of work (i.e. written work, handling of callers, standard of interviewing etc.) does not form part of regular management information statistics. A quality of service package has, however, been developed in which these areas and others are tested in a sample of offices. The system is currently being improved by putting sampling on a firmer statistical basis.

In addition, the administrative costs of each of the main benefits is monitored as a percentage of the benefit expenditure and per benefit payment.

Further information on policy issues, and figures for the performance indicators quoted above, will be found in Chapter 3.12 of Volume II of the Public Expenditure White Paper for 1985 (*The Government Expenditure Plans 1985–86 to 1987–88*, Cmnd 9428-II).

## 14.4.12 Health Service

The Department of Health and Social Security has been working on performance indicators (PIs) for the NHS since 1981, in close collaboration with health authorities. A first package of performance indicators covering clinical activity, finance, manpower and estate management was published by the Department in September 1983.

The PIs were developed further (see *A report of the Joint Group on Performance Indicators to the Secretary of State for Social Services*, DHSS, January 1985) and a revised set was issued to the NHS in the Summer of 1985.

There are now some 450 PIs covering acute services, support services, manpower, estate management, services for the mentally handicapped, mentally ill, children, and elderly.

A very interesting feature of the package is that the ratios have been issued to run on a BBC microcomputer with the aim of making them more easily comprehensible and digestible with graphical presentations. The floppy disks are accompanied by a computer user's manual and a substantial loose-leaf user's guide, *Performance Indicators for the NHS: Guidance for Users*, on sale from the DHSS.

The ratios are intended for use primarily by managers at district level. Districts obviously vary in demographic characteristics and case mix. To allow for this some PIs are 'standardised' and there is a facility to compare with 'similar' districts. The performance indicators are ranked within the national perspective so that managers can compare their performance with that achieved by any other district.

For presentation the PIs have been structured into groups. The PIs contained in each grouping appear on the computer screen together. These groups form part of a hierarchy and are linked by a logical structure. This is shown in a diagram at the beginning of the section and provides a way in which the user can move through the PI information. To start, first line PIs are presented. These are the most important and/or most highly aggregated PIs, and are at the top of the hierarchy. The user then moves down into second and third line PIs which provide either more disaggregation or detail, or complementary information. An example of such a hierarchy is given in Diagram 14–6.

There follows a text which explains how the PIs in the group might be interpreted, and contains cross references to relevant PIs in other groups of the logical structure or

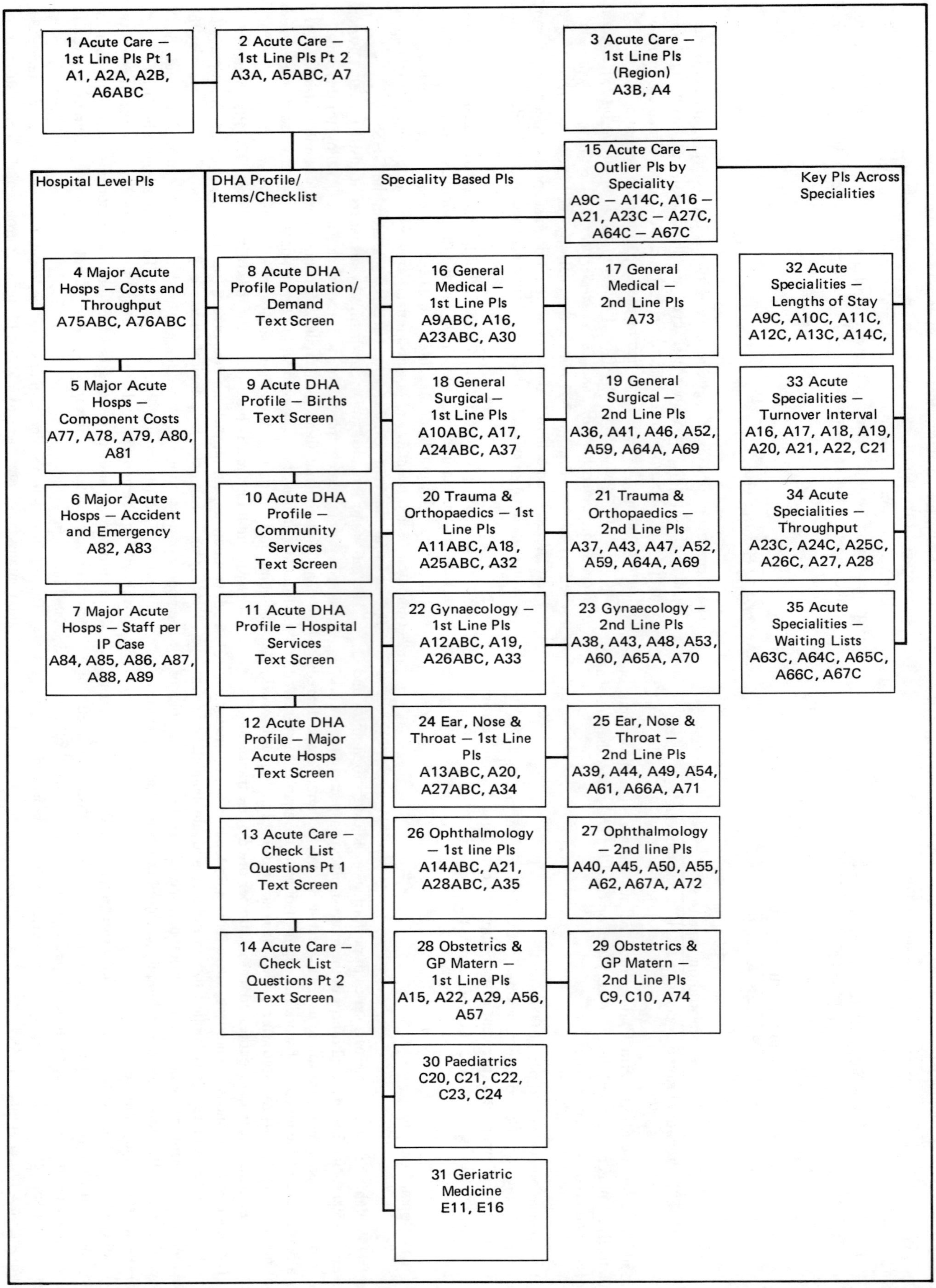

**Key PIs Across Specialities**

**32** Acute Specialities — Lengths of Stay A9C, A10C, A11C, A12C, A13C, A14C,

**33** Acute Specialities — Turnover Interval A16, A17, A18, A19, A20, A21, A22, C21

**34** Acute Specialities — Throughput A23C, A24C, A25C, A26C, A27C, A28

**35** Acute Specialities — Waiting Lists A63C, A64C, A65C, A66C, A67C

**3** Acute Care — 1st Line PIs (Region) A3B, A4

**2** Acute Care — 1st Line PIs Pt 2 A3A, A5ABC, A7

**1** Acute Care — 1st Line PIs Pt 1 A1, A2A, A2B, A6ABC

**15** Acute Care — Outlier PIs by Speciality A9C – A14C, A16 – A21, A23C – A27C, A64C – A67C

**Speciality Based PIs**

**17** General Medical — 2nd Line PIs A73

**19** General Surgical — 2nd Line PIs A36, A41, A46, A52, A59, A64A, A69

**21** Trauma & Orthopaedics — 2nd Line PIs A37, A43, A47, A52, A59, A64A, A69

**23** Gynaecology — 2nd Line PIs A38, A43, A48, A53, A60, A65A, A70

**25** Ear, Nose & Throat — 2nd Line PIs A39, A44, A49, A54, A61, A66A, A71

**27** Ophthalmology — 2nd line PIs A40, A45, A50, A55, A62, A67A, A72

**29** Obstetrics & GP Matern — 2nd Line PIs C9, C10, A74

**16** General Medical — 1st Line PIs A9ABC, A16, A23ABC, A30

**18** General Surgical — 1st Line PIs A10ABC, A17, A24ABC, A37

**20** Trauma & Orthopaedics — 1st Line PIs A11ABC, A18, A25ABC, A32

**22** Gynaecology — 1st Line PIs A12ABC, A19, A26ABC, A33

**24** Ear, Nose & Throat — 1st Line PIs A13ABC, A20, A27ABC, A34

**26** Ophthalmology — 1st line PIs A14ABC, A21, A28ABC, A35

**28** Obstetrics & GP Matern — 1st Line PIs A15, A22, A29, A56, A57

**30** Paediatrics C20, C21, C22, C23, C24

**31** Geriatric Medicine E11, E16

**DHA Profile/Items/Checklist**

**8** Acute DHA Profile Population/Demand Text Screen

**9** Acute DHA Profile — Births Text Screen

**10** Acute DHA Profile — Community Services Text Screen

**11** Acute DHA Profile — Hospital Services Text Screen

**12** Acute DHA Profile — Major Acute Hosps Text Screen

**13** Acute Care — Check List Questions Pt 1 Text Screen

**14** Acute Care — Check List Questions Pt 2 Text Screen

**Hospital Level PIs**

**4** Major Acute Hosps — Costs and Throughput A75ABC, A76ABC

**5** Major Acute Hosps — Component Costs A77, A78, A79, A80, A81

**6** Major Acute Hosps — Accident and Emergency A82, A83

**7** Major Acute Hosps — Staff per IP Case A84, A85, A86, A87, A88, A89

Diagram 14–6  Structure of acute services PIs

other sections (hierarchies) in the guidance. Most PIs are at district level, but there are also PIs at hospital/unit level, regional level, some for ambulance authorities and some for laundries.

The technical difficulties of producing PIs which deal with outcome and quality are well known and explain why few such indicators have been developed so far. However, the new set of PIs includes a checklist of quality questions. These are designed to help assess the quality of care being received by patients, and are intended to be used alongside PIs which point to how economically and efficiently the service is being provided.

The Inter-Authority Comparisons and Consultancy (IACC) at the Health Services Management Centre, Birmingham has been developing PIs for use by the NHS for a number of years, funded by the DHSS and health authorities. The work has proved useful and valuable, and the information is complementary to the PIs published in the new package.

There are problems with the age of the data – the 1985 package of PIs uses 1983/84 data – which it is hoped to ameliorate when new data based on the recommendations of the HS Information Steering Group become available towards the end of the 1980s. Lack of data has also prevented some desirable ratios being calculated.

A brief selection from the circa 450 PIs is included in Appendix 14–2.

The new PIs are outlined in a series of articles in the *Health and Social Services Journal,* 20 June–4 July 1985.

For an interesting and amusing commentary on performance measurement in the NHS see *Performance measurement in the public sector: paving the road to Hell,* A. Williams, University of Glasgow, 1985.

## 14.4.13 Home Office – The Police

The Home Office is developing a financial system that includes output measures. The system is designed to help HM Inspectors of Constabulary assess the efficiency of police forces. The background to this is described in *Progress in Financial Management in Government Departments* (Cmnd 9297, July 1984, p. 70).

While the ultimate effect of police activity is hard to measure, it proved relatively easy to devise more intermediate measures for most functional categories. Indeed the recommended list of measures had to be kept reasonably short by selecting only those measures that seemed clearly relevant to the practicalities of policing and generally applicable to most forces, and the list is likely to be reduced further as experience suggests which measures Inspectors find most useful.

The measures fall into three categories:

(*a*)    indicators of workload;

(*b*)    indicators of effectiveness (the extent to which objectives are met);

(*c*)    indicators of efficiency (a comparison of output and cost).

The proposed ratios include:

    Costs per operational employee
    Costs per 1,000 population

for each of the following categories: patrol, public order, crime, community relations, traffic, other operations, total costs (including training and management),

    Training cost per police officer
    Transport cost per vehicle mile

Patrol
    Cost per incident response

Crime detection
    Cost per crime recorded
    Cost per clear-up

Traffic
    Cost per offence reported
    Cost of motorway and trunk road unit per mile of road policed
    Cost of motorway and trunk road unit per police vehicle mile

Other operations
    Cost per prosecution

Training
    Average cost per day in training
    Cost per officer per year of refresher training

Complaints and discipline
    Cost per complaint investigated.

The measures have been piloted in three forces initially and the system appears to be workable. It will be used as a regular and integral part of inspections, primarily to see if forces are responding to overall policing objectives and their own local objectives by adjusting their deployment of resources, and if and how output alters as a consequence. The system will also be used for year-on-year comparisons within a force, and, cautiously, for identifying and examining differences between forces. For the latter exercise to be effective it will need fully to recognise intrinsic differences – for example, unit cost/mile of vehicle patrol will depend on the amount of motorway, geographical features of the force's area, etc.

Information about performance measurement in a police force will be found in 'The force's better beat', S. Caulkin, *Management Today*, March 1985, and the issues are discussed in *Measures of police effectiveness and efficiency*, I. Sinclair and C. Miller, Home Office, 1984.

### 14.4.14 Inland Revenue

*The Board of Inland Revenue's Annual Report* (HMSO) provides the ratio of the cost of collecting a tax to its yield. In 1983–84 this was 1.72p per £ tax collected (or 1.23p if NIC is included). It varied considerably across the different taxes, ranging from 0.01p from PRT, where a small number of companies pay large amounts, to 5.9p for Schedule D, where an individual assessment has to be made for over 2m individuals. PAYE – the dominant money raiser and which occupied the bulk of the staff – costs 1.6p in the £ to collect. The Revenue point out that these ratios have two severe limitations as management ratios:

1 The cost/yield ratio is affected far more by Budgetary changes in tax rates and reliefs and by changes in underlying economic activity, certainly in the short term, than by administrative changes which either increase the yield by countering evasion more effectively, or reduce collection costs. The introduction of a new relief may not only reduce the tax yield but also increase the cost of collection if new procedures are required to administer it.

2 The ratios for individual taxes should be regarded as no more than broad estimates since much of the Department's work is carried out for the purpose of more than one tax, and many costs cannot be clearly allocated to one tax rather than another.

As guides for day-to-day management of the staff different indicators and ratios have to be used. Since the assessment work in tax districts employs most staff and covers a very wide range of work ranging from clerks shifting files to Tax Inspectors examining the accounts of the largest companies this can be used to illustrate the Department approach. Most indicators are reported at district, region and national level.

*Clerical work (mainly PAYE).* The performance indicators used are timetables for certain regular tasks such as annual coding; the volumes of forms produced or examined; arrears monitoring in the form of uncleared post over two weeks old or cases from previous years still unsettled; error rates. Some of these are in ratio form e.g.

per cent of returns examined by a certain date;
items of uncleared post over 14 days per staff employed;
per cent of previous year's cases still open;
per cent of assessments correct (based on sample surveys).

The task of counting all the outputs of clerical work in the current manual systems have prohibited development of a reliable total work done indicator. Post computerisation and the completion of a formal work measurement programme a productivity indicator may well be achievable at the end of the decade.

*Investigation work.* Since the mid-1970s the Department has run selective investigations to counter tax evasion. The ideal measures of effectiveness would be the change in the amount of evasion or the deterrent effect. Neither are readily measurable. The Department uses the following indicators as proxies:

the percentage of accounts investigated (targeted);
the percentage of successful investigations
the money recovered by individual investigations and the overall programme (not targeted);
the subsequent compliance of investigated taxpayers (by sample surveys).

Two of the above are ratios in themselves. For the various forms of evasion or investigative activity (e.g. self-employed, PAYE non-compliance, moonlighting) the Department calculates yield/cost ratios dividing the money recovered by the cost of the staff employed on the activity. This is useful for resource allocation purposes and monitoring trends in compliance work (but it is not the sole criterion or measure used for the purpose).

A system for quality assessment by examining files has just been launched.

*Technical scrutiny of accounts.* This highly technical work is the most difficult to measure. Inspectors do record the adjustment to profits they make (although these are difficult to interpret in terms of tax yield) and this form of measure is used for limited purposes. The main ratios used are the percentage of companies examined and the percentage of these on which significant adjustments occurred.

It should be stressed that in all the Department's investigation and technical scrutiny work, while the size of the cases are relevant, targets are never set for the level of money recovered by individual officers or offices.

Further information on the plans and performance of the Inland Revenue will be found in *Senior Management System Reports,* Inland Revenue Central Financial Management Unit, December 1984.

## 14.4.15 Chessington Computer Centre, HM Treasury

CCC is a computer centre for 65 government organisations both Exchequer and non-Exchequer. Its services include payroll, Departmental Staff Records (DSRs) and awarding of superannuation. The Management Accounting Information System (MAISY) used by central departments is run and maintained at CCC. CCC also provides computer time for the Civil Service Commission (CSC). It employs 400 staff, 100 of them computer specialists.

CCC uses some 50 indicators describing performance in the areas of computer operations, systems and programming, pay (clerical and computing), DSR, MAISY, superannuation and administration.

The indicators fall broadly into three categories: use of resources, service to users and efficiency. The *use of resources* is measured by, for example, the number of switched on computer hours for each area (e.g. MAISY), expressed as a percentage of total. There are also a number of indicators of use of manpower resources, for example number of data processor days worked, number of working days effort on system programming, and number of COs on pay accounts. The wastage of resources is indicated by the time lost due to the need for reprocessing. This is analysed by reason, for example, computer failure, program failure or operator error.

*Service to users* is measured in a number of ways. Indicators such as computer downtime and MTBSF (mean time between system failure) give an overall impression of the level of *availability*. A more specific example is the on-line computer time actually available to MAISY users in a month which can be compared with the maximum or 'contracted' hours which CCC has offered. It is sometimes useful to consider quality of service in terms of eliminating errors and backlogs and there are various indicators of this type. Timeliness, for example, is indicated by the number of target dates missed for MAISY, backlogs of reported errors and outstanding requests for program enhancement. Measures of *accuracy* include the number of errors in the DSR database, number of program bugs reported and the number of run time errors raised by departments.

There are a number of indicators of *efficiency:* for example, average key depressions per DP day, average job clearance rate for programmers and number of pay accounts cleared per monthly CO.

Chessington management find the system of indicators useful both as a picture of the whole operation and in pinpointing problem areas; it has also generated a spirit of competitiveness amongst sections, with each keen to improve their performance as measured by the relevant indicators.

A subset of key indicators has formed an important part of the centre's description of its performance and plans when these are reviewed in the Treasury's top management system. They are also beginning to provide the basis for setting performance targets.

Comparisons are also made with other public sector computer centres with similar responsibilities.

## Appendix 14.1

## EXAMPLES OF OUTPUT AND PERFORMANCE MEASURES USED IN THE MINISTRY OF DEFENCE

| FUNCTION | MEASURES/INDICATORS |
|---|---|
| Training | Trainee cost statistics |
| | Staff: trainee ratios |
| | Trainee days – actual compared with planned and per cent utilisation |
| | Cost per course and per student week |
| Recruitment | Candidate selection statistics |
| Hospitals | Patient cost statistics, e.g. per in-patient day and per out-patient |
| | Bed occupancy statistics |
| Store depots | Cost per issue/receipt |
| | Utilisation of capacity statistics |
| | Manpower ratios |
| | Vehicle utilisation and availability |
| | Storage and movement statistics |
| Storage depots | Cost per square foot |
| Aircraft repair and maintenance | Analysis of manpower output and cost information e.g. direct hours, overtime hours, efficiency ratios |

| Vehicle repair and engineering workshops | Productivity analysis |
| | Manpower ratios |
| | Analysis of workload |
| | Cost per repair hour |
| | |
| Dockyards | Estimate/outturn analysis of dockyard programme |
| Marine services | Utilisation ratios |
| | Usage downtime hours per vessel |
| | Annual comparison of operating costs per vessel group and costs per hour of usage |
| Transport operations | Vehicle cost per mile |
| | Costs per unit served |
| Service children schools | Cost per pupil |
| | Pupil: teacher ratios |
| Signals units | Message transactions and availability statistics |
| | Workload summaries |
| Operational flying stations | Flying task statistics |
| Weapons production | Costs per working day |
| | Authorised expenditure compared with estimates |
| | Productive hours per working day |
| Proof and testing ranges | Records of staff activity and range usage, e.g. usage as a percentage of range availability |
| Defence accounts | Cost per: |
| | pay account and £'000 paid |
| | superannuation award |
| | travel and subsistence claim |
| | bill paid and £'000 paid |
| | invoice presented and £'000 presented |
| Common services | |
| (a) HQ Typing Services | Total cost per Treasury Typing Unit (TTU) |
| | Staff cost per TTU |
| | Units produced per member of staff |
| (b) HQ Reprographic and Printing Services | Total cost per A4 impression |
| | Staff cost per A4 impression |
| | Units produced per member of staff |
| (c) Records section | Ratio of enquiries: replies |
| | Cost per enquiry/reply |
| (d) Mail services | Total items handled |
| | Average delivery times |
| | Average handling of items by mail/transit staff |
| Data processing services | Cost per unit of mill time |
| | Use of terminals – cost per elapsed minute |
| | Use of peripherals – cost per 100 transfers |
| | Data preparation – cost per 1,000 key depressions |
| | Systems analysis/design/programming – cost per day |

**Appendix 14.2**

**SELECTED PERFORMANCE INDICATORS FOR THE NHS**

ACUTE SERVICES

*1st line PIs*

1   Number of residents treated as in-patient or day cases anywhere in England divided by the resident population
2   Number of patients treated per available bed, actual and standardised

*Hospital level PIs*

3   Cost per case (analysed into its major components)
4   Staff per in-patient case (divided into principal categories of staff)

*Speciality based PIs*

5   Length of stay (analysed by speciality), actual and standardised
6   Consultants in geriatric medicine per resident population aged 75 years and over

*2nd line PIs*

7   Theatre sessions per bed
8   Waiting list per 1,000 catchment population
9   Notional days to clear waiting list (calculated separately for major specialities)

CHILDREN SERVICES

*1st line PIs*

10   Number of nurses allocated to special care baby units per 100 babies weighing 2,500 grammes or less born per year

11   Number of nurses per 100 babies treated
12   Neonatal and post-neonatal mortality rates

*Hospital child care – manpower*
13   Number of senior doctors working in hospital paediatrics related to the catchment population
14   Number of cases per 1,000 children analysed by type of illness
15   Length of stay (per 1,000 children analysed by type of illness)

*Community Child Care*
16   Child clinic attendance rate
17   Immunisation rate (analysed by type of immunisation)
18   Health Visitor contact rate
19   Health visitors per 1,000 under 5
20   School health nurses per 1,000 school population

SUPPORT SERVICES

*Ambulance service*
21   Cost per 1,000 resident population
22   Cost per 1,000 patients carried
23   Cost per patient mile

*Catering services*
24   Catering cost per patient day
25   Provisions cost per patient day
26   Staff cost per patient day

*Domestic services*
27   Total cost per 100 square metres cleaned

*Laundry services*
28   Total cost per 100 articles

*Pathology*
29   Cost/workload analysed by type of speciality

ESTATE MANAGEMENT

30   Cost per unit area
31   Maintenance cost per building area
32   Energy used per heated volume

# Suggestions for Further Reading

For those who want to follow up any aspect of the subjects covered in this book, the following selection of articles and books is recommended. Apart from the first two sections it is set out in the chapter order of this book. Some chapters are sub-divided by topic. Within each section or sub-division publications are in alphabetical order of their title. Some of the books may be out of print but should be obtainable from a library. Use a later edition than that listed if one has subsequently been published. It is not suggested that anyone should read *all* the books under any heading. Several are alternatives and have been listed in case some are not available and to attempt to cater for the different tastes of readers.

## Guides to business books

*Accountants' Reference Library*, D.B. Atkinson, Accountants' Digest No. 173, ICAEW, 1985

*Anbar Yearbook*, Anbar Publications, Annual

*Business and Economic Books and Serials in Print*, R.K. Bowker, 1981

*The Good Book Guide for Business*, Penguin Books Limited, 1984

*Reading Lists on Accounting, Finance and Taxation*, ICAEW, 1983

## General

*Efficiency Comparison Within Large Organisations*, Study Group of B.I.M. member firms, British Institute of Management and The Centre for Interfirm Comparison, 1962*

---

* *contains bibliography*

*The Meaningful Interpretation of Financial Statements*, D.E. Miller, American Management Association, revd. edition, 1979

*Ratio Analysis for Small Business*, R. Sanzo, Small Business Administration, 1957

'Ratios and Performance', Chapter 17 in *Business Planning*, D.R.C. Halford, Pan, 1968

*Successful Managerial Control by Ratio-analysis*, S. Tucker, McGraw-Hill, 1961

*The Use of Ratios in the Study of Business Fluctuations and Trends*, K.W. Bevan, Institute of Chartered Accountants, 1966

## Introduction

'The du Pont Chart System for Appraising Operating Performance', C.A. Kline, Jr. and Howard L. Hessler, *N.A.C.A. Bulletin*, Conference Proceedings, August 1952, pp. 1595-1619

*Financial Ratio Analysis – an Historical Perspective*, J.O. Horrigan, Arno Press, 1978

'Pyramid Structure – a Pattern for Comparative Measurements', H. Ingham and L.T. Harrington, *The Manager*, September 1956, pp. 657-660

'A Short History of Financial Ratio Analysis, J.O. Horrigan, *The Accounting Review*, April 1968

## Chapter 1 – Principles of ratio selection

*The Board and the Presentation of Financial Information to Management,* J. Batty, Business Books, 1978

*Facts from Figures,* M.J. Moroney, Penguin, 1965

'Properties of Accounting Ratios', G. Whittington, *Journal of Business Finance & Accounting,* Summer 1980

'The use of Ratios in Measuring Asset Utilisation', C.A. Westwick, *The Accountant,* 23 December 1967

*Using your Overhead Projector and Other Visual Aids,* C. Waller, Fordigraph Division of Ofrex Ltd., 1983


## Chapter 2 – Standards of comparison

In addition to the books and articles listed here, see also those listed in the Appendices to Chapter 2.

'Accountants' Role in Zero Base Budgeting', B. Neumann, J.D. Suver and R.L. Brown, *CPA Journal,* January 1978

*Balancing Sales and Production,* Herbert Ingham, Management Publications, 1971

*Behavioural Aspects of Budgeting,* D. Otley, ICAEW, 1977

*Business Efficiency: An ABC of Advisory Services,* NEDO, HMSO, 1968

'The Companies Act 1967 and its Implications for Interfirm Comparison,' C.A. Westwick, *Business Ratios,* Spring 1968

*Efficiency Comparisons within Large Organisations,* L. Taylor Harrington, BIM, 1960

*Financial Reporting,* Institute of Chartered Accountants in England and Wales, Annual

*Guidelines to Insider Dealing,* The Society of Investment Analysts, May 1981

*Interfirm Comparison,* Herbert Ingham and L. Taylor Harrington, Heinemann, 1980

*Interfirm Comparison for Management,* Herbert Ingham and L. Taylor Harrington, BIM, 1958

*Introduction to Work Study,* International Labour Office, Geneva, 3rd revd. edition, 1978

*Management Policies and Practices, and Business Performance,* L. Taylor Harrington, R.M.L. Carruthers, G. Hodson et al, The Centre for Interfirm Comparison, 1978

'Measuring Financial Performance', A.H. Seed, *Financial Executive,* January 1982

*Productivity Measurement – a Symposium for the 70's,* R. Allard et al., Institute of Personnel Management, 1971*

*Productivity Measurement Review,* Number 26, August 1961, published by the Productivity Management Advisory Service of the European Productivity Agency.

*Profit Forecasts – How they are Made, Reviewed and Used,* C.A. Westwick (ed.), Gower, 1983

'Simplification for Efficiency', M.J. Glenn, *The Manager,* June 1959

*Sources of British Business Comparative Performance Data,* C.A. Westwick, The Institute of Chartered Accountants in England and Wales, 1980

*A Study of Profitability in the Hosiery and Knitwear Industry,* C.A. Westwick, NEDO, 1971

'To Incorporate or not to Incorporate', R. Pereira, *The Accountant,* 24 July 1985

'What the Chancellor Did for Britain's Small Businesses', *The Accountant,* 28 March and 30 May 1985

'Will ZBB Ever Catch On?', B. McSweeney, *The Accountant,* 4 August 1983

*Work Study,* R.M. Currie, Pitman, 4th edition, 1977

'The ZBA Path to Improved Efficiency', D. Guy and T. Bevington, *Accountancy,* May 1983

*Zero Base Budgeting: A Practical Management Tool for Evaluating Expenses,* P.A. Pyrr, Wiley, 1973


## Chapter 3 – Principles of ratio definition and calculation

See Chapter 13, the sections on Financial accounting, Inflation accounting, Management accounting and Using accounts.

*contains bibliography

## Chapter 4 – Priority ratios for the chief executive

*The Business of Success*, R. Meller, Sidgwick and Jackson, 1982

*The Change Masters – Corporate Entrepreneurs at Work*, R.M. Kanter, Allen and Unwin, 1984

*Competitive Advantage*, M.E. Porter, Collier-Macmillan, 1985

*Competitive Strategy*, M.E. Porter, Collier-Macmillan, 1980

*In Search of Excellence*, Thomas J. Peters and Robert H. Waterman, Harper and Row, 1982

*Managing for Results*, P.F. Drucker, Heinemann, 1964

*Passion for Excellence*, Thomas J. Peters and N. Austin, Collins, 1985

*Top Management Control in Europe*, J.H. Horovitz, Macmillan, 1980

*The Winning Streak*, W. Goldsmith and D. Clutterbuck, Weidenfeld and Nicolson, 1984

## Chapter 5 – Ratios for overall control

*Added Value – the Key to Prosperity*, E.G. Wood, Business Books, 1978*

*Divisional Performance: Measurement and Control*, David Solomons, 1965 (reprinted M. Wiener, 1983)

*How to Survive the Recession*, Jeremy Prescott, The Institute of Chartered Accountants in England and Wales, 1982

*Managing for Profit*, Patrick Mills (ed), McGraw-Hill, 1982

*Practical Corporate Planning*, J. Argenti, Allen and Unwin, 1980

*Problems of Using 'Return on Capital' as a Measure of Success*, L. Taylor Harrington, Manchester Statistical Society, 1961

'Return of Capital Employed as a Measure of Efficiency', R.C. Skinner, *Accountancy*, June 1965

*Value Added – An Appreciation for the Accountant Concerned with Industry*, Bernard Cox, The Institute of Cost and Management Accountants, 1979

*Value Added Reporting: Uses and Measurement*, S. Gray and K. Maunders, Assoc. of Certified Accountants, 1980*

'What the Ratios Saw', D. Beaven, *Management Today*, July 1982

*You Can Profit from Product Life Cycle*, J.S. Bridges, Rydges, April 1971

### Research and Development

*The Financial Side of Industrial Research Management*, L.W. Ellis, Wiley, 1984

*How Companies Manage R & D – A Survey of Major UK Companies*, Niall Lothian, The Institute of Cost and Management Accountants, 1984

*Industrial R & D Management*, A.J. Gambino and M. Gartenburg, National Association of Accountants (U.S.), 1979

*Management of Research, Development and Design in Industry*, T.S. McLeod, Gower, 1973

## Chapter 6 – Ratios for marketing management

*Advertising Cost Control Handbook*, O. Riso, Van Nostrand Reinhold, 1973

*Application of Computers in Physical Distribution Management*, A.G. Slater, Centre for PDM/BIM, 1983

*Application of Management Accounting Techniques to the Planning and Control of Marketing of Consumer Non-durables*, R.M.S. Wilson and A.C. Bancroft, Institute of Cost and Management Accountants, 1983

'Creating a Market', *Learning Systems*, International Labour Office, Geneva, 1968

*Creativity in Marketing*, Remus A. Harris, American Marketing Foundation, Southampton, (N.Y.), 1960

*Distribution*, K. Newton, ICAEW, 1981

*Elements of Export Practice*, A.E. Branch, Chapman and Hall, 2nd edition, 1985

'The Evaluation of Direct Sales Campaigns', W.N.S. Calvert, *Business Ratios*, Spring 1968

*Export Strategy*, N. Piercy, Allen and Unwin, 1982

*Exporting for Profit*, A.J. Day, Graham & Trotman, 1976

---

* contains bibliography

'The Financial Control of Advertising', D. Britton, *Accountancy,* November 1971

*Financial Dimensions of Marketing,* R.M.S. Wilson (ed), Macmillan, 1981*

*Fundamentals of Advertising,* J. Wilmshurst, Heinemann, 1985

*Handbook of Advertising Management,* R. Barton (ed), McGraw-Hill, New York, 1970

*How British Industry Buys: An Enquiry,* H. Buckner, Hutchinson, 1967

*How to Prepare a Marketing Plan,* J. Stapleton, Gower, 3rd edition, 1982

*How to Win Customers,* H.M. Goldmann, revd. edition, Pan 1971

*Is Your Advertising Budget Wasted?,* Economist Intelligence Unit, 1986

*Management Controls and Marketing Planning,* R.M.S. Wilson, Heinemann, 1979*

*Management in Marketing: Text and Cases,* H. Lazo and A. Corbin, McGraw-Hill, 1961

*Marketing,* C. McIver, Business Publications, 3rd edition revised and edited by G.C. Wilson, 1968

*Marketing Classics – A Selection of Influential Articles,* B.M. Enis and K.K. Cox, Allyn and Bacon, 5th edition, 1985

*Marketing and Higher Management,* E. Pearce, Allen & Unwin, 1970

*Marketing Management,* P. Kotler, Prentice-Hall, 5th edition, 1984

*Marketing Management: Analysis, Planning and Control,* P. Kotler, Prentice-Hall, 5th edition, 1984

*Marketing for Profit,* L. Hardy, Longmans Green, 1962

*Marketing – the Sales Manager's Role,* A. & G. Tack, World's Work, 1968

*Physical Distribution Management, Handbook of,* J. Gattorna (ed), Gower, 3rd edition, 1983*

*Planning a Distribution System,* P.R. Attwood, Gower, revised reprint, 1978

*The Practical Approach to Marketing Management,* S. Morse, McGraw-Hill, 1967*

*Pricing,* F. Livesey, Macmillan, 1976

*The Principles of Marketing,* Learning Systems, Business Books, 1969

*Product Management in Action,* R.H. Offord (ed), Business Publications, 1967

*Profit Centre Sales Management,* E. Körlin, Business Books, 1976

*Profitable Marketing for the Smaller Company,* C.G. Roe, Gower, 1969

*Sales Management,* Cunliffe L. Bolling, Pitman Paperbacks, 5th edition, 1971

*Systematic Export Documentation,* SITPRO, 1976 and 1979 Supplement

## Chapter 7 – Ratios for purchasing management

*Cutting Costs by Analysing Values – A Practical Purchasing Programme,* National Association of Purchasing Agents, New York, 1963

*A Guide to Stock Control,* A. Battersby, Pitman, 2nd edition, 1970*

*Improving the Purchasing Function Through Cost and Price Analysis,* C.C. Chauvin, Materials Management Institute, Boston, USA, 1961

*Inventory Control for the Financial Executive,* T.S. Dudick and R. Cornell, Wiley, 1979

*The Lease-Purchase Decision,* W.L. Farrava et al, National Association of Accountants, 1980

*Purchasing Principles and Management,* P. Baily, and D. Farmer, Pitman, 4th edition, 1981*

*Scientific Inventory Control,* C.D. Lewis, 2nd edition, Butterworths, 1981

*Stock Control in Manufacturing Industries,* A.B. Thomas, Gower, 2nd edition, 1980

*Stock Control Systems and Records,* P. Baily and G. Tavernier, Gower, 2nd edition by R.G. Storey, 1984

*Zero Inventories,* R.W. Hall, Irvin, 1983

## Chapter 8 – Ratios for financial management

See also Chapter 13, the sections on Financial accounting, Inflation accounting, Management accounting and Using accounts.

General

*Effective Use of Business Consultants,* W. Seney, Financial Executives' Institute, New York, 1963

* contains bibliography

404

*Parkinson's Law*, C.N. Parkinson, John Murray, 1958

*Up the Organisation*, R. Townsend, Coronet, 1971

## Data processing

*Computer Appreciation*, T.F. Fry, Butterworths, 3rd edition, 1981

*Computers and Commonsense*, R. Hunt and J. Shelley, Prentice-Hall, 3rd edition, 1983

*Developing Microcomputer-based Business Systems*, C. Edwards, Prentice-Hall/ ICMA, 1982

*Effective Use of Computers in Business*, P.A. Losty, Cassell, 1969*

*Electronic Data Processing*, G. Emery, Pitman, 2nd revised edition, 1975*

*Managing with Micros*, C. Lewis, Blackwell, 2nd edition, 1984

## Finance

*Business Finance and the Capital Market*, K. Midgley and R.G. Burns, Macmillan, 2nd edition, 1979

*The Financing of Industry and Trade*, D.J. Darby, Pitman, 1970*

*Fundamentals of Financial Management*, James C. Van Horne, Prentice-Hall, 1977

'Gearing in British Quoted Companies', D. Prusmann and G. Murphy, *Business Ratios*, Winter 1968

*How to Forecast Interest Rates*, M.J. Pring, McGraw-Hill, 1981

*Managerial Finance*, J.F. Weston and E.F. Bringham, Dryden Press, 7th edition, 1981

*Managing Money and Finance*, G.P.E. Clarkson and B.J. Elliott, Gower, 3rd edition, 1983

*The Money Game*, Adam Smith, Michael Joseph, 1968

'Towards a New Measure and Use of Gearing', C.A. Westwick, *Accounting and Business Research*, Winter 1970

## Investment

'Analysing Return on Equity Capital', C.A. Westwick, *The Manager*, January 1965

*Capital Budgeting and Company Finance*, A.J. Merrett and A. Sykes, Longmans, 2nd edition, 1973

*Differential Costs and Management Decisions*, D.R.C. Halford, Pitman, 1959

*Discounted Cash Flow*, A.M. Alfred and J.B. Evans, Chapman & Hall, 3rd revd. edition, 1971

*Financial Futures Markets*, B. Brown and C.R. Geisst, Macmillan, 1983

*An Introduction to Risk and Return from Common Stocks*, R.A. Brealey, Blackwell, 1983

*An Introduction to Stock Exchange Investment*, J. Rutterford, Macmillan, 1983

*Investment Analysis*, D. Weaver, Longmans and the Society of Investment Analysts, 1971

*Investment Appraisal*, D. Lumby, Van Nostrand Reinhold, 2nd edition, 1984

*Investment Appraisal and Inflation*, C.A. Westwick and P.S.D. Shohet, The Institute of Chartered Accountants in England and Wales, 1976

*Investment Arithmetic*, M.S. Rix, Pitman, 1964

*Major Stockmarkets of Europe*, P. Stonham, Gower, 1982

*Managing for Profit: the Added Value Concept*, R.R. Gilchrist, Allen & Unwin, 1971*

*Practical Approach to Business Investment Decisions*, R.J. Briston and J. Liversidge, Macmillan, 1979*

*Profit Management and Control*, F.V. Gardner, MacDonald, 1971

*Take-overs and Mergers*, M.A. Weinberg, Sweet & Maxwell, 4th edition, 1979

*Trading In Financial Futures*, P. Sarnoff, Woodhead-Faulkner, 1985

## Liquidity

*Application of Classification Techniques in Business*, Banking and Finance, E.I. Altman et al, JAI Press, 1981

---

* contains bibliography

'Company Failure – Long Range Prediction Not Enough', J. Argenti, *Accountancy*, August 1977

*Effective Credit Management*, M. Goddard, Graham and Trotman, 1984

'Evaluation of a Company as a Going Concern', E.I. Altman and T.P. McGough, *Journal of Accountancy*, December 1974

*Financial Ratios: Analysis and Prediction*, M. Tamari, Paul Elek, 1978

'Going, Going, Gone – Four Factors Which Predict', R. Taffler and H. Tishaw, *Accountancy*, March 1977

'How to Figure Who's Going Bankrupt', A. Hershman, *Duns Review*, October 1975

'Liquidity Evaluation by Ratio Analysis', H. Fadel and J.M. Parkinson, *Accounting and Business Research*, Spring 1978

*Management of Trade Credit*, T.G. Hutson and J. Butterworth, Gower, 3rd edition, 1984

*A Method of Quantifying Companies' Relative Financial Strength*, D.A.J. Marais, Bank of England Discussion Paper No. 4, July 1979

*Practical Financial Statement Analysis*, R.A. Foulke, McGraw-Hill, 6th edition, 1968

'Predicting Corporate Collapse', A. Bathory, *Financial Times*, 1984

'Predicting Corporate Failure', J. Argenti, *Accountants' Digest* No. 138, ICAEW, 1983

## Pensions

*Accounting for the Cost of Pensions*, C.J. Napier, ICAEW, 1983

*Accounting for Pension Costs, a Consultative Statement of Intent*, ASC, 1984

*Annual Survey of Occupational Pension Schemes*, National Association of Pension Funds

*Disclosure of Pension Information in Company Accounts*, ED32, ASC, 1983

*Occupational Pension Schemes, Survey by the Government Actuary*, HMSO, every five years, latest 1979 published in 1981

*Pension Scheme Accounts: A Discussion Paper*, ASC, 1982

*Pension Scheme Accounts*, ED34, ASC, 1984

*Pensions Terminology*, The Pensions Management Institute, 1984

*Population, Pension Costs and Pensioners' Incomes*, DHSS, HMSO, 1984

'Using Financial Ratios to Analyse Pension Liabilities, F.G. Burianek, *Financial Executive*, January 1981

## Tax

*Practical Tax Saving*, Nicholas R. Noble and David N. Marks, Butterworth, 1985

*Tax in Business*, P. Hardman, Gee/ICAEW, 1984

*Tax Strategy for Companies*, M. Gammie, Oyez, 3rd edition, 1983

## Chapter 9 – Ratios for production management

*Analysis for Production and Operations Management*, E.H. Bowman and R.B. Fetter, Irwin, Illinois, 3rd edition, 1967

*Control Techniques for Production Management*, R.H. Offord (ed), Business Publications, 1967

*Design of Project Management Systems and Records*, A.T. Peart, Gower, 1971*

*Measuring Purchasing Performance*, J. Stevens, Business Books, 1978*

*Modern Production/Operations Management*, E.S. Buffa, Wiley, 6th edition, 1980

*Principles of Production Control*, J.L. Burbidge, MacDonald & Evans, 4th edition, 1978

*Production Control in Practice*, K.G. Lockyer, Pitman, 2nd revd edition, 1975

*Production and Inventory Control – Principles and Techniques*, G.W. Plossl and O.W. Wight, Prentice-Hall, 1967*

*Production Planning*, J.L. Burbidge, Heinemann, 1971*

*Production Planning and Inventory Control*, J.F. Magee and D.M. Boodman, McGraw-Hill, 2nd revd edition, 1967

*Scientific Method in Production Management*, G.R. Gedge, Oxford University Press, 1965*

* contains bibliography

## Chapter 10 – Ratios for personnel management

*Analysis and Costing of Company Training,* J.R. Talbor and C.D. Ellis, Gower, 1969*

*How to Get your Employment Costs Right,* E. Whiting, ICAEW, 1984

*Industrial Relations and Communications,* W. Walsh, Gee, 1970*

*Industrial Relations Handbook,* Advisory Conciliation and Arbitration Service, HMSO, 1980

*Industrial Relations Procedures and Agreements,* J. Muir, Gower, 1981

*Industrial Training Management,* J. Finnigan, Business Books, 1970

*Labour Turnover? Towards a Solution,* P.J. Samuel, Institute of Personnel Management, 1969

*The Manager and Industrial Relations,* T. Owen, Pergamon Press, 1979

*Manpower Planning,* G. Stainer, Heinemann, 1971*

*Manpower Planning and Control,* G. McBeath, Business Books, 1978

*Personnel Administration and Industrial Relations,* J.V. Grant and G.J. Smith, revd edition, Longmans, 1978*

*Personnel and Industrial Relations: A Managerial Approach,* J.B. Miner, Collier-Macmillan, 3rd revd edition, 1970

*The Personnel Management Handbook,* J. Larkcom (ed), Business Publications, 4th edition, 1967*

*Personnel Management – Principles and Practice,* C.H. Northcott, Pitman, 4th edition, 1960*

*The Personnel Management Process,* W. French, Houghton Mifflin & Co., 4th edition, 1978*

*Personnel Systems and Records,* B. Dyer (Industrial Society), Gower, 3rd edition, 1979

*Productivity Agreements and Wage Systems,* D.T.B. North and G. Buckingham, Gower, 1969

*Recruitment Handbook,* B. Ungerson (ed), Gower, 3rd edition, 1983

*Textbook of Personnel Management,* Y. Thomson, 3rd edition, Institute of Personnel Management, 1978*

## Chapter 11 – Operating ratios for non-manufacturing organisations

Professional Firms

'Assessing the Efficiency of an Accounting Firm', M.H. Cabourn Smith, *Accountancy,* December 1970

*Financial Management in the Professional Office,* M. Groom, ICAEW, 1977 (Accountants' Digest, No. 46)

'Interfirm Comparison Between Stockbrokers', *Stock Exchange Journal,* June 1968

*Management Consulting,* M. Kubr, International Labour Office, 1976

*Management and Financial Control in the Professional Office,* P.J. Grant, Business Books, 1971

*Partnership Management,* W. Moberly, ICAEW, 1983

The *Practice Administration Series* of booklets published by The Institute of Chartered Accountants in England and Wales

*Stockbrokers,* M.C. Clarke and J.P. McAleenan, ICAEW, 1985 (Business Briefing, No. 5)

*Stockbroking Today,* J.D. Hamilton, Macmillan, 2nd edition, 1979

Printers

*Cost Accountancy for Printers,* British Federation of Master Printers, 1971

Farms

*Estate Finance and Business Management,* C.W.N. Miles, Estates Gazette, 4th edition, 1981

*Farm Accounting and Management,* F. Sturrock, Pitman, 7th edition, 1982

*Farm Planning and Control,* C.S. Barnard and J.S. Nix, Cambridge University Press, 2nd edition, 1979

*Financial Management for Farmers,* M.F. Warren, Hutchinson, 1982

---

* contains bibliography

## Hotels

*Financial Management in Hotel and Catering Operations,* D.F. Sutton, Heinemann, 2nd edition, 1979

*Hotel Accounts and their Audit,* L.S. Fenton and N.A. Fowler, ICAEW, 1978

*Management Accounting for Hotels and Restaurants,* R. Kotas, Surrey University Press, 1977

*A Standard System of Hotel Accounting,* Hotels and Catering EDC, HMSO, 1969

## Newspapers

*The National Newspaper Industry,* Economist Intelligence Unit, 1966

*Newspaper Accounting and Control,* Institute of Newspaper Controllers and Finance Officers (U.S.), 1966

*Royal Commission on the Press,* Report, HMSO, 1977

## Retailing

*Retailing,* G. Pintel and J. Diamond, Prentice-Hall, 3rd edition, 1983

*Retailing: Management Controls and Performance Improvement,* N.A. Highton and D.L. Chilcot, ICAEW, 1980

## Chapter 13 – Using published accounts

## Auditing

*Analytical Review,* D.G. Smith, Canadian Institute of Chartered Accountants, 1983

*Auditing Research: Issues and Opportunities,* Anthony G. Hopwood, Michael Bromwich and Jack Shaw, Pitman, 1982

*Do the Figures Make Sense? A Practical Guide to Analytical Review,* C.A. Westwick, ICAEW, 1981

*Manual of Auditing,* Coopers & Lybrand, Gee & Co., 4th edition, 1984

*What is an Audit?* Richard Buckley, Auditing Practices Committee of the Consultative Committee of Accountancy Bodies, 1980

## Financial Accounting

*Accounting & Audit Requirements for Small Firms: A Consultative Document,* DTI, June 1985

*Added Value in External Financial Reporting,* M. Renshall et al, ICAEW, 1979

*Advanced Financial Accounting,* J. Samuels, C. Rickwood, A. Piper, McGraw-Hill, 1981

*Analysed Reporting,* Coopers & Lybrand, ICAEW, 1977

*British Accounting Standards,* Sir Ronald Leach and Professor Edward Stamp, Woodhead-Faulkner, 1981

*Burdens on Business,* DTI, HMSO, March 1985

*Comparative International Accounting,* edited by C.W. Nobes and R.H. Parker, Philip Allan, 1981

*The Corporate Report, Accounting Standards Steering Committee,* The Institute of Chartered Accountants in England and Wales, 1975

*Current Accounting Law and Practice,* R. Willott, Quinta, 1985

*Current Issues in Accounting,* Bryan Carsberg and Tony Hope, Philip Allan, 1977

*Debits, Credits, Finance and Profits,* Harold Eady and B.S. Yamey, Sweet and Maxwell, 1974

'Deferred Tax: How Much to Provide Now', C.A. Westwick, *Accountancy,* December 1984

*Essays in British Accounting Research,* Michael Bromwich and Anthony G. Hopwood, Pitman, 1981

*External Financial Reporting,* Bryan Carsberg & Susan Dev, Prentice-Hall, 1984

*Financial Reporting Under the Companies Act 1981,* Allan Hardcastle and Michael Renshall, The Institute of Chartered Accountants in England and Wales, 1985

*Modern Financial Accounting,* G.A. Lee, Nelson, 3rd edition, 1981

*Property Valuation and Accounts,* C.A. Westwick, The Institute of Chartered Accountants in England and Wales, 1980

*Selected Accounting Standards – Interpretation Problems Explained,* The Institute of Chartered Accountants in England and Wales, 1984

*Statements of Source and Application of Funds – A Practical Guide to SSAP 10,* R.W. Knox, The Institute of Chartered Accountants in England and Wales, 1977

*UK Financial Accounting Standards: a Descriptive and Analytical Approach,* R.K. Ashton, Woodhead Faulkner, 1983

*The Value Added Statement,* M.F. Morley, Gee and the Scottish Institute, 1978

## Fraud

*Corporate Fraud,* M.J. Comer, McGraw-Hill, 2nd edition, 1985

*Fraud and Other Irregularities,* APC, May 1985

*Gray's Building Society Investigation,* I.H. Davison and M. Stuart-Smith, HMSO, Cmnd. 7557, 1979

*Report of the Working Party on Fraud* (Chairman Ian Hay Davison), ICAEW, August 1985

'What the Auditor Needs to Know About Fraud', A.M. Rabarts, *Accountancy,* December 1978

## Inflation accounting

*Accounting for Stewardship in a Period of Inflation,* The Institute of Chartered Accountants in England and Wales, 1968

*Accounting Under Inflationary Conditions,* Patrick R.A. Kirkman, Allen & Unwin, 2nd edition, 1978

*Case Studies in Current Cost Accounting,* R.W. Scapens, A.J. Southworth, G.H. Stacy, The Institute of Chartered Accountants in England and Wales, 1983

*Current Cost of Accounting,* P. Raymond Hinton and Chris A. Westwick, Oyez, 1981

*Current Cost Accounting – The Benefits and the Costs,* Bryan Carsberg and Michael Page, The Institute of Chartered Accountants in England and Wales, 1984

*The Debate on Inflation Accounting,* David Tweedie and Geoffrey Whittington, Cambridge University Press, 1984

*Guidance Manual on Current Cost Accounting,* The Inflation Accounting Steering Group, Tolley and The Institute of Chartered Accountants in England and Wales, 1976

*Inflation Accounting,* W.T. Baxter, Philip Allan, 2nd edition, 1984

*Inflation Accounting – A Guide for Non-accountants,* P.R.A. Kirkman, Associated Business Programmes, 1975

*Inflation Accounting – An Introduction to the Debate,* Geoffrey Whittington, Cambridge University Press, 1983

*Inflation and Accounts: Discussion Paper and Fact Sheet,* The Institute of Chartered Accountants in England and Wales, 1971

'The Lessons to be Learnt from the Development of Inflation Accounting in the UK', C.A. Westwick, *Accounting and Business Research,* Autumn 1980

*Reporting under CCA,* Peat Marwick Mitchell & Co., Tolley, 1982

*Understanding Current Cost Accountting,* Derek Mallinson, Butterworths, 1980

## Management accounting

*Casebook on Management Accounting,* J. Sizer, 2 volumes, ICAEW, 1984

*Fundamentals of Management Accounting,* Robert N. Anthony and G.A. Welsch, Irwin, 3rd edition, 1981

*An Insight into Management Accounting,* John Sizer, Pitman, 2nd edition, 1979

*Introduction to Management Accounting,* Charles T. Horngren, Prentice-Hall, 6th edition, 1984

*Management Accountancy,* J. Batty, MacDonald & Evans, 5th edition, 1982

*Management Accounting: Text and Cases,* R.N. Anthony, Irwin, 1956

*Studies in Management Information,* The Institute of Chartered Accountants in England and Wales, 1969

*Topics in Management Accounting,* John Arnold, Bryan Carsberg and Robert Scapens, Philip Allan, 1980

## Using accounts

*Business Ratios: A New Guide to Interpretation,* L. Hopkins, Inter Company Comparisons Limited, 1983

*Do the Figures Make Sense? A Practical Guide to Analytical Review,* C.A. Westwick, The Institute of Chartered Accountants in England and Wales, 1981

*Financial Statement Analysis,* George Foster, Prentice-Hall, 1978

*'How to Read a Financial Report',* Merrill Lynch, Pierce, Fenner & Smith, undated

*How to Understand and Use Company Accounts,* R. Warren, Business Books, 1983

*Interpreting Company Reports and Accounts,* G. Holmes and A. Sugden, Woodhead Faulkner, 2nd edition, 1982

*The Meaning of Company Accounts,* W. Reid and D.R. Myddelton, Gower, 3rd edition, 1982

*Ratio Analysis,* M.F. Morley, Gee, 1984

*Understanding Company Financial Statements,* R.H. Parker, Penguin, 2nd edition, 1982

## Chapter 14 – Ratios in the public sector

### General

*Decision Analysis,* Myra Chapman, HMSO, 1981

*Financial Reporting in the Public Sector,* B.A. Rutherford, Butterworth, 1984

*'Framing Targets for Accountability',* B. Currie, *Public Finance and Accountancy,* August 1978

*Issues in Public Sector Accounting,* A. Hopwood and C. Tomkins (eds), Philip Allan, 1984

*Public Sector Accounting,* R. Jones and M. Pendlebury, Pitman, 1984*

*Public Sector Accounting: a Control,* N.W. Marsland, Polytech, 1981

*Public Sector Accounting and Financial Control,* Sir Douglas Henley, Andrew Likierman, Clive Holtham and John Perrin, Van Nostrand Reinhold, 1983

*Value for Money in the Public Sector* (or The Waste-watcher's Guide), CIPFA, 1980

*Value for Money – the Public Sector,* H. Butt and R. Palmer, Blackwell, 1985*

*Your Disobedient Servant,* L. Chapman, Chatto and Windus, 1978

### Central Government

*Efficiency and Effectiveness in the Civil Service,* Government Observations on 3rd report from Treasury & Civil Service Committee, HMSO, Cmnd. 8616, 1982

*Financial Management in Government Departments,* HMSO, Cmnd. 9058, September 1983

*Health Service Finance,* M.S. Rigden, Heinemann, 1983

*Making Things Happen: A Report on the Implementation of Government Efficiency Scrutinies,* Kate Jenkins, Graham Oates, Andrew Stott, HMSO, 1985

*Output and Performance Measurement in Central Government: Progress in Departments,* Sue Lewis (ed), HM Treasury, 1986

*Policy Work and the FMI: Report by the Cabinet Office (MPO)/Treasury Financial Management Unit,* HM Treasury, June 1985

*Progress in Financial Management in Government Departments,* HMSO, Cmnd 9297, 1984

*Structure and Form of Government Expenditure Reports: Proposals for Reform,* A. Likierman and P. Vass, Certified Accountant Publications, 1984

*'Why Whitehall Reform Takes the Same Old Road',* Sir Kenneth Clucas, *The Guardian,* 22 August 1983

### Education

*The Development of Higher Education into the 1990's,* HMSO, Cmnd. 9524, 1985

*Education: Polytechnic Expenditure,* The Department of the Environment Audit Inspectorate, HMSO, 1983

*Education Statistics,* CIPFA, annually

*School Standards and Spending: Statistical Analysis,* Department of Education and Science, 1983

*Standards in English Schools,* J. Marks, C. Cox, M. Pomian-Srzednicki, National Council for Educational Standards, 1983

*Teaching Styles and Pupil Progress,* N. Bennett et al, Open Books, 1976

*Value for Money in Education,* R. Lord, CIPFA, 1984

* contains bibliography

## Local Government

*Accounting in Local Government,* R.H. Jones, ICMA, 1983

*Economy, Efficiency and Effectiveness,* The audit commission for local authorities in England and Wales, 1983

'The Force's Better Beat', S. Caulkin, *Management Today,* March 1985

*Housing Revenue Account Statistics,* CIPFA, annually

*Improving Vehicle Fleet Management in Local Government,* Audit Commission, HMSO, 1984

*Local Authority Annual Reports,* DOE, HMSO, 1981

*Local Authority Reports and Accounts: A 1985 Survey,* R. Chandler, P. Cox and J. Pearson, CIPFA, 1985

*Local Government Comparative Statistics,* CIPFA, annually

*Local Government Value for Money Handbook,* CIPFA, SOLACE & LAMSACC, 3rd edition, 1985

*Management and Maintenance Statistics,* CIPFA annually

*Measures of Police Effectiveness and Efficiency,* I. Sinclair and C. Miller, Home Office, 1984

*Reducing the Cost of Local Government Purchases,* Audit Commission, HMSO, 1954

*Refuse Collection: Costs and Comparisons,* Barry Lynch, Centre for Environmental Studies Review, April 1980

*Services Administration by Local Authorities,* P. Lloyd, ICSA Publ., 1985

*Social Services: Care of Mentally Handicapped People,* The Department of the Environment Audit Inspectorate, HMSO, 1983

*Social Services: Provision of Care to the Elderly,* The Department of the Environment Audit Inspectorate, HMSO, 1983

*Waste Collection Statistics,* CIPFA, annually

## Nationalised Industries

*Controlling Public Industries,* J. Redwood and J. Hatch, Blackwell, 1982

*Current Cost Accounting and the Nationalised Industries,* M.C. Wells, University of Glasgow, 1984

*The Evaluation of Financial Performance in the Water Industry,* B. Carsberg and S. Lumby, CIPFA, 1983

'Financial Objectives, Production Efficiency and the Regulation of a Subsidised State Monopoly', I. Lapsley, *Accounting and Business Research,* Summer 1984

*The Nationalised Industries,* HMSO, Cmnd. 7131, 1978

*Nationalised Industries' Accounting Policies,* Consumers' Association, 1979

*Nationalised Industries – Policies and Performance Since 1968,* R. Pryke, Martin Robertson, 1981

'Performance Measures for the Nationalised Industries', Andrew Likierman, *Accountancy,* May 1979, p. 117

*Publication of Information by Bus Operators,* Department of Transport code of practice

*The Reports and Accounts of Nationalised Industries,* Andrew Likierman, HMSO, 1979

# Index to ratios

In this index all the ratios described in this book are listed in alphabetical order. All entries have the page number (in Roman type).

Some ratios have a code letter and/or number (eg **AD2, 6.5**) which is in **bold** type. Sometimes ratios have more than one code name because they are of use in more than one situation.

Where ratios have colloquial names (eg stock turnover) these are indexed as well as their more formal description (eg stock/cost of sales).

Public sector ratios have been indexed only under the name of the department or body concerned.

# Subject index